Planet Dog

Books by Sandra Choron

College in a Can
(with Harry Choron)

The Book of Lists for Teens
(with Harry Choron)

1,001 Tips for Caregivers
(with Sasha Carr)

The All-New Book of Lists for Kids
(with Harry Choron)

Elvis: The Last Word
(with Bob Oskam)

The Book of Lists for Kids
(with Harry Choron)

The Big Book of Kids' Lists

Rocktopicon
(with Dave Marsh and Debbie Geller)

Everybody's Investment Book
(with Edward Malca)

National Lampoon's Class Reunion

Planet Dog
(with Harry Choron)

Planet Dog

A Doglopedia

SANDRA AND HARRY CHORON

Houghton Mifflin Company   Boston New York 2005

Library of Congress Cataloging-in-
Publication Data
Choron, Sandra.
Planet dog : a doglopedia / Sandra and
Harry Choron.
p. cm.
Includes bibliographical references
and index.
ISBN-13: 978-0-618-51752-7
ISBN-10: 0-618-51752-9
1. Dogs. 2. Dog breeds. 3. Dogs —
Miscellanea. I. Choron, Harry. II. Title.
SF426.C54 2005
636.7 — dc22   2005013435

For detailed photograph and illustration
credits, please see pages xv–xvi.

Printed in the United States of America
Book design by Lisa Diercks
Typeset in DIN, Chalet, New Bold, and
French Script
MP 10 9 8 7 6 5 4 3 2 1

This book is not intended as a substitute
for professional assistance. The author
and publisher disclaim any responsibility for any adverse effects resulting directly or indirectly from information contained in this book.

This book is not in any way related to, or
sponsored or endorsed by, any business
entity named "Planet Dog," including
Planet Dog of Portland, Maine, and Planet
Dog of Toronto, Canada.

To the dogs:

Coco	**Guy**
Marley	**Dustie**
Roxy	**Abby**
Penny-Belle	**Kasha**
Midnight	**Zuni**
Trafalgar	**Puggie**
Chevy	**Chips**
Señor Esteban	**Mickey**
Bandit	**Miss Lucy**
Elvis *	**Jagger**
Molly	**Kesey**
Annie	**The Puerto Morelos Brat Pack**
Jordy	

* Only part-dog

Contents

PART 2: Top Dogs 🦴 75

PART 3: Breeds and Breeding 🦴 139

PART 4: Tender Loving Care and Training 🦴 233

Acknowledgments

Dog people are a breed unto themselves — generous, thoughtful, supportive, and clever. These kind souls, who assisted us throughout, are our heroes:

Kira Sexton, who worked tirelessly editing our initial draft, fact-checking, and ensuring that our sensibility — our love of dogs and a sincere appreciation of their contributions to society and individuals alike — was present throughout. We are grateful to her for her help.

William O'Reilly, DVM, acted as our medical expert in residence. His professional advice and contributions ensure that *Planet Dog* will be as useful as it is entertaining, and we are grateful to him not only for his kindness in helping with our book but also for always making our little friends feel happy and secure in his care.

Lori Sash-Gail, dog trainer and photographer extraordinaire, was always willing to jump in with advice. Thanks, Lori, for your good cheer throughout and especially for gracing these pages with your amazing photographs.

Shannon Garrahan, Dave Marsh, and Susan Levy are among the most committed dog lovers we know, and being members of their extended families meant spending time with — and getting to love — their dogs. Coco, Trafalgar, Annie, Mollie, and Penny-Belle each had a special lesson to teach us, and we are humbled by their wisdom.

Would that all writers were lucky enough to land editors with the talent and creativity of Susan Canavan. She shared our vision from the start, and her support throughout was always uplifting. We're grateful to Susan; to Sarah Gabert; to Will Vincent; to Alison Miller, our patient and most able copy editor; to the detail-oriented Laura Noorda; and to all those at Houghton Mifflin who have cheered us on and lent their talents to *Planet Dog.*

In designing this book, Lisa Diercks helped turn our text and art into a lively tour of Planet Dog. We thank her for her hard work, for her thoughtful contributions, and for communicating the spirit of our work so perfectly.

Casey Choron and Livnat Hai, Morris and Sonia Choron, Kathi Goldmark and Sam Barry, the Baers, and the Fabulous Cherries made us want to write a book that would make them proud. We hope we did that.

We're grateful to the following contributors for their material, time, expertise, and especially for their dogged enthusiasm:

George and Wendy Rodrigue for "What I've Learned from Painting a Blue Dog"

Martha Thomases for "6 Superdogs"

Mathilde de Cagny for "The Trouble with Moose"

Roy Blount, Jr. for "5 Reasons Why I Can't List My Favorite Dogs"

Sarah Watson and pdsa.org.uk for "Dickin Medal Winners"

Barbara Kolk, AKC librarian, for information about dog show personalities

Alvin Grossman for "3 Kinds of Conformation Dog Shows," "How a Conformation Dog Show Works," and "An Early History of Conformation Dog Shows"

Fiona Pearce and the Kennel Club of London for "All About Crufts," reproduced with the kind permission of the Kennel Club.

David Frei and the Westminster Kennel Club for "The Story of the Westminster Kennel Club," "8 Special Trophies and Awards Given at Westminster," and "Westminster Stats"

Shirley Bell and James Veraldi, of Eden Kennels of Ontario for "Basic Dog Show Terminology," copyright © Bellcrest Web Design (reprinted with permission)

Randi Moore for "20 Things Every Junior Handler Should Know"

Patie Ventre and the World Canine Freestyle Organization, Inc. (WCFO), for "How to Prepare for the Musical Canine Freestyle"

Susan Netboy of the Greyhound Protection League for "6 Greyhound Racing Myths"

Frank Ross and AlaskaStock.com for "Highlights of the Iditarod," "5 Multiple Iditarod Winners," and "5 Recent Iditarod Champions"

G. V. Williams and Dean Fritz, of the Saint Bernard Club of Alaska, for "World Weight Pull Records"

William Harper for "What Is Schutzhund?"

Lorraine Hill and PetWebsite.com for "Basic Biology of the Dog"

Robert Keely and the American Kennel Club (www.ack.org) for "How a Breed Becomes Recognized by the AKC"

Marko Kulik for "Life Expectancy of 68 Popular Dog Breeds." Copyright © 2004 www.pets.ca, Canada's pet information center.

Stacey Wolf for "Astrology for Dog People"

Sharon Maguire and DogBreedInfo.com for "The 45 Best Dogs for Allergy Sufferers," "10 Dogs to Avoid if You Suffer from Allergies," "12 Dogs Who Don't Like Strangers," "34 Dogs for Couch Potatoes," "29 Dogs Who Hate Cats," and "22 Droolers"

Deborah Wood for "The 10 Best Date Bait Breeds" and "The 5 Worst Date Bait Breeds." From *The Dog Lover's Guide to Dating: Using Cold Noses to Find Warm Hearts* by Deborah Wood. Copyright © 2003. Reprinted with permission of Wiley Publishing, Inc., a subsidiary of John Wiley & Sons, Inc.

Jana Seikel and PetsAndPeople.com for "15 Breeds to Avoid if You Have Children"

Stanley Coren for "The 10 (Reputedly) Least Intelligent Dog Breeds," "The 10 Most Intelligent Breeds," "Breeds to Match Your Personality Type," and "Canine Partners for Your Vocation"

Scott Zucker and PetPlace.com for "Top 10 Lap Dogs," "Top 20 Dog Breeds for Outdoor Life," "Top 20 Dog Breeds for Apartment Living," and "Lifetime Costs of Dog Ownership." Reprinted with permission from Intelligent Content Corp. Copyright © 1999–2004 Intelligent Content Corp. All rights reserved.

Betty Corson and AkPharma, Inc., for "The 10 Gassiest Dogs"

The Humane Society of the United States (HSUS) for "What You Can Do About Puppy Mills," "10 Examples of Bad Breeding," "The Top 10 Considerations in Caring for Your Dog," "20 Tips for Preparing Your Dog for a New Baby," "Myths About Spaying and Neutering," "16 Things You Can Do to Keep Your Dog Safe," "10 Ways to Prevent Your Kids from Being Bitten by a Dog," and "What to Do When You Find a Stray Dog." Reprinted by permission of the Humane Society of the United States.

Melissa McMacken and VetCentric.com for "8 Reasons Not to Breed Your Dog"

Barbara Denzer and CrazyPetPress.com for "10 Dog Breeds with the Most Misleading Names"

Lonnie Olson and DogScouts.com for "The 4 Worst Reasons to Get a Dog"

Susan Hosman and Weimaraner Rescue of North Texas (WeimRescueTexas.org) for "How to Buy a Purebred Puppy"

Kathy Podolski and NaturalDogTreats.com for "How to Estimate Your Dog's Age"

Annmarie Mikelski and WhiteShepherdRescue.org for "25 Poor Excuses for Giving Up a Dog"

Margaret Muns and PetLoss.com for "11 Ways to Cope with the Death of Your Dog"

Kenneth Phillips and DogBiteLaw.com for "12 Ways to Avoid Legal Problems with Your Dog" and "Dog Bite Statistics"

Marshall H. Tanick, of Mansfield Tanick & Cohen, National Counsel for the American Dog Owners Association, Minneapolis, Minnesota, for "The 6 Most Misunderstood Aspects of Dog Law"

Kristina Vourax and the Dumb Friends League for "Developmental Stages of Puppy Behavior" and "Tips for Dealing with Doggy Stains and Odors"

Mark Weston and SiriusDog.com for "21 Tips to Help You Socialize Your Puppy"

Andy "The Dog Man" Luper, of A Canine Academy International, and CyberDog.com for "16 Basic Training Tips"

Bash Dibra for "How to Read Your Dog's Body Language." Adapted with the permission of Simon & Schuster Adult Publishing Group, from *Dogspeak: How to Learn It, Speak It, and Use It to Have a Happy, Healthy, Well-Behaved Dog.* Copyright © 1999 by Bashkim Dibra. All rights reserved.

Martin Deeley and DogPro.org for "20 Noted Dog Trainers"

Jennifer Schneider and PickOfTheLitterDogTraining.com for "10 Types of Dog Collars"

Sue Carney, of the New Hampshire SPCA, for "Understanding and Controlling Excessive Barking"

Mary Schilder and the Progressive Animal Welfare Society (Paws.org) for "6 Problems Caused by Isolating Your Dog"

Linda Glass and BlindDogs.com for "13 Tips for Training a Blind Dog"

Susan Cope Becker for "8 Tips for Training a Deaf Dog"

Diane Blackman and Dog-Play.com for "How to Create a Dog Park in Your Community"

Gary Merrick and SouthBayDogParks.org for "Top 10 Reasons Dog Haters Should Support Dog Parks"

Trevor Monk and Dogs-And-Diets.com for "6 Dog Food Choices" and "How Much Should You Feed Your Dog?"

Vicky Dupuis and seefido.com for "5 Great Recipes for Homemade Dog Biscuits"

Richard Webster for "7 Tests to Determine if Your Dog Is Psychic." From *Is Your Pet Psychic? Developing Psychic Communication with Your Pet* by Richard Webster. Copyright © 2002. Reprinted with permission from Llewelyn Worldwide, Ltd., St. Paul, Minn., www.llewellyn.com. All rights reserved.

Laurie Sash-Gail for "How to Photograph Your Puppy"

Tanya Brown for "The Cheap-'n'-Easy Dog Bed." Copyright © 2000 by Tanya A. Brown. Reprinted by permission of the author. All rights reserved.

Dave Barry for "Dave Barry's Deep Thoughts on Dog Behavior." Copyright by Dave Barry. Reprinted with permission.

Tara Kain and DogFriendly.com for "10 Rules of Etiquette for Traveling with Your Dog"

Larry Ash and DoghousePlans.com for "The Ideal Outdoor Doghouse"

Dr. Jeffrey Proulx, of the San Francisco SPCA, and Fawn Pierre for "16 Questions to Ask Before You Hire a Professional Dog Walker." Reprinted with kind permission of the *Oakland Tribune* and ANG Newspapers.

Charlotte Reed for "Choosing a Pet Sitter"

Arden Moore for "5 Ways to Help Your Dog Deal with Divorce"

Lexiann Grant for "Physics for Dogs"

Wendy Brooks and VeterinaryPartner.com for "The Top 10 Major Advances in Dog Health Care"

Kay Swann and LifestyleBlock.co.nz for "13 Dog Wound Treatment Basics"

Brent Ablett, of Animal Control, Christchurch City Council, New Zealand, for "What to Do if You Are Being Attacked by a Dog"

Paula Leahy for "Signs of Distemper." Copyright © 2005 HealthCommunities.com, Inc. Reprinted with permission. All rights reserved.

We owe a special debt of gratitude to these individuals, who assisted us by contributing their time and sharing their valuable professional experiences:

Suzanne Clothier, of FlyingDogPress.com

Maureen Hill-Hauch, of the American Dog Owner's Association

Barbara Kolk, of the AKC Library

Arden Moore, of byarden.com, author of *Happy Dog: How Busy People Care for Their Dogs, Real Food for Dogs,* and *Dog Training: A Lifelong Guide*

William O'Reilly, DVM

Robin Schwartz

Ruth Silverman, noted photographer and former associate curator of the International Center of Photography

Connie Vanacore, author of *Who's Who in Dogs*

Jack and Wendy Volhard, authors of *Dog Training for Dummies*

We are grateful to all those who contributed photographs and artwork:

Please note that unless otherwise indicated the images in this book belong to the authors' private collection and/or are in the public domain. Best efforts have been made to contact the rightsholders in all cases.

Cartoons by Mark Parisi. Copyright © Mark Parisi. Reprinted with permission. For many more dog cartoons, please visit offthemark.com.

George and Wendy Rodrigue for the "Blue Dog" illustration *A Pack of Oak Groves.* Copyright © George Rodrigue.

Cover art from *Bark if You Love Me* by Louise Bernikow. Published in 2000 by Algonquin Books of Chapel Hill. Reprinted by permission of Algonquin Books of Chapel Hill.

Cover art from *Dog Miracles* by Brad Steiger and Sherry Hansen Steiger. Copyright © 2001. Used by permission of Adams Media. All rights reserved.

Cover art from *My Therapist's Dog* by Diana Wells. Published in 2004 by Algonquin Books of Chapel Hill. Reprinted by permission of Algonquin Books of Chapel Hill.

Cover art from *Old Friends* by Mark Asher. Copyright © 2004 by Mark Asher. Used with permission of Chronicle Books L.L.C., San Francisco, Calif. Visit www.ChronicleBooks.com.

The following individuals and Web sites were helpful in providing us with information, ideas, and kind support. The range of information you'll find in *Planet Dog* is largely due to their generous assistance:

Dale Adams

Jan A. Allinder, of Digital Imaging Group

Jane Anderson, of Bluegrace Portuguese Water Dogs

Helga Andresdottir, of the Icelandic Kennel Club

Melissa Bain, DVM, DAVB, of the Companion Animal Behavior Program at UC Davis School of Veterinary Medicine

Mike Banks, of PetFinder.com

Susan Cope-Becker

Lori Blake, of NAHEE.org

Kim Bloomquist

Nicko Christenfeld, of the Department of Psychology, University of California, San Diego

Bill Cook, of the Trenton (New Jersey) Thunder Baseball Club

Carolyn Cusick, of Aberdeen Kennels

Mike Davies, Managing Director of Provet Ltd.

Lawrence Frederick, president of Disc-Connected K9s

Soravia Graziella, of the Federation Cynologique Internationale

Susan Hosman

Ashfaq Ishaq, Ph.D., executive director of the International Child Art Foundation

Steve Kelly, of HollywoodPaws.com

Emily Kerridge, of Nefer-Temu Kennels

Chris Kingsley, of PetsWelcome.com

Dave "The Dog Man" Klein

Dan Lago

Margery Leest

David Lim

Jennifer McClure and Yvonne Taylor, of People for the Ethical Treatment of Animals (PETA)

Julia Marston and Marian Probst, of the Fund for Animals

Jennifer Metzger, of GuideDogs.com

Jeri Moore, president of the Black-and-Tan Coonhound Club

Cathy Nelson

Limor Paldi, of the Israeli Kennel Club

Karen Peak and the Safe Dogs Project

Anna Quigley and Lyn Richards, of DogLogic.com

John Ryan, of *New York Dog* magazine

Evelyn Sanford, of Yankee Golden Retriever Rescue, Inc.

Dale G. Smith, of Flyball.org

Heather Smith, of the United States Dog Agility Association

Wilson Tan, of DogTracker.com

David Tayman, DVM, of PetsHealth.com

Greg Tresan, of the International Disk Dog Handlers Association

Cindy Vierra, of Von Diamant Rottweilers

Dr. John Wedderburn, of the Asian Animal Protection Network

Ben at 4netcom.net

Introduction

The marvelous creature known as *Canis familiaris* occupies a special place in the human heart. In addition to providing companionship and protection, amusement, and labor, dogs work right alongside us, always striving to make our lives better. Military dogs have been joining their humans in battle for thousands of years, and more recently, on September 11, 2001, rescue dogs entered Ground Zero to lead some survivors to safety and dig through rubble to find others. German Shepherd Dogs guide the blind, and Beagles sniff our luggage for illegal contraband. And if we lose our way, Bloodhounds will willingly track us down.

In our homes, parks, and even our places of work, pet dogs have taken over our time, our space, and even our food. No longer relegated to a doghouse in the yard, the dog now occupies prime real estate in our homes, from a perch in the dining room to a cushion on the bed. We dress our pooches in the latest fashions, put them on homemade diets, and provide them with holistic treatments from acupuncture to hydrotherapy. But where did these special helpmates — and roommates — come from?

The dog we know and love today can be traced back 40 million years to a weasel-like animal called the Miacis who thrived during the Euocece epoch. A tree dweller who also occasionally lived in dens, Miacis is also an ancestor of cats, raccoons, walruses, weasels, and the catlike Asian civet, as well as bears, hyenas, wolves, foxes, jackals, and the Australian dingo. During the Oligocene era some 20 million years later, the Miacis evolved into the Cynodictis, an animal with forty-two teeth and the same kind of anal glands that are found in today's domesticated dog.

The Cynodictis later evolved into the Tomarctus, a direct forebear of the genus *Canis,* which includes the wolf, the jackal, and the dog. During the Pleistocene epoch, the members of the genus *Canis* evolved closely to their present form.

Archaeological findings in areas as diverse as China and England suggest that wolves and humans initially shared hearth and home some 400,000 to 500,000 years ago. The first relationship between them was probably based on a mutual need for shelter and protection. As the human race struggled to survive, the intelligence and adaptability of the wolf made life simpler. Hunting became easier, since wolves proved to be wonderful trackers. Unafraid of humans, these wolves eventually evolved into what we now know as *Canis familiaris,* the domesticated dog.

The oldest known dog bones were found in Asia and date as far back as approximately 10,000 B.C., while the first recognizable dog breed appeared about 9,000 years ago and was probably a lanky, Greyhound-type dog used for hunting. By 4500 B.C., five distinct types of dogs existed: wolf-dog hybrids, Mastiffs, Greyhounds, pointers, and herding dogs.

Today there are more than four hundred recognized breeds, each with a distinctive set of characteristics, as well as thousands of mixed-breed dogs — each a true original — and they fit into our lives myriad ways. This book explores them all: how we include them in our culture, how we celebrate them, how we raise them, how we care for them, and even how we grieve for them when they leave us.

Welcome to Planet Dog.

Planet Dog

Part One

The Culture
of Dogs

"Outside of a dog, a book is man's best friend. Inside of a dog it's too dark to read."
—GROUCHO MARX

If you have any doubt about whether dogs have infused every aspect of our consciousness and culture, this chapter should put them to rest once and for all.

From early cave art to superstitions that have survived centuries, dogs have helped us express our fears, our hopes, and our questions about the universe. We think about them in order to make sense of ourselves, giving meaning to their presence in our dreams, and we find their form in the constellations that dot the sky. Lassie, Old Yeller, and Toto, and more recently Beethoven, Hooch, Scooby-Doo, and Skip, are all members of our "Canis Film Festival." In the same vein, writers from Dashiell Hammet and Christopher Morley to Stephen King and Carl Hiassen have made enduring literary heroes of the dogs they have depicted in their stories. Superdogs show up regularly on TV, in advertising, in comics, and in our music. Even our language is canine-conscious; we say, "I'm sick as a dog" and "It's a dog-eat-dog world" to drive home our points, unable to forget about dogs, it seems, even for a moment. Advertisers have always known of this special connection; Francis Barraud tipped them off back in 1899 when he created Nipper, who would go on to be the most recognizable dog of all time and lead the way for dogs who help sell us everything from floor wax to cars.

Just as it would be impossible to include here the thousands of dogs who have sparked our imagination, we cannot possibly list all the ways in which we have been shaped by how we think about dogs. This chapter is about some of the respects in which we oftentimes forget where we end and our dogs begin.

A BRIEF HISTORY OF THE RELATIONSHIP BETWEEN DOGS AND HUMANS

Archaeological findings in China and England, among other sites, tell us that the relationship between man and wolf dates back some 400,000 to 500,000 years and that it was based on the shared need for shelter and protection. As the human race struggled to survive, the intelligence and adaptability of the wolf made life simpler for people. Hunting became easier, since wolves proved to be wonderful trackers. But as the wolves became more and more popular for domestic purposes, humans noticed that some of the cubs were wilder than others. In what we today call selective breeding, the wilder cubs were killed or driven away while the tamer cubs were trained and allowed to remain with humans. By the Stone Age, humans had tamed dogs primarily to help them track game, thus marking the incidence of the first domestication of animals; and by the Bronze Age (4500 B.C.), five different types of dogs existed: Mastiffs, wolf-type dogs, Greyhounds, pointing dogs, and shepherding dogs.

9 Dog Superstitions

1. If you scratch a dog before you go job-hunting, you'll get a good job.

2. A strange dog walking into your house portends a new friendship.

3. Meeting a dog — especially a Dalmatian — is considered good luck.

4. A dog eating grass means it will rain soon.

5. If you see three white dogs together at the same time, you will have good luck.

6. If a newborn baby is licked by a dog, the baby will be a fast healer.

7. A Greyhound with a white spot on her forehead brings wealth.

8. If a dog scratches herself and seems sleepy, there'll soon be a change in the weather.

9. A dog who growls for no apparent reason is growling at a spirit.

4 Children Who Were Raised by Dogs

1. In 1996 Ivan Mishukov, just four years old, was abandoned by his parents. He survived by begging for food in the streets of Moscow. During this time he found that he was most at home living with stray dogs, with whom he shared his food. He told social workers that he was better off with the dogs because they loved and protected him. His bond with these dogs was so strong that it took more than a month for the police to totally separate him and his canine companions.

2. In 1920 two girls living in India named Amala and Kamala were discovered living with a she-wolf. Reverend J.A.L. Singh spotted a mother wolf and cubs, two of which had long and matted hair and looked human. The girls that he discovered were nocturnal, walked on all fours, and had large calluses on their knees and palms. They were partial to raw meat, drank by lapping up liquids with their tongues, and ate in a crouched position. They were eventually taken to an orphanage in Mindapore.

3. A two-year-old by the name of Prateep Chumnoon living in the Thai province of Nakhon Si Thammarat was partially raised by his impoverished grandmother's dog. She would leave him while she went off to work. She left him with the dog so often that Prateep began making dog rather than human sounds. When his plight was revealed, he was sent to a welfare center.

4. A Chilean boy who was abandonded as a baby survived in a cave for eleven years with the aid of a family of fifteen stray dogs who lived near the port of Talcahuano on Chile's Pacific coast and found and adopted him shortly after his birth. They taught him to scavenge for food in the same way they did, and one of the dogs even allowed him to nurse from her.

Barbara Bush's book about her English Springer Spaniel, **Millie's Book**, was on the bestseller list for twenty-nine weeks. Millie was the most popular "first dog" in history.

During the reign of the early Greek and, later, Roman empires, dogs took on new roles, as they began to be raised not only as hunters, herders, and guardians but now as beloved pets. Images of dogs were prominent in the art of these cultures, and early Greek medicine employed dogs to tell whether someone was living or dead (it was believed that a wagging tail indicated life). In Greece, fifty dogs protected the fortress known as Corinth. They saved the city when it was attacked, and the one surviving dog was given a pension for life and a silver collar. The Romans used their dogs for war purposes, often in Europe, and as the dogs traveled around the world to various battle sites, they began mating with European dogs, creating many new breeds. Soon the Romans began collecting dogs from all corners of the world. In A.D. 391, Quintas Aurelis Symmachus, the Roman consul, wrote to thank his brother for seven Irish Wolfhounds, saying that "all Rome viewed them with wonder."

Asiatic breeds appeared in Europe around the fourth century, contributing many of the curly coats we've come to love today. In the Far East, the kind of life a dog led was determined by its breed. The Chow Chow was routinely employed as a hunter, and the Shar-Pei found favor as a fighter and as dinner. Pekingese and Japanese Chins were considered so important that they had their own servants. Then, as now, they were often carried along trade routes as gifts for kings and emperors. In nearby Tibet, the Tibetan Terrier was so loved for the good luck it purportedly brought that it could not be bought or sold for any price.

"Beware of silent dogs and still waters."
— PORTUGUESE PROVERB

After the fall of the Roman Empire, when human survival became more important than breeding and training dogs, abandoned dogs commonly roamed the streets in search of food, and these, in packs, often terrorized townspeople, resulting in the many superstitions that arose around dogs. Legends of werewolves emerged during this period, as the uneducated began blaming dogs for their misfortune.

But dogs prevailed; with their proficiency at so many skills, monasteries started to see dogs as a source of revenue and began to breed them, most notably Bloodhounds, for sale to the nobility. Dogs became expensive, and hunting became the province of only the rich. The mixed breeds of peasants were required to wear heavy blocks around their necks to prevent them from breeding with "noble" dogs.

"Ever consider what dogs must think of us? I mean, here we come back from a grocery store with the most amazing haul —chicken, pork, half a cow. They must think we're the greatest hunters on earth!"
— ANNE TYLER

During the Crusades, dogs taken from the Holy Land were bred with others there, resulting in the hounds and spaniels of today. Further breeding produced dogs that could hunt a wide variety of animals, and peasants pursued small, ferocious breeds that were able to control the rat population.

In Europe, the Middle Ages saw the purebred dog become the prized possession of kings, noblemen, and church officials as a new use was developed for the dog when hunting for sport became popular. The Bloodhound traces back to the St. Hubert hounds of the seventh century A.D., when everybody who was anybody kept his own pack of hounds. The English Mastiff and Greyhound became standardized, recognizable breeds at this time, as did a few of the herding breeds. The lap dog finally became popular in Europe as the ladies of

The most dogs ever owned by one person were 5,000 Mastiffs owned by Kubla Khan.

the court took to them as "comforters." Even the dog collar became a measure of the dog's importance; some were made of gold, silver, white leather, and velvet. The Great Dane and the Mastiff accompanied their masters into battle fitted with spiked collars and, occasionally, their own suits of armor. A number of breeds were developed for sport of another kind — bull and bear baiting, as well as rat catching and pit fighting.

Early church documents from this period show that it was common for parishioners to bring their dogs to church with them as foot warmers. Those churches that didn't welcome animals required parishioners bearing them to sit outside for services. Thus began the custom of the Blessing of Animals on church steps, a practice that is still popular today. Dogs figured prominently enough in daily life that they became the objects of a number of laws. For instance, the ownership of a Scottish Deerhound or Greyhound was kept off-limits for all but the nobility. And there were laws on the books that decreed that certain sizes of dogs kept near the king's forests had to be crippled to prevent their being used for poaching. Only dogs small enough to jump through a hoop of a set size were allowed to go unharmed.

Dogs were especially popular with the nobility during the Renaissance for their value as companions, and this period saw many new breeds, as monarchs developed their favorite types. King Charles had spaniels named after him, and when Charles IX of France lost his beloved Griffon, he declared a royal day of mourning.

But after the French Revolution, when many monarchs were killed, the specialty breeds went into decline and gun dogs (developed by crossing Greyhounds with Braques) and pointing dogs replaced them in popularity, as peasants were now able to hunt and move about freely.

Many-headed dog, gouache on linen, ca. 1800

In the nineteenth century, an interest in creating lost breeds and developing new ones for specific purposes led to the emergence of many new breeds. The first dog show was held in 1859, ensuring the longevity of the most popular breeds and the permanence of an international dog lovers' community.

DOGS IN ANCIENT CULTURES

Dogs played a major role in ancient cultures and religions, so it's no surprise that today you can have your dog blessed at a church during the feast day of St. Francis of Assisi, the patron saint of animals, or that some clergy go beyond blessing animals and actually perform weddings and other religious rituals for them. The first dog chapel was established in 2001. It was built in St. Johnsbury, Vermont, by Stephen Huneck, a folk artist and children's book author whose five dogs helped him recuperate from a serious illness. The chapel is dedicated to them and is operated according to its official doctrine: "All creeds, all breeds, no dogma."

In 2003, the American Academy of Religion offered a scholarly discussion of the roles of animals in religion at their annual convention, a first, and in 2004, an edict in the Middle East declared that dogs — just like the women there — must wear burquas covering all but their eyes and ears. Following is an abbreviated history of the tradition from whence such ideas have sprung.

Fu Dog, ca. 1900

The Far East

Dogs were important participants in early Chinese religion, folklore, and mythology. In Asian superstitions, black dogs hold the eerie, slightly sinister role that black cats have long held in Europe. The "Fu Dog," a mystical part-lion, part-canine creature, recurs in Chinese culture as a protector of the home and of small children. In contemporary life, Fu Dog statues are very popular with practitioners of Feng Shui. These statues are placed next to windows and doorways (either inside or outside) to keep success close and evil at bay.

In the ancient Far East, a dog's life depended entirely on his breed. The noble Chow Chow was a hunter, and the Shar-Pei was popular as a fighter. Dogs with

10 Characteristics of People Born in the Year of the Dog

According to Chinese astrology, people born during the Year of the Dog (1922, 1934, 1946, 1958, 1970, 1982, 1994, 2006) exhibit the following characteristics.

1. Have a fierce sense of loyalty to those they love

2. Are honest in all things

3. Are generous with themselves and with their time

4. Have selfish tendencies

5. Don't particularly care about money but always seem to do well

6. Can be aloof and standoffish at parties

7. Exhibit great leadership qualities

8. Can be overly critical

9. Have a strong sense of duty

10. Don't adjust well to change

42 Celebrities Born in the Year of the Dog

Andre Agassi 1970

Candice Bergen 1946

Buddha 563 B.C.

George W. Bush 1946

Susan Canavan 1970

Mariah Carey 1970

Cher 1946

Harry Choron 1946

Connie Chung 1946

Winston Churchill 1874

Bill Clinton 1946

Confucius 551 B.C.

Matt Damon 1970

Rodney Dangerfield 1921

Claude Debussy 1862

Sally Field 1946

Benjamin Franklin 1706

Zsa Zsa Gabor 1917

Judy Garland 1922

George Gershwin 1898

Alexander Hamilton 1703

Ethan Hawke 1970

Herbert Hoover 1874

Michael Jackson 1958

Al Jolson 1888

Jennifer Lopez 1970

Sophia Loren 1934

Madonna 1958

Norman Mailer 1923

Liza Minelli 1946

David Niven 1909

Gary Oldman 1959

Prince 1958

Linda Ronstadt 1946

Claudia Schiffer 1970

Norman Schwarzkopf 1934

Socrates 469 B.C.

Sylvester Stallone 1946

Sharon Stone 1958

Mother Theresa of Calcutta 1910

Uma Thurman 1970

Shelly Winters 1922

short muzzles and stylized ears who resembled today's Pekingese, Pugs, and Japanese Chins held a special place at court. Even today, one kind of Pekingese is referred to as a "sleeve" because in the royal court of China, these dogs were bred extra small to fit into an empress's sleeve, which is how they were commonly carried around the palace.

A great deal of the dog's early domestication took place in ancient China, where the first pack-hunting dogs were bred. Both dwarfing, as seen today in the Dachshund and Basset Hound, and miniaturization, as exemplified by breeds as disparate as the Miniature Poodle and the Shetland Sheepdog, first occurred in China. The Chinese created companion breeds as well as lap dogs whose sole purpose was to warm the lap of their people, usually individuals of high status. Dogs even received a prominent place in the Chinese and Japanese zodiacs as the eleventh of twelve creatures. Those born under the sign of the dog in Chinese astrology are considered to be loyal and discreet, if a little temperamental. The next three years of the dog begin in 2006, 2012, and 2018.

Greece

During the early Greek empire the dog was kept as a hunter, herder, guardian, and beloved pet. Homer wrote about the dog's fidelity in *The Odyssey,* when the hound Argus is the only one who recognizes his long-lost master, Odysseus, upon his return to Ithaca. In the city of Pompeii, destroyed when Mount Vesuvius erupted in A.D. 79, the bones of a real dog named Delta were discovered stretched out beside the remains of a child. Delta was identified by the silver collar around his neck.

Many early Greek myths feature dogs. Cerberus, the Greek guard dog of Hades, had three heads. The center head was in the shape of a lion's, while the other two were in the shape of a dog's and a wolf's, respectively. Xanthippus, the father of Pericles (the King of Athens), had a dog who swam beside his master's ship to the city of Salamis when the Athenians were forced to abandon their city. Upon his death, Xanthippus's dog was buried beside him. Other dogs or dog-related figures in Greek mythology include Hecate, Laelaps, Marea, Sirius, and Scylla.

Cerberus, from an amphora, ca. 510 B.C.

According to ancient Greek literature, when Odysseus arrived home after an absence of twenty years, disguised as a beggar, the only one to recognize him was his aged dog, Argus, who wagged his tail at his master and then died.

The Near East

The ancient Egyptians revered dogs. The god Anubis, whose responsibility it was to accompany souls of the deceased to the afterworld, was often depicted with a human body and the head of a dog. (When the Greeks invaded Egypt, they merged their dog-god Herms with Anubis to create a new god, Hermanubis, a human figure with the head of a dog who also presided over death.) When a pet dog died, his owners shaved off their eyebrows, smeared mud in their hair, and mourned aloud for days. Even commoners tried to scrape together the small fortune it took to embalm and mummify their dogs and have them buried in one of Egypt's many animal necropolises. At Abydos, the ancient burial ground for royalty, a part of the cemetery was set aside for the graves of dogs.

A tale from the ancient Near East tells of the Seven Sleepers, good Muslim boys who, in flight from the wicked emperor Decius, fall asleep in a cave. A faithful dog named Katmir remains alert and guards the entrance to the cave while the boys sleep—for 309 years!

One of the volumes of Zoroastrianism's Zend Avesta, the sacred books of the religion, is devoted to the care and breeding of dogs. The book warns: "Whosoever shall smite . . . a . . . dog . . . his soul when passing to the other world shall fly howling loudly and more sorely grieved than the sheep does in the lofty forest where the wolf ranges. . . . No soul will come and meet his departing soul and help it, howling and grieved in the other world; nor will the dogs that keep the Kinvad bridge help his departing soul howling and grieved in the other world" (from the *Vendidad*).

A celestial dog-demon, ca. 1900

"If I have any beliefs about immortality, it is that certain dogs I have known will go to heaven, and very, very few persons."
—JAMES THURBER

Muslims believe that Allah created animals and, therefore, each animal has been created for a specific purpose. It is considered the duty of human beings to respect Allah's creations and to protect, employ with dignity, and promote the well-being of the animals in his care. By doing so, humans thank Allah for his blessings.

Islam, though, is practiced mainly in a region of the world where rabies has always been endemic. Therefore, dogs aren't allowed to be kept in the house. In fact, in the current Islamic Republic of Iran, it is against the law to own a dog as a pet. If, however, you can prove that your pet is actually a guard dog (whether she's a Mastiff or a Chihuahua), this restriction doesn't apply.

According to Muslim custom, if the saliva of a dog touches you or any part of your clothing, you must wash the body part and the item of clothing that was touched by the saliva. It is necessary for every Muslim who owns animals, whether for work purposes or as pets, to provide adequate shelter, food, water, and, when needed, veterinary care for his animals. It is not permissible to use one's dog for dog fighting, as this causes them harm and violates their nature.

Europe

Christianity in Europe was greatly influenced by Roman mythology. By the third century A.D., Christian lore was rife with canine imagery: St. Dominic, St. Bernard of Menthon, and St. Christopher were often painted by Byzantine artists as having dog heads.

Folktales about the loyalty of the dog appeared throughout northern Europe. The Norse saga of Olaf Triggvason contains descriptions of the faithfulness of dogs, as does the story of Cavall, the favorite hound of the English king Arthur. In the saga of Gelert, the Welsh prince Llewellyn's great hound (proba-

Doggie Dreams and What They Portend

Dogs and images of them invade not only our consciousness and culture but our subconscious as well. These dream interpretations, based on both scientific findings and folklore, are further evidence that dogs will forever stir our imagination.

1. A vicious dog: You are facing unalterable misfortune.

2. You own a dog with fine qualities: You will soon possess wealth.

3. A Bloodhound is tracking you: You will succumb to a temptation.

4. A dog bites you: You will have a quarrel with a business or love relationship.

5. A lean, filthy dog: You have a bad conscience.

6. Barking dogs: Difficulties will follow.

7. Growling dogs: You are at the mercy of manipulative people.

8. The lonely baying of a dog: You will be separated from a friend.

9. Puppies: You will be happy in a relationship.

10. A dog show: You are about to enjoy good fortune.

11. A fancy pet dog: You will marry a fool.

12. Dogs and cats are fighting but then they stop and are able to get along: A disaster in your love life isn't far off.

13. A friendly white dog: For men, you will soon face a victory; for women, you will marry early.

14. Swimming dogs: Expect good fortune.

15. A dog kills a cat: A happy surprise is near.

16. Hounds are following you: You will have many admirers but no luck in love.

17. Getting bitten by a poodle: You are about to do something foolish.

18. A black or red dog: You are dreaming about a faithful friend.

19. Being led by a dog: You are aware of your inner strength.

20. A many-headed dog: You are taking on more responsibility than you can handle.

21. You are traveling somewhere and a dog is following you: You are in the company of loyal friends.

24 Biblical References to Dogs

The Bible has nothing good to say about dogs, and, interestingly, it references them only twenty-four times. The following are from both the Old Testament and the New Testament.

1. "For dogs have compassed me: the assembly of the wicked have inclosed me: they pierced my hands and my feet." (Psalms 22:16)

2. "Deliver my life from the sword, my precious life from the power of the dogs." (Psalms 22:20).

3. "That thy foot may be dipped in the blood of [thine] enemies, [and] the tongue of thy dogs in the same." (Psalms 68:23)

4. "As a dog returns to its vomit, so a fool repeats his folly." (Proverbs 26:11)

5. "Watch out for those dogs, those men who do evil, those mutilators of the flesh." (Philippians 3:2)

6. "Speaking of the New Heaven Jesus said, 'Outside are the dogs, those who practice magic arts, the sexually immoral, the murderers, the idolaters and everyone who loves and practices falsehood.'" (Revelation 22:15)

7. "And ye shall be holy men unto me: neither shall ye eat [any] flesh [that is] torn of beasts in the field; ye shall cast it to the dogs." (Exodus 22:31)

8. "Him that dieth of Jeroboam in the city shall the dogs eat; and him that dieth in the field shall the fowls of the air eat: for the LORD hath spoken [it]." (Kings 14:11)

9. "Him that dieth of Baasha in the city shall the dogs eat; and him that dieth of his in the fields shall the fowls of the air eat." (Kings 16:4)

10. "And thou shalt speak unto him, saying, Thus saith the LORD, Hast thou killed, and also taken possession? And thou shalt speak unto him, saying, Thus saith the LORD, In the place where dogs licked the blood of Naboth shall dogs lick thy blood, even thine." (Kings 21:19)

11. "And of Jezebel also spake the LORD, saying, The dogs shall eat Jezebel by the wall of Jezreel." (Kings 21:23)

12. "Him that dieth of Ahab in the city the dogs shall eat; and him that dieth in the field shall the fowls of the air eat." (Kings 21:24)

13. "And [one] washed the chariot in the pool of Samaria; and the dogs licked up his blood; and they washed his armour; according unto the word of the LORD which he spake." (Kings 22:38)

14. "And the dogs shall eat Jezebel in the portion of Jezreel, and [there shall be] none to bury [her]. And he opened the door, and fled." (2 Kings 9:10)

15. "Wherefore they came again, and told him. And he said, This [is] the word of the LORD, which he spake by his servant Elijah the Tishbite, saying, In the portion of Jezreel shall dogs eat the flesh of Jezebel." (2 Kings 9:36)

16. "But now [they that are] younger than I have me in derision, whose fathers I would have disdained to have set with the dogs of my flock." (Job 30:1)

17. "His watchmen [are] blind: they are all ignorant, they [are] all dumb dogs, they cannot bark; sleeping, lying down, loving to slumber." (Isaiah 56:10)

18. "Yea, [they are] greedy dogs [which] can never have enough, and they [are] shepherds [that] cannot understand: they all look to their own way, every one for his gain, from his quarter." (Isaiah 56:11)

19. "And I will appoint over them four kinds, saith the LORD: the sword to slay, and the dogs to tear, and the fowls of the heaven, and the beasts of the earth, to devour and destroy." (Jeremiah 15:3)

20. "Give not that which is holy unto the dogs, neither cast ye your pearls before swine, lest they trample them under their feet, and turn again and rend you." (Matthew 7:6)

21. "But he answered and said, It is not meet to take the children's bread, and to cast [it] to dogs." (Matthew 15:26)

22. "And she said, Truth, Lord: yet the dogs eat of the crumbs which fall from their masters' table." (Matthew 15:27)

23. "But Jesus said unto her, Let the children first be filled: for it is not meet to take the children's bread, and to cast [it] unto the dogs." (Mark 7:27)

24. "And she answered and said unto him, Yes, Lord: yet the dogs under the table eat of the children's crumbs." (Mark 7:28)

bly a burly Irish Wolfhound) was left at home with his son, Owain. Llewellyn returned to find blood on the dog's face and his son missing. He killed the dog, only to discover his son safe beside the body of a slain wolf. Llewelyn had a statue cast in Gelert's memory.

The Americas

Dogs play a variety of roles in many North and South American cultures. According to the Kato Indians of California, the world was created by the god Nagaicho, who afterward took a walk and made each living creature. But nowhere does the legend mention the creation of the dog, so the Kato, who cannot conceive of a world without dogs, came to the conclusion that Nagaicho must already have had a dog by his side when he set out to create the world.

The Mayans and Aztecs symbolized every tenth day with the dog; those born under this sign were believed to have outstanding leadership skills. The ancient Mbaya Indians of the Gran Chaco in South America believe that humans originally lived underground and saw the light of day only when dogs dug them up.

Guardian hounds occur commonly in shamanic otherworldly lore. The Altaic shaman encounters a dog that guards the underworld. When the Yukaghir shaman follows the road to the kingdom of shadows, he finds an old woman's house guarded by a barking dog. In Koryak shamanism, the entrance to the land of the dead is guarded by dogs. In Eskimo shamanism, a dog with bared teeth guards the entrance to the undersea land of Takakapsaluk, Mother of the Sea Beasts.

The Kankanai Igorots in the Philippines practically worshiped dogs and

A Dog Creation Theory

1. On the first day of creation, God created the dog.

2. On the second day, God created man to serve the dog.

3. On the third day, God created all the animals of the earth (especially the horse) to serve as potential food for the dog.

4. On the fourth day, God created honest toil so that man could labor for the good of the dog.

5. On the fifth day, God created the tennis ball so that the dog might or might not retrieve it.

6. On the sixth day, God created veterinary science to keep the dog healthy and the man broke.

7. On the seventh day, God tried to rest, but He had to walk the dog.

"If there are no dogs in heaven, then when I die I want to go where they went."
— UNKNOWN

"A dog has the soul of a philosopher."
— PLATO

"Heaven goes by favour. If it went by merit, you would stay out and your dog would go in."
— MARK TWAIN

Will All Dogs Go to Heaven?

A poll conducted by ABCNews/Beliefnet in 2001 revealed that as many as 40 percent of those questioned think heaven is reserved for people only. Theologians seem to disagree. In September 2003, the editors of *Dog Fancy* magazine put the question to various religious leaders and experts in what it termed an extension of the debate over "animal theology." Here are some of their thoughts on the subject.

1. "Heaven was designed for humans. The reason dogs may be there is for us, not for themselves. Dogs will go to heaven perhaps because of our relationship with them. I would think a loving God wants us to be happy and allows us to have animals that shared love with us."
— Rev. Brian T. McSweeney, vice chancellor of the New York archdiocese

2. "Everything, humans and animals, every blade of grass, all are endowed with a spirit and every spirit returns to its creator. . . . Every animal based on how it lives in this world will reap its reward, its divine bliss in the world to come."
— Rabbi Gershon Winkler, an exponent of mystical Judaism who lives in Cuba

3. "Dogs are subject to reincarnation . . . as well as the law of karma, which determines the form of the reincarnation. Dogs can go to heaven or dogs can go to hell. A dog's actions decide where it goes, like a human's actions."
— Lama Pema Wangak, director of New York's Tibetan Buddhist Center

4. "The vast majority of Southern Baptists believe only humans have souls, which most likely precludes dogs from reaching heaven. But the Bible notes that someday the lamb will lie down with the lion, which would lead you to believe that heaven may be somewhat like it is here, and there may be animals."
— Herb Hollinger, a spokesman for the Southern Baptist Convention

5. "I think the species as a whole is a natural shoo-in."
— Stephen H. Webb, associate professor of religion and philosophy at Wabash College and the author of *On God and Dogs*

gave them amulets to wear against sickness and danger. However, among some neighboring Igorot tribes, the dog, while considered sacred, was killed and eaten during sacrifices. This very different treatment was often a source of hostility among Igorot people.

Africa

African legends concerning dogs usually assign them extraordinary powers and therefore respect. A legend from the Nyanga people of the Congo tells of Rukuba, who, like all dogs at the time, could talk. When Rukuba was offered a permanent job as a messenger, he declined, fearing a future of servitude; from that day on, he and all dogs after him simply stopped talking. In other African cultures, dogs have always been believed to inhabit the world of the dead just as they do the living.

"Dogs are our link to paradise. They don't know evil or jealousy or discontent. To sit with a dog on a hillside on a glorious afternoon is to be back in Eden, where doing nothing was not boring — it was peace."
— MILAN KUNDERA

Judaism

According to the Old Testament, dogs guarded the flocks of the tribes of Israel, but nothing suggests that there was a bond between them and man. Most likely they were regarded as unclean scavengers.

Judaism places great stress on the proper treatment of all animals; pets are to be fed before people are fed. Animals are also entitled to a day of rest, so it is not permissible to have a dog, for instance, turn light switches off and on during the Sabbath. Pets may be fed nonkosher food. Since castrating males of any species is prohibited, as it represents unnecessary cruelty to animals, neutering of male and female dogs is prohibited.

The Old Testament book of Tobit tells us that when Tobias set off on a great journey, he was led by the angel Raphael and a small dog. After many years' travel, the dog ran ahead to herald his Tobias's return. The dog later preceded Tobias into Heaven.

The Hebrew Talmud recommends that dogs be respected because they miraculously refrained from barking (thereby not alerting the Egyptian guards) during the night the Israelites escaped from bondage in Egypt.

The first dog chapel was established in St. Johnsbury, Vermont, by Stephen Huneck, a folk artist and children's book author whose five dogs helped him recuperate from a serious illness. The chapel is dedicated to them and is operated according to its official doctrine: "All creeds, all breeds, no dogma."

A History of Dogs in Art

From 12,000-year-old cave paintings in Spain and North Africa to the graffiti art of the late Keith Haring, humans have been drawing, painting, sculpting, and photographing dogs throughout history. Perhaps it's because they provide so much inspiration; or maybe it's because in them we see so much of ourselves. Here is a vastly abbreviated history of the ways in which dogs have captured our collective artistic imagination.

JACKSON POLLOCK AND HIS ASSISTANT.

The Hittites and Assyrians depicted dogs on lion hunts on their sculpted reliefs.

The sophisticated early Chinese civilization embraced the dog in the form of the Fu Dog, a figure that was half dog and half lion who was thought to bring happiness and good fortune and who was often depicted in paintings, sculptures, and tapestries.

Another ancient people whose culture contains an extensive mythology about dogs were the Parsees of Persia. The Zoroastrianism religion was introduced to the Parsees — in what is now Iran — by a religious figure, Zarathustra, about 2,750 years ago. One of the volumes of the Zend Avesta, the sacred books of Zaroastrianism, is devoted entirely to the care and breeding of dogs.

Egyptian wall paintings and hieroglyphics appear to depict specific dog breeds. These mostly resemble our contemporary Mastiffs and Greyhounds. But there are some hieroglyphics that even resemble terriers and spitz-type dogs (dogs similar to our Samoyeds and Shiba Inus). Anubis, the dog-headed (jackal-headed, some argue) god of the dead, was also featured in many early Egyptian hieroglyphics.

Classical Greek pottery and sculpture featured stylized images of dogs; pictures of Cerberus, who guarded the gates of hell, is shown to have three wild-dog heads, along with a dragon for his tail and the heads of snakes all over his body. In ancient Greek frescoes, the goddess Diana is often shown accompanied by her hunting hounds.

By A.D. 1066, dogs had become a favorite subject among European artists. Tapestries depicting dogs were particularly popular. These were often associated with religious subject matter, as exemplified by various paintings of the Last Supper, in which Judas Iscariot often has a dog at his feet.

The Middle Ages produced bestiaries — illuminated manuscripts using animals to elucidate moral messages — and dogs featured prominently in these, as they did in the first treatises on hunting, which also appeared during this time. The most famous of these, *The Book of the Hunt,* by Gaston III, dates to 1405. Prayer books with illuminated calendars included domestic scenes of dogs and their people.

During the Renaissance, nobility and royalty often sat for portraits with their dogs — men with their hunting hounds to boast of wealth and stature; women with their lap dogs to show refinement and fidelity. Portraits of dogs became highly detailed, as is seen in the work of Leonardo da Vinci (1452–1519), who produced scientific and anatomical studies of dogs. Veronese (1528–1588) painted exquisite Greyhounds but never as the main subject of his paintings. Diego Velasquez (1599–1660) painted portraits of dogs often accompanied by children. Jan Van Eyck (1390–1441) and Albrecht Durer (1471–1528) were also fond of depicting canines.

By the beginning of the eighteenth century, British dog portraiture had come into its own, with some artists specializing in it. The paintings of George Stubbs (1724–1806), Thomas Gainsborough (1727–1788), John Boultbee (1753–1812), John Emms (1843–1912), and Sir Edwin Landseer (1726–1806) — probably the best-known animal painter of all time — became popular during this period. In addition to representing wealth and stature, dogs came to embody loyalty and sympathy. Dramatic paintings of suffering and bereavement often included a doleful dog. On the other side of the Atlantic, dogs were popular among American folk artists such as Amni Phillips (1837–1941).

In France, the earliest and most famous sculptor of the nineteenth-century Animalier School was Antoine-Louis Barye (1796–1876). His sculptures were usually of individual dogs or of dogs in hunting scenes. Paintings from this period often show Mastiffs pulling milk carts and working as beasts of burden.

Throughout the second half of the nineteenth century and through the early years of the twentieth, impressionists such as Pierre-Auguste Renoir (1840–1919) and Toulouse-Lautrec (1864–1901) created romantic visions of dogs. Charles van den Eycken (1859–1923) is considered one of the leading animal artists of the nineteenth century; his paintings depict playful puppies in domestic scenes. It was during this period that Francis Barraud (1856–1924), a photographer turned painter, cre-

Summer Snow Storm, Little Bear Ranch, McLeod, Montana, 1992 features Bruce Weber and Nan Bush's Golden Retrievers.

ated a portrait of Nipper, the Bull Terrier mix who had belonged to his late brother. The Royal Academy rejected "His Master's Voice" for exhibition, but it was later sold for use in advertising to the Gramophone Company in 1899. The portrait of Nipper has since become one of the most famous dog images of all time.

Victorian artists expressed many of their satirical messages and social comments through anthropomorphism, carrying it to a new extreme. They painted dogs dressed up and playing musical instruments, putting out fires, and, thanks to an otherwise unnotable artist of the period, Cassius Marcellus Coolidge, playing poker.

Dog portraiture played a smaller role in twentieth-century art when naturalism lost its popularity and modernism came into vogue. The ascendancy of

"If a picture wasn't going very well, I'd put a puppy dog into it."
— NORMAN ROCKWELL

photography also threatened the market for paintings of dog portraits. Nonetheless, modern artists from Pablo Picasso (1881–1973) to the painters Otto Dix (1891–1969) and Joan Miro (1893–1993), as well as the sculptor Alberto Giacometti, often used the canine form to explore abstraction. At the same time, realists such as Andrew Wyeth (b. 1917) and Alex Colville (b. 1920) and the bold pioneers Roy Lichtenstein, Andy Warhol, Alex Katz, and David Hockney all used dogs in their work.

Today, images of dogs are more popular than ever. Photographers from Bruce Weber to William Wegman keep dogs in the forefront of both fine and commercial art. George Rodrigue created a pop art idol when he first painted his Blue Dog in the 1980s, while Stephen Huneck immortalized his beloved Sally in popular woodcuts and children's books. Dogs are prominent in advertising, animation, and films. Whatever direction art takes, dogs always seem to follow along.

What I've Learned from Painting a Blue Dog

George Rodrigue's famous "Blue Dog" in a painting entitled *A Pack of Oak Groves*, 2004

George Rodrigue (b. 1944), famed pop artist, originally found inspiration in the cutting-edge creations of artists such as Andy Warhol and Roy Lichtenstein, as well as the dark folklore of Louisiana. It was a myth about a werewolf known as the *loup garou* that inspired Rodrigue to create his signature image, which has appeared in hundreds of his paintings. Rodrigue's work has been collected and exhibited around the world, and his books (including *The Art of George Rodrigue, Blue Dog,* and *Blue Dog Man*) are popular with children and adults alike. We're grateful to the artist for sharing some of his insights here.

1. True art can be anything I want it to be.

2. The older I get, the more young people relate to my work.

3. The Blue Dog is many things to many people, often having nothing to do with my intentions. Leonardo had his Mona Lisa. I have my Blue Dog.

4. Everyone knows dogs and everyone knows the color blue, but together they become magical. As many times as I've painted the Blue Dog, I'm still inspired to paint it again. Painting the Blue Dog exclusively has expanded my imagination and creativity.

5. It's not really a dog at all; Blue Dog might be ME!

6 Man-Bites-Dog Stories

1. According to the *South China Morning Post,* a man bit a dog to death in eastern China on April 12, 2004. The drunken man was on his way home after a night of carousing with his buddies when a dog attacked him by nipping at his fingers and face. He responded by pouncing on the dog and repeatedly biting him. The man's fate was unknown at the time of this writing.

2. On November 13, 2004, the *Kansas City Star* reported a story of Soty, a German Shepherd police dog that nearly lost an ear. Soty and his partner, Officer David Magruder, were both bitten while trying to arrest a man who had committed a minor crime. The suspect began punching Officer Magruder, who immediately called on Soty for

grabbed Renny, a German Shepherd Dog, by the throat and began choking her on the side of her neck. It was only after Officer Foster punched Russell in the face a couple of times that the dog was released. Renny was later treated by a vet, who insisted that he have a couple of days off to recuperate.

5. According to DogsInTheNews.com, in August of 2001 a Winston-Salem, North Carolina, man by the name of Nakia Miguel Glenn, suspected of driving under the influence, was apprehended by a police officer, who asked if he could search the vehicle. A fight broke out as the officer attempted to conduct the search, and he was bitten on the hand by Glenn. A police dog on the scene was re-

> ## "Revenge is often like biting a dog because the dog bit you."
> ### —AUSTIN O'MALLEY (1858–1932), AMERICAN OCULIST

help. When Soty arrived and bit the suspect, the man bit back, nearly amputating Soty's ear with his teeth. A Taser was finally used to subdue the suspect.

3. According to CNN.com, on December 14, 2004, a Gainsville, Florida, man apparently punished his Jack Russell Terrier, Lady, by allegedly biting one of her front paws. Police arrested him and charged him with animal cruelty. He explained that biting the dog was a way of training it not to bite. Duh!

4. On Monday, April 21, 2003, a thirty-three-year-old man was charged with biting a police dog outside a bar in Syracuse, New York. According to the Associated Press, Paul Russell was charged with assaulting and injuring a police animal. Russell

leased to help the officer but was bitten on the face by Glenn when it approached him. Glenn eventually went into seizures and required CPR after he ingested a bag of cocaine.

6. Another story from DogsInTheNews.com suggests that August of 2001 was an auspicious month for "man bites dog." A woman was walking her Scottish Terrier puppy, Alex, near her Tallahassee, Florida, home. Another terrier named Holly was out in the street and confronted the pair. Holly attacked Alex and locked her jaws around Alex's head. Margaret Hargrove tried unsuccessfully to pry Holly's teeth apart to release Alex. When that didn't work, Ms. Hargrove got down on all fours and bit Holly on the back of the neck. Alex and his mommy sustained minor injuries.

"Any man who does not like dogs and want them about does not deserve

Dogs and Their Presidents

Dogs have been helpful image boosters during election campaigns and faithful companions to our leaders. Only Millard Fillmore, Franklin Pierce, James Buchanan, Andrew Johnson, and Chester Arthur did not have pets while in office; others adopted not only dogs but also alligators, snakes, raccoons, and zebras. The dogs listed here all made it to the White House. For a lively, illustrated history of those dogs who bestowed their special gifts on the East Lawn, read *First Dogs: American Presidents and Their Best Friends,* by Roy Rowan and Brooke Janis.

Franklin Delano Roosevelt and Fala

"Children and dogs are as necessary to the welfare of the country as Wall Street and the railroads." —HARRY S. TRUMAN

George Washington — Mopsey, Taster, Cloe, Tipler, Forester, Captain, Lady Rover, Vulcan, Sweetlips, and Searcher, all Foxhounds

Thomas Jefferson — Briards and Foxhounds

James Monroe — unnamed spaniel

John Tyler — Le Beau, a Greyhound

Abraham Lincoln — Jip and Fido, breeds unknown

Ulysses S. Grant — Faithful, Jesse Grant's Newfoundland

Rutherford B. Hayes — Grim, a Greyhound; Duke, an English Mastiff; Hector, a Newfoundland; Dot, a terrier

Grover Cleveland — Unnamed Japanese Poodle

Benjamin Harrison — Dash and various dogs of unknown breeds

Theodore Roosevelt — Pete, a Bull Terrier; Sailor Boy, a Chesapeake Bay Retriever; Skip, a mixed breed; Manchu, a Pekingese; terriers named Jack and Peter

Woodrow Wilson — Davie, an Airedale

Warren Harding — Laddie Boy, an Airedale; and Old Boy, a Bulldog

Calvin Coolidge — Peter Pan, a terrier; Paul Pry, an Airedale; Rob Roy, a white Collie; Prudence Prim, a white Collie; Calamity Jane, a Shetland Sheepdog; Tiny Tim and Blackberry, both Chow Chows; Ruby Rough, a Collie; Boston Beans, a Bulldog; King Kole, a German Shepherd Dog; Bessie, a Collie; and Palo Alto, a setter

Herbert Hoover — King Tut, a German Shepherd Dog; Big Ben and Sonnie, both Fox Terriers; Glen, a Scottish Collie; Yukonan,

The largest and the smallest dogs to live in the White House both resided there during the tenure of James Buchanan. The president had a Newfoundland named Lara, and his niece, Harriet Lane (who served as White House hostess because the president was unmarried), had a tiny toy terrier named Punch.

to be in the White House."
— CALVIN COOLIDGE

"I care not for a man's religion whose dog and cat are not the better for it."
—ABRAHAM LINCOLN

John-John with Shannon on the White House lawn, March 1963

an Eskimo Dog; Patrick, a wolfhound; Eaglehurst Gillette, a setter; Weejie, a Norwegian Elkhound; and Pat, a German Shepherd Dog

Franklin Delano Roosevelt — Fala, a Scottish Terrier; Majora, a German Shepherd Dog; Meggie, a Scottish Terrier; Winks, a Llewellyn Setter; Tiny, an English Sheepdog; President, a Great Dane; and Blaze, a Mastiff

Harry S. Truman — Feller, a Cocker Spaniel; and Mike, Margaret Truman's Irish Setter

Dwight D. Eisenhower — Heidi, a Weimaraner

John F. Kennedy — Charlie, Caroline Kennedy's Welsh Terrier; and Shannon, an Irish Cocker Spaniel; plus Charlie's puppies: Blackie, Butterfly, Streaker, and White Tips. Also, Pushinka, a gift from the premier of Russia, who was the daughter of Laika, the first dog in space

Lyndon B. Johnson — Him and Her, both Beagles; Freckles, Him's

puppy; Blanco, a white Collie; Yuki, a mixed breed; J. Edgar, a mixed breed

Richard Nixon — Checkers, Nixon's dog while vice president; Vicky, a Poodle; Pasha, a Yorkshire Terrier; and King Timahoe, an Irish Setter

Gerald Ford — Liberty, a Golden Retriever

Jimmy Carter — Grits, a mixed breed (who lost his White House privileges for refusing to be housebroken)

Ronald Reagan — Lucky, a Bouvier des Flandres; and Rex, a Cavalier King Charles Spaniel

George Bush — Millie, a Springer Spaniel; Ranger and Spot, two of Millie's puppies

Bill Clinton — Buddy, a Chocolate Labrador

George W. Bush — Spot, Millie's daughter, an English Springer Spaniel; Barney, a Scottish Terrier; and Mrs. Beasley, a Scottish Terrier.

The Kennedys on vacation in August 1963 with their K-9 corps: Caroline with Irish Spaniel Shannon and Welsh Terrier Charlie; John-John with Pushinka's pups; Jackie with Clipper

"If you want a friend in Washington, get a dog." — HARRY TRUMAN

A History of War Dogs

When we go to war, our dogs also go to war, and this has been the case throughout history. From ancient times to modern ones, dogs have engaged in active service at the sides of their owners. They have been heroes and companions, displaying bravery under fire and saving our lives. The following list represents a vastly abbreviated history of canine contributions to the war effort.

Who first thought of using dogs to guide blind people? At the end of World War I, the German government trained the first guide dogs to assist blind war veterans.

Attila the Hun used giant Molossian dogs (precursors of Mastiffs), as well as Talbots (ancestors of the Bloodhound), in his campaigns, circa A.D. 500.

In Europe during the Middle Ages, Great Danes and Mastiffs were outfitted with armor and spiked collars. They frequently defended supply caravans.

An English Poodle named Boyce was the first famous war dog, accompanying his owner, Prince Rupert, throughout the English Civil War. He was so famous that Oliver Cromwell's opposing troops used pamphlets to vilify the dog.

During the Seven Years' War, the army of Frederick the Great used Russian dogs as messengers. Dogs became associated with national identity at this time to such an extent that in Holland the human "Keezens," who rose up against the House of Orange, were named after the national dog of Holland, the Keeshond.

British postcard from World War II

In the early part of the fourteenth century, the French navy used attack dogs in St. Malo, France, to guard naval dock installations. Such use of dogs was abolished in 1770 after a young naval officer was killed by one of these dogs.

Dogs, probably Mastiffs, helped the Spaniards conquer the Indians of Mexico and Peru. Later on, native North American Indians trained dogs for pack and draft work, as well as for sentry duty.

The first recorded American Canine Corp was formed during the Seminole (Indian) War of 1835, when the army used Cuban-bred Bloodhounds to track any Indians and runaway slaves in the swamps.

Early in the nineteenth century, Napoleon posted dogs as sentries at the gates of Alexandria, in Egypt, to warn his troops of attack. During the Napoleonic Wars, a Pug named Moustache delivered messages between the empress Josephine and Napoleon. Moustache was later decorated for his valiant service.

During the American Civil War, dogs were used as messengers, guards, and mascots (See "11 Civil War Dogs," page 78).

In 1884, the German army created the first organized military school to train war dogs at Lechernich, near Berlin. Thus, "Schutzhund," a very strict form of dog training (for mostly Doberman Pinschers and German Shepherd Dogs), was established. (See "What Is Schutzhund?" page 136.)

In 1898, during the Spanish-American War, Theodore Roosevelt's "Roughriders" used dogs as scouts in the jungles of Cuba.

By the early part of the twentieth century, most European countries were using dogs in armies and for police work.

In 1904, imperial Russia used ambulance dogs during the Russo-Japanese War. These dogs were trained by a British dog fancier who established England's first army dog at the start of World War I.

The United States didn't have an official dog training program when World War I broke out. Their forces bartered with the French, Belgian, and English armies for trained sentry and courier dogs. The most famous war dog of World War I was Stubby, a Pit Bull Terrier who became the mascot of the 102nd Infantry and distinguished himself in various battles in France. It was at this time that an American soldier rescued a German Shepherd Dog puppy who went on to become the matinee idol Rin Tin Tin. (See "The Rin Tin Tin Story," page 54.)

As dogs continue to shape our folklore, they become associated with issues of national identity and patriotism. In the United States and in Great Britain after World War I, the German Shepherd Dog was renamed the Alsatian in order to disassociate it from the enemy.

By World War II, American forces were ready. The army's K-9 Corps was established in 1942 and quickly set up facilities across the country, beginning with a station at Fort Royal, Virginia. The U.S. Marines and the Coast Guard quickly followed suit. Dogs had already proven to be of considerable value on the front lines, not only as sentries and couriers but also for the companionship they provided to soldiers. The canines performed brilliantly, with many achieving legendary status (see "Canine Heroes of World War II," page 79).

Almost all military dog training centers were closed by 1944 due to budget considerations and a general lack of interest. The army's Twenty-sixth Scout Dog Patrol was the only military dog training center active during the Korean War. All told, its members were awarded more than forty-five commendations for meritorious service. York, a German Shepherd Dog, was the most famous service dog of the era. He completed 148 combat patrols.

In 1965, dogs trained by the army, the air force, and the Marines began arriving in Vietnam. More than 4,000 canine sentries, scouts, and trackers acted as successful deterrents to Vietcong attacks on military installations.

When the Berlin Wall came crashing down on November 9, 1989, the Communist East German government used more than 5,000 dogs just to patrol the wall.

During the Gulf War, at least 1,177 highly trained German Shepherd Dogs were used by the French forces to guard and protect their troops, supplies, and aircraft.

In 2004 the AKC organized a relief effort to aid the working canines serving in Iraq after receiving word from a military veterinary technician overseas that "rest and relaxation" supplies were greatly needed. While the dogs are provided for in terms of basic care, many were without recreational toys and treats, which help alleviate stress and anxiety through play. Thirty boxes of various items — collected from the Hartz Mountain Corporation, Nylabone, the Iams Company, and Cherrybrook Pet Supply — were sent to kennels in two U.S. Army units, which maintain large kennels of K-9 teams. Items included disc flyer toys, AKC Christmas stockings, pull toys, rawhide chews, rubber chew toys, AKC-licensed treats, and glow-in-the-dark Frisbees, as well as blankets, cool-down towels, and water dishes.

Cat People
vs. Dog People

1. Cat people go on diets.
   Dog people work out.

2. Cat people leave a message and tell you when they'll be calling back.
   Dog people hang up.

3. Cat people drink white wine spritzers with a twist of lime.
   Dog people drink beer.

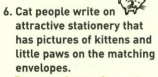

4. Cat people smoke Virginia Slims.
   Dog people gave up smoking.

5. Cat people swim.
   Dog people surf.

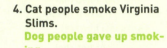

6. Cat people write on attractive stationery that has pictures of kittens and little paws on the matching envelopes.
   Dog people send a postcard.

7. Cat people go to Broadway shows.
   Dog people go to rock concerts.

8. Cat people go on the South Beach Diet.
   Dog people are on Atkins.

9. Cat people get pulled over for driving 45 mph in a 35-mph zone.
   Dog people can outrun the cop.

10. Cat people shop in department stores.
    Dog people know someone who can get it wholesale.

11. Cat people invest in money-market funds.
    Dog people can get a 3 percent bonus in addition to the regular annuity on their investments by rolling over their IRAs into short-term corporate accounts.

12. Cat people visit usps.com and print out their own postage.
    Dog people use FedEx.

13. Cat people plant annuals.
    Dog people plant perennials.

14. Cat people warn you that if you don't pay the bill within thirty days, they will turn your name over to their collections department.
    Dog people sue.

15. Cat people love *Old Yeller.*
    Dog people love *Cujo.*

16. Cat people listen to lite FM.
    Dog people listen to Sirius radio.

17. Cat people own PCs.
    Dog people have Macs.

18. Cat people will name it Ashley if it's a girl and Maximillian if it's a boy.
    Dog people just hope it's healthy.

19. Cat people turn off the TV at ten o'clock and read a book.
    Dog people fall asleep clutching the remote.

20. Cat people know how to tape shows automatically.
    Dog people have TiVo.

21. Cat people send Hallmark cards.
    Dog people send e-greetings.

22. Cat people patiently wait behind you as you purchase fourteen items at the six-items-and-under checkout line.
    Dog people will follow you to your car, tailgate you all the way home, and then yell, "I know where you live," as they speed off.

23. Cat people voted for Clay.
    Dog people voted for Reuben.

12 Urban Dog Legends

Urban legends spread quickly and are usually designed to horrify us, usually in fun. Tellers of these tales swear that these things really happened to a friend of a neighbor who lived next door to the second cousin of a guy who saw the whole thing. We don't vouch for any of these.

1. A widowed trapper returns home due to heavy snow and discovers that his large sled dog, who was entrusted with guarding the trapper's infant son, has fresh blood all over its mouth and the floor of the cabin is also drenched in blood. Believing that the dog killed his son, the trapper takes an ax to the dog, thereby killing it. He later hears his son crying and discovers a dead timber wolf clutching some of his dog's fur in its teeth. This tale originated in Wales during the Middle Ages.

2. An elderly woman accidentally kills her dog by attempting to dry it in a microwave oven.

3. A young woman, alone in her apartment, goes to bed with her dog on the floor beside her. Sometime during the night she wakes up to a strange sound. She is frightened but reaches down and, feeling her hand being licked by her dog, is comforted that the dog is still at her bedside. The next morning she discovers that her bloodied dog has been hung in the shower and a note that reads, "Humans can lick, too."

4. A man tries to impress his date by playing ball with her dog while she is getting ready for their first date. The dog, usually a Great Dane, goes out the open window of a high-rise in an attempt to retrieve the ball. It is possible that this legend began with a story Truman Capote told on a late-night talk show. In another version of the story, a man is killed when he is hit on the head by the falling dog.

5. A dog is killed after he bites into a tennis ball that has been laced with an explosive. This one might actually be true. On November 25, 2000, a Labrador Retriever in Portland, Oregon, was reportedly killed when he bit into an exploding tennis ball. Why the ball had explosives in it in the first place is unclear. Police explained that explosive tennis balls were not that uncommon in urban areas. Agassi beware!

6. A Las Vegas woman brings her choking Doberman to the vet, only to be told that the dog has human fingers stuck in his throat. Apparently a burglar broke into her home and was attacked by the dog. The intruder was discovered in a closet with three fingers missing. This story was sent to the *Las Vegas Sun,* but investigations by the paper revealed that there was no evidence that this ever really happened.

7. A group of inebriated ice fishermen pack up a jeep with their gear and a Labrador Retriever and head out to the lake to do some fishing. When they get to the lake they decide to create a hole in the ice by using dynamite. As soon as they toss the dynamite, the dog rushes out to retrieve it and is killed when the explosive goes off.

8. An evil Seeing Eye dog named Lucky causes the deaths of four of his blind owners by leading one into the path of a speeding bus, another into the path of an oncoming train, another down a flight of stairs, and the last out an open window. No one ever suspects the dog of murder, and so he is reassigned to new owners.

9. A nervous young student visiting the dean's office at her college doesn't notice a dog asleep on a chair in the office and accidentally sits on the dean's dog, killing it instantly.

10. A man notices his dog dragging a dead rabbit under his fence. Afraid that his next-door neighbor's daughter might blame his dog for killing her pet, he cleans up the rabbit and places it back in the neighbor's cage. After a few hours he hears his neighbor scream, "What kind of sicko would dig up a little girl's rabbit and put it back in its cage?"

11. A couple touring the Far East with their dog stop for dinner in a Hong Kong restaurant. Being unfamiliar with the waiter's language, they use hand motions to explain that they want to order food for themselves and that they want their dog to be fed as well. The waiter takes the dog back into the kitchen and returns a half-hour later — with the dog fully cooked and served on a platter.

12. An eagle captures and flies away with a prized Poodle. This legend relies on the mental image of a tiny little Poodle being whisked away by a predatory bird. In reality, eagles are not able to fly with more than three or four pounds in their clutches, making this story virtually impossible. We're guessing it was really a Chihuahua.

Circus Poodles

Even to this day, nary a circus is complete without a dog act. Poodles, most popular as tricksters for their intelligence and love of performing, were especially popular in nineteenth-century England; spaniels were second in popularity.

1. Marquis of Gaillerdain and Madame de Poncette were the stars of "The Ball of Little Dogs," a troupe owned by a trainer named Crawley. The dogs performed for Queen Anne earlier in the eighteenth century, "greatly to Her Majesty's delight."

2. Munito was a Standard Poodle well known as the "learned dog." He entertained all levels of society by playing dominoes, counting, reading, and writing. His sidekick was an "educated" goat. Munito had many imitators, including the "scientific bitch," a Poodle who could read, count, and tell time; and Bianca, who could write in nineteen languages.

3. Jojo and Toto entertained circus crowds in Paris in the 1890s. They were large white Standards clipped in what was described at the time as "fantastic fashion": each tail sported six pompoms. Their act included dancing, a fire rescue vignette, and a battle reenactment in which red-coated Poodles defended themselves against green-coated Poodles.

4. In the early twentieth century, Rols, from Darmstadt, was trained as an opera buff and would bark when a wrong note was played. He was also taught to "sing" in a chorus with other Poodles.

5. American audiences as well as British enjoyed the troupe trained by Charles Prelle, who assembled twelve large Poodles to look like miniature ponies ridden by tiny Poodle jockeys. Dressed as ladies and gentlemen, the dogs would even talk and sing (Prelle was an accomplished ventriloquist).

Dan, "the original drunken dog," and his circus troupe, ca. 1920

"I have seen a poodle turn a double somersault, others turn somer-saults either backwards or sideways at the will of their trainers; they can 'take a hand' both at cards and dominoes, and their tight-rope walking on the hind legs, or on all fours with a monkey on their backs, and their steeplechases with monkey riders, are certainly ahead of anything in the way of poodle training presented before the public in olden times. Only the other day I saw two little poodles on stage at Westminster Aquarium that gave an excellent bout at boxing, standing on their hind legs, the gloves being placed on their fore paws, and spar-ring and striking each other in the face and neck with as much pugnac-ity as two bipeds might display. As I write, I should say there are now in 1893 at least half-a-dozen troupes of performing dogs in the metrop-olis, and each contains several poodles."

— RAWDON B. LEE, A HISTORY AND DESCRIPTION OF THE MODERN DOGS OF GREAT BRITAIN AND IRELAND, 1894

7 Real Dog Ads

All of these really appeared in newspapers around the country.

1. Dog for sale: Eats anything and is fond of children.

2. Great Dames for sale.

3. Free puppies: ½ Cocker Spaniel, ½ Sneaky Neighbor's Dog.

4. Found: Dirty white dog. Looks like a rat. Been out awhile. Better be a reward.

5. Female Boston Terrier puppies, 7 wks old, perfect markings, 555-1234. Leave mess.

6. Lost: small apricot Poodle. Reward. Neutered. Like one of the family.

7. For Sale — Eight puppies from a German Shepherd and an Alaskan Hussy.

13 Legendary Black Dogs of Great Britain

The British term "black dog" is used to refer to apparitions or creatures who typically resemble black dogs, although it is also refers to canine apparitions of other colors and types. Black dogs, also referred to as shuck dogs, have been widely reported throughout Great Britain.

1. Shuck, Black Shuck, or Old Shuck, as it is called in Norfolk, is said to be one of the oldest phantoms of Great Britain. The name is derived from the Anglo-Saxon word *scucca* meaning "demon or devil." *Shuck* is said to be a word that imitates the sound of chains being dragged across the ground. Black Shuck was the inspiration for Sir Arthur Conan Doyle's *Hound of the Baskervilles.* Conan Doyle is best known, of course, as the creator of Sherlock Holmes.

2. During the days when Charles II was king of England, Moddey Dhoo, or Mauthe Doog, was often seen by the soldiers of Peer Castle, laying himself down by the hearth of the military barracks.

3. Trash, as the dog is referred to in Lancashire, makes a sound like heavy shoes splashing through mud.

4. Skriker, another name for the Lancashire black dog, is said to emit screaming sounds.

5. Morphing Shuck of Bristol was seen to climb out from a hedge before transforming into a donkey and standing on his hind legs.

6. Barghest, Barghaist, Barguest, Barguest, or Barn-ghaist of Yorkshire was reputed to have large, saucer-shaped eyes.

7. Capelthwaite of Westmorland had shape-shifting abilities and was as large as a calf.

8. Padfoot in Staffordshire was as big as a calf and haunted lonely roads.

9. Suicide Shuck, as it is called in Tivington, is thought to contain the soul of a local man who committed suicide.

10. Lost travelers in Somerset were led to safety by Gurt Dog.

11. The black dogs of Wales are called Gwyllgi. The name means "wild dog" or "dog of darkness."

12. Muckle Black Tyke ("Choin Dubh" in Gaelic) is a fairy dog of Scotland who appears either in green or in white.

13. Pooka, a great black fairy dog of Ireland, was generally seen at the gloaming (dusk) at bridges, riverbanks, and crossroads.

Dogs Who Went Postal

Even the history of stamp collecting reflects our love for dogs. In the 1960s, only a few postage stamps depicted dogs. Today, worldwide, there are more than 4,000 of them, and almost every breed of dog is represented. Newfoundland has the distinction of being the first country, in 1887, to feature a dog on a stamp; quite naturally, it shows a Newfoundland dog. This timeline features the highlights of dogs on U.S. issues.

1893: The United States issues one of its earliest stamps depicting a dog. The thirty-cent stamp of the Columbian Exposition shows Columbus at the monastery of La Rabida, discussing his plans, while a dog is at his feet. The stamp is currently worth approximately $325.

1898: A dog accompanying western mining prospectors is shown on a U.S. fifty-cent stamp. The value of this stamp today is approximately $800.

1959: A four-cent stamp for Arctic Explorations shows sled dogs and their value to the explorations there.

1963: A stamp to commemorate the centenary of free city mail delivery shows a mailman with a boy and a dog running alongside him.

1966: A mixed-breed dog is shown for the Humane Treatment of Animals issue.

1972: The Mail Order Business issue features a rural post office with a dog in the foreground.

1973: A dog is shown in the Postrider stamp of the Bicentennial issue.

1979: The Fiftieth Anniversary of the Seeing Eye Dogs issue shows a German Shepherd Dog leading a blind man.

1982: A thirteen-cent stamp features a puppy, and the year's Children's Christmas issue shows children and dogs.

1984: A block of four twenty-cent stamps picturing eight different dogs is released in recognition of the founding of the American Kennel Club. (The AKC did not choose the dogs, neither was the AKC mentioned on the stamps.) The dogs were paired on the four stamps: a Black-and-Tan Coonhound with the American Foxhound; the Beagle with the Boston Terrier; the Chesapeake Bay Retriever with the Cocker Spaniel; and the Alaskan Malamute with the Collie.

1984: The cartoon character Detective McGruff, the official mascot of the National Crime Prevention Council, appears on a twenty-cent anticrime stamp.

1986: The Love Theme issue features a sad-looking dog.

1990: Toto, of *Wizard of Oz* fame, appears on a twenty-five-cent stamp.

1995: The Yellow Kid, a cartoon character, is shown riding on his dog on a thirty-two-cent stamp, and an environment issue shows a family at the beach with their dog.

1996: The Christmas stamp for this year shows a dog with a family in front of a fireplace.

1998: A set of four thirty-two-cent stamps features various pets — a goldfish, a gerbil, a cat, and a Basset Hound.

2001: A first-class Neuter or Spay stamp is issued featuring a dog and cat, both of whom were rescued from an animal shelter.

6 Superdogs

We're grateful to Martha Thomases, our supergirl in residence, for this list of canine superheroes.

1. Krypto

Superman's pet, Krypto, is a white terrier from the planet Krypton, with all the powers and abilities of the Man of Steel, and he was featured in Superman comics right alongside his human counterpart. He can fly, and he has superstrength, superspeed, super-vision, and a super sense of smell. Bullets bounce off him, and cats can't scratch his invulnerable hide. "The Dog of Tomorrow" can fetch sticks thrown to the moon and go for romps in space; plus, his superintelligence made him easy to housebreak. Krypto was the leader of the Legion of Super-Pets, a group that included Streaky, the Super-Cat; Beppo, the Super-Monkey; Comet, the Super-Horse; and Proty, the protoplasmic shape-changing pet of Chameleon Boy of the Legion of Super-Heroes.

2. Underdog

Like Mighty Mouse, Underdog was a cartoon superhero inspired by Superman. Underdog had a

"There's no need to fear — Underdog is here!"

secret identity, a secret love for a beautiful female, Polly Purebred, and an arch-nemesis, the evil scientist Simon Bar Sinister. The voice of Underdog was supplied by the actor Wally Cox, whose comic persona of a nervous coward was very similar to Clark Kent.

3. G'Nort

A member in good (but not great) standing of the Green Lantern Corps, G'Nort, from the planet G'Newt, was originally assigned to patrol Sector 2112 by the Guardians of the Universe. After several adventures with the Justice League of America, he settled on Earth. He is friends with Green Lantern's Guy Gardner and Kyle Rayner.

4. Ace the Bat-Hound

Batman's dog, Ace, was a canine sleuth who helped the Gotham Gladiator in a few adventures in the comics of the 1950s. Like his master, Ace wore a mask to conceal his identity. He appeared in only a few adventures. We'd like to think he found a nice police officer to take care of instead of hanging out in a drafty Batcave.

5. Scooby-Doo

Like Ace the Bat-Hound, Scooby-Doo solves mysteries. Unlike Ace, Scooby can talk — albeit in a dialect heavily weighted to the letter *r*. With his slacker master, Shaggy, and Shaggy's friends, Scooby fights monsters, ghosts, and the forces of evil who masquerade as these scary creatures. Scooby and Shaggy are more like two guys sharing a dorm room than pet and human, which is probably a superpower itself, especially if Scooby ever orders the pizza.

6. Yankee Poodle

Yankee Poodle has the useful power of being able to emit repelling stars with one hand and attracting stripes with the other. Her secret identity is gossip columnist Rova Barkitt, and she gained her powers after being exposed to the rays of a mysterious meteor. She works together with a superteam that includes Captain Carrot (a rabbit with superstrength), Alley-Kat-Abra (a wizard cat), Rubberduck (a mallard with a stretchable body), Pig Iron (a pig who can change his body to steel), Fastback (a turtle with superspeed), and Little Cheese (a mouse who can shrink). Among their enemies is another superpowered dog, Bow-Zar the Barbarian!

13 Dog Haikus

I lift my leg and
Whiz on each bush. Hello,
Spot — Sniff this and weep.

Today I sniffed dog
behinds — I celebrate my luck
By kissing your face.

I lie belly-up
In the sunshine, happier
Than you'll ever be.

How do I love thee?
The ways are numberless as
My hairs on the rug.

Dig under fence — why?
Because it's there. Because it's
There. Because it's there.

I am your best friend,
Now, always, especially
When you are eating.

I sound the alarm!
Mailman fiend — come to kill
     us:
Look! Look! Look! Look! Look!

I sound the alarm!
Paper boy come to kill all!
Look! Look! Look! Look! Look!

I hate my choke chain —
Look, world, they strangle me!
     Ack
Ack Ack Ack Ack Ack!

My human is home!
I am so ecstatic I
have made a puddle.

I love my master;
Thus I perfume myself with
this long-dead squirrel.

Look in my eyes and
Deny it. No human could
Love you as I do.

My owners' mood is
Romantic — at their feet I
Fart out a big one.

"Oh, what is the
matter with poor
Puggy-Wug?
Pet him
and kiss him and
give him a hug.
Run and fetch him
a suitable drug.
Wrap him up
tenderly all in
a rug.
That is the way
to cure
Puggy-Wug."
— WINSTON CHURCHILL,
ON HIS DAUGHTER
MARY'S PET PUG

How to Say Dog in 131 Languages

Consult the next edition of this book for a pronunciation key.

1. Abenaki (Algonquin family of Native American languages) — alemos, adia
2. Ainu (a Japanese language) — seta
3. Afrikaans — hond
4. Albanian — qen
5. Amharic (Ethiopian) — wv
6. Apache — góshé
7. Arabic — Calb
8. Aramaic — Oblkd
9. Armenian — shoon
10. ASL (American Sign Language) — tap your right hip, raise your right hand up at shoulder level, and snap your fingers
11. Asturian (spoken in the western part of Cantabria and northern Castilla-Leon, Spain) — perru
12. Ayapathu (Australian aboriginal language) — ku'a
13. Aymara (Andean language) — anu
14. Basque or Euskara — zakur
15. Belarusian — sabaka
16. Bemba — imbwa
17. Bengali (Bangladesh) — kukur

18. Berber (a group of Arabic languages) — aqjun, eydi, ijji
19. Bicol (a language of the Philippines) — ayám
20. Blackfoot — imitáá
21. Breton (Celtic language) — ki
22. Bulgarian — kuche
23. Catalan (a language spoken in northeastern Spain, in the Balearic Islands, in Andorra, and in a small part of France) — Gos
24. Catawba (a language of the Sioux Indians) — ta'si
25. Cebuano or Bisaya (a language of the Philippines) — ero
26. Chamorro — ga'lagu
27. Chechen (a very old language indigenous to the Caucasus) — zhwala
28. Cherokee — gi li
29. Cheyenne — oesˇkeso
30. Chinese — gau
31. Cornish — ky´
32. Creole (Haitian) — chen
33. Czech — pes
34. Danish — hund
35. Dutch — hond

36. Ecuadorian Quechua — allcu
37. Eskimo — kringmerk
38. Esperanto — hundo
39. Estonian — koer
40. Faeroese — hundur
41. Farsi (a Persian language) — kuche
42. Finnish — koira
43. French — chien/ne
44. Frisian (an Indo-European language spoken in Germany and the Netherlands) — hûn
45. Breton (Celtic language) — ki
46. Gamilaraay (language of the Kamilaroi people in northern New South Wales, Australia) — buruma
47. Ganda (a Bantu language) — 'ddogo'jjo
48. German — hund
49. Greek — skylos
50. Guarani (spoken by the people of the eastern lowland area of South America) — jepe
51. Hawaiian — 'Ilio
52. Hausa (a Chadic language, spoken by the people of northern Nigeria) — kàr.ee
53. Hebrew — kelev
54. Hiligaynon (Austroniesian language spoken by in the Iloilo and Capiz provinces of the Philippines) — ido
55. Hmong (spoken in Laos and Thailand) — dev
56. Hindi — kuttA or shvAna
57. Hungarian — kutya
58. Icelandic — hond
59. Indonesian — mengikuti
60. Ingush (the language of the Sunni Muslim people living in the North Caucasus) — zhwala
61. Inuktitut — qimmiq
62. Irish — madra
63. Italian — cane
64. Japanese — œú
65. Kapampangan (a Malayan language) — asu
66. Karelian (spoken by the people of northwestern Russia and by emigrants in neighboring Finland) — koir
67. Khmer (official language of Cambodia) — sunx
68. Kongo — mbwa
69. Korean — gae

70. Latin — canis

71. Latvian — suns

72. Lithuanian — sunis

73. Lozi (language of Zambia) — bya

74. Macedonian — kuche

75. Maltese — kelb

76. Maori (indigenous language of New Zealand) — kelb or kurii

77. Malay — anjing

78. Manx — moddey

79. Mayan — pek'

80. Mohawk — erhar

81. Mongolian — noqai

82. Navajo — lha-cha-eh

83. Norwegian — hund

84. Ojibwe (Native American language) — animosh

85. Pahlavi (an Iranian language) — en

86. Papago — gós, chin

87. Papiamen — cachó

88. Pashto (language of the Kanadahar region of Afghanistan) — spay

89. Pidgin (the language of Papua, New Guinea) — dok

90. Pig Latin — ogday

91. Polish — Pies

92. Portuguese — cão

93. Rasta — dog

94. Romanian — câine

95. Romany (Gypsy language) — Rikono

96. Roviana (spoken in the Western Province of Solomon Islands) — siki

97. Ruanda — inbwa

98. Russian — cobaka

99. Samoan — maile

100. Sardinian — cane

101. Scottish — cù

102. Sepedi (spoken in a Northern Province of South Africa) — mpaa

103. Serbian — pas

104. Serbo-Croatian — psec´i

105. Shona (the language of the Shoshoni) — imbwa'

106. Sicilian — cani

107. Slovak — pes

108. Somali — eey

109. Spanish — perro

110. Swahili — mbwa

111. Swazi — î-njá

112. Swedish — hund

113. Tagalog (a Philippine language) — áso

114. Taiwanese — kao and kaw'ar

115. Tiano (spoken in the islands throughout the Greater Antilles) — ao'n

116. Thai — ëáò

117. Tibetan — khyi

118. Tocharian (an ancient Indo-European language) — ku

119. Turkish — köpek

120. Ukrainian — sobaka, pes

121. Umbrian (an ancient Indo-European language) — katel (puppy)

122. Urdu (an Indo-European language) — kutta

123. Vietnamese — chó

124. Vulcan — Valit (a Vulcan burrowing animal, perhaps a Jack Russell Terrier)

125. Wagiman (Australian Aboriginal language) — lamarra

126. Welsh — ci

127. Wolof (the language of Senegal) — hatch

128. Yiddish — hunt or kelef

129. Yucatec — pek'

130. Zarma (language of Niger) — hansi

131. Zulu — inja

"My neighbor has two dogs. One of them says to the other, 'Woof!' The other replies, 'Moo!' The dog is perplexed. '"Moo"? Why did you say, "Moo"?' The other dog says, 'I'm trying to learn a foreign language.'"
— MOREY AMSTERDAM

28 Dog Idioms

In ancient times, the Romans named the hottest of their summer months *"dies caniculares"* ("dog days") and believed that the heat was intensified during that time by Sirius, the Dog Star. Some believed it was this heat that drove dogs mad; in Britain, Victorian law required dog owners to refrain from letting their dogs run free during what has come to be known as the dog days of summer.

1. **A dog in a manger:** A mean-spirited person who prevents others from enjoying themselves.

2. **A dog is for life, not just for Christmas:** Reap what you sow.

3. **Every dog has his day:** Bad luck never lasts.

4. **The black dog walked all over him:** Refers to someone suffering from depression.

5. **To blush like a black dog:** Not to blush at all.

6. **Three-dog night:** A night so cold that sleeping with one dog for warmth won't do; you'd need three dogs to do the job.

The phrase "raining cats and dogs" originated in seventeenth-century England. During heavy downpours of rain, many of the poor animals who roamed the streets unfortunately drowned, and their bodies would be seen floating in the rain torrents that raced through the streets. The situation gave the appearance that it had literally rained "cats and dogs" and led to the current expression.

7. **Hair of the dog that bit you:** A hangover remedy that includes whatever you got drunk on in the first place.

8. **To see a man about a dog:** An excuse to leave present company without offering an explanation: "I have to go see a man about a dog."

9. **Doggone:** Euphemism for "goddamned."

10. **Dog tired:** Exhausted.

11. **Dog's age:** A very long time.

12. **Dog's breakfast:** A mixture of many things.

13. **A dog's life:** Hard times.

14. **Doggie bag:** Leftovers from a restaurant.

15. **Dog-eat-dog:** Relentlessly competitive.

16. **Fight like cats and dogs:** To argue violently.

17. **Dog-and-pony show:** An event during which someone attempts to sell their wares.

18. **A dog with two tails:** Someone who is very happy.

19. **A dog's chance:** No chance at all.

20. **Put on the dog:** To seem more prosperous than you really are.

21. **Shaggy-dog story:** A very long joke with a silly ending.

22. **Sick as a dog:** Very sick.

23. **The tail is wagging the dog:** An unimportant aspect of a situation is controlling the entire situation.

24. **Top dog:** The most important person in a group.

25. **To work like a dog:** To work very hard.

26. **Let sleeping dogs lie:** Leave a potentially volatile situation alone.

27. **To be in the doghouse:** To be in someone's bad graces.

28. **Iron dog:** A car. This term originated in Alaska at the time when automobiles replaced, at least in part, the sled dog.

How to Communicate with Your Dog in 36 Languages

We bet you didn't know that dogs spoke foreign languages. Well they do, sort of. Each country has its own special way of describing a dog's bark. So if your dog says "Vov" instead of "Bow-wow," don't worry — he might be Danish. Here's a sampling of how dogs bark around the world.

1. Afrikaans: Woef-woef
2. Albanian: Ham-ham
3. Arabic: Haw haw
4. Bengali: Ghaue-ghaue
5. Catalan: Bup-bup
6. Chinese: Wang-wang
7. Croatian: Vau-vau
8. Danish: Vov-vov
9. Dutch: Woef-woef
10. English: Rrrrf-ruf, Bow-wow, or Arf-arf
11. Esperanto: Boj-boj
12. Estonian: Auh-auh

23. Japanese: Won-won or Kyan-kyan
24. Korean: Mung-mung or Wang-wang

"If dogs could talk it would take a lot of the fun out of owning one." —ANDY ROONEY

25. Norwegian: Voff-voff or Vov-vov
26. Philippine: Ow-ow
27. Polish: Hau-hau
28. Portuguese (Portugal): ão-ão
29. Russian: Gav-gav or Guf-guf
30. Slovene: Hov-hov

"No one appreciates the very special genius of your conversation as the dog does." —CHRISTOPHER MORLEY

13. Finnish: Hau-hau or Vuh-vuh
14. French: Whou-whou or Vaf-vaf
15. German: Vow-vow
16. Greek: Gav-gav
17. Hebrew: Haw-haw or Hav-hav
18. Hindi: Bho-bho
19. Hungarian: Vau-vau
20. Icelandic: Voff-voff
21. Indonesian: Gong-gong
22. Italian: Bau-bau

31. Spanish (Spain, Argentina): Guau-guau
32. Swedish: Vov-vov
33. Thai: Hoang-hoang
34. Turkish: Hav-hav
35. Ukrainian: Haf-haf
36. Vietnamese: Wau-wau

"No animal should ever jump up on the dining room furniture unless absolutely certain that he can hold his own in the conversation." —FRAN LEBOWITZ

27 Songs About Dogs

1. In 1787 Ludwig von Beethoven wrote a song entitled *"Elegie auf den Tod eines Pudels"* ("Elegy on a Dead Poodle"). The song reflected his love for his loyal companion and the hope that the dog would live on joyfully in his memories.

2. It was the antics of one of the writer George Sand's Poodles that served as the inspiration for Frédérick Chopin's famous "Minute Waltz," which he composed in 1847.

3. "One Man and His Dog," traditional English folk song

4. "Old Dog Tray," written by Stephen Foster in 1853

5. "Police Dog Blues," by Blind Blake, written and recorded between 1926 and 1932

6. "How Much Is That Doggie in the Window?" written by Bob Merrill, was a number one hit for Patti Page when she recorded it in 1953.

7. "Hound Dog," by Leiber-Stoller. The record topped the pop, country, and black charts when Elvis Presley sang it in 1956, and it went on to become one of the most popular songs ever recorded.

8. "Old Shep," words and music by Foley-Westparas, recorded by Elvis Presley in 1956

9. "The Fang," written and recorded by Nervous Norvus (aka "Singing" Jimmy Drake) in 1956

10. "Bird Dog," written and recorded by the Everly Brothers in 1958

11. "Old Tige," written by M. and R. Burke, recorded by Jim Reeves in 1961

12. "The Dog Song," words and music by James Bevel and Bernard Lafayette, recorded by Harry Belafonte in 1967

13. "Martha My Dear" (for Paul's sheep-dog), by John Lennon and Paul McCartney, who recorded it in 1968*

14. "Me and You and a Dog Named Boo," written and recorded by Roland Kent LaVoie, using the alias "Lobo," in 1971

15. "Jet" (Jet was another one of Paul's dogs), written by Paul McCartney and recorded by him in 1973

16. "Put the Bone In," written and recorded by Terry Jacks in 1973

17. "Nanook Rubs It," from Frank Zappa's album *Apostrophe,* 1974

18. "Sick as a Dog" written by Aerosmith, recorded in 1978

19. "Poodle Party," written and recorded by the Dickies in 1979

20. "Fluffy," written by Richard van Dorn and Davey Sayles, recorded by Gloria Balsam in 1979

21. "Children and Dogs," written by Graham Parker, recorded in 1991

22. "Dixie, the Tiny Dog," written and recorded by Peter Himmelman in 1991

23. "Old King," written by Neil Young, recorded in 1992

24. "Youth Culture Killed My Dog," written by They Might Be Giants, recorded in 1997

25. "Who Let the Dogs Out?" by the Baha Men, recorded in 2000

26. "Shoot the Dog," written and recorded by George Michael in 2002

27. "Walkin' the Dog," written and recorded by Wayne Hancock in 2003

*Paul again paid tribute to Martha when, at the end of "A Day in the Life," he added an ultrasonic whistle audible only to dogs.

18 Rock-'n'-Roll Dogs

1. "When you call my name, I salivate like Pavlov's dog."
— The Rolling Stones, "Bitch"

2. "The bigger the city, the brighter the lights. The bigger the dog, the harder they bite."
— Lynyrd Skynyrd, "I Know a Little"

3. "The reason a dog has so many friends is that he wags his tail instead of his tongue."
— Aerosmith, "The Reason a Dog"

4. "Mice pie, dog-eye, eagle on the wind, I'm searching through this garbage looking for a friend."
— T. Rex, "Baby Boomerang"

5. "Today I saw a car crush my little dog under its wheel."
— Todd Rundgren, "Sometimes I Don't Know How to Feel"

6. "He's a bird, he's a dog, he's a bird dog." — Everly Brothers, "Bird Dog"

7. "You ain't nothing but a hound dog, cryin' all the time." — Big Mama Thornton; Elvis Presley, "Hound Dog"

8. "There goes a dogfish chased by a catfish." — B-52s, "Rock Lobster"

9. "Crazy Chester . . . said, I'll fix your rack, if you'll just jack my dog." — The Band, "The Weight"

10. "He took a dog-doo snow cone and stuffed it in my right eye." — Frank Zappa, "Nanook Rubs It"

11. "I set my monkey on the log, and ordered him to do the Dog." — Bob Dylan, "I Shall Be Free #10"

12. "If you want to pet that old hound dog, make sure he ain't rolled in shit." — Neil Young, "Don't Spook the Horse"

13 "I'm the dog who gets beat, shove my nose in shit." — Alice in Chains, "Man in the Box"

14. "In a dog's brain a constant buzz of low-level static, one sniff at the hydrant and the answer is automatic." — Rush, "Dog Years"

15. "Livin' with Louie dog's the only way to stay sane." — Sublime, "What I Got"

16. "Puss and dog, they get together. What's wrong with you, my brother?" — Bob Marley, "So Jah She"

17. "The dog has not been fed in years, it's even worse than it appears." — Grateful Dead, "Touch of Grey"

18. "The dogs of doom are howling more." — Led Zeppelin, "No Quarter"

73 Popular Performers with Dog Names

1. 4 Dog Pile-Up
2. 7 Year Bitch
3. Angry Dogs
4. The Arrogant Sons of Bitches
5. Big Dog Band
6. Bitch Boys
7. The Bloodhound Gang
8. The Blue Dogs
9. The Bonzo Dog Doo-Dah Band
10. Bow Wow Wow
11. Cat Rapes Dog
12. Coyotes
13. Crime Scene Dog
14. Devil Dogs
15. Diamond Dogs
16. The Dirty Dogs
17. Dog and Everything
18. Dog Eat Dog
19. Dog Fashion Disco
20. Dog Food Five
21. Dog Lips
22. The Dogs
23. The Dogs D'Amour
24. Dogs Undecided
25. Dog Toffee
26. Dogs with Jobs
27. Four Dog Night
28. The Hangdogs
29. Hank Dogs
30. High Heel Horn Dogs
31. High Grass Dogs
32. The Ho'Dogs
33. Jackal
34. Jack Russell
35. Johnny Underdog
36. The Lane Dogs
37. The Love Dogs
38. Love That Dog
39. My Dog Has Hitler's Brain
40. Naugahyde Chihuahuas
41. The Old Dog Band
42. Ol' Dogs New Trix
43. Peace, Love & Pitbulls
44. Pet Shop Boys
45. Poi Dog Pondering
46. The Poodles
47. Poundhound
48. Pretentious Flamedogs
49. Rabid Dogs
50. Rain Dogs
51. Red Dogs
52. Saturn Flea Collar
53. The Screaming Bulldogs
54. Seasons of the Wolf
55. Skip Towne & The Greyhounds
56. Slice Hound
57. Slutpuppies
58. Snoop Dogg
59. Steppenwolf
60. Stray Dogs
61. Temple of the Dog
62. Three Dog Night
63. Three-Legged Dog
64. Toto
65. Ugly People and Their Dogs
66. Wardog
67. Wasted Dogs
68. Wolf
69. Wolfcry
70. Wolfenmond
71. Wolf's Moon
72. Wolfsbane
73. Wolverine

"Did you hear about the dyslexic agnostic insomniac who stays up all night wondering if there really is a Dog?" — UNKNOWN

A History of the American Kennel Club

The AKC has undergone a great amount of growth and change over the past century — from its first registered dog in 1885, to 1.2 million dogs and 555,000 litters in 1998; from a small office, to the forefront for information about anything and everything concerning purebred dogs. These are the most important developments in the history of the AKC:

1884: The American Kennel Club was founded in a meeting held at Madison Square Garden in New York City on October 22. Major James M. Taylor became the AKC's first president. No official headquarters were established. The organization would combine various dog shows and field trials that had been held on local levels to create a national "club of clubs."

1887: A small office was established at 44 Broadway in New York City, sparsely furnished with a desk, a filing cabinet, and a few chairs.

1889: A publication entitled the *AKC Gazette,* sponsored by August Belmont, Jr., the club's fourth president, made its first appearance. More than a century later, it remains one of the oldest dog magazines in existence.

> The last member of the famous Bonaparte family, Jerome Napoleon Bonaparte, died in 1945, of injuries sustained from tripping over his dog's leash.

1900: The AKC broke with the traditional dog show scoring system established in England and a new point scale emerged. One point would be awarded to a dog that won a competition in a show with fewer than 250 dogs, up to a five-point maximum for a show of more than 1,000 dogs. A total of ten points became required for the title of champion.

1908–1910: The AKC adopted a new constitution and bylaws as well as new rules governing dog shows. The ten-point scoring system gave way to a fifteen-point system and was to be scored by three judges. In addition, a dog had to win at least three points at any given show to be considered a candidate for a championship title.

1911–1917: Definite rules for classified and unclassified special prizes were established. This led to the establishment of the Best of Breed and Best in Show awards.

1920: AKC-approved competitions took place for the first time.

1924: Comprehensive new rules for groups and Best in Show judging were adopted. Breeds were separated into six groups — sporting, hounds, working dogs, terriers, toy breeds, and nonsporting breeds. Winners in each group would vie for the Best in Show title. The Westminster Kennel Club was first to adopt this new format.

1930: The AKC began requiring exhibitors to have a license, which led to the formation of the Professional Handlers Association in 1931.

1932: The first book of AKC rules was published.

1936: The AKC published the first official *Regulations and Standard for Obedience Test Field Trials.*

1941–1945: Hardships during the Second World War led the AKC to relax rules governing dog shows. Even the size of the *AKC Gazette* was reduced in order to conserve paper for the war effort.

1947: A judges' directory entitled "Licensed Judges" was issued.

1950: An attempt was made to seat female delegates, but no one seconded the motion and it failed.

1951: A rule was established that limited judges to judging twenty dogs per hour. This was later changed to twenty-five dogs per hour; the total number of dogs a judge could see in a day was two hundred.

1969: New streamlined obedience rules went into effect, and an important new approach to approving conformation and obedience judges was enacted a few months later. The Board of Directors of the AKC also adopted a system that would be used in rating judges and new applicants for judgeships.

1974: A motion to allow women to serve as delegates was seconded and carried by a vote of 180 to 7. The first women delegates were elected in June.

Mid-1970s: Due to gas shortages, cluster shows begin to spring up, at which all breed clubs were able to hold their events at the same time and place, making it more convenient for traveling exhibitors.

1978: The AKC stops the practice of licensing professional handlers. This change allows anyone to show a dog for a set fee.

1982: The Dog Museum of America opens. The original museum is located in New York City, but five years later it moves to its permanent location in St. Louis, Missouri. The museum's name is changed to the American Kennel Club Museum of the Dog.

1984: The American Kennel Club celebrates its one hundredth anniversary at the Centennial Show in Philadelphia.

1985: Dr. Jacklyn Hungerland, the first female director of the AKC, is elected.

The 1990s: The AKC establishes the Canine Health Foundation and the Canine Good Citizen program. The Companion Animal Recovery program is initiated in 1995.

1998: The AKC moves several of its departments from the New York City office to Raleigh, North Carolina. The Raleigh location is named the American Kennel Club Building.

1998: DNA testing becomes a recognized method of insuring the integrity of the AKC's registry.

2005: Almost 2 million dogs are competing in more than 15,000 member, licensed, and sanctioned events. Having registered more than 1.2 million dogs and 550,000 litters, the AKC is recognized as the top authority in American dogdom.

The 25 Most Common Male Dog Names in the United States

1. Max	10. Duke	19. Barney
2. Jake	11. Charlie	20. Winston
3. Buddy	12. Jack	21. Bennet
4. Bailey	13. Harley	22. Lucky
5. Sam	14. Rusty	23. Kernal
6. Rocky	15. Toby	24. Dylan
7. Buster	16. Murphy	25. Millhouse
8. Casey	17. Shelby	
9. Cody	18. Sparky	

The 24 Most Common Female Dog Names in the United States

1. Maggie	9. Sasha	17. Sophie
2. Molly	10. Sandy	18. Bo
3. Lady	11. Dakota	19. Coco
4. Sadie	12. Katie	20. Tasha
5. Lucy	13. Annie	21. Lassie
6. Daisy	14. Chelsea	22. Honey
7. Ginger	15. Princess	23. Misty
8. Abby	16. Missy	24. Samantha

The Canis Film Festival: 66 Great Dog Movies

The damsel in distress, the lonely nerd, the family struggling to make it through the Depression, the homeless hobo — where would these characters be without the four-footed heroes who, more often than not, manage to steal the show? Dogs have been gracing the silver screen for almost as long as humans have: in the early twentieth century, Teddy the Labrador cross-worked on dozens of silent films for the Keystone Company before Strongheart, Flash, Rin Tin Tin, and Lassie started getting top billing. The following movies are among the most notable dog films of all time.

1. *Rescued by Rover* (1905) Cecil Hepworth's seven-minute film featured a Collie named Blair who saves a baby from kidnappers. The film was so popular that several sequels were made, but Blair's career — and life — ended in 1910. Upon the dog's death, Hepworth recalled the great friend and companion he had been, saying, "Every morning in life he jumped up on a washing basket by my dressing table and waited for a dab on the nose with my shaving brush." Blair is recognized as the first canine film star.

2. *A Dog's Life* (1918) Probably the most famous of the early films in which dogs appeared, it introduced filmmakers to one of the greatest obstacles to using dogs in film: Mutt, who played Charlie Chaplin's dog Scraps, grew quickly during the filming, and no double could be found to match him. For purposes of continuity, different camera angles and oversize props were used.

3. *Funny Side of Life* (1925) One of the shortest comedies in this compilation of Harold Lloyd's films pits Lloyd against Mike, a dog, as he tries to teach his pet to retrieve a ball.

4. *Jaws of Steel* (1927) Rin Tin Tin was played by Rinty, the German Shepherd Dog who was already a star when this film was released; Warner had unleashed him in the 1922 movie *The Man from Hell's River*. Rinty was paid $1,000 a week and was served Châteaubriand for breakfast every day. (See "The Rin Tin Tin Story," page 54.)

5. *The Kennel Murder Case* (1933) A Philo Vance mystery in which a murder is tied to wealthy rivals whose dogs are competing in a Long Island dog show. A fine old standard film.

6. *Peg o' My Heart* (1933) Marion Davies, who starred in this old-fashioned comedy, became so fond of Mutt, who played the dog Michael, that she complained when he was ignored in reviews.

7. *The Thin Man* (1934) Skippy, the Wire Fox Terrier who helped William Powell and Myrna Loy out of more than one tight spot, became so well known as Asta that his owners changed his name. In 1937 Asta appeared in *The Awful Truth,* a comedy in which a divorce court judge allows the dog to choose his owner. He then had a chance to reprise his role as the sleuth-dog in the television version of *The Thin Man* and won two PATSY (Picture Animal Top Star of the Year) Awards for his performances in 1959 and 1960.

8. *The Call of the Wild* (1935) A Saint Bernard named Buck played the lovable canine in this film, based on Jack London's famous book about a dog's survival during Alaska's Klondike gold rush. Buck was trained by Carl Spitz, one of the most celebrated animal trainers at the time. By the late 1930s, Americans were so interested in trained animals that Spitz took an entourage of dogs on the road and made public appearances throughout the country. Buck was accompanied by Musty, the Mastiff who appeared in a film called *Wild Boys of the Road* (1900); Prince, the Great Dane from *Wuthering Heights;* and Terry, the Cairn Terrier who achieved fame and fortune as Toto from *The Wizard of Oz.*

9. *The Wizard of Oz* (1939) Terry the Cairn Terrier was so indispensable to the filming of Dorothy's adventures that he was paid a whopping $150 a week, while the Munchkins received only $50 each. Once Terry achieved fame as Toto, his name was legally changed.

10. *The Biscuit Eater* (1940) Two boys, one black and one white, have so much faith in an unwanted dog that they name him Promise and train him to be a champion bird dog. Promise competes in a championship where the favorite is Georgia Boy, bred and trained by the boys' fathers, and the competition takes on new proportions.

11. *Reap the Wild Wind* (1942) When Cecil B. DeMille first saw Rommy, a Cairn Terrier, he knew immediately that he wanted the dog for his next film. Rommy easily gained the admiration of his co-stars; Humphrey Bogart once called him "the best actor in Hollywood."

12. *Lassie Come Home* (1943) A magnificent British Collie struggles to cover the hundreds of miles that separate her from the family she loves in what many consider to be the best of the Lassie movies. Hundreds of dogs have played Lassie in the many film and TV incarnations of this famous story by Eric Knight, but the original was a male Collie named Pal. Apparently no female Collie was right for the part, thus making this film the first one to star a cross-dressing dog.

13. *The Courage of Lassie* (1946) A young girl adopts a dog who has been traumatized by his combat experiences in World War II. Despite the film's title, the dog in this movie is named Bill. Initially released as *Blue Sierra,* this film starred the same Collie as the other Lassie films.

14. *Hills of Home* (aka *Master of Lassie*) (1948) An elderly village doctor is tricked into buying a sheepdog who is afraid of water, and he must then teach him to swim. At the same time, the doctor must prepare a younger physician to eventually take his place. The film features the growing love of the trio as they battle death, nature, and time.

Wire Fox Terrier Skippy often stole the show when he appeared with William Powell and Myrna Loy in *The Thin Man* as the famous Asta.

15. *You Never Can Tell* (1951) Rex, a German Shepherd Dog and an ex-police/army dog, inherits a fortune from an eccentric millionaire. But someone kills him for his fortune, and he gets to go back to Earth as a human detective to bring his killer to justice. To add to the fun, his sidekick used to be a horse! In 1980's *Oh, Heavenly Dog,* the plot is reversed: Rex was a human private eye who comes back to Earth as a dog. The dog here is played by the one and only Benji; this was his third film.

16. *Lady and the Tramp* (1955) *Lady and the Tramp* is Disney's most enduring animated classic ever. It's a song-filled adventure about Lady, a lovingly pampered Cocker Spaniel, and Tramp, a roguish mutt from across the tracks. Lady learns what it means to be footloose and leash-free — and discovers romance. This was the first Disney film to appear in CinemaScope.

17. *Old Yeller* (1957) When famous animal trainer Frank Weatherwax rescued Spike, a large, clumsy yellow puppy from an animal shelter, he wasn't sure the dog would be useful. He was slow to respond to training and his bark was just a weak yelp; Walt Disney himself wondered whether this gentle animal would be able to play the scenes in which he needed to be vicious. Nevertheless, Spike won their hearts — and the part — and helped make this movie a top box office success. Based on Frank Gipson's popular novel, the film realistically evoked life in Texas in 1869 as it told the touching story of a boy and his dog.

18. *Anatomy of a Murder* (1959) Danny, the Cairn Terrier who played Muffy in this film, was a film vet: he had played Little Ricky's dog, Fred, on *I Love Lucy* and had appeared in the film *Pal Joey.*

19. *The Shaggy Dog* (1959) Through an ancient spell, a boy finds that he is changed into a sheepdog for short periods at — of course — the most inopportune times; he must break the spell through an act of bravery. This was the first of Disney's two Shaggy Dog movies, still loved today for pure situation comedy.

20. *Nikki, Wild Dog of the North* (1961) In this third production of this story, Nikki, a Malamute, is separated from his master, a Canadian trapper, and undergoes a series of adventures — both dangerous and charming, as when he befriends a bear cub — before they can be reunited. The film features informative nature commentary and marvelous footage of the Canadian wilderness.

21. *Greyfriars Bobby* (1961) Based on the true story of a Skye Terrier who refused to leave his master's side, even in death. Famous throughout Scotland, a statue of Bobby in Edinburgh bears the inscription "Let his loyalty and devotion be a lesson to us all."

22. *Big Red* (1962) Big Red, an Irish Setter, is valued by his owner only as a show dog until a young boy comes into his life and the two become attached emotionally. But Big Red manages to remain loyal to both owners. A charming family film based on the popular novel by Jim Kjelgaard.

Spike, star of *Old Yeller*

23. *The Incredible Journey* (1963) The original version of the story of three pets who make their way across Canada to be with their human family. The film is as well loved for its story as it is for the wonderful action and exciting photography. (See *Homeward Bound: The Incredible Journey*, page 45.)

24. *Benji* (1974) If the dog-actor Higgins could talk, he would tell you his rags-to-riches story: He was rescued from a shelter, went on to star in TV's *Petticoat Junction*, and was happily retired when, at fifteen, he charmed movie audiences as "America's most huggable hero." The dog earned several million dollars before retiring. This story about an irresistible dog that saves two children from kidnappers became an instant classic when it was released.

25. *Where the Red Fern Grows* (1974) Set in 1930s Oklahoma, this fine drama is the story of a boy who purchases a pair of hunting dogs and the lessons about responsibility that the dogs teach him. The film, based on a novel by Wilson Rawls, explores themes of love, loss, and self-reliance.

26. *A Boy and His Dog* (1975) A post-apocalyptic sci-fi/fantasy based on Harlan Ellison's novella. In 2024 Earth is a devastated wasteland after the nuclear holocaust of World War IV: it now looks like a desert, and water and food are extremely scarce. A man and his faithful sidekick, a mangy telepathic dog named Blood, travel this desolate terrain together.

27. *Rocky; Rocky II* (1976; 1979) Sylvester Stallone was so poor that he was on the verge of giving up his dog, a Bullmastiff named Butkus, when he finally was able to sign a deal for the first of these well-loved stories about a down-and-out boxer who beats the odds. The films made stars of both of them: Butkus plays himself in both movies.

28. *The Shaggy D.A.* (1976) In this sequel to *The Shaggy Dog*, a successful lawyer running for district attorney is transformed into an English Sheepdog and must retrieve a stolen ring in order to become human, win the election, and save the day.

29. *For the Love of Benji* (1977) In this second Benji film, one of the most expressive pooches ever explores Athens while covert agents hunting for the secret formula tattooed on his paw follow in hot pursuit.

30. *The Fox and the Hound* (1981) One of Disney's finest and most underrated motion pictures is this animated story of a fox cub and a hound pup who become friends, only to have their natural instincts cause them to turn on each other in later years. A thoughtful film that makes a powerful statement about racism.

31. *Annie* (1982) So well loved was Sandy the dog in the Broadway musical version of the comic strip come to life that his role was expanded for the film version, in which Annie, played by Aileen Quinn, sings two songs directly to him: "Dumb Dog" and "Sandy."

Walt Disney's family dog was named Lady. She was a Poodle.

For the movie version of Stephen King's **Cujo** (1983), five Saint Bernards were used, along with one mechanical head and an actor in a dog costume, to play the title character.

During the late 1980s, Bud Light spokesdog Spuds McKenzie didn't just help sell beer; he also helped popularize his breed, the Bull Terrier, when he made his debut in a Bud Light beer commercial during the 1987 Super Bowl. As a marketing sensation, Spuds was especially popular with sports crowds, as he was shown water-skiing, skateboarding, lounging by a pool with a bevy of beautiful women, and generally giving people the impression that his life was more exciting than theirs.

32. *Never Cry Wolf* (1983) This is the true story of the author Farley Mowat, who was sent to the Canadian tundra area to collect evidence of the grievous harm the wolf population was doing to the caribou herds. In his struggle to survive in that difficult environment, he studies the wolves and realizes that the old beliefs about their supposed threat are almost totally false and that humans represent a far greater threat to the land than the wolves ever could.

33. *Ladyhawke* (1985) By day she is human, by night she is a hawk; by day he is a wolf, by night he is human. Thus the star-crossed lovers are caught in an evil spell in this entertaining medieval fantasy adventure.

34. *The Journey of Natty Gann* (1985) A dark story that takes place during the Great Depression and tells of the hardships of a young girl traveling cross-country to find her father, under the unlikely protection of a lone wolf.

35. *Down and Out in Beverly Hills* (1986) Scruffy Matisse, one of the most neurotic dogs in movie history (the scenes with Matisse and his shrink are hilarious), is played by Mike, a forty-two-pound black and white Scottish Border Collie with one blue eye and one brown. He appeared in hundreds of commercials and in Little Richard's music video "Great Gosh a' Mighty, It's a Matter of Time" before he passed away.

36. *The Accidental Tourist* (1988) Geena Davis trains Edward, a Welsh Corgi, in this adaptation of a best-selling novel by Anne Tyler about a grieving man who falls for an eccentric animal lover. In real life, his trainer is Boone Narr, one of the most celebrated Hollywood animal trainers and the winner of numerous film awards.

37. *Oliver and Company* (1988) Disney's animated version of *Oliver Twist* — with a twist. The characters are all dogs, except for Oliver, who's an orphaned kitten. The Chihuahua voiced by Cheech Marin steals the show. Good animation, story line, characters, and music, but not one of Disney's best.

38. *K-9* (1989) The lovable partner of vice cop Thomas Dooley, played by Jim Belushi, was really a Kansas City police dog named Jerry Lee. Shortly after the filming of the movie, Jerry Lee was returned to regular duty and became famous again when he sniffed out some $1.2 million worth of cocaine. The movie wasn't much of a success; critics pretty much dubbed it "a dog."

39. *Turner and Hooch* (1989) The hound behind Hooch is Beasley, a Dogue de Bordeaux, the same rare breed of dog that appeared in *Payback* (1999) with Mel Gibson. The multifolded star got rave reviews — "a great actor," "Oscar caliber" — in a Tom Hanks police comedy that was otherwise unnotable.

40. *Bingo!* (1991) Originally a circus dog, Bingo finds a family, only to be separated from them accidentally. Here are his adventures in reuniting with Chuckie, his human, and overcoming numerous obstacles along the way. The dog in this movie was played by four extraordinarily well-trained dogs.

41. *White Fang* (1991) Disney's version of Jack London's classic adventure story about the friendship between a Yukon gold hunter and the mixed dog-wolf he rescues from the hands of a man who mistreats him. Two other versions of the film precede this one (1936, 1972); this one's the best. The real White Fang is Jed, who is half dog and half wolf. In the scene in which the dog is shown setting upon the body of a rabbit, he's really attacking a mixture of dog food and chicken.

42. *Beethoven; Beethoven's 2nd* (1992; 1993) Charles Grodin tries unsuccessfully to resist the cute little runaway Saint Bernard puppy that has charmed his whole family. But the puppy grows into a slobbering giant with pups of his own, who make their appearance in the sequel. Filming the movie was difficult, and delays led to an eight-month-long schedule, during which scads of puppies, five Saint Bernards, and a guy in a Saint Bernard costume were used to portray Beethoven and his brood.

43. *A Far Off Place* (1993) Percois Patch of Shagara, a champion pedigree Rhodesian Ridgeback, played Hintza in this South African adventure story about children fleeing from poachers. Filming lasted for eight months, after which Percois retired in South Africa.

Set in Alaska during the gold rush, in 1936 *White Fang* was the popular sequel to Jack London's *Call of the Wild.*

44. *Homeward Bound: The Incredible Journey* (1993) In this version of 1963's *Incredible Journey*, Shadow, a Golden Retriever, and Chance, an American Bulldog, travel with Sassy the cat on a journey across the country. Trainers employed numerous tricks — and plenty of patience — to help the dogs achieve their memorable performances. Shadow was especially clever: not only did he tolerate the muzzle that he had to wear in the film, but he even learned to take it off between scenes when it grew cumbersome.

45. *Lassie* (1994) A city family moves to the country, where Lassie "adopts" them and teaches the troubled young son remarkable lessons about life. Much of this is predictable, yet the film manages to charm audiences again and again with endearing moments and Lassie's endless feats.

46. *The Little Rascals* (1994) The dog Petey in the 1930s *Our Gang* comedies really had a black circle around his right eye. For this remake, the filmmakers had to settle for a fake — they used nontoxic vegetable dye to make the new Petey (that's the dog's real name, too) look like the original.

47. *Babe* (1995) The story of an orphaned pig was based on the book *The Sheep-Pig* by Dick Kings-Simth and became an instant "family" hit, rife with endearing moments and great special effects. But the scenes in the movie where Babe snuggles with Fly, his adopted Collie mom, were for real: production on this film lasted so long that the animals actually became attached to one another.

Today Petey, the famous friend of the Little Rascals, rests at the famous Pet Memorial Cemetery in Calabasas, California. He's in great company: Steven Spielberg's Jack Russell; Rudolph Valentino's dog, Kabar; and Hopalong Cassidy's horse, Topper, are there as well.

48. *Far from Home: The Adventures of Yellow Dog* (1995) A boy and his dog must battle nature and the elements after their boat capsizes. So sweet a dog was Dakota, the Labrador who plays Yellow in this film, that in the scenes between the dog and a wolf, the wolf refused to growl at Dakota. Luckily, Dakota's stand-in, Tyler, was not nearly as good-natured.

49. *Fluke* (1995) A young family man is killed and reincarnated as a dog in this touching story. The shaggy mongrel here is really a beautiful Golden Retriever named Comet, a regular on TV's *Full House.* Comet was the wrong color for the part but landed the role anyway, provided he wear brown makeup on the set. There's no business like show business.

50. *The Truth About Cats and Dogs* (1995) It took the Great Dane Hank three months to train for his side-splitting roller-skating scene. Even so, he had to have help from his trainer, who pulled him along on a hidden lead in this romantic comedy about a radio host of a pet-advice call-in program.

51. *Michael* (1996) The movie about an archangel who teaches people to believe in miracles wasn't one of John Travolta's biggest successes; some critics claimed that Sparky, the Jack Russell that Travolta revives after he's run over by a car, was the best actor in the film. Others sniff that the part wasn't all that demanding.

52. *101 Dalmatians* (1996) Cruella de Vil makes her debut here as the evil dog-napper in a story that's told from the dogs' point of view. The adorable puppies used in this film and its 2000 sequel, *102 Dalmatians,* grew so fast that trainer Gary Gero had to get a fresh batch of them each week. After their duties had been fulfilled, the puppies were all adopted, many by members of the cast and crew.

53. *As Good As It Gets* (1997) A Brussels Griffon named Jill played Verdell, the irresistible pooch who captures Jack Nicholson's dog-hating heart in this hilarious film. Jill was smart — but not that smart: the scene in which Verdell walks down the street stepping over the cracks had to be accomplished largely through animation techniques.

54. *Air Bud* (1997) Buddy was a Golden Retriever stray when he was found by his trainer, Kevin Di Ciccio, who actually taught the dog to play basketball. When you see this film, which is based on a true story, bear in mind that there are no special effects or trickery at work here — Buddy can really shoot baskets!

55. *Men in Black; Men in Black II* (1997; 2002) Mushu the Pug got the part of Frank the talking alien dog because director Barry Sonnenfeld thought he was "ugly and strange" and "looked like an alien." The same dog was used in both films.

56. *Doctor Doolittle* (1998) The reason Sam, a dog shelter mixed breed, was able to give such a convincing performance as a talking dog is that he's incredibly intelligent. He's also patient and tolerant; Eddie Murphy, who stars in the film, is very nervous around animals.

"You beasts! But I'm not beaten yet. You've won the battle, but . . . all of you will wind up as sausage meat. . . . Cruella de Vil has the last laugh!"

— CRUELLA DE VIL, 102 DALMATIANS

57. *Dog Park* **(1998)** After twenty-seven dogs auditioned for the part of the dog in this movie, the writer/director Bruce McCulloch finally decided to use his own Standard Poodle, Kelsey. The film pokes fun at post-breakup behaviors and features a deadpan dog therapist who is uncomfortable with people.

58. *Family Dog* **(1998)** Based on Wolters's dog training book *Family Dog*, this film depicts a family in the process of training their amazing Lab, only to be upstaged by Pierre, the dog next door who can do everything from getting Cokes out of the refrigerator to carrying letters to the mailbox, mailing the letters, and then nosing up the flag before returning to the house.

59. *K-911* **(1999)** This time around (see *K-9*, page 44) there's also a Doberman whose human partner just happens to be an attractive female police officer.

60. *Best in Show* **(2000)** The owners of five show dogs head for the Mayflower Kennel Club Dog Show in this comic "mockumentary." A film crew interviews the eccentrics as they journey to the competition, all the while exhibiting behavior far quirkier than that of their lovable pets. A laugh-out-loud comment about the unconditional love that dogs provide.

61. *My Dog Skip* **(2000)** A shy boy is unable to make friends in Yazoo City, Mississippi, in 1942, until his parents give him a terrier puppy for his ninth birthday. Skip becomes well loved throughout the community and enriches Willie's life as he grows toward manhood. Have tissues ready for the scene in which Willie leaves for college, with Skip staring forlornly as the bus takes off into the distance. The older version of Skip in this movie is played by Moose, the same Jack Russell Terrier who played Eddie on TV's *Frasier*. The younger Skip is played by Moose's son Enzo and three other Jack Russells. The film is based on the memoir of the noted author and editor Willie Morris.

62. *Little Nicky* **(2000)** The devil's son must go to Earth and save his errant brothers in this original but ill-conceived Adam Sandler comedy. Beefy, the Bulldog who serves as Little Nicky's guide to Earth, was played by three dogs: Harvey, Harley, and Roo, one of whose puppies was later adopted by Sandler and named Meatball.

 **The Dogs of Best in Show**

1. "Beatrice" the Weimaraner is played by Can. CH Arokat's Echobar Take Me Dancing

2. "Winky" the Norwich Terrier is played by Can. CH Urchin's Bryllo

3. "Hubert" the Bloodhound is played by CH Quiet Creek's Stand By Me

4. "Miss Agnes" the Shih Tzu is played by Can. CH Rapture's Classic

5. "Tyrone" the Shih Tzu is played by Can. CH Symarun's Red Hot Kisses

6. "Rhapsody in White" the Standard Poodle is played by Can. CH Exxel Dezi Duz It With Pizaz

> "Women and cats will do as they please, and men and dogs should relax and get used to the idea."
> —ROBERT A. HEINLEIN

63. *Cats and Dogs* (2001) In the first "Great War of the Pets," cats and dogs slug it out to see who will control the universe. The four-legged stars of this film are helped along the way by animation techniques, but at the heart of it all, real dogs and cats were needed to do the job. The starring dogs included Butch, an Anatolian Shepherd who had been rescued from a shelter; Lou, an adorable Pocket Beagle who measures just ten inches high; Ivy, a Saluki; Peek, a Chinese Crested; and Sam, an English Sheepdog.

64. *Snow Dogs* (2002) It would have been impossible to find eight Siberian Huskies to play those in the film, whose roles called for winking, smiling, and various comical expressions. Special effects to the rescue.

65. *Scooby-Doo* (2002) Based on the old TV cartoon series, this film brought to life all of the original characters — except for Scooby-Doo, for whom we had to settle for state-of-the-art animation.

66. *Good Boy!* (2003) Twelve-year-old neighborhood dog walker Owen meets Hubble, an interplanetary agent from the Dog Star Sirius, sent to Earth on a mission to make sure that dogs are ruling the planet. Appalled to find out dogs are being kept as mere pets, Owen and Hubble set out to rectify the situation.

The Trouble with Moose

According to Mathilde de Cagny, who trains the lovable Jack Russell on *Frasier,* Moose (his real name) wouldn't last even one round at Westminster. On the upside, Moose is a spirited dog who is happiest when he is working. The downside:

Moose with his beloved human, Mathilde de Cagny

1. He picks fights with other dogs.

2. He's pigeon-toed and would be disqualified as soon as the judges saw him walking.

3. He would embarrass everyone by going after the ladies.

4. He would act like any other Jack Russell — only worse!

Moosisms
1. "If your bark is worse than your bite, you're not biting hard enough."

2. "He who learns fast gets fewer treats."

3. "Request to veterinarians: If it ain't broke, don't fix it."

4. "If you got 'em, lick 'em."

5. "Carpe Kitty!"

4 Genesis Award Winners 2004

The Genesis Awards were launched in 1986 by the animal advocate and actress Gretchen Wyler, who now heads the Humane Society of the United States Hollywood office. Every year, the Genesis Awards pay tribute to the major news and entertainment media for producing outstanding works that raise public understanding of animal issues. During a three-hour ceremony, Genesis Awards are bestowed on members of the media whose artistry and journalistic integrity have increased public awareness of animal issues. The following winners contributed to the safety, appreciation, and well-being of dogs.

1. Feature film: *Legally Blonde 2* (MGM). For boldly placing an animal advocacy message at the heart of a mainstream Hollywood movie, with the unstoppable Elle Woods taking on animal testing and Capitol Hill, proving that animal issues can make it big at the box office.

2. Reality programming: *Cell Dogs* (Animal Planet). For an inspiring series focusing on an extraordinary prison program teaming unwanted shelter dogs with death row inmates whose task of rehabilitating their new canine friends gives new meaning to the lives of these hardened criminals and puts the dogs back on track for adoption.

3. Television movie/children's programming: *Bike Squad* (Showtime). For raising the bar in presenting serious animal cruelty issues to children, with an engaging story about the pervasive yet rarely acknowledged crime of stealing and selling dogs to laboratories for research.

4. Series of newspaper articles: *Charlotte Observer* three-part series "Death at the Pound" by Scott Dodd and Michelle Couch. For galvanizing city officials and the public into seeking ways to reduce the staggering and above-average number of dogs and cats ending up at Charlotte's local shelter, destined for euthanasia.

5 Really Bad Dog Movies

1. *The Brain from Planet Arous* (1957) An evil alien brain matches wits with a good alien brain who takes the form of a dog. Totally preposterous and very funny.

2. *The Hills Have Eyes* (1977) Cave-dwelling cannibal mutants attack a vacationing family from Cleveland in this Wes Craven cult favorite. Lots of violence, including the bloody demise of the family dog.

3. *Zoltan . . . Hound of Dracula* (1978) Zoltan, an undead Doberman, and a creepy vampire track down Dracula's last descendant in a vacation camp. Zoltan recruits other vampire dogs, and together they tear up the place. Short on plot but with plenty of doggie drama.

4. *Frankenweenie* (1984) Tim Burton, who wrote this comedy, added cartoonlike images here not unlike those he would use later in *The Night Before Christmas*. The "weenie" is Sparky, who is hit by a car and resurrected by his owner during an electrical storm.

5. *The Hills Have Eyes, Part II* (1985) This ill-conceived sequel contains a ludicrous flashback that is the dog's recollection of what happened in the first movie.

And Toto, Too!

When the Cairn Terrier who played Toto in *The Wizard of Oz* was chosen for the role, he was already a Hollywood veteran, having appeared in eleven movies between 1934 and 1942. The terrier's name was Terry, and he was trained by Carl Spitz, a famous animal handler. MGM offered the shy dog $300 a week to play the role of Toto. But Spitz was so unsure of Terry's ability to perform that he accepted only $150. Terry, whose name was eventually changed to Toto, went on to create a role as memorable as those of the Tin Man, the Scarecrow, and the Cowardly Lion.

Toto was originally drawn into life in 1901 with the publication of L. Frank Baum's *The Wonderful Wizard of Oz.* The first edition of Baum's book was playfully illustrated by the artist William W. Denslow. He envisioned Toto as a Cairn Terrier. The other thirteen volumes, however, were illustrated by R. A. Neill, who depicted Toto as a French Bulldog. When the movie version of *The Wizard of Oz* was in preproduction, MGM cast a Frenchie named Captain to play Toto. But the Frenchie turned out to be an uncooperative actor, so the studio went with Denslow's depiction. Toto the scrappy little Cairn Terrier became firmly embedded in our collective consciousness.

Dorothy might have had an easier time of it if not for Toto's shenanigans, but she wouldn't have had nearly as much fun.

In the 1902 musical version of the *Wizard of Oz,* two actors played Toto as a spotted calf named Imogene. This was because, as Baum explained, "We found Toto an impossibility from a dramatic point of view." He felt that a calf would amuse children as much as a dog would.

Philosophers, sociologists, and even students of religion have long argued over the metaphysical interpretation of Toto. One theory postulates that Toto represents Anubis, the dog-headed Egyptian god of death. After all, it's *Toto's* fault that Dorothy never makes it to the Kansas storm cellar — and to safety. It's also Toto who exposes the wizard, and it's Toto who keeps Dorothy from returning home by leaping out of her arms at the worst possible moment. Thus, it is because Dorothy faces death at every corner that she must finally draw on her own inner strength — her spirituality, which is symbolized by her ruby slippers.

In his book *The Wizard of Oz,* Salman Rushdie refers to Toto as a "yapping hairpiece of a creature; that meddlesome rug."

The Story of Lassie

Lassie's saga has touched books, film, TV, comics, merchandise (remember those beloved lunch boxes?), and almost every other pop culture medium. She is credited with popularizing the rough-coated Collie and has become an icon representing courage, loyalty, and an uncanny ability to "get help."

1938: Eric Knight publishes his short story "Lassie Come-Home" in the *Saturday Evening Post.*

1940: An expanded version of the story appears in book form and becomes a popular bestseller. Set in Knight's native Yorkshire, *Lassie Come Home* tells the story of a loyal Collie who travels hundreds of miles to return to the boy she loves.

1941: MGM purchases the film rights to Knight's story for $10,000. Simultaneously, Robert "Rudd" Weatherwax, a respected Hollywood dog trainer, acquires Pal, a rambunctious male Collie who had frustrated the training efforts of his previous owner.

1943: *Lassie Come Home,* featuring the beautiful young Elizabeth Taylor and Pal, is released in theaters and goes on to become one the top-grossing films of the year.

1940s–1960s: Dell Comics publishes a bimonthly Lassie comic that has America's favorite Collie living with her new family in South America, which is where these comics are sold. In 1956, however, Lassie suddenly develops an allergy to a certain kind of South American plant, and she is tearfully shipped to the Miller family in the United States, much to the relief of the publishers, who felt they could sell more copies if they tied their story line into the successful TV series. These comics are highly collectible today, as is much Lassie memorabilia and merchandise that was manufactured during this time, including action figures, lunch boxes, dolls, clocks, candy molds — you name it.

1945–1953: Lassie continues to resonate with U.S. and British audiences as the film gives birth to a litter of six sequels plus various other nonsequel films starring Lassie which continue to be released well into the 1980s (many are available on DVD), and the Collie becomes the mythic embodiment of the kind of faith and determination for which audiences hungered in postwar years. Lassie's talents knew no bounds as she (Pal and all the succeeding Collies who played Lassie have been male) took on social roles, facilitating romances and rescuing orphans, in addition to performing daring rescues and part-time jobs as

The actor John Barrymore became an eccentric animal collector in his later years. His beloved menagerie consisted of three hundred different birds, dozens of Siamese cats, and nineteen dogs, of which there were eleven Greyhounds, several Saint Bernards, and a few Kerry Blue Terriers. Barrymore also had a monkey, a few opossum, and mouse deer.

babysitter, shepherd, messenger, firefighter, and others. At the height of his career, Pal was earning $4,000 a week.

1947–1950: A Lassie drama hits the radio airwaves. The fifteen-minute weekly anthology had Lassie playing a different dog each week. Aired first on the ABC radio network before being moved to NBC, the program featured the real Lassie, who provided the barking and growling, while an actor handled the whining and other dog noises.

1954: Whereas up to this point the Lassie stories have taken place in Great Britain, she becomes a full-fledged American idol as *Lassie* the TV series, about a farm family struggling through hard times, debuts. The show's rural setting and moving rescue stories touched the hearts of viewers, many of whom could identify with the hearth-and-home values and themes that *Lassie* espoused, and the depiction of an American boyhood helped further shape the coming of age of baby boomers. Jeff Miller (played by Tommy Retig until 1957) played the dog's original owner, eventually turning over the leash to the orphaned Timmy Martin (Jon Provost). Once Timmy outgrew the role in the midsixties, Lassie became the province of a series of park

rangers, and she spent the rest of her TV career in civic service.

1971: The program's relevance diminishes during a time of intense social and political change, and the *Lassie* TV series is canceled, airing only in syndication for the next three years.

1975: Cartoon rights to the character of Lassie are sold, and almost two dozen animated features are produced for TV programming.

1981: An attempt to revive the TV series, to be based on Earl Hamner's made-for-TV *Lassie: A New Beginning,* fails.

1994: *Lassie,* the last of the films, is released, and although it has more substance that the sequels of recent years, it becomes lost among special-effects and action blockbusters. The moving story tells of a boy who must make a traumatic move from the city to the country and the Collie who helps him make the adjustment. This same year, PBS airs the best of many film salutes to Lassie, called *The Story of Lassie,* to celebrate Lassie's fortieth year on television. It is a well-produced tribute to a dog whose stature in film history is eclipsed only by her status as a symbol of family values.

"Histories are more full of examples of the fidelity of dogs than of friends."
— ALEXANDER POPE

8 Weird Laws About Dogs

1. In Palding, Ohio, a police officer may bite a dog to quiet him.

2. It is illegal for anyone in Zion, Illinois, to give lighted cigars to dogs, cats, and other domesticated animals kept as pets.

3. Cats and dogs are not allowed to have sex without a permit in Ventura County, California.

4. People who make "ugly faces" at dogs in Oklahoma may be fined and/or jailed.

5. The animal code of Northbrook, Illinois, stipulates that a dog may not bark for more than fifteen minutes at a time.

6. Since the 1980s, a council ordinance has explicitly prohibited defecation in Cuyahoga Falls, Ohio, by any animal, including dogs. Constipated canines were thrilled when this law was repealed in 2002.

7. In Hartford, Connecticut, it is illegal to educate dogs.

8. In North Carolina, it is against the law for dogs and cats to fight.

"My dog can bark like a congressman, fetch like an aide, beg like a press secretary, and play dead like a receptionist when the phone rings."

— GEROLD SOLOMON, U.S. CONGRESSMAN

"We are alone, absolutely alone on this chance planet: and, amid all the forms of life that surround us, not one, excepting the dog, has made an alliance with us."

— MAURICE MAETERLINCK

The constellation Canis Major

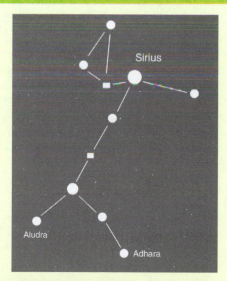

Sirius

Aludra

Adhara

3 Dog Constellations

1. Sirius, the Dog Star, is the brightest star in the constellation Big Dog, also known as Canis Major, the Greater Dog, and the Dog of Orion.

2. Canis Minor, also known as the Lesser Dog, is Orion's second hunting dog, much smaller than its mate. Its brightest star is Procyon.

3. Canes Venatici is an obscure constellation that represents two dogs, Asterion and Chara, both held on a leash by Boötes the hunter as they chase the Great Bear around the North Pole.

The Rin Tin Tin Story

Rin Tin Tin and his descendants have been inspiring and entertaining audiences for more than eighty years. Today he is among the most beloved dogs ever in both fact and legend. His story has inspired books, films, cartoons, board games, and merchandise, and his name has come to be associated with the very best qualities in dogs. Rin Tin Tin progeny continue to entertain audiences through their inspiring story and personal appearances. All of Rin Tin Tin's earnings are donated directly to ARFKids, a group that supplies terminally ill and disabled kids with service dogs trained especially for them.

"Rinty" is the most recognized German Shepherd Dog in history and descends from the oldest continuous bloodline in the breed, thereby fulfilling his first owner's dream that "there will always be a Rin Tin Tin." For more information, write to Rin Tin Tin Incorporated, Box 27, Crockett, Texas, 75835; 936-545-0471.

September 15, 1918: Corporal Lee Duncan, in Lorraine, France, with his battalion during World War I, visits a bombed war dog kennel and discovers the only survivors: a German Shepherd Dog named Betty and her litter of five ten-day-old puppies. The family is rescued, but only one of the puppies ultimately survives: the one named Rin Tin Tin.

1918: Duncan brings his beloved dog back home to Los Angeles and attends dog shows, where filmmaker Darrell Zanuck sees Rin Tin Tin jump 13.5 feet and uses the dog to try out his new moving camera.

1922: Rin Tin Tin appears in a film called *The Man from Hell's River* after filmmakers, experiencing difficulty with a scene involving a wolf, take Duncan up on his boastful promise that his dog could do the scene in one take. A canine star is born.

1923–1932: Rin Tin Tin saves Warner Bros. from the brink of bankruptcy and goes on to make twenty-six pictures for the studio. At the height of his career he earns a record (for a dog, anyway) $2,300 a week.

August 10, 1932: Rin Tin Tin dies just as he is scheduled to begin shooting a new film. At the peak of his career, Rin Tin Tin received more than 10,000 fan letters a week and was the only dog in Los Angeles to be listed in the telephone directory. As a gesture of honor to the dog's home country, Duncan has the dog buried in Paris, France, where his black onyx, gold-leafed headstone reads, "Star of Cinema."

1933: Having abandoned the film project of the previous year, Warner Bros. sends Duncan, devastated by the loss of his pet, on the road with one of Rin Tin Tin's puppies, Junior, who is now dubbed Rin Tin Tin. The dog wins the hearts of audiences wherever he goes, most notably that of his owner: when Duncan's wife files for divorce, she cites Rin Tin Tin as a co-respondent, claiming her husband loves the dog more than he loves her.

1941–1953: Duncan continues to study and breed German Shepherd Dogs, attending shows and participating in the development of the breed as Rin Tin Tin's progeny continue to perform in films and elsewhere.

1954: In the first episode of a new TV action series, the U.S. Cavalry comes upon the only survivor of an attack by Apache Indians — a little boy named Rusty (played by Lee Aaker) and his German Shepherd Dog, Rinty. They are taken to Fort Apache in Arizona, and Rusty is made an honorary corporal so he can remain at the fort with the soldiers whose hearts he has won.

1954–1959: *The Adventures of Rin Tin Tin* dominates TV programming, and Rin Tin Tin becomes established as a household name once and for all. Two dogs share the lead role: the dogs that Duncan had registered as Rin Tin Tin II and Rin Tin Tin IV.

1956: Janiettia Brodsgaard Propps acquires Rin Tin Tin IV's son and Duncan's blessing for her breeding program to continue the dog's lineage.

1960: Duncan dies on September 20, leaving Rin Tin Tin's bloodline in the hands of Ms. Propps and her granddaughter, Daphne Hereford, who maintains it still. She does so abiding by the primary concerns Duncan had for the dog's progeny: intelligence and a sound working environment. Today's Rin Tin Tin puppies are identical to Rin Tin Tin II and Rin Tin Tin IV. The breeding program is closed, which means that all puppies are adopted under a nonbreeding agreement to protect "not only . . . the integrity of the lineage," says Ms. Hereford, "but the Rin Tin Tin name."

1999: Ms. Hereford founds the ARFKids ("A Rinty for Kids") in cooperation with Rin Tin Tin Incorpo-

rated after learning about the many children who are on waiting lists for assistance dogs. The foundation provides service dogs to disabled children at no cost; these include dogs of the Rin Tin Tin lineage as well as qualified dogs from other breeders of German Shepherd Dogs. ARFKids is staffed by volunteers and funded completely by grants and donations; for more information or to make a contribution to this worthy organization, visit arfkids.com.

2003: A petition is circulated by fans requesting that the U.S. Postal Service issue a stamp featuring Rin Tin Tin.

At the height of Rinty's popularity, Rin Tin Tin merchandise was all the rage: everything from stuffed dogs, a cavalry mess kit, and beanies, to a 3-D color televiewer and a Wonderscope kit that included a compass, a mirror, action figures, and other goodies. Today Rinty's collectibles fetch a small fortune. A Shredded Wheat box with Rin Tin Tin premium offers goes for $175, while a Rin Tin Tin Nabisco gun and leather holster can sell for up to $575.

45 Dogs Who Appeared on <u>The Simpsons</u>

In a 1995 episode called "Two Dozen and One Greyhounds," the family dog, Santa's Little Helper, runs away to the dog track from which he came, where he meets and falls in love with She's the Fastest. The twenty-five resulting puppies, along with some twenty other dogs who found their way to the Simpson household, are listed here.

Dog	Episode	Description
Always Comes in Second	"Two Dozen and One Greyhounds"	Greyhound that raced against She's the Fastest
Blitzen	"Two Dozen and One Greyhounds"	One of She's the Fastest's puppies
Bobo	"There's No Disgrace Like Home"	Tracking dog used to investigate "a family of peeping toms who have been terrorizing the neighborhood"
Buddy	"Bart's Dog Gets an F"	One of Santa's Little Helper's fellow students
Branford	"Two Dozen and One Greyhounds"	And Branford II; two of She's the Fastest's puppies
Cleo	"Two Dozen and One Greyhounds"	One of She's the Fastest's puppies
Dave	"Two Dozen and One Greyhounds"	And Dave II; two of She's the Fastest's puppies
Dinner Dog	"The Day the Violence Died"	One of the original Itchy & Scratchy characters
Dog O' War	"Simpsons Roasting over an Open Fire"	Greyhound that raced against Santa's Little Helper
Dogkid	"Radioactive Man"	One of the comic book heros seen on the shelves at "The Android's Dungeon"
Donner	"Two Dozen and One Greyhounds"	One of She's the Fastest's puppies
Dopey	"Two Dozen and One Greyhounds"	One of She's the Fastest's puppies
Fickler	"Dog of Death"	The old guard dog that Mr. Burns retires and replaces with Santa's Little Helper; some argue the name is Crippler
Fido	"Simpsons Roasting over an Open Fire"	Greyhound that raced against Santa's Little Helper
	"Two Dozen and One Greyhounds"	And Fido II; two of She's the Fastest's puppies
Flatulent Fox	"The Day the Violence Died"	One of the original Itchy & Scratchy characters
Geech	"The Brother from Another Series"	The hick construction crew's "smell hound" that gets sealed in cement at the Terwilligers' dam
Ghost Mutt	"The Day the Violence Died"	Marge's idea for a new cartoon hero
Grumpy	"Two Dozen and One Greyhounds"	And Grumpy II; two of She's the Fastest's puppies
Hercules	"Homer Defined"	Mr. Smithers's Yorkshire Terrier
I'm Number Three	"Two Dozen and One Greyhounds"	Greyhound that raced against She's the Fastest
Jasper	"Treehouse of Horror II"	Bart uses his telekinetic powers to turn senior citizen Jasper into a dog
Jay	"Two Dozen and One Greyhounds"	And Jay II; two of She's the Fastest's puppies
King	"Two Dozen and One Greyhounds"	One of She's the Fastest's puppies
Laddy	"The Canine Mutiny"	Bart uses a phony credit card to buy this amazing Collie
Lao-Tzu	"Bart's Dog Gets an F"	Martin Prince's Shar-Pei and fellow student of Santa's Little Helper
Little Monty	"Two Dozen and One Greyhounds"	Puppy chosen to be spared from Burns's tuxedo because he reminded him of Rory Calhoun

McGriff	"The Springfield Connection"	Marge shows Lisa a "McGriff" hand puppet who says, "Help me bite crime."
Number 8	"Simpsons Roasting over an Open Fire"	Santa's Little Helper's racing number; when Lisa asks, "What's his name?" Homer replies (at first), "Number 8."
	"Two Dozen and One Greyhounds"	She's the Fastest's racing number
Paul	"Two Dozen and One Greyhounds"	And Paul II; two of She's the Fastest's puppies
Poochie	"Itchy & Scratchy & Poochie"	Short-lived addition to Itchy & Scratchy, voiced by Homer
Prince	"Two Dozen and One Greyhounds"	And The Puppy Formerly Known as Prince; two of She's the Fastest's puppies.
Quadruped	"Simpsons Roasting over an Open Fire"	Greyhound that raced against Santa's Little Helper
Queenie	"Two Dozen and One Greyhounds"	One of She's the Fastest's puppies
Rex	"Marge in Chains"	On the show *I Can't Believe They Invented It*, the "Doggie Doorman" greets the incoming pooch by saying mechanically, "Good morning, Rex."
	"Two Dozen and One Greyhounds"	And Rex II; two of She's the Fastest's puppies
Rover	"Two Dozen and One Greyhounds"	And Rover II; two of She's the Fastest's puppies
	"Homerpalooza"	Rover Hendrix; when leaving the vet's office, Homer asks him, "Got any messages for Jimi Hendrix?" The vet replies, "Yes: 'Pick up your puppy!'" and points to Rover.
Santa's Little Helper	various episodes	The Simpsons' Greyhound
Santos L. Halper	"The Canine Mutiny"	The credit card company's butchered version of "Santa's Little Helper," which Bart uses as his name when he fills out the application
She's the Fastest	"Two Dozen and One Greyhounds"	Santa's Little Helper's Greyhound girlfriend and the mother of his numerous children
Sleepy	"Two Dozen and One Greyhounds"	One of She's the Fastest's puppies
Smithers	"Bart Gets Hit by a Car"	Burns and Smithers peer at the Simpsons through eyeholes in a painting; Smithers uses the dog's eyeholes.
	"Rosebud"	In Burns's vision of the future (A.D. 1,000,000), Smithers's head is attached to a robot-dog body.
	"Homer Goes to College"	Smithers is sleeping on the floor by Burns's chair
Spot	"Two Dozen and One Greyhounds"	One of She's the Fastest's puppies
Sprinkles	"The Canine Mutiny"	The name given to Santa's Little Helper by the blind man
Timmy O'Toole	"Radio Bart"	Dr. Marvin Monroe says Timmy has reverted "to a feral, or wolf-like state" after they hear him "growling"; they show an artist's conception of a wolf-boy.
Two by Two	"Simpsons Roasting over an Open Fire"	Racing Greyhound that placed against Santa's Little Helper
Whirlwind	"Simpsons Roasting over an Open Fire"	Greyhound that Barney bet on (and who won)

"Well, crying isn't gonna bring him back . . . unless your tears smell like dog food. So you can either sit there crying and eating can after can of dog food until your tears smell enough like dog food to make your dog come back or you can go out there and find your dog." —HOMER SIMPSON

Dogs in Print

Whatever role they play in our lives — whether it be that of pet, playmate, confidante, or professional assistant — we tend to give them story lines: now they love us, now they are mad at us, now they can't live without us. So it's no surprise that they have made their way into thousands of books, including novels of romance, mystery, intrigue, humor, and horror. The following lists only scratch the surfaces of their categories. For a list of the best books on dog health and behavior, see Part 4, "Tender Loving Care and Training."

Literary Dogs

Timbuktu, by Paul Auster (Picador, 2000).
This is the poignant story of Brooklyn-born poet/saint Willy G. Christmas and his empathetic canine companion, Mr. Bones. Though unable to speak, Mr. Bones understands every nuance of human "Ingloosh" and is able to provide a dog's-eye view of his owner's alternately troubled and beatific existence. Tubercular and knowing that his days are numbered, Willy sets out with his four-legged friend on a last, quixotic adventure — to Baltimore, and the last known address of his revered high school English teacher.

Lives of the Monster Dogs, by Kirsten Bakis (Farrar Straus Giroux, 1997).
This disturbingly charming novel follows the saga of a master race of dogs created in the eighteenth century by Augustus Rank, a mad Prussian scientist. The narrator, Cleo Pira, befriends the dogs after they make their way (via Canada) to New York City circa 2008. There they settle down to lead civilized lives. With the help of technology, the monster dogs — mostly Rottweilers, Doberman Pinschers, and German Shepherd Dogs — can talk, walk, read, and even enjoy the opera. This unbelievable novel is so utterly enthralling, and ultimately convincing, that you will never look at your dog in the same way again.

Heart of a Dog, by Mikhail Bulgakov (Grove Press, 1987 reprint edition).
First published in 1925, this absurdist parody of the Russian Revolution follows a rich and respected Moscow professor as he implants the testicles and pituitary gland of a man into a mixed-breed dog. Chaos follows, of course.

That Pup, by Ellis Parker Butler (Doubleday & Co., 1988).
This novel consists of two stories: "The Education of Fluff" and "Getting Rid of Fluff." Together, they tell the rib-tickling saga of a mixed-breed dog and the man determined to train him.

Top Dog, by Jerry Jay Carroll (Ace/Berkley, 1996).
One morning, a Wall Street executive wakes up as a dog. No more cocktail parties, stock reports, or limo rides for him. Instead, "Bogey" has to deal with magical creatures and hideous monsters. In this new world, called Fair Lands, things are either completely good or completely evil. Bogey decides to explore both sides before deciding which one he wants to join. While the cover art hints that the dog in this novel is a Golden Retriever, the author says he actually pictured a very large German Shepherd Dog.

Dog Days, by Mavis Cheek (Simon & Schuster, 1990).
When Patricia Murray decides to divorce her husband of eleven years, she has one major problem: how to tell their daughter. So Patricia buys a mixed-breed dog

The English Romantic poet Lord Byron had the following inscribed on the headstone of his beloved Newfoundland, Boatswain: "Beauty without vanity, strength without insolence, courage without ferocity, and all the virtues of man without his vices."

named Brian to ease the transition. But the dog proves to be a handful, especially for a woman who is rejoicing — for the moment, at least — in her newfound freedom.

Must Love Dogs, by Claire Cook (Viking Penguin, 2002).

This engaging book is about Sarah Hurlihy, a preschool teacher from a big and happy family who answers a personal ad from a gentleman seeking a lady "who enjoys elegant dining, dancing and the slow bloom of affection." The clincher is that he's a man who "loves dogs." But there's a surprising twist at the end of this sweet novel.

Crazy for You, by Jennifer Crusie (St. Martin's Press, 2000).

Quinn McKenzie, living what she calls a boring, "beige" life, decides to change it all by adopting a stray dog, over the objections of just about everyone. Now she must cope with dognapping, breaking and entering, seduction, sabotage, stalking, more secrets than she really wants to know, and two men who are suddenly crazy for her.

A Dog's Head, by Jean Dutourd, translated by Robin Chancellor (University of Chicago Press, 1998).

Much to the horror of his bourgeoisie parents, Edmund Du Chaillu is born with the head of a Spaniel and the urge to carry around a newspaper in his mouth. Needless to say, his classmates tease him. Translated from its original French, this magical realist novel has been likened to works by Jorge Luis Borges, Voltaire, and Gabriel García Márquez.

Redeye: A Western, by Clyde Edgerton (Penguin, 1995).

Set more than a hundred years ago among the cliff dwellings of Colorado, this comical novel features a colorful mix of opportunistic characters, including the local rancher who wants to protect the newly discovered cliff-dwelling site, an Englishman who is writing about it, a Mormon saint looking for proof that Jesus once visited 2,000 years ago, and a drifter who wants revenge for the Mountain Meadows Massacre of 1875. And oh, yes: there is also a talking Pit Bull named Redeye.

Dumb-bell of Brookfield, Pocono Shot, and Other Great Dog Stories, by John Taintor Foote (Lyons Press, 1993).

First published in the early 1920s, these are among the best dog stories ever written. They're tightly plotted and filled with warmth and shrewd perception, and they portray unforgettable relationships between humans and canines. Anyone who loves dogs or loves reading about dogs will enjoy these classics.

The Curious Incident of the Dog in the Night-time, by Mark Haddon (Doubleday, 2003).

Christopher John Francis Boone loves dogs and numbers but hates to be touched. He's also autistic. One day Christopher discovers the neighbor's dog, Wellington, impaled on a garden fork. Falsely accused of the crime, Christopher sets out to find the real killer. This highly emotional story is told seemingly without emotion, making for a fine, dark comedy that delivers a poignant statement about those who interpret the world literally.

Fluke, by James Herbert (New English Library, 1978).

In the novel on which the film was based, Fluke is a mixed-breed dog with a secret past — he was once a human, and he's back to reveal his killer. The story is somewhat predictable, but Fluke's wit and wisdom make this book memorable.

Sick Puppy, by Carl Hiaasen (Warner Books, 2001).

In typical Hiaasen fashion, this story involves corrupt, crazed, and power-hungry Florida politicians accidentally pitted against quirky but innocent individuals. Twilly Spree and the Stoats family's feud evolves into mayhem that includes, among other things, a dognapping, kinky sex, hit men, a big-game hunt, and an ex-governor turned ecoterrorist.

Toyon: A Dog of the North and His People, by Nicholas Kalashnikoff, illustrated by Arthur Marokvia (Harper-Collins, 1950).

Set in czarist Siberia, this adventure story stars Toyon, a Siberian hunting dog who protects his people (native Shamanistic locals) and brings them good luck. This novel is based on the author's real-life experiences while in exile in Siberia.

"A dog teaches a boy fidelity, perseverance, and to turn around three times before lying down."
— ROBERT BENCHLEY

"A dog's best friend is his illiteracy."
— OGDEN NASH

To Dance with the White Dog, by Terry Kay (Pocket Books, 1993).
A mysterious white dog joins the recently widowed Sam on a trip to his sixtieth college reunion. Stray dog, ghost dog, or guardian angel, we never really know, but the white dog remains Sam's companion until just before his own death.

Cujo, by Stephen King (Viking, 1981).
A rabid, two-hundred-pound Saint Bernard terrorizes a woman and a little boy who are trapped in their stifling car. This tightly wound drama is especially frightening in its depiction of the dark side of a once-lovable pet, a theme King visited again in *Pet Semetary*.

Dog People, by Cris Mazza (Coffee House Press, 1997).
This emotionally charged novel explores the sad reality that people who can't get along with dogs often can't get along with humans, either. The narrator's pooch, Lacy, however, may be the only one with enough gumption — and animal instinct — to straighten out the mess.

Where the Blue Begins, by Christopher Morley (Telegraph Books, 1986).
Back in print after many generations, this sweet satirical novel is about a noble dog named Gissing, a bachelor who lives in a suburb known as Canine Estates. When Gissing becomes a father, everything about him changes. An outré classic.

A Dog of Flanders, by Marie Ouida (de la Ramée) (Dover, 1992).
Originally published in 1872, this sentimental classic is considered to be the first modern dog story. It tells of a young boy named Nello who wants to be a painter, and his Belgian working dog. Boy and dog endure hunger and cruelty until they meet a tragic, bittersweet end.

The Dogs of Babel, by Carolyn Parkhurst (Little, Brown, 2003).
When Paul Iverson's wife, Lexy, is found dead in their yard, the only witness to her death is the couple's loyal dog, Lorelei. Numb with grief, Paul leaves his job as a linguistics professor to take on the impossible task of teaching his dog to communicate. With Lorelei by his side, he flashes back to the pivotal moments of his life with Lexy, and eventually becomes desperate enough to connect with a bizarre cult intent on teaching dogs to talk, however inhumane their methods. Paul's journey leads him to the secrets of Lexy's burdened heart, while Lorelei teaches him that the truest forms of love don't need words at all.

A Girl's Best Friend, by Elizabeth Young (Avon, 2003).
After her most recent disaster with the King of the Unrepentant Jerks, Isabel "Izzy" Palmer is finally convinced that the only male she truly needs in her life is Henry, her lovable part wolfhound, part who-knows-what. Henry's faithful, he adores her madly, and he's great fun to sleep with. So who needs the additional heartache? Enter the handsome vet.

> "The poor dog, in life the firmest friend,
> The first to welcome, foremost to defend."
> — LORD BYRON

According to the American Pet Products Manufacturers Association, pet spending has doubled from $17 billion in 1994 to a projected $34.3 billion in 2004. Sales in 2003 exceeded projections and reached $32.4 billion. The numbers put the pet industry at 60 percent larger than the toy industry ($20 billion) and 33 percent larger than the candy industry ($24 billion).

Snoop Dogs: Detectives and Their Canine Partners

There's something about a dog that makes an independent woman seem even more independent. Perhaps it's that she can obviously take care of both herself and a creature of another species. Or maybe it's the skulking protectiveness that dogs — even little ones — project around their people, creating an even greater aura of self-sufficiency. In any case, the heroines in mystery novels always seem extremely capable. They can shoot a gun, change a tire, find the bad guy. Okay, so most of them have too many bad hair days and can't sustain a personal relationship with a human male. No bother. The women in the books listed below can do it all, and they do it in the company of a panting, four-pawed sidekick. These are among the best of the woman-and-her-dog detective books.

Laurien Berenson. Berenson's cozies focus on the personal and professional travails of their multitasking protagonist, Melanie Travis, a teacher, a prizewinning Poodle breeder, and an amateur sleuth. Most of the crimes in this series take place in the seemingly genteel world of dog shows and dog people. Melanie stars in the series alongside her two black Standard Poodles, Faith and Eve. And while the humans in these books are engaging enough, it's the canines — in all sizes, colors, and ages — who provide the most amusement. In *Hot Dog,* the ninth installment in the series, Melanie explains that her life is pretty dull. Unless, of course, you count her tangled personal life. First, her former fiancé returns after leaving town for six months to "find himself." Then her ex-husband moves back to reconnect with their seven-year-old son — bringing along his new twenty-something girlfriend and a pony. A divorced couple battle over their Dachshund puppy, and somehow Melanie has gotten herself smack into the thick of things. Other notable titles in the series include Berenson's initial entry, *A Pedigree to Die For* and *Jingle Bell Bark*.

Susan Conant. Dog fans are sure to devour Conant's Dog Lovers series featuring dog magazine columnist Holly Winter and her trustworthy Alaskan Malamutes, Rowdy and Kimi. Holly is a plucky narrator who has learned to rely on the instinct of her dogs to solve crimes. Particularly interesting titles in the series include Conant's very first entry, *A New Leash on Death.* This book contains a mystery along with a plethora of information on dog obedience training. Conant does a good job of illustrating the dynamics of dog training classes. In the fifteenth title, *Bride and Groom,* local dog lovers are being murdered. All of the victims are women and they all have some connection to Holly Winter, who fears that she's next on the villain's agenda. With characteristic courage, Rowdy and Kimi help solve the gruesome mystery.

Sue Henry. This series stars Alaskan detective and kennel owner Jessie Arnold and her lead sled dog, Tank. The mysteries draw heavily from their exotically snowy setting, with dogsled racing taking a central role, along with the quirky locals and Jessie's rugged love interest. But it's the heroine's relationship to her dog, Tank, that's most important to these mysteries. Jessie relies on Tank to help her solve crimes and also to help guide her sled teams. In the first book in the series, *Murder on the Iditarod Trail,* the top contestants in this grueling test of endurance are dying in strange and gruesome ways. Jessie Arnold and Tank must solve the mystery so that they can go on to compete. In the ominous *Deadfall,* Jessie is stalked and one of her sled dogs is hurt by a steel trap.

Virginia Lanier. Even if you aren't a fan of books set in the South and aren't yourself a Bloodhound fancier, this wonderful series is worth looking into. Six books feature Jo Beth Siddon, a Bloodhound breeder and trainer. When Jo Beth isn't tending to her dogs, she's helping local law enforcement find lost children and pets as well as missing criminals and contraband from the alligator-infested Okefenokee Swamp. Jo Beth is a talented tracker, and her dogs are as lovable as all get out — especially the blind Bobby Lee, who stars in *A Brace of Bloodhounds* and *Blind Blood Hound Justice,* the third and fourth titles in the series. Lanier is as talented an author as Jo Beth is a tracker, and the details in these books — such as the diet needed to raise healthy Bloodhound puppies, and all the gear a tracker has to carry along on missions with her — are fascinating.

17 Aesop Dog Fables

We know that dogs have been respected as teachers since at least as early as the sixth century B.C., when Aesop, a freed slave, employed them in many of the stories he wrote. Even today, these tales are told to thousands of schoolchildren daily as basic lessons in humanity.

1. The Dog and the Shadow

A dog crossing a bridge over a stream with a piece of flesh in his mouth sees his own shadow, and, taking it for that of another dog with a piece of meat double his own in size, he lets go of his own and fiercely attacks the other "dog" while his dinner is swept away in the stream. Thus he learns about the losses that come with envy.

2. The Dog in the Manger

A dog lies in a manger, and by his growling and snapping, prevents the oxen from eating the hay that has been placed for them. "What a selfish Dog!" says one of them to his companions; "he cannot eat the hay himself, and yet refuses to allow those to eat who can." The phrase "a dog in a manger" has since come to mean a selfish person who prevents others from enjoying themselves.

3. The Donkey and the Lap Dog

A man who owns a donkey and a Maltese lap dog favors the dog, who knows many tricks and provides companionship. The donkey laments his life as a beast of burden, and in an attempt to win his master's love, he gallops into his house and tries to imitate the behavior of the little dog. He succeeds only in causing a ruckus and annoying the man. The donkey, nearly beaten to death, is led back to his stall, lamenting: "I have brought it all on myself! Why could I not have been contented to labor with my companions and not wish to be idle all the day like that useless little lap dog!"

4. The Mischievous Dog

A dog who runs up on the heels of everyone he meets to bite them is outfitted with a bell around his neck so that he might give notice of his presence wherever he goes. Thinking it a mark of distinction, the dog proudly wears his bell and shows it off to the other dogs, until an old hound dog explains that the bell is a mark of disgrace — and that notoriety is often mistaken for fame.

5. The Man Bitten by a Dog

A man who has been bitten by a dog goes about in quest of someone who might heal him. A friend suggests, "Take a piece of bread and dip it in the blood from your wound, and go and give it to the dog that bit you." The man who had been bitten laughs at this advice and says, "Why? If I should do so, it would be as if I should beg every dog in the town to bite me." The moral: Benefits bestowed upon the evil-disposed increase their means of injuring you.

6. The Two Dogs

A man had two dogs: a hound, trained to assist him in his sports, and a house dog, taught to watch the house. When he returned home in the evening after hunting, he always gave the house dog a large share of his spoil. The hound, feeling dejected, reproached his companion, saying, "It is very hard to have [to] labor while you, who do not assist in the chase, luxuriate on the fruits of my exertions." The house dog replied, "Do not blame me, my friend, but

find fault with the master, who has not taught me to labor, but to depend for subsistence on the labor of others." Children cannot be blamed for the faults of their parents.

7. The Wolf and the House Dog

A wolf, meeting a big well-fed Mastiff with a wooden collar around his neck, asks him who it was that fed him so well and yet compelled him to wear the heavy weight wherever he went. "The master," he replies. Says the wolf: "May no friend of mine ever be in such a plight; for the weight of this chain is enough to spoil the appetite."

8. The Master and His Dogs

A man detained by a storm in his country house first kills his sheep, and then his goats, for the maintenance of his household. The storm still continuing, he is obliged to slaughter his yoke oxen for food. On seeing this, his dogs decide: "It is time for us to be off, for if the master spares not his oxen, who work for his gain, how can we expect him to spare us?" He who mistreats his own family is not to be trusted as a friend.

9. The Old Hound

An old hound, who in the days of his youth and strength had never yielded to any beast of the forest, encounters a boar. The hound seizes him boldly by the ear but cannot retain his hold because of the decay of his teeth, so the boar escapes. His master, who watches the incident, is disappointed and fiercely punishes the dog. The hound tells him, "It was not my fault, master: My spirit was as good as ever, but I could not help my infirmities. I rather deserve to be praised for what I have been, than to be blamed for what I am."

10. The Brazier and His Dog

A brazier has a little dog that is a great favorite with his master and his constant companion. While the man hammers away at his metals the dog sleeps; but when the man goes to dinner and begins to eat, the dog wakes up and wags his tail, begging for a share of his meal. One day, pretending to be angry and shaking his stick at him, the master says, "You wretched little sluggard! What shall I do to you? While I am hammering on the anvil, you sleep on the mat; and when I begin to eat after my toil, you wake up and wag your tail for food. Do you not know that labor is the source of every blessing, and that none but those who work are entitled to eat?"

11. The Wolves and the Sheepdogs

A group of wolves address a group of sheepdogs: "Why should you, who are like us in so many things, not be entirely of one mind with us, and live with us as brothers should? We differ from you in one point only. We live in freedom, but you bow down to and slave for men, who in return for your services flog you with whips and put collars on your necks. They make you also guard their sheep, and while they eat the mutton throw only the bones to you. Give us the sheep, and we will enjoy them in common, till we all are surfeited." The dogs, ignoring the very nature of the wolves, enter the den, where they are immediately set upon and torn to pieces.

12. The Dog and the Hare

A hound pursues a hare on a hillside for some distance, at one time biting her with his teeth as if he would take her life, and at another fawning on her, as if in play with another dog. The hare says to him, "I wish you would act sincerely by me, and show yourself in your true colors. If you are a friend, why do you bite me so hard? If an enemy, why do you fawn on me?" No one can be a friend if you know not whether to trust or distrust him.

13. The Dog, the Rooster, and the Fox

A dog and a rooster who are good friends agree to travel together. At nightfall they take shelter in a thick wood. The rooster, flying up, perches himself on the branches of a tree, while the dog finds a bed beneath in the hollow trunk. When morning comes, the rooster, as usual, crows very loudly several times, attracting the attention of a fox in search of food. The fox stands under the branches of the tree and compliments the rooster, saying how much he would like to meet the owner of this fine voice in person. The rooster, suspecting his civilities, says: "Sir, I wish you would do me the favor of going around to the hollow trunk below me, and waking my porter, so that he may open the door and let you in." When the fox approaches the tree, the dog springs out and catches him and tears him to pieces, proving his everlasting loyalty to his friend.

14. The Blind Man and the Dog

A blind man is accustomed to distinguishing different animals by touching them with his hands. A young wolf is brought to him with a request that he feel it and say what it was. He feels it and, being in doubt, says: "I do not quite know whether it is the cub of a fox, or the whelp of a wolf, but this I know full well. It would not be safe to

admit him to the sheepfold," thus demonstrating that evil tendencies cannot be hidden for long.

15. The Dogs and the Fox

A group of wild dogs, finding the skin of a lion, begin to tear it to pieces with their teeth. A fox, seeing them, says, "If this lion were alive, you would soon find out that his claws were stronger than your teeth." It is easy to kick a man that is down.

16. The Dog and the Oyster

A dog who eats eggs sees an oyster and swallows it down with the utmost relish, supposing it to be an egg. Soon afterward, suffering a terrible stomachache, he says, "I deserve all this torment, for my folly in thinking that everything round must be an egg." They who act without sufficient thought will often fall into unsuspected danger.

17. The Dog and the Cook

A rich man gives a great feast for his many friends and acquaintants. His dog decides to invite another dog, a friend of his, saying, "My master gives a feast, and there is always much food remaining; come and sup with me tonight." The invitee boasts to the other street dogs of his good fortune and then goes to the party. Seeing the grand preparations, he declares his gratitude and goes about consuming as much food as he can. But the cook sees him sauntering among the other guests and immediately bundles him without ceremony and tosses him out. The humiliated dog howls, attracting the attention of the other street dogs, who come up to him and inquire how he enjoyed his supper. He replies, "Why, to tell you the truth, I drank so much wine that I remember nothing. I do not know how I got out of the house." Pride goeth before the fall.

14 Memoirs About Dogs and Their People

1. *Dog Is My Co-Pilot: Great Writers on the World's Oldest Friendship.* **From the editors of** *The Bark* **(Crown, 2003).**
Imagine a magazine that is a cross between *Dog Fancy, The New Yorker,* and *ArtForum* with a splash of *Harper's Magazine* thrown in. That magazine would be *The Bark,* the preeminent dog magazine for artsy, sophisticated, literary dog lovers everywhere. The editors of *The Bark* (who started their magazine in a Berkeley garage as an off-leash newsletter) and others have banded together to produce this fun and poignant collection of contemporary dog stories and essays. These include Stephen Kuusisto's touching "Blind Date," about a man meeting his Seeing Eye dog for the first time; Erica Jong's story about her Bichon Frisé; Jon Billman's humorous recounting of the Australian Cattle Dog who won't work cattle; Lama Surya Das's "God Is Dog Spelled Properly," an essay on what dogs teach us; and Lee Forgotson's lovely "Sit. Stay. Heal: One Dog's Response to 9/11." Dog lovers are sure to treasure this collection.

2. *Bark if You Love Me,* **by Louise Bernikow (Algonquin Books, 2000).**

Writer Louise Bernikow doesn't set out to adopt a stray dog from a New York City park. Neither does she expect to fall for him, warts (a metal plate in one leg and a tendency to fart — a lot) and all. But that's exactly what happens in this unconventional love story of Bernikow and the macho Boxer she takes home with her and names Libro. The independent Bernikow and the very dependent Libro form an alliance that's stronger than either of them has ever had before.

3. *If Only They Could Speak: Stories About Pets and Their People,* **by Nicholas H. Dodman (Tufts University School of Veterinary Medicine, 2003).**
Dodman, a veterinary behaviorist, explores human-animal (mostly canine) relationships from both points of view in fourteen stories of problem pets, their owners, and the solutions that made them all happy. Dodman is interested in finding out why good dogs (and cats) do bad things. He examines animals to discover what species characteristics and personality traits might be influencing their behavior, and then bases his solutions on everything from behavior modification, to changing their diets, to putting them on puppy pills.

4. *Amazing Gracie: A Dog's Tale,* **by Dan Dye and Mark Beckloff (Workman Publishing, 2000).**
Gracie is an albino Great Dane puppy with an incredibly sensitive stomach. Dan Dye is a guy looking to adopt a dog. The two meet, move in together, and, along with a Dalmatian named Dotty and a black Labrador named Sarah and Dye's partner, Mark, form a happily blended family. But when Gracie turns her nose up at commercial dog food, Dye starts cooking for her — with amazing results: the Three Dog Bakery. This well-written book is a joy to read.

5. *Bandit: Dossier of a Dangerous Dog,* **by Vicki Hearne (Trafalgar Square Publishing, 2002).**
This story of a Pit Bull ordered put to death by the state of Connecticut in 1987 is infused with the wisdom of poet, philosopher, and animal trainer Hearne. The author earned a reprieve for the dog by training him. This thoughtful book uses the sociological dimensions of the case against Bandit to shed new light on the politics of disenfranchisement.

6. *James Herriot's Dog Stories: Warm and Wonderful Stories About the Animals Herriot Loves Best,* **by James Herriot (St. Martin's Press, 2005).**
This unforgettable collection of stories is just what you would expect from America's favorite veterinarian and the author of the classic *All Creatures Great and Small.* Here, Herriot writes about big dogs and small dogs, quiet dogs and loud dogs. Each of the fifty entries is about a dog, but throughout all, readers are treated to Herriot's philosophies and reminiscences about the many dogs he has known. An enlightening history of animal doctoring emerges as well, as Herriot describes the progress of treatments since the 1930s. This book is, simply, a treasure.

7. *A Dog Year: Twelve Months, Four Dogs, and Me,* **by Jon Katz (Random House, 2003).**
This irresistible memoir of a year with two Labs and two Border Collies features an appealing cast of characters. There are the Labs: easygoing Julius and mischievous Stanley. There is Devon, a supersmart two-year-old Border Collie who is also high-strung and suffers from low self-esteem, along with a Border Collie puppy named Homer. Homer is as sweet and uncompli-

cated as Devon is difficult and complicated. Katz writes with great depth and warmth: "Dogs . . . make me happy, satisfy me deeply, anchor me in an elemental way. Sometimes it's hard for me to trust people, or to find people I can come to trust. I trust my dogs, though. They would do anything for me, and I for them. That's a powerful relationship, no matter what the species."

8. *Clara: The Early Years,* by Margo Kaufman (Plume, 1999).

The irreverent, irrepressible Clara is a Pug puppy who isn't at all fond of being treated like a dog and, for instance, made to sleep on the floor while the human gets the bed. Clara is all id, but she's a loving scamp, and the havoc she creates in Kaufman's home is truly uproarious. Kaufman writes about how Clara enters her life like a whirling dervish, transforming the other two dogs in Kaufman's charge, not to mention Kaufman's career — and Clara's — her love life, and her parental urges.

9. *Pack of Two: The Intricate Bond Between People and Dogs,* by Caroline Knapp (Delta Books, 1999).

Knapp's mother and father died in quick succession right after she ended her affair with alcohol. The author was left wondering who she was without parental attachments and with an unhealthy obsession with drink. Enter Lucille, the Shepherd mix whom Knapp adopts from the local animal shelter. Lucille teaches Knapp about responsibility, loyalty, and love. But this beautifully written book transcends the personal as it tries to explain how — and why — humans and canines have forged such strong and intimate bonds.

10. *Out on a Leash: Exploring the Nature of Reality and Love,* by Shirley MacLaine (Atria Books, 2003).

"If a dog will not come to you after having looked you in the face, you should go home and examine your conscience."

— WOODROW WILSON

Shirley MacLaine has found a perfect love in the furry bundle of irresistible canine charms that is Terry. With her winning terrier ways and an endless wellspring of love, Terry succeeds where no one ever has before: she slows down Shirley's peripatetic travels, shifting the actress/author's global axis from "out there" to hearth and home. Now there are few greater pleasures for Shirley than being with Terry, who, she says, helps her see the world in ways she never thought possible.

11. *What the Dogs Have Taught Me: And Other Amazing Things I've Learned,* by Merrill Markoe (Viking, 1992).

This book is just what you would expect from Markoe, co-creator of the television show *Late Night with David Letterman.* The author depicts her very funny life among not-so-funny mere mortals as she cavorts with members of the opposite (human) sex and has heart-to-heart talks with her (canine) dogs. Among the things Markoe's dogs have taught her are how they *really* spend their time, that they can't stop following her around the house, and that "going for pens means food" while her purse means "ball."

12. *The Cruelest Miles: The Heroic Story of Dogs and Men in a Race Against an Epidemic,* by Gay and Laney Salisbury (W. W. Norton & Company, 2003).

Isolated by geography and blizzard conditions in the winter of 1925 as the ravages of diphtheria threatened to take a deadly toll, Nome, Alaska, desperately needed help that was only accessible via dogsled. This book tells the story of the courageous men and canines who braved incredible adversity to save the town. The real heroes were the dogs, especially the team leaders, and their interaction with and interdependence on humans make tales of the Iditarod pale in comparison. (A statue in New York's Central Park honors Balto, one of these dogs.) Another version of this story, *Race to Nome,* written by Kenneth Ungermann, Salisbury's cousin, is a carefully researched and well-written account of this event.

13. *Dog Miracles: Inspirational and Heroic True Stories,* by Brad Steiger and Sherry Hansen Steiger (Adams Media Corporation, 2001).

More than sixty stories of ordinary canines who have proven themselves to be miraculous: tiny purebred dogs who thwart muggers; powerful ones who save entire families from life-threatening fires; tenacious travelers who return home after roaming hundreds of miles; and some who even manage to connect with their owners from beyond the grave . . .

14. *My Therapist's Dog,* **by Diana Wells (Algonquin, 2004).**

Diana Wells's intriguing exploration into the rewards of relationships — both the canine and human varieties — begins when she reluctantly starts seeing a psychologist during a difficult time in her life. With no insurance to pay for counseling, she agrees to become part-time caretaker to the therapist's dog, Luggs, a sweet, clumsy black Labrador Retriever. As Wells examines her past, she becomes curious about the connections that dogs and humans have shared for centuries — and what these bonds tell us about our own psyches. Her studies and wise observations lead her to agree with Diogenes, the original Greek cynic (the word *cynic* comes from the Greek *kuon,* meaning "dog"), who said that unless we think like dogs, happiness will elude us.

The name of the dog on the Cracker Jack box is

Bingo.

13 Books "Written" by Dogs

Given the remarkable range of talents that dogs possess, is it any wonder that some have actually written their own books?

1. *King,* **with the help of John Berger (Vintage, 2001).**
Narrated by the dog King, this thought-provoking story takes place in England and tells of a group of homeless people who are both dispossessed and dehumanized. This is an odd story in which the substance is more impressive than the drama.

2. *Millie's Book: As Dictated to Barbara Bush* **(Quill, 1992).**
The Springer Spaniel Millie is perhaps the most successful of all the dog writers. Her book was a national bestseller, describing a day in the life of President George Bush and family: morning briefings, adventures in the Oval Office, and, of course, squirrel hunting.

3. *I, Toto: The Autobiography of Terry, the Dog Who Was Toto,* **with the help of Willard Carroll (Stewart, Tabori and Chang, 2001).**
Terry, the famous terrier who changed his name to Toto to cash in on his "overnight" success in *The Wizard of Oz,* "wrote" this book posthumously, giving us the inside scoop on the grueling before-scenes enemas, snafus on the set, and the great difficulty of playing a scene with flying monkeys. Toto tells it like it was: "I don't mean this to sound full of myself but this Wizard of Oz story? It's all about me!!! I'M IN ALMOST EVERY SCENE IN THE PICTURE!"

4. *My Life As a Dog,* **with the help of Brian Hargrove (HarperCollins, 2000).**
Moose, the famous Jack Russell who por-trays TV's Eddie on *Frazier,* took time out from his busy schedule to pen the story of how a pound-bound puppy achieved superstardom. Moose imparts page after page of the kind of wit and wisdom that only a dog can really appreciate: "If it's worth chasing, it's worth shaking till it's dead"; "The best things in life are worth licking."

5. *Unleashed: Poems by Writers' Dogs,* **with the help of Amy Hempel and Jim Shepard (Three Rivers Press, 1999).**
A charming collection of poems by the dogs of celebrated writers and poets whose love of woofs and words goes beyond their own work, including Edward Albee, Lynda Barry, Roy Blount, Jr., Cynthia Heimel, John Irving, Anne Lamott, Gordon Lish, Arthur Miller, William Wegman, and many others.

6. *The Dog Who Spoke with Gods,* **with the help of Diane Jessup (St. Martin's Press, 2002).**
This finely told thriller depicts the relationship between a young medical student and the Pit Bull research dog she befriends. When the student realizes that the dog is capable of limited speech, she determines to save him from those who would capitalize on his abilities. Time and again, dog and medical student demonstrate their loyalty toward each other as the "writer" seeks to set us straight on his much-maligned breed.

7. *Rover's Tales,* **with the help of Michael Z. Lewin (St. Martin's Press, 1998).**
In this charming collection of short sto-

ries, Michael Z. Lewin gives Rover, his canine narrator, a voice that speaks for dogs everywhere. Rover is spunky, intelligent, and compassionate, if not a little raffish with females. He responds only to the dictates of his nature, imparting his unique philosophy all along the way.

8. *A Dog's Life,* with the help of Peter Mayle (Vintage Books, 1996).

A hilarious canine confessional by "Boy," a stray who was adopted by the author in Provence and who displays a condescendingly sophisticated French voice that throughout the book provides us with witty, entertaining commentary on human nature. "My story is based on actual events," he tells us. "However, following the current autobiographical custom adopted by politicians in their memoirs, I have adjusted the truth wherever it might reflect unfavorably on myself."

9. *Shakespeare's Dog,* with the help of Leon Rooke (Knopf, 1983).

Mr. Hooker, a perspicacious mixed breed, reveals the Bard's early life in canine-inflected Elizabethan English. Rather than focus on Shakespeare's literary pursuits, this book is a randy romp of domestic squabbles told in "canine Elizabethan."

10. *Beautiful Joe,* with the help of Marshall Saunders (Buccaneer Books, 1998).

Beautiful Joe was a real dog (circa 1893) who was cruelly abused by his original owner, and he tells his story in a book that is as relevant today as it was in 1893, when it was first written. In his own words, Joe tells of his brutal existence at the hands of seemingly heartless humans. In fact, it was common for writers of the period — the Industrial Revolution — to write about cruelty to animals as a way of exploring our cruelty to one another. Luckily, Joe was later adopted by a good family, and in this book he recounts his sorrows and joys.

11. *Angus: A Novel,* with the help of Charles Siebert (Three Rivers Press, 2001).

A lovingly written "autobiography" of the author's beloved Jack Russell Terrier, *Angus* is the delicate tale of a warm and aggressive puppy and his sadly abbreviated life on Earth. Lucy, an elderly dog in his new home, is in poor health — and not at all happy about the rambunctious puppy in her space, but Angus likes her and guards her with his life while embarking on his own adventures: puppy basic training, an international airplane flight, and an exploration of Brooklyn.

12. *The Captain's Dog: My Journey with the Lewis and Clark Tribe,* with the help of Roland Smith (Harcourt, 2000).

This is the story of the Lewis and Clark expedition as witnessed by Seaman, the massive Newfoundland dog that accompanied the two captains. The book is thoughtful and humorous, as when Seaman offers insight into a dog's life: "Dogs know humans better than they will ever know us." Seaman also tells his story for young adult readers in *Dog of Discovery: A Newfoundland's Adventures with Lewis and Clark,* with the help of Laurence Pringle (2002).

13. *Dog Stories,* with the help of Jon Weber and Dylan Schaffer (Chronicle Books, 1997).

Thirty-seven very short stories (by Schaffer), illustrated with photographs (by Weber), are told from a dog's point of view. But the pooches here are much more than faithful companions; they are witty, wry, and wise to the ways of the world.

Gidget, the rescued pooch known as the Taco Bell Chihuahua, doesn't work as hard as you might think. The entire ad campaign was actually shot in four days, as Gidget posed in a variety of costumes and positions. From there, the images were taken to a graphics boutique in Abeline, Texas, where they are turned into commercials as the need arises.

Say "Kibble": 9 Noted Dog Photographers

According to Ruth Silverman, the former associate curator of the International Center of Photography, the following photographers are noted for their work in the photography of dogs. Her books, *The Dog Observed* and *Athletes,* each won the Photography Book of the Year Award and were organized as traveling exhibitions by the Smithsonian Institution. She is the editor of the amazing *The Dog: 100 Years of Classic Photography* (Chronicle Books, 2000).

1. **Mark Asher** operates a pet portraiture firm in Ashland, Oregon. His duotone portraits capture the golden years of man's best friends. He manages to capture not only the dogs' age and grace but also their more humorous sides. His book *Old Friends: Great Dogs on the Good Life* (Chronicle, 2003) is a marvelous collection of photos that capture tender moments along with the dogs' secrets for a long and happy life.

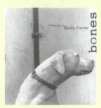

2. **Keith Carter** is an internationally recognized photographer and educator. He is the recipient of two National Endowment for the Arts Regional Survey Grants and the Lange-Taylor Prize from the Center for Documentary Studies at Duke University. In 1997 Keith Carter was the subject of an arts profile on the national network television show *CBS Sunday Morning*. His book *Bones* (Chronicle, 1996) is a thoroughly handsome collection of dog photos.

3. **Elliott Erwitt** is possibly more famous now for his amusing and widely reproduced photos of dogs than for the impressive balance of work he's done during his almost fifty years as a photographer. His book *Dog Dogs* (Phaidon, 1998) contains five hundred black-and-white pictures and is a miraculous blend of composition and content, placing Erwitt right up there with the other postwar, twentieth-century masters of moment and meaning.

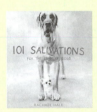

4. **Rachel Hale** is the youngest person in New Zealand to have received a fellowship with the New Zealand Institute of Professional Photographers. But her most valuable qualification is her passion for the animals she works with, a characteristic that shines through in all her pictures. She is the author of *101 Salivations: For the Love of Dogs* (Bulfinch, 2003), and a calendar of her dog photos was published in 2005.

5. **Tony Mendoza** bought his first camera at age eleven and continued photographing through grammar school, high school, Yale University, and the Harvard Graduate School of Design. Although Mendoza is most noted for his photos of his cat Ernie, he has devoted a great deal of time photographing dogs. He is the author of five books, including *Dogs: A Postcard Book* (Capra, 1995).

6. **Diane Pearce** has specialized in canine photography for more than thirty years and as an official photographer for *Dog World* and *Our Dogs* magazines has attended many important dog shows. A pictorial record of her successful career, capturing important changes in dog showing and the evolution of breeds, is on display at The Kennel Club in London.

7. **Robin Schwartz**'s photographs are in several museum collections, including the Metropolitan Museum of Art, the Museum of Modern Art, the National Museum of Art, Washington, D.C., the San Francisco Museum of Modern Art, and the Bibliotheque Nationale in Paris. Her wonderful book *Dog Watching* (Takarajama, 1995) explains why dogs do what they do, offering reasons for such behaviors as sniffing and tail wagging.

8. **Valerie Shaff** has gained renown for her commissioned dog portraits. Her photos appear in Roy Blount, Jr.'s *If Only You Knew How Much I Smell You: True Portraits*

of Dogs (Bulfinch, 1998), a whimsical book with more than fifty doggy photos that seem to reveal their innermost thoughts. In *I Am Puppy, Hear Me Yap: The Ages of Dog* (HarperCollins, 2000), also with Blount, Valerie Shaff's photography showcases our four-legged friends in many of their finest moments — chewing on slippers, rolling in the clover, and shaking the water off their fuzzy puppy fur are just a few of the classics captured here.

9. **William Wegman** is perhaps the most famous dog photographer in the United States, widely respected for his photographs of the majestic Weimaraner dog. One of his first models (and longtime companion) was a pooch named Man Ray, who passed away in 1982. This beautiful dog plays a starring role in *Man's Best Friend,* in which he is caught posing, napping, and playing in more than forty (mainly color) photographs. Wegman dresses his dog in a variety of costumes — transforming him into a strange new creature, half man, half canine. Each exquisite portrait is a testament to Man Ray's beauty — and the strong bond between dog and master.

> "I've seen a look in dogs' eyes, a quickly vanishing look of amazed contempt, and I am convinced that basically dogs think humans are nuts."
> — **JOHN STEINBECK**

Irresistible Photo Books for Dog Lovers

Old Friends: Great Dogs on the Good Life, by Mark Asher (Chronicle, 2003).
Old dogs know plenty of tricks for staying young at heart — and here they are! This humorous and loving collection of duotone portraits by Ashland, Oregon, pet portraitist Asher captures the golden years of humanity's best friends. Sage and tender moments are paired with captions that reveal each dog's age and their secrets for a long and happy life: "Lift and pee, lift and pee, lift and pee on every tree"; "Never let little dogs with bows in their hair get the best of you." These are dogs who know how to live life fully, and they share their lessons happily.

Bones, by Keith Carter (Chronicle, 1996).
Sometimes charming, sometimes mysterious, Carter's dog portraits convey the grace, character, and playfulness of their subjects. Carter, an acclaimed photographer whose works appear in many public and private collections, follows his dogs everywhere — under porches, down cotton rows, and down dirt roads. This collection of duotone portraits comprises a passionate tribute to the spirit and intelligence of dogs.

Southern Dogs and Their People, by P. S. Davis and Roberta Gamble (Algonquin, 2000).

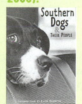

Dogs and southerners have a lot in common: They know when it's time to eat and when it's time to be quiet, when to move slow and when to bare teeth. In southern literature, dogs have taken prominent roles as muses and characters, confessors and conspirators, and this book celebrates that relationship by featuring the endearing photos that P. S. Davis has been taking of dogs around her home of Greenville, Alabama, for many years. Her photographs chronicle the lives of dogs and their owners, from the Poodles of a rich widow to the mixed breed of a homeless veteran. Editor Roberta Gamble has brought together a wide-ranging collection of quotations from great southern writers, including William Faulkner, Eudora Welty, Zora Neale Hurston, James Dickey, Anne Tyler, James Tate, Flannery O'Connor, Bobbie Ann Mason, and many others.

Dogography, by Jim Dratfield (Rizzoli, 2002).
The unspoken fidelity of the eyes, the earnest greeting of a wagging tail, the eager bark that beckons us to run, throw, leap, and play — they're all celebrated here in a book-plus package that proves once and for all that more than any other animal, the dog is our companion on life's long road. The renowned pet photographer Jim Dratfield has compiled an irresistible ode to the dog in a boxed set that includes a keepsake book that pairs images with quotes celebrating the dog, an illustrated journal to record your own dog's life story, and six note cards.

101 Salivations: For the Love of Dogs, by Rachael Hale (Bulfinch, 2003).
Rachael Hale's signature style catches the eye of everyone who comes across it. Featuring color photographs of Chihuahuas, Great Danes, and everything in between, *101 Salivations* presents dogs in all sorts of wonderful poses that bring out their

19 Definitions for the Word Dog

1. A highly variable domestic mammal closely related to the common wolf.

2. A worthless person.

3. A mechanical device for holding, gripping, or fastening that consists of a spike, bar, or hook; an andiron, which is also known as a firedog.

4. A wooden sawhorse used on a race track near the rail to keep horses out of the mud.

5. Uncharacteristic or affected stylishness or dignity, as in "putting on the dog."

6. Ruin, as in "going to the dogs."

7. To annoy someone.

8. To hunt or track.

9. To run away.

10. To fail to do one's best.

11. To loaf on the job.

12. An inferior version of something; a worthless piece of merchandise.

13. An unattractive person, especially a girl or woman.

14. A human foot, as in "my dogs are killing me."

15. A promissory note.

16. An animal, especially a race horse, that does not perform well.

17. A poor-quality automobile.

18. A theatrical flop.

19. A friend, as in "dawg."

most endearing characteristics. Hale's secret to capturing a dog's soul is to focus on his eyes — whether they are wide and shining or heavy-lidded, in the throes of slumber. The book is peppered with humorous and touching quotations from well-known authors. A whimsical compilation that celebrates the quirky character of our canine companions.

The Tao of Pug, by Nancy Levine (Studio Books, 2003).

Wilson the Pug is the apotheosis of the breed dog lovers can't get enough of. That he is irresistible goes without saying — but Wilson is also a descendant of the Chinese philosopher Lao-tzu's beloved companion, Pug-tzu, and he spouts his wisdom in the form of his own take on quotations from the Tao Te Ching: "A pug is a pug is a pug. I'm just me, Wilson the Pug. And I'm okay with that." Veteran dog photographer Nancy Levine captures the essence of Pugs in whimsical words and captivating pictures.

Second Chances: More Tales of Found Dogs, by Elise Lufkin and Diana Walker (Lyons Press, 2003).

Every year, millions of dogs are abandoned — at animal shelters, racetracks, or on the side of the road. Many of these animals end their days without ever knowing a caring human hand, but some are fortunate enough to be found and given a second chance. These dogs, often rescued from death's door, seem to have even more than the usual canine capacity for love and loyalty. They are celebrated in Walker's wonderful collection of photos and words by people who have adopted dogs in myriad ways — celebrities from Julio Iglesias, Mikhail Baryshnikov, Donna Shalala, and Oscar de la Renta to everyday heroes. A moving tribute to the power of the love that passes between dog and man.

Dog, by Deborah Samuel (Chronicle, 2001).

Here's a heart-tugging collection of stunning portraits that celebrates the beauty and spirit of humankind's most devoted companion. Focusing her lens on purebred dogs, the photographer Deborah Samuel has uniquely captured the ever-changing moods and peculiar eccentricities of dozens of different breeds. Through her closely observed photographs we come to understand the vitality of an Irish Setter,

 the roguish humor of a Jack Russell, the diffident elegance of a Greyhound. Ultimately, each irresistible image reveals not just the character of the breed but the heart and soul of a beloved pet. Samuel's personal anecdotes, collected at the end of the book, reveal the often hilarious behind-the-scenes stories of each photo session.

 ### If Only You Knew How Much I Smell You, by Valerie Shaff and Roy Blount, Jr. (Bulfinch, 1998).

Who hasn't looked into a dog's eyes and wondered what's going on in that furry head? What do dogs make of us? The answers are found in this hilarious book of fifty evocative canine countenances giving voice to their inner dog. This charming collection teams up dog portraits by Valerie Shaff with verse by humorist Roy Blount, Jr., to give us an original and entertaining portrayal of what dogs really think. Blount's verses — written from the dog's point of view — tell us the meaning of the quizzical expressions and soulful looks Valerie Shaff's camera catches so well: "What does that mean, 'expensive shoe'?/I ate it because it smelled like you." From adorable Dalmatian puppies, to mournful hounds, to soulful setters, each dog conveys the befuddlement, heartbreak, and simple joys of a dog's life. This team went on to bring us a second delightful collection, *I Am Puppy, Hear Me Yap* (HarperCollins, 2000).

The World According to Dog: Poems and Teen Voices, by Joyce Sidman, with photographs by Doug Mindell (Houghton Mifflin, 2003).

Teen voices explore the funny, comforting, surprising rewards of our lives with dogs: dogs who befriend us; dogs who annoy, perplex, and accept us. Honest and forthright essays combine with Joyce Sidman's insightful poems to express the bond between dog and teen: how days of crowded hallways, pointless assignments, and blinding crushes are brought to balance by our dogs. Doug Mindell's winning photographs confirm that at the end of the day, waiting at home, there is always Dog — full of hope and companionship.

The Dog: 100 Years of Classic Photography, by Ruth Silverman (Chronicle, 2000).
Ruth Silverman was associate curator at the International Center of Photography in New York from 1978 to 1984, and her expertise is evident in this historic collection

of dog photos from the greatest photographers of our time. From the earliest daguerreotypes to captivating portraits from photographers on the forefront of today's art scene, the images here are as stunning as the dogs are endearing. In Robert Capa's 1943 photo a young soldier gingerly places a small puppy into his combat helmet. Robert Doisneau brings to light a Paris that is at once familiar without being trite, simply by photographing a dog looking into the camera while his owner turns away on the Pont des Arts. Each photograph in this remarkable collection reflects a unique moment in time, as well as the sometimes surprising, occasionally humorous, always intimate relationship people have with their dogs.

William Wegman. Anything by him! William Wegman's interest in painting ultimately led him to become one of the most beloved dog photographers of all time. Man Ray, Fay Ray, and his other famous Weimeraners, known in the art world and beyond for their endearing deadpan presence, have graced his books, calendars, videos, and photography, which is represented in museums and galleries internationally. His books for kids — including *Wegmanology* (Hyperion, 2001), *ABC* (Hyperion, 1994), *Dress Up Batty* (Hyperion, 2004) — and adults — *Fay* (Hyperion, 1999), *William Wegman's Polaroids* (Abrams, 2002), and others — all document the career of one of the most central figures in the popular dog world.

Roy Blount, Jr.'s "5 Reasons Why I Can't List My Favorite Dogs"
We asked Roy Blount to describe his favorite dog. He failed miserably.

1. They have all been good. Not all ideal — Bobby, for instance, kept disappearing and showing up at the pound surrounded by dogs of low character. (I don't know how he kept falling in with them.) But all good.

2. They have all been willing to do more for me than I have had occasion to ask them to do, so, okay, being at loose ends, they got into trouble sometimes.

3. One of my sentimental favorites was Pie, who probably never knew it, especially after I got so mad at her when just before I took her to the kennel because I had to go to Peru she ate an entire bag of candy corn and while I was driving her to the kennel she threw up candy corn all over the back seat.

4. Dogs transcend mathematics.

5. See 4, above.

84 More Literary Dogs

Dog	Literary Source	Author	Description
Arlo	Erma Bombeck books	Erma Bombeck	Bombeck's Irish Setter
Argos	*The Odyssey*	Homer	Odysseus's faithful hound
Asta	Nick and Nora North	Dashiell Hammet	The little Wire Fox Terrier dog sleuth
Auld Mustard and Auld Pepper	*Guy Mannering*	Walter Scott	Terriers were actually named after the main character Dandie Dinmont
Banga	*The Master and the Margarita*	Mikhail Bulgakov	Pontius Pilate's dog
Bastard	*And the Ass Saw the Angle*	Nick Cave	Bum's roan mongrel
Beautiful Joe	*Beautiful Joe*	Margaret Marshall Saunders	The author based the dog on a real dog that she saw being mistreated
Big Red	*Big Red* and others	James Kjelgaard	Heroic Irish Setter
Blood	*A Boy and His Dog*	Harlan Ellisan	Telepathic pooch
Bluebell	*Animal Farm*	George Orwell	The mother of one of Napoleon's puppies
Boatswain	*Typee*	Herman Melville	Dog aboard the whaling ship *Dolly*
Bob	*Tale of Little Pig Robinson*	Beatrix Potter	Retriever
Bob	*Watership Down*	Richard Adams	Black Labrador Retriever
Bodger	*The Incredible Journey*	Sheila Burnford	White Bull Terrier
Boots	*Thy Servant a Dog*	Rudyard Kipling	The story's narrator
Buck	*Call of the Wild*	Jack London	The protagonist
Bullseye	*Oliver Twist*	Charles Dickens	Bill Sykes's dog
Cabal or Cavall	*Idylls of the King*	Alfred Lord Tennyson	King Arthur's dog
Champion	Ellery Queen, Jr., Mysteries	Ellery Queen, Jr.	Djuna's old black Scottie
Charley	*Travels with Charley*	John Steinbeck	Steinbeck's Poodle
Copper	*The Fox and the Hound*	Daniel P. Mannix	The hound
Cujo	*Cujo*	Stephen King	Rabid Saint Bernard gone berserk
Enrique	*Tortilla Flat*	John Steinbeck	Pet of the pirate
Fairy Wogdog	*Watership Down*	Richard Adams	Messenger of the great dog spirit
Fluffy	*Harry Potter and the Sorcerer's Stone*	J. K. Rowling	Hagrid's dog, a Neapolitan Mastiff
Flush	*The Barrets of Whimpole Street*	Rudolph Besier	Cocker Spaniel
Gaspode	Discworld novels	Terry Pratchett	A stalking dog
Ginger Pye	*Ginger Pye*	Eleanor Estes	Protagonist
Gissing	*Where the Blue Begins*	Christopher Morley	Protagonist
Greyfriars Bobby	*Greyfriars Bobby*	Eleanor Atkinson	Skye Terrier
Gyp	*Only One Woof*	James Herriot	Mostly silent sheepdog
Howard the dog	*Bunnicula Books*	James Howe	A howling "werewolf" Dachshund
Huan	*The Silmarillion*	J.R.R. Tolkien	Dog of Baren
Jack	*Little House on the Prairie*	Laura Ingalls Wilder	Laura's Bulldog

Jip	*David Copperfield*	Charles Dickens	Dora's dog
Jip	*Dr. Doolittle*	Hugh Loffing	The doctor's dog
Jock	*Jock of the Bushveld*	Sir Percy FitzPatrick	The author's dog
Josephine	*Every Night Josephine!*	Jacqueline Susann	French Poodle
Knave	*Lad: A Dog*	Albert Payson Terhune	Lad's Collie
Kojak	*The Stand*	Stephen King	Saves protagonist's life
Krypto	Superman Comics	Jerry Siegel and Joe Shuster	The Superdog from the planet Krypton
Lad	*Lad: A Dog*	Albert Payson Terhune	Protagonist
Lassie	*Lassie Come Home*	Eric Knight	World's smartest Collie
Leo	*Dogsbody*	Diane Wynne Jones	Protagonist
Misha	*The Hidden Lives of Dogs*	Elizabeth Marshall Thomas	One of the main characters
Montgomery	*Three Men in a Boat*	Jerome K. Jerome	Unruly Fox Terrier
Mr. Bones	*Timbuktu*	Paul Auster	Willy's empathetic companion
Mutt	*The Dog Who Wouldn't Be*	Farley Mowatt	Protagonist
Nana	*Peter Pan*	J. M. Barrie	The family Newfoundland dog
Nero	*Sylvie and Bruno, Concluded*	Lewis Carroll	Newfoundland
No-Sitch	*No-Sitch, the Hound*	Phil Stong	Bulldog/shepherd/spaniel/Saint Bernard mix
Old Yeller	*Old Yeller*	Fred Gipson	Yellow Labrador Retriever
Oscar	*Topper*	Thorne Smith	The Kirby's Saint Bernard, called Neal in the TV series and Mr. Atlas in the movie
Pajarito	*Tortilla Flat*	John Steinbeck	The pirate's pet
Patrasche	*A Dog of Flanders*	Ouida	Belgian work dog
Pickles	*The Tale of Ginger and Pickles*	Beatrix Potter	Terrier
Pilot	*Jane Eyre*	Charlotte Brontë	Rochester's dog
Pitcher	*Animal Farm*	George Orwell	Farm dog
Precious	*Silence of the Lambs*	Thomas Harris	The psychopath's Miniature Poodle
Queen	*Watership Down*	Rich Adams	The great dog spirit Dripslobber
Ribsy	*Henry Huggins* and others	Beverly Cleary	Henry's constant companion
Rowf and Snitter	*The Plaque Dogs*	Richard Adams	Protagonists, escape experiments
Sharik/Sharikov	*Heart of a Dog*	Mikhail Bulgakov	The dog/man
Sheilah	*Big Red* and others	Jim Kjelgaard	Irish Setter
Sigmund	*The Dream Master*	Roger Zelazny	Talking Seeing Eye dog
Sirius	*Dogsbody*	Diane Wynne Jones	The Dog Star is reborn and named Leo
Sirius	*Sirius*	Olaf Stapledon	A dog with the intelligence of a human

"Sir, this is a unique dog. He does not live by tooth or fang. He respects the right of cats to be cats although he doesn't admire them. He turns his steps rather than disturb an earnest caterpillar. His greatest fear is that someone will point out a rabbit and suggest that he chase it. This is a dog of peace and tranquility."

—JOHN STEINBECK, ON CHARLEY

Smoky	*Yorkie Doodle Dandy*	Bill Wynne	Yorkshire Terrier
Snarleyyow	*The Dog Friend*	Capt. Frederick Marryat	A reprehensible cur
Sounder	*Sounder*	William Armstrong	Coon dog
Spot	*Slaughterhouse Five*	Kurt Vonnegut	Billy Pilgrim's traveling companion
Spunky	*Spunky*	Dori Brink	Terrier narrator
Swizzle	*Dr. Doolittle* books	Hugh Lofting	Circus dog
Sylvester Boy	*Big Red*	Jim Kjelgaard	Irish Setter
Tee Tucker	*Mrs. Murphy* books	Rita Mae Brown	Corgi
Timmy the dog	*Famous Five series*	Enid Blyton	One of the famous five
Toby-Chien	*Sept Dialogues de Bêtes*	Collete	Bulldog
Togo	*Nancy Drew books*	Carolyn Keene	Nancy's Bull Terrier
Top	*The Mysterious Island*	Jules Verne	Cyrus Smith's pet
Wolf	*Rip Van Winkle*	Washington Irving	Rip Van Winkle's dog
Woola	*Martian Series*	Edgar Rice Burroughs	Capt. Carter's Martian hound
Yellow Dog Dingo	*Just So Stories*	Rudyard Kipling	The ever-hungry dog in "The Sing-Song of Old Man Kangaroo"

Shakespeare on Dogs

The only dog to ever appear in a Shakespearean play was Crab in *The Two Gentlemen of Verona*. The Bard may have been a cat person, but he managed to contribute to the canine lexicon: the word *watchdog* is first found in *The Tempest*: "The watch-dogs bark!" (act 1, scene 2).

"Talks as familiarly of roaring lions as maids of thirteen do of puppy-dogs!" (*King John*, act 2, scene 1)

"France is a dog-hole." (*All's Well That Ends Well*, act 2, scene 3)

"My hounds are bred out of the Spartan kind; So flew'd, so sanded; their heads are hung With ears that sweep away the morning dew." (*A Mid Summer Night's Dream*, act 4, scene 1)

"I had rather be a dog, and bay the moon, than such a one." (*Julius Caesar*, act 4, scene 3)

"The little dogs and all, Tray, Blanch, and Sweetheart — see, they bark at me." (*King Lear*, act 3, scene 5)

"Thou hast seen a farmer's dog bark at a beggar? . . . And the creature run from the cur. There thou mightst behold the great image of authority — a dog's obeyed in office." (*King Lear*, act 4, scene 5)

"When night dogs run all sorts of deer are chas'd." (*The Merry Wives of Windsor*, act 5, scene 5)

"Hope is a curtal dog in some affairs." (*The Merry Wives of Windsor*, act 2, scene 1)

"Poison more deadly than a mad dog's tooth." (*The Comedy of Errors*, act 5, scene 1)

"Thou call'dst me dog before thou hadst a cause." (*The Merchant of Venice*, act 3, scene 3)

"But, since I am a dog, beware my fangs." (*The Merchant of Venice*, act 3, scene 3)

"Dogs, easily won to fawn on any man!" (*King Richard the Second*, act 3, scene 2)

"They call'd us for our fierceness English dogs." (*King Henry the Sixth*, act 1, scene 5)

"Cry Havoc! and let slip the dogs of war." (*Julius Cæsar*, act 3, scene 1)

"The cat will mew and dog will have his day." (*Hamlet*, act 5, scene 1)

"Thou hadst been better have been born a dog." (*Othello*, act 3, scene 3)

Part Two

Top Dogs

STEVE DONAHUE

"If you think dogs can't count, in your pocket and then giving

They have changed history by traveling into space, influencing presidential elections, and saving lives on the battlefield.

They forged trails through the Alaskan wilderness to bring medical supplies to otherwise unreachable corners of the globe, and they have warmed our hearts with impossibly competent film performances. They are born for recognition, or so it seems as they accept the thousands of awards, honors, and accolades we bestow on them for their achievements.

It would be impossible, in this chapter — or in any one book, for that matter — to list all the accomplishments of the millions of dogs who deserve to be celebrated for their special contributions to humankind. This chapter, then, can cast a spotlight on only a few of those deserving canines, and provide just a sampling of the ways in which we recognize them.

Though thousands of dog shows and competitions are held

try putting three dog biscuits Fido only two of them."

— PHIL PASTORET

throughout the world each year, none is as anticipated or as prestigious as the Westminster Dog Show. Steeped in history and tradition, Westminster and the other conformation dog shows you'll read about here comprise a culture unto itself, complete with its own jargon, etiquette, and super-stars. This is the higher ech-elon on which serious com-petitors set their sights. On the other hand, a day at West-minster is hardly representa-tive of the world of show dog competition. The grueling Idit-arod race over some of the roughest terrain in the world, the captivating musical canine freestyle compe-titions, and the let-it-all-hang-out Great American Mutt Contest all give dogs a chance to put their best paws forward.

"He is your friend, your partner, your defender, your dog. You are his life, his love, his leader. He will be yours, faithful and true, to the last beat of his heart. You owe it to him to be worthy of such devotion." — UNKNOWN

Whether we give them blue ribbons for the breed characteristics they sport, the races they run, or the laughter they elicit, we do it because we love them and because we know that each one, in her own special way, is a top dog.

11 Civil War Dogs

Civil War soldiers often brought their dogs along to battle, mostly as companions. Typically, each company had its own canine mascot, and each unit thought its dog was the most talented and the most loyal. Soldiers formed strong bonds with their canine friends, who in turn provided their owners with inspiration and love. These dogs were not formally trained to participate in fighting, but that didn't stop the following canines from leaving their very special paw prints on the battlefields of history.

1. In October 1859, John Brown took nine Harpers Ferry, Virginia, citizens hostage. But Brown wasn't counting on Bob, the dog who belonged to the hostage Lewis W. Washington. When Washington was abducted, Bob followed his master doggedly; not even John Brown could elude him. Bob stayed with Washington until all the hostages were released one day later.

2. Sallie was a mascot of the Eleventh Pennsylvania Infantry when the battle of Gettysburg broke out. As the Union soldiers were forced to retreat, Sallie became separated from her beloved friends. She was eventually discovered, exhausted and starving, lying among the dead on the battlefield. Sallie was returned to her troops and, a true hero, served with them until February 1865, when she was shot through the head during the battle of Hunter's Run, Virginia. A statue of Sallie stands in Gettysburg today, directly in front of the monument that commemorates the Eleventh Pennsylvania Infantry.

3. Major, the mixed breed who "fought" with the Twenty-ninth Marine Infantry, was said to snap at — and catch — deadly airborne bullets (called minie balls) before they reached their mark.

4. Stonewall Jackson was a little mixed breed who was found on a battlefield near Richmond, Virginia, in 1862. He became a "trained" member of the Richmond Howitzer Battalion and a constant companion of the chief of the gun crew, Sergeant Van. Van taught Stonewall Jackson some tricks of soldiering, including how to stand at attention during roll call.

5. A Bull Terrier named Jack was a well-known, dependable member of the volunteer firemen of Niagara, Pennsylvania. He searched out dead and wounded soldiers after battles in Virginia and Maryland. Jack's remarkable life is well documented, most notably in the book *Dog Jack,* by Florence Biros. Jack escaped capture by Confederate soldiers and survived the battle of Antietam in 1862, in which 23,000 soldiers were killed and wounded. When Jack was eventually captured by Confederate soldiers, he was exchanged, according to wartime protocol, for a Confederate prisoner and returned to his regiment.

6. Captain Werner von Bachelle of the Sixth Wisconsin Brigade brought his dog with him to battle and taught him how to do clever tricks, including performing a military salute. The captain was mortally wounded in the battle of Antietam, but it wasn't until the next day, when soldiers hunted for the dead and wounded, that Bachelle's little dog was discovered on the battlefield, guarding his owner's body.

7. Harvey was the mascot of the 104th Ohio Infantry, beloved for the companionship and humor he provided the troops. Harry showed his love for music by swaying from side to side as the soldiers sang campfire songs in the evening. Harvey was wounded in two different battles but survived each time. Today, Harvey is remembered by the West-

"Dogs are us, only innocent."

— CYNTHIA HEIMEL

ern Reserve Historical Society in Cleveland, where a portrait of the troop features a proud Harvey posing with his fellow soldiers.

8. Widow Pfieff was determined to recover the body of her husband, Lieutenant Louis Pfeiff of the Third Illinois Infantry, after he was killed in the battle of Shiloh in 1862. Traveling to the site of the battle was difficult, and searching for her dead among so many casualties — 10,000 on each side — proved fruitless. Mrs. Pfieff was about to give up when a large dog came bounding toward her. Sure enough, it was the dog her husband had brought with him to battle. The dog promptly led Mrs. Pfieff to a distant section of the battlefield and a single unmarked grave where the body of Lieutenant Pfeiff lay. The widow learned later that her husband was killed more than twelve days earlier and that his dog stayed by his side the entire time, leaving only long enough to eat and drink.

9. When Confederate general Robert E. Lee crossed the narrows between Fort Hamilton and Staten Island, New York, he spotted a dog in the waters and rescued him, took him home, and named him Dart. One of Dart's puppies, Spec, became famous for his insistence on accompanying the family to church every Sunday.

10. Libby Prison in Richmond, Virginia, had especially tight security. It was guarded by a Russian Bloodhound named Hero who was brought to the United States in 1859. Hero was believed to be the largest dog in the world, and he had the strength to match. People claimed Hero weighed 198 pounds and was seven feet and one and a half inches tall. He won many fights with local bears.

11. The Sixty-ninth New York used the Irish Wolfhound as its regimental mascot and displayed him on its coat of arms. Two Irish Wolfhounds were adopted by the unit, and dressed up in green coats with the number 69 written on them in gold letters, and then they marched immediately to the rear of the regimental color guard.

Canine Heroes of World War II

Although dogs have taken part in our wars for centuries, a dog named Stubby is still recognized as America's first trained war dog. Stubby served eighteen months on the front during World War I, saved his regiment from surprise mustard gas attacks, located and comforted the wounded, and even caught a German spy by the seat of his pants. Back home, Stubby's exploits made the front page of every major newspaper. Two different presidents invited the dog to the White House, and he was personally decorated by General John Pershing. But perhaps Stubby's most important contribution is the inspiration he provided in the creation of the U.S. "K-9 Corps," just in time for World War II. The first K-9 Corps training center was in Fort Royal, Virginia. There, dogs were taught to be scouts, trackers, messengers, and detectors of mines and booby traps. Although these heroes don't have the medals and ranks they deserve, their patriotism and sacrifice are widely recognized throughout the armed forces. They are true heroes.

1. Andy. This beloved Doberman Pinscher saved a tank platoon pinned down on the island of Bougainville by flushing Japanese machine-gunners from their nest. His platoon knew him as "Gentleman Jim" because of his aristocratic demeanor.

2. Blackie. In 1945, while on a two-day patrol with Company F, 123rd Infantry, Blackie, handled by Corporal Technician Kido, helped his patrol successfully complete their mission without detection by the enemy, locating an area where five hundred Japanese were bivouacked.

3. Bob, a Collie mix, led more forays into German territory than any other U.S. soldier in World War II, human or canine.

4. Bobo. Sergeant John Coleman, Bobo's handler, led a reconnaissance patrol safely into German-held territory, then started back toward his own lines to safety. But Bobo alerted his owner that a German regiment was in the act of surrounding the outpost, saving not only Coleman's life but also those of his entire patrol.

In 1942, "Dogs for Defense" mobilized dog owners to donate quality animals to the army's Quartermaster Corps. This photo was part of the campaign.

5. Bruce. In 1945, during a banzai attack against "E" Company Twenty-seventh Infantry in Northern Luzon, Bruce attacked three Japanese infantrymen who were advancing with fixed bayonets toward a foxhole containing two wounded American soldiers. Because of his bravery, the lives of the two wounded men were saved. And by discouraging the advance of these particular Japanese, Bruce likely prevented more casualties.

6. Buster. While operating as a messenger dog with "F" Company 155th Infantry Regiment on Morotai Island, Buster saved the lives of an entire patrol of seventeen men. His determination carried him through heavy enemy machine-gun and mortar fire on two excursions, bringing back with him instructions for the patrol to hold its position. Reinforcements arrived thanks to Buster's efforts and these reinforcements, in turn, were responsible for the destruction of the enemy's entire force.

7. Caesar. During a Marine raid in the South Pacific, when radio communications became impossible in the thick jungle, Caesar, one of the canine members of the troop, was dispatched with vital information. He traveled back and forth between his two handlers, always under heavy fire. Another time, Caesar alerted one of his handlers to a grenade thrown at his feet. The soldier was able to throw the device back in the direction it came from, where it exploded. The next morning, eight Japanese bodies were discovered. On the third day of this encounter, with the team under attack, Caesar leaped at Japanese soldiers. His handler called him back, but as Caesar turned to obey, he was shot twice. Caesar survived, but because surgery to remove the bullet would have been too risky, he spent the rest of his life with the chunk of lead lodged behind his left shoulder. Caesar is credited with conveying the first war dog message in actual combat.

8. Chips. The most famous of all canine heroes was part shepherd, part Collie, and part northern sled dog. Chips was affectionate and had particularly keen senses. He was also a bit of a rebel. After wading ashore with the Third Division of General Patton's Seventh Army, Chips sensed impending danger and bounded off toward an enemy machine-gun nest. The firing stopped, and Chips was soon discovered holding on to the throat of the enemy gunner while nearby, five terrified men raised their arms in surrender. Chips went on to act as a sentry for President Roosevelt and Prime Minister Churchill at their historic conference in Casablanca in 1943. About this time it was also revealed that Chips, unimpressed with rank, had taken a nip at General Eisenhower. Chips died of complications from war injuries when he was only six. He was eventually awarded a silver star and a purple heart. The film about him, *Chips the War Dog,* was released in 1990.

9. Daisy. The mascot of a Norwegian merchant ship torpedoed in the North Atlantic, she dove into the icy sea with the surviving crewmen and swam from man to man throughout the night, licking their faces and giving them comfort and encouragement. They were rescued the following morning.

10. Dick. This famous German Shepherd Dog discovered a camouflaged Japanese bivouac and then alerted his patrol, enabling a surprise attack that resulted in the annihilation of the enemy with only a single U.S. Marine casualty.

11. Duchess. Duchess was a member of the Thirty-ninth Infantry Scout Dog Platoon. In 1945, while on patrol with the Third Battalion, 123rd Infantry, she helped inspect enemy cave installations on Luzon in the Philippines. On approaching the entrance to one cave, Duchess let out an unmistakable alert that led to the elimination of thirty-three enemy troops. Duchess performed similar feats throughout her career as a war dog.

12. Kurt. This brave Doberman Pinscher saved the lives of 250 marines when he alerted them to Japanese soldiers lying in wait on a steamy jungle hillside above the Asan Point beachhead.

13. Pal. This celebrated hero was killed by enemy action in 1945 at San Benedetto Po, Italy. In blocking a shrapnel charge with his own body, Pal prevented the serious wounding of several men.

14. Peefke. While on patrol during a mission in 1945, Peefke discovered a wire and alerted his handler, who, upon examination of the wire, found three enemy "S" mines, which were then neutralized. Had these mines not been discovered, they could have wiped out the entire patrol.

15. Sandy. This canny canine was a natural for messenger training, contributing valuable service throughout the Cape Gloucester Campaign. During one battle, Sandy had to travel through the tall Kunai grass, swim a river, and make his way beneath a curtain of mortar and tank fire. He finally jumped over a barbed-wire fence and delivered a message that allowed American units to advance.

16. Smoky, a four-pound Yorkshire Terrier, spent eighteen months in combat during World War II. She flew with the Third Emergency Rescue Squad on twelve long combat missions, each up to twenty-two hours nonstop, and covered strikes to Borneo and the Southern Philippines.

17. Wolf. Committed to combat with the Twenty-seventh Infantry battling through the Corabello Mountains in Italy toward the strategic Balate Pass, Wolf scented the presence of the enemy entrenched on a hillside about 150 yards distant in time to allow the members of the patrol to take cover and resist attack. Wolf performed similar feats over the course of the war and was eventually wounded. In spite of expert medical care and emergency surgery, the Twenty-fifth Division's casualty list after the battle included, among others: "Wolf, US Army War Dog, T121, Died of Wounds, Wounded in action."

"Dogs are our link to paradise. They don't know evil or jealousy or discontent. To sit with a dog on a hillside on a glorious afternoon is to be back in Eden, where doing nothing was not boring — it was peace."
— **MILAN KUNDERA**

5 Dogs Who Changed the Course of History

These dogs didn't receive the awards they deserved. They weren't show dogs, and they didn't compete with other dogs. But they left their mark on history.

1. **Fala**, Franklin Roosevelt's Scottish Terrier, entered the political ring when, in 1944, as Roosevelt ran for a fourth term, his political enemies accused him of sending a destroyer to the Aleutian Islands just to pick up his dog. It was a mud-slinging campaign on both sides, but what seems to have tipped the scale in Roosevelt's favor was the speech in which the president gave voice to his little dog: "These Republican leaders have not been content with attacks on me, my wife, or my sons. . . . They now include my little dog Fala. . . . I don't resent the attacks, and my family doesn't resent the attacks. . . . But Fala does resent them. His Scotch soul was furious. He has never been the same dog since." Lucky Fala went on to witness the historic signing of the Atlantic Charter, which set the foundation for the United Nations, along with Winston Churchill's Poodle, Rufus.

2. In what became known as the famous **Checkers** speech in 1952, Richard Nixon, vice-presidential candidate on the political chopping block for accepting private donations, attempted to garner public sympathy by decrying the many hardships his family had to suffer, including his wife's cloth coat (sadly, fur was not affordable for the Nixons). That only made the public laugh. What did get to them was Nixon's plea on behalf of Checkers, the black-and-white-spotted Cocker Spaniel that had been given to his daughter as a gift. "And you know, the kids," he said, "like all kids, loved the dog, and I just want to say . . . that regardless of what they say about it, we are going to keep it." Checkers is credited with having revived Nixon's career, only to have passed on by the time Nixon made it to the White House in 1970.

3. A three-year-old stray part Siberian Husky named **Laika** (Russian for *bark*) with a calm temperament and easygoing personality became the first living being in space when, in 1957, the Soviets launched *Sputnik II*. Americans were dis-

In the early 1940s, the Swiss inventor George de Mestral went on a walk with his dog. After arriving home, he saw that his pants and his dog's coat were covered with cockleburs. When he looked at the burs under a microscope, he discovered they had a natural hooklike shape, which became the basis for his invention of a unique, two-sided fastener—one side with stiff "hooks" like the burs, and the other side with the soft "loops" like the fabric of his pants. The result was Velcro brand hook-and-loop fasteners, named for the French words **velour** and **crochet**.

Three dogs survived the sinking of the **Titanic**. A Pomeranian and a Pekingese boarded early lifeboats in the arms of their owners. A third dog, the first officer's large Newfoundland, swam between another lifeboat and the rescue ship. The sound of his bark guided the survivors to safety.

heartened to have missed this "first," as the race into space had been a heated one. So hurried were the Russians to send a creature into space that no provisions were ever made for returning Laika, who, it was recently revealed, died of fright shortly after takeoff. In 1997, a memorial to Laika was established at the Institute for Aviation and Space Medicine in Moscow.

4. **Saur** belonged to the King of Norway, who was deposed in the eleventh century but soon returned to power. When he did, he punished those who had insulted his dignity by crowning Saur king for three years and demanding that he be treated like royalty.

5. When weather conditions prevented a much-needed diphtheria serum to be transported from Nenan to Nome, Alaska, a team of Siberian Huskies, led by **Balto**, the most famous of them all, came to the rescue. The team's accomplishment became the famous annual Iditarod race.

A Russian postcard commemorates the first two dogs in space: Laika and Strelka.

13 Russian Dogs Who Were Launched into Space

Russians prepared for sending men into space by sending dogs first. All of the following participated in the Sputnik series of satellite launchings between 1957 and 1961.

1. Laika
2. Bars
3. Lisichka
4. Belka
5. Strelka
6. Pchelka
7. Mushka
8. Damka
9. Krasavka
10. Chernushka
11. Zvezdochka
12. Verterok
13. Ugolyok

18 World Trade Center Dogs

Within hours of the September 11, 2001, attack on the World Trade Center, specially trained search and rescue dogs were on the scene. Little mixed breeds, big mixed breeds, German Shepherd Dogs, Labs of all kinds, Collies, Rottweilers, spaniels — and even a few feisty little Dachshunds — aided in rescue efforts after the tragic events. These dogs climbed and searched places that were too dangerous for humans, and they did so without the aid of gas masks or protective clothing. On Monday, February 11, 2002, the 126th Annual Westminster Kennel Club Dog Show in Madison Square Garden honored the dogs that worked at the World Trade Center and Pentagon immediately after the terrorists attacks. Here are the stories of only a few of these heroes.

1. **Ammo**, a German Shepherd Dog from Florida, has traveled the world and has helped rescue 2,000 people. He worked with his handler for almost forty-eight hours and then collapsed at the scene from shock, dehydration, and exhaustion. Fortunately he made a complete recovery after receiving treatment.

2. **Apollo**, a German Shepherd Dog, and his handler, Peter Davis, were at the site of the disaster fifteen minutes after the World Trade Center towers collapsed. Apollo was nearly killed when he became completely engulfed in flames because of falling debris but was lucky because he had just emerged from a pool of water and did not catch on fire. Davis just brushed the embers off him, and Apollo kept right on working. Apollo was awarded Britain's PDSA Dickin Medal.

3. **Bear**, a Golden Retriever, was the first dog on the scene at the World Trade Center. Bear and his partner, the Maryland firefighter John Gilkey, worked at the wreckage site for three months, trying to locate people buried in the rubble. Sadly, Bear died of cancer on September 26, 2002, at the age of twelve.

4. **Git Ander**, a seven-year-old German Shepherd Dog, returned to duty as a member of the Union County Sheriff's Department K-9 Unit after having served as a search and rescue dog at the World Trade Center. Tragically, even though he was wearing a police badge, he was shot to death when a couple of policemen mistook him for a "vicious stray" after an incident involving a car chase.

5. **Jac** found a living survivor and identified the locations of several bodies, including those of two New York City firemen. While he worked to find the bodies, Jac became ill from inhaling fumes and particles, and was injured when he fell through some of the debris. With the help of a Connecticut State Police escort, it took Jac's handler only fifty-five minutes to reach the Rowley Memorial Animal Hospital in Springfield, Massachusetts, where he responded well to treatment. Jac was back on the job three days later.

6. **Jackson**, a three-year-old German Shepherd therapy dog, served at the World Trade Center in a very special way. A young boy whose parents had been killed in the tragedy was inconsolable and refused to allow anyone to help him. Jackson's trainer spotted the boy and became determined to draw him out, so he began playing ball with Jackson. The ball rolled back and forth between them, and then finally, the trainer rolled the ball to the boy. The child hesitated, but then pushed the ball back toward Jackson. Soon enough, Jackson and the boy were playing ball, and the boy took his first steps toward healing.

7. **Lucy**, a little Border Collie who was only ten and a half months old, was able to locate numerous remains and help bring closure to several families. She also located the remains of a firefighter. Lucy's handler, Lynne Engelbert, a veteran rescue worker from the Oklahoma City bombing, whispered "Bones" in Lucy's ear as her cue to go to work. Lucy was nominated for an ACE award by the AKC in 2002.

8. A German Shepherd Dog named **Miranda** was trained as a police dog for years but had only a few months of experience when she arrived at Ground Zero. Miranda found dozens of bodies during her five days of service at the site. She was injured in the course of duty and was taken home by her handler, police sergeant Dale Warke. Miranda eventually developed serious health problems and was euthanized on August 2, 2002, at age fourteen.

9. **Ricky the Rat Terrier**, age three, was the smallest (at 17" tall) of the dogs at the World Trade Center. He was able to wiggle his way into areas that nothing else

It costs up to $10,000 to train a federally certified search and rescue dog. To make a donation to the National Disaster Search Dog Foundation, call (888)4K9-HERO.

could reach. He and Thunder (see below) located the remains of several victims.

10. **Roselle** and **Dorado** (aka **Riva** and **Salty**) were guide dogs at work with their blind owners in different locations in the towers. They guided their owners through crowded, smoke-filled stairs to safety. Roselle and Dorado were awarded the Dickin Medal "for their service to humanity."

11. **Servus** (aka **Wuss**), a nine-year-old, seventy-pound Belgian Malinois, fell twenty feet down, face-first, into a pocket of jagged rebar, glass, and powdered concrete while working at the site with his partner, Chris Christensen, a police officer from Illinois. Rescuers immediately came to Servus's aid. He was given oxygen and intravenous fluids and was rushed to an animal hospital in an ambulance, along with a three-motorcycle escort. Officer Christensen returned to the site, hoping to do some rescue work by himself, but Wuss was so eager to help that he jumped out of the police cruiser, tail wagging, ready for action. He later died of pancreatitis.

12. **Sirius**, a four-year-old yellow Lab, and his trainer, Officer David Lim, were in the basement of the World Trade Center when the first explosion hit Tower One. Lim put his partner in his crate while he raced up forty-three flights of stairs

to help guide fleeing people to safety. His last words to Sirius were "You stay there. I'll be back for you." Sirius, one of New York's own K-9 police dogs, died in his crate when the building collapsed. He was the only dog to die on September 11. A memorial held at Liberty State Park in Jersey City for Sirius was attended by some 250 officers of the Port Authority and NYPD. Dozens of service dogs from around the country attended the service as well. Officer Lim was presented with Sirius's water bowl at the ceremony. It had been inscribed to read: "I gave my life so that you could save others."

13. **Sweetheart** suffered second- and third-degree burns after children set her on fire in Apple Valley, New York, in September 1990. Despite these injuries, Sweetheart, aptly named, was trained as a therapy dog. Along with Jackson (above), she was used to escort victims' family members to Ground Zero, giving them and rescue workers a chance to pet them and relieve some of their stress. Once these suffering people heard Sweetheart's story, seeing how happy she is gave them hope to carry on.

14. **Thunder**, a five-year-old Golden Retriever, and his owner, Kent Olson of the Washington Task Force of Puget Sound, Washington, were among the first rescuers to arrive at the World Trade Cen-

ter disaster site. Thunder, along with Ricky (above), also from the Puget Sound Task Force, worked together to locate bodies trapped in the debris. Rescuers played fetch with Thunder to help them relieve some of the tension of the day.

15–16. **Tivka**, a two-year-old Keeshond, and **Kate**, a three-year-old yellow Lab, were part of the Hope Crisis and Response Team that work for the American Red Cross. After the events of 9/11, Tivka and Kate were brought to Ground Zero in their role as therapy dogs. They were able to provide emotional support and a smile to emergency crew workers, police officers, and firefighters.

17. **Trakr**, an eight-year-old German Shepherd Dog, was brought out of retirement by his trainer, Jamie Symington of the Halifax Regional Police, to help with the efforts at Ground Zero. Rescuers, who had found little else but body parts, noticed that Trakr began to show interest in one particular area of the rubble, and this led to the discovery of a survivor.

18. **Worf**, a twelve-year-old German Shepherd Dog from Ohio, located the bodies of two missing firefighters on the first day. However, he was so overwhelmed at Ground Zero and so badly traumatized that his partner, Mike Owens, made the decision to retire him from search and rescue duty permanently.

"God . . . sat down for a moment when the dog was finished in order to watch it . . . and to know that it was good, that nothing was lacking, that it could not have been made better." —RAINER MARIA RILKE

22 Jobs That Dogs Have Performed

Above: Bubi and Pfiffi were popular acrobats in Germany early in the twentieth century.

Right: British postcard ca. 1915

Below: British postcard from the turn of the twentieth century

THIS LITTLE DOG HAS COLLECTED OVER 10,000 PENNIES FOR SOLDIERS' AND SAILORS' COMFORTS.

1. Assistance for the disabled, including guiding, fetching, alarming humans to certain events such as a telephone ringing or a baby crying, and even sniffing out oncoming epileptic fits or diabetic comas

2. Carting

3. Conservation: sniffing out rare birds that can then be bred and saved from extinction

4. Earthquake detection

5. Farm work

6. Cattle herding

7. Bovine estrus detection, in which dogs "sniff out" the cows that are ready for mating

8. Military and police service

9. Sniffing out truffles

10. Guides

11. Hunting, flushing out game

12. Lifeboat rescue, in which dogs locate floating survivors

13. Prison guards and prisoner assistance

14. Police tracking

15. Drug sniffing

16. Guard patrol

17. Racing

18. Search and rescue

19. Therapy and companionship for the elderly

20. Water rescue

21. Performance

22. Scat sniffing (sniffing out scatological remains for genetic research)

The Lagotto Romagnolo is the only dog to have specialized in finding truffles on any type of ground whatever, the only breed recognized as having this ability.

4 Famous Guide Dogs

Guide Dogs for the Blind is a nonprofit, charitable organization with a mission to provide guide dogs and training in their use to visually impaired people throughout the United States and Canada. Their dogs and services are free to those they serve, thanks to the generosity of donors and the support of volunteers. The organization is devoted to promoting the human/animal bond. It operates two training facilities, in San Rafael, California, and in Boring, Oregon. To learn more about Guide Dogs for the Blind, call (800) 295-4050, or visit www.guidedogs.com. Here is their list of four of the most distinguished guide dogs.

1. **Buddy**. After World War I, dogs were trained to assist blind veterans. It was the enthusiasm of Morris Frank, a blind young American, that inspired Dorothy Eustis to train a guide dog for him in Switzerland. The dog was called Buddy. Morris and Dorothy then established the first guide dog school in the United States, calling it "The Seeing Eye." In 1931, Guide Dogs for the Blind was founded in Britain and spread from there throughout the world.

2. **Blondie**. In 1942, a German Shepherd Dog named Blondie, who had been rescued from a Pasadena dog pound, was one of the first dogs trained at Guide Dogs for the Blind. She was later paired with Sergeant Leonard Foulk, the first serviceman to to safety from his office on the seventy-eighth floor of Tower One. As World Trade Center survivors and as a guide dog team, they were thrust into the international limelight. Michael and Roselle were featured on *Larry King Live, The Early Show,* and *Regis and Kelly.* Michael and Roselle have since become well known as representatives of the strength of the human/animal bond and have been successful in communicating the power of that bond in many media interviews and public presentations all over the world.

4. **Barley**. This lovable black Labrador has taken the dedication, spirit, and service that exemplify Guide Dogs for the Blind to a new level. Barley's blind partner, Stephanie Salaz, is a multiple-organ

The First Seeing Eye dog was presented to a blind person on April 25, 1938.

graduate from the school. They are significant and even famous because the Guide Dogs for the Blind school was founded to provide mobility dogs for the servicemen who were returning blind from World War II, and Sergeant Foulk and Blondie were used in the first publicity campaigns throughout the country to educate the visually impaired about the services available to them.

3. **Roselle**. Michael Hingson and his guide dog, a yellow Labrador, escaped the World Trade Center attack on September 11, 2001. Roselle led Michael transplant survivor whose weakened immune system resulted in several amputations, including a leg and some fingers. Barley is the "eyes" of her partner, guiding her through her life on a daily basis. Barley's instincts protect her partner as well. If there's a pothole, Barley will guide her around it; if her partner wants to cross the street but there's danger, Barley won't allow her to cross. Barley also provides motivation and inspiration, encouraging her partner, who wears a prosthetic device, to walk and keep walking. They now often walk as many as three miles a day.

11 ACE Award Winners

In 2000, the American Kennel Club presented its first Award for Canine Excellence. These awards were given to five individual dogs who distinguished themselves above and beyond the call of duty. These amazing dogs have performed acts that have benefited either their families or community in some manner. The ACEs are now an annual event that truly honors our bond with our canine friends. Winners receive a cash award of $1,000 and an engraved sterling silver collar, as well as having their names engraved on a plaque that is on permanent display at AKC headquarters in New York City. Here presented in five different categories are recent ACE winners.

1. Exemplary Companion Dog, 2002. Bullet, a Golden Retriever, alerted the parents of a three-week-old infant boy named Troy who was literally turning blue and about to suffocate. Because of Bullet's vigilance and continuous barking, Troy's father was able to get to his son in time to administer CPR. Doctors reported that Bullet's actions saved Troy's life.

2. Search and Rescue Dog, 2002. Topper, a Belgian Tervuren, worked at both the Oklahoma City bombing site and Ground Zero at the World Trade Center after 9/11. He not only helped locate victims but served as an inspiration to exhausted firefighters and other rescuers.

3. Therapy Dog, 2002. Cara, a Standard Poodle, was serving as a therapy dog when she was diagnosed with a form of bone cancer. An operation was performed and Cara lost a front leg. Despite this handicap Cara continued to visit numerous health care facilities as well as a summer camp for kids with cancer.

4. Law Enforcement Dog, 2003. Ordi, a German Shepherd Dog, and his partner, Sergeant Tom Otten, have worked as a team for more than six years, during which time Ordi has helped not only the local drug task force but the FBI as well. Ordi was the recipient of the United States Police Canine Association's "Catch of the Quarter" and "Catch of the Year" awards. The USPCA also awarded Ordi with three obedience trophies and named him their Top Dog for two years in a row.

> "The dog has seldom pulled man up to his level of sagacity, but man has frequently dragged the dog down to his."
> — JAMES THURBER

5. Service Dog, 2003. Brock, a six-year-old male Golden Retriever, is the companion and partner of Marc Jeffrey Grobman, an actor with cerebral palsy. Brock helps Marc get to auditions, rehearsals, and jobs. Before Brock came along, Marc had to rely on friends to help him. Now he only has to rely on one.

6. Therapy Dog, 2003. Josie, a six-year-old female Cardigan Welsh Corgi, along with her people, Betty Jean and Dale Greig, has visited the Ronald McDonald House and rehabilitation centers in Cleveland, Ohio, more than five hundred times. Josie seems to have a special affinity for kids who are seriously ill or handicapped.

7. Exemplary Companion Dog, 2004. Stormy, a ten-year-old Anatolian Shepherd Dog, was only twelve weeks old when she was stricken with meningitis. Although she survived the disease, she was left paralyzed from her shoulders back. This brave and determined puppy finally regained full use of her limbs. She went on to become the first female Anatolian Shepherd AKC Champion of Record.

8. Law Enforcement Dog, 2004. Justice, a five-year-old German Shepherd Dog, received his certification from the USPCA for his abilities as a bomb and explosives dog. In just two years, Justice and his partner, Deputy Brian Litz, have helped in close to five hundred arrests and fifteen bomb searches. Although Justice is a tough character when at work, he is extremely gentle with kids.

9. Search and Rescue Dog, 2004. Saber, a ten-year-old Collie, a member of Texas Task Force One, a statewide disaster response team, has been crossed-trained in water search, cadaver location, urban disaster, and wilderness work. Saber's searching abilities were employed after the Force 5 tornadoes in Oklahoma and the *Columbia* space shuttle tragedy. He is a member of the Oklahoma Veterinary Animal Hall of Fame.

10. Service Dog, 2004. Kelsie, a five-year-old West Highland White Terrier, is a certified medical response service dog. She has been trained to monitor her owner's medical condition. Kelsie is able to activate medical alert systems and retrieve resuscitating medication. Her owner, Lt. Commander Loren Marino, a former dog trainer for the military, was wounded in the line of duty. She trained Kelsie to perform more than two hundred tasks that enable Kelsie to help her.

11. Therapy Dog, 2004. Saydee, a twelve-year-old Miniature Schnauzer, and her owner, Virginia Hyatt, have logged almost 20,000 hours of service to the communities in the Dallas/Fort Worth area. They have visited hospitals, rehab centers, nursing homes, and schools for mentally and physically challenged kids. Saydee and Virginia often visit as many as four facilities a day.

2 Baseball Diamond Dogs

Hot dogs aren't the only kind that are associated with baseball. Two dogs made diamond history:

I HAVE ADVISED MY CLIENT NOT TO FETCH ANY BASEBALL WITHOUT A CONTRACT SECURING ONE MILLION OUNCES OF GOURMET DOG FOOD WITH BONUS BELLY-SCRATCHINGS AND *THE* OPTION TO RENEGOTIATE AFTER FOURTEEN YEARS...DOG YEARS, OF COURSE...

1. **Jake the Diamond Dog**, trained by Jeff Marchal of Lima, Ohio, is a lovable Golden Retriever who spends his summers visiting and performing in minor-league baseball parks nationwide. Jake chases down foul balls, delivers liquid refreshment to the umpires, serves as batboy, and entertains the fans with his Frisbee-catching prowess in between innings. Jake even "signs" paw prints for the kids. During the off-season Jeff takes six-year-old Jake to various nursing homes in Nashville, Tennessee, and lets him show off his talents to older people who can't make it out to the ballpark. Jake not only entertains these folks with his bag of tricks but also doles out a lot of individual, uplifting affection.

2. A three-year-old Golden Retriever by the name of **Chase** became the newest addition to the **Trenton Thunder** baseball team family, an AA affiliate of the New York Yankees. Chase, also trained by Jeff Marchal, loves to play fetch, catch Frisbees, and play with kids. He also likes to collect bats and serves as the Thunder's batboy. For every home game, Chase arrives at Waterfront Park early in the morning and often stays until midnight. He delivers water bottles to the umpires and entertains the fans by catching Frisbees. In addition to his duties on the field, Chase is also involved with It's Your Turn, a program offered by the Trenton Thunder and the New Jersey Educational Association for Kindergarten and First Grade Students. Chase and members of the Thunder staff visit with children and read *It's Your Turn,* a children's book about the Thunder mascot, Boomer.

"The noblest dog of all is the hot dog; it feeds the hand that bites it." — LAURENCE J. PETER

© MARK PARISI

8 Talking Dog Jokes

1. A man sees a sign in front of a house: "Talking Dog for Sale." He rings the bell and the owner tells him the dog is in the backyard. The man goes into the backyard and sees a black mutt just sitting there.

"You talk?" he asks.

"Yep," the mutt replies.

"So, what's your story?"

The mutt looks up and says, "Well, I discovered this gift pretty young and I wanted to help the government, so I told the CIA about my gift, and in no time they had me jetting from country to country, sitting in rooms with spies and world leaders, because no one figured a dog would be eavesdropping. I was one of their most valuable spies eight years running. The jetting around really tired me out, and I knew I wasn't getting any younger and I wanted to settle down.

"So I signed up for a job at the airport to do some undercover security work, mostly wandering near suspicious characters and listening in. I uncovered some incredible dealings there and was awarded a batch of medals. Had a wife, a mess of puppies, and now I'm just retired."

The man is amazed. He goes back into the house and asks the owner what he wants for the dog.

The owner says, "Ten dollars."

The guy says, "This dog is amazing. Why on earth are you selling him so cheaply?"

The owner replies, "He's such a liar. He didn't do any of that stuff."

2. A dog walks into a bar. He hops up on a stool and puts his front paws on the bar. He looks the bartender right in the eye and says, "Hey, guess what? I'm a talking dog. Have you ever seen a talking dog before? How about a drink for the talking dog?"

The bartender thinks for a moment and says, "Okay. The toilet's right around the corner."

3. A guy walks into a bar with a dog under his arm, puts the dog on the bar, and announces that the dog can talk and that he has a hundred dollars he's willing to bet anyone who says he can't. The bartender quickly takes the bet and the owner looks at the dog and asks,

"What's the thing on top of this building that keeps the rain from coming inside?"

The dog answers, "ROOF."

The bartender says, "Who are you kidding? I'm not paying."

The dogs owner says, "How about double or nothing and I'll ask him something else?"

The bartender agrees and the owner turns to the dog and asks, "Who was the greatest ballplayer of all time?"

The dog answers with a muffled "RUTH."

With that the bartender picks them both up and throws them out the door. As they bounce on the sidewalk the dog looks at his owner and says, "DiMaggio?"

4. A wealthy man decided to go on a safari in Africa. He took his faithful pet Dachshund along for company. One day, the Dachshund started chasing butterflies and before long the little dog discovered that he was lost. So, wandering about, he noticed a leopard heading rapidly in his direction with the obvious intention of having lunch.

The Dachshund thought, "Okay, I'm in deep trouble now!" Then he noticed some bones on the ground close by and immediately settled down to chew on them with his back to the approaching cat.

Just as the leopard was about to leap, the Dachshund exclaimed loudly, "Boy, that was one delicious leopard. I wonder if there are any more around here."

Hearing this, the leopard halted his attack in midstride. Terrified, he quietly disappeared back into the forest.

"Whew," said the leopard. "That was close. That Dachshund nearly had me."

Meanwhile, a monkey who had been watching the whole scene from a nearby tree figured he could put this knowledge to good use and trade it for protection from the leopard. So, off he went to strike a bargain. But the Dachshund saw him heading after the leopard with great speed and figured that trouble was afoot.

The monkey soon caught up with the leopard, spilled the beans, and struck a deal. The leopard was furious at being made a fool of and said, "Here, monkey, hop on my back and see what's going to happen to that conniving canine."

Now the Dachshund saw the leopard coming with the monkey on his back, and thought, "What am I going to do now?" But instead of running, the dog sat down with his back to his attackers, pretending he hadn't seen them yet, and just when they got close enough to hear, the Dachshund said aloud, "Where's that monkey? I sent him off half an hour ago to bring me another leopard."

5. The scene: It's 1882 and a hot, dusty summer's day in Dodge City. Suddenly at the edge of town appears a three-legged dog astride a large white horse. Women and children run in fear. The three-legged dog rides up to the saloon and goes inside. He walks to the bar and says, "Gimme a shot of red-eye."

Shaking and quivering, the bartender pours a glass of whiskey. The three-legged dog throws it back and says, "Gimme another." Shaking and quivering, the bartender pours another. The three-legged dog slams it down and turns to look at the crowd.

The sheriff makes his way through the people and faces the three-legged dog. "We don't get many three-legged dogs around here — what's your business?" The three-legged dog pushes away from the bar and says, "I'm looking for the man who shot my Paw."

6. A local business was looking for office help. They put a sign in the window, stating the following: "Help Wanted: Must be able to type, must be good with a computer, and must be bilingual. We are an Equal Opportunity Employer."

A short time afterward, a dog trotted up to the window, saw the sign, and went inside. He looked at the receptionist and wagged his tail, then walked over to the sign, looked at it, and whined. Getting the idea, the receptionist got the office manager.

The office manager looked at the dog and was surprised, to say the least. However, the dog looked determined, so he led him into the office. Inside, the dog jumped up on the chair and stared at the manager.

The manager said, "I can't hire you. The sign says you have to be able to

7. A salesman dropped in to see a business customer. Not a soul was in the office except a big dog emptying wastebaskets. The salesman stared at the animal, wondering if his imagination could be playing tricks on him.

The dog looked up and said, "Don't be surprised. This is just part of my job."

"Incredible!" exclaimed the man. "I can't believe it! Does your boss know what a prize he has in you? An animal that can talk!"

"No, no," pleaded the dog. "Please don't tell! If that man finds out I can talk, he'll have me answering the phone, too!"

type." The dog jumped down, went to the typewriter, and proceeded to type out a perfect letter. He took out the page and trotted over to the manager and gave it to him, then jumped back on the chair.

The manager was stunned but then told the dog, "The sign says you have to be good with a computer." The dog jumped down again and went to the computer. The dog proceeded to enter and execute a perfect program, which worked flawlessly the first time.

By this time the manager was totally dumbfounded. He looked at the dog and said, "I realize that you are a very intelligent dog and have some interesting abilities. However, I still can't give you the job."

The dog jumped down and went to a copy of the sign and put his paw on the sentence that told about being an Equal Opportunity Employer. The manager said, "Yes, but the sign also says that you have to be bilingual." The dog looked at the manager calmly and said, "Meow."

8. Two women who are dog owners are arguing over which dog is smarter:

First woman: My dog is so smart. Every morning he waits for a paperboy to come around, and then he takes a newspaper and brings it to me.

Second woman: I know.

First one: How?

Second one: My dog told me.

15 World's Record-Breaking Dogs

1. Oldest Dog
An Australian Cattle Dog named Bluey, owned by Les Hall of Rochester, Victoria, Australia, was obtained as a puppy in 1910 and worked among cattle and sheep for nearly twenty years. He was put to sleep on November 14, 1939, at the age of twenty-nine years, five months.

2. Smallest Dog
The smallest dog on record was a matchbox-size Yorkshire Terrier owned by Arthur Marples of Blackburn, England. This tiny creature, which died in 1945 at the age of nearly two years, stood two and a half inches tall at the shoulder, measured three and a half inches from nose tip to tail, and weighed only four ounces.

3. Tallest Dog
The tallest dog on record was a male Great Dane named Shamgret Danzas. He was forty-two inches tall (at the shoulder!) and weighed 238 pounds.

4. Heaviest and Largest Dog
The world's heaviest and longest dog ever recorded was an Old English Mastiff named Aicama Zorba of La-Susa. In 1989, "Zorba," who was born on September 26, 1981, and owned by Chris Eraclides of London, England, weighed 343 pounds, stood thirty-seven inches at the shoulder, and was eight feet, three inches long from nose to tail.

5. Longest Jump
A Greyhound named Bang jumped thirty feet while chasing a hare at Bre-con Lodge in Glouchestershire, England, in 1849. He cleared a four-foot, six-inch gate and landed on a hard road, damaging his pastern bone.

6. Best Tracker
In 1925, a Doberman Pinscher named Sauer, trained by Detective Sergeant Herbert Kruger, tracked a stock thief one hundred miles across the Great Karroo, South Africa, by scent alone.

7. Drug Sniffing
Snag, a U.S. Customs Labrador Retriever trained and partnered by Jeff Weitzmann, has made 118 drug seizures worth a canine record $810 million.

> **"Don't accept your dog's admiration as conclusive evidence that you are wonderful."**
> — ANN LANDERS

8. Dog with the Largest Repertoire of Tricks
Chanda-Leah, a champagne-colored Toy Poodle, enjoys bow-wowing audiences with a record-breaking repertoire of 469 tricks. The pooch can perform on the piano, fetch a Kleenex if you sneeze, and even untie the knot in your shoelace. She's the perfect house pet, too, even clearing away her toys when she's finished playing.

9. Fastest Time by a Dog in Opening a Car Window
The world record for the fastest time a dog has unwound a nonelectric car window is thirteen seconds and belongs to Striker, a Border Collie owned and trained by Francis V. Gadassi of Hungary. The record was set on August 14, 2003, in Quebec City, Canada.

10. Highest Jump
The world record for the highest jump cleared by a dog is 167.6 centimeters (66 inches), achieved by Cinderella May a Holly Grey (aka Cindy), a Greyhound owned by Kathleen Conroy and Kate Long of Miami, Florida, at the Purina Dog Chow Incredible Dog Challenge show held at Gray Summit, Missouri, on October 3, 2003.

11. Largest Dog Litter
Three dogs have given birth to twenty-three puppies each. An American Foxhound bore her pups on June 19, 1944; a Saint Bernard gave birth to twenty-three — of which fourteen survived — in February 1975; and a Great Dane had a litter of twenty-three in June 1987.

12. Most Jump Rope Skips by a Dog
The most revolutions of a jump rope "skipped" by a dog in one minute is sixty-three, performed by Olive Oyl, a Russian Wolfhound owned by Alex and Paula Rothacker of Grays Lake, Illinois, on July 8, 1998.

13. Most Tennis Balls in a Dog's Mouth
The world record for the most tennis

> ## "My goal in life is to be as good a person as my dog thinks I am."
> — **UNKNOWN**

balls held in the mouth by a dog at one time is five. Augie, a Golden Retriever owned by the Miller family in Dallas, Texas, successfully gathered and held all five regulation-size tennis balls on July 6, 2003.

14. Most Golf Balls Swallowed
In April 2004, a German Shepherd Dog named Libby scoffed no fewer than twenty-eight golf balls, setting a new world record for the most golf balls swallowed during one golf tournament. The previous record of seventeen golf balls swallowed had stood since 1978.

15. Longest Ears
In November 2002, a Basset Hound named Mr. Jeffries broke the record for the longest ears in the dog world with ears measuring 29.2 centimeters. They have been insured against damage for £30,000.

A total of 4,372 dogs took part in the "Great North Dog Walk" on Tyneside in England on Saturday June 21, 2003, a new world record for the largest dog walk.

"REXIE"
The Sensational High Diver 40 feet

A vintage postcard celebrates Rexie, "the sensational high diver."

3 Dogs Who Have Won Acting Awards

The Palm Dog Award, which takes the form of a gold-studded collar, is the canine counterpart to the Cannes Film Festival's top prize, the Palme d'Or.

1. The first Palm Dog Award for the most outstanding performance by a four-legged actor was scooped by **Otis**, the canine lead in *The Anniversary Party*, starring and directed by Jennifer Jason Leigh and Alan Cumming. This award was presented at the Cannes Film Festival in 2001.

2. **Moses**, the mixed breed who is drawn in chalk on the stage floor of the Nicole Kidman film *Dogville*, won the Palm Dog Award for his brief appearance at the end of the film, when, in the very last shot, the chalk drawing is morphed into a living dog. His presence was simply too powerful for the judges to ignore.

3. The United Kingdom's Shadows Awards presented its best dog actor award to **Jill**, the rare Brussels Griffon who portrayed Verdell in the film *As Good As It Gets* in 1997. In actuality, the role of Verdell was played by six different dogs: Timer, Sprout, Debbie, Billy, Parfait, and Jill, but as Jill was considered the star dog by other members of the cast, she got the prize.

Dickin Medal Winners

The United Kingdom's PDSA (People's Dispensary for Sick Animals) founder Maria Dickin introduced the Dickin Medal in 1943 in order to honor animals who displayed conspicuous gallantry and devotion to duty associated with or under the control of any branch of the armed forces or Civil Defence units. It is considered the animal equivalent of the Victoria Cross. Thirty-two pigeons, three horses, one cat, and (before September 11, 2001) nineteen dogs had received the award.

1. The first dog to receive the Dickin Medal was **Bob**, a white mixed breed who saved members of his infantry unit from capture during World War II.

2. **Antis**, a German Shepherd Dog, served with his Czech owner in the French air force and Royal Air Force from 1940 to 1945 in both North Africa and England.

3. **Sheila**, a sheepdog, received the Dickin Medal for assisting the rescue of four American airmen lost in a blizzard after an air crash in December 1944 in Scotland. Sheila was the first civilian dog to be awarded the Dickin Medal.

4. **Jet**, who served with the Civil Defence, was responsible for the rescue of people trapped under blitzed buildings while serving in London during World War II.

5. **Irma** received her medal for serving beside Jet.

6. **Rob**, also known as War Dog No. 471/322, took part in landings during the North African campaign with infantry and later with the Special Air Unit in Italy.

7. **Thorn**, who served with the Civil Defence during World War II, received the medal for locating air raid casualties in spite of thick smoke in burning buildings.

8. **Tich**, a mixed breed, displayed loyalty, courage, and devotion to duty under hazardous conditions of war while serving in North Africa and Italy.

9. **Rifleman Khan** received the medal for rescuing an officer from drowning while under heavy shell fire at the battle of Walcheren in November 1944.

10. **Rex** was recognized for outstanding good work in the location of casualties in burning buildings. Undaunted by smoldering debris, thick smoke, intense heat, and jets of water from fire hoses, this dog displayed uncanny intelligence and outstanding determination in sniffing out casualties.

11. **Rip**, a mixed breed that was picked up by the Civil Defence Squad in London, received the Dickin Medal for locating air raid victims buried by rubble during the blitz of 1940.

12. **Peter**, a Collie, located victims trapped under blitzed buildings.

13. **Punch** and **Judy**, both Boxers, were awarded the Dickin Medal in November 1946 for saving the lives of two British officers in Israel by attacking an armed terrorist who was stealing up on the men, and thus warning them of the danger; Punch and Judy were both wounded in the process.

14. **Ricky**, a Welsh Sheepdog, was cited for clearing the shoulder of a canal bank in Holland. Ricky found all the mines, but during the operation one of them exploded. Ricky was wounded but remained calm and kept on working.

15. **Brian**, a German Shepherd Dog, was a patrol dog attached to a parachute battalion. He landed in Normandy and after doing the required number of jumps became a fully qualified paratrooper.

16. **Gander**, a Newfoundland, was awarded the Dickin Medal in August 2000, fifty-five years after the last medal had been awarded. He is the only dog from

Canada to have received the medal. His citation reads, "For saving lives of Canadian infantrymen during the battle of Lye Mun on Hong Kong Island in December 1941."

17. **Buster**, an English Springer Spaniel British army dog, was awarded the Dickin Medal in 2003 for heroism and outstanding devotion to duty during the recent conflict in Iraq. In March 2003, in Safwan, southern Iraq, Buster located a hidden cache of arms, explosives, and bomb-making equipment in buildings thought to be the headquarters of extremists responsible for attacks on British forces.

18. On Tuesday, March 5, 2003, the guide dog **Roselle** received her PDSA Dickin Medal in New York, close to Ground Zero, at the waterfront memorial to the rescue workers who lost their lives on September 11. Roselle and her owner, Michael Hingson, were on the seventy-eighth floor of the World Trade Center, Roselle sleeping peacefully under Michael's desk, when the first plane struck fifteen floors above them. In accordance with emergency exit procedures, Roselle led Michael to safety.

19. **Salty**, a yellow Lab guide dog, was awarded the medal at the same time as Roselle. Salty and his owner, Omar Rivera, who is employed by the Port Authority, were on the seventy-first floor of the World Trade Center when the first plane struck. Salty refused to leave Mr. Rivera's side, and, accompanied by Miss Donna Enright, Omar's supervisor, the pair walked down a smoke-filled stairway crowded with terrified people. Despite the overpowering stench of jet fuel, the splinters of glass and debris underfoot, and ankle-high water, Salty never hesitated or faltered.

20. **Apollo**, a German Shepherd police dog, received the Dickin Medal on behalf of the more than three hundred search and rescue dogs who worked at Ground Zero and the Pentagon following the terrorist attacks on New York and Washington on September 11, 2001. Apollo proudly accepted his award with his handler, the police officer Peter Davis, at his side.

21. A Royal Army Veterinary Corps guard and patrol dog, **Sam**, was awarded the Dickin Medal posthumously at a special ceremony in January 2003 in recognition of Sam's outstanding gallantry during the conflict in Bosnia Herzegovina in April 1998 while he and his handler were assigned to First Battalion, Royal Canadian Regiment in Drvar. Sam's handler, Sergeant Carnegie, accepted the medal on behalf of the brave German Shepherd Dog, who had been nominated for the award by his army colleagues.

The World's 7 Wealthiest Dogs

You can't leave money to a pet legally, because pets are considered property, and property can't own property. If you do leave your fortune to your dog, the money will go to your alternate beneficiary or to your closest relatives. You can, however, open a trust fund for your dog and appoint a human trustee, whose job it will be to follow your written instructions.

1. Countess Karlotta Libenstein of Germany left approximately **$106 million** to her Alsatian, Gunther III, when she died in 1992. Her trustees invested the money and tripled the fortune for Gunther's own heir, Gunther IV, making him the wealthiest dog in the world with a treasure in the neighborhood of **$318 million**.

2. Toby Rimes inherited about **$80 million** from New York owner Ella Wendel.

3. Frankie was endowed with **$5.3 million dollars**. He currently resides in a mansion in San Diego, California.

4. Moose, the Jack Russell Terrier that starred as Eddie on the TV show *Frasier*, is worth approximately **$3.2 million**. He earned more than $10,000 per episode.

5. The heiress Diana Myburgh rescued her dog Jasper from a shelter and endowed him with nearly **$700,000**.

6. In 2002, the actress Drew Barrymore followed through on her promise to reward her life-saving pooch Flossie with a new doghouse. She placed her entire Beverly Hills home, valued at **$3 million**, in trust with her yellow Lab mixed breed.

7. Eighty-nine-year-old Norah Hardwell, who passed away in July 2004, left more than half of her **£800,000** estate to her two Collie-cross dogs, Tina and Kate. She also left a portion of her estate to the Animal Health Trust in England.

3 Kinds of Conformation Dog Shows

Dr. Alvin Grossman, an international dog show judge, began his judging career in 1973. Since that time he has judged at English Setter, Golden Retriever, and Vizsla National Specialties and has been approved by the AKC to judge all the breeds in the Sporting Group as well as Best in Show. He was the publisher of Doral Publishing and is the author of five books about dogs. The following explanation of the basic three types of conformation shows was provided by Dr. Grossman.

1. All-breed shows are sponsored by all-breed clubs. As you probably guessed from the name, all AKC-approved breeds may be exhibited at an all-breed show. AKC championship points are awarded to Winners Dogs and Winners Bitches. It takes 15 points to become a champion. Points are awarded on the basis of the number of dogs in competition. AKC establishes the point schedule each year based on the number of dogs competing in that breed in that area for the past year. To become a champion a dog must win two majors, shows that have enough entries to make up a 3-, 4-, or 5-point major.

2. Specialty shows are sponsored by specialty clubs and are the most common type of dog show in the country. Any breed club that is licensed by the AKC can sponsor this type of show. Only a single breed, such as a Brittany Spaniel or a German Shepherd Dog, is exhibited at a specialty show; this makes the competition for points intense. Championship points are awarded to the Winners Dogs and Winners Bitches. Naturally, exhibitors consider winning at a specialty show to be a significant event.

3. The third type of show is the match. There are both all-breed and specialty matches. Most of these are held under AKC sanction, but no championship points are awarded to the winners. Matches provide a practice ground for novice exhibitors, experienced breeders breaking in their newest show prospects, dog clubs working toward being approved by the AKC, and prospective judges who want to become approved AKC judges. This type of show is fun to attend, because it's a great place to learn how to exhibit your dog, and for the dog to learn proper ring manners.

"A dog is like an eternal Peter Pan, a child who never grows old and who therefore is always available to love and be loved."
— AARON KATCHER, AMERICAN EDUCATOR AND PSYCHIATRIST

How a Conformation Dog Show Works

Dr. Alvin Grossman writes, "Dog shows can be a whole new way of life. At first, you'll be exposed to sights and sounds and terms that may confuse your senses. Just remember that dog shows are set up somewhat similarly to the NCAA final basketball tournament. There is Breed competition (dogs of the same breed), which is like the preliminary rounds of play in a tournament. In this example, the best dog from each of approximately 140 breeds is selected to go on to compete in the next higher round, the group competition. You can compare this to a combination of quarter- and semifinal rounds." The following list is Dr. Grossman's description of the dog show process:

1. The show begins with the Puppy Class for six-to-nine-month-old puppies. The judge chooses the top four puppies in each breed and awards them first through fourth place. The next class that is judged comprises the nine-to-twelve-month-old puppies. Judges will then go through the Novice Class; the Bred-by-Exhibitor Class; the American Bred Class, which is open to all dogs bred in America; and Open Class, which is open to all dogs, including puppies. Awards from first to fourth place are given for all classes.

2. After each separate class has been judged, the first-place pooches from each of these classes are brought back into the ring, where they compete in the Winners Class. The judge now selects the Winners Dog, which is always a male dog. The second-place finisher receives the Reserve Winners Dog Award, which is important because if the Winners Dog is disqualified for any reason, the Reserve Winners Dog will receive the championship points, but this hardly ever happens.

3. This entire process is then repeated for the female dogs, culminating in the selection of a Winners Bitch and a Reserve Winners Bitch. The Winners Bitch is the only female of the breed to gain championship points at this show.

> "Man is an animal that makes bargains; no other animal does this — no dog exchanges bones with another."
> — ADAM SMITH

4. The Best of Breed competition is next. All the AKC breed champs are entered in this phase of the show, along with the Winners Dog and Winners Bitch. The judge will now select the Best of Breed winner. The judge will

also compare the Winners Dog and the Winners Bitch and award one of them Best of Winners.

5. Last, the judge selects the Best of Opposite Sex to Best of Breed or Variety — that is, if a male is selected Best, then the judge seeks his opposite sex winner from among the females. If a female is awarded Best, the judge then makes his selection for Best Opposite Sex from among the males.

6. In an all-breed show the Best of Breed or Variety winner will go on to compete against all the other dogs in his group. For example, the winner of the Cocker Spaniels will go on to compete against the winner of the American Pointers, English Setters, Golden Retrievers, and others in the Sporting Group.

7. Each group selects its winners in the same way. Within the group competition the judge awards four placements. The first-place winner is the group winner, and he moves on to the next level of competition — Best in Show. Seven dogs compete for this final award, but only one can win the coveted title.

14 Prestigious All-Breed Conformation Dog Shows

1. AKC/Eukanuba National Invitational Championship (formerly the AKC/Eukanuba American Dog Classic) is dedicated to showcasing the top dogs in each breed in America. The event is by invitation only to the top twenty dogs of their individual breeds during the current calendar year and is held at a different venue every year. More than 3,600 dogs compete for $225,000 in cash and prizes, making it the largest prize-money dog show in the world. A great deal of attention is also given to breeders, who have devoted their lives to improving their favorite breed. The show committee consists of AKC staff and officers and a representative from the Iams Company.

2. The Crufts Dog Show, held in England, is considered by many to be the greatest dog show in the world. It attracts more than 21,000 dogs competing to achieve the title of Best in Show. The event lasts for four days and since 1990 has been held at Birmingham's National Exhibition Centre. BBC's television coverage of the event routinely attracts millions of viewers worldwide.

3. The Detroit Kennel Club Show, dating back to 1916, is one of the six AKC benched confirmation shows. While the DKC has throughout its long history strived to put on an extraordinary dog show that is rewarding for exhibitors and spectators alike, their primary goal has been to educate the public about the sport of purebred dogs. The conformation competition is just a small part of what makes the DKC Show so special. Spectators and dog lovers are invited to visit the benching area, where they can meet the dogs and speak to their handlers up close. Demonstrations in agility, obedience, rescue, hunting, and herding, as well as pet first aid, make this event highly entertaining.

4. The Golden Gate Kennel Club held its first bench show in May 1910. Now, this two-day benched show, which is held at the Cow Palace in San Francisco, is one of the most highly regarded dog shows in the country. More than 2,200 dogs are entered, and all, with the exception of puppies, are on exhibit for the public on both days. Agility, herding, and flyball demonstrations are another popular feature of this event.

5. The International Cluster of Dog Shows draws approximately 100,000 spectators over the four-day period at the enormous McCormick Place convention center. The International is a successor to the old Chicago Kennel Club, which was founded in 1900. The Chicago Kennel Club Show had long been considered one of the premier shows in America, but became a casualty in the 1980s of the other clubs' holding shows on the same weekend.

6. The Japanese Kennel Club Show, held in Tokyo, was established in 1949. The JKC has 1,100 affiliate clubs with 160,000 members and an annual registration of 1,523,530 dogs representing 147 breeds. The club's first dog show was held at Ueno Ikenohata Park in 1950.

7. The Kennel Club of Philadelphia is the host to Purina's National Dog Show, which is held on Thanksgiving Day. It has 1,770 entries representing 144 breeds, with twenty-three judges determining the best specimens. After breed and group judging, seven dogs compete for Best in Show in the final stages of the telecast. In general, the broadcast of the show differs from traditional dog show coverage, with unique elements about various breeds and family pets, including Purina-inspired pieces on pet health and wellness.

8. The Kentuckiana Cluster of Dog Shows or the **Louisville Cluster** is held every March and attracts more than 4,000 dogs each day, making it the largest entry of any dog show in the United States. The event, which is conducted over a period of a few days,

> **"Rambunctious, rumbustious, delinquent dogs become angelic when sitting."**
> —DR. IAN DUNBAR

takes place in three or four different cities and on successive days. The finals, which involve as many as 5,000 dogs, are always held at the state fairgrounds in Louisville.

9. **The Monaco Dog Show**, until recently under the patronage of H.S.H. Prince Rainier and officially titled Exposition Canine Internationale, is usually held during the last week of March or the first week of April at Monaco's Espace Fontvieille. This event gives out the International Beauty Champion certificate (CACIB) and the Monegasque Beauty Champion certificate (CACM), judged by a jury of fifteen international experts. For more information, call the Société Canine de Monaco (+377) 93 50 55 14.

10. **The Sydney Royal Dog Show**, held annually in early April, is Australia's premier dog show event. There are more than 4,000 dogs entered, and judges from all over the world officiate. Conformation titles are awarded, but the main draw is actually the sheepherding competitions. There is an agricultural show as well, for stock animals and produce (vegetables).

11. **UKC Premier United Kennel Club** conformation shows are similar to AKC shows but with a more relaxed, family atmosphere. There are no professional handlers showing dogs, just the true owners or co-owners or the breeders of the dogs. To enter a UKC show you must first have a UKC-registered dog who is intact and neither blind nor deaf. While the focus of this show is primarily on performance events, awards are given out to Best in Group and Best in Show winners.

12. **The Westchester Weekend** takes place at Lyndhurst Castle, a Gothic mansion in Tarrytown, New York, a National Trust Historic site. This highly prestigious event, begun eighty-seven years ago, offers dog lovers the chance to see an exceptional array of dogs. More than 2,000 gorgeous dogs are judged by top-rated judges during this one-day September event.

13. Established in 1877, the **Westminster Kennel Club** is America's oldest organization dedicated to the sport of purebred dogs. There is only one Westminster, and in its long and prestigious existence just about every superlative imaginable has been used to describe the club, the show, and its impact on the world of purebred dogs. The Westminster Kennel Club "has had great effect in improving the quality of the dogs owned for use or companionship. Of this there can be no doubt," wrote one reporter. True then, true today.

14. **The World Dog Show**, run by the the Fédération Cynologique Internationale, which is the World Canine Organization, is held in different countries each year that showcase many of the rare and important breeds of Europe. This includes judging of all ten FCI groups with special emphasis on rare and unusual breeds and including agility and many interesting demonstrations. The 2004 World Dog Show will be held in Rio de Janeiro, and the 2005 show will be held in Argentina. Future hosting countries include Poland, Mexico, and Sweden.

5 Ways to Find Dog Shows

1. Dog shows are handled by licensed superintendents who are hired by kennel clubs. You can locate three of the country's top superintendents online: **Jack Onofrio Dog Shows,** www.onfrio.com **Jim Rau,** www.raudogshows.com **Roy Jones,** www.royjonesdogshows.com

2. Consult magazine listings in publications such as *Dog World* and *Dog Fancy* and training magazines such as *Front and Finish* and *Off-Lead*. All UKC shows are listed in *Bloodlines,* and the AKC announces their events in the *Events Calendar.*

3. Check local event listings in newspapers and penny-saver publications.

4. Consult the local kennel club, a breed club, or a dog trainer, especially one who teaches conformation classes, as many do.

5. Companies that manufacture dog products often publish events calendars that you can locate online or at pet discount chain stores.

Who's Who at the Dog Show

The **superintendent**'s responsibilities are enormous. He or she basically runs the show and is in charge of the massive amount of paperwork involved in getting the show under way. This person is also responsible for printing and distributing the premium list and overseeing the printing of the show's catalogue. It is also the role of the superintendent to report all results of the show to the kennel club. Some noted dog show superintendents are Jack Onofrio, Roy Jones, and Jim Rau.

The **show chairman** and **assistant chairman** are the CEOs of the event. They are responsible for renting the venue and communicating with both the AKC and the show superintendent when necessary. They arrange to have a vet at the show and hire the dog show photographer. They also supervise the trophy chairman, the hospitality chairman, the grounds chairman, the vendor chairman, the chief ring steward, and the judge's transportation chairman.

The role of the **judge** is paramount at the dog show. The judge, an expert in the breed that he or she is assigned to, will examine each dog and place them according to his or her mental image of the perfect dog as set down in the breed's official AKC standard. These standards include the dog's structure, temperament, and movement. Every judge must prove his or her knowledge of each individual breed and be tested on this knowledge before the AKC will license him or her to judge a breed.

The role of the **handler** is to present his or her dog in the show ring and in the best possible light. The handler will try to display the dog's strongest points and downplay his weaknesses. A good handler will have a thorough knowledge of the breed he or she is exhibiting, will train the dog for the show ring, will groom the dog prior to showing, and make the experience as exciting for the dog as possible. A great handler will virtually fade into the background and go unnoticed. Professional handlers are hired by dog owners to exhibit their dogs and will often exhibit as many as a dozen dogs at a show.

Owner-handlers are obviously owners who exhibit their dogs themselves. While it is generally felt that judges will favor a professional handler in a judging situation, good owner-handlers can and often do win at the dog show. If you are interested in showing your dog and can afford a good professional handler, your chances for success are greater. Choosing the right handler for your dog should start with a recommendation. You can ask your breeder for some names.

The **steward** is a volunteer worker and is usually a member of the dog club that sponsors the show. The steward's job is to take care of little details while the show is being conducted. The steward sees to it that each exhibitor has his or her armband and then escorts and positions the exhibitor in the show ring, and also cues the exhibitors when it is their turn to show their dog. The steward also sees to it that the judge has the judging book and that all records are kept. The steward may also be in charge of organizing ribbons presented to the winners. Being a steward is a great way to learn how the show operates and gives you an opportunity to see all those beautiful dogs up close and personal.

The **chief ring steward** is responsible for making sure there are enough stewards to supervise each ring who are either club volunteers or from a professional organization. For shows including obedience trials, there is often a chief conformation steward and a chief obedience steward.

Junior handlers are youngsters who are often newcomers to the sport of dog showing. Juniors are eligible to show from the day they are ten years old until they turn eighteen years old. Junior handling is a great way for kids to enter the dog show world, learn about their favorite breeds, make friends, and learn how to lose and win gracefully.

What the Judges Look For

Judges are usually a fair-minded breed, and there are some excellent ones around the world. The ideal judge has a professional manner in the ring and is respectful to both dog and handler. Although there are exceptions, it's good form to accept a judge's placement gracefully no matter how much you disagree with the decision; if you must challenge a placement, go through formal channels.

Your dog will be judged not against other dogs but against his or her own breed standard — a set of rules that dictates how a breed should look. This is why dogs of different breeds can be judged alongside one another.

Dogs are judged in two ways: overall appearance, which includes grooming your dog to the required standards, and movement, or the pace he has to move to produce the desired gait.

In order to have your dog's overall appearance judged, you will be asked to "stack" your dog, which refers to the dog's standing square. This will require practice for both you and your dog. You will need to learn how to "free stack" (in which your dog poses himself) and "hand stack" (in which you arrange the position). During the competition, you will need to be able to stack your dog in less than ten seconds.

The judge will examine the dog to make sure he is "suitably equipped." At one end, he'll check that a dog has two proper testicles, and at the other, he'll check the mouth for the correct number of teeth and a proper bite.

The judge will feel various parts of the dog for shoulder and hip angles, the planes of the head, and the spring of the ribs, allowing him to ascertain information that a coat often hides. With some breeds, the judge will also check the arch of the dog's neck to make sure that the ears are the correct length.

You will be required to run your dog around the ring in what's called a "gaiting pattern." Various shows use different patterns, but the most common is the triangle, which allows the judge to ascertain the movement of the dog in three different ways.

Your dog should demonstrate an even and friendly temperament and be animated. The judge will be looking to see how interested your dog is in what is going on around him. Many a ribbon has been lost because the dog was too complacent to show the required animation. It is perfectly legal for you to use a small piece of dried liver in your hand or a small toy to show the judge that your dog can be animated, although some judges frown on this practice.

Seven out of ten British dogs get Christmas gifts from their owners.

An Early History of Conformation Dog Shows

Throughout history, dogs were primarily bred for their skills as hunters, trackers, herders, or draft dogs. It wasn't until the nineteenth century that dogs began to be appreciated for their beauty and individuality. As the times changed and people no longer looked upon dogs as workers, they began to see dogs in a different light and bred them as companions. Eventually consistent physical appearance became an important factor for breeders.

1859. The very first organized conformation show was held in Newcastle-on-Tyne, England. Prior to this date there had been informal matches called "Pot House Shows" at which hunters could compare and discuss their dogs. The 1859 show was the first that took pre-show entries and offered a printed catalogue. Only sixty dogs participated, all of them pointers or setters.

1860. A show was held in Birmingham the following year and the number of dogs involved grew to 267. Two divisions were established in an attempt to categorize the dogs. One division was for sporting dogs, while the other included sheepherding, nonsporting, toy, and terrier dogs. This was the precursor of the group divisions that we see today.

1863. More than a thousand dogs were entered at the Birmingham show, and by 1892 the public was so enthralled by seeing dogs exhibited that more than two hundred different shows took place throughout England.

1873. As the popularity and interest in dogs grew, the Kennel Club was formed.

Twelve men got together and made up a committee that set down a code of rules to regulate shows, and all the dog clubs or societies that abided by these rules would be eligible for the Stud Book, which covered shows from 1859 to 1873.

1874. The first dog show held in the United States took place in Chicago.

1877. At the first Westminster Show, thirty-five breeds were represented. This show is now the second-oldest sporting event held in the United States, second only to the Kentucky Derby.

1884. The American Kennel Club was founded. The AKC's aim was to establish and maintain breeding records on pure-bred dogs in the United States. The AKC is the second-oldest amateur sports organization in the United States, the first being the U.S. Lawn Tennis Association.

1888. The Canadian Kennel Club was founded as a response to Canadians' not wishing to have their dogs judged under AKC rules.

1911. The Fédération Cynologique Internationale or FCI was established in Belgium. This organization, comprising seventy-five member countries, licenses and conducts shows around the world. The World Show, as it is called, is held in a different member country every year.

All About Crufts

For four days each year since 1990, 20,000 top pedigree dogs and their owners have gathered in Birmingham, England, for what is considered by many to be the greatest dog show in the world. The show is named after its founder, Charles Cruft, who began his career in dogs shortly after leaving college in 1876 and whose entrepreneurial talents and dedication to dogs eventually led to the first Crufts show in 1891. Here are some interesting milestones in the history of this event, provided by the kind folks at Crufts.

1. Crufts's first show was booked into the Royal Agricultural Hall, Islington, in 1891 and was the first in a long series of shows there. During this era it was possible for individuals to run shows for personal profit, an aspect that appealed mightily to its founder, who ran his shows with considerable profit to himself. Today there are no privately owned dog shows and permission to hold shows is granted by the Kennel Club, which licenses only noncommercial organizations.

2. In 1938 Charles Cruft died, and his widow ran the 1939 show. Three years later Mrs. Cruft felt the responsibility for running the show too demanding and, in order to perpetuate the name of the show her husband had made world famous, she asked the Kennel Club to take it over and sold it to them.

3. The first show under the Kennel Club's auspices was conducted in 1948. It took place at Olympia and proved an immediate success with both exhibitors and the public. Since then Crufts has increased in stature year by year.

4. In 1979 it was decided to change the venue from Olympia to Earls Court, as the increasing entries had the show bursting at the seams. In 1982 the show ran for three days and in 1987 for four days to accommodate the increasing numbers of dogs and spectators.

5. 1991 saw the Crufts Centenary Show being held at the Birmingham National Exhibition Centre, this being the first time the show had moved from London.

6. 2005 will be the fifteenth year that the show has been staged at the NEC.

A Cocker Spaniel holds the world's record for the most persistent barking. It barked 907 times in ten minutes.

The Story of the Westminster Kennel Club

Before there were light bulbs, automobiles, or the World Series, there was Westminster. The Westminster Kennel Club is America's oldest organization dedicated to the sport of purebred dogs. Established in 1877, Westminster's influence has been felt for more than a century through its famous all-breed, benched dog show held every year at New York's Madison Square Garden. Here are some interesting historical facts about this prestigious club:

1877: A group of hunters who routinely met to discuss and compare their dogs form a club, which they name after their favorite hotel, the Westminster. Also this year, the First Annual New York Bench Show of Dogs is held at Gilmore's Garden in New York City, drawing an entry of 1,201 dogs. This is the first Westminster show.

1888: It is established that all dogs eligible for competition be certified by the AKC, which was founded in 1884. This is also the first year that a woman, Anna Whitney, serves as a judge.

1905: By this time, Westminster is the largest dog show in the world; 1,752 dogs appear at the Crystal Palace in London for the annual competition.

1907: The award of Best in Show is given for the first time at Westminster. A panel of ten judges makes the decision.

1918 and 1919: Profits from these annual shows are donated to the American Red Cross in support of the war effort.

1924: The first Westminster show is held under the new rules for groups and Best in Show judging. Five group

winners (sporting, working, terrier, toy, and nonsporting) compete for the final award of Best in Show.

1926: Madison Square Garden becomes the official and permanent venue for the Westminster shows.

1933: Geraldine Rockefeller Dodge becomes the first woman to be the sole judge of Best in Show. Mrs. Dodge became legendary in the dog show world as the force behind the Morris & Essex Kennel Club and the benefactor of St. Hubert Giralda Animal Shelter in New Jersey.

1934: The Children's Handling Grand Challenge Trophy is first awarded. This event was later to be called Junior Handling and is still part of the Westminster show today.

1937: The number of dogs entered at Westminster grows to 3,140.

1941: The show is changed from a three- to a two-day event.

1941 and 1942: Proceeds from these shows are donated to the American Red Cross. During the next few years, proceeds benefit Dogs for Defense and the National War Fund.

1948: Westminster receives television coverage for the first time.

1968: The Westminster Kennel Club Dog Show is the final event of any kind held at Madison Square Garden III, which later relocated to its present site.

1992: Westminster becomes the first champions-only dog show held under AKC rules. During this year's event, awards of merit are given out for the first time.

2002: Westminster honors the search and rescue dogs who performed with distinction at the World Trade Center on September 11, 2001.

Top, left: An Irish Wolfhound is evaluated by a Westminster judge. **Lower, right:** A Newfoundland struts her stuff at Westminster.

8 Special Trophies and Awards Given at Westminster

The Westminster Kennel Club awards silver-plated trophies for all individual winners. However, there are also special awards given to dogs and owners who have won on multiple occasions. They are as follows:

1. Permanent possession of the **James Mortimer Memorial Silver Trophy** goes to the Best in Show winner if the dog is American bred and has repeated the win five times with the same owner. A sterling silver plaque is given for each win.

2. **The McGivern Challenge Bowl**, a sterling silver bowl, goes to the winner of the Sporting Group. Permanent possession is awarded if the dog has won three times with the same owner. A silver-plated replica is given to commemorate each win.

3. **The St. Hubert's Giralda** is a sterling silver trophy in memory of Geraldine R. Dodge. It goes to the winner of the Hound Group. Permanent possession is awarded after three wins with the same owner.

4. **The Louis F. Bishop III Memorial Trophy** is awarded to the winner of the Working Group if won three times by the same owner. A sterling silver trophy is given for each win.

5. **The William Rockefeller Trophy** is given to the winner of the Terrier Group. This award is presented by Rockefeller's children in his memory. Permanent possession is given if there have been three wins by the same owner. A silver-plated replica is awarded for each win.

6. **The Walter M. Jeffords, Jr., Trophy** is offered to the winner of the Toy Group. Permanent possession is given if there have been three wins by the same owner. A sterling silver trophy is awarded for each win.

7. **The James F. Stebbins Trophy** is awarded to the winner of the Nonsporting Group. Permanent possession is given if there have been three wins by the same owner. A sterling silver replica is awarded for each win.

8. **The Strathglass Trophy** is offered in memory of Mr. and Mrs. Hugh J. Chisolm to the winner of the Herding Group. Permanent possession is given if there have been three wins by the same owner. A silver-plated replica is awarded for each win.

The Top Winning Groups at the Westminster Kennel Club Best in Show

Terrier Group — 43

Sporting Group — 16

Working Group — 15

Nonsporting Group — 10

Toy Group — 9

Hound Group — 3

Herding Group — 1

Junior Showmanship Winners, 2000–2004

2000, Nicholas Urbanek, Glenshaw, Pennsylvania

2001, Elizabeth Jordan, San Jose, California

2002, William Ellis, Reddick, Florida

2003, Chad Malinak, Harvey, Louisiana

2004, Katie Shepard, Kansas City, Missouri

Westminster Kennel Club Show Winners, 2000–2004

The winners, listed by group, are given with breed, dog's name, and owners.

2004

Best in Show. Newfoundland, CH Darbydale's All Rise Pouchcove, owned by Peggy Helming and Carol A. Bernard Bergmann.

Herding. Welsh Corgi (Pembroke), CH Hum'nbird Keepn Up'Pearances, owned by Samuel and Marion Lawrence.

Hound. Ibizan Hound, CH Luxor's Playmate of the Year, owned by Wendy Anderson, Leslie D. Lucas, G. E. Brand, and C. T. Woods.

Sporting. Sussex Spaniel, CH Clussexx Three D Grinchy Glee, owned by Cecilia Ruggles and Beth Dowd.

Nonsporting. Standard Poodle, CH Ale Kai Mikimoto on Fifth, owned by Karen LeFrak and Wendell J. Sammet-Alekai.

Toy. Pekingese, CH Yakee Leaving Me BreathlessAtFranshaw, owned by John Shaw and Maria Francis.

Terrier. Norfolk Terrier, CH Cracknor Cause Celebre, owned by Pamela Beale, Stephanie Ingram, and Elisabeth Matell.

Working. See Best in Show entry.

2003

Best in Show. Kerry Blue Terrier, CH Torums Scarf Michael, owned by Marilu Hansen.

Herding. German Shepherd Dog, CH Kismets Sight for Sore Eyes, owned by B. and D. Wood, J. and N. Bennett, A. Howells, and M. Kish.

Hound. Ibizan Hound, CH Luxor's Playmate of the Year, owned by Wendy Anderson, Glen E. Brand, L. Lucas, and H. Goldberg.

Sporting. Brittany Spaniel, CH Magic Sir-ly You Jest JH,

Westminster Stats

Through 2003, 281,217 dogs have been entered at Westminster's 127 shows.

There have been 1,614 judges to officiate at Westminster at least once, with some judging as many as twenty-two times.

Only once has the offspring of a Best in Show winner duplicated the feat. In 2000, the English Springer Spaniel CH Salilyn N' Erin's Shameless repeated the 1993 accomplishment of her sire, CH Salilyn's Condor.

Two Best in Show winners, Norwich Terriers, had the same sire: 1994's CH Chidley's Willum the Conqueror and 1998's CH Fairewood Frollic were offspring of CH Royal Rock Don of Chidley (making them half brother and sister).

The Papillon CH Loteski Supernatural Being is the only dog to capture the Best in Show crown at the World Show (1998 in Helsinki) and at Westminster (1999).

Two dogs have won Best in Show at both Westminster and Crufts in England. They are the Lakeland Terrier CH Stingray of Derryabah in 1968 and the Kerry Blue Terrier CH Torums Scarf Michael in 2003.

owned by C. Douglas, N. Otterson, J. Bates, and B. Callier.

Nonsporting. Standard Poodle, CH Ale Kai Mikimoto On Fifth, owned by Karen LeFrak and Wendell J. Sammet-Alekai.

Toy. Pekingese, CH Yakee Leaving Me BreathlessAtFranshaw, owned by John Shaw and Maria Francis.

Terrier. See Best in Show entry.

Working. Newfoundland, CH Darbydale's All Rise Pouchcove (2004 Best in Show winner), owned by Peggy Helming and Carol Bernard Bergmann.

2002

Best in Show. Miniature Poodle, CH Surrey Spice Girl, owned by Ron L. Scott and Barbara Scott.

Herding. Pembroke Welsh Corgi, CH Foxlor Shafrhaus Sammy Sosa, owned by Beth G. Dowd, Sandra Mottes, and Lori Sawyer.

Hound. Rhodesian Ridgeback, CH Wetu Of Kalahari, owned by Sandra C. Fikes, Darlene Stewart, M. Well, and C. L. Well.

Sporting. Brittany Spaniel, CH Magic Sir-ly You Jest, owned by Carolee Douglas, N. Otterson, J. Bates, and B. Callier.

Nonsporting. See Best in Show entry.

Toy. Affenpinscher, CH Yarrow's Super Nova, owned by Dr. and Mrs. William Truesdale.

Terrier. Kerry Blue Terrier, CH Torums Scarf Michael (2003 Best in Show winner), owned by Marilu Hansen.

Working. Standard Schnauzer, CH Charisma Jailhouse Rock, owned by Constance C. Adel.

2001

Best in Show. Bichon Frisé, CH Special Times Just Right, owned by Cecelia Ruggles, E. McDonald, and F. Werneck.

Herding. Pembroke Welsh Corgi, CH Coventry Queue, owned by Steven Leyerly and Mrs. Alan R. Robson.

Hound. Bloodhound, CH Ridge Runner Unforgettable, owned by Susan LaCroix Hamil and Lori Burch.

Sporting. Flat-Coated Retriever, CH Flatford Zeus The Major God JH, owned by Dr. Robert and Sonja Rickert and Mary and Marv Farwell.

Nonsporting. See Best in Show entry.

Toy. Shih Tzu, CH Charing Cross Ragtime Cowboy, owned by Gilbert S. Kahn.

Terrier. Kerry Blue Terrier, CH Torum's Scarf Michael, owned by Marilu Hansen. (2003 Best in Show winner).

Working. Standard Schnauzer, CH Charisma Jailhouse Rock, owned by Constance C. Adel.

2000

Best in Show. English Springer Spaniel, CH Salilyn 'N Erin's Shameless, owned by Carl Blain, Fran Sunseri, and Julia Gasow.

Herding. Pembroke Welsh Corgi, CH Coventry Queue, owned by Steven Leyerly and Mrs. Alan R. Robson.

Hound. Basset Hound, CH Moonbeam's Astronomer, owned by Maria Elisa Martinez.

Sporting. See Best in Show entry.

Nonsporting. Standard Poodle, CH Lake Cove That's My Boy, owned by Mrs. Allan Robson.

Toy. Shih Tzu, CH Charing Cross Ragtime Cowboy, owned by Gilbert S. Kahn.

Terrier. Bedlington Terrier, CH Willow Wind Tenure, owned by Carol C. Greenwald.

Working. Doberman Pinscher, CH Ravenswood Southern Cross, owned by Don and Betty Clark.

All About the AKC/Eukanuba National Championship

Though the AKC is the nation's oldest and only not-for-profit dog registry, the AKC/Eukanuba National Championship is a fairly new development, first held in Orlando, Florida, in 2001. It has quickly earned points toward being one of the most exciting shows in dogdom, and it is televised on Animal Planet and the Discovery Channel.

1. Although the AKC sponsors thousands of annual events, this is the only show organized and held solely by the AKC.

2. Show attendance is by invitation only. The top twenty-five dogs in every AKC-recognized breed and variety, as well as every Bred-by-Exhibitor Champion and Best in Show winner during the qualification period, are invited to compete.

3. This international competition attracts contestants from the world over. Recent events included entrants from countries as far away as Belgium, Hong Kong, and Chile.

4. The prize money is significant — a total of more than $225,000, plus special money awards for AKC Bred-by-Exhibitor Champions.

5. The show honors breeders with the coveted AKC Breeder of the Year Award. Seven breeders who have dedicated their lives to improving the health, temperament, and quality of purebred dogs are honored.

6. The event actually encompasses three different events, all of which are held under the same roof. The AKC National Agility Championship and the AKC National Obedience Championship are held in conjunction with the show.

7. The AKC/Eukanuba National Championship is the only all-breed qualifying show in America for the entry into Crufts, which is the world's largest dog show. Winners of Best of Breed, Best of Opposite Sex, and Best Bred-by-Exhibitor, as well as recipients of an Award of Merit at the show, are qualified to enter Crufts.

8. Junior handlers are celebrated here, too. Youngsters between the ages of ten and eighteen have a chance to demonstrate their talents and win a $2,000 scholarship.

The Role of the AKC

The American Kennel Club (AKC), founded in 1884, is a quasi-private corporation with a multimillion-dollar annual budget. It was established to promote the interests and well-being of purebred dogs. It is run by delegates who are chosen by their local dog clubs all around the country. These delegates, in turn, elect a board of directors from their own ranks. Besides policy formulation and other standard business functions, the board hires a president, who functions as the chief executive officer, directing the staff and carrying out the policies of the board. According to Dr. Alvin Grossman, international dog show judge, the major functions of the AKC are as follows:

1. Registering purebred dogs

2. Publishing a monthly journal, the *AKC Gazette*, which lists championship points by each dog, offers a wide variety of statistics about the status of the dog show game, month by month, and provides informative articles.

3. Authorizing dog clubs as show-giving entities

4. Educating the public about purebred dogs

5. Sponsoring medical research relating to purebred dogs

6. Sanctioning dog shows and approving dates and locations of shows

7. Approving dog show judges

8. Overseeing dog shows

9. Representing the United States at international meetings and seminars

To contact the AKC, write to American Kennel Club, 51 Madison Ave., New York, New York 10010 or visit them online at www.akc.org.

Basic Dog Show Terminology

For the ordinary spectator or for someone who plans on showing dogs, the terms used at dog shows can often be confusing, and be forewarned: the world of dog shows is a culture unto itself, with its own rules, taboos, and jargon. The very best introduction to the subject is Cheryl Smith's *The Absolute Beginner's Guide to Showing Your Dog* (Three Rivers, 2001). The following list is an explanation of some of the most basic and essential terms anyone interested in dog shows should know.

Agility. An obstacle race for dogs. Dogs and handlers complete a course made up of jumps, A-frames, dog walks, weave poles, tunnels, and other apparatus at a controlled pace.

All-breed club. An organized group of dog fanciers recognized by the Canadian Kennel Club (CKC) and/or the American Kennel Club (AKC) to hold all-breed dog shows and performance events within a geographic boundary.

All-breed show. An event at which dogs are judged as to how closely each *conforms* (hence the term *conformation*) to his own breed's written standard of perfection.

American Kennel Club. Organized in the late 1800s, the AKC is a body of licensed clubs whose stated mission is to maintain a registry for purebred dogs and preserve its integrity, and sanction dog events that promote interest in and sustain the process of breeding for type and function of purebred dogs.

Armband. A number printed on paper that an exhibitor wears to indicate the entered dog's reference number in the judge's book and catalogue.

Article. Items that are used in obedience trial competitions in exercises testing retrieval on command or scent discrimination. These can be wooden, leather, or metal dumbbells.

Baiting. When used as a verb, as "to bait the dog" or "to freebait," this refers to using an item of food or toy to gain the dog's attention; showing expression and animation to the judge.

Benched show. An all-breed show specifically designed for public education and enjoyment, wherein all dogs are required to stay in an assigned "benching area" for the duration of the show (except when being exercised, groomed, or exhibited), in order for the public to easily view the exhibits up close and talk to the breeders, owners, and handlers.

Best in Show. A coveted award given to the *one* dog who, at the end of an all-breed dog show, has successfully defeated *all* other dogs of all breeds entered that day.

Bitch. A female dog. *Not* a dirty word. Get used to it.

Brace. Two dogs of the same breed and exact same ownership being shown together as a pair in order to display the breeder's consistency in their breeding program. Brace competition is a non-regular competition, and no points are awarded.

Breed. Used to describe a particular subspecies of animals of similar type and heritage who have been carefully and intentionally bred to meet certain functional, temperamental, and physical characteristics. "Breed competition" or "in the breed ring" are also common references to competing in the conformation classes at a dog show.

Breed standard. A written standard of excellence agreed upon as the official description of perfection for a particular breed, describing functional, temperamental, and physical attributes.

Campaign (conformation). To enter and compete in a large number of shows with a Champion of Record (a "Special") — in order to obtain national rankings by way of defeating the greatest number of other dogs.

Campaign (obedience). To enter and compete in a large number of obedience trials at the Open or Utility level. Points are accumulated with the scores achieved. An overall "top ten" list is accumulated of the dogs and handlers who achieve the highest point totals in their respective countries during a calendar year.

CKC. The Canadian Kennel Club.

Catalogue. A document sold at shows listing each entered dog's entry number, class entered, registered name and number, breeder, owner, sire, dam, and date of birth. Excellent tool for following along with the competition and looking for patterns in breeding that you prefer, as well as breeders and exhibitors to contact.

Champion. In AKC competition, a Champion of Record ("CH") title is given to a dog or bitch who has won a total of 15 points at licensed AKC shows. At least 6 of these points must have come from "major" wins. A Champion of Record may then enter and compete in the Best of Breed competition, and the "CH" becomes an official prefix to the dog's registered name.

Choke. A metal, nylon, or leather collar consisting of a straight piece of the material, usually joined by looping it through one of two rings on each end. This is the most common collar worn by dogs in the breed ring.

Classes. The term used when referring to the different class divisions available to show your dog in when entered at a dog show.

Closing date. The last date by which entries must be received by the show superintendent or secretary in order for an entry to be valid and included in the show's competition.

Conformation. How well a specific dog's structure, type, and temperament conform to his breed's written standard of excellence.

Crate. A containment unit used to safely transport and house a dog during rest periods.

Croup. The lower spinal region of a dog, from the back of the pelvis to the root of the tail.

Crufts. *The* international dog show of the year, held outside London each March.

Cut. A handful of dogs whom the judge wishes to further consider for placements. Those who don't make the cut are typically dismissed.

Dog. Used specifically, a term to describe a male canine. Generally, a term used to describe the canine species.

Ex. An abbreviation for the verb "to exercise (potty) one's dog" — allowing them to eliminate, stretch their legs, and so on. As in, "I'm going to ex the dogs before bed."

Ex-pen. A portable wire fencing unit taken to shows to allow dogs a safe, clean place to eliminate and stretch out.

Finish. In conformation competition, to finish means to have won enough points to be awarded the title of Champion of Record. In obedience, a finish is a transitional movement the dog makes between the completion of a recall and the return to the heel position.

Flexi. Flexi-Lead is the common brand name of a retractable, spring-loaded lead that allows a dog to wander and traverse at a distance from the handler without getting caught up in the lead itself.

Free bait. To use food, a toy, or some other enticement to get the dog to stack properly (without physical interaction from the handler) and show alert, animated expression while standing in the breed ring being judged. The term "free" comes from "hands-free."

Gait. The most efficient way of moving for a particular dog. Most breeds are gaited at a trot or jogging speed.

Garden, the. Slang for the Westminster Kennel Club's high visibility, prestigious, and well-respected benched show held in New York City's Madison Square Garden each February.

Get. The offspring of a stud dog.

Groom. To bathe, dry, comb, and clip a dog to best exhibit his virtues.

Group(s). Groupings of dogs by their traditional functional similarities. The AKC and CKC currently have seven groups; sporting, hound, working, terrier, toy, nonsporting, and herding.

Handler. The person presenting the dog in competition.

Judge. An adjudicating official tasked with evaluating and comparing how well, in his or her opinion, and in comparison to the other dogs entered in the class that day, a dog conforms to his breed's written standard of excellence.

Junior. A young person between the ages of ten and eighteen who competes with other juniors of similar age and experience levels in exhibiting his or her technical skills in handling dogs, ring conduct, and sportsmanship.

Junior handling. The actual competitive classes offered for juniors exhibiting their handling skills, which are usually offered at dog shows and matches. The AKC and CKC offer classes for two age groups, each divided by skill.

Lead. A thin leather, nylon, or cotton piece of material, usually with a metal snap or clip connector on one end to attach to the dog's collar, and a loop on the other end for the handler to hold on to, leading the dog around the show ring.

Loin. The area of the body between the last rib and the beginning of the pelvis. (In human terms, this would be the waist). The lower portion of the loin is known as the "tuck-up."

Major. "A big win for a class dog who has defeated enough dogs that day by going Winners Dog or Winners Bitch, to earn either 3, 4, or 5 points toward its championship.

National. An annual specialty show hosted by the breed's national parent breed club. Usually considered that breed's most important, competitive, and prestigious event to win or in which to place well.

Obedience. A competitive performance event in which the dog and handler are judged on their ability to execute a predetermined set of exercises that display the dog's ability to adhere to certain commands.

Occiput. A bony section of the skull located at the back of the head, also known as an occipital protuberance. During puberty, or if not situated properly in an adult, this bone creates an unattractive bump (or protuberance) in the shape of the headpiece. Situated properly, it creates a slight dome to the skull.

Open. This is usually the largest and most competitive class at the dog show and is open to all AKC-registered dogs.

Opposite. Refers to the winner of the Best of Opposite Sex award.

Parent club (aka national breed club). The officially recognized national organization governing each specific breed's independent specialty clubs. Parent clubs or "national breed clubs" are tasked with being the official

guardians of their breeds and their written standards and stud book in this country, and to protect the welfare and integrity of their respective breeds.

Pastern. The area between a dog's paws and his lower arm, which in the front relates to a human wrist area, and in the rear relates to the sole of a human's foot.

Patella. The knee joint of a dog's rear leg, which allows the dog's leg to bend and flex as it moves.

Points. In conformation ("breed") competition, the CKC and the AKC award between 1 and 5 points toward their Champion of Record title — depending on the regional point schedule and/or how many dogs defeated — to both the Winners Dog and Winners Bitch of each breed entered at a show.

Poststernum. The "breastbone" on a dog.

Premium list. A publication created by the show superintendent or secretary that is mailed to prospective exhibitors, listing the club giving the show, the date and location of the show, the judges, classes and awards ("premiums") being offered, and so on. Premium lists contain forms and fees for entering and give the closing date by which entries must be received.

Produce. The offspring of a brood bitch.

Regional. A grouping of states with similar numbers of entries, which the AKC designates as a region for calculating point schedules.

Reserve. Refers to the Reserve Winners Dog or Bitch.

Ringer. A substitute for; a dog closely resembling another dog.

Ring steward. A judge's assistant who is tasked with coordinating the logistics of getting the exhibitors and their dogs into and out of the rings efficiently.

Roadwork. Form of exercise and dog conditioning, usually walking, jogging, or biking.

Secretary. A show official (usually an individual person) licensed by the CKC or the AKC and hired by the show-giving club to act as the coordinating management for the show. The secretary usually generates and distributes the premium lists, receives the entries, creates the catalogues, provides the equipment and materials needed, keeps all the records, and generates the reports for CKC.

Setting the back. This is done after the front is set. Move to the back legs and set them so that the pastern is perpendicular to the ground and the feet are slightly outside the front feet.

Setting the front. Placing your dog's front feet first so that the legs are aligned directly under the withers.

Setup. The area on the show grounds in which you establish your home base for grooming and holding your dogs while you are not in the ring. Pray for a space close to the rings, with an electrical outlet!

Sidegait. The movement of a dog as it is seen from the dog's side. Look for how effectively he tracks, and how appropriately he reaches with his front legs and drives off his rear.

Six to Nine. This refers to the Puppy Class in which the puppies between six to nine months old are exhibited. Note: Nine to Twelve and Twelve to Eighteen refer to pups in the nine-to-twelve-month and twelve-to-eighteen-month ranges.

Slicker. A small grooming tool with a rectangular head containing fine teeth with bent tops, which is used to separate and brush out the topcoat and furnishings such as hock hair.

Special. Slang for a Champion of Record who is being actively shown and campaigned.

Specialty. A show consisting of only one breed, given by a "specialty club." Specialty clubs are groups of individuals (breeders, exhibitors, pet enthusiasts, etc.) who share a passion for a specific breed of dog and who host events specific to promoting that breed.

Stack. To cause your dog to stand in a manner that best displays his virtues. In most breeds, the dog's forelegs are stacked in alignment with the withers, and the rear pasterns are squarely aligned and presented at a 90-degree angle from the floor. Note: a free stack is the show dog's natural pose without being touched or influenced by the handler.

Standard. The officially recognized written description of an ideal specimen of a specific breed. This is the document judges are tasked to interpret when judging in the breed ring.

Stifle. The curved area on a dog's rear legs containing the thighs and patella (knee). The actual bend of stifle regulates how much flexibility the dog will have to drive off his rear.

Stop. The skeletal junction on the skull's foreface between the back of the muzzle and the beginning of the top-skull. Collies and Afghans have very little stop, and Chihuahuas, Labrador Retrievers, and Saint Bernards have a great deal of stop.

Superintendent. A show official (usually a professional show managing company) licensed by the CKC/AKC and hired by the show-giving club to act as the coordinating management team for the show.

Sweepstakes. A nonregular class, usually offered at specialty shows, specifically designed to recognize outstanding young dogs and puppies.

Tack. Equipment (collars, leads, grooming products, combs, brushes, shears, etc.) used to prepare and show a dog.

Topline. The spinal section of a dog from his withers (top of shoulder blades) to the end of his croup (at the tail root).

Veterans. A nonregular but competitive class for dogs at least seven years old, designed to honor those dogs who have maintained their structural integrity, health, vigor, and love of showing into their golden years.

Westminster Kennel Club. A very prestigious all-breed/all-champions limited-entry benched show held in New York City's Madison Square Garden each February. The Westminster Kennel Club show is legendary. The WKC show is the second-oldest sporting event in the United States, younger only than the Kentucky Derby.

Whelp. To give birth to a litter of puppies. A pregnant bitch is considered to be "in whelp." When she is giving birth, she is said to be "whelping."

Winners Dog. The class (aka "unfinished" or "nonchampion") dog who has defeated all other class dogs of that breed at that show is the *one* male of that breed to be awarded points toward his championship. The term *Winners Bitch* is the same but refers to a female dog.

Withers. The point at which the shoulder blades (scapulae) meet. This critical structural point and its adjoining muscles and ligaments regulate how effectively a dog is able to cover ground with the rest of his front assembly.

Show Dogs Aren't Like Pets

Pets shed.	Show dogs "blow coat."
Pets are in heat.	Show dogs "come into season."
Pets trot.	Show dogs "gait" or "move."
Pets stand.	Show dogs "stack."
Pets get baths	Show dogs "are groomed."
Pets beg for food.	Show dogs "express desire for bait."
Pets jump the fence.	Show dogs "have natural jumping ability."
Pets poop.	Show dogs "toilet."
Pets bark at other dogs.	Show dogs "display excitement before the big event."
Pets chew up the trash.	Show dogs "possess a natural tendency for scent articles."

19 Luminaries of the Dog Show World, Past and Present

Choosing which personalities to include on this list was a challenge. There are so many wonderful and accomplished owners, handlers, and judges who have made significant contributions to the dog show world, and mentioning them all was not possible in this volume.

Another difficulty we encountered was the lack of information on even some of the most famous of dog show personages — very little written information exists for Dr. Samuel Milbank, for example. The names we did choose were based on suggestions from judges that we interviewed, from biographical information provided by the American Kennel Club, and from the wonderful book *Who's Who in Dogs* by the award-winning author Connie Vanacore.

The following list, therefore, represents a partial sampling of some of the most renowned folks ever to have graced the show ring.

1. **Nigel Aubrey-Jones** has had an illustrious career as a judge, breeder, and dog owner. During his forty-six-year career, he has bred, judged, and owned more than eight hundred Best in Show winners, including two that won at Westminster (1960, 1982). In addition to his success in the show ring, he has also been a prolific writer for dog magazines and newspapers. In 1990 Howell Book House published his book *The New Pekingese.* Although he rarely works in the ring anymore, his business, the Bibliography of the Dog, keeps him busy handling the purchase and sale of dog-related, pre-1940 oil paintings, bronze statues, porcelains, prints, and books.

2. **Richard G. Beauchamp** grew up with field dogs and began breeding and exhibiting when he was only a teenager. During his illustrious career he was a breeder, exhibitor, professional handler, writer, and judge. He purchased the *Kennel Review* and developed it into one of the leading dog magazines for breeders-exhibitors, and he also went on to write several breed books. He was instrumental in gaining AKC recognition for the Bichon Frisé in the early 1970s and has bred more than sixty champion Bichons himself. He served as an all-breed judge for the Fédération Cynologique Internationale and has judged shows all over the world. The UKC licensed him to judge most of the 250 breeds the organization registers.

3. **Michele L. Billings** began her judging career in 1972. She is now one of only ten women who have been approved as all-breed judges in the United States. She has judged several major shows around the world. She is a winner of the Gaines Fido Award for Woman of the Year in 1983, and a winner of the Kennel Review award for Judge of the Year in 1986. She was inducted into the New York Sports Museum Hall

"Most dogs don't think they are human; they know they are."
— JANE SWAN

"My little dog — a heartbeat at my feet."
— EDITH WHARTON

of Fame in 1993 and the Nature's Recipe Hall of Fame in 1998. She has been selected to head the panel as Best in Show judge for the 2005 AKC/Eukanuba National Championship.

4. **Marsha Hall Brown** has been one of the leading advocates for junior handling in this country. During her career, which began in 1949 when she won her first children's handling class, she has lectured extensively in the United States, Canada, and Australia. She has served on the AKC Junior Showmanship Rules Committee, and she cofounded and chaired the San Francisco Bay Judges Workshop. She created the first instructional video for junior handlers. Ms. Brown is also the author of *The Essence of Setters: A Study of English, Gordon, Irish and Red and White Setters* and *The Junior Showmanship Handbook.*

5. **Anne Rogers Clark** is certainly one of if not the most famous and respected of show judges. Anne became handler in the late 1940s. As a breeder-exhibitor-handler, Anne has had three dogs go Best in Show at Westminster, and she has bred three Westminster group-winning Poodles. She is the past president of the Poodle Club of America and the English Cocker Spaniel Club of America. The many awards won by Mrs. Clark include Handler of the Year, the Mark Morris Lifetime Award, and Dog Writer of the Year. She is a regular columnist for the *AKC Gazette* and is the coauthor of the *International Encyclopedia of Dogs.* Along with her many accomplishments during her twenty-one years as a judge, Mrs. Clark holds the distinction of being the only person to have judged six groups at Westminster.

6. **Dr. Josephine Deubler**'s career was inspired by five family members who were veterinarians, all male. Despite becoming totally deaf in early childhood, she overcame her disability and went on to earn a master's and Ph.D. from the University of Pennsylvania and became the first woman to be admitted to the Pennsylvania Veterinary Medical Association. She later gained international renown as a breeder, exhibitor, and judge of dogs — even judging Best in Show at Westminster. She has been the show chairman of both the Montgomery County Kennel Club and the Bucks County Kennel Club for the past twenty-five years.

7. **Geraldine Rockefeller Dodge** was a famous breeder of Bloodhounds, German Shepherd Dogs, and as many as eighty-five other breeds. It was the English Cocker Spaniel, however, that really captured her fancy. She is credited with developing the breed in the United States and was responsible for the breed's recognition by the AKC. Mrs. Dodge was a remarkable woman, and once a year she opened her home in rural Madison, New Jersey, to the public at her Morris and Essex Ken-

The 10 Dog Show Ribbon Colors and What They Mean

Each winning dog is awarded a ribbon by a judge. The color of the ribbon signifies the type of award the dog has won. Here are the ribbon and rosette colors used by the AKC.

1. **Blue:** first place in each group

2. **Red:** second place in each group

3. **Yellow:** third place in each group

4. **White:** fourth place in each group

5. **Purple:** to each winner of the Winners Dog and Winners Bitch classes

6. **Purple and White:** the Reserve Winners

7. **Blue and White:** the dog or bitch that wins Best of Winners

8. **Purple and Gold:** the dog deemed Best of Breed in each separate breed competition

9. **Red and White:** the Best of Opposite Sex in each individual breed

10. **Red, White, and Blue:** the dog judged Best in Show

8 Qualities of a Good Dog Show Person

If you are interested in showing your dog but are a newcomer to the sport, you will have to decided whether you have what it takes to get involved. Here are some attributes every good competitor should have:

1. You will need to have a great deal of patience with your dog. Be willing to spend the time that it takes to train your dog for the show ring.

2. Enjoy the show even if your dog doesn't win. Be mentally prepared to lose, because you will lose often, and if you do win it will probably be out of sheer luck. So, be prepared to lose and do it with a smile and remember to congratulate the winners.

3. Know your self-worth. Don't let your dog's performance determine how you feel about your own skills. She may have an off day, but you need to perform well despite it.

4. You should be friendly and outgoing. Dog people are wonderful and usually more than willing to give you advice. Don't be afraid to ask questions and let others know that this is your first time in the show ring.

5. Be willing to study. Read all you can about your breed and about how dog shows operate.

6. Be willing to take criticism gracefully. A good critique will only make you stronger and wiser in the show ring.

7. Be flexible in your beliefs and methods, and be willing to change even if it means swallowing your pride.

8. Respect your dog. She's your buddy, not an asset or possession.

nel Clubs dog show. It is said that these shows, last held in 1957, have never been equaled in elegance or splendor and were internationally known as the world's largest and most prestigious.

Mrs. Dodge also spent years devoted to the animal welfare and the animal protection movement in this country. She established the St. Hubert's Giralda Animal Shelter on her estate and provided for it in her will: proceeds from the sale of some of her vast collection of animal art was used to keep the shelter going after her death at age ninety-one.

8. **Melbourne T. L. Downing**, of Baltimore, Maryland, is one of the dog world's most distinguished personalities. He grew up with a variety of dogs raised in his parents' famed Holly-Lodge Kennel. He was so immersed in the dog world that he once said, "You can say I grew up in a dog kennel." He began breeding his own dogs in the early 1930s and is credited with producing and exhibiting the first American-bred Pekingese to win an all-breed Best in Show and was also responsible for the first winners in Pugs. During the course of his illustrious career he has judged in every state in the United States and almost every country in the world. He has judged twenty-one Westminster shows, and Best in Show at the world's fair in Seattle. He has also been both president and show chairman of the Baltimore County and Catonsville Kennel Clubs in Maryland. He founded the Senior Conformation Judges Association and served as its president. He was named Dogdom's Man of the Year in 1995 and is a recipient of the American Kennel Club Lifetime Achievement Award.

9. **Bob Forsyth** has spent his entire life devoted to dogs. During World War II he served with the U.S. Marines in the first war dog platoon. Bob has won the Kennel Review handlers award and is a two-time winner of the Gaines Handler of the Year Award. He has bred pointers for forty years, producing approximately twenty-five champions. He has judged at every important venue in the United States, and, as an FCI "all-rounder" judge since 1981, has had assignments in Australia, Italy, Japan, Finland, Sweden, Canada, Mexico, and several South American countries. He judged the Sport-

ing Group at the 2002 AKC/Eukanuba National Championship. He and his wife, Jane, are the authors of *The Forsyth Guide to Successful Dog Showing*, which was awarded Best Technical Dog Book by the Dog Writers' Association of America.

10. **Jane Forsyth** began her career in dogs sixty-four years ago. Before she married Bob, she, Bob, and Anne Rogers Clark worked at shows together while each operated a separate kennel. Jane has been named the Kennel Review Handler of the Year three times. She has won three Gaines Awards, including Woman of the Year, and was inducted into the American Boxer Club Hall of Fame in 2001. After forty-three years of handling, Mrs. Forsyth retired in 1981 to become a judge. She now judges all breeds in the United States, as well as all breeds for the FCI. She has judged in England, Finland, Sweden, South America, Puerto Rico, Canada, Italy, and Mexico. She and her husband are the only couple to have each had a Best in Show winner at Westminster.

5 Things You Should Know About Hiring a Professional Dog Handler

If you're pressed for time, not physically up to the difficult tasks of handling, or simply not temperamentally suited for showing, consider hiring a professional handler, who has the expertise to help Madame Varushka achieve her true potential. Top handlers are powerful people in the dog world and can be invaluable in helping you network and negotiate your way through the dog world.

1. Learn about handlers in your area by asking for references from breeders you trust. Look for one who is licensed by one of the three organizations that do so: the AKC, the Professional Handlers Association (PHA), and the Dog Handlers Guild (DHG).

2. Before you hire a handler, watch him or her in the ring. Are his dogs well groomed and happy? Does he have a good rapport with them? Does she practice good sportsmanship by avoiding gossip and accepting placements gracefully?

3. If you're happy with what you've seen in the ring, make an appointment with the handler at his or her kennel facility. You'll have a chance to see if the dogs are kept clean and are well cared for, how the dogs are exercised, etc. Ask whatever questions come to mind. Also, find out if the handler already handles a dog of your dog's breed.

If so, there might be a conflict at certain shows and an assistant will be asked to show your dog.

4. Your arrangement with the handler can take a variety of forms. You might want a professional to handle your dog only at shows, or you may decide to have the handler take over everything, including full-time boarding of the dog. Think about what's important to you and your dog before you decide. If being with your dog is really important to you, don't let anyone convince you that that's not an important consideration.

5. When you hire a handler, be sure to discuss all costs up front. Find out what's included in the fee you're quoted. There will be other charges for handling your dog in the ring in addition to expenses for traveling, grooming, and any special dietary or medical needs your dog may have. Find out what these are up front and ask for a detailed written agreement.

14 Reasons for Disqualifications at the Dog Show

There are several reasons that a judge will disqualify a particular dog or handler at a conformation show.

1. A dog who attacks a judge can be disqualified from the conformation competition and any other scheduled event. The dog may be reinstated, but if it misbehaves again, a "two strikes and you're out" policy applies.

2. A dog who exhibits aggressive behavior in the ring on two separate occasions will be forever barred from conformation, obedience, and agility events.

3. A dog who has violated the breed standard (height, weight, coloring, etc.) can be barred from further conformation competitions if it has been disqualified on three different occasions and by three different judges.

4. A dog who does not have two healthy and properly positioned testicles will be disqualified.

5. A dog who is either blind, deaf, castrated, or spayed will be disqualified.

6. A common reason for disqualification is lameness. Sadly, a dog who leaps off a grooming table can pull a muscle, only to completely ruin her chances in the ring.

7. A dog who either has or was exposed to distemper will be disqualified.

8. Dogs must have the correct number of teeth in order to compete. Missing teeth call for disqualification.

9. A dog who has had certain surgical alterations such as the correction of harelip or the removal of skin patches to change markings will automatically be disqualified, as well as any dog who has been chalked, powdered, or dyed to alter a faulty coat.

10. A handler will be disqualified if he slaps or hits his dog.

11. A handler can be disqualified for receiving instructions from ringside.

12. A handler can be disqualified if he shows poor sportsmanship.

13. A handler can be disqualified for arguing with or being rude to the judge.

14. Awards are disallowed if it is discovered that a dog was not eligible for the class in which he was registered. Make sure you read the class descriptions carefully so that you don't, for instance, register your dog as a novice even though he has already won three first-place prizes. In such instances, any ribbons or trophies won and points earned are awarded to the second-place winner, also known as the Reserve Winners Dog.

11. **David Frei** is a familiar face to millions of TV viewers as the longtime co-host of USA Network's annual telecast of the popular Westminster Kennel Club Dog Show. He has appeared on *The Today Show* (NBC), *Good Morning America* (ABC), *The Early Show* (CBS), *Charlie Rose* (PBS), National Public Radio, Fox News Channel, MSNBC, CNN, and others. In addition, David also cohosts the NBC television coverage of the National Dog Show every Thanksgiving Day. As a breeder he has had much success with his Afghan Hounds and Brittany Spaniels. His Afghan CH Stormhill's Who's Zoomin Who was the top-winning female in the history of the breed.

12. **William Kendrick** was a legendary all-breed judge. He began his judging career when he was a twenty-year-old junior at Princeton University. He later acquired the Queensbury Kennel that his uncle, the former mayor of Philadelphia, had owned. Kendrick was president of the Kennel Club of Philadelphia for thirty years and was an exhibitor at the AKC of Philadelphia's sesquicentennial show in 1929 and served as a judge at the centennial show in 1984.

13. **Michael J. Lafave**'s career spans more than thirty years. He has served as president of the Pilgrim Basset Hound Club, vice president of the Worcester County Kennel Club, and president of the Wachusett Kennel Club. In addition, LaFave is a member of the Eastern Dog Club, where he has served in a number of leadership roles including group ring announcer, chief steward, show chairman, vice president,

and president. Michael was named show announcer at the Westminster Kennel Club Dog Show in 2001.

14. **Dr. Samuel Milbank** was the chairman of Westminster Kennel Club between 1935 and 1937 and judged Best in Show in 1940 and 1948. His reputation in the dog world is legendary, but unfortunately little biographical information exists about him.

15. **Louis Murr**, breeder, exhibitor, and judge, was a major figure in the dog world for more than fifty-six years. His Romanoff Kennels bred championship Borzois. He appeared on the panel of Westminster for twenty-one consecutive years, and in 1969 judged Best in Show. His last show was in 1976, when he was eighty-two, in Vineland, New Jersey.

16. **Anna Katherine Nicholas** received her first dog, a Pekingese, when she was seven. Her interest in dogs centered around writing and judging. Her first book, *The Pekingese*, was published in 1930. Since then she has written more than seventy books, including *The Nicholas Guide to Dog Judging*, which won the Dog Writers' Association of America award for Best Technical Book. She judged her first show in 1934 and was approved to judge all hounds, terriers, toys, and nonsporting breeds, plus many of the sporting dogs. She has been on Westminster's panel eighteen times and judged Best in Show in 1970. Ms. Nicholas has won the Gaines "Fido" award for Dog Writer of the Year and in 1996 was honored by Heinz Pet Foods as an inductee into their Hall of Fame.

17. **Percy Roberts**, a renowned all-breed judge, was born only five years after the AKC was established. He was born in England and emigrated to the United States in 1913. In 1919 he opened his famous Revelry Kennel and began breeding Whippets and Greyhounds, but it was his abilities as a professional handler and importer of dogs that helped establish his reputation. Percy, who wore a mustache that was curled on each end and heavily waxed, went on to become an all-breed judge. He judged every major show in the United States, including Westminster and the Sidney Royal in Australia. He holds the distinction of handling more Westminster Best in Show winners than any other person for his wins in 1926, 1927, 1934, and 1937. He also judged Best in Show in 1967. Percy Roberts is considered by those who knew him to be one of the greatest figures in the sport of dogs. He is credited with the now famous quote, "The breed standard is the blueprint, the breeder is the builder, and the judge is the building inspector."

Dog Show Point System Basics

The point system used at AKC conformation shows is very complicated and varies from one region of the country to another. It will therefore not be covered here in detail. There are, however, some general facts that can give you a better basic understanding of how the point system works.

1. At one show, a dog can earn from 1 to 5 points toward a champion title, depending on the number of males or females actually in competition for the breed.

2. Points awarded at a major show are based on the number of dogs a contestant will compete against. A dog will win anywhere from 3 to 5 points at a major, depending on the number of dogs it has defeated.

3. An AKC-registered dog must garner 15 points in order to become a champion. However, the dog must win two major events and with two different judges.

4. Generally speaking, the more dogs likely to be present, the more that must be beaten to earn points. If a dog beats two to three dogs, he will usually be awarded 1 point, if he beats four to five dogs he will earn 2 points, 3 points are awarded if he beats six to seven dogs, 4 points for beating eight to eleven, and 5 points for beating twelve or more dogs.

"There are three faithful friends—an old wife, an old dog, and ready money."
—BEN FRANKLIN

"Dogs are not our whole life, but they make our lives whole."
—ROGER CARAS

18. **Mr. Alva Rosenberg** was a legendary all-breed judge known for his gentle manner with dogs. It is said that he could not touch a dog without having the dog like him. He was perhaps the most influential judge in the early decades of the twentieth century. He attended his first dog show at the age of eight and fell in love with dogs. He judged his first show in 1910 at the age of eighteen and spent the next seven decades judging shows in the United States and around the world. In 1946 he was chosen *Kennel Review*'s Dog Man of the Year, an honor that was repeated in 1947 and 1948. He served as judge at Westminster for twenty-one years. He has been described as one of the finest if not the finest dog man America has had and will ever have.

19. **Burton J. Yamada** started judging in 1989 and has judged all over the world, including Japan, Taiwan, and Costa Rica. In his thirty-five years in dogs, Mr. Yamada has been active in breed and all-breed clubs and has served as president and director for many of them, including the Standard Schnauzer Club of America and the Standard Schnauzer Club of Southern California. He is currently president of the Orange Empire Dog Club and has served as show chairman for more than twenty years. He judged Best in Show at Westminster's 128th show in 2004.

4 Qualities of a Good Show Dog

Good temperament is considered by many judges to be the key ingredient to a dog's success in the show ring. Here are some attributes your dog must have if you are thinking of entering her in a show.

1. She should be properly socialized and accustomed to being handled, especially by strangers. Getting her used to being around children is a great way to accomplish this. If she can tolerate being fawned over and prodded by kids and comes back for more, you probably have a good dog show candidate.

2. She should be able to travel and be around other dogs and people without feeling or exhibiting any stress. Taking her to a local show can help her get used to being around other dogs, handlers, and judges and will help build up her confidence.

3. She should have an outgoing personality and should love the sort of attention that she may receive at the show. Some dogs seem to have an instinctive flair for this sort of thing.

4. She should show "attitude" and a desire to perform under the pressure of the show ring. She must exhibit an "up and ready" attitude at all times. She's not going to win if her ears are down or if she seems distracted and unfocused.

19 Things to Bring to the Dog Show

This list will give you some idea of the amount of paraphernalia required for showing your dog — and this is just a basic list. As you become more experienced, this list will most likely grow. Oh, and don't forget to bring the dog!

1. Your tack box, containing grooming supplies such as combs, brushes, scissors, clippers, Tacky Foot (a great product that increases traction for your dog's pads), and any other articles you'll need for Bjorn to look his best

2. A grooming table or a plastic crate

3. A collar

4. A lead, plus an extra if it breaks

5. A water bowl or bucket, and a water supply, so you won't need to go running around trying to find water at the show

6. Bait (either food or a toy)

7. A crate or exercise pen (called an "ex-pen") with a canopy or umbrella to keep out the sun

8. A grass mat, a pad, or a blanket for the ex-pen, or a dog bed

9. Towels for wiping away drool and dirt

10. A spray bottle — great for dampening your dog to wipe away dirt right before your showing

11. An equipment dolly for carting all your supplies (especially useful for a long trek through a crowded parking lot)

> "Some days you're the dog, and some days you're the hydrant." — UNKNOWN

12. A pooper-scooper and some plastic bags for easy cleanup

13. Your entry confirmation and admission tickets

14. Your parking pass

15. An apron or a beautician's cape

16. A folding chair (seating at the show is always limited)

17. An armband holder or a rubber band to secure your credentials

18. A camera

19. Ice chest for drinks, snacks, and bait

> "The average dog is a nicer person than the average person." — ANDREW A. ROONEY

The Care and Feeding of Judges

Judges are a breed unto themselves, and they take a lot of heat in the dog world. Their placements are constantly second-guessed; they are the target of irate losers; and even during their precious few free moments at the show, they are barraged with pleas for advice. Know that the judges did not arrive at their position of power easily. The AKC requires their judges to have at least ten years of experience as an owner, breeder, and exhibitor; and he or she must have bred and raised at least four litters, passed written and oral exams, and judged at least six AKC matches in addition to completing other assignments. Remember, too, that those qualified as "all-breed" judges must study each of the breeds separately. It is possible for a judge to be approved only for a specific breed or group. However you fare at the show, remember to treat these special beings with just the right amount of TLC.

1. Judges rule the rings. There are channels for challenging a placement, but in general, what they say goes. It is wise to accept all decisions gracefully and to remember that once you start showing, you are likely to encounter the same faces many times over. You don't want to wear out the judge's welcome mat early on.

2. When you enter a show, you automatically reserve time with the judge. Use it wisely; don't squander it asking questions that you could have answered for yourself by doing a little research. Neither do you want to waste his time telling him about the night the Christmas tree caught fire and Virgil dialed 911.

3. If you feel you must know more about why your dog may have been placed out of the running at any point, you can do so. Ask the judge when she might have a few moments, and when the time comes, pose general questions about your dog rather than challenge her decision. Be prepared for brutal honesty and thank her for her time no matter what you think of her advice. If you have more questions, join one of the classes she might be teaching or attend a seminar.

4. When the judge is engaged in examining your dog, you want to make sure he has a chance to appreciate all of Connery's good qualities, don't you? So distracting him with little details about his past wins and feats can only work against you. Judges abhor this kind of verbal interference during a show. The polite ones will ignore you; others are likely to put you in your place with barbs that they reserve for just such occasions.

5. Of course, there are judges who make mistakes, have quirks, and simply lack experience. Consult the registry's rules for filing questions. Do try to forgive them their shortcomings when you can. Remember that they are only human.

Dress for Ring Success

No, it's not all about you, but your appearance at the show is still important. You don't want to upstage Chips, but you don't want to embarrass him, either. Here are some general guidelines.

1. The dress code for most events is fairly conservative. Women show up in pantsuits, dresses, and skirts, while men wear mostly sports jackets, with ties, or suits. The more prestigious shows call for more formal dress, with women in floor-length outfits and men in tuxedo attire.

2. Women's skirt lengths are conservative for a purpose: you don't want to reveal too much when bending over to tend to your dog. Neither do you want the hemline to hit the dog's face. An A-line skirt is usually best, as it allows free movement without billowing out when you stride beside your dog. Similarly, low-cut necklines should be avoided.

3. Men should keep their jackets on — and buttoned — unless the judges have removed theirs, as they often do in warm weather.

4. Look for washable clothing (you'll probably have to wash it after each show) with plenty of

pockets for bait (unless you're at a UKC show, where baiting is not allowed) and grooming tools. But keep those pockets empty of loose change, keys, and anything else that's likely to make a lot of noise when you move about. If you're anticipating an especially messy day, you might want to dress in layers, which you can remove as they become soiled.

5. Because you want Jupiter to really stand out for the judges, you'll want to wear clothing that provides some contrast to his coat. If you're showing a white Poodle, you might look for a medium blue tone. You can experiment by taking some photos of you and your dog to see what works best. Remember that some of the show photos will probably be printed in black-and-white (in which case bright blue and red will both appear to be black).

6. Keep accessories to a minimum. Avoid noisy, dangling jewelry (even a small piece of jewelry might throw off a glint and distract a dog at the worst mo-

ment) and scarves that can flap in the wind or interfere when you bend down. Long hair should be pinned up.

7. Choose comfortable shoes with good traction that don't make noise when you move on a hard floor. Women should wear flats or low-stacked heels.

> "All knowledge, the totality of all questions and all answers, is contained in the dog."
> — FRANZ KAFKA

A Dog Show Dictionary

1. Great stud dog	Mounts anything that can fog a mirror.
2. Excels in movement	If he gets loose, run like hell.
3. Personality plus	Wakes up if you put liver up his nose.
4. Good bite	Missed the judge, got the steward.
5. Large-boned	Looks like a Clydesdale.
6. Good obedience prospect	Smart enough to come in from the rain, but ugly.
7. Quiet and good-natured	In his kennel.
8. Excels in type and style	However, moves like a spider on speed.
9. Won in stiff competition	Beat four puppies and a nine-year-old Novice dog.
10. Multiple group winner	At two puppy matches.
11. Pointed	His head is shaped like a carrot.
12. Noted judge	He put up our dog.
13. Respected judge	He put up our dog twice.
14. Esteemed judge	He puts up anything that crawls.
15. Specialty judge	Puts up anything that looks like his own breeding.
16. Won in heavy competition	The other dogs were revoltingly overweight.
17. Shown sparingly	Only when we had it in the bag.
18. Show prospect	He has four legs, two eyes, two ears, one tail.
19. Finished in five shows	And eighty-nine where he failed to win a ribbon.
20. Well-balanced	Straight as a stick, front and rear.
21. Handled brilliantly by	Nobody else can get near him.
22. At stud to approved bitches	Those bitches whose owner's check is good.
23. Linebred from famous champions	CH Whoozitz appears twice sixth generation.
24. Terrific brood bitch	Her conformation is the pits, but she conceives big litters.
25. Wins another Best in Show	His second, under the same judge, his owner's uncle.

20 Things Every Junior Handler Should Know

Junior Showmanship is a class in which the juniors' handling ability is evaluated. It was originally designed to "prepare" kids to enter the breed ring successfully and to teach good sportsmanship, how to lose or win gracefully. Juniors are eligible to show dogs from their tenth birthday until they turn eighteen years old. Competitors are evaluated on their grace, knowledge of procedures, and ability to present their barker to the best of their ability. The winner is awarded a Best Junior Handler trophy. Since its inception at Westminster's 1934 show, forty-nine girls and twenty-two boys have won this prestigious title. If you are interested in becoming a junior handler, you can find out more about this exciting sport by calling the AKC's Event Records Department, (212) 696-8281, or by visiting the Minnesota 4-H Dog Project online at www.fourh.umn.edu.

1. In AKC the juniors are divided into age groups: juniors (ten to fourteen) and seniors (fourteen to eighteen). Within each age group there is a division based on experience. Novice is for juniors just starting and Open is for the more experienced handlers. When first competing, you will begin in Novice Classes.

2. You must receive three first placements in the Novice Class (with competition) before you are eligible to move into the Open Class. If you receive two Novice wins as a junior and then reach your fourteenth birthday, you will need to win one more first placement to move into Open Class. Once you are eligible for Open Classes you do not need to go back to the Novice Class.

3. Under AKC rules, a puppy is eligible for Junior Showmanship if he is six months of age.

4. Any puppy shown in Junior Showmanship must be owned by either you or your father, mother, brother, sister, uncle, aunt, grandfather, or grandmother (this includes half and step relations and any member of the junior's household). The junior's dog must be in your control and may not be aggressive.

5. Your puppy does not need to be a Champion of Record to compete in Junior Showmanship, but a correctly groomed, well-trained dog is a big plus for juniors competition.

6. As long as you practice and have a good bond with your furry pal, you should make a great team. Remember that all breeds are shown a bit differently and that as long as you and your baby show correctly for your breed, you should do well.

7. It is a big help to go to shows and watch and talk to juniors outside the ring. Also, you might want to attend conformation handling lessons until you understand showing. Another good choice is to enter a fun match. It is less expensive and gives you experience. Local All-Breed Clubs can help you find a training class, and some 4-H Clubs offer training classes. You may also learn from handlers, parents, books, and videotapes.

8. You must first get a premium list for the show you are interested in entering, from the show-giving club or the show superintendent. The premium list will tell you the judge, date, and cost of the show.

9. Your dog can be substituted with another as long as you complete an AKC entry form for the new dog and turn it in to the superintendent of the show at least one half-hour before Junior judging. Your new puppy should meet all other requirements for Junior Showmanship competition.

10. Your doggie needs to be washed, brushed, and groomed to the standard for the breed.

11. Appearance and neatness do count. You'll be expected to be neat and clean and with your hair out of your face. A grooming smock will help keep you clean and free of loose dog hair prior to ring time.

12. Boys should wear a shirt and tie with a tie tack in place so it won't flop around, slacks, and comfortable, clean shoes. A sports jacket or a sweater is appropriate, and pockets for bait are a must. For girls, culottes, skirts, or dresses that are knee to midcalf length (to accommodate your bending over) are all good choices. Make sure the length of the outfit does not interfere with your dog (a long flowing skirt flying in the face of a toy dog is not a good idea!). Find comfortable shoes that will not slip off or cause you to lose your footing. Try to find pockets in your show clothes, or use a bait bag. Do try to make your clothing complement your dog (do not wear a dark skirt with a dark dog). You want the dog to stand out.

13. In order for a junior to qualify for Westminster, he or she must have eight first places in the Open Class during the preceding year.

14. For AKC Junior Showmanship the age limit is eighteen. But if you qualify for Westminster before your eighteenth birthday you may compete at Westminster.

15. The judge is supposed to evaluate the juniors in four different areas: 1) proper breed presentation; 2) skill in presenting the individual dog; 3) knowledge of ring procedures; and 4) appearance and conduct. The judge looks for economy of motion (no over- or underhandling) and correct breed presentation, and she could be asking herself the following questions: Do the dog and handler work as a team? Is the dog posed and interested at all times? Is the dog under control? Is the dog moved correctly? Are the dog's main faults minimized? Are the dog and handler relaxed? Does the junior know proper ring procedure? Is the dog correctly groomed? Is the handler's appearance suitable?

16. Junior handlers should know all the patterns a judge might ask for: out-and-back (or "I"), a triangle, an "L", a "T," and perhaps a "reverse triangle." Juniors should have a good knowledge of their dog so they can present him correctly, minimizing faults and accentuating strengths. They should know how to stack their dog correctly, as well as bait him. They should know how to show a dog's bite and expression. They should be prepared to do a courtesy turn and also avoid coming between the judge and their dog.

17. Junior Showmanship classes proceed in this order: Novice Junior, Novice Senior, Open Junior, and then Open Senior.

18. Juniors are usually called in catalogue order. So wait outside the ring with your armband on. When the ring steward calls your number, enter the ring, go to the designated position, and stack your dog. You should always remember not to crowd the team in front of you, to pay attention to the judge, and to have FUN!

19. Once you've won your class, you get to do the whole thing all over again for Best Junior Handler, and there will be only the division winners in the ring. Do your best, and maybe you will win the coveted award.

20. Once you've reached the age of eighteen you are able to advance and apply for your license to judge Junior Showmanship.

11 Great Dog Sports

The popularity of dog sports has grown in recent years, and TV shows featuring these canine events have gained huge audiences worldwide. Whether you want to enter serious competitions with your buddy or just have some fun, here are some sports that you can consider. Regardless of what your goals are, one thing is for sure: you and your dog will strengthen your bond by practicing and playing together.

1. Agility is one of the most exciting dog sports to watch, and chances are you've already seen it on television. Dogs race against the clock on an obstacle course comprising tunnels, seesaws, weave poles, and ramps while their human leads the way, giving directions. The dog with the fastest time combined with the fewest number of mistakes or faults is the winner. Titles awarded range from Novice Agility (NA) to Master Agility Excellent (MX). Border Collies usually rule, but you always have to watch out for those Jack Russells. To find out more about this sport, visit the North American Dog Agility Council at www.nadac.com.

2. Earthdog events feature the "going to ground" skills of the terriers and Dachshunds. No training is required of an Earthdog; its performance is based on instinct and a willingness to enjoy the hunt. During a typical run a dog is sent down a man-made tunnel that is thirty feet long and contains either one 90-degree turn or a series of three of them, depending on the dog's skill level. To get the terrier's attention, the tunnel and its entrance are sprinkled with water that has been scented with rat poop. At the end of the tunnel are one or two rats, safely contained in a cage. Doggies are released ten feet from the den and must reach a caged rat within thirty seconds. After reaching the quarry, the dog must "work" the rat by either barking, pawing, pushing, snapping, growling, or anything that shows the dog's urge to get close and personal with the rat inside. If the dog works for one full minute, it passes.

The AKC has responded to the popularity of Earthdog Trials by instituting its own testing program for Earthdogs. Their dogs are tested in the Junior, Senior, and Master divisions and are awarded JE, SE, or ME, respectively.

3. Field trials are competitions that demonstrate each breed performing the skills that it was bred for, whether it be hunting, retrieving, pointing, or scenting. Retrievers, pointers, spaniels, Beagles, Basset Hounds, and Dachshunds all have trials especially developed to test the skills of their particular breed. If you have ever watched a field trial exhibition on TV, you know that this event is just as challenging and intense as any major conformation show. The communication between the dog and his human during an event is a wonder to behold. Winners receive the Field Champion (FC) title.

People who are involved in this sport all have one thing in common: they love to watch a good dog work. If you think your dog has what it takes and you want to get him involved, contact the Amateur Field Trials Clubs of America online at www.aftca.org or e-mail them at aftca@aol.com.

4. Flyball is, in essence, a canine relay race in which each dog, in a team of four, races over a series of jumps, grabs a tennis ball, and races back. When one dog crosses the finish line, the next dog in the team starts. Because the size of the jump is set so that the smallest dog on the team can get over it, most flyball teams include one small but very fast dog. Flyball doggies can accumulate anywhere from 100 points, which leads to a Flyball Dog Excellent title (FDX), all the way up to 30,000 points, which earn the dog the title of Flyball Grand Champion (FGRCh). Of the top one hundred flyball dogs, forty-five are Border Collies, fifteen are mixed breeds, and ten are Jack Russell Terriers. The North American Flyball Association was founded to administer the sport of flyball racing in North America. For more information about this fast-growing sport, visit the NAFA Web site at www.flyball.org.

5. Flying disc is a sport at which the truly athletic dogs shine. They leap into the air, often vaulting off their humans, trying to catch a flying disc. Three types

of events make up flying disc, namely, the Freestyle, the Mini-Distance, and the Long Distance. Freestyle is the event that is usually featured on TV telecasts. During Freestyle the dog and his human perform a routine with an accompanying musical score. The result is a combination of doggie dance, flying catches, vaults, and flips that will amaze you. Incidentally, you may be interested to know that Mark Molnar and his Malinois, Falco, set the outdoor world distance record on May 21, 2004, at 321 feet, 2 inches.

Dogs participating in this sport have to be at the top of their game and in the very best of health since they often land hard while twisting and turning in every direction, making injury a serious risk. If you want to train your dog for this sport you'll have to check with your vet first to determine if your pooch's body can withstand the rigors of this sport. For more information, contact the International Disc Dog Handlers' Association at www.iddha.com or Lawrence Frederick of K9Frisbee.com.

6. Herding is an equal-opportunity sport: many competitions allow any dog to participate, including a mixed breed. To qualify, a dog needs merely to demonstrate that he has the appropriate behavior and skills of a herding dog. And, despite the common belief that a herding dog must live in the country with animals that need to be controlled, all herding dogs have a natural instinct that allows even "city folk" to get their pooches involved. If your dog has a heritage of herding, you may want to see just how well he will do when tested, especially if he's a Bor-

der Collie. Once you and your dog get started in this sport, you may never want to stop. The titles awarded range from Herding Tested (HT) to Herding Champion (HCH). To learn more about this sport you can contact the American Herding Association by visiting them at www.ahba-herding.org or the Australian Shepherds Club of America Trial Program at www.asca.org.

7. Lure Coursing is a sport in which beautiful and sleek sight hounds such as the Greyhound, Whippet, and Borzoi participate. This sport re-creates the chase of the rabbit by using a lure that simulates a rabbit. This lure, which is made up of strips of white plastic, is attached to a series of pulleys that are set up to bring the lure through a zigzag path simulating that of a rabbit fleeing a predator. The dogs are judged for their enthusiasm, agility, accuracy on the path, and overall endurance. The titles range from Junior Courser (JC) to Field Champion (FC). To find out more about this exciting sport you can visit the American Sighthound Field Association online at www.asfa.org or contact either the AKC or CKC, which both offer programs in lure coursing.

8. Musical freestyle is an activity that

involves you and your dog dancing to a choreographed program. Competitors get a chance to express their creativity by innovating dance routines,

Lawrence Fredericks gives Sprite a great workout at the 2004 Dixie Disc Dog Championship in Macon, Georgia.

choosing their own music, and creating matching costumes for themselves and poochie. Performers are judged on the basis of teamwork, artistry, interpretation of the theme of the music, and costuming. This exciting sport has also been referred to as "extreme obedience." The points awarded at a competition are based on technical merit and artistic impression. So if your pooch is a budding Ginger Rogers and you like to boogie, this might be the perfect activity for you

Patie Ventre and Dancer, a Border Collie, perform "God Bless America" at the Off-Lead Disco Doggie Dance Invitational.

and your dog to share. To learn more about freestyle, contact **Patie Ventre**, the founder of the World Canine Freestyle Organization, at her Web site, www.worldcaninefreestyle.org, or call (718) 332-8336.

9. Obedience is a sport where you get to see the teamwork of the dog and trainer in action. Basic commands such as sit, down, stay, heel, and come are all requirements for a pooch that is just starting out, whereas more experienced dogs retrieve a scented object and perform a series of exercises to signals alone. If you are interested in this sport and are experienced with dogs you can probably train your dog toward one of the obedience titles, or you can always take poochie-pie to an obedience class. This is generally a great idea regardless of whether your dog is going to compete or not. Obedience titles range from Companion Dog (CD) to Companion Dog Excellent (CDX). If you are interested in this sport or wish to find an obedience instructor near you, visit the National Association of Dog Obedience Instructors at www.adoi.org or write to them at PMB 369, 729 Grapevine Hwy, Hurst, Texas 76054.

10. Tracking is a truly challenging sport that explores the limits of a dog's capability to follow a scent. Every dog is born knowing how to follow a scent trail, but the challenge in this sport is getting your dog to follow only the one you want him to. Although training methods for tracking competitions are the same regardless of the breed, some breeds of dogs, such as hunting Beagles and other hounds, have a bit of an edge because of their extra-keen noses. Beagles are especially good at this sport because they have been selectively bred for many centuries to be one of the world's greatest scenting and tracking dogs. Dogs are not judged against each other or awarded points; their titles are based on a simple pass-or-fail system. If you think this sport is something you will enjoy, starting off with a puppy is a great idea, since this is an instinctive activity and no prior obedience training is required. To find out how you can get started, you can learn more by going to the AKC Web site, www.akc.org.

11. Water rescue is a sport that was originally designed to test the skills of the purebred Newfoundland dog, which has historically been acknowledged for its heroic rescues. However, organizations such as Wet Dog now grant Water Dog titles to all breeds, including mixed-breed dogs. During this event the teamwork between the dog and its human are put to the test. To receive a title the dog must display willingness and enjoyment of the task at hand. Of course, it is the job of the human to be in the water with his dog and help it along. At the Junior skill level a Water Dog must demonstrate basic obedience, show retrieving skills, tow a boat, and swim with its human. Awards range from Water Education and Training Tested (WETT) for a Junior dog to Water Education and Training Excellent (WETX) for a Senior dog. If you feel like getting your feet wet at this sport, you can dive right in by visiting the Newfoundland Club of America online at www.newfdogclub.org.

How to Prepare for the Musical Canine Freestyle

Musical Canine Freestyle or just Canine Freestyle is simply dancing with dogs to music. You and your dog will be able to strut your stuff and showcase your teamwork, artistry, athleticism, and style in interpreting the theme of music you have selected for this challenging sport. Timing, costuming, routine development, and showmanship make this a fun and often hilarious sport for you, your pooch, and the audience. The World Canine Freestyle Organization, a nonprofit corporation, was founded to promote the joy and fun of responsible pet ownership through musical canine freestyle throughout the world. The WCFO's founder, Patie Ventre, has provided us with a guide to this exciting "tail-wagging" sport.

1. Get out your record collection and pick a song that excites both you and your pooch. Elvis may already have his own favorite tune. Pick something that has a great beat and runs anywhere from three to six minutes.

2. Once you've selected music the next step is to choreograph your routine. Design steps that both of you can easily perform and that show some variation in speed and footwork. You can always pop a Fred and Ginger movie into your VCR if you need some choreography tips or ideas.

3. The next step is to choose costumes for you and your dog. Your outfits should coordinate with the theme of the music you have selected and be pleasing to an audience. You'll be able to wear as elaborate a costume as you like, but your dog can wear only a decorative collar and ankle bands. In fact, you can dress up like Ginger and dress your pooch as Fred. Picture yourself dancing with a bow-tied Boston Terrier and you'll get an idea of how much fun performing or even just watching this sport can be.

4. Points for technical merit are awarded as follows:

Content: 3

Precise execution of all moves by dog and handler: 2

Flow of movements from one to the other by dog and handler: 2

Difficulty of routine: 2

Dancing in time to the music: 1

Total technical points possible: 10

Points for artistic impression are awarded as follows:

Animation, attitude, attention, and interaction of dog and handler: 2

Quality and creativity of choreography: 2

Ring space (75 percent minimum, 50 percent minimum for small dogs under 14" and juniors): 1

Coordination of routine with music and team: 1.5

Costume coordination with music and routine: 1.5

Costumes on handler and dog suit the music: 1

Spectator appeal: 1

Total artistic impression points possible: 10

6 Greyhound Racing Myths

The Greyhound Protection League (GPL) is a national nonprofit organization dedicated to protecting Greyhounds from the exploitation and abuses inherent in the Greyhound racing industry. Through education and continued media exposure, they hope to change the public perception of Greyhound racing from that of being a harmless spectator activity to its brutal reality — being a blood sport responsible for immense animal suffering and the routine killing of thousands of young, healthy dogs each year for the simple crime of being unfit for racing. Susan Netboy of the GPL lists some of the myths that the racing industry would have us believe, and then dispels them with the facts.

15 States with Active Greyhound Racetracks

1. Alabama
2. Arizona
3. Arkansas
4. Colorado
5. Connecticut
6. Florida
7. Iowa
8. Kansas
9. Massachusetts
10. New Hampshire
11. Oregon
12. Rhode Island
13. Texas
14. West Virginia
15. Wisconsin

Greyhounds

1. **Myth.** Greyhound racing is a humane and harmless sport.
   Fact. Greyhound racing is responsible for the death of an estimated 20,000 Greyhounds each year.

2. **Myth.** Racing Greyhounds are prized athletes who receive the best of care. These dogs wouldn't be out there running if they were not well cared for.
   Fact. Greyhound adoption groups routinely receive race dogs riddled with external and internal parasites, open sores, and untreated broken bones. Race dogs are caged for up to twenty-two hours a day. The standard industry feed is 4-D meat from diseased livestock. Moreover, running is instinctual for Greyhounds. In fact, it is not uncommon for a Greyhound to finish a race in spite of having suffered a serious injury.

3. **Myth.** Cases of abuse and killing of racing Greyhounds are rare isolated incidents.
   Fact. Over the past two decades, hundreds of cases of abuse have been documented, including Greyhound dogs that were shot, starved, electrocuted, and sold for research. Industry insiders report that this is only the tip of the iceberg.

4. **Myth.** Critics of the Greyhound racing industry are animal rights extremists who are opposed to the use of animals for any useful purpose.
   Fact. The killing and abuse of Greyhounds is a mainstream issue that has been taken to heart by the American public. Opposition to industry practices has been publicly stated in newspaper editorials, by government officials, and by mainstream animal welfare groups.

5. **Myth.** Since humane societies routinely euthanize thousands of unwanted dogs, eliminating Greyhounds is justified.
   Fact. Humane societies do not breed dogs knowing that they will be put to death. By purposely overbreeding, the Greyhound industry saddles charitable organizations and private citizens with the responsibility of caring for even more unwanted animals.

6. **Myth.** Greyhound racing is a highly regulated sport with high standards of animal care in the states that have dog tracks.
   Fact. In most states, dog track regulations are primarily concerned with gambling rules; breeding and training farm operations are virtually unregulated.

Highlights of the Iditarod

You can't compare it to any other competitive event in the world! Mushers and their dog teams race over 1,150 miles of the roughest, most beautiful terrain Mother Nature has to offer: jagged mountain ranges, frozen rivers, dense forest, desolate tundra, and miles of windswept coast. Add to that temperatures far below zero, winds that can cause a complete loss of visibility, the hazards of overflow, long hours of darkness, and treacherous climbs and side hills, and you have the Iditarod, a race extraordinaire, a race possible only in Alaska.

The Iditarod Trail had its beginnings as a mail and supply route. In 1925, part of the Iditarod Trail became a life-saving highway for epidemic-stricken Nome. Diphtheria threatened and serum had to be brought in, again by intrepid dog mushers and their faithful, hard-driving dogs.

Running the Iditarod is a grueling test that can last as long as three weeks and involve head-on encounters with some of the most forbidding weather and terrain on Earth.

A U.S. mail team in Nome, Alaska, 1906

Nevertheless, any musher worth his or her salt wants to run the Iditarod someday, just as runners want to complete the Boston Marathon, even if they have no chance of winning.

Since it was first held in 1973, the race has grown every year despite financial ups and downs. The Iditarod has become so well known that the best mushers now receive thousands of dollars a year from corporate sponsors, and dog mushing — once all but forgotten — has recovered to become a North Country winter mania. With an annual budget of almost $2 million, the Iditarod Trail Committee depends on a hard-working force of volunteers and supporters to raise funds. To find out more or to get involved in this exhilarating sport, visit iditarod.com.

1. From Anchorage in south-central Alaska, to Nome on the western Bering Sea coast, each team of twelve to sixteen dogs and their musher cover more than 1,150 miles in ten to seventeen days. The route encompasses large metropolitan areas and small native villages. A complex communications network is set up to cover the course, offering logistical support, emergency communications, and an information source for race officials. The race causes a yearly spurt of activity, and everyone from very young schoolchildren, for its educational opportunities, to the old-timers, who relive the colorful Alaskan past, gets involved.

2. Although must of the race is regulated, each musher has a different strategy — some run in the daylight, some run at night. Each one has a different training schedule and his own ideas on dog care, dog stamina, and his own personal ability.

3. While the Iditarod has become by far Alaska's best-known sporting event, there are a dozen other major races around the state every winter, such as the grueling thousand-mile Yukon Quest, the Kobuk 440, the Kusko 300, the Klondike 300, and the Copper Basin 300. In a revival of age-old tradition, some entire villages and towns in rural Alaska become swept away in the frenzy of sled dog racing, and sled dogs are now common in many rural areas where they were eclipsed by "iron dogs" only a few decades ago.

4. Each Iditarod team is limited to sixteen dogs. Together they constitute an incredibly powerful pulling machine fully capable of dragging a pickup truck with its brakes set on packed snow. Hooked up in pairs, a six-teen-dog team stretches more than eighty feet from the leader's nose to the musher on the back of the sled — longer than a highway eighteen-wheeler.

5. The musher's only real form of control of this juggernaut is voice commands to the lead dogs (the sled has a brake, but it is sometimes not much more effective than dragging a foot in the snow). This setup cleverly takes advantage of the dogs' wolf heritage: a dog team is basically a pack, and a pack always follows the leader, who in turn follows the commands of the driver. Most mushers run a pair of leaders (superbly well-bred, smarter-than-average dogs) up front, but a few run a solo leader. The dogs just behind the lead dogs are called the swing dogs, and then just in front of the sled are the wheel dogs, who are very important in helping to guide the sled through turns. Wheel dogs, who are usually a little larger or more muscular than the other dogs on the team, have as much re-

"Life is like a dogsled team. If you ain't the lead dog, the scenery never changes." — LEWIS GRIZZARD

sponsibility as leaders in that they must keep the sled from hitting trees or boulders when making turns or just bring the sled around without tipping it over.

6. No one special breed of dog is used on the Iditarod. Some mushers run specific AKC-recognized breeds such as Malamutes and Siberians, but most sled dogs are called by the generic term "Alaska husky," which means any critter with four legs and a tail capable of pulling a sled. Over the years, mushers have mixed all sorts of breeds in attempts to find the perfect sled dog, making the average Iditarod sled dog basically a mutt — albeit a carefully bred and highly prized one.

7. Mandatory gear for the Iditarod (and most other races) includes essential survival items: snowshoes, an ax, an arctic sleeping bag, at least two pounds of food and two sets of booties for every dog, and an alcohol stove with a four- or five-gallon pot (for melting snow and making hot water for dog food). Mushers will also include warm clothing items (temperatures can range from 40 above to 60 below), medicine and ointments for the dogs, food for themselves, spare lines and snaps, a small tool kit, and a sewing kit to repair harnesses. A Thermos of drinking water is critical. Dehydration is a major threat in the cold, dry climate. Most mushers will also include a camera and a Walkman with their favorite cassettes to help fight the interminable hours of boredom on the long, wide-open stretches of the trail.

The 5 Basic Sled Dog Commands

Only in Hollywood do dogs respond when a driver yells "mush," which comes from *marchon*, the French word meaning "to move." The basic commands are the following:

"Hike"	Start running
"Gee"	Turn right
"Haw"	Turn left
"On by"	Pass, or go straight
"Whoa"	Stop

5 Multiple Iditarod Winners

Rick Swenson, 5 wins	1977, 1979, 1981, 1982, 1991
Susan Butcher, 4 wins	1986, 1987, 1988, 1990
Doug Swingley, 4 wins	1995, 1999, 2000, 2001
Martin Buser, 4 wins	1992, 1994, 1997, 2002
Jeff King, 3 wins	1993, 1996, 1998

Cats, not dogs, are the most common pets in America (roughly 66 million cats to 58 million dogs, with parakeets a distant third at 14 million).

5 Recent Iditarod Champions

2000 Doug Swingley	Simms, Mont., 9 days, 58 minutes
2001 Doug Swingley	Simms, Mont., 9 days, 19 hours, 55 minutes
2002 Martin Buser	Big Lake, Ark., 8 days, 22 hours, 6 minutes
2003 Robert Sørlie	Hurdal, Norway, 9 days, 15 hours, 47 minutes
2004 Mitch Seavey	Sterling, Ark., 9 days, 12 hours, 20 minutes

10 Silly Dog Contests

These contests aren't about champions, breeding, or pedigrees. They're about tail-wagging, happy human and canine faces, and raising money for great causes. If you live in these areas or are just passing through, don't miss a chance for you and Jokerman to enjoy a memorable day of fun.

1. **Woof-a-Palooza** is held each year in Pittsboro, North Carolina, to benefit Chatham Animal Rescue and Education. It's a full day of fun that begins with a mile-long dogwalk and features a fairlike atmosphere including refreshments, vendors, and exhibitions. Dogs compete in a variety of contests such as the Weenie Toss, the Musical Sit, and the Owner-Pet Look-Alike event. The highlight of the day is the Best-Dressed Dog Fashion Show. For more information, visit chathamanimalrescue.org.

2. If you and Buddy are up for a "grave encounter," you'll want to attend the annual **Fright Fest Pet Parade and Costume Contest** held at the Six Flags Elitch Gardens in Denver, Colorado, right around Halloween to raise funds for the local Dumb Animal League. The event is open to all pets — snakes and goats included — so if you have other pets, you might want to pair them up: Bunny and Clyde? Starsky and Pooch? Visit sixflags.com to find out the exact date of the event.

3. In Long Beach, California, some doggie dads spend their Father's Day competing along with their dogs at the **Dog Beach Zone**, which permits off-leash and unfenced beach access for dogs. In the "Who's Your Daddy?" Contest, ten dogs are held at a start line while their daddies wait at the finish line. The first dog that comes to

her daddy wins. Other contests include the Ugly Tie Contest (the dog has to wear the tie), the Ugly Dog Contest, the Best Legs Competition (dog's and dad's cumulative best), and the Best Belly Flop Contest, in which the dog who does the best entry into the surf, usually chasing a ball, wins. Prizes are also given out for the longest ears, the longest tail, and the best smile.

4. Does Garcia miss the sixties? Take him to **Woofstock**, a doggie love-in held in Toronto each June. More than 30,000 dog lovers and their four-footed friends converge for exhibitions in the latest pooch food, fashion, and furnishings, and, of course, the zany contests, after which furry fashionistas take to the runway for the Miss and Mr. Canine Canada Pageant. Prizes are not to be sniffed at: vacations, doggie makeovers, hand-painted portraits of your dog, and more. Learn more at woofstock.ca.

5. **Ralph's Bay Area K9 Games**, held in conjunction with the Marin Humane Society in Marin County, California, conducts a silly dog contest where you can test your puppy's skills at the fifty-yard dash, see if he is the fastest eater, and let him bob for hot dogs or show off his silly pet tricks. The hilarious Marathon Beg Award is given to the dog that can sit up the longest. In addition to the parades and dog-sport

events, the fair offers educational seminars on subjects such as managing leash aggression and treating canine injuries. The event is held in late spring. For exact dates, visit marinhumanesociety.com.

6. At the **Northern Nevada Dog Days of Summer Dog Tricks Contest** held in Capitol City, Nevada, dogs compete in Bob for a Water Dog (a hot dog–eating contest); the Fastest Tail Wagger event, during which your dog will be given thirty seconds to wag his tail as many times as possible; and the Best Kisser Contest, in which each dog has thirty seconds to show off her kissing power on her human, a contest in which everyone is a winner.

7. **Snowfest**, an annual festival held at the Kings Beach Elementary School in Truckee, California, features the Dress Up Your Dog Contest, sponsored by the Wylie Animal Rescue Foundation. There are Most Like a Rock Star, Looks Like a Famous Person, and Looks Most Like Owner competitions for your pooch, along with a pancake breakfast, face painting, and clowns that everyone can enjoy. Visit kidznsnow.com.

8. **The Groom Expo**, the largest grooming trade show in the world, is held each September in Hershey, Pennsylvania. The popular Groom-Olympics attracts contestants to its

various breed-specific conformation events not only for the fun that's offered but also for the $60,000 in prize money. But all seem to agree that the highlight of the gala is the stunning Dancing with Dogs Dinner and Contest, offering $600 in prize money and a spectacular dinner besides. For information, visit groomexpo.com.

9. The Denton Main Street's **Annual Dog Days of Summer Celebration**, held in June in Denton, Texas, is an annual pageant in which dogs and their people can strut their stuff in the dog parade led by Sparky the Fire Dog or compete in the pet tricks contest, a dog singing contest, or the official Spokesdog Pageant. The show also gives Kasha the chance to compete in such prestigious categories as Curliest Tail, Best Pedicure, and Most Caninely Challenged. Consult dentonmainstreet.org for details.

10. Join hundreds of other animal lovers from the Maryland region for the annual **Walk-n-Wag**, the Frederick County Humane Society's day of fun to benefit area animals. The festivities kick off with a dog walk and include live music, games and prizes, a canine barkery, and dozens of informational exhibits and sponsor tables. Games include doggie musical chairs, a flying disc competition, and silly pet trick contests. For more information, visit walk-n-wag.com.

Virtual Dogs: 4 Online Dog Shows and Games

1. **Best of Breed** is a very sophisticated canine, feline, and equine simulation game in which you get to create your own pets. The goal of the game is to own the best show and stud animal around. You'll be able to start up your own virtual kennel to breed, show, own, and care for your very own pet without the fuss or expense! All players start with $100,000 and five created dogs. Your dogs will age one year for every month that you play. You won't be able create your kennel until you've been playing for at least one month. This means you must board your animals for the first month of game play. To get started or to find out more about this challenging competition, visit www.geocities.com/bestofbreedsim.

2. **Furry Paws** is an online dog simulated game. You enter their world with $30,000 and little else. It's now up to you to make your fortune in dogs. You'll train, raise, and show virtual dogs, gaining as many wins and prestigious titles as possible, in this virtual canine dog world. Although this game has its complexities, most of the stuff on the site should be self-explanatory. If you are someone who's never played this type of game before, FP offers a tutorial to help you along. So, if you want to test your entrepreneurial skills you can contact Furry Paws at Furry-paws.com.

3. **ShowDog.Com** gives you the opportunity to raise, feed, groom, train, breed, and show cyber dogs through this inventive dog simulation game. You get to manage and budget the rations of food your dogs receive, how you breed your dogs, which shows you enter, and much, much more. Join hundreds of other kennel owners as you get your own dogs and bitches ready to compete in the show ring. You can choose from 158 different breeds; whether it be Great Dane, Beagle, Whippet, or Poodle, there is a breed for you. See them grow from puppy to champion! So, whether you've been showing real dogs for years, have never shown a dog in your life, or have never even owned a real dog, this game is fun, challenging, and a unique experience. Visit ShowDog.com for information on how to get started.

4. **The Virtual Dog Show**, the creation of Liz and Kynn Bartlett of Idyll Mountain Internet, takes place entirely on the Internet — just as in a real show, your dog will be judged by knowledgeable, experienced judges using photos. However, you won't need to go through the experience of bathing, grooming, loading the dog and family into the car, and driving for hours! Just look for your favorite photos (or take some new ones) and enter!

The first show was held in the fall of 1995, and the VDS has become a recognized institution among the dog-loving members of the Internet public. For more information, visit www2.dogshow.com.

4 Reasons to Compete in the Great American Mutt Contest

"There's no animal that's more faithful, more loyal, more lovable than the mutt," says Bill Murray in the movie *Stripes.* The folks at New York–based Tails in Need, a nonprofit group that celebrates and promotes awareness about mixed-breed, unwanted, abandoned dogs, agree; each year they sponsor a nationwide competition open to any mixed-breed dog that has been rescued, all in the search for America's most lovable mutt. The contest takes place in New York's Central Park and routinely attracts entrants from all over the United States.

1. A chance to network. The 2004 event attracted more than 1,500 entrants of a dozen dominant breed mixes, with Labs, shepherds, and terriers at the top of the list. Others included Collies, Beagles, Pit Bulls, Chows, Chihuahuas, Boxers, and even one Queensland Heeler mix. This variety alone makes the contest an excellent place to connect with other enthusiasts, make new friends, and delve into your mutt's background. Just think — Rocky may discover his true lineage!

2. Original contest events. Where else can Leticia compete against other mutts in events such as "What Else Am I?" Traditional events also include competitions for Best Trick, Highest Jumper, and Best in Show, which was snatched up in 2004 by Brandon, an eleven-year-old German Shepherd Dog/Whippet or Greyhound/terrier mix.

3. Great prizes awarded by celebrity judges. Winning pooches become instant celebrities — their photos and bios are featured in *Animal Fair* magazine. Past prizes have included custom portraits of winners painted by celebrated animal artists and baskets of original and useful "I ♥ MUTT" accessories. In 2004 these were awarded by the fashion designer Isaac Mizrahi

and the NBC news anchor Chuck Scarborough.

4. It's free. To enter (and check annual contest dates), visit tailsinneed.com and read the rules. You can register by mail or online. You'll be asked to send in two photos of your mutt along with a short essay that explains why he is so special, how he has changed your life, or how he came to be a treasured member of your family.

4 Winners of the Great American Mutt Contest

2004: Toby lives with his family on a U.S. Army base in Germany. He was born without eyes and was found wandering around a shelter in the Virginia countryside. He was adopted by a loving family, who immediately fell in love with Toby's sweet spirit and intelligence. He underwent surgery to close his open eyelids and settled quickly into his new home, where he amazed everyone with his amazing radarlike ability to get around. He learned basic obedience very quickly with the help of hot dogs and encouragement. He is always quick to give kisses, sit in a lap, or snuggle, making each day a joy for those around him. Toby is a portrait of canine courage

and perseverance. Meeting him for the first time, you don't even notice, until told, that he has no eyes. His performance at the 2004 Great American Mutt Contest was an inspiration to both dogs and humans.

2003: Tricky was rescued from a shelter on the day he was to be euthanized. A man who came to the shelter to drop off some baby birds spotted Tricky and just had to have him. This was a match made in heaven. Tricky, his human, and his human's girlfriend really hit it off. After discovering what a wonderful dog they had, Tricky's parents decided to enter him at the Great American Mutt Contest in the Best Mystery Breed competition. He seemed to be an interesting mix of Australian Shepherd, Brittany Spaniel, pointer, and Chow, with perhaps a smidgen of some other breeds. Tricky became the regional winner of Best in Show in Toledo and went on to win Best in Show at the national event in 2003.

2002: Brandon, an emaciated, depressed, and frightened little creature, was huddled up in a corner of a cage at the North Shore Animal League on Long Island when a woman visiting the shelter came to his rescue. As the woman approached the cage, Brandon crawled over to greet her and lick her

fingers. It was love at first lick! Once home, Brandon's new mom nursed him back to health. Brandon's once dingy coat was now shiny and bright. Brandon now revealed his bushy shepherd tail, Doberman markings, and some terrier features. Brandon also discovered his "inner puppy" and his high level of acrobatic ability, especially at Frisbee. Brandon's spins, twists, and flips earned him the coveted Best in Show award at the Great American Mutt Contest in 2002.

2001: C.J., a Pit Bull/Rhodesian Ridgeback mix, was eighteen months old when he was adopted. C.J.'s previous owners were very cruel to him. They had actually burned him with cigarettes, and traces of gunpowder were found in his blood. C.J. was only hours from being euthanized when he was rescued. C.J.'s training was long and arduous. His new human spent five years undoing the effects of all the abuse to which C.J. had been subjected. During the course of rehabilitation, C.J.'s new daddy discovered that the dog loved learning tricks. He was entered at the Great American Mutt Contest in New York and won the competition for the Most Creative Pet Trick and went on to also win Best in Show in 2001.

World Weight Pull Records

At the World Championship Dog Weight Pull[SM], held annually every February in Anchorage, Alaska, since 1969, dogs in different weight divisions compete against one another for the coveted title of champion. Each dog, regardless of size, must pull as much weight as he is able for a distance of twenty-five feet in under sixty seconds. The following profiles of these astounding winning-record holders have been provided by Dean Fritz and Glen Williams of the Saint Bernard Club of Alaska[SM].

1. Ultra-Lightweight Class (0–55 lbs.). Frank, a nine-time world champion in this division, set the record in 1995 by pulling 2,450 pounds. As he was the son of a stray, his breed mix has been the subject of much conjecture. Frank earned his caretaker more than $30,000 in prize money during his career. He made his last pull at the age of fourteen during the World Championship Dog Weight Pull[SM], where he again won the Ultra-Lightweight Division. He placed first in 1987, 1989, 1990, 1992, 1993, 1994, 1995, 1997, and 1999. In the early morning of June 14, 2000, at the age of fifteen, Frank passed away peacefully in his sleep.

2. Lightweight Class (55–85 lbs.). In 1987, LT, handled by Norm Stoppenbrink, broke the previous record by pulling 2,600 pounds in 18.79 seconds. Like all the records of this competition, his has not been approached in many years.

3. Middleweight Class (85–125 lbs.). In 1976, Grumpy, owned by Sharon Hess, set the standard at 3,000 pounds. This record has been approached many times but has never been beaten.

4. Heavyweight Class (125 lbs. and over). Susitna Von Thor, a Saint Bernard, died many years ago but still lives on in the hearts and memories of dog weight pull enthusiasts. His pull of 5,220 pounds at the event has not been equaled since and seems insurmountable to the many competitors who have since followed. Susitna won the event six times in a row.

The World Championship Dog Weight Pull[SM] is a Service Mark registered exclusively to the Saint Bernard Club of Alaska, Inc.

What Is Schutzhund?*

We're grateful to Jim Harper at dvg.com for this fascinating glimpse at a little-known sport.

The Germans call it *"hundesport,"* meaning dog sport. For generations, people from Europe and North America have been drawn into this unique idea of participating in an active sport with a dog. Schutzhund offers this in a way that no other sport can. It is outdoors. It is physical. It is mental. The demands are great, but the sport also offers competition and new friendships. In short, it is what all recreational sports should first be: good exercise, fun, and full of rewards.

Schutzhund started at the beginning of the twentieth century as a test for working dogs. Its initial purpose was to determine which dogs could be used for breeding and which had true working ability. The growing demand for working dogs made more sophisticated tests and training necessary. These dogs were needed for police training, border patrol, customs, military purposes, and herding. As these tests evolved, more people participated just for the sheer enjoyment of seeing if their pet dogs could be trained as effectively as these "professional dogs." Now, more than sixty years after the first formal Schutzhund rules were introduced, tens of thousands of people participate in the sport each year.

Schutzhund tests three specific areas of a dog's training and behavior. The first, tracking, requires the dog to track footsteps over mixed terrain, change direction, and show absolute accuracy and commitment to finding the track. He must also find dropped articles and indicate their locations to the handler. Often this is done under less than ideal circumstances with difficult cover, bad weather conditions, and an aged track. Many find tracking, when only the handler and dog are working together, to be the most satisfying experience in training. It is certainly the most peaceful part of Schutzhund.

The second phase is obedience. Those who are familiar with AKC obedience will feel more comfortable in this area, as many of the exercises are similar to those in Open and Utility. There is heeling, both on- and off-lead. The sit, down, and stand are also done, except when the dog is moving. But Schutzhund applies its own style to this work. Instead of on a forty-foot ring, the handler and dog work on a soccer-size trial field. Some exercises require the dog to work under the noise of a firing gun. In addition to the normal dumbbell retrieval, the dog must retrieve over a one-meter jump and a six-foot wall. Down stays and a long send away conclude the test.

The final test is the most misunderstood by the general public. This is protection. The most important point to understand when watching a protection routine is the relationship between dog and handler. The dog must never bite the trial helper, unless either the dog or the handler is attacked. Then it must attack fully and without hesitation. But here the real difference becomes apparent. The dog must stop biting on the command of the handler and guard the trial helper without further aggression. Often people confuse Schutzhund protection training with police dog or personal protection work. The Schutzhund dog is capable of the feats of never being aggressive except under those specific situations it is trained to face, and even then it must always be under the absolute control of the handler.

The above tests are difficult enough, but to make it even more demanding, they all happen in one day during competitions held all over the country. These trials are held by local clubs or in regional and national championships. Each dog is judged by a complex point system that determines the winner of the trial.

When a dog successfully completes the first trial, he is awarded a title of Schutzhund I. The dog can then progress to Schutzhund II and, the ultimate, Schutzhund III. Each level makes ever greater demands on the dog and training in all three areas. Any Schutzhunder will tell you that a high-scoring Schutzhund III dog is the ultimate working dog: one in a thousand of all working dogs.

In addition to the Schutzhund I, II, and III titles, other titles in advanced tracking, temperament tests, police training, and agility work are awarded.

Today, Schutzhund is more than the small group that started in Germany so long ago. Its organizations have several hundred thousand members scattered across Europe, North America, and several other continents.

* *Schutzhund* has been changed to *VPG* (in German — Vielseitigkeitspruefung für Gebrauchshunde), which roughly translates into "versatility test for working dogs."

21 Weird Dog News Items

1. London, December 2002. Harvey, a portly Bulldog, was out for a ride with his owner in his Maserati 3200GT when his owner suspected he had a sore tummy. The driver hopped out of the car to walk over to the passenger side and let Harvey out for a walk, but before he got there, Harvey had leaped over to the driver's seat, pushed the gearshift into drive, and pressed down on the accelerator. Harvey and the Maserati were off—straight into the back of a parked van. Although Harvey was guilty of speeding, reckless driving, and car theft, charges were dropped providing he never drove again.

2. Philippines, December 2002. Hundreds of people went without Christmas dinner when police intercepted three vans en route to an illegal slaughterhouse, containing 175 caged and muzzled dogs who were scheduled to become Christmas meals. Ninety-one of the dogs survived and were rescued by the Criminal Investigation and Detection Group.

3. Berlin, July 2003. A lost Dachshund was found—swallowed whole—in the belly of a giant 1.5-meter-long catfish named Kuno the Killer.

4. Nepal, February 2004. Following a practice prevalent in the Tharu community, which believes that a man who regrows teeth must take a dog as his bride for good luck, a seventy-five-year-old man was wed to his dog—and died three days later.

5. Australia, February 2001. A man who was arrested for drug possession argued that the drug-sniffing dog who discovered his stash had violated his civil rights by assaulting him when he nuzzled his crotch. A judge dismissed the charges, but they were reinstated by a Supreme Court judge when a prosecutor pointed out that in the animal kingdom, crotch-nuzzling could be interpreted as a friendly gesture.

6. Kansas, November 2003. A Wichita family was especially grateful this Thanksgiving as their dinner was interrupted by the arrival of Bear, their beloved dog who had disappeared—some six years before!

7. Norway, December 2003. Searchers had given up on recovering a four-year-old boy who had become separated from his mother while shopping. But Agathon, a Dachshund, was undaunted. He led his owner to a slippery rock, where the rain-drenched boy was holding on for dear life. Agathon was celebrated as a national hero for his efforts.

8. Chile, November 2003. Dog owners in Santiago will no longer have to put up with paunchy pooches now that the first gym exclusively for dogs has opened, complete with doggie treadmills, personal training services, and a beauty parlor.

9. Australia, September 2003. More than eight hundred dogs gathered together to create the world's biggest doggie bath in Sydney Olympic Park as part of an effort to raise funds for animal health and welfare.

10. Romania, August 2003. A dog named Vasile carried a bundle two miles to his home after finding it abandoned in the woods. The dog's owner was shocked to open the bundle to find an otherwise healthy baby boy.

11. Colorado, September 2003. A man who spent six days trapped in his bathtub was kept alive by his dog. The Highlands Ranch, Colorado, resident, who suffers from multiple sclerosis and uses a wheelchair, could not reach the safety handles to rescue himself, and the phone that the dog, Libby, retrieved was not charged. As the days stretched on, he would drift in and out of consciousness. Libby would lick his face to get his attention and slap her paws on the floor to wake him up.

12. California, July 2003. Rock legend Ozzy Osbourne saved Pipi, his wife Sharon's Pomeranian, from being killed by a coyote outside their Beverly Hills mansion. He tackled and then wrestled with the coyote until it released the dog, which was held firmly in its mouth.

13. West Virginia, July 2003. An injured black Labrador made his own way to Beckley Appalachian Regional Hospital after being hit by a car. He hobbled through the sliding glass doors and waited for assistance in the hallway. Hospital workers gave the dog water and called a vet.

14. Russia, June 2003. Residents of Togliatti raised $8,000 to erect a bronze statue commemorating Faithful, a German Shepherd Dog who had refused to move

cluding shampoo, rinse, delousing, and blow-dry features. The owner said, "Washing a dog at home can be a nightmare, and this is proving to be a popular alternative."

18. Minnesota, March 2003. A burglar who took his dog to rob a butcher's shop was caught after the hound refused to leave. Lumpi was so busy devouring the sausage that the burglar had opened for him that when the police turned up, he stayed where he was instead of running for it.

19. Germany, March 2003. An artist announced plans for opening the first brothel for dogs in Berlin. Explaining that his own Jack Russell, Karlchen, was having a hard time satisfying his sexual cravings while being

The owner said, "Washing a dog at home can be a nightmare."

from the spot where his owners were killed in a car crash. Faithful stood vigil on the same spot for seven years, surviving on the food and water that people began bringing him after he refused their attempts to find him a new home.

15. Austria, May 2003. Officials announced that stainless steel toilets were being installed in Vienna in an attempt to keep the city's pavements free of the forty tons of excrement left behind daily by the city's 100,000 dogs.

16. Gulf of Mexico, April 2003. A Doberman puppy by the name of Jet flung himself on a two-meter-long shark in order to rescue another dog — a three-year-old Kelpie named Honey Girl who was being pulled underwater when Jet sprang into action.

17. United Kingdom, March 2003. The first automatic "dogwash" opened, featuring a twelve-minute cycle in-

taken for walks, this imaginative entrepreneur gives new meaning to the phrase "doggie style."

20. Great Britain, March 2003. The dog expert Dr. Roger Mugford has invented a device that can tell a dog's exact mood by measuring the wag of his tail. Called the wagometer, the contraption attaches to the dog's back and has sensors that connect to the tail. Details such as the speed, direction, and arc of the wag can then be analyzed to judge how the dog is feeling.

21. On February 26, 2003, it was reported that a man accused of punishing his stepson by forcing him to sleep in a dog kennel has agreed to the same punishment in a plea deal. The Texan agreed to plead guilty in exchange for a choice of punishments — thirty days in jail or thirty nights inside a doghouse. Prosecutors said the plea deal also included eight years' probation and a $1,000 fine.

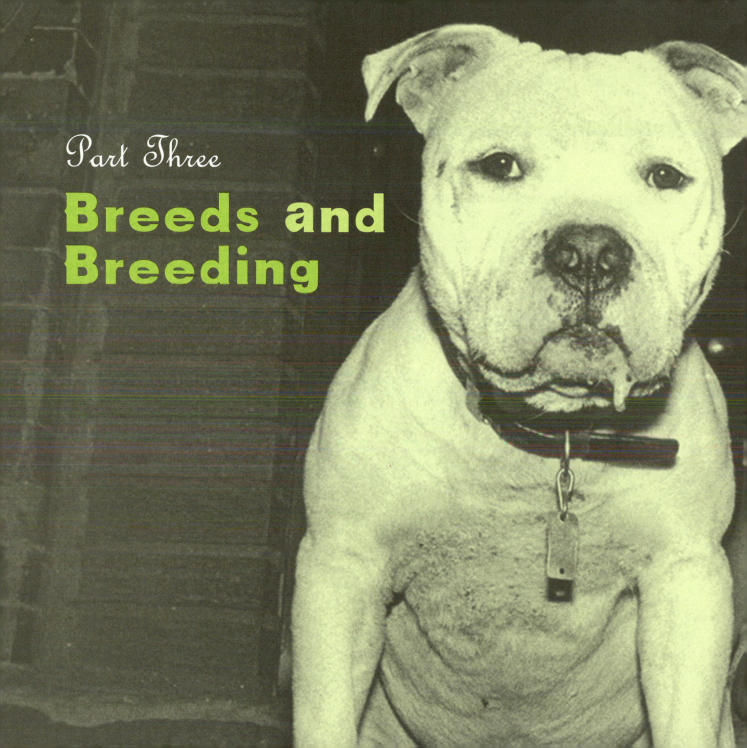

Part Three

Breeds and Breeding

"Things that upset a terrier may pass virtually unnoticed by a Great Dane."

— SMILEY BLANTON

Happily, Planet Dog is inhabited by a wide variety of breeds that come in a wider variety of shapes, sizes, temperaments, and talents. Whether you abhor noise, suffer from allergies, live life in the fast lane, or just enjoy watching it go by on TV, there's a dog for you.

This chapter explores the range of dog breeds and provides the information you need to make an intelligent choice about which dog might be right for you. Although purebred dogs offer myriad forms of companionship and abilities, bear in mind that there are exceptions to every rule. A Shih Tzu is not always the lap dog she was bred to be, and every once in a while you'll encounter a Golden Retriever who is the exception to the rule of "athletic, easygoing, and friendly." Your German Shepherd Dog might be lazier than most members of this naturally industrious breed, or you may wind up with the only subdued Jack Russell on the planet. So when we make generalizations about breeds, keep in mind that each dog of a particular breed may not have all the characteristics of that breed.

Of course, when it comes to variety, mixed-breed dogs have it all. Perhaps because so many of these dogs are rescued, or maybe because their own personal makeup makes each one a true original, mixed-breed dogs seem to come complete with their own brand of love, and so they, too, are celebrated here.

Whether you're a fan of purebred or mixed-breed dogs, the rules of good breeding apply to all, so we hope you'll pay special attention to the lists here that encourage us all to live on Planet Dog with a responsible attitude toward acquiring and raising dogs, and to demonstrate for our dogs, in the choices we make about breeding, the kind of deep concern that they routinely have for us.

> **"She had no particular breed in mind, no unusual requirements. Except** the special sense of mutual recognition **that tells dog and human they have both come to the right place."**
> **—LLOYD ALEXANDER**

Basic Biology of the Dog

Order — **Carnivora**

Family — **Canidae**

Genus — **Canis**

Species — **familiaris**

Size — **varies according to breed**

Weight — **varies according to breed**

Body temperature — **ranges from 100.4 to 102.2° F**

Heart rate — **70–130 beats per minute (puppies and smaller dogs having a higher heart rate than medium or large dogs)**

Respiratory rate — **10–30 breaths per minute**

Toes front — **4**

Toes rear — **4**

Adult food consumption — **varies according to breed**

Adult water consumption — **varies according to breed**

Gestation period — **60–67 days average**

Chromosomes — **78**

Life span — **varies according to breed, from approximately six to twenty years**

Characteristics of the 7 Different Dog Groups

1. Herding — When early human herders discovered that they needed an equal helpmate to round up sheep and other livestock and bring them to pasture, they developed the herding dog. There is great variety in this group, from the short Pembroke Welsh Corgi to the Smooth Collie to the brilliant Australian Shepherd. These dogs adapt easily to their surroundings, allowing them to work in small, mountainous regions, as with the Shetland Sheepdog, or making it difficult for predators to get a grip on their coats, as with the heavily corded Hungarian Puli. Herding dogs are confident, courageous, and active. Having been bred for their decision-making capabilities, these dogs are adept problem solvers. Members of this group do have a strong chase instinct, with a tendency to gently herd other family pets as well as their owners and small children. They are generally intelligent, make excellent companions, and respond well to training. Herding dogs require plenty of exercise.

2. Sporting — Sporting dogs make hunting (for both entertainment *and* dinner) easier for humans by searching out and retrieving game birds and waterfowl. A few of these dogs even hunt small mammals. Included in the Sporting Group is the Labrador Retriever, the most popular dog in the United States, with more than 144,000 puppies registered with the AKC in 2003. The Spinone Italiano, an Italian pointer, was recently recognized by the AKC and is gaining in popularity every year because of his joyous attitude and carefree appearance. Sporting dogs are very energetic, friendly, tractable, focused, fun-loving, and nonterritorial. Dogs in this group have a strong desire to please, and they make great family pets. Sporting dogs need regular, invigorating exercise.

3. Toy — Dogs in the Toy Group are our companions and lap warmers. They share our chairs, our meals, and, often, our beds. Their personalities and looks vary widely, from the monkey-faced Affenpinscher to the aristocratic, butterfly-eared Papillon. Toy dogs are usually excellent companions for the elderly but are sometimes too delicate for families with small children. Some toy dogs, such as the Italian Greyhound, can be shy, while others, like the Pug, are full of bravado. As with all purebred dogs, make sure you get your pet from a reputable breeder. Owning a dog from the Toy Group has many advantages: they are loving, playful, and always up for cuddling. Another plus — it's easier to manage a ten-pound dog than one ten times that size.

4. Nonsporting — All dogs were once classified as sporting, so when the breeds currently in this category arrived on the scene, they were promptly dubbed *Nonsporting*. Because dogs in the Nonsporting Group were developed for so many different reasons, they really don't have much in common with one another — which makes them all the more interesting to see. This is especially true at dog shows, where you have the chance to observe a Dalmatian follow quickly on the heels of a Chow Chow. The Nonsporting Group contains a variety of personalities, instincts, and characteristics, from the large, intelligent Standard Poodle (once a water dog) to the medium-size American Eskimo Dog (once a circus performer).

5. Terriers — Terriers were bred to hunt and kill vermin. They typically have little tolerance for other animals, including other dogs. They're feisty, energetic, confident, curious, courageous, tenacious, and dominant. They also retain a keen prey instinct. Though their personalities tend to be similar, there is great variety of appearance within the Terrier Group, from the tiny, longhaired Yorkshire Terrier to the long-limbed, short-

"About the only thing on a farm that has an easy time is the dog."
— EDGAR WATSON HOUE, AMERICAN JOURNALIST

coated Airedale. In order to keep Wire Fox Terriers looking neat and trim, their coats need to be stripped. This can be time-consuming and expensive if you're paying a groomer. But though coat stripping is a requirement for the show ring, it certainly isn't for the family pet. What *is* required when you have a charming terrier in the house is an owner with as much determination as her dog.

6. Hound — The Hound Group includes both scent hounds, who track their prey by air or ground scent, and sight hounds, who sight and chase a fleeing animal. Hounds are independent, nonterritorial, and nondominant. Scent hounds are adaptable, accepting, bold, and social with other dogs and people, but they may view cats and other small animals as prey. Sight hounds — a group that includes Greyhounds and Whippets — are the swiftest dogs around. Both kinds of hounds tend to be quiet, placid, and aloof. Some also share the ability to produce a unique sound known as baying. Be sure to sample this sound before you fall in love with a hound dog.

7. Working — These dogs were bred to guard flocks, patrol estates, pull loads and sleds, aid fishermen, and rescue people. Alert, loyal, courageous, hardy, confident, territorial, protective, persistent, and dominant, they take their jobs seriously and prefer work to leisure. Their size and strength, as exhibited by the Kuvasz and the Great Pyrenees, make many working dogs unsuitable pets for the average family. The Great Dane, however, is a gentle giant famously at home in small apartments. Other working dogs, such as the Doberman Pinscher and the Alaskan Malamute, are recognized for their brains more than their brawn. All in all, working dogs are intelligent, capable animals who make steadfast companions.

First Prize Dog Power.

No. 16924. This power can be operated by a dog, goat or sheep; yields 25 per cent. more power from a given weight of animal than any other, and with adjustable bridge to regulate the required power and motion, a 30 pound animal will do the churning; if you keep a dog, make him "work his passage." The power can be connected to any churn sold by us. Price **$15.00**

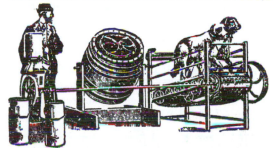

The illustration above shows how the double dog power can be used in operating a cream separator. When the separator is not in use and you desire to churn, connect it to tumbling rod sent with machine. A corn sheller, fan mill or sawing machine can be connected by belt from balance wheel. Separators require a high gear, and for this purpose we recommend our steel pulley, 3½x36 inches. This we can furnish at $6 extra. If iron coupling rod and coupling as shown in illustration are desired to connect and run cream separator, we can furnish them at $3 extra.

From the 1897 Sears, Roebuck Catalogue

2003 Breeder of the Year Awards

In 2002 the American Kennel Club (AKC) began an awards program recognizing outstanding purebred dog breeders with a Breeder of the Year award. Individual breeders, chosen from each of the seven groups, are honored with awards for their contributions in the improvement of the health, temperament, and quality of purebred dogs. The Breeder of the Year is then awarded to one of these individuals. Here is a list of 2003 winners.

1. Sporting Group: Helen K. Szostaks of Plymouth, Massachusetts, has worked with Flat-Coated Retrievers for more than thirty years, resulting in numerous champions and group winners. One of her dams has produced twenty championship offspring. She has served in various capacities with the Flat-Coated Retriever Society of America including as National Specialty show chair. Dr. Szostaks is a veterinarian with her own private practice.

2. Hound Group: Patricia Craige Trotter of Antioch, Tennessee, had bred the top sire and dam in the history of the Norwegian Elkhound breed. Her distinguished career has included multiple *Kennel Review* Breeder of the Year awards, and her breeding column for the *AKC Gazette* has earned her the 1997 Maxwell Medallion from the Dog Writers' Association of America. She has judged numerous national specialty shows as well as the Westminster and AKC/Eukanuba National Invitational Championship.

3. Working Group: Mary M. Rodgers of Hamilton, Montana, has worked with Dobermans since 1963 and has produced more than a hundred champions. She has won seven Best of Breed titles at the Doberman Pinscher Club of America's national competitions. In 2002 her Doberman was named the Number One Working Dog. In 2003 she was also named Breeder of the Year.

4. Terrier Group: Capt. Jean L. Heath and William H. Cosby, Jr., of Pleasanton, California, have been breeding Lakeland Terriers for more than twenty-three years, resulting in 144 champions from their Black Watch kennel. They are past recipients of Breeder of the Year awards from *Kennel Review* and *Dogs USA* magazines.

5. Toy Group: Thomas O'Neal of Genoa City, Wisconsin, has bred eighty-eight Cocker Spaniel champions along with his partner, Ron Fabis. They began breeding English Toy Spaniels in 1975 and developed what they call the "Dreambridge" lines. Tom has had more than seventy Dreambridge champions, including the top-producing Toy Spaniel in the history of the breed.

6. Nonsporting Group: Joseph D. Vergnetti of Medina, Ohio, began breeding all three varieties of Poodles in 1972. He is best known for his distinctive type of Miniatures and Standards. His Dassin Kennel Poodles are among the top-producing sires and dams in the breed's history and have won Best of Breed at the Poodle Club of America's National and Regional Specialties a grand total of nine times.

7. Working Group: Jere Marder of Chicago, Illinois, began her work with Old English Sheepdogs in the 1970s and bred the top-winning bitch in the history of the breed. She is responsible for producing some of the most noted dogs in the breed, including the number one dog in the history of the breed with an outstanding record of sixty-four Best in Shows.

2004 Breeder of the Year Awards

1. Sporting Group: Sandra Bell of Statesboro, Georgia, has been breeding Cocker Spaniels for more than twenty years. Her efforts have resulted in sixty-eight champions. She has sat on the board of the Carolina and Chattanooga Cocker Spaniel Specialty Clubs. In 2004 Ms. Bell's Parti-Color Cocker, CH San Jo's Born to Win, won Best of Breed at Westminster.

2. Hound Group: Gayle Bontecou of Clinton Corners, New York, operates Gayleward Scottish Deerhounds. She is currently on the board of directors of the AKC Museum of the Dog. Gayle has served as judge of the Hound Group competitions numerous times. Her Deerhound CH Gayleward's Gray Gucci won Best of Breed at the 128th Westminster show in 2003. She has been assigned as a judge in the Hound Group for the 2004 Westminster show.

3. Working Group: Patricia Turner and Anna M. Quigley of Chehalis, Washington, have been involved with Komondors for more than thirty years, striving to preserve the temperament of a true working breed. Their Komondor CH Lojosmegyi Dahu Digal won Best in Group at Westminster's 1993 show. He also won three National Specialties and contributed to their breeding program by producing two National Specialty winners. In total Pat, Anna, and their Komondors have won ten National Specialty shows. Pat and Anna have both served on the board of the Komondor Club of America.

4. Terrier Group: Catherine B. Nelson of Potomac, Maryland, has been the breeder/owner/handler of Pennywise Dandie Dinmont Terriers since 1974. Past president of the Dandie Dinmont Terrier Club of America, she has owned or bred seventy champions (including five all-breed Best in Show winners), and eight Dandies who have won Best of Breed at eleven National Specialties, and she has bred, owned, and handled the number one Dandie in breed standings for twelve of the past fourteen years. In 2004 she was also named AKC Breeder of the Year.

5. Toy Group: Dale Adams of Palm Beach Gardens, Florida, has been one of the top breeders of Japanese Chins for twenty years. She consistently has been the breeder/owner/handler of the top Chins in the United States, as well as Breeder of the Year. Under her two-year leadership of the Japanese Chin Club of America, the standard was revised, an AKC video was produced, and Japanese Chin Rescue was started. Her Chin Tai a Little Knot SOD (Tommy) was a breed winner and group placer at Westminster. Tommy is a top producer in the breed and the holder of numerous other records, and his son "Digger" retired as the top winning Chin in the history of the breed.

6. Nonsporting Group: Cody T. Sickle, Oyster Bay Cove, New York, has been involved with Bulldogs for more than forty years. He has bred or owned 120 champions. His dogs have won 28 All-Breed Best in Show titles, 297 Specialty Best in Show titles, 3 National Specialty Best of Breed titles, and 9 Westminster Best of Breed titles. Cody is also an AKC-approved judge.

7. Herding Group: Thomas W. and Nioma S. Coen of Alford, Massachusetts, owned and operated the Macdega Kennel. Their first litter was whelped in 1964, and all their dogs trace to their pillar sire, CH Halstor's Peter Pumpkin. Their Registry of Merit (a male who has sired ten or more champions and females who have produced five or more champions) is the breed's top sire with 160 American champions. Sires and dams bred or owned by Macdega have produced about seven hundred champions. The Coens have owned a great number of special Shelties who have contributed to the breed. Among them are four of the top ten sires, somewhere around eighteen ROM sires and dams, numerous National Specialty winners, and eight All-Breed Best in Show winners.

Also Known As . . .
22 Breeds and Their Nicknames

Dog breeds come by their nicknames based on a variety of traits, including countries of origin, original purposes, and special talents. Here are a few of our favorites.

1. Affenspinscher: "The Monkey Dog," because he looks like one!

2. Airedale Terrier: "King of the Terriers," for having all the best qualities of terriers: versatility, agility, and outstanding performance in search-and-rescue police and military work.

3. Basenji: "The Barkless Dog," for her quiet nature.

4. Bearded Collie: "Beardie," for obvious reasons.

5. Boston Terrier: "The American Gentleman of Dogs," for his handsome black and white coloring.

6. Bullmastiff: "The Gamekeeper's Night Dog," originally bred from the Mastiff and the Bulldog to guard English estates.

7. Bull Terrier: "The White Cavalier," originally a strain of pure white terrier bred by James Hicks. Despite the color changes in the breed, the name has stuck.

8. Cairn Terrier: "The Best Little Pal in the World," because he seems to be everyone's fun-loving favorite.

9. Chinese Shar-Pei: "The Sharkskin Dog," for her rough, sandpaper-like coat. She's also known as "The Chinese Fighting Dog" and "The Chinese Bulldog."

10. Collie: "The Lassie Dog," named for the literary and film legend that made this breed famous throughout the world.

11. Dalmatian: "The Plum Pudding Dog," perhaps so nicknamed for her spots. Used in England to run beside horses, the Dalmatian is also some- times known as "The Carriage Dog," "The English Coach Dog," or "The Firehouse Dog."

12. Great Dane: "The Apollo of Dogs," named for the most beautiful of the Greek gods.

13. Havanese: "The Cuban Silk Dog," because she has silky soft hair instead of fur.

14. Keeshond: "The Dutch Barge Dog," originally bred to guard barges and provide companionship for the crews.

15. Lhasa Apso: "The Lion Dog of Tibet," because he guarded Tibetan temples possibly as far back as 800 B.C.

16. Manchester Terrier: "The Gentleman's Terrier," named for his popularity in Victorian England.

17. Old English Sheepdog, Pug, and Irish Water Spaniel: "The Clown Dog of the World."

18. Papillon: "The Butterfly Dog," for her large, fluffy ears like butterfly wings.

19. Petit Basset Griffon Vendéen: "The Happy Breed," because he always seems to sport a smile and a wagging tail.

20. Pug: "Multim in Parvo," Latin for "a lot of dog in a small space," or "a lot in a little."

21. Weimaraner: "The Grey Ghost," because her silver gray coloring gives her a ghostly appearance.

22. Whippet: "The Poor Man's Racehorse," originally bred to hunt rabbits, the Whippet was later used in Northern England among the working class as a racing dog.

2004 National Animal Control Association Award Winners

The National Animal Control Association (NACA) presents four annual awards for achievements and accomplishments to those individuals and organizations working in or for the animal control field. Prizes were awarded to the following in 2004.

1. Bill Lehman Memorial Award: The recipient of this award is not directly employed in the animal control field but has shown exceptional awareness of animal control matters. The 2004 winners were Richard and Christine Camp, whose efforts resulted in bringing air conditioning to all the animal shelters in St. Louis, Missouri. Their nonprofit organization, called Adopt-A-Stray, has helped hundreds of dogs in St. Louis find new families. The Camps currently run three storefront adoption centers in shopping malls around that city.

2. Animal Control Employee of the Year Award: The recipient of this award must be directly employed in the animal care profession for a minimum of five years and must be a current member of NACA or his or her affiliated state association. The 2004 winner was Debby Leddy, the assistant director at the Williams County Animal Control in Franklin, Tennessee. At the shelter, Debby oversees the volunteer and educational programs, as well as undertaking a variety of other duties. It was Debby's work in developing Maggie's Bark Park and Rascal's Run Around, the very first off-leash parks in the state of Tennessee, that garnered her this award.

3. Diane Lane Memorial Award: This award is for outstanding volunteer service in animal welfare–related fields. The recipient has demonstrated exceptional dedication or has performed outstanding work far and beyond the requirements of her volunteer position. The 2004 recipient, Mary Robertson of Edmond, Oklahoma, is the president of and one of the founders of the volunteer program at Paws for Life. She herself has spent numerous hours walking and bathing shelter dogs and has helped with the Home for the Holidays program, for which she has solicited numerous contributions for the shelter and has spent hours contacting prospective volunteers.

4. Outstanding State Association Award: The recipient of this award must be a current agency member of NACA. Selection criteria include effective training programs for personnel, outstanding/innovative public education programs, active community involvement, and average response time to calls for assistance. The 2004 recipient was the Missouri Animal Control Association. The MACA's dedicated staff have networked supplies, space and manpower, and numerous shelters. It has also developed a scholarship program for those agencies that cannot otherwise afford to participate in training. Through persistence they have obtained a not-for-profit status that allows donations to their association to be tax exempt.

Before the enactment of the 1978 law that made it mandatory for dog owners in New York City to clean up after their pets, approximately 40 million pounds of dog excrement were deposited on the streets every year.

The 50 Most Popular Breeds in the United States

According to the AKC, the following fifty dog breeds are the most popular ones in the United States. These brief descriptions are intended to offer a quick overview of each breed. Their characteristics are general in nature. Dog breeds are listed in descending order of popularity. Heights and weights are given for male dogs. Females are generally a few inches shorter and three to ten pounds lighter than males of the same breed.

1. The Labrador Retriever is a large, lively, and good-natured dog who is easy to train. Labs love everyone but can be reserved with strangers if they aren't well socialized. Labrador Retrievers are excellent water dogs: they have a weather-resistant coat, a heavy-set body, strong legs, and an "otter tail," all of which enable them to swim with great power. Frequent exercise is needed to keep this breed healthy and occupied. A playful companion and a calm house pet, the Labrador Retriever is currently the most popular dog in America.

Group: Sporting
Height: 22–24"
Weight: 60–75 pounds

2. The Golden Retriever is large, loyal, intelligent, and eager to please. Though too gentle and friendly to be successful watchdogs, Goldens, with their alert manner and desire to please, do extremely well in obedience training. Active and sweet, they can also be overenergetic and distractible. A Golden needs to be with her people; she may get into trouble if left alone too long. Golden Retrievers are heavily muscled, with a dense coat and a thickly feathered tail. These highly trainable sporting dogs have a confident and alert personality; they need

constant attention to be happy. Gentle and loving, the Golden Retriever makes an excellent family pet.

Group: Sporting
Height: 22–24"
Weight: 60–80 pounds

Beagle

3. The Beagle is a small, curious, happy tail-wagger. Beagles are sweet and spirited, but put them in contact with an interesting scent and they are likely to follow it wherever it may take them. Beagles should always be kept on-lead or in a safe, fenced-in area. Because they can be willful, Beagles require patient, firm training. They don't like to be left alone, which, in conjunction with another Beagle trait — their loud, baying cry — can keep this dog from being everyone's ideal pet. Beagles may be difficult to housebreak and many have a "houndy" odor. When on scent, this tenacious dog breed will block out everything around it — including you. But their charming,

upbeat personalities make Beagles excellent family pets.

Group: Hound
Height: 14–16"
Weight: 22–25 pounds

4. The German Shepherd Dog (known as an Alsatian in many parts of the world) is large, intelligent, loyal, fearless, alert, bold, cheerful, and obedient. This breed can be trained for many different tasks. They have strong protecting instincts and need an owner who shows leadership. German Shepherd Dogs are often reserved with strangers. They do shed constantly. At certain times of the year, their shedding increases dramatically. German Shepherd Dogs are strong and agile, and they possess one of the keenest noses in the dog world. Unsurpassed as working dogs, they were the first dogs trained to sniff out drugs, and they adapt easily to both protection and police work. Smart and protective, the German Shepherd Dog develops strong bonds with his family and can suffer from severe separation anxiety.

Group: Herding
Height: 24–26"
Weight: 77–85 pounds

5. The Dachshund is a small, affectionate, curious, lively, and proud dog with a pleasant and energetic expression. They can be difficult to housebreak and they like to dig and bark. Dachshunds come in two sizes, standard and miniature, and three coat types: smooth, longhaired, and wirehaired. The Dachshund is agile, with a low, long, and muscular body, enabling her to move freely in a tunnel or a den.

Group: Hound
Height: 14–18"
Weight: 20 pounds

6. The Yorkshire Terrier or **"Yorkie"** is a tiny dog with plenty of spirit and energy. Among the world's smallest dogs, they are affectionate and always willing to please. The Yorkie's intelligence, fearlessness, and self-confidence — combined with his stubbornness — can make him a challenging dog to own. Yorkshire Terriers, like all terriers, love to bark and can be snappish if irritated or frightened. Early socialization and obedience training and will reduce any tendency toward timidity and nipping.

Group: Terrier
Height: 6–7"
Weight: 7 pounds

Boxer

7. The Boxer is as large as she is devoted. This breed is also playful, energetic, highly intelligent, and obedient. Boxers are good with children and reserved with strangers. This is the Virgo of the dog world, with a fierce desire to stay clean and a tendency to groom herself, like a cat. Boxers are alert and protective. Because of their strength and exuberance, this breed needs a dominant owner. Some Boxers slobber, while others may drool or snore. They are thickly muscled, with a short coat and a docked tail. Boxers make good family dogs because they get along well with children and other pets.

Group: Working
Height: 22–25"
Weight: 60–70 pounds

Standard
Poodle

8. The Standard Poodle is an extremely intelligent dog who is very easy to train and makes a great family pet. He is a noble, graceful, and kind dog. The Standard variety of Poodle is far more manageable than the Miniature and Toy versions of this breed. Standard Poodles are squarely built and well proportioned. They have a proud carriage and elegant appearance, with a springy, effortless gait that can be reminiscent of a horse's canter. Poodles need a great deal of grooming. Interestingly enough, the Poodle's highly stylized grooming is a vestige of their past as water dogs, when their joints had to be covered with a fair amount of fur to protect them from the cold while the rest of their fur was trimmed off so the dogs could move easily in the water.

Group: Nonsporting
Height: 15"
Weight: 45–70 pounds

9. The Shih Tzu is devoted, beguiling, self-assured, and proud. This little dog craves attention and needs to be with her family to be happy. Friendly, playful, and full of life, she can also be difficult to housetrain. Shih Tzus have compact, sturdy bodies with long, flowing double coats that require a great deal of grooming.

Group: Nonsporting
Height: 11"
Weight: 9–16 pounds

10. The Chihuahua is the smallest of all dog breeds, but he is nonetheless a bold, fast, and strong-willed little dog. Chihuahuas are very loyal. They give attention and affection freely and expect the same in return. This breed often bonds strongly with one person and can become fiercely protective of that person. Chihuahuas are feisty and may snap if teased or irritated. A note to the sound-sensitive: this breed *loves* to bark. Chihuahuas can become easily chilled (they wear those little sweaters for more than just a fashion statement). Like many small breeds,

"I wonder if other dogs think Poodles are members of a weird religious cult." — RITA RUDNER

this one can be difficult to housetrain. There are two breed types: short-coated and long-coated. The Chihuahua is known for his saucy expression and alert attitude. Despite their tiny size, Chihuahuas make excellent watchdogs.

Group: Toy
Height: 6–9"
Weight: 2–6 pounds

11. The Miniature Schnauzer is as intelligent and trainable as she is diminutive in size. Lively, playful, cheerful, and alert, this breed requires plenty of human companionship. The Miniature Schnauzer is a robust, sturdily built, energetic, and affectionate little dog who can sometimes forget her petite frame and become dog-aggressive. The long hair on her muzzle and eyebrows enhances her strikingly keen facial expression.

Group: Terrier
Height: 12–14"
Weight: 10–15 pounds

12. The Pug has a big attitude and lives in a small-size body. These dogs *think* they have the courage of a German Shepherd Dog, the athleticism of a Weimaraner, and the speed of a Greyhound. What they *do* have is a frisky, clever, affectionate, playful, cheerful, and rambunctious nature. Pugs are happiest when spending time with their people. They have a tendency to snore and wheeze, so make sure you get your

Pug from a reputable breeder, whose goal is to reduce such problems. The Pug has a square, stubby, and compact body and communicates by making nasal noises. This breed makes a wonderful family pet.

Group: Toy
Height: 12–14"
Weight: 13–20 pounds

13. Pomeranians or **"Poms"** are very small, spitz-type dogs. They are lively, brave, excitable, alert, curious, happy, and occasionally stubborn. Their love of barking makes Poms excellent watchdogs. This breed learns best under the tutelage of a firm-handed trainer. The Pomeranian has a rounded, cobby body, an alert, foxlike expression, and a signature ruff of hair around her neck.

Group: Toy
Height: 7–12"
Weight: 3–7 pounds

14. The Cocker Spaniel is a small, playful, devoted dog. He needs to be with his family to be totally happy. A wonderful companion dog for a child, a Cocker must be socialized while he is young to avoid timidity. Cocker Spaniels can be difficult to housebreak. They are quite energetic and have a tendency to bark.

Group: Sporting
Height: 15.5"
Weight: 15–30 pounds

15. Rottweilers or **"Rotties"** are large, brave, loyal, and devoted. Generally a calm, mellow dog, she will fight to the death to protect her family. The Rottweiler needs competent training to remedy any overaggressive tendencies. They have great strength and endurance. With proper training, Rotties make excellent guard dogs. Because of their bulky frame and immense strength, it isn't a good idea to leave them alone with small children (Note: *Always* supervise children when dogs are around. Accidents can happen, no matter what breed your dog is).

Group: Working
Height: 24–27"
Weight: 95–130 pounds

16. The Bulldog is medium-size, loyal, and affectionate. They are friendly but can be dog-aggressive if they aren't well socialized as puppies. Bulldogs want to please their people more than anything, and they need an owner who will show leadership. Bulldogs are prone to health problems relating to

"The pug is living proof that God has a sense of humor."
— MARGOT KAUFMAN

their low-slung, yet extremely muscular, body and short muzzle. They also tend to drool and slobber, and, like many other short-muzzled dogs, they may snore. Don't be fooled by the tiny, adorable puppies of this breed; they grow up to be very powerful, strong adults with a dense, wide-shouldered body and a massive head. The Bulldog is almost always gentle and good-natured. Because of their even disposition and sturdy build (which isn't easily toppled by young children), Bulldogs make excellent family pets.

Group: Nonsporting
Height: 12–16"
Weight: 53–55 pounds

17. Shetland Sheepdogs, or **"Shelties"** as they are often known, are small, highly trainable dogs who are loving, lively, gentle, and graceful. They are also very smart and eager to please. Shelties are wonderful with children and wary of strangers. Their propensity to bark is so extreme, however, that many show dogs have their voice boxes removed (ouch!). Shelties are fast runners and nimble jumpers, exhibiting great speed and endurance. This intelligent little dog is both a great herder and an excellent family pet.

Group: Herding
Height: 13–15"
Weight: 14–18 pounds

18. The Boston Terrier is a small, well-mannered indoor dog. Because they are so alert — and like to bark — Bostons make fine watchdogs. Their gentle nature can make them a good choice for elderly pet owners. Be careful, however, to temperament test Boston puppies. This breed can be hyper, with an ability to leap to great heights. Otherwise a quick study, Bostons can be difficult to housetrain. They may also wheeze, drool, or snore, and they can overheat easily in hot weather. Some Bostons can be dog-aggressive. The Boston Terrier is a compact, well-muscled, and clean-cut dog who rarely sheds. Determined, strong, and sturdy yet affectionate and loving, the Boston Terrier is intelligent and lively. An aside: Boston Terriers aren't really terriers; instead, they're members of the Nonsporting Group.

Group: Nonsporting
Height: 15–17"
Weight: 10–25 pounds

19. The Miniature Pinscher or **"Min-Pin"** is small, intelligent, active, hardy, demanding, proud, and brave. Contrary to popular belief, the Min-Pin isn't a miniaturized version of the Doberman Pinscher. Instead, it is believed that Min-Pins, a far older breed, were bred with Rottweilers and Greyhounds to create a larger dog, the Doberman. Because they are so intelligent, Miniature Pinschers require a confident, experienced trainer. Otherwise, they won't deign to obey. If spoiled, this breed has a tendency to become bossy, even tyrannical. Min-Pins are best known for their high-stepping gait and blissful self-assurance. They are upstanding and alert, loyal to their owners, and make excellent companions.

Group: Toy
Height: 10–12"
Weight: 8–10 pounds

20. The Maltese is a very small and highly intelligent animal who loves to learn tricks. He is brave, active, lively and playful, gentle, loving, and trusting. Maltese like to bark and can be reserved with strangers. Some dogs may be difficult to train, while others can be picky eaters. The Maltese has a compact and petite body with a silky white coat. Their jaunty, flowing gait makes them appear to float as they move. The Maltese makes an excellent companion dog, and he thrives in small living spaces. Because of their petite frames and fragile demeanor, how-

"Every dog is a lion at home." — H. G. BOHN

ever, these dogs don't do well in families with young children.

Group: Toy
Height: 8–10"
Weight: 6.5–9 pounds

21. The German Shorthaired Pointer is a large, intelligent, friendly dog who needs to be with people in order to be happy. Smart and easily trainable, the German Shorthaired Pointer is also an agile, athletic hunting dog with superior scent ability. Exercise is extremely important for this highly energetic dog breed.

Group: Sporting
Height: 23–25"
Weight: 55–70 pounds

22. The Doberman Pinscher is large, intelligent, and very versatile. She is an outstanding guard dog who is determined and fearless. Dobermans (or "Dobies") thrive on daily exercise and need consistent obedience training. This breed is extremely loyal, noble, protective, and affectionate with her family. Dobermans have a compact, muscular, and powerfully athletic body capable of great endurance and speed.

Group: Working
Height: 26–28"
Weight: 66–88 pounds

23. The Siberian Husky is a medium-size dog who is smart, gentle, loving, good-natured, and great with kids. Siberians (never call them "Huskies") love everyone, making them a poor choice for guard duty. Because of their lineage — Siberians were bred to be self-determining sled dogs, able to make life or death decisions independently of their people — Siberians can be stubborn. Some are difficult to housetrain. Their success as sled dogs is due to their great strength, speed, and endurance. These dogs can have varying eye color; brown and blue are predominant, sometimes one of each. The Siberian Husky makes a great family companion if she is properly trained.

Group: Working
Height: 21–23.5"
Weight: 45–60 pounds

24. Pembroke Welsh Corgis are small, highly intelligent, trainable, and obedient. They are so courageous that they often forget their own size. This loyal and loving dog is a long, moderately low to the ground, small dog breed with large, pointy ears and a docked tail. As a member of the Herding Group, the Pembroke Welsh Corgi has a lot of stamina and makes a great working dog. With an intelligent, somewhat fox-like expression, she is an obedient dog who is very loyal to her master.

Group: Herding
Height: 10–12"
Weight: 25–30 pounds

25. The Basset Hound is a medium-size dog who is affectionate, devoted, gentle, naturally well behaved, and even-tempered, but he can be stubborn. Basset Hounds have a tendency to get fat if they don't have enough exercise. Because they are scent hounds, there is always the possibility that your dog will pick up a tantalizing scent and wander off. He may also snore and howl. Some dogs of this breed have a "houndy" odor, while others do not. Heavy-boned and thick-bodied, the Basset Hound moves slowly, though he is reputed to be an excellent climber. This breed makes a good hunting dog and an obedient, loyal family companion.

Group: Hound
Height: 14–16"
Weight: 50–70 pounds

26. The Bichon Frisé is small, cheerful, happy, charming, and lively. This dog sheds lightly, but frequent grooming of her fine, white coat is needed. The Bichon is a good choice for allergy sufferers. She can, however, be difficult to housebreak. The Bichon Frisé

> ## "Did you ever walk into a room and forget why you walked in? I think that is how dogs spend their lives." — SUE MURPHY

is a small and sturdy dog who loves to be the center of attention. She is merry and agile and does extremely well with small children and other pets. In 2001, the Bichon CH Special Times Just Right (or J.R.) won the Westminster Kennel Club Dog Show.

Group: Nonsporting
Height: 9–12"
Weight: 7–12 pounds

27. The Great Dane is an extremely large dog who is brave, loyal, gentle, dignified, and kind. Affectionate and sweet by nature, this dog can be dog-aggressive and should be trained while she is a puppy to avoid this tendency. Unfortunately, this giant breed has a short average life span (usually only six to eight years). The Great Dane needs to be around her people. Because of their majestic carriage, Danes are known as the Apollo of dogs. Great Danes make excellent family pets and they are remarkably tender with children. Despite their large size, Danes don't require as much exercise as many smaller breeds — they also thrive in smaller houses and apartments.

Group: Working
Height: 30–34"
Weight: 120–200 pounds

28. The English Springer Spaniel is a medium-size tail-wagger who loves everyone. He is brave, playful, gentle, and energetic. This breed needs a lot of exercise to be happy and can be destructive if left alone for too long. This breed has a compact body, upstanding and with proud carriage. His build suggests a combination of endurance, strength, and agility. Very eager to please, the English Springer Spaniel makes a good family pet and working dog.

Group: Sporting
Height: 19–21"
Weight: 45–55 pounds

29. Weimaraners, sometimes called the "gray ghosts," are large, intelligent, and easy to train. Some can be stubborn, but generally they are happy, loving, courageous, and devoted. Rambunctious by nature, these dogs have a very strong prey instinct; don't ever leave your Weimaraner alone with your cat. Combining endurance and speed, the Weimaraner is an outstanding hunting breed and, if trained with a steady hand, a great family dog.

Group: Sporting
Height: 24–27"
Weight: 55–70 pounds

30. The Brittany Spaniel or **"Brittany"** is a medium-size dog who is a very trainable hunter. This breed is gentle, alert, passionate, and active. They are affectionate and cheerful, with a good nature. Brittanys do like to roam, so keep a close eye on her whenever she's off-lead. These dogs need

regular, vigorous exercise and they do best with an active, outdoorsy family. Some Brittanys are hyperactive or nervous, so make sure you get your pet from a reputable breeder. The Brittany has an alert and eager expression, with fairly heavy eyebrows. They make excellent hunting dogs, as their diminutive size allows them to go where larger dogs cannot.

Group: Sporting
Height: 17–21"
Weight: 35–40 pounds

31. The West Highland White Terrier is small, cocky, playful, lively, enthusiastic, and outgoing. He is devoted to his family and is a bit more manageable than other terriers, although he is still a digger and barker. Westies love other dogs but can sometimes be a bit aggressive. Westies are elegant-looking dogs with compact, sturdy bodies. They are very affectionate and love human and animal companionship.

Group: Terrier
Height: 10–12"
Weight: 15–22 pounds

32. The Collie is a large and extremely intelligent dog who is loyal, kind, and very devoted to his family. He will respond only to gentle, respectful training. Puppies of this breed may nip at people's heels in an attempt to herd them. The Collie is easily housetrained. There are two varieties of Collie:

"Money will buy you a pretty good dog, but it won't buy the wag of his tail." — UNKNOWN

rough-coated and smooth-coated. Both kinds need to be brushed regularly to keep their fur mat-free and healthy. Collies shed a lot, but heavily only for three weeks out of the year. Thanks to Lassie, the rough variety of Collie is perhaps the most widely recognized of all dog breeds. Collies are strong, active dogs who combine speed and strength with plenty of grace. The expression of the Collie's refined face always shows alertness and intelligence.

Group: Herding
Height: 24–26"
Weight: 50–65 pounds

33. Mastiffs are very large dogs who are surprisingly calm, docile, and eager to please. They are also brave, loyal, and very protective — in short, born guard dogs. Mastiffs use their size to intimidate intruders, but they generally will not attack. These dogs are notorious droolers. Combining endurance with strength, Mastiffs are one of the heaviest of all dog breeds, sometimes reaching over two hundred pounds. Affectionate and intelligent, the Mastiff makes an excellent family pet.

Group: Working
Height: 27–30"
Weight: 150–160 pounds

34. The Australian Shepherd or "Aussie" is a medium-size, easygoing dog who loves to play with children, though he may try to herd them. Naturally protective, courageous, loyal, and affectionate, he is also highly intelligent. Aussies can get into trouble if they don't have a job to do and a lot of space to exercise in. Boredom leads many Aussies to become destructive and nervous. This breed requires a lot of interaction with their people. The Australian Shepherd is athletic, fast, and agile, with plenty of stamina. Because of their herding instincts, Aussies don't do too well with smaller dogs and other pets.

Group: Herding
Height: 22"
Weight: 50–70 pounds

35. The Cavalier King Charles Spaniel is a small lap dog who needs human companionship to be happy. This breed should not be left home alone all day long. She is a well-behaved dog who wants to please her master. Obedience training should be gentle and considerate. Cavaliers are natural-born chasers who love to play outdoors, although they don't do well in very warm temperatures. The Cavalier King Charles Spaniel has long ears and beautiful dark eyes. This breed has noteworthy senses of smell and vision, and she can successfully be used for short hunts. Loving and good-natured, the Cavalier King Charles Spaniel adores both people and other dogs.

Group: Toy
Height: 12–13"
Weight: 10–18 pounds

36. The Papillon is a tiny dog full of fun, mischievousness, and charm. This breed is easily trained for competitive obedience. They are very affectionate and love to cuddle, becoming easily attached to their owners and potentially jealous of visitors. *Papillon* means "butterfly" in French and aptly describes the appearance of this breed's ears, which look like beautiful butterfly wings.

Group: Toy
Height: 8–11"
Weight: 8–10 pounds

37. The Pekingese is a very small dog who is loving, sweet, and affectionate with his owner, but who can be distrustful of strangers. He is a loyal, calm, demanding lap dog, but not high-strung. This is a big dog in a little dog's body and is fearless to the point of folly. This little barker is very territorial and possessive of food and toys. The Pekingese has a compact, stocky, heavily built body. His flowing mane — and staunch courage — gives him a leonine appearance.

Group: Toy
Height: 6–9"
Weight: 8–10 pounds

38. The Lhasa Apso is a small, active, devoted and loving pet. In Tibet, Lhasa

While small dogs are gaining in popularity, the top dogs are still the big ones. The Labrador Retriever, Golden Retriever, and German Shepherd Dog are first, second, and third on the list of the American Kennel Club's most popular breeds.

Apsos were palace watchdogs. Dogs of this breed don't like to be teased, and they are wary of strangers. Lhasa Apsos can snap if surprised or irritated. They do best with a dominant master. Lhasa Apsos have long, sturdy bodies with long, flowing coats, which give them a leonine presence. A strong dog despite her diminutive size, the Lhasa Apso is very loyal to her family.

Group: Nonsporting
Height: 10–11"
Weight: 13–15 pounds

39. The Saint Bernard is very large, obedient, highly loyal, peaceful, and dignified. Patient with children and eager to please, this breed drools, slobbers, snores, and wheezes. Yet having a Saint Bernard in your life is more than worth the bother. This "gentle giant" is a sweet and friendly dog with a strong sense of smell. There are two varieties of Saint Bernard: longhaired and shorthaired. These large dogs require a lot of space and exercise.

Group: Working
Height: 25–27.5"
Weight: 110–200 pounds

40. Chinese Shar-Peis are medium-size dogs who are devoted and loyal to their family. Although very intelligent, Shar-Peis can be willful and require plenty of positive behavioral training. These dogs are reserved with strangers

and have strong guarding instincts. Once used as a fighting dog, the Chinese Shar-Pei has a muscular build. The signature wrinkles on the Shar-Pei's face and body enabled her to twist away when grabbed by another dog in a fight. No longer enlisted in dogfights, Shar-Peis are friendly and good-natured despite their scowling expression. Translated from Chinese, the name *Shar-Pei* literally means "sand skin."

Group: Nonsporting
Height: 18–20"
Weight: 40–55 pounds

41. The Chesapeake Bay Retriever is a large, intelligent, brave, enthusiastic, and trainable dog. He is great with children but can also be more aggressive and willful than other retrievers. The "Chessie" requires a dominant trainer with a firm hand. This dog loves to swim and retrieve and needs daily, vigorous exercise to keep him happy. Powerful retrievers with strong and muscular bodies, Chessies make good waterfowl hunters because of their extraordinary swimming ability and a tender bite, which enables them to carry (but not crush) birds under adverse conditions such as strong tides and rough water.

Group: Sporting
Height: 24–26"
Weight: 65–80 pounds

42. Cairn Terriers are very small. They are lovable, friendly, alert, and independent. Fearless, hardy, and extremely curious, Cairns are also patient and love to play with children. This breed needs a lot of attention; otherwise they may bark extensively or become destructive. Cairn Terriers require firm but gentle discipline and training. They have compact, strong bodies with water-resistant coats, and their faces have foxlike expressions. Cairn Terriers are effective watchdogs. They are also very affectionate and make superb family dogs.

Group: Terrier
Height: 10–13"
Weight: 14–18 pounds

43. The Scottish Terrier is an intelligent, lively, courageous, and charming little dog, full of character. The "Scottie" responds well to gentle and experienced training, although this alert little dog is a digger and barker at heart. The Scottie is a sturdy, strong, compact dog with short legs and erect ears. These dogs love to be coddled and make wonderful family pets. Scotties were hugely popular in the 1940s (partly due to FDR's dog, Fala), and their graphic-looking visage still graces many fashion items, from purses to jewelry.

Group: Terrier
Height: 10–11"
Weight: 19–23 pounds

> "The Airedale . . . an unrivaled mixture of brains, and clownish wit, the very ingredients one looks for in a spouse."
>
> — CHIP BROWN, CONNOISSEUR

44. The Akita is large, dignified, good-natured, alert, bold, courageous, and loyal. This breed can also be docile, intelligent, fearless, and willful. Akitas need firm training while they are still puppies. They can be very aggressive with other dogs and should be supervised. Akitas are good with *their* (human) children but may not accept unfamiliar ones. Akitas can be food-possessive. Originally bred in Japan to hunt bears, this breed is large and powerful, with heavy bones, a muscular body, and a strong muzzle. He has a powerful, brisk gait. Faithful and affectionate, the Akita loves human companionship.

Group: Working
Height: 27"
Weight: 80–120 pounds

45. The Vizsla is a lightly built, muscular medium-size dog. She is intelligent, loving, friendly, and gentle. Vizslas thrive with extensive daily exercise and can become neurotic if they don't get outside enough. This breed possesses great speed and grace in her gait. The Vizsla is a very energetic dog who is most happy when she has something to do. Alas, these Hungarian beauties are also notorious chewers.

Group: Sporting
Height: 22–26"
Weight: 45–60 pounds

46. The Newfoundland or **"Newfie"** is a very large, loyal, devoted, calm, gentle, good-natured, sweet, and brave drooler. They become very attached to their owners and are patient and playful with children. Newfies love water and despite their burly size they are excellent swimmers. In fact, Newfies have been known to rescue drowning victims with seemingly little effort. The Newfoundland is a wonderful family dog.

Group: Working
Height: 27–29"
Weight: 130–150 pounds

47. The Bernese Mountain Dog is large, gentle, loyal, affectionate, quiet, and very devoted. Like many working dogs, she is willing and very trainable. Bernese Mountain Dogs can be slow to mature, remaining puppylike for many years. This breed isn't suited to backyard kennel life; she needs to be with her people and requires vigorous daily exercise. Bernese Mountain Dogs have a black coat trimmed with symmetrical markings of white and rust. They shed heavily and seasonally. The Bernese Mountain Dog's thick coat does not fare well in hot or humid climates. Sadly, this beautiful animal is susceptible to certain canine illnesses and has a relatively short life span.

Make sure to get your dog from a reputable breeder to reduce this risk.

Group: Working
Height: 25–28"
Weight: 80–115 pounds

48. The Bullmastiff is a huge and powerful dog who is affectionate and very devoted to his family. This breed is especially loyal and makes a fearless guard dog. Bullmastiffs are good-natured, but they can be stubborn. Make sure your Bullmastiff receives obedience training and has a dominant owner who can show leadership. These dogs should socialize with other animals and people while they are still puppies. The Bullmastiff is more aggressive than one of its hereditary progenitors, the Mastiff. The Bullmastiff has a broad, wrinkled head and a tapering tail. They do tend to drool, slobber, and snore. True to his name, the Bullmastiff is descended from Bulldogs and Mastiffs, creating a very vigilant, strong dog with endurance and stamina to spare. The Bullmastiff is a natural guardian of home and family.

Group: Working
Height: 25–27"
Weight: 110–132 pounds

49. The Bloodhound is a large, friendly dog who loves everyone. He is good-natured, patient, docile, lovable, and excellent with children. Bloodhounds are very energetic dogs who love the outdoors. Because they can be willful, this breed needs firm but gentle training. Bloodhounds like to bay and may take off after an interesting scent, so make sure that this superior scent hound has a fenced-in, secure space. Bloodhounds drool, slobber, and snore. This large and powerful dog has wrinkled skin and drooping ears, both of which aid his natural ability to scent and track. Because of these skills, Bloodhounds are often used in police searches and investigations. A gentle dog breed, the Bloodhound does well with children and other family pets.

Group: Hound
Height: 25–27"
Weight: 90–110 pounds

50. The Airedale Terrier is a medium-size dog. Playful and rowdy as a puppy, the Airedale is dignified and courageous as an adult. This terrier is protective, with a strong desire to please his people. Dogs of this breed do, however, have a tendency to be scrappy with other animals. Though sensitive and responsive, Airedales still need firm and consistent obedience training. Airedale Terriers are independent and territorial. They make good watchdogs and excellent hunting dogs.

Group: Terrier
Height: 22–24"
Weight: 50–60 pounds

The 15 Least Common Breeds in the United States

In descending order of popularity:

1. Sealyham Terriers
2. Canaan Dogs
3. Dandie Dinmont Terriers
4. German Pinschers
5. Plott Hounds
6. American Foxhounds
7. Komondor
8. Pharaoh Hounds
9. Skye Terriers
10. Finnish Spitz
11. Ibizan Hounds
12. Irish Water Spaniels
13. English Foxhounds
14. Harriers
15. Otterhounds

"Not Carnegie, Vanderbilt, and Astor together could have raised money enough to buy a quarter share in my little dog."
— ERNEST THOMPSON SETON, AMERICAN WRITER AND NATURALIST

152 AKC-Recognized Breeds

The term *breed* is defined by the AKC as "a homogeneous group of animals within a given species . . . developed and maintained by man." Although there are hundreds of dog breeds, the AKC recognizes only upwards of 150 specific breeds. These are divided into seven distinct groups indicating the purpose for which each dog was bred — herding, retrieval, or hunting, for example. The list of recognized breeds below is divided into the groups to which they belong.

Working Dogs

Portuguese
Water Dog

Akita
Alaskan Malamute
Anatolian Shepherd
Bernese Mountain Dog
Black Russian Terrier
Boxer
Bullmastiff
Doberman Pinscher
German Pinscher
Giant Schnauzer
Great Dane
Great Pyrenees
Greater Swiss Mountain Dog
Komondor
Kuvasz
Mastiff
Neapolitan Mastiff
Newfoundland
Portuguese Water Dog
Rottweiler
Saint Bernard
Samoyed
Siberian Husky
Standard Schnauzer

Herding Dogs

Belgian Malinois

Australian Cattle Dog
Australian Shepherd
Bearded Collie
Belgian Malinois
Belgian Sheepdog
Belgian Tervuren
Border Collie
Bouvier des Flandres
Briard
Canaan Dog
Cardigan Welsh Corgi
Collie
German Shepherd Dog
Old English Sheepdog
Pembroke Welsh Corgi
Polish Lowland Sheepdog
Puli
Shetland Sheepdog

Terriers

Norwich Terrier

Airedale Terrier
American Staffordshire Terrier
Australian Terrier
Bedlington Terrier
Black Russian Terrier
Border Terrier
Bull Terrier
Cairn Terrier
Dandie Dinmont Terrier
Irish Terrier
Glen Imaal Terrier
Kerry Blue Terrier
Lakeland Terrier
Manchester Terrier
Miniature Bull Terrier
Miniature Schnauzer
Norfolk Terrier
Norwich Terrier
Parson Russell Terrier
Scottish Terrier
Sealyham Terrier
Skye Terrier
Smooth Fox Terrier
Soft-Coated Wheaten Terrier
Staffordshire Bull Terrier
Welsh Terrier
West Highland
Wire Fox Terrier

The smallest breed of dog recognized by the American Kennel Club is the Chihuahua, which stands six to nine inches at the top of the shoulders and weighs two to six pounds. The tallest is the Irish Wolfhound, which stands thirty to thirty-five inches at the top of the shoulders and weighs 105 to 125 pounds.

Toy Dogs

Chihuahua

Affenpinscher

Brussels Griffon

Cavalier King Charles Spaniel

Chihuahua

Chinese Crested

English Toy Spaniel

Havanese

Italian Greyhound

Japanese Chin

Maltese

Manchester Terrier

Miniature Pinscher

Papillon

Pekingese

Pomeranian

Pug

Shih Tzu

Silky Terrier

Toy Fox Terrier

Toy Poodle

Yorkshire Terrier

Nonsporting Dogs

American Eskimo Dog

Bichon Frisé

Boston Terrier

Bulldog

Chinese Shar-Pei

Chow Chow

Dalmatian

Finnish Spitz

French Bulldog

Keeshond

Lhasa Apso

Löwchen

Schipperke

Shiba Inu

Standard Poodle

Tibetan Spaniel

Tibetan Terrier

Hounds
Sight Hounds

Greyhound

Afghan Hound

Borzoi

Greyhound

Ibizan Hound

Rhodesian Ridgeback

Saluki

Whippet

Scent Hounds

Bloodhound

Basenji

Basset Hound

Beagle

Black-and-Tan Coonhound

Bloodhound

Dachshund

Foxhound

Harrier

Irish Wolfhound

Norwegian Elkhound

Otter Hound

Petit Basset Griffon Vendéen

Pharaoh Hound

Scottish Deerhound

Sporting Dogs
Pointers

English Setter

German Shorthaired Pointer

Gordon Setter

Irish Setter

Pointer

Viszla (or Hungarian Pointer)

Wirehaired Pointing Griffon

Retrievers

Chesapeake Bay Retriever

Curly-Coated Retriever

Flat-Coated Retriever

Golden Retriever

Labrador Retriever

Weimaraner

Spaniels

American Water Spaniel

Brittany Spaniel

Clumber Spaniel

Cocker Spaniel

English Cocker Spaniel

English Springer Spaniel

Field Spaniel

Irish Water Spaniel

Sussex Spaniel

Welsh Springer Spaniel

The 3 Breeds Most Recently Recognized by the AKC

1. **The Black Russian Terrier** is a large dog initially developed by the Soviet military to withstand harsh Russian winters. Her abilities are comparable to those of the German Shepherd Dog, but she does not have any of the Shepherd's tendencies toward aggression. This breed received full AKC acceptance on September 1, 2001.

2. **The Glen of Imaal Terrier** is a small dog who resembles the Welsh Corgi in that he has a long and slender body. This terrier originated in Glen of Imaal, in County Wicklow, Ireland. He also attained full AKC recognition on September 1, 2001.

3. **The Neapolitan Mastiff** is an immense dog with an enormous head and a wrinkled face. She was originally bred by the Romans for use in war and arena spectacles. The Neapolitan Mastiff gained AKC acceptance on May 1, 2004.

How a Breed Becomes Recognized by the AKC

According to the American Kennel Club, the recognition of a new breed begins with a written request to compete in what is known as the Miscellaneous Class. Once a dog has been accepted into this class (by meeting the criteria listed below), he can then be assigned to one of the seven groups.

To be eligible for consideration to become an AKC-recognized breed, the following general criteria must be met:

1. A demonstrated following and interest (minimum of one hundred active household members) in the breed in the form of a national breed club.

2. A sufficient population in this country (minimum of 300–400 dogs), with a three-generation pedigree. Dogs in this pedigree must all be of the same breed.

3. The breed must have populations in twenty or more states.

4. The AKC must review and approve the club's breed standard as well as the club's constitution and bylaws. Breed observations must be completed by the AKC's field staff.

5. If there is sufficient interest and work being done in the development of breed, it can then be submitted to the AKC board of directors for consideration to compete in the Miscellaneous Class.

6. It generally takes between one to three years of competition in the Miscellaneous Class before a new breed can be considered. By the end of the first year, the national breed club or parent club for this breed must provide the AKC with the number of dogs and litters recorded as well as the number of dogs who have been competing. The club must prove that a sufficient number of local and national shows have been judged and that breed seminars have been conducted. Once all these criteria are met, the breed can be presented to the AKC board of directors for official recognition.

The Canary Islands were not named for a bird called a canary. They were named after a breed of large dogs. The Latin name was **Canariae insulae**—"Island of Dogs."

31 Extinct Dog Breeds

The following dog breeds are commonly believed to be extinct. Very little has been written about them and the dates of their extinction are largely unknown. As with all creatures who become extinct, there can be a variety of reasons that a particular dog breed suddenly ceases to exist. Sometimes it's physical — the result of a disease that a particular breed is susceptible to, or a weakness in their constitution that makes caring for them difficult, causing people to lose interest and instead focus on other breeds. Extinction can also be caused by drastic cultural change, such as when the Cuban Revolution almost rendered the adorable Havanese extinct. In Japan, the Akita almost became extinct due to excessive dogfighting during the Meiji period (the late nineteenth century and early twentieth century). This noble breed was threatened again during World War II when starving Japanese citizens relied on his meat to sustain them. But extinction isn't always the result of calamity. The particular traits inherent in one dog breed may no longer be valued by society. Without active breeding programs, these domesticated animals no longer have viable populations. While certain breeds such as the New Guinea Singing Dog and the Manchester Terrier have been brought back from near extinction, many others are lost to history. Listed here are the names of extinct breeds and their (former) countries of origin:

1. Bärenbeisser (Central Europe)
2. Basketmaker Dog (United States)
3. Black Bobtail (Australia)
4. Bouvier de Moerman (France, Belgium)
5. Bouvier de Paret (France, Belgium)
6. Brabantse Bullenbijter (Netherlands, Belgium)
7. Bullenbeiser (Germany)
8. Céris Hound (France)
9. Chincha Bulldog (Peru)
10. Chinese Happa Dog (China)
11. Cordoba Bulldog (Argentina)
12. Dogo Cubano (Cuba)
13. Dogue du Midi (France)
14. Drover's Cur (United Kingdom)
15. Dutch Mastiff (Holland)
16. English Red Decoy Dog (United Kingdom)
17. English Staghound (United Kingdom)
18. Garpehund (Norway)
19. Gawi (Afghanistan)
20. Havanese Silk Dog (Cuba)
21. Hubert Hound (United Kingdom)
22. Indian Hairless Dog (India)
23. Mâtin Corse (France)
24. Mordashka (Russia)
25. Old English Black-and-Tan Terrier (United Kingdom)
26. Renegade Bulldog (United Kingdom)
27. Reznicky Pes (Czech Republic)
28. Tahltan Bear Dog (Canada)
29. Tengger Dog (Java)
30. Tesem (Egypt)
31. Tweed Water Spaniel (United Kingdom)

The Dingo of Australia and the New Guinea Singing Dog are the oldest breeds — the last existing representatives of early dogs developed in southwestern Asia including Israel and Iran. These dogs are thought to have eventually traveled to Southeast Asia, Australia, and New Guinea.

Life Expectancy of 68 Popular Dog Breeds

The average life span of the North American and European dog is 12.8 years, a large increase in life span over the past hundred years, mostly attributable to improvements in diet and medical care. In general, larger dogs live shorter lives than smaller dogs, mostly because the bodies of large dogs must work harder (and are therefore more stressed) than the bodies of small dogs. That said, the life expectancy of any one dog in particular is also determined by the stresses in his life (both physical and psychological), what he eats, and how well he is cared for.

In descending order:

Bichon Frisé (15)

Boston Terrier (15)

Miniature Pinscher (15)

Papillon (15)

Toy Poodle (14.4)

Bedlington Terrier (14.3)

Tibetan Terrier (14.3)

Whippet (14.3)

Petit Basset Griffon Vendéen (14)

Border Terrier (13.8)

Parson Russell Terrier (13.6)

Chow Chow (13.5)

Shih Tzu (13.4)

Beagle (13.3)

Cairn Terrier (13.2)

Pekingese (13.3)

Shetland Sheepdog (13.3)

Greyhound (13.2)

Border Collie (13.0)

Chihuahua (13.0)

Dalmatian (13.0)

English Springer Spaniel (13.0)

Wire Fox Terrier (13.0)

Bull Terrier (12.9)

Irish Red and White Setter (12.9)

Basset Hound (12.8)

West Highland White Terrier (12.8)

Yorkshire Terrier (12.8)

Labrador Retriever (12.6)

Cocker Spaniel (12.5)

Vizsla (12.5)

Bearded Collie (12.3)

German Shorthaired Pointer (12.3)

Dachshund (12.2)

Rough Collie (12.2)

Afghan Hound (12.0)

Golden Retriever (12.0)

Pug (12.0)

Scottish Terrier (12.0)

Standard Poodle (12.0)

English Cocker Spaniel (11.8)

Irish Setter (11.8)

Old English Sheepdog (11.8)

Welsh Springer Spaniel (11.5)

Corgi (11.3)

Gordon Setter (11.3)

Airedale Terrier (11.2)

English Setter (11.2)

Samoyed (11.0)

Cavalier King Charles Spaniel (10.7)

Boxer (10.4)

German Shepherd Dog (10.3)

English Toy Spaniel (10.1)

Norfolk Terrier (10.0)

Staffordshire Bull Terrier (10.0)

Weimaraner (10.0)

Doberman Pinscher (9.8)

Rottweiler (9.8)

Flat-Coated Retriever (9.5)

Scottish Deerhound (9.5)

Rhodesian Ridgeback (9.1)

Japanese Chin (9)

Saint Bernard (9)

Bullmastiff (8.6)

Great Dane (8.4)

Bernese Mountain Dog (7.0)

Bulldog (6.7)

Irish Wolfhound (6.2)

> The smallest of the recognized dog breeds, the Chihuahua, is named for the region of Mexico where they were first discovered in the mid-nineteenth century. The Chihuahua can live anywhere from eleven to eighteen years.

Bernese Mountain Dog

30 American Dog Breeds

With her origins dating back more than 20,000 years, the domestic dog boasts more different varieties than any other mammal. Throughout her history, the domestic dog's skill as a hunter, tracker, herder, guardian, or companion helped to nurture the relationship she had with man. It was primarily humans' desire to improve and modify the characteristics of their dogs that led to the great variety of breeds we see today. But other factors, such as war, geographical change, politics, religion, and trade routes, also played significant roles. The following list comprises breeds who originated on the Northern American continent, or breeds from other countries who served as the foundation for what are now considered classic American dog breeds.

1. **American Bandogge Mastiff.** The word *Bandog* originates with the Saxon word *Banda,* which means "chain," and a chain was used to tie down this powerful breed. A cross between an American Pit Bull Terrier and a Neapolitan Mastiff, this is a huge dog with a menacing appearance who first appeared in the 1960s.

2. **American Black-and-Tan Coonhound.** This breed is sometimes called "the black-and-tan." With their droopy skin and long pendant ears, these dogs resemble Bloodhounds but are not as heavily boned. They are, in fact, descended from the Talbot Hound, who was common in England during the eleventh century — and America's Virginia Foxhound. Simon Kenton and the Poe brothers, who were noted scouts and Indian fighters, were the first to foster this active, powerful hound in the late 1700s.

3. **American Blue Gascon Hound.** Also known as "Big 'n' Blue" and "Bluetick," this dog is the result of crossing an American Foxhound with a Mastiff. These large, agile dogs have droopy ears and a well-balanced gait. They are often recognized by their long, deep bawl and bugle voices.

4. **American Bulldog.** In an effort to save this uncommon breed from extinction, a breeder named John D. Johnson gathered these dogs from around the rural South and began mating them. The American Bulldog is an intelligent, extremely sturdy breed who is very protective and has great stamina. They resemble the English Bulldog but are larger, with more speed and agility.

5. **American Bullnese.** The American Bullnese was developed in 1989 by a breeder named Robert E. Rice of Florida by crossing the French Bulldog with the Pekingese. The resulting dog has a short nose, stumpy legs, an elongated body, and a wonderful, clownish personality.

6. **American Cane Corso.** This breed originated from Neapolitan Mastiffs brought to America in 1988 from Italy by a man named Michael Sottile who wanted to breed a smaller and more athletic Mastiff-type dog by crossing three individual litters from different parts of Italy. The Cane Corso has an elegant, powerful body and a massive head. His expression is almost always dignified and proud.

7. **American Cocker Spaniel.** This breed dates back to the landing of the *Mayflower* in 1620 when field and water spaniels were first brought to America. These small, compact dogs were commonly used by game bird hunters. Their long hanging ears, rounded heads, and silky, medium-length feathered coat make them extremely attractive dogs who can easily retrieve birds in heavy brush.

8. **American Eskimo Dog** or **"Eskie."** This breed is descended from White German Spitz dogs who originated around 3,000 years ago, and not from working sled dogs as is commonly believed. German immigrants brought this breed to America in the 1600s. The name of the breed was changed from German Spitz to American Eskimo Dog because of anti-German sentiment during World War I. The "Eskie" often performed in circus acts in the early part of the twentieth century. They are extremely intelligent dogs who like to please their people.

9. **American Feist.** This breed dates back to the American Indians and the early colonial period. A small dog who re-

sembles a Rat Terrier, the American Feist has an extraordinary sense of sight, hearing, and smell and thus developed a reputation as an excellent squirrel-hunting dog.

10. **American Foxhound.** European settlers brought Foxhounds to America in the mid-1600s. George Washington took an active role in breeding these dogs (he was an avid hunter) and is largely responsible for their popularity today. American Foxhounds are larger than their English counterparts, with broad pendant ears and pleading eyes that give them a compelling expression.

11. **American Hairless Terrier.** This breed arose by accident when a hairless Rat Terrier puppy was born into an otherwise normal litter in 1972. The female, named Josephine, eventually gave birth to a male and female puppy who were later bred. This breed is still under development.

12. **American Indian Dog.** This indigenous breed can be traced back more than 30,000 years in both North and South America. Used as pack animals, they were valued for their hunting, herding, and guarding abilities, as well as for their fur. Once almost extinct, this dog — with his long, pricked ears — is now being selectively bred to improve his natural balance, his primitive instincts, and his abilities as a good worker.

13. **American Lamalese.** This is a crossbreed between a Lhasa Apso and a Maltese. The breed was first developed in San Francisco in the 1960s, and these dogs quickly gained popularity because of their sweet temperament.

14. **American Lo-Sze Pugg™.** A dog breeder named Rebecca Manns developed this breed. Her interest in modern-day Chinese Pugs led her to try to recreate the long-extinct ancient Chinese dog known as the Lo-Sze. Manns felt that her new breed of Lo-Sze was more akin to the Lo-Sze of ancient China.

15. **Alaskan Malamute.** This large breed, with his coarse double coat and wolflike eyes, dates back to prehistoric man and his migration from the Asian continent to Greenland. Many varieties of this dog were developed over thousands of years and have appeared in Greenland, Canada, and other northern regions. The name of this breed refers to an Alaskan tribe called the Mahlemut.

16. **American Mastiff.** This breed resulted from a cross between an English Mastiff and either an Anatolian Mastiff or Anatolian Shepherd. She is identical to the English Mastiff in every way except that the American variety doesn't drool as much. Fredericka Wagner of Piketon, Ohio, is credited with developing this dry-mouthed Mastiff.

17. **American Mastiff (Panja).** Originally bred by drug dealers to protect their homes and property, this dog first appeared in Detroit and was the result of crossbreeding Mastiffs with Rottweilers and Pit Bulls.

18. **American Pit Bull Terrier.** Crosses between Bulldogs and various terriers led to the development of this breed, first brought to America in the early 1800s by immigrants from Ireland, England, and Scotland. They were originally bred for use as farm dogs.

19. **American Pointer.** This breed originated with pointers who were brought to England after the War of Spanish Succession in 1713. These Spanish Pointers were then crossed with Italian Pointers, creating the American variety. Pointers first appeared in America around the time of the Civil War. They are typically solid-colored in orange, liver, black, or lemon, or with these colors in combination with white.

20. **Australian Shepherd.** The Australian Shepherd or "Aussie" isn't from Australia at all. Instead, he probably originated in the mountainous Basque regions between France and Spain but came from Australia to the United States with Basque sheepherders in the 1800s. He is, however, a purely American breed. Also known as pastor dogs, bobtails, and heelers, Aussies are attentive and loyal. They make amazing farm and ranch dogs. The breed has four different and very striking coat variations with white markings around the face, neck, chest, belly, and legs.

Dogs can hear sounds that are too faint for us to hear, and they also can hear noises at a much higher frequency than we can. **Their hearing is so good that they probably rely more on sound than on sight** to navigate their world.

21. American Staffordshire Terrier or "AmStaff." This dog has her origins in the early nineteenth century. Cross-breeding between Bulldogs and terriers resulted in this breed, first developed for farm work, hunting, and guarding. Though the history of the AmStaff includes her training as a fighting dog, today she is a successful family companion. The AmStaff closely resembles the American Pit Bull Terrier, but unlike the Pit Bull she is recognized by the AKC.

22. American Staghound. This breed originated from the Scottish Deerhound and the Greyhound. He has been bred for more than a hundred years to be a strong and fast runner. These make wonderful hunting dogs, able to bring down even the largest deer. In appearance, the American Staghound resembles a shaggy Greyhound.

23. American Tundra Shepherd. This breed was produced by crossing the Alaskan Tundra Wolf with the German Shepherd Dog as part of a 1970s government project called the "Superdog" project, the goal of which was to produce a superior shepherd dog.

24. American Water Spaniel. Although the origins of this breed are vague, she is known to be one of only five breeds completely indigenous to the United States. The breed first appeared along the Wolf and Fox river valleys of Wisconsin and is believed to be a cross between an Irish Water Spaniel and a Curly-Coated Retriever. She has a tightly curled or wavy outer coat and a protective undercoat. The American Water Spaniel is the state dog of Wisconsin.

25. American White Shepherd. This breed is a direct ancestor of the German Shepherd Dog and has not been mixed with any other breeds. His white color is attributed to a genetic mutation of German Shepherd Dogs.

26. American Wolfdog. The earliest records of a wolf-dog crossbreed dates back 8,000 years and were found primarily in what is now the state of Wyoming. There has also been evidence of wolf-dogs in the Ukraine.

27. Boston Terrier. This breed originated in the United States, through a mixture of the English Bulldog and a white English Terrier. They have been referred to as "American gentlemen" because of their black-and-white tuxedo-type markings. This is a friendly, comical dog.

28. Chesapeake Bay Retriever. A true American breed, the Chesapeake Bay Retriever is traced back to 1807 when two Newfoundland puppies were rescued from a British shipwreck and were then crossed with local retrievers. Excellent swimmers even in frigid waters, these big, beautiful dogs are ideal for retrieving ducks. "Chessies" are light to medium brown in color, with intense yellow- or amber-colored eyes. The official dog of Maryland, the Chesapeake Bay Retriever has webbed toes.

29. Plott Hound. This breed dates back to the late 1700s and is classified as a Coonhound. The Plott, with her long, large ears, has a legendary reputation as a hunting dog, a courageous fighter, and tenacious tracker. Her webbed toes make her an excellent swimmer. She is the official state dog of North Carolina.

30. Toy Fox Terrier. These dogs are descended from the larger Smooth Fox Terriers who originated in England during the mid-1800s. American owners of this breed discovered that the smallest dogs of a litter turned out to be the feistiest, and so they proceeded to breed miniatures. Breeders have reduced this dog's size down from twenty pounds to seven.

17 Royal Breeds

Throughout history, dogs have found favor with royalty and in noble households. Some of these dogs became the favorites of royals because of the specific tasks they could perform, while some of them became so revered that they were actually deified. The following dogs have received a great deal attention at various royal courts during various times in history.

1. The **Beagle** came into prominence in the 1300s and 1400s, during the days of King Henry VII of England. Henry kept packs of Glove Beagles that were so small they could actually fit into a glove. The breed's popularity further increased during the reign of Elizabeth I, who was fond of Pocket Beagles who were only nine inches high. Charles II and George IV used Beagles for hunting. Later on, Prince Albert hunted rabbit with his Beagles.

2. The **Bichon Frisé** first appeared in France during the reign of Francis I in the early 1500s. The popularity of the Bichon grew under Henry III in the later part of the sixteenth century. It is said that King Henry loved his Bichon so much that he took him everywhere he went. The dog was placed in a basket that Henry wore around his neck. This practice was then adopted by everyone at his court.

3. The **Brussels Griffon** gained her first notoriety in the court of Brussels when Queen Henrietta Maria took a liking to this breed and became its patroness. The breed found favor with the nobility and eventually gained popularity in England and other countries in Europe. The Brussels Griffon almost became extinct after World War I, but thanks to the efforts of Belgium's Queen Astrid, she regained her popularity.

4. The **Cavalier King Charles Spaniel** got his name from Charles I and Charles II of England, but these kings certainly weren't the only admirers of this gentle breed. Other royal fans included Mary, Queen of Scots, the Duke of Marlborough, and, later on, Queen Victoria, whose dog Dash gained national notoriety and was given the royal treatment by everyone at her court.

5. The **Coton de Tulear**, a Bichon-like dog, appeared in Madagascar during the seventeenth century at the slave-trading port of Tulear. He was favored by the Merina, a tribal monarchy that existed at the time. The Coton de Tulear was named the "Royal Dog of Madagascar." Ownership of this breed was restricted to royal families. It was a criminal offense for anyone other than a noble to own one.

6. The **Dachshund** first arrived in Germany when Maximillian, the heir of the Hapsburgs, came to marry the Duke of Burgundy's daughter in the mid-fifteenth century. His future father in-law, also known as Charles the Bold, kept thousands of these hounds. In the mid-1800s, Prince Edward of Sax-Weimar sent a number of these dogs to England.

7. The **Great Pyrenees** is considered an aristocratic relative of the Saint Bernard and the Newfoundland. She became popular among the French nobility because of her ability as a guard dog. In 1675, Louis XIV named her the Royal Dog of France.

8. Although named the **"Japanese" Chin**, this breed was actually developed in an area close to Beijing, China. In the first century A.D. Japanese Chins were known as lion dogs, and they were the prized companions of Emperor Ming Ti, who abandoned his faith and converted to Buddhism. Ming Ti believed that lion dogs were touched by Buddha, and, hence, the white spot on their forehead is called "Buddha's Thumbprint."

9. The **Lhasa Apso**, one of the world's most ancient breeds (possibly dating as far back as 800 B.C.), was developed in Tibetan monasteries. Because they symbolized the lion, the Lhasa Apso was thought to protect the Buddha and the monasteries' treasures. These dogs also participated in religious ceremonies and were enthroned on small silk cushions. Only a Lama or a high-ranking dignitary could own one of these "lion dogs."

10. The **Maltese** lived in ancient Egypt, and Phoenician traders may have

brought them to Malta and the surrounding Mediterranean countries. These delightful little animals were owned by kings and queens and were a favorite at the Maltan court. They were first imported to England during the reign of Henry VIII and became one of the favorite breeds of Queen Elizabeth I.

11. The Papillon, once known as the Continental Toy Spaniel, dates back almost seven hundred years in continental Europe. It is believed that Marie Antoinette changed the breed's name to Papillon, likening its ears to the wings of a butterfly. These dogs were a favorite of the French court, and they were especially popular with Henry III and Madame de Pompadour. The Papillon is featured in many Renaissance paintings.

12. The origins of the Pekingese, or "Peke," dates back as far as 2000 B.C. This dog was worshiped in the temples of China for centuries. An emperor would choose four Pekes as his bodyguards. Two of these dogs would precede him, and by barking would signal his arrival. At the same time, the other two dogs would follow the emperor and gently hold the hem of his royal robe in their mouths. When an emperor died, his dogs were killed so that they could accompany their master to the afterlife.

13. The Pug first appeared in the courts of Europe during the sixteenth century and reached the peak of his popularity during the Renaissance. This breed was a favorite of Henry II of France and Marie Antoinette. A Pug is actually

credited with saving the life of William, Prince of Orange, by barking and alerting him to attacking Spaniards. Empress Josephine used her Pug, Fortune, to deliver messages to Napoleon while he was in prison. The Pug was introduced to England by William and Mary.

14. The Saluki, the royal dog of Egypt, is considered a sacred gift from Allah. Her origins go back to the time of the Pharaohs. These dogs were often found mummified along with the Pharaohs themselves. Salukis were held in high regard by their masters and were called "el hor," which means "the noble." A pair of Salukis was given to Lady Florence Amherst in the late 1800s, and she was so enamored of these dogs that she sponsored their recognition in England.

15. The Shih Tzu is an ancient cross between the Lhasa Apso and the Pekingese. Dalai Lamas would on occasion present a number of Lhasa Apsos as gifts to the emperors of China during the Manchu dynasty in the seventeenth century. In the Forbidden City, Chinese royalty crossed this dog with the Pekingese and developed the Shih Tzu. This breed remained unknown to the West until the early twentieth century.

16. The Scottish Deerhound or "royal dog of Scotland" commanded such respect by the great lords during medieval times that no one ranking below earl was permitted to own this breed. Queen Victoria became a fan of the Scottish Deerhound. Sir Walter Scott loved his dog Maida so much that he

described her as "the most perfect creature of heaven."

17. The Welsh Corgi is known the world over for his patronage by the current British royal family. A great deal has been written about the hold these dogs have on Queen Elizabeth II. The Pembroke Welsh Corgi, a generally calmer and gentler dog, became the favorite of the royal family at the expense of the popularity of the Cardigan Welsh Corgi.

His Majesty King Edward VII with Caesar, ca. 1908

39 Breeds of the British Isles

1. The **Airedale Terrier**, a large terrier with a harsh and wiry coat, was originally known as the Waterside Terrier and sometimes as the Bingley Terrier. Developed in the early twentieth century, this breed was created by crossing the Old English Black-and-Tan Terrier with the Otterhound.

2. It is believed that the **Bedlington Terrier**, which in many ways resembles a sheep, may have been brought to England by gypsies—hence his nickname, "gypsy dog." Lord Rothbury of Bedlington was responsible for fostering and improving this breed by using the Otterhound and possibly the Dandie Dinmont Terrier.

3. **Bloodhounds** are believed to date back more than 1,000 years and were perfected by the Monks of St. Hubert in Belgium. This large and powerful breed, with her long ears and loose, wrinkled skin, was brought to England by William the Conqueror in 1066. The Bloodhound is credited with being the forerunner to numerous other hound breeds, including the American Coonhound and the Brazilian *Fila Brasileiro.*

4. In 1830, the **Bull Terrier** was created by crossing the Bulldog with the Old English Terrier. She was originally bred to be a fighting dog but eventually proved to be a better pet than a fighter. The white-coated variety, nicknamed the "white cavalier," is especially popular. Spuds MacKenzie was a Bull Terrier.

5. The **Cairn Terrier**, or **"Toto" dog**, is now the most popular terrier in England. He is also thought to be one of the oldest dog breeds, having originated in the highlands of the Western Isles of Scotland. Cairn Terriers served as the foundation stock for the Scottish Terrier.

6. The **Cardigan Welsh Corgi**, distinguished by her long and erect ears, is descended from Swedish Vallhunds who were brought to Wales by the Celts in about 1200 B.C. She is believed to be in part descended from the early Dachshund. The name Corgi is derived from the Celtic word for dog.

7. **Clumber Spaniels** were first developed in France in the late 1700s by the Duke of Noailles. When the French Revolution broke out, the duke, fearing the destruction of the breed, sent his dogs to England's Duke of Newcastle. This short, thickset, and heavy dog is believed to have been a cross between the Alpine Spaniel and several other ancient breeds.

8. The **Dandie Dinmont Terrier** was named after a character of the same name in Sir Walter Scott's novel *Guy Mannering.* He is one of the oldest terrier breeds and appeared during the early 1700s in the border country between England and Scotland. He has a large, round head and a body that is longer than it is tall.

9. The **English Bulldog** traces his roots back to the thirteenth century B.C., when the ferocious Alaunt, a powerful and vicious dog, was brought to Britain by Phoenician traders. The Alaunt served as the foundation for the English Bulldog, who was initially bred for bull baiting in the bull-fighting ring. An aside: This dog was also expected to fight bulls.

10. **English Cocker Spaniels**, as with all the dogs in the spaniel family, originated in Spain. They were used as hunting dogs in England, where they were bred into seven distinct breeds: the Clumber, the Sussex, the Welsh Springer, the English Springer, the Field, the Irish Water, and the Cocker. The English Cocker Spaniel is the smallest of all spaniels.

11. **English Mastiffs** are the descendants of Mastiff dogs who were brought to England by the Romans between 50 B.C. and A.D. 400. British landowners used these massive dogs, originally bred as fighting dogs, to ward off game poachers.

English Pointer

12. The **English Pointer** has a powerful, graceful, and aristocratic appearance. This breed arose from crossing

Spanish pointers with a variety of other breeds including the Foxhound, Greyhound, Newfoundland, Spanish Setter, and Bull Terrier. This breed can be traced back to 1650s England.

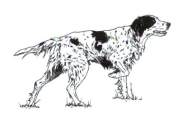

English Setter

13. The **English Setter**, with his elegant and uniquely speckled coat, can be traced to France in the 1500s when the first basic setter was developed. French and Spanish pointers were bred to create the first rudimentary setter, which was bred in England in the 1800s by Sir Edward Laverack. The modern-day English Setter owes his appearance to the efforts of the breeder R. Purcell Llewellin.

14. The **English Springer Spaniel** traces her history back to before the 1500s when spaniels were brought to Britain from Spain. The English Springer Spaniel was bred to serve as a land dog, unlike the water variety. She has served as foundation stock for all other land spaniel breeds except for the Clumber Spaniel.

15. The **English Toy**, or **Cavalier King Charles**, **Spaniel** is believed to derive from Asian spaniels and possibly the Pug. Bred entirely in Britain, the English Toy became the favorite of King Charles II. At first the dog took on the appearance of a small Cocker Spaniel. Centuries of crosses with various Asian breeds, however, resulted in a smaller dog with a rounded head, flattened face, and prominent eyes.

16. The **Irish Setter** or **"Red Setter,"** with her silky, highly feathered mahogany-colored coat, was achieved by crossing various spaniels, setters, and Spanish pointers. The Red and White Setter was also used in the breeding of the Red, which eventually surpassed the Red and White in popularity.

17. The **Irish Water Spaniel**, with his curly coat but hairless face, is the largest of all spaniels. He was developed in Ireland prior to the mid-nineteenth century. Two theories surround his origins: one holds that he was the result of a cross between the North and South Country Water Spaniels; another is that he originated from crossing the Poodle with the Curly-Coated Retriever.

18. The exact origin of the **Glen of Imaal Terrier** is not known, but she first appeared in county Wicklow, Ireland. She is an ancient breed who has been likened to the Kerry Blue Terrier and the Soft-Coated Wheaten and Irish Terriers, but she actually predates all of these breeds. Some breeders believe that she was the result of crossing native Irish Terriers with dogs who were brought to Ireland by Hessian soldiers fighting the exiled King James.

19. The **Gordon Setter** was developed by Alexander, the fourth Duke of Gordon, at the Gordon Castle kennel during the early 1800s. Using Black-and-Tan Setters and Bloodhounds, he was able to achieve a larger and heavier setter. The Gordon Setter is the only sporting dog developed in Scotland.

20. The **Jack Russell Terrier**, or **Parson Russell Terrier**, as he is now called, was developed in the nineteenth century by a clergyman named Jack Russell. He is a conglomeration of several breeds including the Old Fox Terrier, the Beagle, the Foxhound, the Bedlington Terrier, the Border Terrier, the Bull Terrier, the Cairn Terrier, the Dachshund, and several other terrier breeds. This fearless canine is often characterized as a big dog in a small dog's body. Eddie on the television show *Frasier* is a Jack Russell Terrier.

21. While the exact origins of the **Kerry Blue Terrier** are unknown, she is believed to have been bred by peasants in the mountainous area of Lake Killarney by crossing existing terriers with Irish Wolfhounds. These dogs were used by Irish nobility to guard against poachers on their estates. Her soft, wavy dark blue coat distinguishes the Kerry Blue from all the other terriers.

22. The **Lakeland Terrier** shares his lineage with the Bedlington Terrier, the Old English Wire Fox Terrier, and the Dandie Dinmont Terrier. He was developed in the mountains of the Lake District of northern England to hunt and kill the Westmoreland fox and was originally called the Patterdale Terrier. He is similar to the Welsh Terrier but is slightly smaller.

23. The **Manchester Terrier**, originally known as the Black-and-Tan Terrier, dates back to the sixteenth century. This

breed was crossed with the Whippet and Greyhound as well as various terriers to produce the dog we know today. The Manchester looks somewhat like a small Doberman Pinscher but isn't as thin as a Miniature Pinscher.

24. The origin of the **Old English Sheepdog** or **Bobtail**, as he is sometimes known, dates back about two hundred years, most likely from a cross between a Bearded Collie and the Polish Owczarek Nizinny, or Polish Lowland Sheepdog. Some people believe that he is related to the Briard and the Bergamasco. This shaggy-looking dog was developed by farmers for sheep- and cattle herding. His heavy coat is difficult for predators to grab.

25. The **Norwich Terrier** and **Norfolk Terrier** started out as the same breed, with the Border Terrier and the Cairn Terrier as his ancestors. It wasn't until 1964 that by breeding they were separated into two distinct breeds. How to tell the difference between them? The Norfolk has dropped ears and the Norwich has pricked ears (ears that look like a witch's hat). The Norfolk became the mascot at Cambridge University in the 1800s.

26. The history of the **Pembroke Welsh Corgi** is unknown, but many people believe that he is completely unrelated to the Cardigan Welsh Corgi, having more in common with the spitz family of dogs, which includes breeds like the Schipperke, the Pomeranian, and the Keeshond. Another theory holds that the Pembroke was introduced into Wales about A.D. 1107 by Flemish weavers.

27. The **Sealyham Terrier** originated in Wales and was developed by Captain John Tucker Edwardes around 1860. Edwardes crossed the Dandie Dinmont Terrier, the Basset of Flanders, the West Highland White Terrier, the Cardigan Welsh Corgi, and the Wire Fox Terrier to achieve this completely white terrier.

28. The **Scottish Deerhound**'s ancestor, the African Greyhound, is believed to have been brought to Scotland more than 3,000 years ago by Phoenician traders. This Greyhound was then crossbred with longer-coated dogs to achieve a thicker and more weather-resistant coat. These dogs became so prized that only nobility were allowed to own them, and they were known as the "royal dog of Scotland."

29. The **Skye Terrier** is considered to be the oldest of all the Scottish Terriers, dating back to the sixteenth century. A shipwreck in the Scottish Hebrides brought Maltese dogs to Scotland, and these were mated with the Scottish Terrier and Cairn Terrier to produce the Skye. He is distinguished by a long coat that parts down the back and hangs over the ears and face.

 30. The **Smooth Fox Terrier**, with her elegant body that typically has a white coat with black or brown markings, is the result of crossing the smooth Black-and-Tan Terrier, the Greyhound, and the Beagle. Her ancestors are quite unlike those of the Wire Fox Terrier, to whom she is often compared.

31. **Staffordshire Terriers** were originally bred in seventeenth-century Staffordshire, England, for bull-baiting purposes. Bulldogs and various terriers were crossed to produce a dog with great strength and agility. Staffordshire Terriers were known as the "pit dog."

32. The **Scottish Terrier**, or **"Scottie,"** originated in Scotland in 1770. He was first known as the Aberdeen Terrier and served as the foundation for the Cairn Terrier, the West Highland White, and the Dandie Dinmont. The Scottie, as well as the other terrier breeds, was not recognized as a distinct breed until 1800. He is a small dog with a coarse coat that is usually black in color.

33. The **Soft-Coated Wheaten Terrier** hails from Ireland. Although it is not clear how the dog was developed, she does seem to share her lineage with Kerry Blue and Irish Terriers and dates back centuries in Ireland. It wasn't until 1937, however, that this terrier became known as the Wheaten. When Wheatens are puppies, they resemble bear cubs.

34. The **Smooth and Rough Collie** is basically the same dog with only his coat length varying. His specific origins are not known, but he is believed to be derived from the same stock as the Border Collie. The name Collie was taken from the Gaelic word for "useful" or from the Scottish black-faced sheep, the colley, which it was assigned to guard.

35. The **Sussex Spaniel** has her origins in southern England and is believed to be the result of a cross between the Clumber Spaniel and the

Bloodhound. A Mr. Fuller of Rosehill, Sussex, is credited with the creation of this breed in 1795. The Sussex Spaniel resembles the Clumber but has a golden-liver-colored coat instead of one that is predominantly white with lemon or orange markings.

36. **Welsh Terriers** are believed to be an extension of the old British Black-and-Tan Terrier and were sometimes referred to as the old Reddish-Black Wire Fox Terrier. He is one of the oldest terrier breeds, dating back to the middle of the eighteenth century. Sadly, because of their color, these dogs were often mistaken for the foxes they were hunting and many were accidentally shot.

37. **West Highland White Terrier** or **"Westie"** is a relatively recent breed. They were derived from white Cairn Terrier puppies in Scotland. These white puppies were bred to develop the West Highland variation. The Westie is basically a white Cairn Terrier — and an extremely popular breed.

38. While some think they are the same breed, most experts believe that the **Wire Fox Terrier** and **Smooth Fox Terriers** were developed independently. John Russell, who developed the Jack Russell Terrier, was also considered the father of the Wire Fox Terrier. The Wire was achieved by crossing rough-coated Black-and-Tan Terriers with Beagles.

39. The **Yorkshire Terrier** or **"Yorkie"** breed is only about a hundred years old. They were most likely created by crossing the Maltese with Black-and-Tan, Manchester, and Dandie Dinmont Terriers. Originally a larger dog, the Yorkie has been miniaturized over the years and is now the smallest of all terriers.

How Many Dogs Does It Take to Change a Light Bulb?
Well, that all depends on what kind of dog it is. . . .

Golden Retriever: "The sun is shining, the day is young, we have our whole lives ahead of us. What are you doing inside, worrying about a light bulb?"

Border Collie: "Just one! And I'll replace any wiring that's not up to code!"

Dachshund: "I can't even reach the stupid lamp."

Toy Poodle: "I'll just blow in the Border Collie's ear and he'll do it. By the time he's finished rewiring my house, my nails will be dry."

Rottweiler: "Go ahead! Make me!"

Shih Tzu: "Puh-leeze, dah-ling! Let the servants do it."

Labrador Retriever: "Oh me, me, pleeeeeeze let me change the light bulb! Can I? Can I, huh? Huh? Can I?"

Alaskan Malamute: "Let the Border Collie do it. You can feed me while he's busy."

Cocker Spaniel: "Why change it? I can still pee on the carpet in the dark."

Doberman Pinscher: "While it's still dark, I'm going to sleep on the couch."

Mastiff: "Mastiffs are NOT afraid of the dark."

Hound dog: "ZZZZZZZZZZZZZZZZZ."

Chihuahua: "Yo quiero taco bulb."

Pointer

Pointer: "I see it, there it is, it's right there. . . ."

Greyhound: "It isn't moving; who cares?"

Cairn Terrier: "I'll attack it!"

Australian Shepherd: "Put all the light bulbs in a little circle . . ."

Old English Sheepdog: "Light bulb? LIGHT BULB? That thing I just ate was a light bulb?"

10 Sight Hounds

Sight hounds, also known as gazehounds, have extremely acute vision. Their long jaws and necks aid them in sighting their quarry. These elegant dogs, with long strides, agile bodies, and powerful chests and lungs, can chase and even kill their quarry. The swiftest of the sight hounds can attain speeds of faster than forty miles per hour. These dogs are excited by the sight of any possible "prey" that runs fast. Beware! The sight hound's chase instinct is very strong. He will easily take off after anything from a rabbit to a rodent, leaving his home or yard without a backward glance.

1. The **Afghan Hound** is a very old breed. She was once used to hunt the large cats — including leopards and panthers.

2. The **Basenji**, which originated in ancient Egypt, is a small dog with excellent eyesight. He was once used to drive game into nets or to track wounded

> ## "They never talk about themselves but listen to you while you talk about yourself, and keep up an appearance of being interested in the conversation."
> ### — JEROME K. JEROME, HUMORIST

prey. Quiet and deliberate, Basenjis have been described as a cat in a dog's body. This is a very active pack-hunting dog of small game.

3. The **Borzoi**, or **Russian Wolfhound**, is a large dog who gets his name from the Russian word *borzii*, meaning "swift." These dogs were valued by Russian nobility for their ability to hunt wolves. Russian hunters used the Borzoi in pairs, allowing them to attack the wolf from both sides.

4. The **Greyhound**, able to attain speeds of forty-five miles per hour, is the fastest four-legged animal in the world, second only to the cheetah. As a sight hunter, she was able to catch and bring down wild boar and deer without even stopping.

5. The **Ibizan Hound** was bred to hunt rabbit, small game, and gazelle. This breed dates back to ancient Egypt and hunts by sight, although his senses of smell and hearing are also well developed.

6. The **Irish Wolfhound** is an extremely large dog who can attain a height of seven feet when standing on her hind legs. She was used to hunt wolves, elk, and wild boar. These dogs often accompanied Irish noblemen into battle.

7. The **Pharaoh Hound**, a truly ancient breed, was used to hunt and chase down small game using his keen eyesight, sharp sense of smell, and acute hearing. This friendly and affectionate dog possesses great speed and agility.

8. The **Saluki**, or **Persian Greyhound**, was named after an ancient Arabian city of Saluq. This dog was an amazing sight hunter whose great speed and agility over rough terrain enabled her to hunt gazelle, the fastest of all antelopes. Salukis were also used to hunt fox, jackal, and hare.

9. The **Scottish Deerhound** is a very large dog closely related to the Greyhound and Irish Wolfhound. Although classified as a sight hound, this dog also uses his fine sense of smell. Scottish noblemen used Deerhounds in packs for the sport of "deer driving."

10. The **Whippet** looks like a small Greyhound. She is extremely agile and is unsurpassed in her ability to accelerate to top speed. Whippets were originally bred to chase and capture small game.

16 Scent Hounds

Scent hounds are hunting dogs who have an exceptional sense of smell. Typically these dogs are long-muzzled and have well-defined nostrils. Scent hounds are among the oldest dog breeds, first appearing around 3000 B.C. They have historically been a fierce group of dogs, easily capable of holding their own against a variety of wild animals including boars and wolves. Due to selective breeding, these dogs now have some of the gentlest and most laid-back personalities in the canine world. Scent hounds can be difficult to train because they tend to follow their noses instead of any set of commands. Scent hounds have long, droopy ears, which stir up scents from the ground and surrounding foliage.

1. The **Basset Hound** is a chunky, short-legged scent hound. His sense of smell for tracking is second only to that of the Bloodhound. The name Basset is derived from the French word *bas* meaning "low" or "dwarf."

2. The **Beagle** is a medium-size dog similar in appearance to the larger Foxhound. The term Beagling referred to the hunting of hare using a pack of thirty to forty Beagles. They have incredible noses and are now used as sniffer dogs for drug detection.

3. The **Bloodhound** is a large dog who is capable of following a scent for many days over large distances. Her ability to follow a scent in the air as opposed to on the ground makes her the most formidable scent hound of all. The Bloodhound's sense of smell is more than a million times better than a human's.

4. The **Black-and-Tan Coonhound** is a large dog with great agility who was bred to hunt raccoon. Once he has "treed" his quarry, this dog howls. He has also been used to hunt bear, deer, and mountain lions.

5. The **Bluetick Coonhound** was also bred to hunt raccoon. Though these dogs originated in France, they were developed in Louisiana. Bluetick Coonhounds are patient, persistent trackers primarily used in the Ozark Mountains and other remote areas of the South.

6. **Dachshund** literally means "badger dog" in German. Besides hunting badgers, the Dachs-hund, with his short legs and elongated body, was also employed to hunt fox and rabbit. Hunting in packs, they were even capable of hunting wild boar.

7. The **English**, or **Red Tick**, **Coonhound** was most commonly used to hunt fox, not raccoon as her name implies. These dogs were also capable of hunting cougars and bears.

8. **Foxhounds** are large hunting hounds who look a lot like Beagles but are much larger. Foxhounds hunt in packs and have a very strong sense of smell, as well as great stamina. As their name implies, they were used primarily to hunt foxes. This dog has an excellent nose and terrific speed, and makes a musical baying sound.

9. In size, the **Harrier** is midway between the Beagle and English Foxhound. They were primarily used to hunt hare, though the breed has also been used to hunt fox. She has a keen sense of smell and is extremely cunning and brave. Prey chased by a Harrier will generally collapse from exhaustion.

10. The **Ibizan Hound** is both a scent and sight hound. He possesses great speed and uses his scenting ability — along with his great sense of sight and hearing — to enable him to hunt at night as well as during daylight hours. Ibizan Hounds are similar in appearance to the Pharaoh Hound but is larger and multicolored.

"To a dog the whole world is a smell." — UNKNOWN

11. The **Norwegian Elkhound** tracks her quarry best at night. She has been used to hunt badger, lynx, cougars, bears, wolves, and reindeer. This is an ancient breed that has been helping hunters since the time when they used slingshots to kill their prey.

12. The **Otterhound** has long pendulous ears with folds that enable scent to be pushed forward to the dog's nose, thus enhancing his ability as a scent hound. The Otterhound's sense of smell is so acute that he can smell an otter long after it has passed through water.

13. **Petit Basset Griffon Vendéen**, or **PBGV** as she is commonly known, is a small scent hound who uses her nose to follow small game over rough and difficult terrain. She shares some of the characteristics of the Basset Hound and Wire-haired Griffon.

14. The **Plott Hound** is a true American scent hound whose claim to fame is cold-trailing bears and raccoons in the Appalachian, Blue Ridge, and Great Smoky Mountains of the eastern United States.

15. The **Rhodesian Ridgeback** hails from South Africa. When used in packs, these dogs are able to hunt deer and lions. Ridgebacks are known to be ferocious in the hunt.

16. The **Treeing Walker Hound** has an excellent sense of smell and a distinctive howl. She trees her quarry and can sometimes even climb the tree to get at it. These dogs have great stamina and drive and have been used to hunt raccoon, squirrel, and possum.

12 Russian Dog Breeds

1. The **Caucasian Ovtcharka (Shepherd)** is a descendant of the prehistoric Molossur. This dog aided Russian herders for at least six centuries in Caucasia, a mountainous region located between the Caspian and Black Seas. Despite her enormous size — she can weigh as much as 150 pounds — the Caucasian Ovtcharka is a very athletic dog and is favored by the Russian military due to her innate aggression toward strangers.

2. **Central Asian Shepherd Dogs** have existed for at least 4,000 years and are believed to be descended from the Tibetan Mastiff. This flock guardian is virtually unseen outside Russia and has been declining in numbers due to the growing popularity of the Caucasian Ovtcharka. Because of severe extremes of climate, this breed's puppies needed to be very hardy to survive. These conditions led to the evolution of a very strong and brave breed.

3. The **East Siberian Laika** is a spitzlike dog who originated in the Baikal Lake region of eastern Siberia. There are no specific characteristics that define this dog. He is merely a combination of various dog breeds that passed through this part of Siberia from Europe, China, and Mongolia.

4. The **Karelo-Finnish Laika** is similar to the spitz dog of Finland. The Russian version is found in an area called Karelia in northwestern Russia. *Laika* is the Russian word for "barker." This dog was invaluable to Russian fur hunters, who relied on her bravery and speed.

5. **Middle Asian Ovtcharkas** first appeared in the Urals in Siberia and Mongolia. They served as flock guardians for the herds kept by the nomads who lived in this bleak region. Virtually unknown outside Central Asia, Middle Asian Ovtcharkas are descended from the Tibetan Mastiff. These dogs

Samoyed

are a strong, brave breed that can withstand the harsh weather conditions of Siberia. They were sometimes crossed with the Borzoi to fashion a shepherd who could also hunt.

6. The **Russian Bear Schnauzer**, or **Black Russian Terrier**, originated in the 1940s in the army-controlled Red Star Kennels of the Soviet Union. It is believed that at least twenty dog breeds were used to create this breed. Giant Schnauzers, Airedale Terriers, Russian Water Dogs, and Rottweilers are just a few of the contributing breeds. Black Russian Terriers are excellent guard dogs, with a thick coat that allows them to withstand the harsh Russian winters.

7. The **Russian Wolfhound**, or **Borzoi**, originated in seventeenth-century Russia. Arabian Greyhounds were crossed with native Russian coursing hounds to produce this magnificent and popular Russian breed. Built for speed, the Borzoi was designed to chase wolves. He is a very tall and aristocratic-looking white dog with a long, narrow head and a slightly shaggy coat.

8. **Russo-European Laikas** were developed in both Russia and Finland during the 1700s by crossing the courageous Karelian Bear Laika with the Utchak Sheepdog. These amazing spitz-type dogs, who are predominantly black with patches of white, are capable of hunting bear, elk, wolf, and wild boar.

9. The **Samoyed** traces her history back to an ancient nomadic tribe called the Samoyedes who lived in the north-central part of Siberia. This indigenous Russian breed was used to pull sleds and herd reindeer. Samoyeds — with their perpetual smiles and beautiful white coats — are cheerful, obedient companions.

10. The **Siberian Husky** was developed over a period of 3,000 years by the Chukchi people who lived along the coasts of the Arctic and Pacific Oceans of Siberia. Siberians were used primarily as sled dogs, reindeer herders, and watchdogs. They have a great deal of stamina, allowing sled teams to often travel one hundred miles in a single day.

11. The **South Russian Shepherd Dog**, or **Ovtcharka**, probably descended from similar Tibetan or Chinese dogs and first appeared in Russia in the eighteenth century. They were then crossed with Spanish shepherd dogs to produce the modern-day heavy-coated South Russian Ovtcharka.

12. The **West Siberian Laika** is a primitive breed developed by Khantu and Mansi hunters in the Ural Mountains. This dog was bred for hunting deer and elk in cold weather conditions. Hunters depended on the West Siberian Laika for survival in the Arctic. To this day, they are the most popular hunting dog in Russia.

"They are better than human beings, because they know but do not tell." — **EMILY DICKINSON**

20 Asian Breeds

1. The **Ainu Dog**, or **Hokkaido**, is considered Japan's oldest breed. Her ancestors are not known, but this spitzlike dog was brought to Japan by the Ainu tribe more than 3,000 years ago. The Ainu were forced to settle in Hokkaido. This breed has changed very little over the centuries.

2. The ancestors of the **Akita**, or **Akita Inu**, came to Japan before Japan and the European continent were separated by the Sea of Japan approximately 10,000 years ago. The modern-day Akita evolved from a hunting dog of the Matagi people, who hunted on the Northern Honshu Island. The Akita is considered a national treasure in Japan. He is the largest of the Japanese spitz-type dog breeds.

3. The **Chongqing Dog** is a quite old and now quite rare Chinese breed. She is believed to have first appeared in southwestern China during the Han dynasty, some 2,000 years ago. The Chongqing Dog has been bred in China for centuries and hasn't lost any of her natural characteristics, including a reddish brown coat and her trademark short "bamboo stick" tail.

Chow Chow

4. The **Chow Chow**, with his leonine appearance, originated in China about 3,000 years ago. He is believed to have been the result of crossing Tibetan Mastiffs with Samoyeds. Others claim that the Chow Chow is actually ancestor to the Samoyed, Pomeranian, and Keeshond. One Chinese emperor was so enamored of this breed that he kept 5,000 of them.

5. The **Chinese Crested** first appeared in China in the 1500s. Her ancestry is vague, but it is believed that she shares her origins with other hairless breeds. Chinese explorers are credited with the spread of hairless dogs throughout Asia, Africa, and Central and South America. There are two types of "Cresteds," the hairless and the powderpuff.

6. The **Chinese Fu Dog**, who resembled a lion, was held sacred in all of Asia and was used to guard Buddhist temples. The breed can be traced as far back as 200 B.C. His name is derived from the word *Fo,* the Chinese name for Buddha. The Fu Dog is commonly depicted in Asian art.

7. The toy dog breed known as the **Japanese Chin** is actually native to Korea. Once brought to Japan, however, he was developed further and became a favorite of Japanese royalty. He was also a favorite of Queen Victoria, a huge dog lover, who received a pair of Chins as a gift from Commodore Perry after his return from Japan. It is believed that the Japanese gave these dogs sake to drink in an effort to stunt their growth. The Chin is related to both the Pug and the Pekingese.

8. The **Japanese Spitz** closely resembles the American Eskimo Dog. She is thought to be either a descendant of, or a variation on, the Siberian Samoyed, a dog who was imported to Japan in the early part of the twentieth century. It is believed that the Samoyed was bred smaller and smaller, finally resulting in the toy breed known as the Japanese Spitz.

9. **Japanese Terriers** are descendants of the Smooth Fox Terrier and were brought to Japan by the Dutch in the early 1700s. This terrier was mated with existing Japanese breeds. The Japanese Terrier, with her Whippet-like elegance, was perfected in the coastal towns of Yokohama and Kobe.

10. The **Jindo Dog** was named after the island of Chindo in South Korea. He is believed to be the result of crossing native Korean breeds with dogs brought by invading Mongols during the thirteenth century. These spitzlike dogs were then brought to the island of Jindo by Korean soldiers, and it was there that they were bred to perfection.

11. Not much is known or written about the **Kai**, or **Lion Dog**, but she is believed to be descended from medium-size dogs that existed in ancient Japan. She was developed in the mountainous Kai district of Honshu, where she was bred to hunt deer and wild boar. This breed is distinguished by her brindled coat. She is very rare, even in Japan.

12. The **Lhasa Apso**'s roots can be traced back to 800 B.C. Tibet. This breed was so treasured by the Dalai Lama that it was forbidden to sell him. It wasn't until the beginning of the Manchu dynasty in 1583 that the Lhasa Apso was even seen outside of Tibet. The Dalai Lama sent Lhasa Apsos as gifts to the Manchu emperors of China. The breed's name is derived from his city of origin, *Lhasa*, combined with the word *rapso*, which means goatlike.

13. The history of the **Pekingese** dates back 4,000 years. She was the imperial dog of China and was believed to ward off evil spirits. Chinese commoners had to bow to this toy dog, and Chinese emperors were buried with them with the hope that they would serve as protection in the afterlife. The theft of one of these dogs was punishable by death.

14. The ancestry of the **Pug** dates back to 400 B.C. Asia. The actual origins of this breed are the subject of much speculation. Some people believe that he is descended from a short-haired Pekingese, while others think the dog is either a miniaturized Mastiff or the result of a small Bulldog cross. In Europe, he reached the height of popularity during the Victorian era.

15. The **Shar-Pei** is another ancient breed and is considered by some to be a descendant of the Chow Chow, since he is the only other breed who also has a purple tongue. It is thought that Shar-Peis, with their multitude of folded skin, developed in the village of Tai Li in the Kwangtung province around 200 B.C. The word *Shar-Pei* literally means "sand-skin" in Chinese.

16. The **Shiba Inu** can be traced back to Japan's Joumon period (10,000 to 300 B.C.). She is the oldest Japanese breed and is also the smallest of the Japanese spitz breeds. The Shiba Inu we see today is the product of crossing the Shinshu Shiba, Mino Shiba, and Sanin Shiba, all from different regions of Japan.

17. The ancestor of the **Shih Tzu**, whose name means "lion," is thought to be the smallest and most ancient of the Tibetan "holy dogs." This dog was given to Chinese emperors as tribute and was then further developed by crossing him with the Pekingese to produce the modern-day Shih Tzu.

18. The **Tibetan Mastiff** is one of the oldest dog breeds in existence. Her origins may date back as far as the Bronze Age, possibly even to the

"In order to keep a true perspective of one's importance, everyone should have a dog that will worship him and a cat that will ignore him."

— DEREKE BRUCE

Stone Age. Tibetan Mastiffs have changed little over thousands of years. This breed is a descendant of the noted Tibetan Dog, ancestor to most of the Molussuses and Mastiff breeds throughout the world. It is thought that Alexander the Great brought these dogs along with him on his conquests. Great Danes, English Mastiffs, Newfoundlands, and Saint Bernards are all descended from Tibetan Dogs.

19. The **Tibetan Spaniel** or **"Tibbie"** is an indigenous Tibetan breed and dates back at least 2,000 years. He is thought to be the product of crossbreeding the Pekingese, Pug, and Japanese Chin. Tibetan Spaniels made excellent watchdogs for Tibetan monks because they could sit on very high walls, spotting intruders from great distances. Allegedly, these dogs could be trained to turn their master's prayer wheels.

20. **Tibetan Terriers** originated in the Lost Valley of Tibet about 2,000 years ago. Known as holy dogs, they were treated with a great deal of love and respect. It was considered an honor to receive a Tibetan Terrier as a gift; they were often presented to show gratitude. Because of his squarely proportioned body, this little dog resembles a sheepdog more than a terrier.

Dogs may not **have as many taste buds as we do (they have fewer than 2,000 on their tongues, whereas we humans have about 9,000), but that doesn't mean they're not discriminating eaters. They have more than 200 million scent receptors in their noses (we have only 5 million), so it's important that their food smells good and tastes good.**

An Asian Love Story

Eisaburo Uyeno and his Akita, Hachiko, were inseparable friends from the start. Each day, "Hachi" would accompany Eisaburo, a professor at the Imperial University, to the train station when he left for work. Upon returning, the professor would find the dog patiently waiting for him, tail wagging. This happy routine continued until one fateful day in 1925, when the professor became sick at work and died before he could return home. Nevertheless, Hachiko continued to wait each day at Shibuya Station for the friend who would never again return. The Akita was a familiar sight to commuters as he kept his vigil for more than ten years. On March 8, 1935, Hachiko finally joined his master. He died on the very same spot where he had last seen his friend alive. Today, a life-size bronze statue of Hachiko is nestled amid hoards of harried commuters and a variety of shops at Tokyo's busy Shibuya Station. The tale is lovingly retold for children by Pamela Turner in *Hachiko: The True Story of a Loyal Dog* (Houghton Mifflin, 2004), with lush watercolors by Yan Nascimbene that provide their own inspiration.

6 Middle Eastern Breeds

1. The **Afghan Hound** is a very ancient dog. Depictions of these dogs in cave paintings in Afghanistan date back more than 4,000 years. This elegant sight hound, with his long, feathered coat, is arguably one of the most beautiful of all dog breeds. Afghan Hounds were used both as hunting dogs and as shepherds. The Western world didn't discover these thin, elegant beauties until the nineteenth century.

2. The graceful, long-legged **Azawakh** has her origins in the southern Sahara region of Africa. This sight hound is named after the Azawakh valley. She was highly prized by nomads for her ability to ward off hyenas as well as for her loyalty and friendship.

3. The **Canaan Dog** was developed by the selective breeding of feral Pariah dogs who were once prevalent in the Middle East. This dog, whose origins date back more than 3,000 years, served to guard and protect livestock. He is the native dog of Israel and one of the only indigenous breeds in existence.

4. The **Pharaoh Hound**'s origins date back to 4000 to 3000 B.C. She is believed to hail from Egypt, where she was valued for her hunting ability and steadfast nature. The Island of Malta, however, is credited with preserving this breed for the past 2,000 years. Pharaoh Hounds are elegant-looking sight hounds with erect ears, small amber eyes, and a short coat that is generally a glossy red or tan color.

5. Among the world's most ancient breeds, the **Saluki** dates back as far as 5000 B.C. His visage is depicted on everything from tomb paintings to the hieroglyphics on Egyptian pyramids. This breed was held in such high esteem by Arab nobility that he became the royal dog of Egypt. Salukis are strikingly beautiful dogs who have a Greyhound-like body with long, silky feathering on their ears and tail.

6. The **Sloughi** or **Arabian Greyhound** dates back perhaps to 7000 to 8000 B.C. This breed hails from Asia, where she was often presented as a tribute to the Pharaohs of Nubia. She may be the ancestor to all the lop-eared sight hounds of the Middle East.

> An ancient tale of the Near East tells of seven good Muslim boys who, in flight from the wicked emperor Decius, fell asleep in a cave. Their faithful dog Katmir remained alert and guarded the entrance of the cave to keep the boys safe — for 309 years!

15 French Dog Breeds

1. The **Beauceron** is a breed of French shepherd dog. It is believed that her origins date back to the late 1500s. Extremely obedient and able to follow commands promptly, this dog was commonly employed as a messenger during World Wars I and II. She is distinguished by having six toes on each of her hind paws.

2. **Berger de Picard** is perhaps the oldest of the all French shepherds, named for the Picardie region of northeastern France. He is believed to date back to A.D. 800. The Berger de Picard nearly became extinct after World War II. Today, there are only approximately 3,000 of these dogs in existence.

3. The **Bouvier des Flandres**, a cattle-herding dog, may have resulted from a cross between the Griffon and Beauceron. The breed suffered near extinction as a result of his exposure to warfare during World War I, but enough dogs were saved so that breeding could continue. The Bouvier des Flandres is a powerful dog with a massive head, long eyebrows, and prominent whiskers that resemble a mustache.

4. The **Braque Saint-Germain** is a cross between an English Pointer and a Continental Pointer. It is believed that the breed first appeared around 1830 in the royal kennels at Compiègne, then in Saint Germain en Laye. She reached the height of her popularity in the early twentieth century. These dogs are used primarily to hunt fowl.

5. The **Briquet Griffon Vendéen** is a rare breed, even in France. Originally from La Vandée, in France, she is basically a copy of the Grand Griffon Vendéen but is bred to be a smaller, medium-size dog. Nearly brought to extinction after World War II, the breed was revitalized by a well-known French dog show judge named Hubert Dezamy.

6. Some believe that the **Brittany Spaniel** may have first appeared as long ago as A.D. 150, possibly resulting from a cross between an Orange and White Spaniel and a French dog of unknown origin. Though an orange and white coat is characteristic of this intelligent-looking dog, they do appear in numerous other color combinations.

7. The **Chien D'Artois** is a small hound with very long, flat ears. He was once referred to as the Picardy dog and was a favorite of Louis XIII in seventeenth-century France. In England he is considered one of the forerunners of the Beagle. He's an excellent hunter of hare.

8. The **Dogue de Bordeaux**, also known as the French Mastiff, is one of France's oldest dog breeds. It is believed that the Dogue de Bordeaux is descended from the Roman Molossus and the Spanish Mastiff, as well as various other unknown breeds. Raymond Tri-

quet, a French breeder, and his Dogue de Bordeaux Club were responsible for saving this breed from extinction during the early 1970s. This dog's trademark is her massive head.

9. The **Gascons-Saintongeois** was created by Baron de Virelade and is sometimes referred to as the Virelade. After the French Revolution, the hounds of the Saintongeois region nearly disappeared. In the 1840s, the baron crossed the few remaining Saintongeois hounds he could find with the Grand Gascony Hound to produce today's Gascons-Saintongeois. This dog is extremely rare.

10. The **Grand Griffon Vendéen** is a descendant from the so-called King's white hound and the "griffon fauve de Bretagne" during the early part of the sixteenth century. He arose in the district of La Vendée on the west coast of France. This large version of the Petit Basset Griffon Vendéen has droopy ears that are covered with long hair.

11. The **French Basset Hound** was bred by monks during the Middle Ages. They are believed to be a cross between the Basset Artois and the Basset Normand. Basset Hounds appear to have the head of a Bloodhound, the coloring of a Foxhound, and the legs of a Dachshund.

12. The **French Bulldog** arose from the crossbreeding of miniature English Bulldogs with French terriers in

the 1860s. The French Bulldog became a favorite of prostitutes in France and was often pictured on postcards with Parisian streetwalkers. This comical little Bulldog, with her batlike ears and Pug nose, makes a great pet.

13.The earliest evidence as to the origins of the **Great Pyrenees** dates back to 1800–1000 B.C. and the Bronze Age. But it is believed his lineage dates back even further and most likely originated in either Asia or Siberia. The Great Pyrenees is a descendant of the Hungarian Kuvasz and the Italian Maremmano-Abruzzese. In 1675, the future Louis XIV proclaimed this breed the royal dog of France. This is a huge, bearlike dog who usually has a white coat.

14. The **Petit Basset Griffon Vendéen** is an ancient French breed that originated in the coastal Vendée area of western France. She first appeared in the sixteenth century and can be traced to the larger and more powerful Griffon Vendéen. The PBGV, as she is often known, was bred to hunt hare, fox, and deer. This small dog has an unkempt and natural-looking wiry coat.

15. The **Petit Bleu de Gascongne** was created through selective breeding of the Grand Bleu de Gascogne, a descendant of the original scent hounds of Gaul. The Petit Bleu was produced by breeders who desired a smaller dog who could handle smaller quarry.

6 Spanish Breeds

It may seem as though there aren't many Spanish dog breeds in existence today. Certainly, more hounds hail from Germany than from Spain. Spain, however, is the country of origin for all the spaniel breeds, a numerous lot that includes the Cavalier King Charles Spaniel, Clumber Spaniel, American Cocker Spaniel, English Cocker Spaniel, English Springer Spaniel, English Toy Spaniel, Field Spaniel, Sussex Spaniel, and Tibetan Spaniel. Additionally, Spain is the home to the Ibizan Hound (from the island of Ibiza) and the Maltese (from the island of Malta). The following are some uncommon Spanish dog breeds.

1. The *Alano Español*, or **Spanish Bulldog**, did not originate from any breed known today. He did, however, become the foundation for numerous modern breeds such as the Great Dane and the Dogue de Bordeaux. This ancient breed was brought to the Iberian Peninsula by the Alans, a nomadic group who spoke an Indo-Iranian language, in A.D. 406.

2. The *Perro de Presa Canario*, or **Canary Dog**, got her name from the Canary Islands, a possession of Spain, and from its ferocious indigenous dogs. The Presa Canario is descended from these indigenous dogs, called *Bardino Majero*, who were bred with old-style Bulldogs and Mastiffs brought over by English settlers in the nineteenth century.

3. The **Spanish Mastiff**, or *Mastin de Español*, is a gentle giant whose origins can be traced back to 2000 B.C., when he was brought to the Iberian Peninsula by the Phoenicians. He was developed primarily in Estremadura in the southwestern region of Spain and is believed to be a cross between the Mastiff and the Roman Molossus.

4. The rare **Spanish Water Dog**, sometimes referred to as the Turkish Dog, is an ancient variety of the Barbet, a water dog. The dog's origins are sketchy, but this very shaggy dog was bred to herd sheep and retrieve waterfowl.

5. **Spanish Greyhounds** originated in ancient times and were possibly descendants of Arabian Greyhounds who were brought to Spain by the Moors in the ninth century. This sight hound was bred purely for racing and is ancestor to several other Greyhound breeds who later appeared in England and Ireland between the sixteenth and eighteenth centuries.

6. **Spanish Pointers** are believed to be the original pointers, though they are far heavier set than the modern-day variety. Indigenous to Spain, the Spanish Pointer was brought to England after the War of Spanish Succession in the early eighteenth century by returning British soldiers. She was then most likely crossed with the English Foxhound to produce the English Pointer, or the Pointer, as she is known in the United States.

9 German Dog Breeds

1. **The German Hunt Terrier**, also known as the *Jagdterrier*, originated in the 1940s when four German hunters decided to create an all-purpose terrier. The Hunt Terrier resulted from a cross between Patterdale Terriers and the German Wire Fox Terriers. This is a remarkable hunting dog, but due to his aggressive temperament, he doesn't make a good house pet.

> French Poodles did not originate in France but in Germany. Poodles were originally used as hunting dogs. The dogs' thick coats were a hindrance in water and thick brush, so hunters sheared the hindquarters, with cuffs left around the ankles and hips to protect against rheumatism. Each hunter marked his dogs' heads with a ribbon of his own color, allowing groups of hunters to tell their dogs apart.

2. **German Longhaired Pointer**, or *Langhaar* ("long hair"), is the oldest of the German pointer breeds. Although little is known about the origins of this breed, she is believed to have appeared first during the sixteenth century, the result of crossing German and English Pointers.

3. The **German Pinscher** can be traced back to the Middle Ages to a breed known as the Rattler. The smooth-coated variety of this breed was the forerunner to the German Pinscher, who is herself the forerunner of both the Doberman Pinscher and Affenpinscher.

4. The **German Shepherd Dog**, or *Deutsche Schäferhunde*, as a breed has existed only since the early twentieth century. She is the result of crossing various long-, short-, and wirehaired shepherd dogs from various regions of Germany. Captain Max von Stephanitz is the founder of the modern German Shepherd Dog.

5. **German Shorthaired Pointers** first appeared during the middle of the nineteenth century, a product of crossing Old Spanish Pointers, Hounds of St. Hubert, the Foxhound, and the English Pointer. Prince Albrecht zu Solms-Brauenfels's dogs served as the foundation for this breed. They are usually liver and white in color and have webbed toes.

6. The **German Spitz** is descended from Nordic herding dogs such as the Samoyed and the Lapphund who were brought to Europe by Vikings in the fifteenth century. This dog is the forerunner of today's Pomeranian.

7. **German Wirehaired Pointers**, with their short and wiry coats, were developed in Germany during the last half of the nineteenth century from the German Shorthaired Pointer and several other pointing breeds. Breed stock included the *Pudelpointer,* who was a cross between a Poodle dog and an English Pointer bitch.

8. The **German Wolfspitz**, or **Keeshond**, originated in the Arctic. He is related to the Samoyed, Chow Chow, Pomeranian, and Elkhound. He was, for a time, referred to as the symbol of the common man in Holland. The Keeshond's coat is typically gray with black tips that stand away from the body, giving him a puffed-up look.

9. The **Standard Poodle** has been popular in Europe for at least four hundred years. Her exact origins are debatable, but many believe that she is a German breed, though France is officially recognized as her country of origin. The term *Poodle* is derived from the German word *Pudel*, meaning "one who plays in water." It is also believed that the Poodle resulted from a cross between a rare French breed, the Barbet, and the Hungarian Water Hound.

The Planet's Favorite Dogs

Which dog is the most popular in the world? This distinction belongs to the beloved mutt, or mixed-breed dog. But when it comes to purebreds, there certainly seem to be some trends and similarities around the world. We asked dog clubs worldwide to give us the names and rankings on their country's ten most popular breeds. We were surprised to find that dogs indigenous to a country didn't necessarily make the list and that certain dogs (the Labrador Retriever, the Golden Retriever, the German Shepherd Dog, and the Rottweiler) are popular the world over.

The 10 Most Popular Dogs in the United States

1. Labrador Retriever
2. Golden Retriever
3. German Shepherd Dog
4. Dachshund
5. Beagle
6. Poodle
7. Chihuahua
8. Rottweiler
9. Yorkshire Terrier
10. Boxer

The 10 Most Popular Dogs in Canada

1. Labrador Retriever
2. Golden Retriever
3. German Shepherd Dog
4. Poodle
5. Shetland Sheepdog
6. Miniature Schnauzer
7. Yorkshire Terrier
8. Beagle

9. Bichon Frisé
10. Shih Tzu

The 10 Most Popular Dogs in England

1. Labrador Retriever
2. German Shepherd Dog
3. Cocker Spaniel
4. English Springer Spaniel
5. Staffordshire Bull Terrier
6. Golden Retriever
7. West Highland White Terrier
8. Cavalier King Charles Spaniel

Great Dane

9. Boxer
10. Rottweiler

The 10 Most Popular Dogs in France

1. German Shepherd Dog
2. Labrador Retriever
3. Yorkshire Terrier
4. Brittany Spaniel
5. English Setter
6. Rottweiler
7. Belgian Shepherd
8. Golden Retriever
9. Dachshund
10. Berger de Beauce

The 10 Most Popular Dogs in Germany

1. German Shepherd Dog
2. Dachshund
3. German Wirehaired Pointer
4. Labrador Retriever
5. Standard Poodle
6. English Cocker Spaniel

7. Great Dane

8. Boxer

9. Golden Retriever

10. Rottweiler

The 10 Most Popular Dogs in Belgium

1. German Shepherd Dog

2. Belgian Shepherd Tervuren

3. Golden Retriever

4. Labrador Retriever

5. Bernese Mountain Dog

6. Bouvier des Flandres

7. Boxer

8. Doberman Pinscher

9. Border Collie

10. Rottweiler

The 10 Most Popular Dogs in Sweden

1. German Shepherd Dog

2. Golden Retriever

3. Labrador Retriever

4. Swedish Elkhound

5. Wirehaired Dachshund

6. Cocker Spaniel

7. Rottweiler

8. English Springer Spaniel

9. Cavalier King Charles Spaniel

10. Flatcoated Retriever

Belgian Tervuren

The 10 Most Popular Dogs in South Africa

1. Yorkshire Terrier

2. Labrador Retriever

3. Bulldog

4. Bull Terrier

5. Rottweiler

6. Golden Retriever

7. Staffordshire Bull Terrier

8. Siberian Husky

9. Rhodesian Ridgeback

10. Shar-Pei

The 10 Most Popular Dogs in Finland

1. Finnish Hound

2. Norwegian Elkhound

3. German Shepherd Dog

4. Golden Retriever

5. Labrador Retriever

6. Carelian Bear Dog

7. Finnish Spitz

8. Finnish Lapphund

9. Swedish Elkhound

10. Cavalier King Charles Spaniel

The 10 Most Popular Dogs in Argentina

1. German Shepherd Dog

2. Rottweiler

3. Boxer

4. Labrador Retriever

5. Toy Poodle

6. Yorkshire Terrier

7. *Dogo Argentino*

8. Beagle

9. English Cocker Spaniel

10. Golden Retriever

The 10 Most Popular Dogs in Ireland

1. Cavalier King Charles Spaniel

2. Labrador Retriever

3. West Highland White Terrier

4. Boxer

5. Yorkshire Terrier

6. Labrador Retriever

7. Golden Retriever

8. German Shepherd Dog

9. English Springer

10. Beagle

The 11 Most Popular Dogs in Israel

1. German Shepherd Dog
2. Labrador Retriever
3. Golden Retriever
4. Shar-Pei
5. Dogue de Bordeaux
6. Miniature Pinscher
7. Boxer
8. English Bulldog
9. American Cocker Spaniel
10. Doberman Pinscher
11. Yorkshire Terrier

The 10 Most Popular Dogs in Iceland

1. Icelandic Sheepdog
2. Cavalier King Charles Spaniel
3. American Cocker Spaniel
4. Boxer
5. Chihuahua
6. Doberman Pinscher
7. German Shepherd Dog
8. Labrador Retriever
9. Bichon Frisé
10. English Cocker Spaniel

The 10 Most Popular Dogs in Japan

1. Dachshund
2. Chihuahua

3. Pembroke Welsh Corgi
4. Shih Tzu
5. Labrador Retriever
6. Yorkshire Terrier
7. Papillon
8. Poodle
9. Golden Retriever
10. Pomeranian

The 10 Most Popular Dogs in the Netherlands

1. German Shepherd Dog
2. Labrador Retriever
3. Golden Retriever
4. Rottweiler

A Japanese postcard from 1910

English Bulldog

5. Bernese Mountain Dog
6. Boxer
7. Bouvier des Flandres
8. West Highland White Terrier
9. Jack Russell Terrier
10. Cavalier King Charles Spaniel

The 10 Most Popular Dogs in Norway

1. German Shepherd Dog
2. Norwegian Elkhound
3. English Setter
4. Border Collie
5. Golden Retriever
6. Gordon Setter
7. Labrador Retriever
8. Bichon Frisé
9. Wirehaired Dachshund
10. Rottweiler

Astrology for Dog People

Stacey Wolf, the author of *Stacey Wolf's Psychic Living, Secrets of the Signs, Get Psychic!,* and *Love Secrets of the Signs,* has been featured on *The Other Half, The View, The Late Show with David Letterman, The Roseanne Show,* and ABC's *World News Now.* Stacey is known for her spot-on readings and her celebrity, sport, and political predictions. With her experience of standup comedy, Stacey Wolf is one of the hippest and coolest psychics and astrologers around. Here's Stacey's take on what dog breed's characteristics you have based on your astrological sign:

Aries: Jack Russell Terrier. You are really friendly, very feisty, and completely untrainable! You have boundless energy to run around and mess things up! You also like to be the center of attention.

Taurus: Saint Bernard. You are a big, mushy, lovable, slobbery kind soul. You love to work, in any condition, and help people with a lick and a smile. Let's not forget your stubborn streak: once you get your paws into something, you're not likely to let go soon!

Gemini: Yorkie. You are really cute and bouncy, very yappy, and best of all, you have really well-groomed hair — with accessories to match!

Cancer: Chihuahua. Everyone thinks you're all cute and cuddly, until they get into your space and you want to bite their head off. "Ruff, don't touch my bone!"

Leo: Great Dane. The king of all dogs. You do everything larger than life, from the way you walk to the way you play. You command attention and have a big loud bark!

Virgo: Westie. The dog in you is stubborn and pleasing. You are one of the cutest and best-groomed pooches around, and you love to work, too. Once you get into a good bone, you can dissect the thing for hours with energy and determination.

Libra: Greyhound. Your inner dog is both graceful and classic. If you had it your way, you wouldn't use your speed for racing — you'd run from one party to another. You don't like to work — just to play!

Scorpio: German Shepherd Dog. As the master of the universe, you are the most intense breed. You inspire both awe and fear. You are cautious around strangers but *love* your best friends. You strut with an air of mystery — what are you thinking today?

Sagittarius: Golden Retriever. One of the friendliest breeds, you love everyone you come in contact with equally. You are always up for a new adventure — a hike in the woods or a dip in someone else's pool — but love to come home for a good nap at the end of the day.

Capricorn: Pug. You are cute and cuddly but balance that with a feisty independent streak. You are mostly good-natured, but every once in a while you give a loud snort if something isn't going your way.

Aquarius: Miniature Schnauzer. You've definitely got a mind of your own, but no one can really understand what's going on in there! You are cautious with strangers and like to bark a lot — sometimes about nothing. Opinionated and adventurous, you are always up for a good sniff.

Pisces: Toy Poodle. You just want to cuddle up to someone you love all day long, do nothing, get carried everywhere, and never let your feet touch the ground. Being treated like a princess (or prince) isn't bad either.

Jack Russell Terrier

11 Sled Dog Breeds

Long before sled dog racing became an established sport, sled dogs were bred and used by people indigenous to the polar regions around the world. These dogs helped people to survive in harsh climates. Polar explorers such as Roald Amundsen and Robert Peary used sled dogs to take them to areas that were until then unreachable. Snowmobiles and airplanes now traverse these remote areas and have replaced the sled dog.

1. **Alaskan Husky** — Considered a hybrid dog (possibly part setter, part wolf, and part Siberian Husky) rather than a distinct breed unto itself. This breed is not officially recognized.

2. **Alaskan Malamute** — This Nordic dog is an ancestor of the Arctic wolf. His name is derived from the Mahlemuts, an Alaskan tribe who raised and cared for these beautiful Arctic dogs. The Mahlemut used these dogs as long as 2,000 to 3,000 years ago for transportation. Alaskan Malamutes accompanied Admiral Byrd on his expeditions to the North Pole; they have amazing strength, endurance, and fidelity.

3. **Canadian Eskimo Dog** — This is one of Canada's only indigenous dog breeds, with a history dating back more than 2,000 years. This dog has been known by many names throughout history, including Gronlandshund and Inuit Husky. The Inuit word for *dog* is *Qimmiq*.

4. **Chinook** — The Chinook is a northern breed derived from a single ancestor. The father of this breed, named Chinook, was born on the Wonalancet, New Hampshire, farm of the author/explorer Arthur Walden in 1917. Chinook was one of three puppies born to a Northern Husky bitch, sired by one of the dogs on Robert Peary's North Pole team. He was bred with German Shepherd Dogs and Belgian Sheepdogs.

Their offspring were then bred back with Chinook to create this breed.

5. **Greenland Dog** — The ancestors of this spitz-type dog date back well over 12,000 years, with a lineage that can be traced to Siberia. The Greenland Dog is similar to the Canadian Eskimo Dog, but she is taller and thinner. Today, these rare dogs can be found only in Greenland.

6. **Inuit Sled Dog** — The Inuit Sled Dog originated on the Asian continent, possibly in what is present-day Mongolia. Accompanied by their dogs, the Tunit people crossed the Bering Strait in continuous waves of migration between A.D. 900 and 1100. The Inuit Sled Dog is a working dog who is able to pull one and a half times his own weight over great distances.

7. **Mackenzie River Husky** — This term describes several overlapping local populations of Arctic and sub-Arctic sled dogs. They were created by crossing local freighting huskies with large European breeds such as the Saint Bernard, Newfoundland and Staghound.

8. **Norrbottenspets** or **Nordic Spitz** — Originating in Sweden, the Norrbottenspets is a member of the spitz family of dogs. He was originally used as an all-purpose farm dog who also hunted small game and pulled sleds.

9. **Samoyed** — Since ancient times, a population of hunters and fishermen known as Samoyedes have lived in Siberia. And for centuries, these people have used a beautiful, robust white dog to pull their sleds, the dog known to this day as the Samoyed.

10. **Scandinavian Hound** — This sled dog was established by crossing the German Shorthaired Pointer and English Pointers with Alaskan Huskies.

11. **Siberian Husky** — Siberian Huskies originated with the Chuckchi, a Stone Age people from northeastern Siberia. The Chuckchi used Siberians for herding reindeer and pulling heavy loads. These dogs are smaller and faster than their counterpart, the Alaskan Malamute.

Siberian Huskies

5 Pit Bulls

10 Biters

The Centers for Disease Control (CDC) and many local jurisdictions issue yearly dog-bite statistics. The following dog breeds are the ones the CDC considers the highest risk.

1. Pit Bulls
2. Rottweilers
3. German Shepherd Dogs
4. Siberian Huskies
5. Alaskan Malamutes
6. Doberman Pinschers
7. Chow Chows
8. Great Danes
9. Saint Bernards
10. Akitas

Pit bull was once merely a canine job description and not the name of a particular dog breed. Small, sturdy dogs were used to bait the bulls brought to market under the theory that this activity somehow "tenderized" the bull's meat. Bull baiting then became a sport, and these small bulldogs were heralded for their tenacity and courage in the ring. Unfortunately, in 1835, when bull baiting was banned, the vicious sport of dogfighting soon took its place. People who were impressed with these brave bull-baiting dogs then bred them with terriers to create the Bull and Terrier, a dog known for his bravery, dog-on-dog aggression, and docility toward humans.

Today, the dog commonly referred to as a Pit Bull is usually an American Pit Bull Terrier, the descendant of the Bull and Terrier. The APBT, as he is often known, is generally brave, sweet-tempered, courageous, and loyal. Pit Bulls, with their sturdy physiques and calm demeanors, make good family pets for households with older children. But because of the Pit Bull's strong prey drive — the result of their terrier heritage — these dogs don't do well in homes with babies or toddlers. It is unfortunate that this much-maligned breed has been the victim of so much bad press. When it comes to dog bites, it is usually an owner's fault and not his dog's. The combination of dogfighting history, however, and the corruption of Pit Bulls as watchdogs for criminal activity has generated a frantic rush of politicians' trying to "do something" to assuage their constituents' mass hysteria. This uproar has led to misguided breed-specific legislation and a general condemnation of Pit Bulls, whether purebreds, crossbreeds, or mixed breeds. All the dogs listed below participated at one time or another in the sport of dogfighting.

1. **American Staffordshire Terrier**
2. **American Pit Bull Terrier**
3. **Staffordshire Bull Terrier**
4. **Bull Terrier**
5. **Boston Terrier**

Doberman Pinscher

The 45 Best Dogs for Allergy Sufferers

There is no dog breed that can truly be considered hypoallergenic, because all dogs produce dander. Dander can be found in the shed skin cells, saliva, and urine of dogs. There are breeds, however, who produce less dander than others. Many people who are allergic to dogs have an easier time with these breeds. According to DogBreedInfo.com, the following dogs are generally recommended for allergy sufferers because they have a single coat of fur and as a result produce less dander than double-coated breeds.

1. American Hairless Terrier
2. Basenji
3. Bedlington Terrier
4. Bergamasco
5. Bichon Frisé
6. Bichon/Yorkie crossbreed
7. Bolognese
8. Border Terrier
9. Cairn Terrier
10. Chinese Crested (hairless)
11. Cockapoo
12. Coton de Tulear
13. Dachshund
14. Doodleman Pinscher (crossbreed)
15. Giant Schnauzer
16. Hairless Khala
17. Havanese
18. Irish Water Spaniel
19. Kerry Blue Terrier
20. Labradoodle
21. Lagotto Romagnolo
22. Löwchen
23. Maltese
24. Malti-Poo
25. Miniature Poodle
26. Miniature Schnauzer
27. Native American Indian Dog
28. Peruvian Inca Orchid
29. Portuguese Water Dog
30. Puli (Pulik)
31. Schnoodle
32. Schnauzer
33. Shepadoodle
34. Shichon
35. Shih Tzu
36. Soft-Coated Wheaten Terrier
37. Spanish Water Dog
38. Standard Poodle
39. Standard Schnauzer
40. Tibetan Terrier
41. Toy Poodle
42. West Highland White Terrier
43. Wire Fox Terrier
44. Xoloitzcuintle
45. Yorkshire Terrier

10 Dogs to Avoid if You Suffer from Allergies

The degree to which people are allergic to dogs varies a great deal. And though there are some dogs who are more easily tolerated than others, some breeds are a definite no-no for people with even the mildest allergic tendencies. DogBreedInfo.com makes these recommendations.

1. Afghan Hound
2. Basset Hound
3. Shar-Pei
4. Cocker Spaniel
5. Collie
6. Dachshund
7. Doberman Pinscher
8. German Shepherd Dog
9. Irish Setter
10. Springer Spaniel

Schnauzer

12 Dogs Who Don't Like Strangers

1. Akbash Dog — This is an elegant, rare breed from the area we now call western Turkey. It was developed 3,000 years ago by shepherds who selectively bred for white-colored guarding sheepdogs, perhaps to differentiate them from predators. They are naturally dog-aggressive. In town, with sights and sounds everywhere, barrier frustration and aggression are common.

2. Anatolian Shepherd Dog — Independent, very watchful, proud, and self-assured, these dogs are affectionate with their own family but suspicious of strangers, especially after reaching adulthood. Strangers should be formally introduced before the mature dog is asked to accept them. The Anatolian Shepherd Dog is possessive with respect to his home and property and will not allow anyone onto the family property if the owner is not home unless it has had frequent contact with the person, but he is fairly friendly with those people the family accepts.

3. Boerboel — Boerboel are protectors and can be very aggressive to people passing on the street. They will guard their family, friends, and property with their life. When the owners are not home they will not allow anyone to enter the home, unless they know them very well. In their native South Africa they are known as "Boerdogs."

4. Caucasian Ovtcharka — The Caucasian Ovtcharka is most popular in Russia. *Ovtcharka* means "sheepdog" in Russian. The typical Caucasian Ovtcharka is assertive, strong-willed, and courageous. Unless properly socialized and trained, the Caucasian Ovtcharka may exhibit ferocious and unmanageable tendencies. It is very brave, alert, strong, and hardy.

5. Central Asian Ovtcharka or **Mid-Asian Shepherd** — This is a calm, fearless flock guardian. Independent dogs, they stand their ground and do not back down. Outside the home they may try to dominate other dogs and are wary of strangers; they are guardians and will act as such. This independent and aloof breed, believed to be of Tibetan origin, has protected nomadic herdsmen and their flocks for centuries.

6. Chinese Chongqing Dog — This breed is noble, alert, intelligent, and dignified. If his owners are not with him and a stranger approaches, the Chongqing Dog will heighten watchfulness and prepare for action. But if his owners are on the scene, it is different. When he sees that a stranger is friendly with his owners, he will

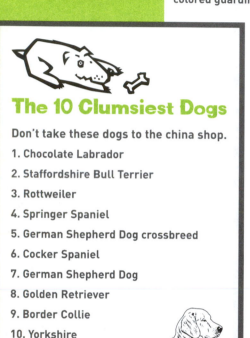

The 10 Clumsiest Dogs

Don't take these dogs to the china shop.

1. Chocolate Labrador

2. Staffordshire Bull Terrier

3. Rottweiler

4. Springer Spaniel

5. German Shepherd Dog crossbreed

6. Cocker Spaniel

7. German Shepherd Dog

8. Golden Retriever

9. Border Collie

10. Yorkshire Terrier

Golden Retriever

be nice to the stranger, even if his owners leave. The Chinese Chongqing Dog is an ancient and unique breed, thought to have been in existence since the Han dynasty in China.

7. *Fila Brasileiro* or Brazilian Mastiff — Extremely dedicated to his owner, a *Fila* will protect you without a moment's hesitation. Bold and very wary with strangers, this breed makes an amazing guard dog. They can be trained to tolerate strangers, but their natural inclination is to attack. With an adult weight of 90–110 pounds, this is an imposing-looking dog.

8. Kangal Dog — The Kangal Dog, weighing 110–145 pounds, is alert, territorial, and defensive of the domestic animals or the human family to which she has bonded. This breed is very suspicious of strangers, and it is therefore necessary to provide a secure fenced yard. The Kangal District of the Sivas province in central Turkey is where she probably originated.

9. Kuvasz — Very territorial with strong protective instincts, the Kuvasz is quite reserved with and even suspicious of strangers. Some authors claim that the Kuvasz has been known since the age of the Huns. Others describe him as a sheepdog that accompanied the Turkish refugees and their flocks fleeing the Mongols into Hungary in 1200. His name in Turkish means "protector."

10. Mioritic Sheepdog — The Mioritic Sheepdog, originating in the Carpathian Mountains in Romania, is vivid and balanced, alert and vigilant, disciplined, and very attached to her owner but suspicious with strangers. Fearless and very courageous, she is the perfect protector of her owner and the herds. She is a courageous and aggressive dog, but she obeys her owner with calm and discipline.

11. Mountain Cur — These dogs have a strong desire to please their master. Very protective of the property and family, they can sometimes be overprotective. The Mountain Cur is noted for his courage. The dog in the book *Old Yeller* was a Mountain Cur, but in the film the dog was portrayed by a Labrador Retriever.

12. Slovensky Cuvac — He is a fearless defender of his territory and "pack," whether it be made up of humans or animals. These dogs have been known to be dramatically affectionate with members of their own family but reserved with and even suspicious of strangers. The Slovensky Cuvac is well documented as far back as the seventeenth century. As wolves slowly disappeared from the European mountains and modern herding practices came about, the Cuvac almost became extinct.

5 Hairless Dogs

1. American Hairless Terrier
2. Chinese Crested (hairless variety)
3. Hairless Khala or Pila
4. Peruvian Inca Orchid
5. Xoloitzcuintle or Mexican Hairless Dog

Chinese Crested

The 10 Best Date Bait Breeds

Deborah Wood, writer, dog trainer, and the pet columnist for the *Oregonian,* appears regularly as the pet expert on ABC radio's *Satellite Sisters.* Wood was named Newspaper Person of the Year in 2001 and 2002 by the Dog Writers' Association of America. After a year of interviewing scores of people for her book, *The Dog Lover's Guide to Dating* (Howell, 2004), Ms. Wood was able to figure out the right dogs for attracting Mr. or Ms. Right.

1. **Golden Retriever.** Friendly and nonthreatening, the Golden is the ideal date bait dog. With their happy face, glistening fur, and wagging tail, these dogs make humans feel good — and brave enough to say hello to the person at the other end of the leash.

2. **Scruffy Terrier Mix.** Small terrier mixes can be the cutest dogs in the world. Bright eyes, an adventurous soul, and the waifish tousle of hair compel people to come over and coo. Bonus points if the dog came from a shelter with a sad story — and has a fabulously happy life with you.

3. **Collie.** One word: Lassie. Who doesn't have childhood memories of yearning for this dog? Especially if you're looking for a love over forty, this dog will bring people to your side.

4. **Afghan Hound.** Elegant, aloof, and hairy, this exotic breed isn't the kind dog people will hug. However, they will stop in their tracks and say, "Wow!"

5. **Labrador Retriever.** There's a reason Labs are the number one dog in America — we just can't help but love these mugs. Half of America has a story about a Labrador they once loved — and will share it as they pet your dog.

6. **Pug.** Very hip thanks to the *Men in Black* movies, Pugs are friendly, happy, comical dogs who invite a conversation. They're small enough to be portable but big enough to be sturdy pals. Note: At Pug parties around the globe, lots of people seem to feel compelled to dress their Pugs in clothes — especially giving female Pugs highly feminine outfits reminiscent of Miss Piggy. Don't dress your Pug in clothes if you're hoping to meet a normal human.

7. **Saint Bernard.** Nothing has quite the "awwwww" factor as a big, sweet, lovable Saint Bernard. They've got the big eyes and round heads that we're genetically programmed to respond to the way we respond to babies. They have giant size without intimidation and are a guaranteed conversation starter. (Get used to people asking, "How much does that dog eat?!")

8. **Tiny dogs with big-dog confidence.** A lot of people are turned off by Yorkies, Maltese, Toy Poodles, and other pint-size pooches. However, if one of these tiny toy dogs is a confident, friendly little guy who looks people in the eye and sort of shrugs as if to say, "What's your problem?" you and your dog will soon have a small army of admirers.

9. **Beagle.** There's no friendlier face than a Beagle's. This breed seems simple and straightforward, a kind of Midwestern working-guy dog in a convenient package.

The 5 Worst Date Bait Breeds

1. **Pit Bull.** There are lots of sweet, gentle Pit Bulls in the world, and most Pit Bulls love people and are great with kids. No matter how nice your Pit Bull may be, understand that, with the breed's fierce reputation, lots of people won't come near these dogs. Some communities have banned Pit Bulls and related breeds. Expect people to cross the street to avoid you if you have a Pit Bull, even if your dog is a wonderful, friendly, sweet soul.

2. **Rottweiler.** Like Pit Bulls, too often Rottweilers are given a bad rap, unfairly. These loyal, intelligent, trainable dogs can be fabulous pets for singles and families alike. But here's a hint: any breed that is the subject of a cult classic movie named *Rottweiler: Dogs of Hell* may lose you more friends than he wins you.

10. Old English Sheepdog. Fuzzy, furry, and funny, Old English Sheepdogs invite a hug. And you'll spend hours answering the question "How does that dog see anything through all that hair?"

3. Yapping little dogs. Some people don't like little dogs, period. No one likes yapping little dogs. These dogs can irritate even their owners.

4. Dogs with elaborate hairdos. People who show their Poodles learn to love all the fluff and pompons. Not the rest of the world. If your Poodle or other breed is trimmed like topiary, expect derisive laughter, not love.

5. Chinese Crested. These dogs are usually born naked, except for tufts of hair on their heads, feet, and tails. No matter how smart, funny, and just plain lovable these little guys are, even many of their owners will admit they look a little bit like space aliens. It doesn't help that Chinese Cresteds are the perennial winner of the World's Ugliest Dog Contest, held annually in Petaluma, California. In fact, a Crested named Chi Chi is in the *Guinness Book of World Records* for winning this dubious title the most times — seven in all.

34 Dogs for Couch Potatoes

They're sedate enough to sit beside you for a *Twilight Zone* marathon on television, and you can even teach them how to use the remote during commercials. Just remember that all dogs — and their humans — need some exercise, even if it's just a jog to the kitchen for more popcorn. Here are the best boob tube companions, according to DogBreedInfo.com.

1. Affenpinscher
2. American Bullnese
3. Basset Hound
4. Basenji
5. Beagle
6. Bichon Frisé
7. Bolognese
8. Boston Terrier
9. Brussels Griffon
10. Bulldog
11. Chihuahua
12. Chinese Crested (hairless)
13. Clumber Spaniel
14. Cockapoo
15. Cocker Spaniel
16. Dachshund
17. English Toy Spaniel
18. French Bulldog
19. Havanese
20. Italian Greyhound
21. Japanese Chin
22. Maltese
23. Miniature Pinscher
24. Papillon
25. Pekingese
26. Pomeranian
27. Pug
28. Shih Tzu
29. Silky Terrier
30. Sussex Spaniel
31. Toy Fox Terrier
32. Toy Manchester Terrier
33. Toy Poodle
34. Yorkshire Terrier

Pug

MARK ASHER/CHRONICLE BOOKS

15 Breeds to Avoid if You Have Children

According to Kenneth Phillips at Dogbitelaw.com, these breeds are good choices for experienced dog owners and should be considered only if you have careful, considerate, respectful children.[1] Training and professional help (for the dog, not the children) might be essential, especially for larger breeds. As always, do not leave dogs and children alone together unsupervised, no matter how much you trust your dog.

1. **Pit Bulls** — Most Pit Bulls adore children, but these dogs have steel-trap jaws, so when they're bad, they're awful.

2. **Lhasa Apso** — Most are very cross with children and also with some adults.

3. **Toy Poodles** — Since these dogs are so tiny, children may accidentally injure them, and they then might bite out of self-defense.

БЪЛГАРИЯ • BULGARIA
7.00
ЧАУ ЧАУ • CHOW CHOW

4. **Dachshunds** — Impatient with little ones.

5. **Rhodesian Ridgeback** — A very dominant breed.

6. **Miniature Pinschers** — This is a big dog in a little body; he can be fierce.

7. **Australian Blue Heelers** — Nip at children's heels and tend to herd them.

8. **Pekingese** — Can be intolerant of children.

9. **Chihuahuas** — These tiny dogs almost always prefer adults. They tend to be intolerant of children, especially unpredictable toddlers.

10. **Rottweillers** — Rotties can be great if they are raised with children, but generally they consider themselves superior to youngsters.

11. Some **Malamutes** — Like Rottweilers, these dogs can get along with the children they are raised with. Generally, though, they prefer adult company.

12. **Chow Chows** — Can be very cranky with the little ones. These are one-person dogs who usually bond with an adult and might not appreciate a tiny usurper (no matter how cute).

13. **Giant Schnauzers** — This very dominant breed often challenges even adult authority.

14. **Dalmatians** — Members of this breed are very excitable and prone to jump a lot, even on the kids.

15. Some **Dobermans** — These smart dogs don't seem to have much use for little ones.

Dachshunds

[1] In which case you should contact us immediately and tell us your secret!

33 Breeds That Are Great with Kids

These are by no means the only dogs that are liable to form strong bonds with little ones, but they are all commonly known to be gentle, protective, and not prone to jealousy issues. They are fun-loving and won't mind the frenzy that children can bring into their lives.

1. American Cocker Spaniel
2. Australian Shepherd
3. Basset Hound
4. Beagle
5. Bearded Collie
6. Bernese Mountain Dog
7. Bichon Frisé
8. Bloodhound
9. Boston Terrier
10. Boxer
11. Brittany Spaniel
12. Bulldog
13. Collie
14. Coonhound
15. English Setter
16. Foxhound
17. Golden Retriever
18. Gordon Setter
19. Great Dane
20. Irish Setter
21. Keeshond
22. Labrador Retriever
23. Mastiff
24. Newfoundland
25. Old English Sheepdog
26. Portuguese Water Dog

27. Pug
28. Saint Bernard
29. Samoyed
30. Siberian Husky
31. Springer Spaniel
32. Standard Poodle
33. Vizsla

> "The dog was created especially for children. He is the god of frolic."
> — HENRY BEECHER WARD

ROBIN SCHWARTZ

Dogs who are great with kids come in all shapes and sizes.

The 5 Most Challenging Dogs to Own

According to *PetLife* magazine there are five breeds of dogs who pose a number of potential problems for their owners. These problems can make them difficult to raise, maintain, and train properly. The following dogs have been selected because they present a combination of challenging personality traits as well as potentially serious health problems.

1. **Akitas** by nature are extremely willful and need expert training and handling, especially during their puppyhood. They also tend to be aggressive toward other dogs and are capable of great ferocity, which makes them an excellent guard dog but not necessarily an excellent family dog. It is suggested that you never leave an Akita alone with another animal. Additionally, if your Akita is unfriendly with children she doesn't know, she will probably bite when teased — so keep your Akita away from unfamiliar people and always, always supervise her when she is around small children. Furthermore, never take food away from your Akita! This breed does not respond well to harsh discipline. In fact, it is only through positive, gentle training that Akitas can become wonderful household pets. The Japanese say of the Akita that she is "tender in heart and strong in strength."

2. While there are exceptions to any rule, **Chow Chows** are generally bossy, suspicious, willful, and extremely independent. This breed needs a dominant owner if he is to meet his potential as a family companion. Chow Chows are eager to please, but they require a firm and patient trainer. This breed is loyal to their people and will guard their family to the death. Strangers, however, can be seriously threatened if they don't approach a Chow Chow carefully. Chow Chows must be appropriately socialized with other household animals from puppyhood in order not to behave aggressively toward them. If properly managed, this breed can make an excellent family dog.

3. **Shar-Peis** ordinarily are wonderful companions and watchdogs, but they do

---

Cats have better memories than dogs. Tests conducted by the University of Michigan concluded that whereas a dog's memory lasts no more than five minutes, a cat's can last as long as sixteen hours — exceeding even that of monkeys and orangutans.

The 10 (Reputedly) Least Intelligent Dog Breeds

The psychologist Dr. Stanley Coren, author of *The Intelligence of Dogs* (Bantam, 1995), developed a canine intelligence scale as the result of surveying more than two hundred dog obedience judges around the country. The rankings on this list — and on the one that follows — are based on these dogs' needing to have a command repeated anywhere from between eighty to one hundred times before they were able to obey.

1. Afghan Hound
2. Basenji
3. Bulldog
4. Chow Chow
5. Borzoi
6. Bloodhound
7. Pekinese
8. Beagle
9. Mastiff
10. Bassett Hound

not always follow directions. They can be quite dominant and unfriendly toward strangers but do well with children and other animals they are familiar with. This breed requires gentle and consistent training; otherwise she won't deign to obey. Shar-Peis were developed to be hunters, guardians, and fighting dogs. In fact, the loose skin that is characteristic of this breed enables the Shar-Pei to turn on an opponent even when he is grasped firmly in the enemy's teeth. Potential owners of this breed should meet their puppy's sire and dam in order to get an idea of what their dog's future disposition may be like.

4. The **Rottweiler** is a powerful and courageous dog, and to a great extent she is impervious to pain. This breed needs to be trained properly to ensure that she doesn't exhibit aggressive tendencies. If raised *and* trained properly from early in her life, the Rottie can be an excellent, affectionate pet and guard

The Plutocrats toured the United States early in the twentieth century.

dog. This breed is usually friendly to people she knows but shouldn't be approached by strangers. If an owner raises his Rottweiler improperly, however, he can easily find himself dominated by his dog. And believe us: you don't want to be dominated by one hundred pounds of aggressive animal.

5. **Dalmatians** are extremely active dogs and require a great deal of exercise on a daily basis. These dogs can behave destructively if they don't receive adequate exercise. Dalmatians also crave human attention and can get depressed without it. If they aren't properly socialized when they are puppies, Dalmatians can act nervous or high-strung. This breed also has a tendency toward dog-on-dog aggression. Health problems such as hip dysplasia, deafness, and bladder stones often arise in this breed. Dalmatians are also susceptible to distraction by either smells or sounds. This dog is not a good choice for a sedentary family or a family with small children.

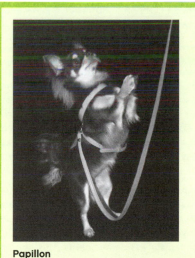

Papillon

The 10 Most Intelligent Breeds

1. Border Collie
2. Poodle
3. German Shepherd Dog
4. Golden Retriever
5. Doberman Pinscher
6. Shetland Sheepdog
7. Labrador Retriever
8. Papillon
9. Rottweiler
10. Australian Cattle Dog

Top 10 Lap Dogs

No, we certainly don't endorse a sedentary lifestyle. But you might want to think about curling up with one of these breeds after some brisk exercise. They'll love to get petted and pampered while you relax and lazily channel-surf. Each dog's weight — which helps determine their suitability for different-size laps — is included here, courtesy of PetPlace.com.

1. **Bichon Frisé.** Not only is the Bichon Frisé a great lap dog, but this curly-coated white breed is also recommended for people with allergies. The Bichon Frisé loves attention and is very affectionate. Lap weight: 7 to 12 pounds.

2. **Cavalier King Charles Spaniel.** King Charles II was almost never without two or three of these spaniels. He once ordered that they be admitted to all public places — even courtrooms (this decree is still in place in Great Britain). With large eyes and a slightly rounded head, the Cavalier is absolutely adorable. Their hair coat is moderately long and most often is white-and-chestnut-colored. Cavaliers get along in almost any household — they even like cats — although your lap may get a little crowded. Lap weight: 10 to 18 pounds.

Shih Tzu

3. **English Toy Spaniel.** This breed is a cousin to the Cavalier King Charles Spaniel. The Toy Spaniel has a shorter muzzle than the Cavalier, and their moderately long, wavy coats are most often red and white. This breed has a merry disposition like his cousin, but they are a little shyer with strangers and in unfamiliar situations. Lap weight: 9 to 12 pounds.

4. **Japanese Chin.** Elegant yet comical, the Chin is rare in the United States. In Japan he is known as the Japanese Spaniel and was a historic favorite of royalty. The Chin has a large head, wide-spaced almond-shaped eyes, and an amazingly luxuriant coat. The most common colors for this breed are black and white. This is a dog whose function is strictly that of a companion. On your lap, a Chin is excellent at keeping your lower extremities warm. Lap weight: about 7 pounds.

5. **Lhasa Apso.** Hailing from Tibet, where this dog is called *apso seng kye* ("bark lion sentinel dog"), the lovable Lhasa's keen hearing and intelligence make her a good watchdog, but this breed has had even more success as a lap dog. The longhaired coat of the Lhasa is usually tan in color and needs daily brushing. These very friendly dogs are easy to train. They truly do make ideal companion pets. Lap weight: 13 to 15 pounds.

6. **Maltese.** As their name suggests, the small Maltese originated on the island of Malta in the Mediterranean. This breed is believed to be more than 2,800 years old and has been depicted on Greek ceramics and in Roman poems. This diminutive dog may look fragile, but he is actually quite

"**Among God's creatures** two, the dog and the guitar, have taken all the sizes and all the shapes, in order **not to be separated from the man.**"

— ANDRE SEGOVIA

resilient. His long, flowing white coat needs daily care. Maltese are smart and extremely affectionate. Lap weight: about 3 to 7 pounds.

7. **Pomeranian.** If you are looking for a spunky, perky little dog, look no further than the Pom. Believed to have originated in Pomerania, Germany, the Pomeranian is an alert, lively companion. This compact little dog has very fuzzy fur and resembles a cuddly teddy bear. Lap weight: about 3 to 7 pounds.

8. **Pug.** For a dog of such small stature, there's an awful lot of love stuffed into the Pug. Clowns by nature, Pugs demand attention and adoration, but they also return these affections in great measure. Pugs are short-muzzled dogs with large eyes and wrinkled foreheads. In ancient times, these wrinkles were emphasized to resemble the Chinese symbol for "Prince." Pugs have short coats (fawns are double-coated; blacks single-coated) that need little care beyond daily brushing. Beware: these dogs shed a lot! Pugs are more energetic than most toy breeds, and they love a rewarding play session. They are always ready, however, to sit on a nice comfortable lap. Lap weight: 15 to 20 pounds.

9. **Shih Tzu.** Proud and intelligent, the Shih Tzu hails from Tibet and China, where the breed's name means "lion dog" because of the tufted mane of fur around their face. Shih Tzus are also called "chrysanthemum-faced dog" because their hair tends to grow in all different directions, just like a chrysanthemum's petals. This breed is alert, curious, and gentle. Shih Tzus bond closely with their people and exhibit fierce loyalty to their families.

Show dogs typically have a long, flowing multicolored coat. Companion Shih Tzus are usually trimmed, which means that they need regular trips to the groomer to keep them in tip-top shape. But don't be fooled by this breed's fancy exterior: Shih Tzus are fun-loving party animals. Lap weight: 8 to 10 pounds.

10. **Toy Poodle.** As a distinct breed, Poodles have existed for quite some time; paintings representing them date as far back as the thirteenth century. Poodles hate to be left alone and usually prefer the company of people to other dogs. This breed hates to be ignored and does not like being thought of — or treated as — "just a dog." The Toy Poodle is the smallest member of the Poodle family and, like her larger cousins, she needs daily grooming to keep her curly coat tangle-free. Lap weight: under 10 pounds.

Seventy percent of people sign their pet's name on greeting cards and 58 percent include their pets in family and holiday portraits, according to a survey done by the American Animal Hospital Association.

Top 20 Dog Breeds for Outdoor Life

We don't recommend that a dog ever be forced to live outdoors. Dogs need a secure and safe haven inside the house. Dogs who are separated from their families not only fail to thrive but can also become listless, fearful, and sometimes even vicious. Certain dogs, however, were bred for outdoor living and are far better suited and able to adapt to life outside than other breeds. Keep in mind that even when they are out-of-doors, these dogs should always be provided with some kind of shelter from the elements — a doghouse, if you will. Here are the top twenty outdoor dogs recommended by PetPlace.com:

1. **Alaskan Malamute.** Bred to pull sleds over frigid terrain, the Alaskan Malamute is ideally suited for life outdoors, though not in hot temperatures. This dog's thick, heavy coat is far better suited to cold climates.

2. **Australian Cattle Dog.** Unlike the Australian Shepherd, the Australian Cattle Dog truly is from Australia. Developed to herd cattle, this dog needs lots of mental stimulation and physical activity. Australian Cattle Dogs can do well outside if they are provided with large yards that are securely fenced.

3. **Australian Shepherd.** Despite his name, the Australian Shepherd is an American-made dog. Used in many different ways, the Aussie is very intelligent and craves activity. Outdoor life can work well for dogs of this breed as long as they have plenty of things to do.

4. **Bearded Collie.** The Bearded Collie may not be as popular as some other breeds, but she has plenty of admirers. A hardy dog who works as a sheepdog in Scotland, this breed has a thick coat that allows her to thrive in cold, outdoor weather.

5. **Belgian Sheepdog.** As one of the representative breeds of Belgium, this dog is cherished as a police dog, guard dog, herding dog, and companion. With a thick coat, this breed can live outdoors, provided he is given a lot of attention.

6. **Bernese Mountain Dog.** As with the Greater Swiss Mountain Dog, the Bernese was developed to be a draft dog. Hardy and strong, the Bernese is at home both indoors and out. He thrives in cold weather.

7. **Chow Chow.** This is one of the most easily recognized breeds. Popular because of his thick fluffy coat, Chow Chows can thrive outdoors, even in the coldest weather. During the hot summer months, outdoor Chows appreciate a drastic haircut.

8. **Curly-Coated Retriever.** This retriever is a hardy dog who loves water. Her thick coat provides protection from harsh weather. Additionally, she is a faithful and devoted guard dog.

9. **Foxhound.** As a hound developed to hunt foxes, the American Foxhound thrives with outdoor activities. Not the best apartment dog, this breed needs a sturdy fence and plenty of room to run.

10. **German Shepherd Dog.** Nearly always topping the lists of popular dog breeds, the German Shepherd Dog has innate guarding and protective instincts. His double coat insulates him in cold weather. He can be quite content spending his days and nights outside.

11. **Great Pyrenees.** The Great Pyrenees is happiest when he has a job to do. Whether guarding sheep, pulling carts, or protecting his family, the Great Pyrenees seems to thrive outdoors, especially in winter.

12. **Greater Swiss Mountain Dog.** This breed was developed in Switzerland as a working dog. Bred to guard, herd, and haul heavy carts, the Greater Swiss Mountain Dog enjoys the outdoor life.

13. **Irish Wolfhound.** This gentle giant was originally developed to hunt wolves in Ireland. Her massive size enables her to enjoy the wide-open spaces of the great outdoors.

14. **Keeshond.** With his thick coat, the Keeshond does well outside as long as his family is nearby and provides him with daily grooming and plenty of companionship.

15. **Mastiff.** This giant and imposing dog was once used as a hunter and protector. Now content to patrol her home and guard her family, the Mastiff can thrive outdoors but needs companionship.

16. **Norwegian Elkhound.** This dog is descended from canines who hunted with the Vikings. Brave enough to track bear and moose, the Elkhound is also hardy enough to live outdoors.

17. **Old English Sheepdog.** Easily recognized by his thick white and gray coat, the Old English Sheepdog can live anywhere. At home in an apartment or outside in the yard, this dog needs a daily grooming to keep his coat healthy.

18. **Rottweiler.** This powerful dog can live indoors or outdoors. Originally bred to be a herding dog, the Rottweiler is now best known as a formidable guard dog.

19. **Samoyed.** This big white dog with the smiling visage is popular mostly because of her gentleness. Sturdy and thick-coated, this breed can live outdoors as long as she has plenty of contact with her family.

20. **Siberian Husky.** Historically, Siberians always lived outside in one of the world's harshest, coldest climates. Bred to pull sleds across frozen terrain, this dog is very hardy and is quite content living outdoors.

Top 20 Dog Breeds for Apartment Living

According to PetPlace.com, the ideal apartment dog should be relatively small, sedate, quiet, and easy to clean up after, and he should have low daily exercise requirements. So if you live in an apartment — and are looking to add a dog to your life — consider one of the following breeds. No barkers need apply!

1. **Bichon Frisé.** This white fluff ball is a happy-go-lucky dog. Faithful and obedient, the Bichon is a wonderful addition to any apartment. Weighing around fifteen to twenty pounds, this breed requires regular grooming to keep his coat tangle-free and looking great.

2. **Boston Terrier.** Bostons are small black and white dogs who love to make you laugh. After brief periods of activity, the Boston loves to curl up on the sofa next to you while you read a good book. Obedient and loyal, the Boston is also a good watchdog.

3. **Boxer.** The Boxer is one of the most successful larger breeds who do well in an apartment. Their short hair and pleasant disposition make them a great choice for an apartment dweller who still wants a dog of substance. Brief daily walks are enough to keep this dog happy and healthy.

4. **Cairn Terrier.** Despite his small size, the Cairn Terrier is a tough little dog. This breed does well in any living situation as long as people are around to give him care and company. As with all terriers, the Cairn needs exercise, but he does not require a large living space.

5. **Chihuahua.** What the Chihuahua lacks in size she certainly makes up for in personality. Faithful and protective, this tiny dog does well in the smallest of apartments. Weighing around five pounds, the Chihuahua is also relatively easy to train and care for.

6. **Cocker Spaniel.** The popular Cocker, with his curly hair and sad eyes, is a good choice for apartment life. He needs only basic exercise and usually spends his days lounging around, waiting for his owner's return.

7. **Dachshund.** With their short legs and long bodies, the Dachshund can do well in an apartment. They appreciate a good walk or run in the park but are most comfortable snoozing in a nice warm bed.

8. **English Bulldog.** Once you get used to her snoring, the Bulldog

will prove to be a cherished family pet. Not big on exercise, this breed just needs to get outside and take a look at some grass a few times a day.

9. **Italian Greyhound.** This toy version of the larger Greyhound usually weighs around ten pounds and is a quick study. Though he does enjoy a good chase, the Italian Greyhound also loves a good nap.

10. **Lhasa Apso.** Hailing from Tibet, this breed makes the perfect lap dog. Weighing less than fifteen pounds, the Lhasa requires regular grooming and expects to be treated like a king, but he nevertheless does well in small living spaces.

11. **Maltese.** This popular breed of European royalty expects to be treated like a queen. With a long, flowing white coat, the Maltese needs routine grooming and prefers being pampered to working for her kibble. These characteristics unite to create a wonderfully docile companion for apartment dwellers.

12. **Pomeranian.** This little fluff ball resembles a tiny fox. Weighing around five pounds, the Pom is an adorable breed who thrives on human companionship. Requiring little space, the Pom is perfect for living in an apartment.

13. **Poodle.** The Miniature and Toy Poodles make excellent apartment dogs. These breeds crave human companionship and need daily walks. Well known for their minimal shedding, the Poodle is one of the more popular canine apartment dwellers.

14. **Pug.** Weighing in at fourteen to twenty-five pounds, the short-muzzled, stocky Pug is a clown at heart. This breed does not need special care, though they do tend to shed a lot. As long as Pugs get enough exercise, they are happy to sleep away the rest of the day. Pugs make loving family members, are good with children, and don't require a lot of space.

15. **Schipperke.** Although not well known, this breed is great for apartment living. A small black dog with a docked tail, the Schipperke generally weighs around ten to eighteen pounds. This is an active dog who likes to be included in all aspects of family life. Daily exercise is a must.

16. **Schnauzer.** The Standard and Miniature Schnauzers are wonderful breeds for apartment living. Eager to keep his family safe and desiring to please, this dog requires regular grooming and daily exercise. Schnauzers thrive with human companionship.

17. **Scottish Terrier.** This working dog from the Scottish highlands weighs around fifteen to twenty pounds. Most often black, the Scottie is highly intelligent and needs daily exercise. Tough and compact, the Scottie makes a loyal and protective family member.

18. **Pembroke Welsh Corgi** and **Cardigan Welsh Corgi.** At about twenty-five pounds, the Corgis are popular pets. These stocky, short-tailed breeds need daily exercise but not necessarily a large living space.

19. **West Highland White Terrier.** This small terrier is playful and lovable but requires moderate exercise to be happy. The perfect size for an apartment, the Westie is also a good watchdog and faithful companion. Her wiry white coat needs some grooming to keep it mat- and tangle-free.

20. **Yorkshire Terrier.** The Yorkie is a tiny, spirited dog who weighs less than ten pounds. Yorkies are happy to spend their days lounging on the sofa with their people. Their long coats, however, should be groomed regularly.

Barkers

Watchdogs are not the same as guard dogs. A *watchdog* alerts his owners when a stranger approaches, but he usually will not attack. A good watchdog doesn't have to be big or aggressive; he just needs to possess a strong bark that lets his family know someone is approaching the house. Often, just hearing a dog's bark will deter would-be intruders. A *guard dog* can do the same, but he is usually large enough to intimidate and, if necessary, attack an intruder. Almost any dog who barks when something abnormal happens can act as a watchdog, but the following breeds are best known for their natural watchdog tendencies.

1. **Airedale.** As the largest member of the Terrier Group, the Airedale can be intimidating. Though he may seem aloof to strangers, the breed is very loving toward his family members, especially children.

2. **Boston Terrier.** Small, muscular, and compact, the Boston Terrier is one of the few truly American breeds. These are gentle, friendly dogs who are very protective of home and family. Most Bostons have a good bark and will alert their people when a stranger approaches.

3. **Chihuahua.** The Chihuahua is a small dog with a big bark. She almost always barks vigorously, as if trying to make up for being just eight inches tall and weighing less than five pounds. A Chihuahua will always make sure you know when someone is approaching your house.

4. **French Bulldog.** The Frenchie isn't a big barker, but he will certainly alert his family to strange noises or people who get too close for comfort. Natural guardians, Frenchies are also devoted companions.

5. **Irish Setter.** An Irish Setter is a beautiful, friendly, energetic dog. She will bark to let you know when someone is at your house, but despite this dog's size, don't expect any more. Setters are friendly enough to invite a stranger inside and show her around.

6. **Miniature Pinscher.** Contrary to popular belief, the Miniature Pinscher was not bred down from the Doberman Pinscher. (Min Pins are the older of the two breeds and are a cross between Greyhounds and terriers.) Always curious, the Min Pin will alert her owner when an unfamiliar person is nearby.

7. **Norwegian Elkhound.** This breed is descended from the Valhund, the first Viking dogs. Brave enough to track bear and moose, the Elkhound makes an excellent watchdog. This breed is bold, courageous, and athletic.

8. **Pekingese.** The Peke is a bold, regal toy dog with an enthusiastic bark to rival the Chihuahua's. This dog loves to be pampered but will do his best to alert his family when strangers come around.

9. **Schipperke** (pronounced "skipperkee"). Skips (as they are nicknamed) were originally bred to be watchdogs, hunters of vermin, and companions. They excel at all three.

10. **Standard** and **Miniature Schnauzer.** Both breeds make excellent watchdogs. Schnauzers hail from Germany and are intelligent, reliable, and protective.

"A watchdog is a dog kept to guard your home, usually by sleeping where a burglar would awaken the household by falling over him."

— ANONYMOUS

Breeds to Match Your Personality Type

According to Dr. Stanley Coren, the author of *Why We Love the Dogs We Do,* choosing a puppy is similar to choosing a spouse. It is important that you understand your own and your dog's personality types in order to make the right match. Type A humans are generally impatient with their time, highly competitive, stressed, and driven by ambition. These people are usually happier when they have a calm, type B dog (although some type A humans also do well with type A dogs). Type B humans, on the other hand, are "laid-back," easygoing, and able to work at a reasonable pace. They know how to relax.

Here are several breeds that work well with each personality type. Keep in mind that like people, dogs are individuals. A particular member of a type B breed might still be very high-strung. That's just his personality! Age and lifestyle are also factors that determine your dog's character.

Type A Dogs (for Type B Humans)		Type B dogs (for Type A Humans)	
Airedale	Irish Terrier	Basset Hound	Great Dane
Belgian Sheepdog	Jack Russell Terrier	Bloodhound	Great Pyrenees
Border Collie	Siberian Husky	Boston Terrier	Irish Wolfhound
Brittany	Springer Spaniel	Bulldog	Newfoundland
Cairn Terrier	West Highland White Terrier	Cavalier King Charles Spaniel	Pekingese
Collie			Pomeranian
Dalmatian	Whippet	Clumber Spaniel	Pug
Fox Terrier	Yorkshire Terrier	French Bulldog	Saint Bernard

"If you want to be liked, get a dog. The people you work with are not your friends."

— DEBORAH NORVILLE

Canine Partners for Your Vocation

According to Dr. Mark Goulston and Dr. Stanley Coren, these breeds are your best bets:

1. **Journalist/Type A:** A busy journalist should have a low-maintenance, type B dog who is perfectly willing to stay at home, says Dr. Coren. And a calm canine wouldn't hurt, either.

2. **Executive Secretary/Type A:** A low-key type B dog is best if he plans to bring his work home or often stays late at work.

3. **Cocktail Waitress/Type B:** A type A/type B canine is best because our cocktail waitress will need a fair amount of quiet time. However, she may want to go out running and get away from it all.

4. **Short-Order Cook/Type A:** Type B pooches are ideal, because when short-order cooks get home, they're usually dog tired. You do not want your dog following you around the house begging for a walk or a game of catch.

5. **Hair Stylist/Type B:** Type B dogs are the best bet for those in this chatty, personalized profession. They're more likely to appear interested while you use them as a sounding board. And they won't mind as much when you braid their hair . . .

6. **Teacher/Type B:** Type A/B dogs are a good bet when you bring your work home with you. They're less likely to interfere with your efforts but will also provide plenty of social interaction, a must for type B people.

7. **Accountant/Type B:** Type A dogs are perfect for you, because your sedentary (and let's face it, predictable) life can really benefit from the sparkle you'll receive from a go-getting type A dog.

8. **Real Estate Broker/Type A:** A type B dog is best — since you're away from home so much, you'll need a classic low-maintenance canine.

9. **Hostess/Type A:** Type A/B is a hostess's surest bet because a restaurant can be a flurry of activity during peak hours but relatively low-key at other times. You need a dog who can adapt the way you are used to adapting.

---

9 Dogs Who Can Raise Your Homeowner Insurance Costs

Insurance companies believe that certain dog breeds are more prone to bite and damage property than others. The AKC points out that these dogs should actually bring premiums down because they guard property and therefore prevent theft. Here is a list of the breeds that insurance companies have characterized as "bad dogs."

1. Akita
2. Alaskan Malamute
3. American Pit Bull Terrier
4. Chow Chow
5. Doberman Pinscher
6. German Shepherd Dog
7. Rottweiler
8. Siberian Husky
9. Staffordshire Bull Terrier

---

10. **Doctor/Type A:** A harried doctor who responds to emergency calls requires a type B dog. Contrarily, a type A pooch works well for the nine-to-five physician, because watching your dog's antics will take your mind off your work.

The 10 Noisiest Dogs

They yap, they bark, they annoy the hell out of your neighbors. (You gotta love 'em!)

1. Beagle
2. Collie
3. Doberman Pinscher
4. Finnish Spitz
5. German Shepherd Dog
6. Norwegian Elkhound
7. Rottweiller
8. Shetland Sheepdog
9. Terriers (almost all of them!)
10. Toy and Miniature Poodle

Shetland Sheepdog

Top 10 Guard Dogs

These breeds are particularly aggressive. Their bulk, strength, courage, and resistance to counterattack combine to make them great guard dogs.

1. **Bullmastiff** — This alert, good-natured guard dog is devoted to her people but can sometimes be willful. Docile unless provoked, the Bullmastiff is fearless and protective, yet affectionate. Although unlikely to attack an intruder, this breed will catch him, knock him down, and hold him in place. The Bullmastiff was once used as a gamekeeper's dog to track down, tackle, and detain poachers.

2. **Doberman Pinscher** — Bred for a century to be an outstanding guard dog, the Doberman Pinscher is intense and energetic, with tremendous strength and stamina. Versatile, highly intelligent, and very easy to train, the Doberman is fearless and assertive but not vicious. The creator of this mixture was a German tax collector named Louis Doberman who needed a dog to protect him when he visited thief-infested neighborhoods.

3. **Rottweiler** — The Rottweiler is calm, trainable, courageous, and devoted to his owners and family. These dogs have a reliable temperament and seem immune to pain. Rottweilers are highly intelligent, natural guard dogs who over the centuries have proven their protective abilities in police, military, and customs work.

4. **Komondor** or **Hungarian Sheepdog** — Descended from Tibetan dogs, the Komondor was brought to Hungary 1,000 years ago by nomadic Magyars to guard flocks of sheep. The Komondor is serious, confident, alert, and commanding. She can be very reserved with strangers and is highly territorial and protective of her family, house, car, and livestock. Implacable against wolves and bears who would attack her flock, this dog can quickly get the best of even the strongest opponent.

5. **Puli** — Pulik crossed the plains into Hungary with the Magyars several thousand years ago, when they were used as sheepdogs. Many shepherds seemed to prefer black dogs, but this was probably because they were easier to view among the white flock. The Puli was prized for her light, agile movements, while the larger Hungarian breed, the Komondor, was more often used as a guard dog for the flocks. Though wary of strangers, Pulik are never aggressive. Instead, they will give a vocal warning if they feel their owner is threatened.

6. **Giant Schnauzer** — The Giant Schnauzer is a large, powerful, compact dog who is very protective and spirited. Steadfast and responsible, the Giant Schnauzer is thought to have been created from crosses between black Great Danes, Bouvier des Flandres, and Standard Schnauzers. The Giant Schnauzer was first used as a cattle-driving

© LORI SASH-GAIL

dog in Bavaria. Later, the police and the military used him as a guard dog.

7. **German Shepherd Dog** — German Shepherd Dogs are direct and fearless, eager and alert. Bold, cheerful, obedient, and eager to learn, this breed is known for tremendous loyalty and courage. They are calm and confident but never hostile. Serious and almost human in his intelligence, the German Shepherd Dog has a high learning potential. These dogs love to be near their families but are very wary of strangers. They have strong protective instincts, so they need to be socialized extensively in order to prevent overguarding when they are adults.

8. **Rhodesian Ridgeback** — This breed is intelligent and cunning. They are loyal to their family yet have something of a mind of their own. Ridgebacks are brave, vigilant, and reserved toward strangers, and they possess considerable stamina. A South African breed, he was imported by Boer settlers in the sixteenth and seventeenth centuries and used for a variety of purposes, including protecting game, retrieving waterfowl, and guarding property. Ridgebacks are also known to be excellent babysitters. South African hunters discovered that the Ridgeback, when used in packs, was very effective at keeping lions at bay. Hence the breed's other name: the African Lion Hound.

9. **Kuvasz** — Bold, determined, brave and fearless, and easy to housebreak, this livestock guardian is very territorial, with strong protective instincts. He makes an excellent guard dog. Traditionally, the Kuvasz was an outstanding herder and defender of the flock against wolves. This breed is not for everyone. His large size and strong protective instincts demand that an owner put in extra time and effort to train him. The Kuvasz will fiercely defend his people and territory. *Kuvasz* means "protector" in Turkish.

10. **American Staffordshire** — Although she is a courageous and persistent fighter if she is provoked, the American Staffordshire Terrier is a good-natured, amusing, loyal, and affectionate family pet. She is gentle with both children and adults. The AmStaff is an extremely courageous and intelligent guard dog. Highly protective of her owners and her owners' property, she will fight an enemy to the death. This breed has a very high tolerance for pain.

10 Quiet Dog Breeds

With the exception of the Basenji, a dog who doesn't bark yet can still make quite a racket (by yodeling, howling, and crowing), all the dogs listed below are capable of producing a barking sound. They remain relatively quiet, however, most of the time.

1. Akbash Dog
2. Basenji
3. Borzoi
4. Bulldog
5. Cane Corso
6. Chesapeake Bay Retriever
7. Greater Swiss Mountain Dog
8. Irish Wolfhound
9. Italian Greyhound
10. Whippet

"It's not the size of the dog in the fight, it's the size of the fight in the dog."
— MARK TWAIN

29 Dogs Who Hate Cats

According to DogBreedInfo.com, most dogs will get along with the family feline providing that the socialization of the new puppy and the cat are done as carefully as possible. This process should occur when the puppy is around three months old. Since most reputable breeders don't let their puppies go home before twelve weeks, this means that you will need to introduce puppy and kitty as soon as you walk in the door with your new bundle of fur. The kind folks at DogBreedInfo.com also point out that it's easier to introduce a kitten into a household that already has dogs rather than the other way around. Still, there are dog breeds that generally don't like cats and shouldn't be left alone with them. They are as follows:

Afghan Hound
Ainu Dog
Alaskan Malamute
American Blue Gascon Hound
American Foxhound
Australian Cattle Dog
Australian Kelpie
Basenji
Beagle

Border Collie
Border Terrier
Bullmastiff
Dandie Dinmont Terrier
English Foxhound
Greyhound
Harrier
Ibizan Hound
Jack Russell Terrier
Norwegian Elkhound

Otterhound
Pharaoh Hound
Plott Hound
Redbone Coonhound
Rhodesian Ridgeback
Saluki
Samoyed
Shiba Inu
Vizsla
Weimaraner

Ocadash, an Afghan Hound

Dandie Dinmont Terrier

25 Dogs Who Don't Like Other Dogs

Some dog breeds — as well as some individual dogs — tend to be more dominant and aggressive than others. According to DogBreedInfo.com, the following breeds are generally considered to be the most dog-aggressive. Training and socialization can sometimes curb this behavior.

1. Airedale Terrier
2. Akita
3. Alaskan Malamute
4. American Mastiff
5. American Pit Bull Terrier
6. American Staffordshire Terrier
7. American Toy Terrier
8. Australian Cattle Dog
9. Basenji
10. Bedlington Terrier
11. Bull Terrier
12. Doberman Pinscher
13. Fox Terrier
14. Giant Schnauzer
15. Irish Terrier
16. Jack Russell Terrier
17. Lakeland Terrier
18. Manchester Terrier
19. Miniature Bull Terrier
20. Miniature Pinscher
21. Sealyham Terrier
22. Smooth Fox Terrier
23. Staffordshire Bull Terrier
24. Wire Fox Terrier
25. Yorkshire Terrier

4 Terriers Who Actually Like Other Dogs

1. Australian Terrier
2. Silky Terrier
3. Tibetan Terrier
4. West Highland White Terrier

22 Droolers

Some dogs drool a lot. They just can't help it. Traditionally, dogs who drool a lot are those who have been bred for certain tasks (such as retrieving game) that make slack jaws, loose skin, and soft bites necessary traits. Of course, any dog will drool on occasion (a chipped or cracked tooth, a sirloin roasting on the barbeque). Some dogs, though, just naturally slobber more than others:

1. Basset Hound
2. Black-and-Tan Coonhound
3. Bloodhound
4. Bluetick Coonhound
5. Boxer
6. Bullmastiff
7. Dogue de Bordeaux
8. English Bulldog
9. English Setter
10. French Bulldog
11. Great Dane
12. Great Pyrenees
13. Irish Water Spaniel
14. Kuvasz
15. Mastiff
16. Neapolitan Mastiff
17. Newfoundland
18. Plott Hound

THAT'S MY BARNEY. HE'S A LOYAL COMPANION, A GUARD DOG, AND A HUMIDIFIER ALL IN ONE...

MARK PARISI

19. Redbone Coonhound
20. Saint Bernard
21. Shar-Pei
22. Spanish Mastiff

Great Jogging Companions

If you're a distance runner and want your dog to come along for the ride, there are some things you need to consider. Before embarking on any exercise regimen, you should have a veterinarian thoroughly examine your dog to determine that she is healthy. **Never push your dog beyond her limit. Don't exercise your dog in extremes of hot or cold temperatures.** And keep in mind that small dogs usually don't fare well on long runs. The following are some common dog breeds that love to run:

Airedale Terrier	Chesapeake Bay Retriever	Golden Retriever	Rhodesian Ridgeback
Alaskan Malamute	Collie	Greyhound	Rottweiler
American Pit Bull Terrier	Dalmatian	Irish Setter	Samoyed
Australian Shepherd	Doberman Pinscher	Newfoundland	Siberian Husky
Bearded Collie	English Springer Spaniel	Old English Sheepdog	Soft-Coated Wheaten Terrier
Border Collie	German Shepherd Dog	Pointer	Weimaraner
Boxer	Giant Schnauzer	Portuguese Water Dog	Welsh Springer Spaniel

"If your dog is fat, you aren't getting enough exercise." — UNKNOWN

Bearded Collie

Tip: The "DogJogger" leash is designed for "hands-off" jogging so that you don't have to hold the leash and miss the full "pump" action of your arms for a good aerobic workout.

22 Poos and Doodles

People appear to be fascinated by Poodle mixes. From Cockapoos to Peek-a-Poos to Labradoodles to Golden Doodles — what's all the fuss about? Largely, it has everything to do with the nature of Poodles themselves. This highly intelligent dog sheds very little, is highly trainable, and possesses great agility and strength. These wonderful characteristics, however, are very often exploited by breeders trying to make money by promulgating new "poo" breeds. To date, the only Poos who have received any serious attention from the AKC are the Labradoodle (Labrador Retriever and Poodle) and the Cockapoo (Cocker Spaniel and Poodle).

Cockapoo

1. **Bich-Poo** — Bichon Frisé/Poodle
2. **Boxerdoodle** — Boxer/Poodle
3. **Cairnoodle** — Cairn Terrier/Poodle
4. **Chi-Poo** — Chihuahua/Poodle
5. **Cockapoo** — Cocker Spaniel/Poodle
6. **Daisy Dog** — Bichon Frisé/Poodle/Shih Tzu
7. **Doodleman Pinscher** — Doberman/Standard Poodle

8. **English Boodle** — English Bulldog/Poodle
9. **Golden Doodle** — Golden Retriever/Poodle
10. **Labradoodle** — Labrador Retriever/Poodle

Labradoodle

11. **Malti-Poo** — Maltese/Poodle
12. **Papoo** — Papillon/Poodle
13. **Peke-a-Poo** — Pekingese/Poodle

Prairie dogs are not dogs at all; they are a kind of rodent.

14. **Pomapoo** — Pomeranian/Poodle
15. **Pugapoo** — Pug/Poodle
16. **Schnoodle** — Schnauzer/Poodle
17. **Shepadoodle** — German Shepherd/Standard Poodle
18. **Shih-Poo** — Shih Tzu/Poodle
19. **Weimerdoodle** — Weimaraner/Poodle
20. **Westiepoo** — Westie/Poodle
21. **Whoodles** — Soft-Coated Wheaten Terrier/Poodle
22. **Yorkipoo** — Yorkie/Poodle

An American Animal Hospital Association poll showed that 33 percent of dog owners admit that they talk to their dogs on the phone or leave messages on an answering machine while away.

24 Wacky Mixed Breeds

What do you get when you cross a . . .

1. Pekingese + Lhasa Apso = **Peekasso**, an abstract dog

2. Great Pyrenees + Dachshund = **Pyradachs**, a puzzling breed

3. Pekingese + Dachshund = **Peking Dach**, owned by Chinese restaurateurs

4. Kerry Blue Terrier + Bloodhound = **Blueblood**, a favorite with society's upper crust

5. Poodle + Great Pyrenees = **Poopyree**, a dog who smells good

6. Pointer + Setter = **Pointsetter**, a traditional Christmas pet

7. Irish Water Spaniel + English Springer Spaniel = **Irish Springer**, a dog fresh and clean as a whistle

8. Kerry Blue Terrier + Skye Terrier = **Blue Skye**, a dog for optimists

9. Smooth Fox Terrier + Chow Chow = **Smooch**, a dog who loves to kiss

10. Airedale + Spaniel = **Airel**, a dog who brings in good TV reception

11. Labrador Retriever + Curly-Coated Retriever = **Lab Coat Retriever**, the choice of research scientists

12. Newfoundland + Basset Hound = **Newfound Asset Hound**, a dog for financial advisors

13. Terrier + Bulldog = **Terribull**, a dog who always makes mistakes

14. Keeshond + Setter = **Keester** — you can't get this dog off his duff . . .

15. Bloodhound + Labrador = **Blabador**, a dog who barks a lot

16. Chihuahua + Whippet = **Chiapet** — order it from television! Three for $19.95!

17. Boxer + German Shorthair = **Boxer Shorts**, a dog never seen in public

18. Basenji + Schipperke = **Baserke**, a dog who's crazy about his owner

19. Malamute + Pointer = **Moot Point**, owned by . . . oh, well, it doesn't matter anyway

20. Collie + Malamute = **Commute**, a dog who lives on the freeway

21. Deerhound + Terrier = **Derriere**, a dog who is true to the end

22. Collie + Lhasa Apso = **Collapso**, a dog who folds up for easy transport (and enjoys Caribbean music)

23. Spitz + Chow Chow = **Spitz Chow**, a dog who throws up a lot

24. Bull Terrier + Shih Tzu = **Ah, never mind!**

Terribull

"I have a great dog. She's half Lab, half pit bull. A good combination. Sure, she might bite off my leg, but she'll bring it back to me." — **JIMI CELESTE**

How to Recognize a Reputable Breeder

You've done your research, you've learned everything there is to know about the breed of dog you want, and now you're ready bring one home. You've heard that pet stores sell unhealthy puppies from puppy mills, and you don't want any part of that. Your next step is to locate a breeder who will guarantee — in writing — that your new puppy was bred properly, is healthy, and conforms to AKC standards. Finding a reputable breeder can be as easy as calling the American Kennel Club or visiting them online and requesting a referral for a local breeder. Here are some positive indications that you have found a reputable breeder.

A reputable breeder . . .

1. . . . keeps her dogs inside the house as part of her family — not outside in kennel runs.

2. . . . has healthy-looking dogs who are eager to meet new people and don't shy away from visitors.

3. . . . shows you where most of his dogs spend their time. This should *always* be in a clean, well-maintained area.

4. . . . encourages you to spend time with your puppy's parents — at a minimum, you should meet the puppy's mother when you visit the breeder (the father is more likely to be a sire for hire — a stud, if you will — than is the dam).

5. . . . breeds only one (two at the most) type of dog and is knowledgeable about the breed standard (how the breed should look).

6. . . . has a strong relationship with a local veterinarian and shows you records of the puppies' veterinary visits. This explains the puppies' medical history and which vaccinations your new puppy has received and which ones he still needs.

7. . . . is well versed in the potential genetic problems inherent in the breed.

8. . . . gives you guidance on caring and training your puppy and is available to assist you after you take your puppy home.

9. . . . provides referrals for other families who have purchased puppies from him.

The 10 Gassiest Dogs

A recent survey of dog lovers, conducted on AkPharma's toll-free CurTail Hotline, reveals that all dogs are not created equal when it comes to pet gas. From shepherds to Poodles, Rottweilers to Beagles, CurTail consumers report pet gas to be the most notorious in a diverse list of canine offenders. Pet gas is definitely a problem that most pet owners encounter, and frequently it's the result of a pet's inability to properly digest the ingredients in pet food. CurTail Drops are designed to prevent pet gas associated with most types of food, from generic store brands to gourmet special diet formulas. Here's AkPharma's list of the ten most serious offenders:

1. German Shepherd Dog
2. Mixed breed
3. Labrador Retriever
4. Boxer
5. Doberman Pinscher
6. Poodle
7. Cocker Spaniel
8. Rottweiler
9. Beagle
10. Dalmatian

10. . . . feeds her dogs high-quality premium-brand food.

11. . . . doesn't always have puppies available but will instead put you on a waiting list for the next available litter.

12. . . . actively competes with his dogs in conformation trials where judges decide just how closely his dogs match the breed standard. Reputable breeders will also work with their local, state, and national breed clubs.

13. . . . provides you with a written contract and health guarantee and allows plenty of time for you to read it through. A breeder should not require that you use a specific veterinarian.

14. . . . asks why you want a dog.

15. . . . asks you questions such as the following: Who will be responsible for the puppy's daily care? Who will attend puppy training classes? Where will the dog spend most of her time?

16. . . . asks you to provide proof from your landlord (or condominium board) that you are allowed to have a dog.

17. . . . insists that you agree (in writing) to spay or neuter your puppy. Unless your puppy is going to a show home (yours), your breeder is likely to provide a certificate of limited registration for your puppy. This means that you can register your dog with the AKC as long as she is spayed or he is neutered. Your veterinarian will sign these papers after your dog's procedure.

18. . . . allows you to sign a contract stating that you will return the dog to the breeder if you are unable to keep the dog at any point in her life.

Breeders to Avoid

1. One who asks to meet you in a parking lot or a public place (as opposed to the facility where the puppies are raised). You *must* inspect the dogs' environment.

2. One who breeds so his kids can witness "the miracle of birth" or so the female "can have one litter before she is fixed."

3. A breeder who is in it just to make some extra money.

4. A breeder who sells more than two different dog breeds.

5. A breeder who overbreeds his dogs. Females should never be bred more than once every two years. A responsible breeder breeds only to produce puppies of excellent quality and to improve on the qualities of the sire and dam in temperament, structure, trainability, and any other breed-specific abilities (such as hunting or tracking or retrieving).

Based on reports from 1,038 facilities around the United States, 56 percent of dogs and puppies entering shelters are killed, according to the National Council on Pet Population Study and Policy.

What You Can Do About Puppy Mills

Every year hundreds of thousands of puppies are brought into the world by mass-breeding operations called puppy mills. Puppy mills provide most of the puppies sold in pet stores, so they continue to be highly profitable and flourish. These mills frequently house dogs in shockingly poor conditions, particularly for "breeding stock" animals who are caged and continually bred for years, without human companionship and with little hope of ever becoming part of a family. When these breeding dogs outlive their usefulness they are commonly killed, abandoned, or sold to another mill. The puppies that are produced in these mills often leave the mill with serious behavior and health problems.

Because a puppy mill is a business, the facility is designed purely for profit, not comfort. Laws are on the books to provide minimum-care standards for puppy mill animals, but enforcement has historically been spotty at best. The U.S. Department of Agriculture (USDA) licenses and inspects puppy mills for violations of the Animal Welfare Act; likewise, some state laws are designed to protect the charges in the average puppy mill. But puppy mills can successfully navigate around these laws, whether by selling directly to consumers (thereby avoiding USDA licensing requirements) or simply avoiding the reach of law enforcement (with so few USDA inspectors and minor fines, it's easy to stay in business).

The Humane Society of the United States has been investigating puppy mills for decades, exposing the cruel realities of the commercial dog-breeding industry. They've lobbied for the current laws as well as for additional money to enforce those laws. They've also educated millions of consumers on the many reasons they should avoid pet store puppies. Here are some of the HSUS's suggestions on how to stop the cruel treatment of dogs in puppy mills.

1. Don't support puppy mills. Puppy mill dogs are sold even in the swankiest of pet stores and through the most picturesque of Web sites. The truth is, unless you personally visit the place where your dog is born and raised, you have no real way of knowing whether you're supporting a puppy mill. Puppy millers have devised slick new methods for hiding their cruel businesses. They regularly place newspaper ads that hawk one specific breed (instead of the old approach of exclaiming, "We have over 20 different breeds!") to fool consumers into thinking the mill is actually a small operation. Rule number one is always *Never buy a puppy without personally visiting the breeder's premises.*

2. Write your legislators. Contact your senators and representatives and let them know that the inhumane treatment of dogs in puppy mills is a concern of yours and urge them to do something about it. Current regulations do not ensure humane treatment, and dogs and consumers suffer for it. Let them know that you want puppy mills to be a priority for Congress, because they're a priority for you.

3. Educate others. What's the most common response we hear when people find out that their animal came from a puppy mill? "I had no idea." That's why this action is so vital. There's no greater tool than education. Order copies of HSUS flyers and distribute them. Be creative in your education campaign. Talk to your groomer. Talk to your veterinarian. Even talk to your pet supply store owner.

4. Write a letter to the editor of your local paper. Use the information contained on these pages to write a letter to your local newspaper — a short, polite letter to inform people about the dog industry's dirty secret.

5. Talk to reputable breeders. The trick to finding a good breeder is knowing the right questions to ask — and walking away if you don't get the right answers. The HSUS checklist, available on their Web site, will help you. You can also ask any breeder you know for help. After all, a small reputable breeder hates puppy mills just as much as you do.

6. Recruit your veterinarian. Veterinary offices are logical places to go when looking for information on adoption or animal breeders. So supply your vet's office with the flyers available from the HSUS. A vet should be your dog's second-best friend — ask him or her to help you help dogs.

7. Donate. You can help the HSUS in its ongoing campaign to stop puppy mills and protect all animals. Go to www.stoppuppymills.org to make a donation.

7 Reasons Not to Buy a Puppy from a Pet Store

Pet store puppies come from puppy mills, and puppy mills are nothing but cruel, inhumane breeding factories. Yes, these dogs deserve our compassion just as much as dogs from a reputable breeder do. Ultimately, though, buying puppies from a pet store only supports the deplorable conditions and practices of puppy mills. *Do not support puppy mills.* If you want to save a dog's life, visit your local chapter of the ASPCA and adopt an all-American mixed breed.

1. All pet shops get their dogs from puppy mills. They may claim that their dogs are from a local breeder, but this generally means they got the puppy from a local mill. No ethical breeder *ever* sells his puppies to a pet store.

2. Pet shop salespeople are on equal par with used-car dealers in terms of selling techniques. Their main interest is in profit margins and the bottom line. They use high-pressure sales techniques and play on your emotions to get you to make a purchase, regardless of whether you and your dog are even suitable for each other.

3. You won't receive customer support, ever! You won't receive help if your puppy develops genetic problems, if you have difficulty housetraining her, or if she gets runny eyes or ear infections or is just "acting strange." Pet store personnel cannot be counted on for advice. An experienced breeder, on the other hand, will make himself available to you and can be relied on to be a reliable source of information.

4. Most pet stores will not give you any kind of health guarantee for your puppy. If you do manage to receive a health guarantee, make sure to read it over carefully. The fine print is likely to be meaningless. Odds are, it isn't a real *guarantee* and it won't cover your puppy if she develops any serious health problems.

5. Pet store salespeople know little if anything about a puppy's parentage aside from the mere basics of the breed. Breeders, on the other hand, will entertain you with stories about the parents of your puppy, their quirks and histories, and the kind of details guaranteed to minimize surprises as your dog grows into adult-

One female dog and her offspring can produce 67,000 dogs in six years. Failure to spay or neuter pets results in hundreds of thousands of offspring being euthanized annually.

hood. Breeders are also excellent sources of referrals for grooming, training, breed clubs, and other breed-specific resources.

6. Many of the puppies sold in pet stores are ill or are incubating diseases (see "What You Can Do About Puppy Mills," page 215). Parvo, distemper, and innumerable genetic defects are all common in pet store puppies. Poor circulation and close quarters in these stores also contribute to the contagious diseases that affect countless numbers of pet shop dogs. Beware! Sick puppies are often made to look presentable for sales purposes, and symptoms of many diseases may not appear right away. Don't play Russian roulette with a pet store pooch. You don't want your family to become attached to an animal who isn't long for this world.

7. Every purchase from a pet store only encourages the store and the puppy mill to produce more dogs, thereby condemning that puppy's mother to a life of continuous mistreatment and abuse.

Each day in the United States, animal shelters are forced to destroy 30,000 dogs and cats.

© LORI SASH-GAIL

 # How Much Is That Doggie in the Window?

Average Prices of Puppies of the Top 50 Most Popular Dog Breeds

The price of a female puppy is generally $100 more than that of a male, and the cost of a show dog can be $1,000 more than that of a pet-quality puppy. There are some instances, however, when an exceptional litter is born to championship dogs. These puppies can command prices of well over $5,000. Such prices are not listed here. The lowest prices listed here are for those of a male pet-quality puppy. The highest prices are the average amount for a show-quality dog. The costs of deworming, vaccinations, and health certificates — and in some cases, microchipping — are included in these prices. AKC registration is not included, since that is left up to the buyer to take care of and generally only costs about thirty dollars. The following prices were obtained from breeders around the United States.

Airedale Terrier — $800–$1,200

Akita Inu — $600–$1,500

Alaskan Malamute — $500–$1,000

American Cocker Spaniel — $300–$750

Australian Shepherd — $350–$800

Basset Hound — $450–$1,000

Beagle — $300–$800

Bichon Frisé — $500–$700

Boston Terrier — $500–$700

Boxer — $500–$1,000

Brittany Spaniel — $325–$600

Bulldog — $1,350–$2,000

Cairn Terrier — $700–$1,200

Chesapeake Bay Retriever — $475–$1,000

Chihuahua — $400–$1,000

Chow Chow — $800–$1,200

Collie — $350–$700

Dachshund — $450–$1,250

Dalmatian — $500–$600

Doberman Pinscher — $350–$900

English Springer Spaniel — $600–$850

German Shepherd Dog — $400–$1,250

German Shorthaired Pointer — $400–$600

Golden Retriever — $400–$1,800

Great Dane — $500–$1,700

Great Pyrenees — $600–$1,000

Labrador Retriever — $400–$900

Lhasa Apso — $495–$1,100

Maltese — $550–$1,500

Miniature Schnauzer

Mastiff — $750–$1,500

Miniature Pinscher — $450–$650

Miniature Schnauzer — $400–$850

Newfoundland — $1,150–$1,250

Pekingese — $500–$1,000

Pembroke Welsh Corgi — $500–$1,500

Pomeranian — $250–$6,000

Poodle (Standard) — $500–$3,000

Pug — $800–$1,200

Rottweiler — $750–$1,250

Saint Bernard — $500–$850

Samoyed — $400–$800

Schipperke — $300–$800

Scottish Terrier (Scottie) — $400–$1,200

Shar-Pei — $500–$1,500

Shetland Sheepdog (Sheltie) — $300–$600

Shih Tzu — $500–$800

Siberian Husky — $450–$1,500

Weimaraner — $400–$800

West Highland White Terrier — $500–$1,000

Yorkshire Terrier — $700–$1,200

Newfoundland

8 Reasons Not to Breed Your Dog

Is your dog so cute you wish you could fill the world with creatures just like her? Many owners feel this way about their pets. Some people even see breeding as a way to make extra money by selling purebred puppies. But breeding requires a serious commitment and plenty of resources. More often than not, people find themselves in over their heads when they decide to breed dogs. Here are some considerations provided by VetCentric.com to take into account before you become a breeder.

1. Not all dogs are built to be bred. Most pets, although lovable, are not breeding quality. They may have genetic defects and other problems that should not be perpetuated. People who breed dogs for a living are very careful about choosing which dogs they will breed together based on their physical characteristics and behavior.

2. There are already too many dogs in the world, and far too many of these end up in shelters instead of good homes. If your breed of dog has large litters, what will you do if you are unable to sell the puppies? Do you really want to contribute to the massive problem of pet overpopulation?

3. Dogs who aren't neutered face serious health risks and special hazards. Consider your dog's own health. Male dogs who are neutered are much less likely to be hit by cars. Unlike neutered males, unaltered ones have a very strong urge to roam and find a fertile female. They will travel under fences, through doors, and into windows. They will pull their leash out of unsuspecting hands in the quest for a mate. Additionally, neutering greatly reduces the incidence of prostate disease and eliminates testicular cancer in males; spaying cuts down on breast cancer in females. The incidence of uterine infections is also eliminated by spaying females.

4. Female dogs used for breeding may have unwelcome visitors. If you spay your bitch, you will not have to constantly chase persistent males out of your yard. You also won't have to worry about cleaning up after messy heat cycles.

5. You will have to work like a dog when your pet goes into labor. Many people do not realize just how much effort and expense are involved in "letting dogs have puppies." Get-

ting the mother through her pregnancy is the easy part. The birth itself, however, is truly laborious for both dog and owner alike. This is especially true when puppies make their entrance at two in the morning and the veterinary hospital is closed.

If your pet develops a problem during delivery, you will have to pay the expense of an emergency veterinary house call. You must be prepared to make some difficult decisions in case these complications are life-threatening. And you need to be ready to pay for an emergency cesarean section if your breed of dog has a particularly broad head, such as in a Pug or a Bulldog. The bills, the worry, and the time this takes

can overwhelm even the most enthusiastic dog lover.

6. It can be devastating when puppies die. There is always the possibility of losing some or all of your litter. A neonatal mortality rate of 10 to 30 percent is considered normal in dogs. Also, it's easy to lose a puppy if you don't have the experience or knowledge to care for newborns properly.

7. Not all dogs make the best mothers. If your female doesn't have enough milk to feed all her puppies or decides that feeding her offspring is not her cup of tea, it's your responsibility to provide the puppies with nutrition every three to four hours, around the clock. You will need to provide manual stimulation for uri-

Using their swiveling ears like radar dishes, dogs can, as experiments have shown, locate the source of a sound in 6/100 of a second.

nation and defecation, both of which Mom normally does until her puppies can manage on their own. (Before puppies are three weeks old they won't void unless directly stimulated.)

8. Good luck in seeing a profit! Your final responsibility before those puppies go to a new home is to have them dewormed, vaccinated, and examined by a veterinarian. You will need to budget for this.

Top 10 Reasons to Breed Dogs

1. You think the house is too orderly.

2. You're already an insomniac.

3. You want your vet to buy a new BMW.

4. Your furniture looks too new.

5. You love the sound of puppies — in the morning, noon, afternoon, evening, midnight, predawn, etc., etc.

6. Your garden and backyard need renovating and you don't want to pay a landscaper.

7. Your neighbors don't complain enough already.

8. The kids aren't really a challenge.

9. If you can train and show one dog, why not ten?

10. You can't think of a better way to test your spouse's loyalty.

BEWARE OF
the Following 12 Phrases in
DOG
Ads

Buying a puppy from a reputable breeder isn't as simple as it seems. *Finding* a reputable breeder isn't even as simple as it seems. The amount of work that you put into selecting a dog breed, a breeder, and a particular puppy all increase your chances of getting the right dog for you and your family. Study classified ads if that's your chosen source. But don't look for the lowest-priced puppies or a kennel closest to your home. Instead, consult a trusted veterinarian, a reliable dog trainer, and your local chapter of the breed's national club for the name of a responsible breeder.

Here are some misleading phrases that may show up in a classified ad. These will tip you off that this *is not* a reputable dog breeder.

1. **"Furry little stocking stuffers."** These puppies were probably bred as nothing more than a money-making scheme. Advertisers such as these prey on clients who forget that "stocking stuffers" can grow up to be eighty-pound giants. Be sure that the puppy you buy is the right one for your family to live with all year long. Never purchase a puppy for a child without clearing it first with her parents. Additionally, any reputable breeder will tell you that a living creature makes a terrible Christmas gift. They're too demanding, they need attention when all you want is eggnog, and, unlike a hangover, they will be with you for much longer than the following day. Getting a dog is a huge consideration. Dogs should never, ever be an impulse buy. And if you get someone a dog, there is always the chance that what she really wanted was a cashmere sweater.

2. **"Full-blooded, no papers."** This is usually an attempt to mislead an inexperienced buyer. "Full-blooded" (a vague term at best) probably means that the parents are of the same breed, but it could also be an attempt to characterize puppies of mixed parentage. For example, two Cockapoos do not produce a purebred litter. It takes generations of careful breeding to produce a new breed. A Cockapoo is probably the result of a onetime breeding between a Cocker Spaniel and a Poodle. Because the puppy is then actually a crossbreed, it cannot be full-blooded. The dogs described in this ad were most likely bred by accident, and not to contribute to the health and stature of their breed.

3. **"Papers"** in an ad might refer to a pedigree or to a registration certificate. A pedigree is a family tree that will tell you something about the quality of the parents, grandparents, and great-grandparents of the puppy. A *pedigree* helps to trace a puppy's background so you can see if he may be carrying a particular genetic disorder. A *registration certificate* will allow the dog's owner to register him with the American Kennel Club, the United Kennel Club, a rare breed registry, or an independent kennel club or breed registry. But this certificate in no way reflects the current health or the genetic fitness of your potential puppy. It affirms only that the puppy's parents are registered members of their breed. Be sure to find out exactly which kinds of papers are available.

4. **"Pups OFA registered"** or **"good hips."** Puppies cannot be registered with OFA (Orthopedic Foundation of Animals) since this certification is given only upon examination of radiographs (x-rays) taken after a dog turns two years old. If one or both of your puppy's parents are less than two years old, they may have had preliminary x-rays that indicate the *absence* of hip dysplasia. They cannot, however, be certified free from this debilitating inherited bone malformation. You do not want to

run the risk of getting a puppy who has hip dysplasia. This is a terrifying, crippling disorder.

5. **"Both parents on premises."** Although potential owners should see the mother and father of their puppy's litter, the presence of both parents is not a guarantee that the puppies were thoughtfully bred. It might still mean that these are backyard breeders with a bitch who is bred every time she comes into heat. The parents may have good temperaments and be genetically healthy specimens of their breed, or they may not be. Instead, investigate further if you are considering this breed. Ask a few simple questions; the answers will tell you if these breeders are reputable. Many responsible breeders choose mates for their bitches from other kennels in order to diversify their breeding programs. In this case, the sire of the puppies may live some distance away, even in another state. If this is true and you are otherwise sure that you've located a responsible breeder, a sire who isn't on the premises shouldn't negatively influence your decision.

6. **"AKC championship background."** If you see this phrase in an ad, ask how far back the champions go and how many there are in the four-generation pedigree. A champion great-great-grandmother means little to the health or genetic fitness of that puppy. OFA registration and a history of eye testing and other genetic testing can make up for the lack of champions in the pedigree.

7. **"Prices lower than the local average for the breed."** This could mean that the price is lower than what puppies cost in a pet store. The average cost of a particular breed should be determined by talking to several breeders, not by looking at dogs in a pet store, where they are usually overpriced. Frequently, even the sale price of a pet store puppy is considerably higher than the price for a puppy from a responsible breeder.

8. **"Rare colors"** is often used to describe an unacceptable-looking coat for a particular breed. Many so-called rare colors are actually disqualifications in the breed because of the genetic problems often associated with them, such as deafness or eye problems. A white Doberman, for instance, is likely to be deaf, as is an albino Great Dane. Red and gray merle, a color pattern with either a reddish or a gray background mottled with darker splotches, can foretell a variety of health problems in certain breeds. In order to maintain the integrity of the breed, dogs of rare colors and patterns should not be bred.

9. **"Needs room to run."** Could mean you'll need a fenced-in yard and some obedience training, either on your own or professionally. (*Avoid dogs that need more exercise than you can provide.*)

10. **"Friendly."** Could also mean overbearing, untrained, undisciplined, obnoxious, or destructive.

11. **"Protective."** Could also mean "overprotective." Better to look for the phrase "good watchdog."

12. **"Free to a good home."** Read: "This dog is driving us nuts."

What to Look for in a Classified Ad

1. "Interested parties only." These breeders are serious, and they're interested in placing their puppies only with families that already know the breed.

2. "Parents OFA, eye-tested." These breeders produce healthy puppies from healthy adults.

3. "Puppies home-raised." These puppies were raised in the house with human contact, not in a kennel. Kennel-raised puppies aren't properly socialized; they are often shy or fearful and can have difficulty relating to people and other dogs.

4. "Health guaranteed." These breeders are realistic and honest enough to admit that they can't guarantee that a puppy won't ever get sick, but they will replace a puppy if she develops a genetic disorder.

The Cost of Breeding

The majority of responsible breeders make very little, if any, money. The only breeders who make a profit are those in the wholesale kennel business. These groups breed dogs in large numbers. It has been well documented that about 75 percent of first-time breeders do not attempt to breed again because of the cost, work, and time involved. Any responsible breeder will tell you that breeding dogs is a labor of love and not a good business decision. So if you're in it for the money, you're going to be disappointed. Instead, you will have added to the problem of canine overpopulation. Let's say that you anticipate selling your puppies for $1,200 each. Here are some of the costs you will incur along the way:

Dachshunds are the smallest breed of dog used for hunting. They are low to the ground, which allows them to enter and maneuver through tunnels easily.

1. Any dog who is being considered for breeding purposes should have her hips x-rayed to rule out hip dysplasia. Tests for cataracts and thyroid disease should also be conducted. Find out which tests are recommended for the breed you are going to be working with. You will spend at least $300 on this.

2. It will be necessary for your veterinarian to perform routine exams to check for uterine or vaginal infections. This needs to be done to ensure that the litter is born alive and healthy. Add another $100 to your expenses.

3. The stud fee for a high-quality dog, unless you're already lucky enough to have one, may cost another $400. This can be even higher if you want a championship-winning stud. Are you getting the picture?

4. If an emergency cesarean section needs to be performed, add at least $350 and possibly more. We're up to about $800–$1,200 at this point.

5. Now you have a nice healthy litter of eight puppies. From the age of about six weeks, you'll need to start feeding them. You'll most likely go through forty to fifty pounds of dog food a week. Premium dog food is the best and the most costly. Add another $30 a week.

6. Now your puppies need their first and second vaccines. This will cost you another $250–$300 per puppy. So far we've spent about $900–$1,000 on each puppy.

7. Now you'll need to advertise the litter. This will cost another $100.

8. If you're unable to sell all the puppies, you'll have to keep them yourself. Ka-ching!

9. The annual maintenance of the mother alone will cost approximately $1,000 a year, not including the initial price you paid for her, training expenses, grooming tools, crates, etc.

"No matter how little money and how few possessions you own, having a dog makes you rich." —LOUIS SABIN

10 Examples of Bad Breeding

Selective breeding can perpetuate physical traits that are themselves harmful. So-called responsible breeders take pride in producing dogs whose looks conform to a set of standards such as those endorsed by the American Kennel Club (AKC) or the United Kennel Club (UKC). Although these organizations claim that their standards represent the ideal dog of each recognized breed, some argue that breed standards often rob dogs of their inherent well-being.

Many dogs suffer from physical deformities due to centuries-old breeding practices that are still carried on today in an attempt to make dogs conform to the standards for their breed. Many purebred dogs have genetic defects that can contribute to a shortened life span or considerably interfere with their quality of life. Here are examples of some breeds with serious difficulties from the Fund for Animals and the Humane Society of the United States.

1. **Basset Hound.** Before breeders arrived on the scene, nature had blessed the Basset Hound with long, straight legs, allowing him to run fast after his prey. Today the Basset Hound's stubby legs bow from the strain of carrying around their elongated, heavy body. This weight knocks their elbows out of their sockets, inviting chronic dislocation.

2. **Bulldog.** An extremely short muzzle doesn't allow the Bulldog sufficient air passage. Many Bulldogs spend their lives fighting suffocation.

3. **Chihuahua.** Because they have been bred to extremely small sizes, the Chihuahua has developed many orthopedic problems. Restricted bone growth can cause loose kneecaps, and this is extremely debilitating. Reduced skull size is also a problem — it restricts the flow of spinal fluid around the brain, which can result in hydrocephalus, a swelling of the brain.

4. **Collie.** This breed is susceptible to genetic eye disorders including inadequate development of the blood vessels to the retina. This is the result, in part, to breeding these dogs for their long snouts.

5. **Dachshund.** The length-to-height ratio that breeders love so much often causes the Dachshund excruciating pain due to the compression of their spinal cords.

6. **Dalmatian.** The same gene that is responsible for the Dalmatian's characteristic spots also carries the trait for deafness. Thirty percent of all Dalmatians are deaf in one or both ears.

7. **Doberman Pinscher** and **Great Dane.** Because of an overly long neck and large head, these dogs are susceptible to "wobblers" disease. In a healthy dog, the spinal cord threads its way freely through the neck vertebrae's central holes. But in a dog with wobblers, these holes narrow; to counter instability between the neck vertebrae, the bone of the vertebrae expands inward, painfully compressing the spinal cord.

8. **German Shepherd Dogs.** Due to the conformation ideal of a GSD to have broad and heavy hips, this breed often suffers from hip dysplasia.

9. **Saint Bernards** and other giant dogs. The trend in breeding these dogs has been to make them larger over generations, often causing them to become lethargic and overheated. Giant breeds can be prone to malignant bone tumors in their overburdened legs.

10. **Shar-Pei.** This breed is susceptible to infections in its skin folds and will often go blind unless you surgically remove part of the heavy eyelid.

6 Advantages of Owning a Mixed-Breed Dog

Besides the unconditional devotion a person gets from building and maintaining a bond with any pet dog, mixed breeds have several advantages:

1. Mixed-breed dogs are generally inexpensive, especially if you get one from a shelter. They may even be free — or nearly so — if you acquired your mixed-breed dog from a neighbor or a newspaper ad. Dogs in a shelter might cost sixty to eighty dollars, but this price often includes vaccinations, a general health exam, and even the cost of having them spayed or neutered. (On the other hand, shelter dogs can have behavioral problems, are often poorly socialized, and may be more susceptible to parasites or infectious disease. Veterinarians, boarding kennels, groomers, and obedience instructors all charge the same fees whether your dog has a pedigree or not.)

2. Mixed-breed dogs have a lower incidence of health defects than poorly bred purebreds. It is not true that shelter dogs are damaged goods and that people leave them at a shelter for a good reason. The greatest number of dogs in shelters are there because their owners didn't properly housetrain them.

3. Owners of purebred dogs often feel the need — and obligation — to participate in their dog's breed, usually by sporting breed-specific clothing and accessories or flashing bumper stickers that declare "I ♥ _____." The owners of mixed breeds, on the other hand, can just sit back and enjoy the company of Bandit or Max without any pressure to conform.

4. You don't need to own a purebred dog in order to compete in agility events. Mixed breeds can compete in agility under the auspices of the U.S. Dog Agility Association and the North American Dog Agility Council. Mixed Breeds can also train as search and rescue dogs, therapy dogs, or service animals. They cannot, however, participate in AKC events. See our list of mixed-breed clubs, page 228.

5. Every one is unique! There's little chance that you'll ever come across a Labrador Retriever/Bulldog/Airedale mix exactly like yours. The only standard for your dog is the one he sets. Although less predictable than purebreds, the all-American mixed breed often has wonderful traits, each one making your dog a true original.

6. By acquiring a mixed breed (it's rare to find a pedigreed dog in a shelter, but it can happen), you will save the life of a dog whose only alternative is euthanasia. It is estimated that 60 percent of all dogs in shelters are eventually euthanized.

7 Advantages of Owning a Purebred Dog

1. If you know exactly which characteristics you want in a dog, you can research breeds to find the right one for you and your family. If you need a dog for a specific purpose — such as herding or guarding — you can more or less predict which breed will do the best job. Whether your variables include allergy sufferers, small children, or close living quarters, you can find "CH Right."

2. Purebred dogs are the result of many years of selective breeding. Their size, temperament, and appearance are wholly predictable. Dog breeds were developed for specific purposes, and documentation is available as to each breed's history and heritage. Studying the ancestry of your dog can be a rewarding hobby in itself.

3. Responsible breeders will answer your questions and share their experience and knowledge with you. They can provide background on the breed and explain the characteristics you can expect when your puppy grows into an adult dog.

4. Purebreds are not just for snobs; there are often pet-quality puppies in litters born to champion show dogs.

5. Contrary to popular belief, purebred dogs are not less healthy than mixed-breed dogs. If you purchase your puppy from a reputable breeder, you will have the assurance of a healthy dog, and you will also have the option of replac-

A dog's whiskers are touch-sensitive hairs called **vibrissae**. They are found on the muzzle, above the eyes, and below the jaws and can actually sense tiny changes in airflow.

6 Disadvantages of Owning a Purebred Dog

1. It may take a lot longer to find the dog you want.

2. You will pay more for your dog, at least initially.

3. Purebred dog owners are often disappointed to learn that there's no money in breeding unless you commit to it full-time and do it responsibly (see "8 Reasons Not to Breed Your Dog," page 218).

4. Although purebred characteristics are easy to predict, some physical features, like "medium-large," "silky coat," and "golden color," can vary. For instance, "medium-large" means anything between fifty-five and eighty-five pounds — that's quite a large range. A "silky coat" can be short and easy to brush or heavily feathered and prone to tangling. "Golden" can mean pale cream, medium gold, or a dark red. Be prepared for variations with each breed.

5. Large dogs with territorial working behaviors come with great legal liability. If anything goes wrong in their breeding, socializing, training, or handling, these dogs are capable of causing tremendous injury to another animal or person. Very few individuals have the knowledge, facilities, or education necessary to manage these breeds, especially in our modern, crowded, and litigious society.

6. Purebred behaviors can be influenced by environment. Even a very energetic Jack Russell Terrier can be trained to avoid certain behaviors, such as digging. On the other hand, some purebred dogs have such strong genetic tendencies that nothing you do will have much effect. For example, most Akitas and Malamutes won't tolerate another dog of the same sex no matter what. This, of course, works both ways. A breed's "good" qualities may also disappear if the dog isn't raised and cared for properly.

ing her if she develops a genetic defect later in life.

6. Breeders of purebred dogs have experience in the breed and can give puppies the care and nurturing they need at early critical stages. This ensures not only a healthy puppy but also one less likely to develop into a difficult adult. Breeders will inform you of breed-specific health issues, and they will continue to provide help to you as your puppy grows up.

7. Owners of registered purebred dogs can participate in a wide variety of obedience and conformation shows, as well as breed-specific activities and events. These activities provide an opportunity for social interaction and sport in which many dogs thrive. Owners can join many breed-specific clubs where mixed breeds aren't welcome.

There are probably no more than 100,000 wolves left in the entire world today. The world's dog population easily exceeds that by a factor of 1,000.

10 Dog Clubs for Purebreds

For information regarding breed-specific dog clubs or associations in the United States, visit PetStation.com. For information on dog clubs in specific countries around the world, visit DogInfomat.com.

1. The **American Kennel Club (AKC)** is the most influential dog club in the United States. It registers purebred dogs, supervises dog shows, and is concerned with all dog-related matters including public education. The AKC offices are located at 51 Madison Avenue, New York, New York 10010. Contact the AKC by phone at 212-696-8200 or visit them at www.akc.org. See "A History of the AKC" on page 38.

For every human born, seven puppies are born.

2. The **Westminster Kennel Club** is America's oldest organization dedicated to the sport of purebred dogs. Established in 1877, Westminster's influence has been felt for more than a century throughout its famous all-breed, benched dog show held every year at New York's Madison Square Garden. Their show is America's second-longest continuously held sporting event, behind only the Kentucky Derby.

3. The **United Kennel Club (UKC)** was established in 1898 and is the largest all-breed performance dog registry in the world, registering more than 250,000 dogs annually from all fifty states and eighteen foreign countries. More than 60 percent of its 10,000 annually licensed events are performance events for working dogs. The UKC prides itself on its family-oriented, friendly educational events for the breeder/owner/handler. Contact this organization at 100 E. Kilgore Rd, Kalamazoo, MI 49002-5584; call 269-343-9020; or visit the UKC Web site at www.ukcdogs.com.

4. The **Fédération Cynologique Internationale (FCI)** is the World Canine Organisation and was founded in May of 1911 by Germany, Austria, Belgium, France, and Holland. It now includes eighty members and contract partners that each issue their own pedigrees and train their own judges. The FCI makes sure that the pedigrees and judges are mutually recognized by all the FCI members.
13 Albert Place,
B-6530 Thuin, Belgium.
Tel : ++32.71.59.12.38;
Fax: ++32.71.59.22.29;
www.fci.be/English.

5. The **Canadian Kennel Club (CKC)** is the primary registry body for purebred dog pedigrees in Canada. Beyond maintaining their pedigree registry, this group also promotes events for purebred dogs. For a dog to be registered with the CKC, the dog's parents must be registered with the CKC as the same breed and the litter in which the dog is born must be registered with the CKC. Once these criteria are met the dog can be registered as a purebred.
89 Skyway Avenue, Suite 100,
Etobicoke, Ontario, Canada M9W 6R4;
800-250-8040;
www.ckc.ca.

6. The **Kennel Club** in England. The Kennel Club was founded in 1870 when it was decided that a controlling body was necessary to legislate in canine matters. Its primary objective is to promote in every way the general improvement of dogs. Their Web site aims to provide you with information you may need to be a responsible pet owner and to help keep your pet safe and contented.
The Kennel Club,
1 Clarges Street,
London, W1J 8AB;
0870 606 6750;
www.the-kennel-club.org.uk.

7. The **Continental Kennel Club** was started in 1991 with the idea that since there were no kennel clubs available for the experimentation in "new breeds," they would make one available to the public so breeders who wanted to "make new breeds" could do so and still have their progeny registered. All that was required in starting these "new breeds" were two purebred dogs of any breed. It now boasts

An estimated 1 million dogs in the United States have been named the primary beneficiary in their owner's will.

more than 100,000 club members and hundreds of thousands of dogs registered "worldwide."
P.O. Box 908,
Walker, LA 70785;
800-952-3376;
www.ckcusa.com.

8. The **American Rare Breed Association** is the leader of rare breed dogs in the United States. They strive to protect and serve the rare breed dog and serve all dog fanciers who are interested in the rare breed dog. The most common definition of a rare breed dog is a breed of dog not recognized by the American Kennel Club.

9921 Frank Tippett Road,
Cheltenham, MD 20623;
301-868-5718;
www.arba.org.

9. The **American Working Dog Federation (AWDF)** originated in St. Louis, Missouri, on June 17, 1989. The AWDF was organized to develop awareness in the United States about the crucial need to provide a broader base to represent the working dog throughout the world and to preserve and protect the heritage of our respective breeds in America.
P.O. Box 523,
Elizabeth, CO 80107;
www.awdf.net.

10. The **Australian National Kennel Council** promotes excellence in breeding, showing, trials, obedience, and other canine-related activities and the ownership of temperamentally and physically sound purebred dogs by responsible individuals across Australia. They also promote responsible dog ownership and encourage state member bodies to put in place programs to that effect. The ANKC acts as spokesperson on all canine-related activities on a national basis on behalf of state member bodies and pledges assistance and support to the respective state member bodies. Visit them online at www.ankc.aust.com.

How Southerners Pronounce Dog Breeds
No offense intended!

German Shepherd Dog — Poh-leece Dawg

Poodle — Circus Dawg

Saint Bernard — Thank Gawd, Here Comes the Whiskey Dawg

Doberman Pinscher — Bad-A** Dawg, or Dob'min Pincher

Beagle — Rabbit Dawg

Rottweiler — Bad-A** and Mean-As-He** Dawg. Good dawg to guard the still.

Yellow Lab — Ol' Yeller Dawg

Black Lab — Duck-Fetchin' Dog

Greyhound — Greased Lightnin' Dawg

Pekinese — Mop Dawg

Chinese Crested — Nekkid Dawg

Dachshund — Wienie Dawg

Siberian Husky — Sled-Pullin' Dawg

Bouvier, Komodor — "What the he** kinda dawg is that?"

Great Dane, Mastiff — Danged BIG Dawg

A dog that raids the henhouse — Egg-Sucking Dawg

A lazy dog — Good-fer-Nothin' Dawg

A dog that's died and been buried — Best Danged Dawg I Ever Had

8 Clubs for Mixed Breeds

If your dog is an all-American mixed breed, there are many forums where she can mix it up with others of her many ilk. The following list includes clubs and organizations that provide mixed breeds and the people who love them with a chance to participate in dog shows, contests, and sporting events.

1. The **Mixed Breed Dog Clubs of America**, with chapters in Missouri, Oregon, California, and Washington, offer owners of mixed breeds the opportunity to compete for titles in obedience, conformation, tracking, and more. The MBDCA is a national registry for mixed breeds, providing them with many of the same opportunities that the American Kennel Club (AKC) offers purebreds. To learn more about the MBDCA, go to mbdca.org or call 740-259-3941.

It has been established that people who own pets live longer, have less stress, and have fewer heart attacks.

2. The **American Mixed Breed Obedience Registration** in New Prague, Minnesota, was established in 1983 to improve opportunities for mixed-breed dogs and to acknowledge the efforts and achievements of their handlers in obedience competition. AMBOR provides support to these handlers and affirms the accomplishments of mixed breeds in their many avenues of service. Members and their dogs can earn obedience titles and participate in a wide variety of activities. Visit www.amborusa.org or call 805-226-9275.

3. At the **North American Mixed Breed Registry** in Ontario, Canada, mixed-breed dogs and their owners can earn titles in obedience and tracking. These complement available activities such as flyball and agility, where there is likewise no distinction between pure and mixed breeds. While the primary focus of NAMBR is mixed-breed dogs, they do, however, welcome both registered and unregistered purebreds. For more information on NAMBR, please visit their Web site at www.nambr.cardoso.ca/index.php. No phone number is available.

4. The **Crossbreed and Mongrel Club** in Colchester, England, was set up by British nonpedigree dog owners who knew that their dogs were every bit as fun-loving, companionable, and useful as those with pedigrees. The club was launched in 1994 and continues to be the only national club in the United Kingdom devoted to mixed-breed dogs. Visit crossbreed.freeserve.co.uk for more information.

5. Located in Idaho, the **North American Dog Agility Council (NADAC)** was formed in 1993 to provide dogs and their handlers with a fast, safe, and enjoyable form of dog agility. The NADAC sanctions agility trials, in which dogs and handlers demonstrate their abil-

Cats have more than one hundred vocal sounds, whereas dogs have only about ten.

ity to work as a smoothly functioning team. With separate divisions for veterans and junior handlers and a variety of games, the NADAC offers something for everyone. Contact the club at nadac.com. No phone number is available.

6. **The United Kennel Club (UKC)** in Kalamazoo, Michigan, was established in 1898 and is the world's largest all-breed performance dog registry. While the UKC recognizes other registries and shares issues and concerns with registries around the world, their rules, regulations, and guidelines are indeed their own and are designed around the UKC mission statement. Unlike the AKC, the UKC allows mixed-breed dogs

to compete in all of their events. Visit their Web site at www.ukcdogs.com or call them at 269-343-9020.

7. The **American Kennel Club Canine Good Citizen** program was started in 1989, and is designed to reward dogs who have good manners at home and in their communities. The Canine Good Citizen Program stresses responsible pet ownership for humans and basic good manners for dogs. All dogs — including mixed breeds — who pass the ten-step CGC test may receive a certificate from the American Kennel Club. This program has caught on internationally, and countries such as England, Australia, Japan, Hungary, Denmark, Sweden, Canada, and Finland now have their own CGC programs. For more information, contact www.akc.org/cgc or call 919-816-3637.

8. The **Great American Mutt Show (GAMS)** is a production of Bunny Williams and Kitty Hawks, two prominent Manhattan interior designers. A few years ago, Hawks and Williams started a foundation called Tails in Need in order to encourage people to adopt animals from shelters. Sponsored by Tails in Need, the GAMS is a great forum for mixed-breed dogs. Now online, this yearly contest celebrates mixed breeds by honoring their individuality, ingenuity, and scrappy all-American-ness. Awards are presented for Best in Show, Best Trick, Highest Jumper, and the "What Else Am I?" award, which is given out to the most intriguing dog mix. You can visit them at www.tailsinneed.com or call them at 212-223-3893.

10 Steps for Choosing a Mixed-Breed Dog

If you want to adopt a shelter dog you can better your chances of finding the right dog if you know what to look for and know which questions to ask. It's best to visit a shelter many times in order to avoid making a hasty decision that you — and your dog — may regret. You certainly don't want to go back to the shelter and return a dog who wasn't quite what you expected.

1. Before you begin the adoption process, visit Petfinder.org. This incredible Web site lists shelters across the United States and also allows you to search for specific breeds or breed mixes. It's also a great idea to ask a veterinarian in your area about the adoption process.

2. Call your local shelter ahead of time to find out what kinds of dogs they are currently offering up for adoption. Many shelters have very few small dogs available at any given time. If your heart is set on a Chihuahua mix, you don't want to waste your time — or the shelter's — meeting a herd of shepherd mixes.

3. Try to evaluate the shelter itself by determining how clean the facilities are and how helpful, knowledgeable, and professional the staff is. The staff is really the key. Even if the shelter seems dark and a little depressing, the dogs are probably going to be well treated if the staff truly cares about them.

4. Ask a lot of questions. Find out the dog's history, who the previous owner was, why she gave up the dog for adoption. Was the dog ever abused? Are there any potential behavior problems? Find out if the dog has been vaccinated and dewormed. If applicable, find out if the dog does well with children and other dogs or cats.

Dogs have far fewer taste buds than people. It is the smell that initially attracts them to a particular food.

There are more than 100 million dogs and cats in the United States. Americans spend more than $5.4 billion on their pets each year.

Ask about the breed characteristics of the dog's parents, if they can be determined. Ask if the shelter will provide you with information on care and training for the dog. Be as thoughtful about adopting a shelter dog as you would be about buying a purebred puppy. And no matter how hard you fall for any particular pooch, be sure to ask about the shelter's return policy.

5. As you walk around the shelter and check out a particular dog, put your hands against his wire cage and see what happens. If the dog comes to you and follows your hand as you move it back and forth, there's a good chance this is a well-socialized and friendly dog.

6. When a shelter worker finally presents you with a dog you are interested in, watch for the dog's reaction to you. Is the dog nervous or is she confident? A nervous dog will tend to be more fearful and less friendly than a confident dog. Don't let an instant bond with a dog, however, influence your final decision. The shelter will have many friendly dogs. The dog should remain

Most pet owners (94 percent) say their pet makes them smile more than once a day.

calm while you pet her. Be sure to pet the dog's entire body and not just her head.

7. When you interact with the dog, make some noise. Jingle your keys or coins in your hand or pocket. Watch the dog's reaction. The best dog to take home is going to be comfortable in both noisy and quiet environments.

8. Ask a shelter worker if you can feed the dog. If this is allowed, place some food in a bowl and gently pet the dog on his back and talk gently to him. Watch for his reaction. If the dog stops eating and looks at you, you've found a dog with a calm disposition. A dog who either growls or glares at you isn't a good adoption candidate.

9. Play with the dog. Bring a toy along with you and see how the dog reacts to it. She should get excited at the prospect of playing. If the dog wants to continue playing after you've stopped and remains excited for about another five to six minutes, don't choose this dog. She might be too rambunctious.

10. Don't be let your emotions get the better of you. Learn about each dog and revisit the shelter as many times as necessary before making your final decision.

Every year, $1.5 billion is spent on pet food, four times the amount spent on baby food.

10 Dog Breeds with the Most Misleading Names

When it comes to naming dog breeds, people have done a pretty good job. For example, the Golden Retriever, with her rich, creamy coat, seems well suited for her name. The same can be said for the Scottish Terrier, whose alert expression and sturdy determination reflects the scrappy character of his native land. But other breeds weren't so aptly named. Here is CrazyPets.com's list of dogs with the most misleading monikers:

1. **Bloodhounds.** Contrary to what some people think, this breed did not get her name because of her vicious or "bloodthirsty" nature. Bloodhounds are, in fact, quite gentle. Neither did this great scent hound get her name because she smells blood when following a trail. One of the earliest breeds in history, these dogs were called "bloodhounds" because only those of royal blood were allowed to keep them. An aside: Bloodhounds were originally called St. Huberts Hound after their original breeder.

2. **Great Dane.** This giant breed is "great," but he isn't from Denmark. A more appropriate name might be the

4. **Poodle.** This seems to be a rather inelegant name for a breed often associated with high society. The name *Poodle* sounds uncomfortably like *puddle,* which is no accident when you consider the breed's origins as a duck-hunting water dog. Isn't it time for the Poodle to have a more upscale name such as "Glamour Hound"?

5. **Bouvier des Flandres.** Names can be deceiving. This breed name sounds as if it should describe a small French lap dog. In reality, the Bouvier is a massively (ninety pounds) powerful dog who has often been used for guard work.

6. **Boxer.** The Boxer's name has per-

breed in the 1860s. His name was Louis Dobermann. Strangely, the breed's name has one fewer *n* at the end. Such sloppy spelling errors should not go unchallenged!

8. **Greyhound.** This very fast dog can be found in a variety of colors, including black, white, red, and tiger. So how come they call him a Greyhound?

9. **New Guinea Singing Dog.** This shy, foxlike little dog is unfairly burdened by its intriguing name. The New Guinea Singing Dog has a peculiar howl sounding like a cross between a wolf's bay and the singing of a humpback whale. It's a beautiful sound, but it's not singing. You can enjoy this dog as a pet,

North America has the highest dog population in the world.

Great German, because the modern version of this breed originated in nineteenth-century Germany.

3. **Australian Shepherd.** Here's another breed that could use some "truth in advertising." Her name notwithstanding, Australian Shepherds aren't from the land down under. They were developed in California in the mid-1800s.

petuated many myths about the breed. The dog did not get her name from her tendency to stand up and assume the position of a boxer when fighting. In all likelihood, the name comes from the German word for "biter."

7. **Doberman Pinscher.** The Doberman Pinscher is named after the German tax collector who developed the

but don't bring him up to a karaoke machine.

10. **Xoloitzcuintle.** Phew! This has to be the most difficult name to pronounce in the dog world. Even Crazy Pets.com finds that this name goes "over the top." Better we should just call this breed by its unofficial name, the Mexican Hairless Dog.

Part Four

Tender Loving Care and Training

"A well-trained dog will make lunch. He will just make you not enjoy it."

Throughout history, animals have brought love, laughter, and companionship to the people whose lives they share. Their friendship and playfulness lift us from depression, and their physical warmth and affection help us to heal in times of stress and pain. On a more practical level, dogs can manage the handicapped, guiding the blind, signing with the deaf, and even helping to administer medications to those who cannot do so themselves.

Given all they do for us, dogs deserve the very best care in return, so being informed about your dog's health issues is important. This chapter explores the considerations that responsible dog owners should be aware of. Yes, those puppies are cute, but do you know how to keep them safe as they begin to wander about their new surroundings? What

no attempt to share your
feel so guilty that you will
— HELEN THOMSON

should you know about keeping dogs cool in the summer? If you travel with your dog, what are the rules of etiquette, and if you choose to leave her behind, how do you evaluate a boarding kennel? You'll find these and other subjects treated here.

While *Planet Dog* is not intended as a medical reference, we have provided the basics in health care, with which we believe every dog owner should be familiar. Knowing how to move an injured dog, administer emergency care to a dog suffering from heat stroke, and remove a tick properly are all skills for which your dog may someday thank you. We, in turn, are grateful to William O'Reilly, D.V.M., for advising us with regard to the medical information you'll find here, and for teaching us the importance of always making our furry friends feel as safe and secure as possible.

Dog's Rules of Possession

1. If I like it, it's mine.
2. If I saw it first, it's mine.
3. If it's in my mouth, it's mine.
4. If I can take it from you, it's mine.
5. If I had it a little while ago, it's mine.
6. If it's mine, it must never appear to be yours in any way.
7. If I'm chewing something up, all the pieces are mine.
8. If it just looks like mine, it's mine.
9. If you are playing with something and you put it down, it automatically becomes mine.
10. If it's broken, it's yours.

"Never trust a dog to watch your food." — PATRICK, AGE 10

Why We Love Dogs

Throughout history and all over the world, animals have brought love, laughter, and companionship to the people whose lives they share. Today, many doctors, social workers, and other health care professionals believe that companion animals are important in helping many people lead healthy, happy lives, especially elderly people. Here are some of the advantages of owning a dog:

1. **Companionship.** Dogs fill many lonely hours for elderly people who live alone or feel isolated from friends and family. Round-the-clock companions eager to give and receive love, pets satisfy the universal human need to be needed.

2. **Acceptance.** Loyal, devoted, and utterly forgiving, dogs accept people as they are. No questions asked.

3. **Touch.** Everyone needs to hug and be hugged. A dog curled in your lap with her friendly muzzle thrust in your hand gives reassurance and satisfaction.

4. **Source of activity.** Dogs are naturally playful and their antics are fun to watch. Having a pet who requires daily exercise gets older people outside into the fresh air and sunshine.

5. **Responsibility.** Feeding, grooming, and exercising a dog help the elderly or the infirm (not to mention the rest of us) establish and/or maintain their own healthy routine. A dog's dependence strengthens everyone's self-esteem and motivation to carry out daily tasks.

6. **Someone to talk to.** Talking to your dog can help relieve a lot of emotional pressure. Having a dog to talk to can make a difference — largely by making you feel less lonely. You are able to talk about anything and your dog will listen (or at least seem to). Better still, she won't disagree, interrupt, argue, or tell anyone your secrets. By talking to your dog you may come up with solutions to your own problems.

7. **Security.** Dogs provide their companions with a very important sense of security and will alert them when someone comes to the door.

8. **Promotes social contact.** Dogs are great icebreakers. They encourage conversation and invite other dog owners to share stories. (See "The 10 Best Date Bait Breeds," page 192.)

9. **Link with nature.** When society was more rural, farm animals served to remind humans of their relationship with the natural world. In today's largely urban, industrialized society, many people are isolated from nature. Dogs help fill this void.

10. **Positive role model.** Dogs live for the moment. They deal with life's little and big obstacles and then forget about them. Dogs can help us focus on the present and enjoy the small pleasures that each day brings. A dog's innocence and unquestioning trust can help the elderly overcome the cynicism that often results from feeling isolated from and rejected by society.

"The more I know about men, the more I like dogs." —GLORIA ALLRED

29 Things You Can Learn from Your Dog

We spend a great deal of time caring for and educating our dogs. If we are lucky and take the time to appreciate our dogs, we can see that they have a great deal of wisdom to offer us. Among their most important lessons is why the simple things in life should be appreciated and cherished. Here are some other lessons we can learn from our adoring companions:

1. When loved ones come home, always run to greet them.

2. Approach each day and each new experience with enthusiasm (even a walk).

3. Play every chance you get.

4. Don't be afraid to show your joy! When you are happy — show it. Wiggle and wag.

5. Take lots of naps and always stretch and yawn before you get up.

6. Never turn down a car ride with someone you love.

7. Be loyal.

8. Run, romp, and play daily.

9. Lounge under a tree in the shade on a hot day.

10. Never pretend to be something you're not.

11. Allow the experience of fresh air and the wind in your face to be pure ecstasy.

12. Have a favorite toy.

13. Don't hold a grudge.

14. When someone is having a bad day, be silent, sit close by, and nuzzle them gently.

15. Never underestimate the power of praise.

16. If you feel like it, let the drool fly.

17. Eat each meal with vigor and enjoy anything that's offered.

18. Sleep in any position you find comfortable.

19. Scratch when and where it itches.

20. Protect and defend the people you love.

21. What you look like doesn't matter — it's what is in your heart (and the way someone rubs your tummy).

22. Enjoy every day to its fullest — even if you are sick, in pain, deaf, blind, or wheelchair (cart)-bound or just not mentally all there.

23. When it's in your best interest, practice obedience.

24. Let others know when they've invaded your territory.

25. Avoid biting when a simple growl will do.

26. If what you want lies buried, dig until you find it.

27. Thrive on attention: let people touch you and never turn down a good belly rub.

28. On hot days, drink lots of water.

29. No matter how often you are criticized, don't buy into the guilt thing and pout. Run right back and make friends — life is too short.

"I think animal testing is a terrible idea; they get all nervous and give the wrong answers." — UNKNOWN

The Top 10 Considerations in Caring for Your Dog

Your dog gives you a lifetime of unconditional love, loyalty, and friendship. In return, she counts on you to provide her with food, water, safe shelter, regular veterinary care, exercise, companionship, and more. According to the Humane Society of the United States, if you take care of these ten essentials it's guaranteed that you will develop a rewarding relationship with your canine companion.

1. Outfit your dog with a collar and ID tag that includes your name, address, and telephone number. No matter how careful you are, there's a chance your companion may become lost — an ID tag greatly increases the chances that your pet will be returned home safely.

2. Follow local laws for licensing your dog and vaccinating your dog for rabies. Check with your local animal shelter or humane society for information regarding legal requirements, where to obtain dog tags, and where to have your pet vaccinated.

3. Follow this simple rule — *off* property, *on* a leash. Even a dog with a valid license, rabies tag, and ID tag should not be allowed to roam outside your home or a fenced-in yard. It's best for you, your community, and your dog to keep your pet under control at all times.

4. Give your dog proper shelter. A fenced yard with a doghouse is a bonus, especially for large and active dogs; however, dogs should never be left outside alone or for extended periods of time. Dogs need and crave companionship and should spend most of their time inside with their family.

5. Take your dog to the veterinarian for regular checkups. If you do not have a veterinarian, ask your local animal shelter or a pet-owning friend for a referral.

6. Spay or neuter your dog. Dogs who have this routine surgery tend to live longer, be healthier, and have fewer behavior problems (e.g., biting, running away). By spaying or neutering your dog, you are also doing your part to reduce the problem of pet overpopulation.

7. Give your pooch a nutritionally balanced diet, including constant access to fresh water. Ask your veterinarian for advice on what and how often to feed your pet.

8. Enroll your dog in a training class. Positive dog training will allow you to control your companion's behavior safely and humanely, and the experience offers a terrific opportunity to enhance the bond you share.

9. Give your dog enough exercise to keep him physically fit (but not exhausted). Most dog owners find that playing with their canine companion, along with walking him twice a day, provides sufficient exercise. If you have any questions about the level of exercise appropriate for your dog, consult with your veterinarian.

10. Be loyal to and patient with your faithful companion. Make sure the expectations you have of your dog are reasonable, and remember that the vast majority of behavior problems can be solved. If you are struggling with your pet's behavior, contact your veterinarian or local animal shelter for advice, and check out the HSUS's Pets for Life campaign information at www.hsus.org.

"What kind of life a dog . . . acquires, I have sometimes tried to imagine then becomes strangely incomplete: one sees little but legs."

The 4 Worst Reasons to Get a Dog

Sandi Dremel, the founder of TheDogInformat.com, writes: The decision to get a dog is not something to be taken lightly. An adorable puppy can tug at our heartstrings, but in the end she will require a major investment of your time and money for a significant number of years. Socializing and training a new puppy is time-consuming and, occasionally, frustrating. The constant supervision, socialization, and training necessary to successfully integrate your new pet into the family can increase stress for all involved. Here are some of the worst reasons to get a dog.

1. For my son/daughter/children. Trust me, this will be *your* dog. The kids will play with him occasionally, then groan and grumble about dog-related responsibilities. They will probably do them only begrudgingly and after significant prodding from you. As children's interests and activities change, their involvement with their dog will most likely be inconsistent. Additionally, children — especially young children — will need to be taught how to behave around the dog and will need to be supervised when they are with him.

2. For protection. Some people may disagree, but the only time to get a dog for protection is in professional or agricultural situations (such as for herds) and only when the owner/trainer is humane and knowledgeable of dog behavior and training and handling of a dominant dog. In all other situations, an alarm system, security fence, or other measures are much more appropriate and effective.

3. To breed puppies. Breeding dogs is a responsibility not to be taken lightly. If it isn't your intention to remain responsible for all your puppies their entire lives — including being willing to take back and care for dogs who may find themselves homeless — do not get into this endeavor. If you are planning to breed dogs for profit, you should know that there are much easier, more profitable, and ethical ways to make a buck. Dogs are living beings, and dog breeding requires a significant investment of time, money, labor, and knowledge — both academic and practical — along with patience and emotional fortitude, to be done responsibly and humanely.

4. Because the breed is cool. One of the worst reasons to get a dog is because their physical appearance is currently in style. Often, television and films feature exotic, rare, or unique breeds who are, in the overwhelming majority of situations, unsuitable companions. This visibility may also draw out breeders whose primary motivation is profit instead of health, temperament, structural soundness, and the welfare of their dogs. And remember to incorporate the same thoughtful consideration of whether or not to get a dog when your friend or coworker offers you one of Fluffy's puppies. Dogs are *never* free or cheap. In reality, dogs *always* require significant financial, physical, environmental, and time resources. Also, keep in mind that if it's difficult for you to find information on a particular breed or its breeders, you will most likely also have difficulty finding help with training, health care, and maintenance for that breed.

by kneeling or lying full length on the ground and looking up. The world
— E. V. LUCAS, ENGLISH WRITER

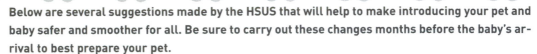

20 Tips for Preparing Your Dog for a New Baby

Below are several suggestions made by the HSUS that will help to make introducing your pet and baby safer and smoother for all. Be sure to carry out these changes months before the baby's arrival to best prepare your pet.

Why Dogs Are Better Than Cats

1. Dogs come when you call them. Cats take a message and get back to you when they are good and ready.

2. Dogs look much better at the end of a leash.

3. Dogs will let you give them a bath without taking out a contract on your life.

4. Dogs will bark to wake you up if the house is on fire. Cats will quietly sneak out the back door.

5. Dogs will bring you your slippers or the evening newspaper. Cats might bring you a dead mouse.

6. Dogs will play Frisbee with you all afternoon. Cats will take a three-hour nap.

7. Dogs will sit on the car seat next to you. Cats have to have their own private box or they will not go at all.

8. Dogs will greet you and lick your face when you come home from work. Cats will be mad that you went to work at all.

9. Dogs will sit, lie down, and heel on command. Cats will smirk and walk away.

10. Dogs will tilt their heads and listen whenever you talk. Cats will yawn and close their eyes.

11. Dogs will give you unconditional love forever. Cats will make you pay for every mistake you've ever made since the day you were born.

1. Take your dog to the veterinarian for a routine health exam and necessary vaccinations.

2. Spay or neuter your pet. Not only do sterilized pets typically have fewer health problems associated with their reproductive systems, but they are also calmer and less likely to bite.

3. Consult with a veterinarian and pediatrician if the thought of your newborn interacting with your dog makes you uncomfortable. By working with these experts before your baby is born, you can resolve problems early and put your mind at ease.

4. Address any training and behavior problems. If Daisy exhibits fear and anxiety, now is the time to get help from an animal behavior specialist.

5. If your pet's behavior includes gentle nibbling or pouncing at you and others, redirect that behavior to appropriate objects.

6. Get your dog used to nail trims.

7. Train Aiko to remain calmly on the floor beside you until you invite her onto your lap, which will soon cradle a newborn.

8. Consider enrolling in a training class with your dog, and practice training techniques. Training allows you to safely and humanely control your dog's behavior and enhances the bond between you and your pet.

9. Encourage friends with infants to visit your home to accustom your dog to babies. Supervise all pet and infant interactions.

10. Accustom your dog to baby-related noises months before the baby is expected. For example,

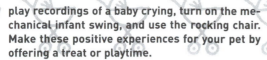

play recordings of a baby crying, turn on the mechanical infant swing, and use the rocking chair. Make these positive experiences for your pet by offering a treat or playtime.

11. To discourage Quinn from jumping on the baby's crib and changing table, apply double-stick tape to the furniture.

12. If the baby's room will be off-limits to your dog, install a sturdy barrier such as a removable gate (available at pet or baby supply stores) or, for jumpers, even a screen door. Because these barriers still allow your pet to see and hear what's happening in the room, she'll feel less isolated from the family and more comfortable with the new baby noises.

13. Use a baby doll to help your dog get used to the real thing. Carry around a swaddled baby doll, take the doll in the stroller when you walk your dog, and use the doll to get your pet used to routine baby activities, such as bathing and diaper changing.

14. Talk to your dog about the baby, using the baby's name if you've selected one.

15. Sprinkle baby powder or baby oil on your skin so your pet becomes familiar with the new smells.

16. Plan ahead to make sure your dog gets proper care while you're at the birthing center.

17. Before you bring your baby home from the hospital, have your partner or friend take home something with the baby's scent (such as a blanket) for your pet to investigate.

18. When you return from the hospital, Peanut may be eager to greet you and receive your attention. Have someone else take the baby into another room while you give him a warm but calm welcome. This is a good time for some doggie treats.

19. After the initial greeting, you can bring your dog with you to sit next to the baby; reward her with treats for appropriate behavior. Remember, you want her to view associating with the baby as a positive experience. To prevent anxiety or injury,

never force your dog to get near the baby, and always supervise any interaction.

20. Life will no doubt be hectic caring for your new baby, but try to maintain regular routines as much as possible to help your dog adjust. And be sure to spend one-on-one quality time with your pet each day — it may help relax you, too. With proper training, supervision, and adjustments, you, your new baby, and your dog should be able to live together safely and happily as one (now larger) family.

7 More Reasons People Love Dogs

1. A dog will bring you the paper without first tearing it apart to remove the sports section.

2. A dog will make a fool of himself simply for the joy of seeing you laugh.

3. A dog will eat whatever you put in front of him. He never says that it's not quite as good as when his mother made it.

4. A dog is always willing to go out, at any hour, for as long as you want and wherever you want to go.

5. A dog will never touch the remote, doesn't give a damn about football, and will happily watch romantic movies with you.

6. A dog is content to get up on your bed just to warm your feet. And you can put him on the floor when he snores.

7. A dog never criticizes your job, and he doesn't care if you are pretty or ugly, fat or thin, young or old. He behaves as if every word you say is brilliant, and he loves you unconditionally — perpetually.

On the other hand, if you want someone who never comes when called, ignores you when you arrive home, sheds on your furniture, walks all over you, runs around at night and comes home only to eat and sleep, and acts as if your entire existence is solely to ensure his happiness, get a cat!

8 Ways to Be the Alpha in Your Home

It is a widely held belief that the domestic dog evolved from the wolf. Because of this genetic makeup, dogs have an instinctual drive to live in a cohesive, highly structured society called a pack. Most dogs are content to accept their position in the hierarchy of the pack and allow the human to be the alpha. However, sometimes a dog will challenge the pack leader. These challenges are normally as simple as resisting commands or not moving out of the way. Sandy Blades, a professional trainer with BestFriends.net, offers the following suggestions for establishing yourself as the alpha in your home:

1. "No free lunch." Your dog should have to earn his treats, his meals, and even his playtime by obeying the simplest commands. He has to learn that being the "cutest dog in the world" does not entitle him to anything. Also, it reinforces that all good things come from you.

2. Don't walk around or over the dog. Make him move out of your way. (You don't have to be a bully and can even be polite about it and say "excuse me" and "thank you" in a happy voice.)

3. Don't allow the dog to initiate play. If she brings you a toy, praise her, tell her to leave it, and then ask her if she wants to play. This teaches her that she is not in control, you are.

4. Don't feed your dog from the table and don't allow begging.

5. Don't play tug of war, wrestle, or play roughly with your dog.

6. Don't allow the dog on your bed. While he should be welcome to stay in your "den," or bedroom, he should not be allowed on the alpha's bed, as this is a privilege reserved for leaders. If he's already accustomed to lounging on your bed, limit his access.

7. Enroll in obedience classes to help establish a relationship between you and your dog in which you give commands and he obeys them.

8. As a last resort, "pin" your dog by placing one hand on the scruff of her neck and the other over her back feet. Tell her "no" if she struggles, and praise her when she settles.

Note: Most dogs will respond appropriately to these corrections. A few dogs, however, may respond with dangerous behaviors, such as growling, snapping, or baring teeth. If your pet shows any of these signs of "dominance aggression," seek the help of a professional trainer immediately.

Finally, always remember to be consistent, fair, and reward good behavior. But the most important rule of dog ownership is to praise and love your pet.

"I like driving around with my two dogs, especially on the freeways.

The Ten Commandments of a Responsible Dog Owner

These wise guidelines are commonly shared among humane societies and dog lovers.

1. Remember that my life is likely to last ten to fifteen years and that any separation from you will be very painful for me.

2. Give me time to understand what you want from me.

3. Place your trust in me. It is crucial to my well-being that you rely on me as I know I can rely on you.

4. Don't be angry with me for long, and don't lock me up as punishment. You have your work, your friends, and your entertainment. I have only you!

> I make them
> **wear little hats**
> so I can use the
> carpool lanes."
> — **MONICA PIPER**

5. Talk to me. Even if I don't understand your words, I understand what the sound of your voice means when you speak to me.

6. Be aware that however you treat me, I'll *never* forget it.

7. Before you hit me, remember that I have teeth that could easily crush the bones in your hand, but I choose *not* to bite you.

8. Before you scold me for being lazy or uncooperative, ask yourself if something may be bothering me. Perhaps I'm not getting the right food, or I've been out in the sun too long, or my heart is getting old and weak.

9. Take care of me when I grow old. You too will grow old.

10. Go with me on difficult journeys. Never say "I can't bear to watch it" or "Let it happen without me." Everything is easier for me if you're there. Remember that I love you.

Bill of Rights for Adopters

Animal shelters throughout the country distribute these recommendations, and they ask all prospective clients to think about these points carefully before they adopt.

1. You have the right to adopt the best dog you have ever met.

2. You have the right to adopt a dog or cat who has not bitten and broken skin on a human.

3. You have the right to adopt a dog who will be safe with the children in your neighborhood.

4. You have the right to adopt a dog who has not killed another dog.

5. You have the right not to be blamed if your adopted dog turns out to be aggressive.

6. You have the right not to be blamed for *not* adopting a dog who has been at the shelter for too long.

7. You have the right not to be pressured into adopting an incompatible dog or a dog who you don't readily connect with because the alternative is euthanasia.

8. You have the right to be informed of the reasons that you are refused an adoption so that you can make the changes necessary to become a conscientious pet owner.

9. You have the right to be treated with respect, courtesy, and professionalism.

10. You have the right to inquire and receive as much prior behavioral and medical history on the dog that is currently available.

11. You have the right to be informed of the dog's actual age, and if the actual age is not known, to receive the best guess from a shelter professional.

12. You have the right to be told about the dog's actual breed or breed mix, and if this isn't known, to receive the best guess from a shelter professional, with no euphemisms to avoid breeds with bad images (e.g., Pit Bulls, Chow Chows, etc.).

13. You have the right to expect the shelter to stand behind its puppies and dogs and to accept them back *at any time* for *any reason* should the need arise in the dog's lifetime.

Myths About Spaying and Neutering

Many people have misconceptions about spaying and neutering dogs, or they may mistakenly believe that a dog who has one litter won't contribute to the pet overpopulation problem. The reality is that millions of dogs are euthanized each year in the United States, and many others suffer as strays. Dog owners who are not registered dog breeders should have their pet spayed or neutered. According to the Humane Society of the United States, these are some common myths concerning spaying and neutering:

1. **Myth:** My dog will get fat.
   Fact: The most likely reason your dog is gaining weight is because you're giving her too much food and not enough exercise.

2. **Myth:** It's better to have one litter first.
   Fact: Medical evidence indicates that the opposite is true. In fact, evidence shows that females who are spayed before their first heat are typically healthier. Many veterinarians now sterilize dogs and cats as young as eight weeks of age. Check with your veterinarian about the appropriate time for your dog's procedure.

3. **Myth:** My children should experience the miracle of birth.
   Fact: Even if children are able to watch a pet give birth — which is unlikely, since it usually occurs at night and in seclusion — the lesson they will likely learn is that animals can be created and discarded as it suits adults. Instead, children should learn that by responsibly preventing their dog's pregnancy they can save the life of another less fortunate animal.

4. **Myth:** But my pet is a purebred.
   Fact: One of every four pets brought to animal shelters around the country is a purebred. Enough said.

5. **Myth:** I want my dog to be protective.
   Fact: Spaying or neutering a dog does not affect her natural instinct to protect home and family. A dog's personality is formed more by genetics and environment than by sex hormones.

6. **Myth:** I don't want my male dog or cat to feel like less of a male.
   Fact: Pets don't have any concept of sexual identity or ego. Neutering will not change a dog's basic personality. He doesn't suffer any kind of emotional reaction or identity crisis once neutered.

7. **Myth:** But my dog is so special, I want a puppy just like her.
   Fact: Your pet's offspring will not be her carbon copy. Not even professional animal breeders who follow generations of bloodlines can guarantee that they will get everything they want out of a particular litter. A pet owner's chances are even slimmer. In fact, it's possible for an entire litter of puppies to receive all of your pet's worst characteristics.

8. **Myth:** It's too expensive to have my pet spayed or neutered.
   Fact: The cost of spaying or neutering depends on the sex, size, and age of the pet, your veterinarian's fees, and a number of other variables. But whatever the actual price, spay or neuter surgery is a one-time cost — a relatively small one when compared to all the benefits. Spaying/neutering is a bargain compared to the cost of having a litter and ensuring the health of the mother and puppies. Delivering and weaning a litter can be prohibitively expensive, especially if significant veterinary bills and food costs are incurred or if complications develop. Most important, spaying/neutering is a very small price to pay for a healthy pet.

9. **Myth:** I'll find good homes for all the puppies and kittens.
   Fact: You may find homes for all of your pet's litter, but each home you find means one less home for the dogs and cats in shelters who need a place to live. Also, in less than one year's time each of your pet's offspring may have his or her own litter, adding exponentially to the problem of pet overpopulation. Let's repeat: The problem of pet overpopulation is created and perpetuated one litter at a time.

How Neutering Affects a Dog's Behavior

There are many myths and misconceptions about having dogs spayed or neutered (see page 244). Only those behaviors that are regulated by male hormones can be reduced or eliminated by neutering. So, in reality, neutering affects only dominance and sexually related behaviors.

1. An intact mature male is very protective of its territory, often marking its boundaries with urine. The trait of territorial aggression can lead to fights between the dog and trespassing animal. Neutering the dog will not affect his ability or need to guard his territory. But he will become significantly calmer and far less aggressive.

2. An unneutered male will actively seek out females with which to mate. This often results in the dog's roaming and escaping his environment, with sometimes serious consequences. These dogs may be injured, hit by a car, or even lost. Neutering will prevent this roaming tendency.

3. Female dogs, during their heat cycles, will actively search out male dogs and may attempt to escape from the house or yard, putting them in the danger of traffic and fights with other animals. An ovariohysterectomy or spay (the complete removal of the female reproductive tract) will not only prevent the dog from becoming impregnated but will also eliminate this biannual heat cycle and help prolong the dog's life. An OHE will also prevent mammary gland (breast) tumors if performed prior to one and a half years of age.

Lifetime Costs of Dog Ownership

Puppies generally cost more to take care of in their first year. This is because they require a menu of vaccinations to prevent trouble later on. Puppies should be vaccinated several times against distemper, hepatitis, parainfluenza, and parvovirus. They should also receive a single rabies injection. Afterward, booster shots for rabies are given either every year or every three years, depending on local laws. Some dogs may also be vaccinated against bordetella and leptospirosis. Most dogs are then vaccinated every year.

Small-to-medium-size dogs (about fifty-five pounds and under) tend to live longer than large-to-giant-size breeds. Remember, the life spans of individual dogs can vary, so the figures given here are only rough averages; how well dogs are taken care of and whether they see a veterinarian for regular checkups is usually the best indicator of their life span.

1. Small-to-medium-size dogs*
   - Estimated life span: 14 years
   - First year: $640 to $1,125
   - Estimated annual costs thereafter: $440 to $775 per year
   - Total cost over a dog's lifetime: about $6,360 to $11,200

2. Large-to-giant-size dogs*
   - Estimated life span: 8 years
   - First year: $640 to $1,125
   - Estimated annual costs thereafter: $440 to $775
   - Total estimated lifetime cost: $3,720 to $6,550

* Of course, a serious illness or injury—especially one requiring hospitalization—can easily inflate this figure by several thousands of dollars. This price tag is also dependent on the creature comforts you lavish on your dog. Doggy daycare and spas (don't laugh—these do a booming business) and regular grooming sessions with Michél for the latest doggy hairdo will quickly add to the tally.

How to Buy a Purebred Puppy

According to Susan Hosman and the wonderful folks at Weimaraner Rescue of Northern Texas, the following list includes the minimum standards you should look for in order to purchase a healthy, quality dog from a responsible breeder (regardless of the dog's breed). They urge you not to settle for less than these minimum standards. Visit them at www.weimrescuetexas.org for more information.

1. **Age.** Puppies must be at least seven weeks old before they are sold. Puppies separated from their mother when they are too young may develop behavioral problems including biting, nervousness, and adjusting to other dogs. Puppies under the age of four weeks should not be handled, since unvaccinated puppies have a very high risk of catching a disease. A breeder who allows you to handle puppies less than four weeks of age is not knowledgeable or responsible.

2. **Genetic problems.** Hip dysplasia (HD) is a malformation of the ball and socket in a dog's hip. Some dogs are very susceptible to HD. Pain and severity of this disease varies from dog to dog. Expensive surgery or euthanasia may be the only option for dogs with debilitating diseases. Avoid hip dysplasia by purchasing a dog from a breeder who provides copies of OFA (Orthopedic Foundation for Animals) certification for both parents of your puppy. The more generations of OFA-certified dogs behind your puppy (parents, grandparents, great-grandparents), the better your chances of avoiding this inherited condition. Increasingly, inherited eye problems are also appearing in some breeds. Ask the breeder about your puppy's parents and have your veterinarian check your puppy for any eye problems.

3. **Health.** The breeder should provide you with a written health record and written guarantee certifying that your puppy has received a parvo and a distemper shot, the puppy has been checked for worms (and dewormed if necessary), and that you will receive a refund if your veterinarian discovers that the puppy is not healthy within seventy-two hours from the date of purchase. Take your puppy to your vet immediately for a healthy puppy checkup. If the puppy is not healthy, return her to the breeder and ask for your money back.

4. **Appearance.** Puppies should be raised inside the home. They should be clean and without fleas or ticks, weepy or crusty eyes, or messy rear ends. They shouldn't have herniated navels ("outie" bellybuttons). Males should have both testicles. If the breed requires, tails should be docked and dewclaws removed.

5. **Temperament.** Puppies should have been well socialized with people. They should be active, playful, curious, and friendly. Avoid buying a puppy who runs and hides from you or one who bites and appears overly aggressive. A responsible breeder breeds for quality, not quantity. If a breeder has an unreasonably large number of dogs, the welfare of the breed is obviously not a

priority. Temperament, sociability, and overall quality suffer when a breeder keeps too many dogs.

6. **Parent dogs.** The sire and dam must be two years old or older to be OFA certified free of hip dysplasia. They should be clean, healthy, and free of allergies and skin irritations, friendly toward people, and not overly shy, aggressive, or high-strung. The breeder should provide a photo of the sire if he is not on the premises and a four-generation pedigree of the puppy. Puppies grow up to closely resemble their parents, so be sure you like what you see.

7. **The breeder.** Do not buy from a pet store, puppy mill, or dog broker (some-

year. A responsible breeder breeds only to produce puppies of excellent quality and to improve on the qualities of the sire and dam in temperament, structure, trainability, and hunting ability. A responsible breeder is knowledgeable and shows deep love and concern for each puppy. Ask the breeder if she will take the dog back at any time during the dog's life, should circumstances prevent you from keeping the dog. The breeder's answer should be "Yes!"

8. **Price.** There should be no difference in price for a male or female. If you are interested in showing your dog in conformation, field trials, or obedience, purchase your puppy from a breeder

pet-quality puppies only under a spay/neuter contract and AKC limited registration.

10. **Paperwork.** The breeder should provide you with a blue AKC registration application for your puppy. Don't buy a puppy from a breeder who promises to send you these papers at a later date. An OFA certification should appear on the AKC registration application. If it does not appear there, the parents have not been certified clear of hip dysplasia. The breeder should provide copies of OFA certification for both parents. You should also receive a written health record from the breeder, which should include vaccination and worming records.

"You can say any foolish thing to a dog, and the dog will give you a look that says, 'My God, you're right! I never would've thought of that!'"

— **DAVE BARRY**

one selling puppies for someone else). You must go to the breeder's house to see the mother and her puppies — not a parking lot. You need to inspect the area where the puppies are kept and raised. Do not buy from a breeder who breeds so his kids can witness "the miracle of birth" or so the female "can have one litter before she is fixed" or from a breeder who is trying to make some money. Do not buy from a breeder who sells more than one or two breeds of dog. Females should not be bred more than once every other

who has a credible record of winning in your area of interest. Expect to pay $800 and up for a puppy who has show dog potential. "Bargain-priced" puppies are usually costlier in the long run because they tend to suffer from health problems that can develop from poor care and irresponsible breeding.

9. **Spay/Neuter.** If your puppy is not going to be used for show or breeding, she should be spayed or neutered at four to six months of age. Responsible breeders now realize the tragic overpopulation problem and sell their

11. **Pedigrees.** The breeder should provide copies of a four-generation pedigree for the puppy.

12. **Health guarantee.** The breeder should give you a written guarantee that you can get your money back within forty-eight to seventy-two hours if your veterinarian says that your puppy isn't healthy. Some breeders will also guarantee that they will replace a puppy within two years if unstable temperament or congenital disorders develop.

11 Reasons to Adopt an Older Dog

"Why on Earth would anyone want to adopt an adult rescue or shelter dog? After all, aren't they similar to used cars? Who wants someone else's problems? If the dog is so wonderful, why would anyone give him away? If he was a stray, why didn't someone try to find him? I'd rather buy a puppy — that way I know what I'm getting. And besides, they're so cute!"

Rescue groups and shelters hear many variations of these sentiments. Prospective dog guardians are not always convinced that owning an older (i.e., six months and older), "preowned" dog is better than buying a puppy. But there are a number of reasons that adopting a pet from a rescue organization that carefully screens and evaluates its dog can provide an even better alternative. We're grateful to Mary Clark at Labrador Retriever Rescue, Inc. (LRR.org), for this list.

1. In a word — **housetrained.** With most family members gone during workdays for eight hours or more, housetraining a puppy and her small bladder can take a while. Puppies need a consistent schedule with frequent opportunities to eliminate where you want them to. They can't wait for the

Mollie, an eleven-year-old Golden Retriever, credits "tennis balls — gnawed, pawed, and wet" to her longevity.

boss to finish his meeting or the kids to come home from their afterschool activities. An older dog can "hold it" much more reliably for longer periods of time, and usually the rescue will housetrain her before she is adopted.

2. **Intact underwear.** With a chewy puppy, you can count on at least ten mismatched pairs of socks and a variety of unmentionables rendered to the ragbag before he cuts all his teeth. And don't even think about buying new shoes! Also, you can expect holes in your carpet (along with urine stains), pages missing from books, stuffing exposed from couches, and at least one dead remote control. No matter how well you watch them, it will happen — this is a puppy's job! An older dog can usually have the run of the house without destroying it.

3. **A good night's sleep.** Even with alarm clocks and hot water bottles, a puppy can be very demanding at two a.m. and four a.m. and six a.m. He misses his littermates, and that stuffed animal will not make a puppy pile with

him. If you have children, you've been there, done that. How about a little peace and quiet for a change? How about an older rescue dog?

4. **Finishing the newspaper.** With a puppy running amok in your house, do you really think you'll be able to relax when you get home from work? Do you really think your kids will feed him, clean up his messes, and take him for a walk in the pouring rain to housetrain him? With an adult dog, only the kids will run amok while your dog calmly sits next to you. Feel your blood pressure lower and your stress dissolve as you pet him.

5. **Easier vet trips.** Puppies require series of shots, and they need to be spayed or neutered. Add in a few frantic phone calls to an emergency veterinary service along with a sudden, scary trip to the vet's when they swallow something you previously thought was unswallowable, and the veterinary costs can add up (on top of what you paid for the dog!). Your donation to the rescue when adopting an older dog

More than a million stray dogs live in the New York City metropolitan area.

should get you an already-altered, heartworm-negative dog with all of his shots current and up-to-date.

6. **What you see is what you get.** How big will that puppy be? What kind of temperament will he have? Will he be easily trained? Will he have a good personality? How active will he be? When adopting an older dog from a rescue, all of these questions are easily answered. You can pick a large or a small dog, an athlete or a couch potato. You will know immediately if your dog is goofy or brilliant, sweet or sassy. The rescue and its associated foster homes can help you pick the right match.

7. **Unscarred children (and adults).** When the puppy isn't teething on your possessions, he will be teething on you and your children. Rescues routinely get calls from panicked parents who are sure their dog is biting the children. Since biting implies hostile intent and would be a consideration whether to accept a "give-up," rescue groups ask questions and usually find out the dog is just being nippy. Parents are often too emotional to see the difference; but a teething puppy (just like a teething baby) is going to put everything from food to clothes to hands in his mouth. As your puppy gets older and bigger, he will definitely hurt more (and it may get worse if your dog isn't corrected properly). Most older dogs

have "been there, chewed that," and moved on.

8. **Matchmaker, make me a match.** Puppy love is often no more than an attachment to a look or a color. That's not much of a basis to make a decision that will hopefully last fifteen or more years. Though the puppy you chose may have been the cutest in the litter, he may grow up to be superactive (when what you wanted was a television-watching buddy); she may be a couch princess (when what you wanted was a tireless hiking companion); he may want to spend every waking moment in the water (while you're a land lover); or she may want to be an only child (while you intend to have kids or more animals). Pet mismatches are one of the top reasons rescues get "give-up" phone calls. Good rescues extensively evaluate both their dogs and their applicants to be sure dogs and families will be happy with each other until death do them part.

9. **Instant companion.** With an older dog, you automatically have a buddy who can go everywhere and do everything with you right *now.* You don't have to wait for a puppy to grow up (and then hope he likes to do what you like to do). Instead, you will be able to select the most compatible dog: one who travels well; one who loves to play with your friends' dogs; one with excellent house

manners whom you can take to your in-laws' house. And, after a long day's work, you will be able to spend your time on a relaxing walk, ride, or swim with your new best friend (rather than cleaning up after a small puppy).

10. **Rescue dog bond.** Dogs who have been uprooted from their happy homes or who have not had the best start in life are more likely to bond very deeply with their new people. Those dogs who have lost their families through death, divorce, or lifestyle change usually go through a terrible mourning period. But once attached to a loving new family, these dogs will want to please you and make sure that they are never homeless again. Those dogs who are just learning about the good life with good people seem to bond even more closely. They know what life on the streets (or on the end of a chain) is all about, and they blossom in a nurturing environment. Most rescues make exceptionally affectionate and attentive pets and are extremely loyal companions.

11. **We believe that there's a special place in heaven for those who love dogs.** But there must be a short line for those who adopt older animals not only for the benefit to the dog but for all the good it does the planet, by helping to curb the dog overpopulation problem and by demonstrating responsible choices to others.

"Acquiring a dog may be the only opportunity a human ever has to choose a relative." — MORDECAI SIEGAL, CONTEMPORARY WRITER

8 Considerations in Naming Your Dog

Choosing the right name for your dog is an important decision. You'll want to capture your dog's personality and at the same time come up with something original-sounding. Here are some ideas that may help you explore dog names far beyond Spot and Fido.

How to Estimate Your Dog's Age

Although the classic formula "one dog year equals seven human years" has crept into popular culture, it is a very poor method of estimating your dog's "human age." This formula is accurate only in the middle of the dog-age spectrum and does not take into account the upper and lower ends of the scale. For example, at one year old, a dog has reached his sexual maturity as well as the maximum height and length (but probably not the weight) for his breed. No one would claim that a seven-year-old human has reached sexual maturity and has stopped growing! At the other end of the scale, you must consider that dogs *routinely* live past the age of fifteen. This means that in human terms, we would be living well into our hundreds! In the case of the world's oldest dog (29 years old), he would be 203!

This formula is a better method:

1. The first year of a dog's life = 15 years.

2. The second year of a dog's life = 10 years.

3. Every year thereafter is equal to 3 "human years." For example, a formula for a ten-year-old dog would be 15 + 10 + (3 x 8) = 49. For a fifteen-year-old dog it would be 15 + 10 + (3 x 13) = 64.

"In dog years, I'm dead."

— UNKNOWN

1. Choose a name that will be easy for your dog to learn. A two-syllable name usually works best. Your puppy should get used to hearing her name often, and it should be spoken in a gentle and happy manner. When she responds to her name by looking at you, praise her and give her a treat.

2. Try to avoid a name with the letter "S" that produces a hissing sound. Puppies find this sound threatening.

3. Don't give your dog a name that sounds like a command. For example, don't name your dog Noel (No!) or Fletch (Fetch!).

4. Your dog deserves a respectful name. The attitude you develop toward your dog can be affected by the name you've given it.

5. Your dog's name should not sound like any other name within the family or a name that belongs to a close friend. You want to avoid confusion or hurt feelings.

6. If your dog is going to be around children or the elderly, names like Killer or Monster may be upsetting.

7. A cute puppy name may not be suitable for your dog once she's grown up. On the other hand, Hagrid of *Harry Potter* fame named his enormous Neapolitan Mastiff Fluffy, and that seemed to work.

8. You may cause a great deal of confusion at the dog park by giving your pooch a common name such as Lucky.

How to Help Your Dog and Cat Get Along

There are many dogs and cats who can get along well with each other. But how do you know whether your cat and dog will become fast friends or instant enemies? For starters, you will want to slowly introduce them in a neutral setting. Here are some tips to help your canine and feline become buddies.

1. From the start, choose a breed of dog that is cat-friendly. Some dogs, such as Greyhounds, have a strong chase instinct and don't do well with cats (or rabbits or guinea pigs). There are also dogs with strong prey drives (such as terriers) who just don't tolerate other pets — they chase them, nip at them, and generally harass them — you'll want to avoid these dogs if you have a cat at home. It isn't fair to your current companion to subject her to that kind of stress. So do your homework. Certain dog breeds are more tolerant of cats than others — that's the kind of dog you'll want to take home with you.

2. Introduce your dog and cat for the first time after they've both eaten and they are relaxed and sated.

3. You need to control the environment and circumstances of the first meeting. Your dog should be on a leash and your cat should be in her crate. You can also keep each animal on opposite sides of a door and have them smell each other first. A lot of people use this method. Since scent is very important to dogs and cats, this will help them get used to the fact that there's a new odor in town.

4. Take it as a warning signal if your dog won't take his eyes off the cat. Try distracting your dog by clapping your hands together loudly and then see what happens next. If your dog does not respond and is totally focused on the cat, you might have a serious problem. In all likelihood, the dog may never tolerate the cat. Your dog's concentration and focus on the cat is a sign that he has predatory intentions.

5. Once your dog and cat have been around each other for a few minutes, leave the room but stay nearby so that you can still monitor their behavior. Be ready to take control if things get out of hand. If they seem a bit aggressive toward each other, you'll have to spend more time with them, encouraging positive behavior.

6. Don't allow your cat to run away from the dog. Your dog will love the chase and look at this opportunity as a reward. Instead, keep them in a small room together.

7. Don't pick up your cat to protect her. This will spark your dog's interest, and his inclination will be to leap up and jump at what you're holding.

8. Try putting your cat in a crate that has a lot of toys and objects she can play with. Let your dog observe the cat's movements, watch her behavior, and smell her scent.

9. Never punish either pet for his or her aggressive behavior. You don't want your dog to think he will be punished every time the cat is around. Your dog's tendency will then be to fend off the cat at all costs.

"Dogs love their friends and bite their enemies, quite unlike people, who are incapable of pure love and always have to mix love and hate."
— SIGMUND FREUD

15 Things About Humans That Annoy Dogs

1. When you run away in the middle of a perfectly good leg-humping.

2. Blaming your farts on me . . . not funny.

3. Yelling at me for barking . . . I'M A FRIGGIN' DOG, YOU IDIOT!!

4. How you naively believe that the stupid cat isn't all over everything while you're out of the house. (Have you never noticed that your toothbrush smells like kitty litter?)

5. Taking me for a walk, then not letting me check stuff out. Exactly whose walk is this, anyway?

6. Any trick that involves balancing food on my nose . . . just stop it.

7. Yelling at me for rubbing my ass on your carpet. Why else did you buy carpet?

8. Getting upset when I sniff the crotches of your guests. Sorry, but I haven't quite mastered my handshake yet.

9. How you act disgusted when I lick myself. Look, we both know the truth — you're just jealous.

10. Dog sweaters. Have you noticed that I have fur?

11. Any haircut that involves bows or ribbons. Now you know why we chew your stuff up when you're not home.

12. Taking me to the vet's for "the big snip," then acting surprised when I freak out every time we go back.

13. The sleight of hand, fake fetch throw. You fooled a dog! What a proud moment for someone at the top of the food chain.

14. Leaving the toilet seat down. How else am I going to get a cool drink of water?

15. Invisible fences. Why do you insist on screwing with us? To my knowledge, dogs have yet to solve the visible fence problem!

6 Reasons People Who Like Dogs Don't Want Them

1. The cost — Some people can't afford the costs of feeding, grooming, and veterinary care for a dog.

2. Limited mobility — Pets can hinder travel if satisfactory pet-sitting arrangements aren't available.

3. Physical demands — Some dogs require more exercise than their owners can provide. Pets who aren't housebroken can soil furniture and carpets. Uncontrolled dogs can cause property damage to neighbors and the entire community.

4. Disease — Although few diseases are transmitted from pets to humans, elderly people in frail health can be susceptible to these diseases.

5. Concern for the dog if the owner becomes sick or dies — Many people are reluctant to have a pet because they're afraid that no one will take care of the animal if something happens to them.

6. Grief over your dog's death — Many people cherish their pets as beloved companions and members of the family. When this animal dies, his owner may be overwhelmed with grief as strong as if she had lost a human companion. For people who are alone in the world, a pet's death can be a devastating loss.

25 Poor Excuses for Giving Up a Dog

According to Whiteshepherdrescue.org, there are many reasons people feel they must give up their animals. Rescue organizations urge you to look for a solution to the problem you are having with your dog and to help make her an invaluable member of the family. By working to solve problem behavior and keeping your pet, there will be one less dog who needs to be rescued. Below is a list of comments people have made when giving up their dogs.

1. "The stupid dog got pregnant."

2. "Because he flattens the grass when he sits on it."

3. "My Dalmatian doesn't match the new furniture."

4. "We love our dog so much that we can't bear to watch her get old."

5. "I hear can we trade our three-year-old in for a puppy."

6. "It grew too big." (This was said about a Doberman Pinscher who was purchased as a puppy by people who lived in an apartment.)

7. "He's just too stupid to be housebroken."

8. "Our new apartment building doesn't allow pets."

9. A shelter worker overheard a mother say to her daughter, "I told you I'd get rid of the dog if you didn't clean up your room."

10. "The dog doesn't match my new carpet."

11. "The dog doesn't like my husband's parole officer."

12. "The dog peed on the floor when we went away for the weekend."

13. "The kids don't want him anymore."

14. "I had the dog tied to the truck. Then I sold the truck."

15. "We're having a baby."

16. "She's gone blind."

17. "My dog doesn't like my new girlfriend."

18. "Barks all night." (So would you if you were tied up in the backyard.)

19. "She's a dog. She won't know any better."

20. "She got lost, and we got a new one by the time she showed up at the pound. So we left her there."

21. "He's too friendly."

22. "Bit my wife when she hit him for getting on the sofa."

23. "She steals the baby's toys."

24. "He always wants to be petted."

25. "It stares at me."

> "A dog is the only thing on earth that loves you more than he loves himself." — JOSH BILLINGS

10 Reasons to Put a Dog to Sleep

Putting your dog to sleep may be one of the most heart-wrenching decisions you ever have to make. Your veterinarian is the most qualified, most experienced person to determine whether or not your dog needs to be euthanized. If your dog is ill, your veterinarian should be able to tell you what can be done to prolong her life. Dr. O'Reilly suggests that you ask yourself the following questions before you even bring your dog to the veterinarian. This way, you can both be better prepared to make an informed decision in your dog's best interests.

1. Is your dog in constant and uncontrollable pain?

2. Has your dog lost her ability to walk without staggering?

3. Is your dog unable to eat and drink without pain and vomiting?

4. Is your dog gasping for air?

5. Has she lost her ability to hold up her head?

6. Has your dog become incontinent?

7. Has your dog lost her ability to see and hear?

8. Does your dog no longer enjoy food?

9. Has your dog become unresponsive?

10. Does your dog have repeated convulsions?

> "One reason the dog has so many friends: He wags his tail instead of his tongue." — UNKNOWN

11 Ways to Cope with the Death of Your Dog

Psychologists have long recognized that the grief suffered by pet owners after their pet dies is the same as that experienced after the death of a person. The death of a pet means the loss of a non-judgmental love source. Dog owners are suddenly without a wet-muzzled friend to nurture and care for. Furthermore, people often lose their contact with the natural world. These emotions can be particularly intense for the elderly, single people, and childless couples.

According to Margaret Muns, DVM, staff veterinarian at the Best Friends Animal Sanctuary, which runs the nation's largest shelter for abused and abandoned animals, there are several things that grief-stricken owners can do to ease the healing process:

1. Give yourself permission to grieve. Only you know what your dog meant to you.

2. Memorialize her. This will make your loss real and help give you a sense of closure. It will allow you to express your feelings and pay tribute to your dear one. It will also give your family and friends an opportunity to support you in your grief.

3. Get lots of rest, good nutrition, and exercise.

4. Surround yourself with people who understand your loss. Let others care for you while you grieve.

5. Take advantage of support groups for bereaved pet owners.

6. Learn all you can about the grief process. This will help you realize that what you are experiencing is normal. Accept the feelings that come with grief.

7. Talk about, write about, sing about, or draw your canine friend.

8. Indulge yourself in small pleasures.

9. Be patient with yourself. Don't let society or anyone dictate how long mourning should last.

10. Give yourself permission to backslide. Your grieving will end and your life will be normal again. And while you will always miss your pet, time will ease your pain.

11. Be sure to consult your own "higher power," whether it be religious or spiritual.

8 Bereavement Helplines

1. Chicago Veterinary Medical Association
708-603-3994
Leave a voice mail message; calls will be returned 7 p.m.–9 p.m., Central Time.

2. Cornell University Pet Loss Support Hotline
607-253-3932, Tuesday–Thursday: 6 p.m.–9 p.m., EST

3. University of California–Davis
916-752-4200, M–F: 6:30 p.m–9:30 p.m., Pacific Time

4. University of Florida
904-392-4700, then dial 1 and 4080, M–F: 7 p.m.–9 p.m., EST

5. Michigan State University
517-432-2696, Tuesday–Thursday: 6:30 p.m.–9:30 p.m., EST

6. Virginia-Maryland Regional College of Veterinary Medicine
540-231-8038, Tuesday and Thursday: 6 p.m.–9 p.m., EST

7. The Ohio State University
614-292-1823, Monday, Wednesday, and Friday: 6:30 p.m.–9:30 p.m., EST

8. Tufts University
508-839-7966, Tuesday and Thursday: 6 p.m.–9 p.m., EST

The Rainbow Bridge

This anonymous essay is commonly shared among bereaved dog owners, and it is has brought comfort to many. These wise and well-loved sentiments have been adapted in many other forms.

Just this side of Heaven is a place called the Rainbow Bridge. When an animal who has been especially close to someone here dies, that pet goes to the Rainbow Bridge. Here there are meadows and hills for all our special friends so that they can run and play together. There is plenty of food, water, and sunshine so our furry friends are always warm and comfortable.

All the animals who have been ill or old are restored to health and vigor; those who were hurt or maimed are made whole and strong again, just as we remember them in dreams of days gone by. The animals are happy and content, except for one small thing; they each miss someone very special who had to be left behind. They all run and play together, but the day comes when one animal will suddenly stop and look into the distance. His bright eyes are intent; his eager body quivers. Suddenly he begins to run from the group, flying over the green grass, his legs carrying him faster and faster.

You have been spotted, and when you and your special friend finally meet, you cling to each other in joyous reunion, never to be parted again. The happy kisses rain upon your face; your hands again caress that beloved head, and you once more look into the trusting eyes of your pet, gone so long from your life but never absent from your heart.

Then you cross Rainbow Bridge together . . . **—AUTHOR UNKNOWN**

A dog cemetery in Hyde Park, London, ca. 1910. From *The Dog: 100 Years of Classic Photography*, edited by Ruth Silverman

8 Dog Owner Support Groups

1. The **Dog Fanciers' Fund** was created in 1993 to answer a growing need in the dog community. The fund is a charitable organization that assists dog owners, breeders, trainers, handlers, and fanciers who find themselves facing a crisis. It provides one-time financial grants to dog enthusiasts who suffer injury, illness, disease, accident, natural disaster, emotional devastation, or just plain bad luck. Visit the fund online at www.dogfanciers-fund.org.

2. **Petdiabetes.org** provides educational information, Internet resources, personal experiences, and support for owners of diabetic pets. Educational information is available for all aspects of diabetes care: basic and advanced diabetes concepts, medications, complications, home care and monitoring, vet relationships, and other diseases your diabetic pet might have. Communicate with others, find emotional support, or find books and other Web sites. There's a memorial section, pet loss poems, and a photo gallery.

3. **Blind Dogs Connections** strives to provide the support and information you need to help both you and your beloved dog, regardless if you're an owner of a newly blinded dog or have been at this for a while. If you're new to this situation, rest assured that it gets much easier. Most blind dogs adjust well and lead happy, near-normal lives. Visit this group at www.blinddogs.com/blind_dogs.htm.

4. **NYC Dog**, as their name implies, is a council of dog owner groups involved with establishing and/or maintaining off-leash recreational opportunities for dog owners and their dogs in New York City. NYC Dog interacts with other canine-related organizations and is happy to count them as affiliates, but their "voting members" must be directly involved with off-leash issues. This means that

members are local dog owner groups focusing on a specific park area, dog run, or other off-leash space. If you are involved with another type of canine-related organization (i.e., adoption/rescue, pet services or business, etc.), please contact them directly to further discuss how you may become affiliated for mutual benefit. To learn more visit their Web site, www.nycdog.org.

5. The **Humane Society of the Willamette Valley** in Salem, Oregon, promotes animal welfare through leadership, education, and action. This independent, private nonprofit corporation introduced a doggie parenting class and a pet loss support group, both meeting monthly at the HSWV facility. Both sessions are free of charge and open to the public. The HSWV classroom is located at 4246 Turner Rd. SE, Salem (503-585-5900 or hswv.org for directions). Call Victoria at Better Best Friends at 503-370-7000 to sign up.

6. **K9aggression.com** is an online support group for owners dealing with their aggressive dogs. Many groups talk about training, but the extent of your effort and compliance to a good treatment program is the most critical factor in determining success in treating your dog's aggression. K9aggression.com invites you to share your experiences dealing with your dog, either with aggressive episodes or with good or bad trainers, behaviorists, and consultants. Sometimes an encouraging word is enough to give you the strength you need to help your dog. Sharing your aggressive dog experiences can relieve the burden for you and can help others. Visit this group online at www.k9aggression.com.

7. The **Rainbow Ark**, located in the Seattle, Washington, area, is a support group for people caring for special needs pets. They provide emotional sustenance, information, resources, guest speakers, and other help to their members. The Rainbow Ark hopes that this goodwill spreads and that other people start groups in their own towns. To sign up, contact Special-Needs-Pets-Support-subscribe@yahoogroups.com.

8. The **American Dog Owners Association (ADOA)** preserves the special relationship between dogs and humankind by protecting and defending the rights of responsible dog ownership, supporting appropriate regulations for dog owners, educat-

8 Signs of a Dog in Mourning

A study by the ASPCA revealed that 66 percent of dogs exhibited four or more behavioral changes after losing a pet companion. Some of these behavioral changes are very similar to those of a human who is grieving. Here are some signs that you may observe if your dog is in mourning.

1. He may become aloof or lethargic.

2. He might eat less than he normally would. The ASPCA suggests that 11 percent of mourning dogs stop eating completely.

3. He can become clingy.

4. He may sleep more than usual.

5. He may become restless or have insomnia.

6. He may become disoriented.

7. He may become more vocal and howl.

8. He may stop playing with his favorite people or favorite toys.

ing the public, and promoting standards for the safe and civilized treatment of dogs. The ADOA speaks to legislators and courts in an effort to protect the rights of responsible dog owners and their dogs. The ADOA's membership is composed of affiliated dog clubs and individual dog owner members representing responsible dog owners from all walks of life and from all over the United States. Visit them at www.adoa.org.

The Celebrity Dog Advocates Hall of Fame

We're delighted to know that thousands of celebrities, publicly and privately, support animal causes. As it would be impossible to list them all, we've selected just a few who have come to the rescue of dogs. These people set great examples for us all, and we hope this list suggests ways in which we can all become heroes.

1. Jenna Elfman, star of films and ABC-TV's *Dharma and Greg,* has recorded public service announcements for the Pets for Life campaign. Jenna and her husband, Bodhi Elfman, share their lives with two Pugs, Willy (adopted from Pug Rescue of Sacramento) and Guinevere. Jenna has also volunteered for charities that help animals.

2. After legendary singer Barbra Streisand lost her Bichon, Sammy, she was contacted by representatives of the HSUS expressing their condolences. As a result Streisand graciously gave the HSUS the rights to her recording of Charlie Chaplin's song "Smile," which she recorded just two days after Sammy died. "Smile" is now the official "anthem of spirit" for those who have experienced the loss of a pet.

3. Comedian Elayne Boosler is a strong supporter of the HSUS First Strike Campaign, which endeavors to educate the public on the connection between cruelty to animals and the violence toward humans. Boosler has donated all the royalties she has earned from tour-related merchandise to animal groups in each city in which she has performed.

4. Actresses Lea Thompson and Dedee Pfeiffer participated in a Homeward Bound public service announcement that has been shown in markets across the United States to raise awareness of pets in need of homes. Pfeiffer is passionate about pets and has two dogs, a cat, five doves, and an iguana. Thompson is also a pet enthusiast and has two dogs, two cats, and a horse — all adopted from shelters.

5. A gift of $500,000 was given by Pearson Television to Harvard Law School in honor of TV game show host Bob Barker, a longtime animal advocate and founder of DJ&T Foundation. The resulting fund, the Bob Barker Endowment Fund for the Study of Animal Rights, supports the teaching and research of animal rights law at Harvard. Barker's DJ&T Foundation in Beverly Hills, California, advocates and helps control the dog and cat population. The foundation was named in memory of his wife, Dorothy Jo, and his mother, Matilda (Tilly) Valandra, both of whom loved all animals.

6. Leeza Gibbons has always been passionate for animals. She has dedicated a number of her TV shows to the welfare of animals. Her "Animal Abuse Caught on Tape" program won her the prestigious Genesis Award. Her program "Attack Dogs: Not in My Neighborhood" discussed the temperaments of various dog breeds and how they can be humanely trained.

7. Baseball legend Mark McGwire donated 15 percent of his earnings for an advertisement he did for Select Toasted Oats cereal to the Animal Rescue Foundation.

8. In August of 2001 the United States Postal Service announced that it

Korea's **poshintang** — dog meat soup — is a popular item on summer-time menus, despite outcry from other nations. The soup is believed to cure summer heat ailments, improve male virility, and improve women's complexions.

would issue two spay and neuter awareness stamps after the USPS received more than 200,000 letters from animal advocates requesting the stamps. Supporters of this movement included various celebrities, including **Alec Baldwin**, **Bob Barker**, **Kim Basinger**, **Bob Dole**, **Eric Harr**, **Tony LaRussa**, **Jack Lemmon**, and **Mary Tyler Moore**, as well as fifty-three members of the U.S. Congress and Senate.

9. Prior to the World Cup football competition held in South Korea in 2002, **Jean-Claude Van Damme**, **Jackie Chan**, **Janet Jackson**, **George Michael**, **Christina Aguilera**, and Italian opera star **Andrea Bocelli** signed PETA's petition asking the South Korean government to end the torment of cats and dogs killed for food.

10. Actor **Christian Bale**, the proud owner of a number of rescued dogs, takes animal rights seriously and is affiliated with the Ark Trust, PETA, the Diane Fossey Gorilla Fund, and many other animal-related organizations.

11. In March of 2001 superstar actress **Brigitte Bardot**, a longtime animal rights advocate, scored an unprecedented victory for dogs. About 100,000 stray Romanian pooches that were scheduled for euthanasia were given a last-minute reprieve, thanks to her diplomatic efforts and almost $150,000, which she agreed to donate. She persuaded Mayor Basescu to redirect the city's $1.5 million "slaughter fund" to instead be used for rounding up and delousing strays. In 1987 she sold off

continued on page 260

16 Reasons to Foster a Dog

Fostering a dog is an extremely important part of dog rescue work. Providing a dog with a good home, albeit temporary, can go a long way in helping a dog adjust to living with a family. Why would someone want to foster a dog? The answer is simple — the adoration you receive when you provide a dog with love, safety, socialization, and nurturing. Here are sixteen reasons that every person should consider fostering a dog. Many dog shelters and breed rescues have canine foster programs through which they carefully screen all applicants to match the appropriate dog with the right person or family. The Internet is also a great place to search for more information on fostering a dog — read all you can before committing to a foster program. If you're feeling at all confused by the fostering process, please contact your local ASPCA chapter for advice or visit them online at www.aspca.org.

1. Fostering gives a dog a second chance at life.

2. Fostering a dog is a wonderful, life-affirming project for the entire family (although singles and couples can foster, too, of course).

3. Fostering a dog costs virtually nothing.

4. Fostering a dog is fun.

5. Fostering a dog results in extra kisses.

6. Fostering can help provide a playmate for your own dog.

7. Fostering a dog is as rewarding for the foster parent as it is for the dog.

8. Fostering can be done anywhere — in a city or suburb, a house or apartment.

9. Fostering a dog enables you to meet new people.

10. Fostering a dog can take place whenever you are ready.

11. Fostering a dog offers you companionship even if you are unable to make a long-term commitment.

12. You get to watch the new owners take their dog home.

13. Fostering a dog gives you the opportunity to learn about the health and grooming of dogs.

14. Fostering dogs helps you satisfy your nurturing instincts.

15. Fostering a dog will ensure that you are getting exercise.

16. Fostering a dog gives you the opportunity to see the joy and feel the gratitude when your foster dog goes to a permanent home.

continued from page 259

many of her jewels to fund and create the animal rights group Foundation Brigitte Bardot.

12. Longtime TV favorite **Mary Tyler Moore** joined with the ASPCA in 2002 in their goal to make New York City a no-kill city. She was elected to the board of the ASPCA. She has encouraged thousands of people to get their dogs from shelters. She and her husband make their home in Manhattan and in upstate New York, where they keep dogs, horses, and goats.

13. Comic genius **Richard Pryor** adopts stray dogs and opposes the use of animals in laboratory testing. He has sent out Christmas cards asking friends not to donate to groups that harm animals.

14. Actress **Alicia Silverstone**, an owner of many dogs, is actively involved with several animal rights groups such as the Ark Trust and PETA, for which she is a spokesperson.

15. Actress **Gretchen Wyler**'s career has been a mixed bag of acting and animal activism. She not only has served as a vice president for HSUS but is also the founder of the Ark Trust, now known as the HSUS Hollywood Office. She has also been a member of thirteen different animal welfare organizations. She is the originator of the Genesis Awards, which acknowledge contributions the media has made toward raising public awareness of cruelty toward animals.

12 Ways to Avoid Legal Problems with Your Dog

According to DogBiteLaw.com, almost 5 million dog bites are reported each year, resulting in some 800,000 victims who require medical treatment and some $1 billion in property damage. These guidelines don't just protect you legally; they also protect your family, friends, and neighbors.

1. **Obey leash laws.** In Los Angeles, for example, a leash must be less than six feet long. It's against the law to use a retractable leash.

2. **Obey licensing laws.** Generally, a dog must be licensed. Check your city and county laws.

3. **Obey laws that require warning signs.** Generally, warning signs are required for aggressive dogs, sentry dogs, and guard dogs. Check your state law, county law, and city law.

4. **Make sure your pets have their rabies shots.**

5. **Identification tags, microchips, and vaccination records are vital** if your dog bites someone or gets lost.

6. **Make sure your dog is spayed or neutered.** Most dog bites come from unneutered male dogs. Intact males are more territorial and dominant than neutered ones. They are more prone to growl, snap, or bite, and are more easily distracted than neutered dogs. An unneutered male might break his leash to pursue a female in heat and then run into the path of an oncoming car or get into a fight with another dog.

7. **Know your dog.** What overexcites him or puts him on guard? Learn his personal language — dogs use certain barks, growls, and whimpers differently. Get to know what each of these means. Learn to read your dog's body language — his tail, eyes, ears, and posture. Taking a dog obedience class will help you understand your pet better.

8. If your dog bites or even snaps at someone, **call your veterinarian and a professional trainer** right away. A snap is a bite that does not connect with skin.

9. **Don't allow your child to take the family dog for a walk** until he is mentally and physically mature enough to handle the dog on his own. He should also know and understand local leash laws.

10. **Never leave infants or young children alone with any dog,** no matter how much you trust him.

11. **Properly socialize and train any dog who comes into your household.**

12. **Do not play aggressive games** with your dog (e.g., wrestling, tug of war).

Dog Bite Statistics

Ken Phillips has been called "the dog bite king of the legal universe" by *The Today Show*. His law practice is devoted exclusively to representing dog bite victims throughout the United States, and he is the author of *Dog Bite Law*, among other books on the subject. He appears frequently on TV and radio, and we're grateful to him for this list.

1. There are almost 5 million dog bites per year.

2. About 800,000 victims per year require medical treatment. Every day, 1,000 dog bite victims are seen in hospital emergency rooms.

3. Dog bites cause losses that exceed $1 billion per year, with $310 million paid by insurance.

4. Kids are the main victims. More than half of the victims who receive medical attention are children — most of whom are bitten in the face.

5. The attacking dog is usually owned by the victim's family, a friend, or a neighbor.

6. For children, dog bites now cause more emergency room visits than anything else except injuries from playing baseball and softball, exceeding injuries brought about by playground accidents, ATVs, in-line skates, skateboards, and volleyball.

7. A ten-year study showed that the number of dog bites rose 37 percent, while the number of dogs kept as pets increased by only 2 percent. For example, there were 4.3 million dog bites reported to authorities in 1996 and 4.7 million in 1999, according to the Insurance Information Institute. The insurance industry paid $310 million on dog bite claims in 2001. Five years ago, the industry paid only $250 million.

"The man who gets bit twice by the same dog is better adapted for that kind of business than any other."
— JOSH BILLINGS

"Keep running after a dog and he will never bite you."
— FRANCOIS RABELAIS (1495–1583), FRENCH HUMORIST

"They say the dog is man's best friend. I don't believe that. How many of your friends have you neutered?"
— LARRY REEB

The 6 Most Misunderstood Aspects of Dog Law

Marshall Tanick is an attorney in Minneapolis–St. Paul, Minnesota, and national counsel for the American Dog Owners Association. He points out that the following dog-related issues most often cause legal contention. For more information, Mr. Tanick can be reached at mtanick@mansfieldtanick.com.

Dogs and Postal Workers

The U.S. Postal Service reported that 3,423 postal workers were victims of dog bites in fiscal year 2003. Dog bites to postal employees peaked during the mid-1980s, when more than 7,000 letter carriers were attacked annually. Through aggressive employee training and public education programs, that statistic has dropped by more than two-thirds. Here's a list of those districts around the United States that reported the highest incidence of dog bites to postal workers.

DISTRICT DOG BITES

1. Greater Indiana **87**
2. Gateway (Missouri, southern Illinois) **77**
3. Long Beach **76**
4. South Florida **73**
5. Houston **72**
6. Santa Ana **71**
7. Northern Illinois **65**
8. San Diego; Connecticut **64**
9. Triboro (Staten Island, Brooklyn, Queens) **62**
10. Van Nuys **61**

1. **Myth:** The owner of a dog cannot be liable in a dog bite case unless the owner knew about the dog's dangerous propensities.
   Fact: In most states, some type of negligence or prior knowledge of a dog's tendencies is necessary for a dog owner to be liable, but about one-third of the states have "strict liability" laws, which means that an owner is absolutely liable regardless of prior knowledge.

2. **Myth:** It is lawful for laws to impose restrictions on specific breeds of dogs.
   Fact: Many courts have ruled that "breed-specific" laws are unconstitutional and invalid under federal and state constitutional provisions.

3. **Myth:** The first time a dog bites someone, it will not affect the owner's homeowners insurance.
   Fact: A growing number of insurance companies will decline to renew a current policy or refuse to extend a new policy to the owner of a dog who has a bite history.

4. **Myth:** Government bodies cannot lawfully limit the number of dogs per household.
   Fact: Actually, they can. Courts have generally upheld "limit" laws affecting ownership of dogs and other household pets.

5. **Myth:** It is not necessary to have a written agreement when two or more people share co-ownership of a dog.
   Fact: Oral agreements are generally difficult to prove in the event a legal dispute goes to court.

6. **Myth:** A person's will may provide money to take care of pets after the owner is deceased.
   Fact: Many provisions of this type are not legally enforceable unless a special trust is established for the benefit of surviving pets.

13 Tips for Bonding with Your Dog

Creating a caring and loving relationship with your dog is emotionally rewarding for both of you. It also goes a long way to helping foster effective dog training. When your dog is secure in your love, she will do everything she can to please you. If you let her know that she is loved, cared for, and respected, the resulting bond created is priceless. Here are some tips to help you create a strong relationship with your dog.

1. Let him know that he is a member of the family. All members of your family should make him feel wanted and should be forgiving of any mishaps that might happen.

2. Speak to him in soft, kind tones. He won't know what you are saying, but he will understand your tone. If he's a puppy, be sure that family members treat him gently and never tease him. After all, he's just a baby.

3. Spend quality time together (not necessarily in front of the TV). Try to set aside a designated time each day and devote it entirely to him. This will help establish a routine that he will look forward to each day.

4. Get him involved in doing daily chores or odd jobs. Whether he is bringing in the newspaper, getting you your slippers, or picking up after the kids, the more jobs he has, the happier he will be — and the more connected he will feel to you.

5. Try to make feeding time special. You are giving him a gift and he loves you for it.

6. Take him out into the world with you. Make him part of your life outside the house, two buddies out to have a good time. He'll love the attention he gets from people, and you'll start making new friends.

7. Enjoy the time that you spend walking him. He appreciates your company.

8. Make bathing time fun. Try to make bathing time fun. Really, really try to make bathing time fun.

9. Spend time training him and be patient. This will help you establish trust with him. Remember to include play-time breaks during your training sessions.

10. Establish boundaries with a firm, fair hand. You will gain his respect and deepen your bond.

11. Teach him to obey basic commands and learn how to read his body language. As this mutual training process proceeds and he begins to understand the difference between good and bad behavior, you'll find that your ability to communicate with each other deepens even further.

12. Exercising your dog every day will help him reduce some of the stress he feels when you have to leave him alone for long periods of time.

13. Housetraining should be done with a great deal of patience and without yelling or hitting or any other harsh corrections. Your dog will appreciate your understanding and will have an easier time learning what's expected of him.

"If dogs could talk, perhaps we'd find it just as hard to get along with them as we do people."
— KAREL CAPEK

11 Helpful Books on Dog Care

Dog care has come a long way since 37 B.C. when the Spanish poet and philosopher Marcus Terentius Varro wrote *De Re Rustica*, the first known documentation about breeding, training, and feeding dogs. A bit later, in fourteenth-century France, Gaston Phoebus (Count of Foix) wrote a carefully observed treatise on the care and preparation of hunting hounds. Nowadays, there are books that cover every aspect of dog care. You can find books about caring for any and every breed of dog, as well as for dogs of all ages, from puppies to senior canines. Here is a selection of the most significant of the general dog care books available today.

1. *Three Dog Bakery Cookbook,* by Dan Dye and Mark Beckloff (Andrews McMeel Publishing, 1998).
It seems that there are almost as many books out there about cooking for your dog as there are dog breeds. But this charming title is from the founders of the Three Dog Bakery chain and comes with some of the best yummy, tried-and-true recipes. You're sure to find these treats, from "German Shepherd's Pie" to "Grandpaw's Spice Cookies," easy to make — and the special dog in your life is sure to find them a cinch to eat. Some are even tasty enough to double as human fare!

2. *New Encyclopedia of the Dog* (revised edition), by Bruce Fogle and Tracy Morgan (DK Publishing, 2000).
With detailed descriptions of more then 420 breeds and varieties of dogs from around the world, this is one of the most complete and lavish dog encyclopedias available. Published by Dorling Kindersley (DK) Publishing, which is known for their detailed, four-color-throughout book treatments, this title includes easy-to-use charts and diagrams.

3. *Dog Owner's Home Veterinary Handbook,* by James M. Giffin and Lisa D. Carlson (Wiley Publishing, 1999).
Drs. Giffin and Carlson have started from scratch, with all-new and updated material on dog health care, including new photos and drawings. Dog owners won't be left scratching their heads in confusion as they look up their sick pooch's symptoms. Instead, they will easily find ailments described along with suggested treatments and knowledgeable advice provided in this eminently readable, comprehensive, up-to-date dog care guide.

4. *The Nature of Animal Healing: The Definitive Holistic Medicine Guide to Caring for Your Dog and Cat,* by Martin Goldstein, DVM (Ballantine Books, 2000).
For two decades, Dr. Martin Goldstein — one of America's most renowned holistic veterinarians — has healed and helped his animal patients with the same natural therapies that benefit humans. The results have been so astounding that today critically sick pets are brought to him from across the country for a new chance at life and health. In this compelling book, Dr. Goldstein explains exactly what holistic medicine is and how it works; how to treat the root of a health problem instead of its symptoms; and how to help your pet to regain and maintain her own health, as nature intended.

5. *How to Housebreak Your Dog in Seven Days,* by Shirlee Kalstone (Bantam Books, 1985).
People swear by this book. And failure to housetrain dogs is the number one reason that people give them up. This title comes complete with sample schedules for you and your pooch and is applicable for both young and old dogs and for dogs who live in apartments as well as houses. Though a little dated, the information is still crucial and helpful. So do yourself, your furniture, and especially your dog a favor and hunker down with this excellent reference.

6. *97 Ways to Make a Dog Smile,* by Jenny Langbehn (Workman Publishing, 2003).
This book is a fount of pleasure for dogs and the owners who love them. Created by a veterinary nurse, it describes ways to rub, massage, scratch, tickle, and knead your pooch. Included are imaginative play scenarios that are just loopy enough to ensure your dog will be amused, whether she's laughing *at*

you or *with* you. Full-color photographs of smiling dogs accompany each entry.

7. *Dr. Pitcairn's Complete Guide to Natural Health for Dogs and Cats,* by Richard H. Pitcairn and Susan Hubble Pitcairn (Rodale Press, 1995).

If there ever were an equivalent to the Bible for dog lovers, this expanded edition of the classic pet care book is it. You'll find yourself using this guide as a cookbook, as a reference to your dog's development, and even as an emergency manual when you notice that your normally healthy puppy has suddenly developed a yucky skin rash. Written with warmth and compassion, "the Pitcairn book" also helps readers select the most compatible dog (or cat) for them and create a healthy and relaxing living space for their pet.

8. *Throw Me A Bone: 50 Healthy, Canine Taste-Tested Recipes for Snacks, Meals and Treats,* by Sally Sampson and Cami Johnson (Simon & Schuster, 2003).

Cooper Gillespie, an extremely intelligent and handsome Welsh Springer Spaniel, is a dog of discriminating taste and strong opinions. Now Cooper, with the assistance of cookbook author Sally Sampson and the transcription services of his favorite human, Susan Orlean (*The Orchid Thief*), has put together fifty delectable recipes for snacks, meals, and treats for your canine companion. Illustrated with more than fifty

endearing black-and-white photographs of Cooper and friends by Cami Johnson, and liberally seasoned with stories, quotes, and nutrition tips, *Throw Me a Bone* makes a dog's dinner something to look forward to.

9. *Your Aging Dog,* by Amy Shojai (New American Library, 2003).

These days, dogs are living longer, healthier lives. To ensure that your pet reaps the benefit of recent advances in veterinary medicine, it's crucial that he receive regular checkups. But you should also keep a book about senior pets handy. This comprehensive title contains valuable in-

formation for older dogs on areas such as exercise, nutrition, and medication.

10. *Animal House Style: Designing a Home to Share with Your Pets,* by Julia Szabo, foreword by Mary Tyler Moore (Bulfinch Press, 2001).

Read this book before you buy that new sofa or invest in an expensive Persian carpet. Though offering ways to accommodate a variety of pets — from cats and ferrets to parrots and rabbits — this original book provides a wealth of information for dog owners, from feeding your canine in style to innovative ways of camouflaging dog hair. You'll never look at a leather sofa in the same way again.

11. *The Veterinarians' Guide to Natural Remedies for Dogs: Safe and Effective Alternative Treatments and Healing Techniques from the Nation's Top Holistic Veterinarians,* by Martin Zucker (Three Rivers Press, 1999).

Giving one's pet natural remedies is all the rage these days. This is a great resource for dog owners who are interested in treating their animals with homeopathy, providing them with Bach Flower Remedies (those with anxious pooches swear by "Rescue Remedy"), or giving them vitamins and antioxidants. While you will certainly want to consult first with a reputable professional, *The Veterinarians' Guide* is a respected and comprehensive compendium of alternative treatments for dogs.

JULIA SZABO/CHRONICLE

11 Good Books on Dog Training

Dog training has come a long way since the days of choke chains and constant reprimands of "Bad dog!" The current trend is toward *positive* dog training. This gentle method uses food rewards instead of reprimands and has dispensed altogether with physical discipline. Clicker training — in which owners reinforce the desired behavior by using a device that makes a clicking noise, followed by a treat — is a popular form of positive dog training. Most people want a happy, well-adjusted, and well-behaved pet, and this doesn't happen without a little work. Therefore, some training is advised for all dogs, both big and small. Below is a selection of the most popular dog training guides around. For more information on dog training, or to find a reputable dog trainer in your area, contact the Association of Pet Dog Trainers (APDT) at 1-800-PET DOGS or via online at www.apdt.com.

1. *Culture Clash,* by Jean Donaldson (James and Kenneth Publishing, 1997).
This book explains why an anthropomorphic approach to dog training is usually unsuccessful in one way or another. It also dispels the notion that dogs act out of spite, stubbornness, or undying loyalty and describes what dog training really means to your dog — and how to get him to crave it.

2. *Before and After Getting Your Puppy: The Positive Approach to Raising a Happy, Healthy and Well-Behaved Dog,* by Dr. Ian Dunbar (New World Library, 2004).
It's fair to say that thirty years ago, British veterinarian Ian Dunbar revolutionized the dog world. Instead of waiting until a dog was six months old (and full of bad habits) to train her, Dr. Dunbar proposed an alternative. Train puppies to do the right thing from the very start, and the training process will be much easier. He espoused gentle methods of teaching puppies and eschewed harsh ones as cruel and unnecessary. These days, most dog train-

ers — and dog writers — are followers of Dr. Dunbar. What's great about this book is that it's a two-in-one deal: the first part contains valuable information about choosing the right puppy for you and your family; the second part includes important lessons to teach your puppy during this, her most impressionable stage.

3. *The Dog Listener: Learn How to Communicate with Your Dog for Willing Cooperation,* by Jan Fennell (HarperResource, 2004).
Jan Fennell's remarkable gifts have earned her the nickname "the dog whisperer." Her unique knowledge of the canine world and its instinctive language has enabled her to bring even the most desperate and troubled dogs to heel. This easy-to-follow guide to Jan's techniques draws on her countless case histories of problem dogs — from biters and barkers to bicycle chasers. *The Dog Listener* is also a moving and inspiring story. Jan tells of the tragic death that first led her to reassess conventional attitudes toward dogs.

4. *The New Work of Dogs: Tending to Life, Love, and Family in a Changing World,* by Jon Katz (Villard, 2003).
Using case studies, Jon Katz, one of the foremost dog authorities in the world, shows that over the past twenty years, the relationship between dogs and humans has changed due to cultural factors. With people having less and less personal human contact because of the Internet, for instance, they've looked to dogs to help fill the relationship void. Playing the perfect, loving companion *is* the new work of dogs.

5. *Good Owners, Great Dogs,* by Brian Kilcommons and Sarah Wilson (Warner Books, 1999).
Brian Kilcommons, one of the world's foremost experts on dog training and animal behavior and the only American to have studied and worked with the renowned (Briton) Barbara Woodhouse, solves all those "bad dog" problems by showing owners how to read dogs' body language and communicate with patience, praise, and clarity.

6. *The Other End of the Leash: Why We Do What We Do Around Dogs,* by Patricia A. McConnell (Ballantine Books, 2003).

An applied animal behaviorist and dog trainer with more than twenty years of experience looks at humans as just another interesting species and muses about why we behave the way we do around our dogs, how dogs might interpret our behavior, and how to interact with our dogs in ways that bring out the best in our four-legged friends.

7. *The Power of Positive Dog Training,* by Pat Miller, introduction by Jean Donaldson (Howell Book House, 2001).

This is one of the best books yet to explain how and why positive dog training works. You'll find an easy-to-read discussion about the philosophy behind positive training followed by specific training tips and exercises. This book is geared toward the dog owner who wants to develop a relationship with her dog based on friendship and positive reinforcement, not fear and punishment.

8. *How to Be Your Dog's Best Friend: The Classic Training Manual for Dog Owners* (revised and updated), by The Monks of New Skete (Little, Brown, 2002).

The Monks of New Skete have achieved international renown as breeders of German Shepherd Dogs and as outstanding trainers of dogs of all breeds. Their unique approach to canine training, developed and refined over three decades, is based on the philosophy that "understanding is the key to communication, compassion, and communion" with your dog. For nearly a quarter century, *How to Be Your Dog's Best Friend* has been the standard against which all other dog training books are measured. This new, expanded edition, with a new design and new photographs, preserves the best features of the original classic while bringing the book fully up-to-date. The result: the ultimate training manual for a new generation of dog owners — and, of course, for their canine best friends.

9. *The Dog Whisperer: A Compassionate, Nonviolent Approach to Dog Training,* by Paul Owens (Adams Media Corporation, 1999).

The gentle, nonviolent training methods and mysteries of "horse whisperers" have recently enlightened the world's consciousness of nonviolent animal training methods. Now trainer Paul Owens applies these methods to dog training. His spiritual approach links sound training principles with intuitive and effective insights. Owens's compassionate training methods teach readers to create deeper bonds with their dogs than many ever thought possible.

10. *Don't Shoot the Dog! The New Art of Teaching and Training,* by Karen Pryor (Bantam Books, 1999).

This book is a best-selling dog training classic thanks to its clear and entertaining explanations of behavioral training methods. This newly revised edition presents more of Pryor's insights into animal — and human — behavior. A groundbreaking behavioral scientist and dynamic animal trainer, Pryor is a powerful proponent of the principles and practical uses of positive reinforcement in teaching new behaviors. This book contains the secrets to changing behavior in pets and kids — and even yourself — without yelling, threats, force, punishment, guilt trips — or shooting the dog.

11. *How to Raise a Puppy You Can Live With,* by Clarice Rutherford and David H. Neil (Alpine Publications, 1999).

This classic, originally published in 1984, is newly revised and offers the latest information, including a discussion of clicker training. Written by a professional dog breeder and veterinarian, this all-in-one guide lays down the rules for raising a puppy in your home. The book makes it crystal clear how to communicate with your puppy, what kinds of things you need to do when training a new dog, and how to properly express verbal commands. Additionally, new puppy owners will find answers to questions about everything from house training to discipline to socializing a puppy in a way that promotes self-confidence and a sound temperament.

The Bloodhound is the only animal whose evidence is admissible in an American court.

10 Great Books on Canine Behavior

1. *Dog Language: An Encyclopedia of Canine Behavior* (third revised edition), by Roger Abrantes and Alice Rasmussen (Dogwise Publishing, 2001).
Dog Language is a book that will benefit anyone interested in what makes our dogs tick. This is a must-read for professional dog handlers and behaviorists, as well as pet owners. *Dog Language* is well organized and written in a clear, easy-to-understand language. The beautiful illustrations help explain what our canine companions are trying to tell us — and each other.

2. *The New Better Behavior in Dogs: A Guide to Solving All Your Dog Problems,* by William E. Campbell (Alpine Publications, Inc., 1999).
A must-read for anyone committed to developing a lifetime relationship with her dog. Using gentle, positive methods, the author teaches owners everything from proper socialization to solving behavior problems such as excessive barking and separation anxiety.

3. *How Dogs Think: Understanding the Canine Mind,* by Stanley Coren (Free Press, 2004).
A best-selling author, psychologist, and world-renowned expert on dog behavior and training, Dr. Coren is always at the forefront of discoveries about dogs. With his ever-entertaining, erudite style, he provides a fascinating picture of the way dogs interpret their world and their owners, how they solve

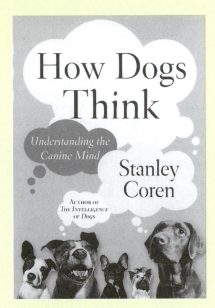

problems, learn, and take in new information. With this book, Dr. Coren lets you experience the world from a dog's perspective.

4. *Dog Behavior: An Owner's Guide to a Happy, Healthy Pet,* by Ian Dunbar (Howell, 1999).
Veterinarian and animal behaviorist Ian Dunbar has written this beginner's-level book on dog behavior. He explores both unseen facets of canine behavior, such as instinct, and visual behaviors, such as play. He focuses on behaviors that humans often define as misbehavior, including digging and chewing. The main solution in preventing misbehavior is through socializing and training puppies. Punishment has no place in Dunbar's world; only reward-based training does. This includes not punishing a dog for growling and *not* correcting her in the same way that an alpha wolf might correct a pack member.

5. *The Dog's Mind: Understanding Your Dog's Behavior,* by Bruce Fogle (Howell, 1992).
Combining more than twenty years of practical experience as a veterinary clinician with a personal knowledge and understanding of the latest international research, Dr. Bruce Fogle has written the most inclusive and relevant book on how the canine mind works. Well written, with bits of dry humor, it describes how a dog thinks and why she does what she does.

6. *Domestic Animal Behavior for Veterinarians and Animal Scientists* (third edition), by Katherine Albro Houpt (Iowa State University, 1998).

Though written for veterinarians, this book is not too difficult for pet owners to understand. Dogs, cats, pigs, horses, cattle, sheep, and goats are all discussed. The nine chapters cover such topics as communication, social structure, biological rhythms, and sexual behavior. This title is recommended for readers with the patience to sort through it and locate the information pertaining to dogs.

"Some dogs live for praise: they look at you as if to say, 'Don't throw balls . . . just throw bouquets.'"
— JHORDIS ANDERSON, AMERICAN PAINTER

7. *Dogwatching: Why Dogs Bark and Other Canine Mysteries Explained,* by Desmond Morris (Three Rivers Press, 1993).
Dogwatching answers fundamental and fascinating questions about man's best friend — questions often overlooked by standard dog books and even by dog owners themselves. This book provides the answers in a clear, concise question-and-answer format.

8. *The Secret Lives of Dogs: The Real Reasons Behind 52 Mysterious Canine Behaviors,* by Jana Murphy (Rodale Books, 2000).
You'll discover what's behind your dog's everyday actions and find intriguing, practical advice on topics such as digging, chewing sticks, eating grass, and getting wet. *The Secret Lives of Dogs* reveals what dogs think, how they feel, and how they see the world and what you can do to make them happy.

9. *The Rosetta Bone: The Key to Communication Between Humans and Canines,* by Cheryl Smith (Howell, 2004).
Packed with unique insights and gentle training advice, *The Rosetta Bone* provides average dog owners with the know-how they need to decipher canine meanings, communicate effectively with their dogs, increase training success, and share a deeper bond. Cheryl Smith reveals how you can use your own body language to send a message to your dog and even teach her the meaning of specific words.

10. *The Canine Good Citizen: Every Dog Can Be One* (second edition), by Jack Volhard and Wendy Volhard (Howell, 1997).
This book provides a wealth of insights for the beginning dog owner as well as the experienced one. The book's best feature is that it gives everyone the means to tailor dog training to their individual pet's character and temperament. This book thoroughly explains what makes dogs different and how these differences dictate the particular training approaches that owners need to take.

How to Set "Strict" Training Limits for Your Dog

1. The dog is not allowed in the house.

2. Okay, the dog is allowed in the house, but only in certain rooms.

3. The dog is allowed in all rooms, but she has to stay off the furniture.

4. The dog can get on only the old furniture.

5. Fine, the dog is allowed on all the furniture, but she is not allowed to sleep with the humans on the bed.

6. Okay, the dog is allowed on the bed, but only by invitation.

7. The dog can sleep on the bed whenever she wants, but not under the covers.

8. The dog can sleep under the covers by invitation only.

9. Fine, the dog can sleep under the covers every night.

10. The humans must ask permission to sleep under the covers with the dog.

Developmental Stages of Puppy Behavior

In order to help your puppy become well socialized, it's important that you talk and play with her — along with constant petting, of course! Well-socialized females are more likely to have well-socialized puppies. Puppies learn from their mother's calm or fearful attitude toward people. Puppies are usually weaned at six or seven weeks, but they are still learning important skills at this stage as their mother gradually spends less time with them. Ideally, puppies should stay with their mother and their littermates for at least twelve weeks.

A puppy separated too early from her littermates doesn't develop appropriate social skills. It is more difficult for her to learn how to interact with other dogs and people. These puppies have a hard time deciphering canine signals, including how far to go in play wrestling and teething. Play helps puppies increase their physical coordination, social skills, and learning limits. Interacting with their mother and littermates helps them learn how to be a dog and is also a way to explore ranking and see who is in charge, or which dog is an alpha and which is a beta.

Skills that aren't acquired during a puppy's first eight weeks may never be acquired at all. While a dog's developmental stages are important and fairly consistent, her mind does remain receptive to new experiences and lessons well beyond puppyhood. Most dogs are still puppies, in mind and body, through their first two years.

The following list, provided by the Dumb Friends Animal League, provides general guidelines for the stages of a puppy's development.

"There is no psychiatrist in the world like a puppy licking your face." — BERN WILLIAMS

0–2 weeks = Neonatal

Most influenced by their mother.

Touch and taste are present at birth.

2–4 weeks = Transitional

Most influenced by their mother and littermates.

Eyes open, teeth erupt, hearing and sense of smell developing.

Beginning to stand, walk a little, wag tail, bark.

By four or five weeks, vision is well developed.

3–12 weeks = Socialization

During this period, puppies need opportunities to meet other dogs and people.

By four to six weeks puppies are most influenced by their littermates and are learning how to be a dog.

From four to twelve weeks puppies are still influenced by their littermates and are also beginning to be influenced by the people in their lives. They're learning how to play and their social skills are developing. They can decipher social structure and ranking, and they are becoming more physically coordinated.

By three to five weeks puppies are becoming aware of their surroundings, including companions (dogs and people) and relationships. They are starting to play more.

By five to seven weeks puppies are exhibiting curiosity and they are exploring their surroundings. At this time, puppies need positive human interaction.

By seven to nine weeks puppies are refining their physical skills and coordination (including housetraining) and they are grasping the full use of their senses.

By eight to ten weeks puppies can experience real fear. This is when puppies can be alarmed by normal everyday objects and they especially need positive reinforcement and training.

By nine to twelve weeks puppies are refining their social skills with littermates and are exploring their environment, spaces, and objects. At this time, puppies begin to focus on people. This is a good time to begin training.

3–6 months and beyond

At three to six months puppies focus mostly on their social order. They are most influenced by their littermates, but playmates may also now include members of other species — usually humans, though some puppies raised with cats will enjoy playing with them. By this time, puppies use rank within the pack to determine their behavior, when and whether they are submissive or dominant. Puppies also determine this behavior with humans, so if you have a strong-willed, independent breed like a Chow Chow or an Alaskan Malamute, this is the time to kindly let them know that you are the dominant leader of the pack.

At three to six months, your puppy will teethe — a lot. Make sure she has many chew toys and chewable bones available.

At seven to nine months, as part of exploring their territory, puppies go through a second chewing phase. They also explore dominance, including challenging humans. This is another opportunity to assert yourself. Despite their many wonderful attributes, a puppy really isn't qualified to run their own — or your own — daily life. If your puppy isn't neutered, he will now exhibit the beginnings of sexual behavior.

At six to eighteen months puppies go through adolescence, when they are most influenced by humans and their other pack members.

21 Tips to Help You Socialize Your Puppy

The most important time to socialize your puppy is during the first three months of her life. Puppies come into the world with no knowledge of humans and the world around them. They need our guidance to become trusting, friendly, good canine citizens. Socializing puppies takes time, energy, commitment, and a lot of patience, but the result is well worth the effort. You will have a happy, secure, and friendly dog. Here are some tips to help you properly socialize your new puppy:

1. Start by introducing her to one new person at a time and then gradually introduce her to more people in noisier situations.

2. Invite friends, relatives, and their pets to come to your house and meet, greet, and play with your puppy. Take her next door and let her meet the neighbors.

3. As soon as your veterinarian says she has been adequately vaccinated, take your puppy on as many walks and outings as possible. She can be introduced to other healthy, vaccinated, friendly dogs (and cats). Avoid situations that might be high risk for disease, such as areas with stray dogs.

4. Let her visit all the rooms of your house, but be sure that she is supervised at all times. Encourage her to explore and investigate her surroundings. She'll feel more like a part of the family the more you let her into your life.

5. Your puppy should meet a variety of people of all ages and appearances. A puppy who grows up with a restricted social group (e.g., all adults or all females) may show fear and aggression

when later exposed to people who appear or act significantly different — such as men with beards. To make any new introduction special, give your puppy a small biscuit whenever she meets a new friend.

6. If you have small children, other dogs, or cats in your family, you are fortunate. Your puppy will become accustomed to the loud noise and active play behavior of children and will also be exposed to other pets. If you don't have kids of your own, invite a well-mannered child and his parent into your home for supervised play with your new puppy. Keep some tasty treats available for the child to give your puppy so she associates kids with yummy food rewards.

7. When you have visitors come to your house — when the mailman delivers mail or the deliveryman brings packages — ask them to hold a dog treat and make your puppy sit for it. They should then reward the puppy with the treat. This will teach your puppy that if she sits for strangers, she will be rewarded. This is an excellent way to prevent your puppy from jumping up on people. Your

"A few weeks after my surgery, I went out to play catch with my Golden Retriever. When I bent over to pick up the ball, my prosthesis fell out. The dog snatched it, and I found myself chasing him down the road yelling, 'Hey, come back here with my breast!'"

— LINDA ELLERBEE

puppy will also learn that visitors come bearing gifts and aren't to be barked at.

8. If your puppy seems particularly fearful when you are trying to socialize her, backtrack. Repeat previous steps that didn't scare her and keep an eye on your puppy. All animals react differently to stimuli — you don't want to force your dog into a situation that scares her.

9. Get your puppy used to riding in the car before you start driving her to the veterinarian's office. She may become fearful of the car if she associates it with a negative experience. The car should be a fun place, so bring along her favorite toys and some treats to reward her for being good. Start with short trips such as local errands and work your way up to longer drives.

10. Take her into town for short on-leash outings. Walk her on a main street with light foot traffic. Let her get used to the sounds of the cars and trucks. Let her experience the movement of people passing by. Be nonchalant about all this and don't forget to praise her. The more time you spend exposing your puppy to the world, the happier and more secure she will feel.

11. In order to prepare your puppy for a visit to the veterinarian, try handling her body on a daily basis. Take her to the vet for a get-to-know-you visit. Ask the office staff to give her treats. This will make her a lot more comfortable when she goes to the veterinarian for treatment.

12. Take your puppy to the pet store with you. Let her browse, but don't give her your credit card.

13. You can help her become comfortable with thunderstorms, fireworks, or any other loud noises by playing with her during a storm and reassuring her that she is not in any danger. Give her a treat as a reward for being good. Don't reinforce a fearful response by picking her up and petting her. Doing this will only reinforce fearful behavior.

14. Make feeding time a happy time for her. Praise her as she eats. Meals can become a bonding experience.

15. Walk her when it is raining and snowing. Avoiding this will only send her the message that rain and snow are something to fear.

16. To help her get used to being bathed, place your puppy in a dry bathtub and give her a toy to play with. As she plays, turn on the faucet gently and get her feet wet. Pet her, praise her, and give her a treat.

17. Get her used to being groomed. Brush her hair, clip her nails, and clean her ears, and perform all the routines of grooming and physical examination. Be very gentle with her and reward her for good behavior.

18. Get her used to being left alone, but do it gradually. Start by leaving the house for short periods of time and then gradually increase the length of your separation. Make sure your puppy has something to either chew on or play with so that she doesn't become bored and destroy your belongings.

19. Another excellent way to promote early socialization is to take your puppy to training classes. Ask your veterinarian about classes in your area. Punishment during the early development stages can impact good people skills. Avoid training methods that involve physical discipline, such as swatting the puppy, thumping her on the nose, or rubbing her face in her mess.

20. Don't rush her. Every puppy is different and learns at her own pace. Remember that she is very eager to please you. So be patient and praise and reward her whenever you can!

21. Don't put any of this off! If socialization does not happen now, it never will.

16 Ways to Make Your Home Safe for a New Puppy

Bringing a new puppy into your home is a very big responsibility. It is now up to you to protect your pooch from all sorts of previously unseen hazards, including dangling wires, toilet bowls, stairs, and the front door. Puppies are like babies, only they have stronger teeth and they're slightly quicker on their paws. So you'll have to get down on your hands and knees and take a look around your puppy's new digs. Anything that Roxy can put into her mouth she will, and this includes objects that may electrocute, poison, or choke her. Make sure you remove toxins and cleaning products from floor and muzzle level and place them on an upper shelf or in a closed cupboard. For extra safety insurance, you may want to invest in a baby gate to keep your puppy from running outside or downstairs. Locks on drawers, closets, and cupboards are never a bad idea. Your new puppy will appreciate some privacy — a crate placed in a quiet corner, containing a chew toy and a water dish and lined with something soft and familiar-smelling, will provide security and comfort.

1. When your new puppy is finally home, you should either monitor her at all times or place her in her crate. This will help her feel secure and keep her out of trouble.

2. Make sure that all electrical outlets have safety plugs in them so she won't get shocked as a result of her own curiosity. According to the National Safety Council, about 5,000 house fires are caused by dogs chewing through electrical cords. So keep these out of reach.

3. Keep your home well ventilated. Both you and your puppy will be healthier.

4. Make sure the paint on your walls does not contain lead.

5. Get rid of small objects that your puppy is likely to chew. Small objects can get lodged in her throat and choke her.

6. If you live in a high-rise apartment or condominium, be sure that there is a safety bar or guard rail so that your dog can't fall off the balcony (or out the window).

7. Keep all objects high and out of her reach, especially sharp ones.

8. Make sure that you put safety latches on cabinets that contain poisonous items. These are often under the kitchen and bathroom sinks. Remember that loosely secured doors can be nudged open by a curious puppy.

9. Keep potentially toxic plants out of her reach or remove these altogether.

10. Make sure that your fenced-in yard is escape-proof. Supervise your puppy the first few times she ventures into the yard (in fact, always keep an eye on pets when they are outside — more than a few dogs have been stolen from their own backyards). After she has spent some time in the yard, do a spot check. Are there any holes in the ground? Did your dog try to tunnel under your (previously) impenetrable fence? Some dogs are ace escape artists, and you don't want to find this out about your pet *after* she performs a vanishing act.

11. Keep potentially dangerous foods, such as chocolate, out of sight.

12. Be sure that she can't get into any garbage or trash cans. Also make sure that your puppy doesn't play with plastic bags — these can suffocate her.

13. Stairs should be inaccessible until the puppy is large enough to go up and down safely.

14. Monitor all of your dog's outdoor activities. This will prevent her from destroying your garden or patio furniture.

15. Keep her away from your swimming pool. When the pool isn't in use, keep it covered. And put a fence of sufficient height around the pool itself.

16. Dogs love the smell and taste of antifreeze. Keep your dog out of the garage!

20 Things You Should Never Do to a Puppy

1. Think carefully before you give your puppy a disrespectful name. The name you give your dog may affect the manner in which he is ultimately treated. A respectful and loving name will result in respectful and loving treatment.

2. Never speak harshly to your puppy. He won't understand what you are saying but he will pick up on the tone of your voice.

3. Puppies should not be teased or mistreated by children. Kids sometimes get so excited around puppies that they may inadvertently harass them. You must closely supervise small children and puppies.

4. Puppies should not be constantly fawned over. They need time away from even the most gentle children and adults. Puppies also need to get used to being by themselves.

5. Puppies should never be hit. Never scold your puppy for something he did at an earlier time. He won't know what you are angry about and will simply learn to be scared of you. Always, always gently correct your puppy when he does something wrong — and keep it in the moment. If you see your puppy poop on the carpet, an emphatic "No" is appropriate. Rubbing his nose in it hours later is not acceptable.

6. Don't bring your new puppy home during the holiday season. The sounds of merriment and the heightened activity in your home may frighten him. A puppy should be introduced to a quiet home at a relaxed time of the year. Besides, a puppy needs your undivided attention, and a celebration of any kind will distract you from giving him the care that he requires.

7. Don't feed your puppy a new type of food. Bring home the same food that the breeder has been giving him. You can then gradually switch over to a preferable brand. A puppy's tummy is very delicate and you don't want to cause him any undue upset.

8. Don't tap on your puppy's nose to stop him from biting. He will learn to become fearful of your hand. And you don't want your puppy to fear the hand that feeds him.

9. Don't pet your puppy after he climbs or jumps on you. Doing this will only reinforce his behavior. Put the puppy back on the floor every single time you pet him.

10. Don't take your puppy outside without a leash. This will teach him that he doesn't have to come when called.

11. Never chase your puppy. Puppies should be encouraged to follow you.

12. Don't play with your puppy when he is mouthing you. Doing so will only reinforce this behavior.

13. Don't overfeed your puppy. The fact that your puppy has devoured his food doesn't mean that he is still hungry and needs more food. An overweight puppy is an unhealthy puppy.

14. Never punish your puppy by forcing him back into his crate. Crates are supposed to be a safe haven for your puppy; you don't want it to have any negative associations.

15. Don't spend more than ten to fifteen minutes at a time training your puppy. You're much better off conducting two or three ten-to-fifteen-minute training sessions than trying to spend an hour of training. Puppies don't have very long attention spans.

16. Don't feed your puppy any table scraps or any kind of meat bones, especially chicken bones, which splinter and may choke him.

17. Don't feed your puppy or dog rawhide bones. Large shank bones are good until they begin to splinter. Once they splinter or chip, throw them out.

18. Don't let your puppy get too much exercise if he is a large-breed dog such as a Great Dane or Saint Bernard. A puppy's bones are still growing and should not be overly stressed.

19. Don't bathe your puppy too frequently. This may result in skin irritation or dryness.

20. Never pick your puppy up by his limbs. Always place your hands beneath his bottom and under his chest to best support him.

16 Basic Training Tips

Andy Luper has devoted himself to the study of animal behaviorism and dog psychology since 1970. A psychology major in college and a dog lover since childhood, he is also a devoted dog owner with extensive breeder and exhibitor experience, all of which helped him to form his philosophy of approaching training in a unique, humane, psychological, and enjoyable manner for both the dog and the owner. It is this approach that has made Luper the subject of numerous articles in publications throughout the state of Arizona and a guest on various local radio and TV shows. Here are his general suggestions for fret-free dog training.

1. Consistency pays. Always use the same words for the same concepts. For example: if you are working on "down," don't say, "Lie down, Prince" one time and "Down, boy" the next time. Keep commands brief. Most of all, make them exactly the same every time. This is also true for hand signals.

2. Introduce commands slowly and only after your dog has performed the behavior you want spontaneously. You wait, he sits. You say, "Good boy, Prince, good sit." In this way the dog learns to associate the command word with the action and with pleasure — the only real winning combination to teach anybody to do anything.

3. Make training sessions pleasurable for both of you. Play with the dog a few minutes before you start any type of work. This doesn't mean you shouldn't be serious about training: you should. Be pleasant, friendly, and animated. The only taboo is laughing at the dog during training. You will either humiliate her or turn her into a clown.

4. Keep sessions short (especially at first). Start with ten-minute sessions and work up to twenty minutes. This is really for your sake. Don't lose your

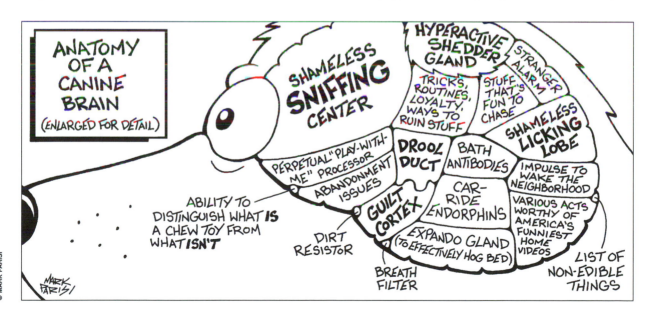

temper and spoil all the effort the both of you have put in.

5. Patience, patience, patience. Not that your dog is a slow learner — far from it — but people are sometimes unreasonable in their expectations. If your attitude is "Let's see what happens today" rather than "Today, Prince, you will learn to sit," you'll have better and faster results. If you are relaxed and patient, you will be rewarded in the short run by a more pleasant training session and have a better-trained dog in the long run.

6. End the session before either of you tire of it. If you feel yourself getting short-tempered, *stop* training — even if you've been at it for only a few minutes.

7. Use praise as a reward, not food. Often, your dog will perform for food only if he's hungry.

8. Be firm, both with your dog and with yourself. If you pay attention to what your dog is doing by praising and rewarding the exact behavior that you want, your dog will learn easily and correctly after only a few repetitions. If you are inattentive or lax, you'll only confuse your dog and make your job harder. Be sure you see exactly what you want your dog to do (or movement toward it) before you praise him. Between sessions, reward desired behavior whenever you see it, but don't be too fanatical. If your dog expects praise every time he performs, he'll be disappointed and confused when you in-

evitably forget to praise him. Rewarding behavior most of the time works better than rewarding it all of the time.

9. Never punish your dog.

10. Use the dog's own name as part of your commands. Say, "Prince, come" or "Prince, heel." There is no sound more pleasant for a dog than the sound of his own name.

11. When you first start training, do it in the same place every day and make sure there aren't any distractions. This is one reason that a group class isn't an ideal place for real training (especially for beginners). After your dog has learned her lessons, you can work him into other surroundings, slowly adding distractions, so he gets used to a variety of situations.

12. Never grab at the dog or run after him. At first, use only coaxing and praise. Later, work the dog on a leash with a training collar. If you chase after or hit him, you can make your dog hand shy and he will be almost impossible to handle.

13. Vary your tones with the appropriate words. Praise, of course, is given in warm, friendly tones. It doesn't matter what you say as long as you say the same thing every time. When a dog is new to an experience, cajole him and coax him along. Later, when he can be expected to understand, use the command tone of voice. The command tone of voice means that you expect obedi-

ence; you demand it. Your dog is better than you are at recognizing changing tones of voice, so beware not just of what you say but of how you say it. Avoid that irritable crabby voice that sounds like whining. If that voice appears, it's time to quit.

14. Be sure your dog is in the same happy mental state of mind when you finish a session as when you started. The simplest way to do this is to be sure *your* frame of mind is good. If you are still "up" and full of enthusiasm, your dog will be also.

15. Remember that commanding and the sharp corrections that go with it come only after your dog has learned to associate certain behaviors with praise and a reward. In the beginning, you must wait for events to occur at random (and learn to induce them) and then reward the ones you want to encourage and correct the ones you want to discourage. Praise teaches dogs what to do — corrections teach the dog what *not* to do. Both are equally important.

16. When we first teach a new command or behavior to a dog, the sequence should be command, demonstration, then praise. Once the dog has learned a command or exercise, the sequence becomes command, correction, then praise. **There is no benefit to correcting a dog for a behavior that he does not associate with it or if he does not understand what the correction is for.**

"**Whoever said you can't buy happiness forgot little puppies.**"   — GENE HILL

7 Schools of Dog Training

There are several schools of thought on how to best train a dog. Some approaches are harsh while others are far more pleasant and effective. Here is an overview on the different approaches that have been employed over the years.

1. **Play training** is an excellent method for motivating your dog to learn commands. Your dog has an enormous play drive, and his learning ability can be enhanced if he is having fun and receiving positive reinforcement. This technique is far more effective than some of the more violent methods used.

2. **Clicker training**, based on the theory of operant conditioning by B. F. Skinner, was developed by noted animal behaviorist Karen Pryor for the training of dogs. This is an excellent approach that will motivate your dog and will provide him with reinforcement for positive behaviors. See page 290.

3. **Target stick training** was developed by Gary Wilkes, a noted trainer and behaviorist. His technique relies on attracting the dog's attention by having her focus on an object referred to as a target stick, although it doesn't have to be a stick; almost any object can be used. Once the dog has learned to focus on the object she will be more willing to learn commands. This method is often used in conjunction with a clicker.

4. **Lure training** employs an object such as a toy or treat to teach your dog obedience commands. The lure is eventually used less and less as your pooch begins to understand each command. Once the command is understood, hand signals will replace the need for a lure. This technique can be useful with timid or sensitive dogs who have not responded to other training methods, and it is especially effective with puppies.

5. **The Jolly Routine**, developed by William E. Campbell, is a method that allows you to retrain your dog to help him get over situations in which he has felt threatened. This is accomplished by substituting a positive device such as a bouncing ball or jingling house keys to change your dog's response from that of fear to acceptance. This technique is designed to make your Murray a happier guy.

6. **The after-the-fact discipline approach** for correcting bad behavior is rarely effective and may even make matters worse than they already are. If your dog has chewed up the family newspaper, disciplining him a minute or even a few seconds later will not work because he won't relate the correction with the offending behavior. And even if he looks guilty, he's not feeling guilty; he's just assuming a submissive posture because he knows you are angry about something.

7. **The Koehler method**, developed by William Koehler, is designed to teach your dog to heel, come, sit, down, stand, and stay in thirteen weeks. However, Koehler's method relies on disciplinary techniques that are rather harsh. Koehler's philosophy, that once a dog anticipates punishment he will stop a bad behavior, is the subject of much criticism.

---

5 Commands Every Dog Should Learn

Being able to communicate with your dog is an invaluable tool that will enable you to have a happier and safer pet. Your pet will be more respectful and better behaved once you have taught her as many words as possible. There are, however, five words or commands that Penny-Belle must learn to ensure her well-being.

1. Sit   2. Stay   3. Come   4. Heel   5. Down

Things to Consider Before You Housetrain Your Dog

These tips, provided by the Dumb Friends Animal League, may influence your decision as to the best housetraining method for you and your dog.

1. You should begin housetraining as soon as you bring your puppy home. Keep in mind that she will need to relieve herself about six times a day.

2. If he was obtained from a reputable breeder, chances are great that his litter area was kept clean. Your chances of successfully housebreaking him are good since he's already used to a clean environment.

3. If you got him by any other means, there's a good chance that he was brought into the world in a puppy mill where sanitary conditions were not high on the list of priorities. He may have grown accustomed to lying in his own waste. This will make crate training difficult, if not impossible.

4. Plan on taking him outside first thing in the morning, then ten to thirty minutes after each feeding, as well as before you settle in for the night and *whenever* he gets excited. Puppies piddle when they get excited. Never yell at or hit a puppy for peeing on the carpet or in any other unacceptable (to you) area. This will only make him think that peeing is bad and he will do his best to hide his business from you in the future.

5. If you live in an apartment and will be away for extended periods of time during the day and can't easily get your dog outside fast enough for her to relieve herself, you will have to use the paper training method until she matures and is able to control her bladder and bowel movements.

6. If you get your dog from a shelter and they tell you she is "almost housebroken," don't believe them. A dog is either completely housetrained or she isn't housetrained at all.

7. You must understand that although he wants to please you, Esteban does not know what is expected when you take him outside. Leaving him in the backyard for a couple of hours is not the way to successfully housetrain a dog. You need to be present when he relieves himself so that you can praise him and reinforce his success.

8. Housetraining should be viewed in the same way as your other dog training exercises. It requires time and patience, because he will make mistakes.

9. You need to be in control. You will need to either watch your puppy at all times or keep him confined in his crate.

10. Do not change your puppy's diet until at least a week or two after you've brought her home. You don't want to surprise her digestive system with food she is not used to.

11. If you are going to crate train, be sure that the crate is the appropriate size for your puppy. A crate that is too large gives your puppy the feeling that it's okay to use a corner of it for toilet relief. If it's too small, he will feel cramped. It is best to buy a crate that will accommodate him as an adult dog. You can add a piece of cardboard to the inside of the crate to restrict the amount of space he has when he is a puppy. As he grows, you can reduce and then remove the size of the barrier as you see fit.

12. Read everything you can about housetraining.

Housetraining Your Puppy

Housetraining a puppy requires time, vigilance, patience, and commitment. By following the procedures below as outlined by the Dumb Friends League, you can minimize house-soiling incidents. Keep in mind that virtually all puppies will have an accident in the house (more likely several). Expect this — it's part of raising a dog. The more consistent you are in following the basic housetraining procedures, the faster your puppy will learn acceptable behavior. It may take several weeks to housetrain your puppy, and with some of the smaller breeds, it might take even longer.

1. Establish a Routine

Like babies, puppies do best on a regular schedule. Take your puppy outside frequently — at least every two hours — and immediately after he wakes up from a nap, after playing, and after eating.

Praise Colonel lavishly every time he eliminates outdoors. You can even give him a treat. You must praise him and give him a treat immediately after he's finished eliminating, not after he comes back inside the house. This step is vital, because rewarding your dog for eliminating outdoors is the only way he'll know that's what you want him to do — and that's what you're rewarding him for doing.

Choose a location not too far from the door to be your puppy's bathroom spot. Always take her on a leash directly to this spot. Take her for a walk or play with her only after she has eliminated. If you clean up an accident in the house, take the soiled rags or paper towels and place them in the bathroom spot. The smell will help your puppy recognize this area as where she is supposed to eliminate. While your puppy is eliminating, use a phrase like "go potty." Eventually, you will want to say this before she eliminates to remind her what she is supposed to do.

If possible, put your puppy on a regular feeding schedule. Depending on their age, puppies usually need to be fed three or four times a day. Feeding your puppy at the same times each day will make it more likely that he'll eliminate at consistent times as well. This makes housetraining easier for both of you.

2. Supervise, Supervise, Supervise

Don't give Maylocks an opportunity to soil in the house. A puppy who isn't housetrained should be watched at all times when she is indoors. You can tether her to you with a six-foot leash or use baby gates to keep her in the room with you. Watch out for signs that she needs to eliminate, like sniffing around or circling. When you see these signs, immediately take her outside, on a leash, to her bathroom spot. If she eliminates, praise her lavishly and reward her with a treat.

3. Confinement

When you're unable to watch your puppy at all times, he should be confined to an area small enough that he won't want to eliminate there. It should be just big enough for him to comfortably stand, lie down, and turn around in. This area could be a portion of a bathroom or laundry room, blocked off with boxes or baby gates. Or you may want to crate train your

"Don't make the mistake of treating your dogs like humans, or they'll treat you like dogs." — MARTHA SCOTT

> "They have dog food for constipated dogs. If your dog is constipated, why screw up a good thing? Stay indoors and let 'im bloat!"
> — **DAVID LETTERMAN**

puppy and use the crate to confine him. If your puppy has spent several hours in confinement, when you let him out, take him directly to his bathroom spot and praise him when he eliminates.

4. Oops!

Expect your puppy to have an accident or two in the house — it's a normal part of housetraining a puppy.

When you catch Trafalgar in the act of eliminating in the house, do something to interrupt him, like make a startling noise (but be careful not to scare him). Immediately take him to his bathroom spot. If he finishes eliminating there, praise him and give him a treat.

Don't punish your puppy for eliminating in the house. If you find a soiled area, it's too late to administer a correction. Just clean it up. Rubbing your puppy's nose in it, taking him to the spot and scolding him, and any other punishment or discipline will only make him afraid of you or afraid to eliminate in your presence. Animals don't understand punishment after the fact, even if it's only seconds later. Punishment does more harm than good.

Cleaning the soiled area is very important because puppies are highly motivated to continue soiling in areas that smell like urine or feces.

It's extremely important that you use the supervision and confinement procedures outlined above to minimize the number of accidents. If you allow your puppy to eliminate frequently in the house, he'll get confused about where he's supposed to eliminate, and this will only prolong the housetraining process.

5. Paper Training

A puppy six months of age or younger cannot be expected to control his bladder for more than a few hours at a time. If you have to be away from home for more than four or five hours a day, this may not be the best time for you to get a puppy. If you're already committed to having a puppy and need to be away from home for long periods of time, you'll have to train your puppy to eliminate in a specific place indoors. Be aware, however, that doing this can prolong the process of teaching him to eliminate outdoors. Teaching your puppy to eliminate on newspaper may create a lifelong surface preference, meaning that even in adulthood he may eliminate on any newspapers he finds lying around the house.

When your puppy must be left alone for long periods of time, confine her to an area with enough room for a sleeping space, a playing space, and a separate place to eliminate. In the area designated as the elimination place, you can use either newspapers or a sod box. To make a sod box, place sod in a container, like a child's small plastic swimming pool. You can also find dog litter products at pet supply stores. If you clean up an accident in the house, take the soiled rags or paper towels and put them in the designated elimination place. The smell will help your puppy recognize that area as the place where she is supposed to eliminate.

> "I wonder what goes through his mind when he sees us peeing in his water bowl." — **PENNY WARD MOSER**

10 Great Dog Training Videos

1. *The Video Dog Trainer* (Goldhil Home Media, 1987). Here's the ideal tool for training puppies, mature dogs, and even problem dogs. This full-color video, one hour and fifteen minutes long, is entertaining and shows you the step-by-step methods used by professional dog trainers. It includes a fifteen-minute-a-day obedience training course to teach your dog basic commands and features the "3-Day Cure," designed to help housetrain your dog, and the "Dirty Dozen," twelve easy methods to help solve the most common behavioral problems pet owners have with their dogs, such as excessive barking, mouthing, and jumping on people.

2. *Dog Training for Children* (Ark Features Ltd., 1997). This video is written and hosted by the veterinarian, animal behaviorist, and author Dr. Ian Dunbar — the world's leading authority on dog behavior and training. Dr. Dunbar is the original creator of off-leash puppy classes, which sparked the revolution in dog training and heralded the era of positive, reward-based obedience training. The program is a bit dated but nonetheless excellent. Dunbar has a wonderful way with the children — clear, gentle, and kind. Kids can be completely successful using this positive method of dog training. Easy to watch and follow, this is an excellent resource for children.

3–6. *Training the Companion Dog: I: Socialization and Beginning Obedience; II: Behavior Problems and Household Etiquette; III: Walking on Leash and Preventing Jumping Up; and IV: Recalls and Stays* (James & Kenneth Publishers, 2004). These specially edited videotapes are based on the popular television series *Dogs with Dunbar*. Dr. Ian Dunbar is the world's leading authority on dog behavior and training, and the original creator of off-leash puppy classes. These award-winning programs, filmed in the enchanting New Forest area of England, are among the most helpful and creative on the market.

7. *Amazing Trick Training* (Tapeworm, 1999). Here's a quick, gentle, and fun way to maximize your play-training experience with your dog. Gather in front of the television with your favorite canine and enjoy! All of the animal lovers in your life will appreciate *Amazing Trick Training* time and time again. It's fast-paced, educational, and highly entertaining. This is the fun way to teach old dogs new tricks.

8. *Smart Training* (Triple Crown Dog Academy, 2000). This program presents dog training and basic obedience for the companion dog and is based on the idea that a well-behaved dog is a pleasure to live with. Learn proven methods for training a dog who will be a good companion, family member, and pet. Professional certified dog trainers demonstrate the obedience exercises and explain how to incorporate a clicker and treats into your training routine.

9. *PuppySmarts: Lessons for a Lifetime* (studio name unavailable, 2003). This easy-to-use training video helps owners and their dogs start off a lifetime together on the right paw. By using the approaches here, you will learn how to best prevent potential behavior problems in puppies and adult dogs. The program includes the most common behavior challenges dog owners face, including housetraining and crate training, obedience, jumping, chewing, and biting.

10. *It's Not the Dog . . . Training You to Train Your Dog* (studio name unavailable, 2001). Learn to be the alpha dog. This video offers the tools you need to teach Rover to come, sit, stay, stop jumping up, and stop chewing. Dogs understand hierarchy and order; this tape will teach you how to be the leader. You and your dog will be much happier once *you* take charge.

"If you are a dog and your owner suggests that you wear a sweater . . . suggest that he wear a tail." — **FRAN LEBOWITZ**

How to Read Your Dog's Body Language

Teaching everything from basic dog training to eliminating destructive habits, Bash Dibra has turned dogs of all breeds and dispositions into well-mannered, obedient companions. Dibra has worked with the four-legged friends of Matthew Broderick, Sarah Jessica Parker, Jennifer Lopez, Mariah Carey, and a host of other celebrities. He is the author of *Dog Training by Bash* (Signet, 1992) and *DogSpeak* (Fireside, 2001), in which he imparts the secret of his $300-an-hour lessons: good communication. Dibra's success is his uncanny ability to speak to dogs in their own language, and it's a skill any pet owner can master. We're grateful to Bash Dibra for sharing with us this basic "dogspeak" primer.

1. The Aggressive Dog

Aggressive

Ears: Either forward or back but always close to her head.

Eyes: Will either narrow her eyes or stare challengingly.

Mouth: Lips will be open and drawn back to expose teeth that are bared in a snarl. You may see her jaw snap as well.

Body: Tense, upright. The hackles on her neck will be raised, and the dog will assume a completely dominant position.

Tail: Straight out from body and fluffed up.

Vocalization: The dog will either snarl, growl, or bark loudly.

2. The Alert Dog

Alert and dominant

Ears: Perked up and turned to catch sounds.

Eyes: Open their normal width or even wider to take in the situation at hand.

Mouth: Either closed or slightly open, but with no teeth showing.

Body: Normal or possibly standing on tiptoe in a slightly dominant position.

Tail: Up, possibly wagging.

Vocalization: There will be either no sound or a low whine or alarm bark.

3. The Anxious Dog

Anxious

Ears: Partially back from her head.

Eyes: Slightly narrowed.

Mouth: Closed or slightly open in a canine grin.

Body: May be tense, and slightly lowered in a submissive position.

Tail: Partially lowered.

Vocalization: Low whine or moaning-type bark.

4. The Dog Who Is About to Give Chase

Chase, beginning stage; predatory

Ears: Perked up, forward-pointing.

Eyes: Wide-open and very alert.

Mouth: Slightly open, with excited panting.

Body: Tense, crouched low in a predatory position,

with legs bent and poised to run.

Tail: Extended straight out from body.

Vocalization: None.

5. The Curious, Eager, or Excited Dog

Friendly, playful, happy, curious, eager, excited

Ears: Perked up and forward-pointing.

Eyes: Wide-open.

Mouth: The mouth will be open but the teeth will remain covered. The dog will possibly pant.

Body: Will assume a normal stance, possibly wiggling, standing on tiptoe, or pacing.

Tail: Up and wagging.

Vocalization: Excited short barking or whining.

6. The Dominant Dog

Alert and dominant

Ears: Straight up or forward.

Eyes: Wide-open and staring.

Mouth/Teeth: Closed or slightly open mouth.

Body: A very tall posture. The hackles may be up.

Tail: Either stiffened and fluffed up or up and straight out from body.

Vocalization: Emitting a low, assertive growl or grunt.

7. The Fearful Dog
Ears: Laid back flat and low on her head.

Eyes: Narrowed, averted, or possibly rolled back in head with the whites showing.

Mouth: Lips will be drawn back to expose her teeth.

Body: Tense, crouched low into a submissive position, with possible shivering or trembling. You may notice a secretion from her anal scent glands.

Fearful, subordinate, submissive

Tail: Down between her legs.

Vocalization: Low, with a worried yelp, whine, or growl.

8. The Dog Who Is About to Flee

Flight, beginning stage

Ears: Back.

Eyes: Wide-open, possibly rolled back with the whites showing.

Mouth/Teeth: Slightly opened mouth with possible drooling.

Body: Tense. The dog may shiver and assume a low position when she is poised to run.

Tail: Low or between her legs.

Vocalization: May be absent or you may hear her yelp or whine.

9. The Friendly Dog

Friendly, playful, happy, curious, eager, excited

Ears: Perked up.

Eyes: Wide-open with an alert look.

Mouth: Relaxed, possibly slightly open and smiling.

Body: Normal or still, or

you may see wiggling of the dog's entire rear end.

Tail: Up or out from body and wagging.

Vocalization: Sounds of whimpering, yapping, or a short, high bark.

10. The Guarding Dog

Guarding

Ears: Perked up and forward on her head.

Eyes: Wide-open and alert.

Mouth: Slightly open, with teeth bared. She may snap or gnash her teeth.

Body: Tense and rigid, standing very tall in an aggressive or dominant stance. Hackles will be up.

Tail: Rigid and held straight out from body and sometimes fluffed.

Vocalization: Emitting a loud, alert bark, growl, or snarl.

11. The Playful and Happy Dog

Friendly, playful, happy, curious, eager; excited

Ears: Perked up and forward, or relaxed.

Eyes: Wide-open. Sparkly and merry-looking.

Mouth: Relaxed and slightly open, with teeth covered. She may pant excitedly.

Body: Relaxed, with front end lowered and rear end up in the air, wiggling in a play bow. She may bounce or jump up and down. She may also circle around and run forward and back in an invitation to play.

Tail: Wagging vigorously.

Vocalization: Barking happily or producing a soft play growl.

12. The Predatory Dog

Chase, beginning stage; predatory

Ears: Alert, held forward or backward to catch sounds.

Eyes: Wide-open, staring and focusing.

Mouth: Closed.

Body: Rigid, low to the ground, and ready to spring forward. She may quietly sniff the air.

Tail: Straight and low.

Vocalization: Not heard; she remains quiet so her prey won't be alerted.

13. The Subordinate or Submissive Dog

Ears: Down and flattened against the head.

Eyes: Either narrowed to slits or open wide with the whites showing.

Mouth: Lips pulled way back from teeth in a "grin." The dog will nuzzle or lick the other animal or person on face.

Body: Lowered to the ground, with a front paw raised. The dog might be lying on her back, belly-up. She will possibly leak or dribble urine. She may also empty her anal scent glands.

Tail: Down between her legs.

Vocalization: Either nonexistent or a low, worried whining sound, or possibly a fearful yelp or whimper.

Fearful, subordinate, submissive

20 Noted Dog Trainers

1. **Carol Lea Benjamin** is a noted author and trainer of dogs. Her award-winning books on dog behavior and training include *Mother Knows Best, The Natural Way to Train Your Dog, Second-Hand Dog,* and *Dog Training in Ten Minutes.* As a former detective, Carol blends her knowledge of dogs with her real-life experiences to create the Rachel Alexander and Dash mystery series. Her latest installment is *The Long Good Boy.* She is recognized in the Dog Trainers Hall of Fame not only for her contribution to dog training but also because of the inspiration she has provided for so many through her dogged enthusiasm and capable writing.

2. **Suzanne Clothier** is a professional dog trainer, a lecturer, and an award-winning author. Her innovative holistic approach focuses on the mind, body, and soul of dogs, emphasizing the importance of the relationship between a dog and her handler. Clothier's seminars — given nationwide — cover a wide variety of topics including the canine athlete, behavior problems, obedience training, relationships, and more. She is the author of *The Natural Jumping Method, Body Posture and Emotions: Shifting Shapes, Shifting Minds,* and *Bones Would Rain from the Sky: Deepening Our Relationships with Dogs.*

3. **Bash Dibra**, author of two best-selling books as well as a new soon-to-be released title on responsible pet ownership, is an expert in the field of animal training. With his numerous contacts in the advertising and movie industry, Dibra knows what it takes to "make your pet a star." His clients include the dogs of such superstars as Mariah Carey, Kim Basinger, and Matthew Broderick and Sarah Jessica Parker, and he is the creator of Star Pet Workshops, an animal actors workshop designed to transform even the most dedicated couch potato pooch into a bono fido performing star.

4. **Jean Donaldson** is the owner of Renaissance Dog Training in Montreal. She and her dogs have won many obedience, tracking, and Flyball titles. Jean is one of the most sought-after speakers on the doggy circuit in both the United States and Canada. Her first book, *The Culture Clash,* is one of the best dog books ever. This seminal title depicts dogs as they really are — stripped of their Hollywood fluff, with their lovable "Can I eat it, chew it, urinate on it, what's in it for me?" philosophy. Donaldson's tremendous affection for dogs shines through at all times, as does her keen insight into the dog's mind. She champions the dog's point of view, always showing concern for their education and well-being.

5. The veterinarian, animal behaviorist, and author **Dr. Ian Dunbar** is director of the Center for Applied Animal Behavior, the founder of the Association of Pet Dog Trainers, and the host of the British TV series *Dogs with Dunbar*. Dr. Dunbar is the author of numerous books and videos, including *SIRIUS Puppy Training* and *How to Teach a New Dog Old Tricks.* Ian lives in Berkeley, California, with a little brown dog named Oliver, a large brown dog named Claude, and a kitty called Mitty.

6. Training famous owners' dogs does not make us better dog trainers, but **Captain Haggerty** has probably trained more famous people and their dogs than any other dog trainer. His clients have included Elijah Wood's Bearded Collies, Leona Helmsley's German Shepherd Dogs, and Brooke Shields's Shih Tzu, among many other celebrity dogs. Haggerty is also known as the "King of Stupid Pet Tricks" on *The Late Show with David Letterman.*

7. **Vicki Hearne** was an author, writer, poet, trainer, and defender of dogs everywhere. She died of cancer at the age of fifty-four. Dog lovers know Hearne mainly from her books *Bandit: Dossier of a Dangerous Dog* and

Adam's Task: Calling Animals By Name, both of which are classics. As a powerful writer, Hearne had the ability to put her finger on the pulse of dogs and their relationship with people. She was able to write and explain our interaction in a way that imparted a heartfelt message and made reading about it fascinating. The International Association of Canine Professionals honored Hearne as the second inductee into the IACP Hall of Fame.

8. **Frank Inn** has worked training movie animals for more than half a century, overcoming great physical challenges due to an automobile accident after which he was mistakenly pronounced dead. Inn has trained some of the world's best-known animals, including Cleo the Basset Hound, who starred with Jackie Cooper on the 1950s television series *The People's Choice,* and Arnold, the pig from *Green Acres.* Today, his best-known animal is that lovable mixed-breed dog, Benji. Inn was the first inductee into the IACP Hall of Fame.

9. **Trish King** is the director of the Animal Behavior and Training Department at the Marin Humane Society in Marin County, California. Department programs include behavior consultations with the public, dog training classes (including classes for aggressive dogs), evaluations of adoption dogs, and training classes specifically geared for dogs up for adoption. King has been instrumental in implementing innovative programs to help screen incoming animals and to train dogs while they wait for adoption. Her staff includes fifteen instructors and behavior counselors and forty-five volunteer assistants.

10. **Robin Kovary** trained dogs and counseled owners for more than seventeen years. She was voted Best Dog Trainer for two consecutive years by *Manhattan File* magazine. Kovary was devoted to helping dogs and their people, and she believed that dog training can and should be fun for everyone involved. She was a cofounding member of the Society of North American Dog Trainers, a charter member of the Association of Pet Dog Trainers, and director of the Canine Resource and Referral Helpline

and the American Dog Trainers Network. She costarred in the video *Children, Dogs and Safety* for the Geisenger Foundation and was a guest on scores of television and radio programs throughout the United States, Europe, and Japan. Kovary died in 2001.

11. **Kay Laurence** designed and taught several new college courses that covered many aspects of dogs, from training and behavior to psychology, history, and care and welfare, as well as for a course called Teaching People, Teaching Dogs. She now runs her own business, Learning About Dogs (www.learningaboutdogs.com), which organizes conferences, offers courses, and publishes *Teaching Dogs* magazine, along with several books and videos on clicker training. Laurence designed a series of competency tests for clicker trainers and is the inventor and initiator of the exciting new sport of Clicker Challenges, now holding regular events in the United Kingdom. She regularly holds workshops in Europe, New Zealand, Australia, Canada, and the United States. She loves spreading enthusiasm for clicker training and encouraging people to learn more about dogs.

12. **Patricia B. McConnell, Ph.D,** is a cohost of Wisconsin Public Radio's *Calling All Pets.* Dr. McConnell gives advice about behavior problems on more than 110 radio stations across the country. She is the behavior columnist for *The Bark* magazine and is a consulting editor for the *Journal of Comparative Psychology.* Dr. McConnell is the author of *The Cautious Canine, The Puppy Primer,* and *The Other End of the Leash,* along with other dog-related titles.

13. **Lois Meistrell** and her husband were involved with training dogs for the military prior to World War II at Mitchell Field, Long Island, New York. Meistrell used techniques that were then new to American dog training. In addition to her training accomplishments, Meistrell is a lifetime member of the Dog Writers Association of America.

14. **Dr. Roger Mugford** is a broadcaster and lecturer, as well as an author of books, including *Dog Training the*

"Only mad dogs and Englishmen go out in the midday sun."
— NOEL COWARD

Mugford Way and *Dr. Mugford's Casebook.* Mugford is an experienced expert witness in law cases relating to animals. His business, the Company of Animals, produces a wide range of products that help dog owners raise better-behaved, happier pets. It is probably most famous, however, for the Kong — possibly the best-known dog toy in the world.

15. **Edi Munneke** had the enviable record, still unbeaten, of having the only dog to score thirty-nine perfect obedience scores. Munneke helped shape the United Kennel Club's obedience rules and judged the very first UKC obedience trial. For years Munneke looked over the AKC obedience regulations before they went to press. She wrote the obedience column in *Dog World* magazine for thirty-two years.

16. **Terry Ryan** is the president of Legacy Canine Behavior and Training, Inc., a business started in 1974. Ryan has been a community dog class instructor since 1968, specializing in motivational exercises that are often presented as games. Ryan was a chairperson for the American Humane Association's Humane Dog Training Project. Her work resulted in a document on humane dog training standards published by the Delta Society. Ryan wrote seven books in Japanese, two in Norwegian, and one in French. Her most recent English-language publication is *The Toolbox for Remodeling Your Problem Dog.*

17. **Pia Silvani** is director of training and behavior at St. Hubert's Animal Welfare Center, Madison, New Jersey. Through research, continuing education, and enthusiasm Silvani was instrumental in developing a pet training curriculum focused on positive, reward-based techniques. These extremely effective techniques enhance the bond between dogs and their human companions. She is a member of the American Humane Association Task Force for Humane Dog Training and a past vice pres-

ident and charter member of the Association of Pet Dog Trainers. Silvani has written five dog training manuals.

18. Known as Ms. German Shepherd of Obedience, **Winifred Gibson Strickland** has received more than 1,500 awards and trophies. Strickland was an AKC obedience judge for eighteen years and judged all classes including Tracking.

19. When they were young boys in 1911, **Frank** and **Rudd Weatherwax** were allowed to raise some puppies on the condition that they train the dogs. The boys' tricks proved quite imaginative, thus inaugurating their dog training careers. In the early 1920s, Frank and Rudd and their dogs received parts in several films. A Wire Fox Terrier named Asta appeared in *The Thin Man,* and a dog named Daisy played in the Blondie movies with Penny Singleton. Another of the Weatherwax brothers, Jack, became a trainer for Carl Spitz, who owned the Cairn Terrier everyone now knows as Toto, helping to work the dog during the filming of the *Wizard of Oz.* And lest a fourth son be outdone, Bill Weatherwax went on to train war dogs, a task he found distasteful, as he objected to the use of dogs for this purpose. In 1940, they formed a partnership business known as the Studio Dog Training School. This partnership produced the dog stars who performed in *Lassie* and *Old Yeller.*

20. **Barbara Woodhouse**, "the lady with the dogs," was familiar to millions of Americans through her appearances on CBS's *60 Minutes, The Tonight Show, Donahue, Merv Griffin, Good Morning America,* and the syndication of her enormously popular television series *Training Dogs the Woodhouse Way.* Born in Dublin in 1910 and raised in Oxford, England, Woodhouse spent three years during the 1930s on a cattle ranch in Argentina, where her extraordinary gift with animals enabled her to break in hundreds of wild horses. She died in 1988.

16 Things You Can Do to Keep Your Dog Safe

Dog theft has reached epidemic proportions in the United States. Nearly 2.5 million dogs are stolen each year, but only 10 percent of these dogs are ever returned home. People who steal dogs either sell them to research labs or to puppy mills, where they can be bred. Stolen dogs are also sold so their fur can be used in ritualistic sacrifices. Others are used as bait in dogfighting matches. Here are ways to keep your dog from being stolen.

1. Teach your dog the "stay" command and be sure she has learned it well.

2. Keep your dog indoors. Don't leave her outside by herself, and don't ever let your dog roam around the neighborhood alone.

3. Know where your dog is at all times.

4. Make sure that your dog has an up-to-date collar and dog tag. Microchips and tattoos are extremely helpful in identifying and locating lost or stolen dogs.

5. Make sure that your dog's license is up-to-date.

6. Keep recent photos of your dog handy.

7. Your dog is more at risk of getting lost on snowy or foggy days when visibility is poor. On days such as these, be particularly vigilant regarding your dog's whereabouts.

8. Keep an eye out for strangers in your neighborhood.

9. Make sure that when your dog is in the backyard, no one can see her from the street.

10. If you are going to leave your dog outside, be sure she is locked safely behind a sturdy gate.

11. Keep your dog on a leash whenever you go outside.

12. Never leave your dog alone in the car.

13. Do not tie your pet up outside a store to wait for you. Never, ever leave your pet outside a store while you run inside. Not even for one second. Just don't do it. Dogs can vanish in an instant, and you'll never forgive yourself if this happens to your dog.

14. Never leave your dog at a boarding kennel unless it has a good reputation, has been in business for several years, and has reported no incidence of lost or stolen dogs.

15. Don't put a dog up for adoption until you have carefully screened the prospective new owner. And never give a dog away for free.

16. Spay and neuter your pets. Altered animals are less likely to stray from home.

"You enter into a certain amount of madness when you marry a person with pets." — NORA EPHRON

How to Teach Basic Commands

If you are using a clicker, you'll click instead of saying "yes" each time it's indicated. (See "8 Advantages of Clicker Training," page 290.)

1. **Sit:** Hold a treat in your fingers and put it near Monk's nose. Slowly move the treat up over his head and slightly backward (toward his tail). As he watches the treat go back over his head, his rear end should naturally go down. When his rear end hits the floor, immediately say "yes" and give him a treat. If your dog doesn't get up after you say "yes," use your release word, such as "OK," "free," or "all done." Let him get up and move around, then repeat. Remember to follow the "yes" with the food reward each time.

2. **Stay:** "Stay" has two components: the stay and the release. These are always performed together. Stay: Have Marley sit. Then tell him "stay" in a firm voice while putting your hand in front of his face. Wait just a couple of seconds, then calmly and quietly reward and praise him. Release: After you have rewarded Marley for the stay, give a release word such as "free," "okay," or "at ease," encouraging him to move out of the stay position. Remember: Always reward the stay first, then release him. If you reward your dog after you have released him, you will reward the release, not the stay.

3. **Come:** With your dog a short distance away and on-leash (or off-leash in a small, confined area), call your dog's name. Using a very positive, happy voice, bend forward and pat your thigh, or get down on your knees and pat the floor. As soon as he looks at you, say "yes." When he comes to you to get his treat, gently take his collar in one hand while you pop the treat into his mouth with the other hand and praise him. Once your dog is reliably coming to you when you get his attention — even if there are a few distractions — add the cue "come" or "here." Say, "Duffy, come," and say "yes" when he starts to come toward you. Gradually increase the number of steps your dog is required to take toward you before you say "yes." Do this until you say "yes" only when he gets all the way to you. (It might be useful to have someone hold your dog loosely while you get into position, then release him when you call.) Remember that coming to you should always result in something positive for your dog.

4. **Heel:** Begin with Dooley sitting at your left side with his ear even with your side pant seam. With the leash gathered or shortened (but not held taut — the leash must be somewhat slack) in your right hand at waist level, hold a treat directly in front of your dog's nose with your left hand. Step out on your left foot as you briskly walk forward with your dog at a trot, and say "yes" and reward with the treat after only one or two steps in the heel position. When you are ready to stop, ask Dooley to sit so that he learns to do so automatically when you halt. Remember: Do not use the leash to keep your dog in heel position. Keep your dog in position by using the treat as a target.

5. **Down:** With Pedro sitting, hold the treat right in front of his nose. Slowly bring the treat straight down to the floor. Your dog's head should follow the treat down to the floor. Pull the treat forward slowly along the floor and the rest of his body should follow naturally. If pulling the treat forward makes your dog stand up to reach the treat, try pushing it back toward his chest. As soon as his body touches the floor, say "yes" and give him the treat. Release him from this position with your release word and take a step back, then give him lots of praise and ask him to sit. Repeat.

8 Advantages of Clicker Training

A clicker is a small plastic box with a metal strip that emits a sharp clicking sound when it's pushed and released. The clicker's use is based on B. F. Skinner's scientific learning theory of operant conditioning. Applied to dog training, operant conditioning occurs when a dog learns that she is rewarded for performing a specific task. Once the dog realizes which of her tasks or behaviors is rewarded (in this case, with a click and a food treat), she will perform that behavior again to get another reward. The clicker simply replaces verbal praise with a more precise signal that the dog can associate with success.

Introduced to the dog world by Karen Pryor, clicker training is a gentle and effective training method. Clickers are not generally available at pet supply stores. If you want to purchase a clicker, contact Karen Pryor's Gear Shop at www.clickertraining.com. Here are some advantages of clicker training:

1. Using a clicker is a precise way to let your dog know immediately that her behavior is correct. In the time it takes to say "Good girl!" a dog may go through a number of other behaviors and may become confused as to which one she is being rewarded for. This does not happen with a clicker.

2. The sound emitted by a clicker is both unique and consistent. Vocal praise and commands often vary in tone, inflection, and volume and can confuse your dog. Because the clicker has a distinct sound, it won't be mistaken for any other sound.

3. Clicker training creates a strong bond between the handler and the dog because the dog is never punished for misunderstanding what the trainer wants.

4. Dogs love clicker training. Their tails wag as soon as they see you with the clicker (not to mention your treat bag). A clicker-trained dog has no reason to be willful because she is motivated to succeed.

5. Clicker training is easier on the handler. Clicker training promotes hands-off training and is more meaningful and memorable to dogs. Dogs learn quickly that the sound of the clicker means that something good is coming. When dogs learn that they can make you click by repeating a positive behavior, they become enthusiastic partners in their own training.

6. Clicker training fosters creativity in dogs. Your dog will try to find different ways to please you so that you use the clicker and then give her a reward. This sense of creativity makes the training progressively easier. It gives trainers many chances to reward their dog and then teach new behaviors.

7. If you've accidentally clicker trained your dog to do something you don't want her to do, **the mistake is easily corrected** by merely taking away the reward.

8. Clicker training rarely results in a dog's acting aggressively. It is also a very safe method for dog trainers and rarely results in injury.

5 Disadvantages of Clicker Training

Here are some of the arguments made against using a clicker as your only training method:

1. Some people find it awkward to use a clicker while they are training and are sometimes intimidated by the apparent complexity of the clicker, mostly because it appears to add an extra step to the training process.

2. Another difficulty is the concept of **taking your dog to a clicker-training class.** Annie may not be able to focus on your clicker alone if she hears several other clickers simultaneously.

3. Many dog trainers believe that dogs should focus on what their people want them to do and not just on an auditory signal (a click).

4. Clicker training is based strictly on using food as a reward. Believe it or not, some dogs aren't interested enough in food to repeatedly perform tasks in order to receive treats. These dogs will easily lose interest in the training process.

5. Clicker training requires a great deal of patience.

---

8 Things to Look For in a Dog Trainer

Professional trainers come in about as many different varieties as dogs themselves. Here's what to look for:

1. A good reputation. Consult your local chapter of the ASPCA, breeders in your area, and your dog's veterinarian for recommendations, as well as other pet owners. Take your time and shop around.

2. Experience. Anyone can call himself a dog trainer; you want someone who has years of expertise behind him. Check references; if the person claims to have worked for an institution, call and make sure the information you have is accurate.

3. A humane, effective approach to dog training. Avoid trainers who use harsh methods of dog training that sometimes don't take the dog's welfare into account. Such techniques are unnecessary and are often counterproductive. Ask specific questions about the trainer's philosophy and note the ways in which he interacts with your dog. Key words and concepts to look for include positive, reward-based training.

4. A love of dogs. You'll know it when you see it. Does the person enjoy her work? Does she talk about dogs with devotion and enthusiasm? How many dogs does she own? What sorts of stories does she tell about them?

5. Comprehensive knowledge of dog behavior. Where did this person study and for how long? More-over, when was the last time he attended one of the many seminars, courses, conferences, or workshops that are held specifically to keep professionals up-to-date on the latest techniques and training methods?

6. Good teaching and communication skills. A dog trainer should be able to communicate with your dog, thereby making the learning process relatively easy and hassle-free. But he also needs to communicate well with you while teaching you how to reinforce everything your dog is learning. Is the dog trainer open and forthcoming in explaining his methods?

7. A sense of humor. It's okay for you and your dog to have fun with the learning process. In fact, it's required! Dog training should be an enjoyable experience for everyone. Don't be fooled into thinking that a stern, severe demeanor is the only way to go. This really isn't the case anymore.

8. Dog training classes. Many trainers teach dogs and their people in groups. This allows dog owners to watch the training process and learn how to do it themselves. It also gives Spot a chance to socialize with other dogs. Groups shouldn't be too large — a good ratio is approximately eight to ten people and dogs per trainer.

10 Types of Dog Collars

Jennifer Schneider, director of PickOfTheLitterDogTraining.com and owner of Pick of the Litter Dog Training in western Washington State, points out that choosing the proper training collar can be extremely confusing. Her list will help you make an informed decision about which training collar is the most effective and humane for your dog:

1. The **regular web collar** is the most common type of collar. This everyday, effective collar comes in either a buckle or quick-snap variety and can be left on your dog at all times without any threat of injury, You can also easily attach your dog's identification tags to this collar. Your dog, however, may be able to slip out of the regular web collar, and it can be difficult for you to effectively grab hold of. These don't function as training collars.

2. The **Martingale collar** is an excellent collar with a loop that tightens and releases around the dog's neck when the leash is retracted. These can be left on at all times and won't hurt your dog. Martingales are escape-proof and easy to get a hold of. They do tend to get caught in longer fur and may not provide enough control with larger, stronger dog breeds.

3. A **harness** wraps around the dog's body at two separate points. These cause no pressure around the neck and are especially good with small dogs because they can't slip out of them. Harnesses are not effective in training larger dogs.

4. The **Gentle Leader nylon head collar** attaches around the dog's neck and muzzle, making it an effective training tool. It does not produce pressure around Cinderella's neck and does not restrict her movements in any way. It is important to note, however, that this collar can injure a dog's neck if it isn't used properly.

5. The **Halti head collar** attaches around a dog's neck and muzzle. This makes an effective training tool because the dog will go wherever his head leads him. Furthermore, the Halti does not create pressure around a dog's neck. It can be a little restricting, and it may take a while for your dog to get used to this collar.

6. The **choke collar** contains stainless steel loops or a nylon cord that tightens around the neck when the leash is retracted. These can be effective training devices with punishment training, and they make a sound that will also get a dog's attention. Choke collars must be used correctly or they can cause breathing difficulties and injury.

7. The **prong** or **pinch collar** is a stainless steel collar with pointed prongs that extend into the neck when the leash is retracted. This is effective with punishment training. Pinch collars can be danger-

From the 1897 Sears, Roebuck Catalogue

ous if they are used incorrectly. They should not be left on an unsupervised dog and can easily injure the neck and surrounding areas. Prong collars can make dogs act more anxiously because they are responding to being in pain.

8. **Electronic shock collars** enable dog handlers to send a mild to moderate shock when a dog incorrectly performs a specific task. This is an effective punishment-based training tool. These collars are effective only about 50 percent of the time, however, and they may frighten your dog and cause her to act submissively.

9. The **snap-around training collar** is different from other training products in that it is placed around the dog's neck as opposed to being fitted over the head like other training products (two-ring training collars). With proper fitting this collar should not slide down the neck but stay in this position, giving the handler better control for more effective teaching. This type of collar is very humane simply because of where it sits on the dog's neck, above the trachea.

10. **Electronic noise collars** emit a tone or a noise when the dog pulls on the leash. These collars don't injure dogs, but they can annoy them. Electronic collars are often easily ignored and therefore they aren't very effective.

Electronic Fence Pros and Cons

In recent years, a lot of debate has centered on electronic fences. Some people say that this sort of fence, which emits a mild shock through a dog's collar, teaches dogs not to wander away from home. Others say that they are inhumane and simply don't work. Electronic fences vary in price according to the size of the area to be contained. Generally, they range from $500 to $1,500. Please consult your veterinarian before you choose an electronic fence. Here are some things you should consider.

Pros

1. An electronic fence will help keep your dog safe by enclosing her in your yard.

2. The shock your dog receives is mild and can be controlled so that if you have a small dog you can reduce the amount of electricity going to her collar.

3. Dogs are able to dig underneath most conventional fences. This won't happen with an electronic fence.

4. A high jumper won't be able to escape from the yard.

5. Since an electronic fence is installed underground, there are no building code restrictions regarding its construction.

6. The system is designed so that both the collar and wires are waterproof and pose no danger to your dog during a lightning storm.

7. People sometimes forget to fully close a gate, allowing a dog to escape. This can't happen with an electronic fence.

Cons

1. Many dog owners and humane societies think pain-inducing collars are inhumane.

2. Some dogs will escape despite the shock they receive. People have reported that their dogs ignored the shocks when chasing animals or when otherwise overexcited. Once they are outside the electronic fence, dogs don't want to cross the fence again to get back into their yard.

3. An electronic fence won't prevent other animals from entering your yard and attacking your dog.

4. People are not prevented from entering your property the way they would be by a conventional fence.

5. You have to make sure the batteries in your dog's collar don't run down, so either you need to have a backup system or you must be extremely vigilant.

Understanding and Controlling Excessive Barking

Sue Carney, manager of behavior and training programs for the New Hampshire SPCA, writes: "Let's face it — dogs bark. Barking in itself is not wrong; it's natural. Excessive amounts of barking, however, or barking at inappropriate times can be a real problem for some owners. In order to successfully teach your dog to control her barking, it's important to determine the motivation behind the noise." In this list Sue provides us with some insights and solutions.

1. **Territorial dogs** are most often unneutered males or dogs who have been encouraged in some way to take an active role in protecting their environment. Whether on purpose or by accident, we play a large role in creating this problem. These dogs are protecting their yard, house, and general "space" from intruders such as the postal carrier, a squirrel, a passing dog, a neighbor, or even a new activity, like mowing the lawn. Neutering will always help any male to "relax" his duties as protector of the universe. The "job" of protector, however, must be reassigned to someone else in order to stop overtly territorial barking behavior.

2. **Bored or underexercised dogs** tend to bark a lot. If you do not provide quality time with your pet more than once a day, then you will have a bored dog. Being tied out on a runner and walked for half an hour before and after work or school is simply not enough exercise for a dog. Dogs need both mental and physical stimulation to create balance and fun in their lives. Give your dog a job — such as retrieving the newspaper — or play Frisbee, fetch, or any number of games (see "19 Games You Can Play with Your Dog," p. 299) with her. Try to do this twice a day for at least half an hour each session.

3. A **fearful or neurotic dog** is undersocialized and coddled too much by her owner. Shelter and rescue dogs may easily fall into neurotic barking because they have experienced so many changes in their short lives. We often make the problem worse by catering to the dogs' shyness or fear. Patting and stroking a fearful dog while the behavior is happening can actually make the problem worse. Do not pet your dog when she is doing anything that you do not want her to do. Wait for your dog to quiet down before you praise her.

If it seems that your dog never quiets down, try this: While your dog is barking, call her to you. Tell her to sit, then reward her for coming and sitting with a pat or a cookie. While she is enjoying the cookie, chances are she'll be quiet. Then praise your dog. If you repeat this every time your dog hears something and starts barking, she will eventually learn that it is better to come to you and sit and wait for a reward than to bark at the door, the person, or whatever she is barking at.

4. **Leaving your dog alone** for more than eight hours at a time can create barking problems. Where is the dog kept when she's all by herself? Often allowing a terrier the run of the house can lead to bad behavior. While you're gone, she will run from window to window alerting the neighborhood that a squirrel has run by and someone better do something because she can't help — she is locked up in the house. A crate will help alleviate pacing and worrying about what is going on outside. You can also simply confine your dog to one room. This will calm her down and relieve the pressure she feels to pace and track activities outside.

5. When **a dog runs to the front door, barking and jumping** on your

guests, it's because she perceives this person to be a trespasser. By using a food reward, you can easily create a friendly greeting. First, each time a person comes to the door and your dog starts barking, say your dog's name and physically get between the dog and the door. Second, tell your dog to sit and then say, "I've got it." When you answer the door, take your dog outside on a leash. Say hi to your visitor and have him ask the dog to sit. When your dog sits, the visitor should give her a treat. By showing your dog that people who come to the front door just might have something to offer her, she will learn that visitors aren't so bad — they may even reward her for sitting and being a good, quiet dog.

6. **Barking at an object or a person outside during a walk** can present a problem. Let Sophie investigate the object. Let her sniff and check it out. Tell your dog "quiet" as you walk slowly toward the object and show her that it's nothing to be scared of. As soon as your dog is quiet, reward her. Even if it's only for a second, use words to reward your dog instead of patting her. If your dog is barking at a person, ask if she can come over to say hello. Be sure to tell the person not to stare at your dog. (By the way, it's rude to stare at any dog you don't know. Dogs often take staring to be confrontational behavior, and they might respond in kind.)

7. If **your dog barks at home when she is alone**, leave a radio or television on. Silence can be a scary thing. A little soothing background music will drown out noise from the outside as well as creaks and squeaks from within the house. Leave the house quietly without saying a long goodbye. If you make a big deal about leaving, so will your dog. The first twenty minutes alone is the worst time for them, so sneak out while your dog is busy or recovering from her morning walk or playtime.

Try this: Buy a new toy and sleep with it or stick it in the dirty laundry so that it smells of you. Use this toy as a special security blanket for your dog while you're gone. Don't get frustrated if you have to replace it often. You want your dog to work out her loneliness and frustration on the toy, not your personal belongings. Toys are for tearing up, so let your dog go at it — that means it's working!

On the weekend or when you don't have to work, imitate your daily departure routine. But leave the house for only one to two minutes. If you normally lock the door with a key, make those same noises, but don't lock the door. You must be able to enter quickly if she stops barking. If you wait for an elevator, ring for it and then get inside. Go one floor down and come right back up. If your dog has not barked, return and *praise, praise, praise* your dog for being good and quiet. If you hear barking, wait for it to stop. As soon as the barking stops, count to ten and go inside. Reward your dog for her "good quiet" behavior. Then turn and leave again. Repeat as necessary.

Remember that barking problems are rarely solved in one day. You should understand that your dog was not born with a tendency to bark too much. Natural behavior in dogs indicates that they generally do not like to draw attention to themselves when they're alone or scared. Chances are, they learned to bark incessantly as a response to the environment in which they live. Take time to understand how dogs behave naturally, and then learn how to acclimate your dog to your way of living. This will take time and is best done when your dog is still an impressionable puppy.

"A door is what a dog is perpetually on the wrong side of."
— OGDEN NASH

10 Ways to Prevent Your Kids from Being Bitten by a Dog

Each year, about 4.7 million people in the United States are bitten by dogs, most of whom they know and are familiar with. More than half of these victims are under the age of thirteen. What's more, children are at least three times more likely than adults to sustain a serious dog bite. Children tend to get excited around dogs, approach them too quickly while talking too loudly, and sometimes even hug them suddenly. Any one of these actions can easily result in a bite. The National Association for Humane and Environmental Education (NAHEE) and the HSUS offer advice on how children should behave around dogs. Here are some simple rules that they suggest all children should follow:

1. Before petting someone's dog, ask the person's permission. Then — and this may seem strange — ask the dog's permission. Don't make direct eye contact, but speak softly to the dog. If the person gives her permission, approach the dog slowly and quietly. Don't try to touch the dog's head — most dogs are head shy. Instead, let the dog sniff you first, then pet her side or back gently.

2. Never sneak up on or pet a dog who is eating or sleeping. Animals may bite when they're startled or frightened, and many dogs will protect their food.

6. Make your child aware of dog body language and teach her to avoid dogs who look angry. A dog with erect ears, one whose fur is standing on end, or one who growls and bares her teeth should always be avoided.

7. Your child should avoid a dog who may shrink to the ground, put her tail between her legs, and fold her ears back. This is a terrified dog in self-preservation mode.

8. If your child sees a stray dog, he should stop walking, stand still, and hold his hands by his sides.

"Properly trained, a man can be dog's best friend."
— COREY FORD, AMERICAN WRITER

3. Never pet a dog who is playing with a toy. Dogs are often protective of their toys and may think a child is trying to take it.

4. Never try to pet a dog who is in a car. A dog in a car is already on edge — she's in a confined space with no visible escape. A stranger's hand will seem doubly threatening to a confined dog.

5. Never pet a dog who is behind a fence. Most dogs naturally protect their property and home.

9. If your child is playing on the ground and a strange dog approaches, your child should lie still and quiet on the ground with his knees tucked toward his stomach and hands over his ears. The dog will most likely just sniff him and go away, but this way your child is protecting his must vulnerable areas — his stomach and his head.

10. Your child should never try to outrun a dog. Instead, he should slowly back away.

7 Reasons to Use a Crate

To put it simply, a crate is a modern version of the den. It's your dog's own space within your house. It's his room — a place where he can relax, sleep, and feel secure. The use of the crate has long been accepted by both trainers and veterinarians as one of the most desirable ways to mold many facets of a dog's behavior and a way to resolve a lot of problems faced by the dog and her owner. Crates are generally available in plastic or metal. The plastic variety is a bit more comfortable and easier to clean. Crates should be just big enough for a dog to stand up, lie down, and turn around in.

1. The crate is a valuable aid in housetraining. Given the dog's natural tendency to keep his sleeping area clean, he will learn to not relieve himself while inside the crate. This tendency, combined with your vigilance, will allow you to find the perfect time to take your dog out of the crate and outside to go potty. To make cleaning up accidents easier, place a waterproof dog pad or bed inside the crate.

2. The crate serves as a way to protect your dog from many dangers in your home. For example, a crate will keep her from chewing on electrical cords or eating foods that are harmful.

3. The crate protects you and your home from some of your dog's destructive tendencies. This is especially true of puppies. Better to invest in a crate than replace that antique coffee table Grandma gave you. If you throw a chew toy or two into the mix, you'll help satisfy your dog's lust for chewing.

> "She was such a beautiful and sweet creature . . . and so full of tricks."
> — QUEEN VICTORIA

4. If you and Wilma have to be apart for a short length of time, the crate can serve as a comfort zone and help her adjust to being by herself.

5. If either you or your dog needs a break from the other, a crate is a great place for your dog to have some privacy. However, never use the crate as a punishment tool. And never leave your dog in a crate for an excessive amount of time.

6. A crate will provide great safety for your dog when she travels.

7. The crate will give your dog a place to which he can retreat in times of confusion and stress — either yours or the dog's. It's a time-out for each of you.

Going into the crate will enable your dog to avoid much of the fear, confusion, and anxiety caused by your reaction to problem behavior.

The Top 10 Dog Tricks Taught in the United States

1. Sit
2. Shake paw
3. Roll over
4. Speak
5. Lie down
6. Stand on hind legs
7. Beg
8. Dance
9. Sing
10. Fetch newspaper

6 Problems Caused by Isolating Your Dog

How often do we see dogs who are left alone in their yard all day long and then sleep in the garage at night with only an occasional hour or two spent in the house with the company of their people? Or worse yet, how many dogs live their entire lives chained or confined in the yard, twenty-four hours a day, with little if any human companionship? Unfortunately for some dogs, many people feel this is an adequate life for their pet. And unfortunately for some dog owners, this type of neglect leads to many behavior problems.

Dogs are social, pack-oriented animals and their owners are members of their pack. Don't endlessly isolate your dog. This doesn't mean that your dog should never be apart from you. It simply means that when you are home your dog should be with you inside the house. Additionally, your dog should sleep in the house and be part of family activities. Often enrolling in an obedience training class will teach both you and your dog how to communicate with each other. It will also give you the means to teach your dog desired behaviors, which in turn will make him more pleasant to have in the house.

The Progressive Animal Welfare Society (PAWS) of Lynnwood, Washington, the leading voice for animals in Washington State and a recognized leader in the nation for its progressive outreach and educational serv-

7 Dog Toys You Can Make

Giving a dog a toy can keep her from exhibiting some of her more destructive tendencies. Dogs use toys as a way to relieve stress, loneliness, and boredom. Playing with a toy will also help your dog work off excess energy. These toys are easy to make and will save you money.

1. Take a tennis ball and drill two holes on opposite sides. Run a scarf or rope through both holes and knot both sides so that there is only one long tail sticking out of the ball. This will make the ball bounce in an unpredictable manner, keeping keep your dog entertained for hours.

2. Put some kibble in a plastic jug in which you have drilled a couple of holes. The holes should be just larger than the treats. Place kibble or any other small treat inside the jug. Shake up the contents. Your dog will love playing with the jug and eating the little bits of kibble when they fall out.

3. Tie a number of heavy-duty rubber bands together to form a chain. Attach a plastic jug to the end of the chain by its handle and suspend the jug in the center of a doorway. Place something noisy in the jug or something that smells really great. Your dog will have fun going after the jug. This is a particularly great toy for a sight-impaired or blind dog.

4. Dip an old ball into a bowl of beef or chicken broth. Need we say more?

5. Most dogs love to play tug of war. Tie a knot at one end of a piece of nylon rope that you can hold on to. Tie an old sock or toy to the other end. Let the games begin.

6. A long piece of nylon rope with big knots at both ends makes a wonderful, long-lasting toy. Dogs seem to prefer ropes when the ends are frayed.

7. Dogs love old hairbrushes. This is one toy you don't even have to make — plus, you'll get your dog to brush her own teeth.

ices, suggests that the following problems can be caused when dogs are isolated for long periods of time. Learn more at paws.org.

1. **Barking.** Bored, lonely dogs often vocalize loudly. This indicates an unhappy animal and leads to angry neighbors.

2. **Digging.** Bored, lonely dogs need an outlet for their frustrations and often resort to digging as a release. Unfortunately, most of us don't want our yards to look like minefields.

3. **Escaping.** Bored, lonely dogs will often try to find places that are neither boring nor lonely. Unfortunately, accidents often happen when dogs escape their enclosures and run free. Most of these accidents are quite expensive for dog owners. Often they are fatal for the dog. Escaping can become a habit for dogs — one that's difficult to break.

4. **Aggression.** Bored, lonely dogs who are isolated from humans and don't receive proper socialization may become aggressive toward humans. This is particularly seen in dogs who are kept chained up.

5. **Chewing.** Bored, lonely dogs will find ways to entertain themselves — often by chewing on patio furniture, garden hoses, and anything else within reach.

6. **Self-mutilation.** Bored, lonely dogs who do not have other means of release will often vent their frustrations by chewing on their own feet, flanks, or other body parts. This can lead to many health problems.

19 Games You Can Play with Your Dog

Playing with your dog can keep both of you healthy by providing stress relief, exercise, and fun. Equally important, playtime gives you the opportunity to reinforce the canine-human bond. If you're playing with a small puppy, just remember to be gentle.

1. Play fetch. This tried-and-true method of entertaining your dog is sure to make her happy.

2. Play peekaboo.

3. Take your dog swimming. Some larger breeds have actually learned to bodysurf.

4. Play bullfight with your dog. All you need is a red cape and some attitude. But never tease a dog — teasing isn't fun!

5. Play hide-and-seek.

6. Play tug of war, at least with a small dog. Such aggressive play with a large dog can lead to aggressive behavior or a power struggle as your dog tries to determine who's the boss.

7. Take your dog for a joy ride. Strap her in. Open the windows. Watch her fur fly and the smile on her muzzle.

8. Give your dog a present. Almost anything will do. Dogs aren't too picky.

9. Leave a trail of small dog treats or popcorn for your dog to follow.

10. Blow bubbles.

11. Juggle — if you drop the balls, so much the better!

12. Play the shell game using large plastic cups. Place a treat under one of three cups, then move the cups around. Your dog gets a treat if he chooses the right cup.

13. Play "Which Hand Is It In?"

14. Play "Clean Your Toys!" Spread a bunch of your dog's toys in a pile and have her put them away in a box.

15. Hold a hula hoop upright on the floor. Have your dog walk through it. Raise the hoop a bit and have your dog jump through it. Keep raising the hoop and see how high she can go.

16. Put peanut butter on your dog's tail and watch her spin with joy.

17. Play "nose ball." Have your dog retrieve a ball for you by pushing it with her nose. This is great for a rainy day.

18. Play soccer with your dog.

19. Teach your dog a new trick — any trick.

13 Tips for Training a Blind Dog

Training a blind dog will give her self-confidence and help to alleviate the depression, dependency, and fear to which she is vulnerable. Proper training will also make it easier, and safer, for your blind dog to participate in everyday activities with you. These training tips are provided by Linda Glass of BlindDogs.com.

1. Try not to move furniture around or leave obstacles (even discarded dog toys) on the floor.

2. Remember that we take things much harder than dogs do and that they also pick up on our feelings, so try to express positive emotions around your blind pet.

The common belief that dogs are colorblind is false. Dogs can see color, but it is not as vivid a color scheme as we see. They distinguish between blue, yellow, and gray, but probably do not see red and green. This is much like our vision at twilight.

3. Emphasize the senses that your dog still has. A blind adult dog or puppy still has a sense of smell, hearing, taste, and touch. A blind and deaf dog has a sense of smell, taste, and touch (they can feel vibrations — especially your movements).

4. Ask people to let your dog smell their hand before they touch her. Most blind dogs' personalities don't change. Some dogs, however, can easily become startled, which can lead to fear biting.

5. Try to treat your dog as normally as possible. Build her confidence by letting her know that she can still do many things and that you still love her. Make sure she understands that she is still the same dog in your eyes. For a blind puppy, this attitude will be the basis for the personality she develops.

6. Coax, encourage, and praise her to do the same things she did before. However, understand and still praise her if she can no longer do those things.

7. Be creative and use different scents to mark areas for your blind puppy — just make sure these scents are safe for dogs. You can use different scents of flavored extracts or even something as simple as a car air freshener or potpourri sachet on a door. Using differently scented candles in each room may also help your dog distinguish the various rooms in your house.

8. Use textured materials to mark areas. Throw rugs and decorative pillows are great (and people won't even realize their real purpose). Out in the yard, indoor/outdoor carpeting, wind chimes, and cedar chips or decorative bricks or blocks can help guide a blind dog.

9. Use bells or jingling tags on your other dogs. This will help your blind dog to follow and locate them, and it will also keep her from being startled by the other dogs. You can also use bells on your shoes to help your blind dog find you.

Dogs' eyes have large pupils and a wide field of vision, making them really good at following moving objects. Dogs also see well in fairly low light.

10. Don't be afraid to walk with a "heavy foot" when approaching a blind or deaf dog. She can still feel vibrations.

11. Don't underestimate the power of touching. Tell your blind dog when you are about to pet her — you don't want to startle her unnecessarily.

12. Be vocal with your dog. Engage in as much conversation with your blind pet as possible. Including her in your daily life will help keep her from feeling isolated and lonely.

13. A tabletop fountain can be used as a water bowl. Get a simple one with a large bowl. The sound of running water will help to orient a blind dog and more easily allow her to locate her water bowl. Additionally, many dogs prefer to drink running water.

8 Tips for Training a Deaf Dog

Susan Cope Becker's book *Living with a Deaf Dog: A Book of Advice, Facts, and Experiences About Canine Deafness* is a must for those new to deaf dog ownership. Here are some of Ms. Becker's basic training tips for your deaf dog:

1. Training a deaf dog requires a major commitment and lots of patience. It is important that you get a copy of an American Sign Language pocketbook. This will open up a world of words for you and your dog. Your deaf dog is going to surprise you. She will learn signs (and facial expressions) instead of words. The first word signs you should concentrate on are *sit, down, stay, come, no,* and *stop.* When your dog understands these words, begin adding a new word occasionally . . . *car, walk,* etc. The first six are enough to start with.

> "If a dog's prayers were answered, bones would rain from the sky."
> — OLD PROVERB

2. Find a trainer who will take you in a basic obedience class. Use standard obedience signs and American Sign Language. Speak the commands; your dog will watch your face and you will have more expression if you are speaking. This should get you to *sit, down, stay,* and *come.* Give the sign and put your dog in the position you want him to be. Reward with food. Repeat. Training sessions should last about fifteen minutes. You train a deaf dog just as

you do a hearing dog, but you sign instead of speaking.

3. From there you will be able to train and teach him as many signs as you want. Some deaf dogs who are five or six years old know up to fifty signs! They learn fast; stay with it.

4. To get your dog's attention, thump on the floor with your fist or foot or wave. Some people use a flashlight or a laser light (you can get one at an electronics store such as Radio Shack). If your dog is outside at night and you want to call him in, turn your porch light on and off.

5. *Important:* When you wake up your deaf dog, always touch her *gently* in the same place. Her shoulder is the best spot. Or put your hand in front of her nose and let your smell wake her up. Give her a treat and/or lots of love every time you wake her. Startling a deaf dog out of sleep can make her very touchy. By giving her a treat, waking up will become less traumatic and she will be eager instead of angry. Tell visitors (especially children) not to touch your dog if she is asleep.

6. Food rewards are the best way for you to reward a deaf puppy, since he can't hear the tone of your voice. You can taper off food rewards as your dog grows older. Replace these with love and enthusiasm. Clapping your hands together is the sign for "Good job!" Some people also use a thumbs-up.

7. The easiest sign for "good" for a dog to see — and the easiest one for you to learn — is the actual sign for the word "Good!" Show this by clapping your hands together. In American Sign Language, this means "good job," or "success." Smile when you do this, and do it often.

8. Always keep your dog on a leash when you walk her or when you are in an unfenced area. This leash — as well as a fenced yard or stake — is a necessity when you have a deaf dog. Buy a dog tag with a statement such as "Midnight is deaf. Please hold him and call the Allens: 508-555-1022." Put a bell on your dog; hunting dog bells are good. This allows you to hear your dog when he is on the move — unless, of course, he falls asleep somewhere out of the way.

> "Both humans and dogs love to play well in adulthood, and individuals from both species occasionally display evidence of having a conscience."
> — JOHN WINOKUR

7 National Dog Foundations

Thousands of organizations benefit dogs, from the well-established national organizations to the efforts of just a few people who band together on a local level to meet the needs of the dogs in their community. They all need — and are worthy of — your support. This list profiles just a few of the many foundations that have paved the way and set the standards for so many other efforts.

1. Founded in 1995, the **American Kennel Club Canine Health Foundation** funds canine health research. They raise money through membership dues, fundraisers, and donations. The foundation conducts surveys of breed clubs to determine which diseases require the most immediate attention. The AKCCHF considers grant proposals from scientists at universities and veterinary colleges throughout the country and funds valuable research efforts. You can reach them by phone at 919-334-4010 or visit them online at donations@akcchf.org.

2. Since 1946, the nonprofit **Guide Dog Foundation for the Blind, Inc.,** has provided guide dogs free of charge to blind people who seek enhanced mobility and independence. They are supported entirely by donations from generous individuals, corporations, and foundations. Your contributions are crucial to the success of this program. You can reach them by phone at either 866-282-8045 or 631-930-9050. You may also contact their Web site at www.guidedog.org.

3. The nonprofit **Morris Animal Foundation** supports humane animal health studies that will advance veterinary medicine. Their work helps animals worldwide enjoy longer, healthier lives. The Morris Animal Foundation subsidizes research in many areas of canine health. Contact them via their Web site, www.morrisanimalfoundation.org.

4. The **National Disaster Search Dog Foundation**, or **NDSDF**, is the country's leader in training search and rescue teams. Its mission is to seek out potential search dogs (many of whom would have otherwise been abandoned or euthanized), provide them with intensive professional training, partner them with handlers/firefighters, and see to their lifetime care. The NDSDF's search teams are the most highly trained in the nation and have become the gold standard in providing first responder disaster search services to local communities across the nation. You can contribute to this worthy organization by calling 888-4K9-HERO ext. 103, or by visiting them online at www.ndsdf.org.

5. The **National Service Dog Center (NSDC)**, a Web-based Delta Society program, provides information and resources for people with disabilities who are considering getting a service dog or who are currently partnered with a service dog. The NSDC also provides resources for people with disabilities who have problems accessing their workplaces and other public places with their service dogs. You can visit the NSDC online at www.deltasociety.org or call them at (425) 226-7357.

6. Over the past ten to fifteen years, the **Orthopedic Foundation for Animals** (or **OFA**) has recognized that a variety of heritable diseases have an impact on animal health. As scientific advancements enhance the ability to diagnose heritable diseases, the OFA has supported development of diagnostic criteria and databases for a number of genetic diseases, including hip dysplasia. The OFA is a not-for-profit foundation that can use your support. Please e-mail them at ofa@offa.org or call 573-442-0418.

7. **Veterinary Medical Assistance Teams (VMATs)** are the national backbone of animal disaster preparedness and response. VMATs provide treatment and aid to animals used in search and rescue efforts and animals hurt or endangered by catastrophic events such as floods, hurricanes, fires, and earthquakes. Comprising highly trained veterinarians, veterinary technicians, and support personnel, VMATs are organized regionally and can be deployed to any state or U.S. territory within twenty-four hours. VMATs operate within the U.S. Department of Homeland Security. All training, preparations, and equipment are made possible through charitable support. To make a contribution to this worthwhile organization, visit them at www.avmf.org or call 800-248-2862 ext. 6689.

How to Create a Dog Park in Your Community

The dedicated dog lovers at the Peninsula Humane Society and SPCA in San Mateo, California, have developed these proven strategies for a successful campaign to creating a dog park in your community:

1. Start with a core group of committed dog park activists. Talk with a half-dozen other dog lovers who are concerned about the lack of off-leash spaces. These may be people you already know — or you can put a notice in the local paper to find more dog-friendly folks.

2. Hold a public meeting. Once the core group is in agreement, a larger community meeting will help you get the word out to supporters and solicit input and suggestions. Encourage people to write letters in support of a dog park to public officials and the media and to make presentations to community groups whose backing would be valuable.

3. Educate your fellow dog owners on the need to be responsible. People who neglect to pick up after their dog or who allow an aggressive or unsocialized animal to run loose can do a lot of damage to your cause and your ultimate chances of success. Your mission should be twofold: establishing an off-leash dog exercise area and promoting responsible canine care.

4. Write a clear mission statement that details the need and purpose of the park, stressing the benefits to dog owners, their canine companions, and the greater community. A suggested statement: "To establish a fenced-in, off-leash dog park where well-behaved canine citizens can exercise in a clean,

Top 10 Reasons Dog Haters Should Support Dog Parks

Gary Merrick of Southaydogparks.org writes, "One of the things that has surprised me since getting involved in promoting dog parks is the fact that dog haters and off-leash advocates are both arguing the same points from two different perspectives. The solution is the same for both parties." Here are some reasons that dog haters should *not* oppose off-leash dog parks:

1. Having well-exercised and mentally stimulated dogs means less barking, less destruction, and generally fewer dog-related problems for your neighborhood. Wouldn't it be nice if your next-door neighbor could do something to quiet Spot's barking?

2. Since dogs would have their own park, parents of young children wouldn't have to worry about dogs in the playground.

3. No more dog poop in the middle of the soccer field.

4. We could finally move one step closer to reducing the number of serious dog attacks by noting that statistics don't change after implementing a dog park. The police and Animal Control can then concentrate their efforts on the aggressive, unsocialized dogs that actually cause these problems.

5. An uninvited canine participant would no longer interrupt your outdoor activities.

6. Dogs behind a fence could no longer bite you, attack you, or run through your yard.

7. Dog-related noise would be limited to park hours (generally seven a.m. to sunset).

8. Depending on the location and circumstance, the presence of dogs may deter crime or loitering. Dogs aren't *all* bad, are they?

9. Dog haters won't have to spend nearly as much time calling Animal Control.

10. Everyone can enjoy a more harmonious existence.

safe environment without endangering or annoying people, property, or wildlife. To develop a beautiful, well-maintained space open to all dog lovers and friends who are willing to uphold the park's rules and restrictions. To view this park as a community project designed to satisfy the needs of dog owners and non–dog owners alike."

5. Demonstrate need. Gather statistics on the dogs and their people in your community. How many dogs would use a dog park? What are the demographics of the people in your city? Who currently uses city parks — and who doesn't? Downplay the "dog factor" and emphasize people issues. Remember, dogs don't pay taxes or vote.

6. Demonstrate support. Activists found that a simply worded request, circulated on a petition, helped convince city officials that there was indeed both a need and widespread public support for a responsibly run dog park. Place petition gatherers at supermarkets, pet supply stores, and other high-traffic areas. Enlist the support of local veterinarians, groomers, dog walkers, and others who have a real interest in having a community filled with healthy, well-socialized dogs. Involve them in gathering petitions, writing letters to the editor of local papers, and generally spreading the word.

7. Create a budget. Determine how much it will cost to construct and maintain the park — include costs for grass, fences, garbage removal, lawn maintenance, drinking water, field drainage, lighting, benches, and a pooper scooper

area. Some cities are willing and able to finance a dog park; others would rather share the cost with a group committed to maintaining the park and ensuring the park's rules.

8. Solicit the input and seek the approval of significant organizations in your community. Talk with the proposed park's neighbors before talking to city hall. As soon as someone puts up a serious red flag, pay attention to it; don't ignore or fight it, and try to come up with a solution. If it really is impossible to resolve, at least you'll know what you are up against.

9. Be prepared to address a range of concerns, including the risk of dog-fights, dog bites, increased noise level, parking and traffic problems, and liability and maintenance issues. Explain why some of these are nonissues and have a plan to address the ones — such as traffic and noise — that are legitimate.

10. Ask your local SPCA for help and for a letter of support.

11. Get to know local officials — your city council members and the director of your Department of Parks and Recreation. Attend meetings, join them at fundraisers. Find out what they need from you to move the dog park forward.

12. When you're ready, **request a hearing with the city government** to discuss your proposal. Have two or three carefully selected, knowledgeable, and articulate members of your group present your plan, clearly expressing its many benefits to the community and calmly addressing any concerns.

13. Be patient. Dealing with city government is rarely a quick deal. Though you may find yourself running with Fido in the dog park of your dreams within a year, it could just as easily take several years to create.

6 Dog Food Choices

All dogs are not created equal. Dogs-and-Diets.com offers these ways to match your dog food choices to your dog's needs. You have several choices of dog food formats. Here are the relative merits and drawbacks of each type:

1. Moist or canned food tastes good, is highly digestible, and has a long shelf life, but it is the most expensive.

2. Dry food is affordable and reduces tartar buildup on your dog's teeth, but it can be a storage problem because the food can get stale and may lose some of its nutritional value.

3. Semimoist food is easy to store, and it tastes good and is digestible. The cost, however, is quite a bit higher than that of dry food.

4. Some homes have strict rules against feeding Rover people food (dog food is more balanced and nutritious). But many of us mistakenly feed our

How Much Should You Feed Your Dog?

Oscar's energy requirements are largely based on his weight and activity level. Check the package and follow instructions carefully. If you feed your dog twice a day, divide the daily requirement by two to get the proper feeding amount. Here's a general guideline as to the quantities of food you should feed your dog, provided by Dogs-and-Diets.com.

1. A puppy's diet should take into account her need for extra nutrients. Avoid enthusiastically overfeeding your pup; follow the directions on bags or cans of trusted puppy food manufacturers. Some breeds are prone to obesity; overfeeding at an early age will have a long-term effect.

2. Generally after age seven, older dogs may benefit from foods specially designed for aging dogs. While some dogs may have failing appetites, others may be prone to obesity because they get less exercise. Visit Dogs-and-Diets.com and click on the Special Needs link if you think your dog is overweight.

3. Dogs such as hunting dogs, racing dogs, guide dogs, and police dogs are all examples of performance dogs. Clearly, they require extra energy from their diets because of both physical exertion and high stress. The professionals who work with them are usually well informed about dietary options for these special canines (a high-energy, high-fat diet is the general rule).

4. Pregnant and lactating bitches undoubtedly need extra energy in their diets. Malnourishment is bad for your bitch and her puppies; follow feeding directions carefully to make sure she has the energy she needs to supply milk for her litter. A nursing mother dog is really a performance dog with respect to her energy needs.

5. Your dog's feeding routine should suit your lifestyle. If your dog is left alone a lot and your comings and goings are random, you might start out with free-choice feeding, meaning you dump a whole day's food in the bowl and let him eat when he's hungry. If you like routines and you're used to feeding once or twice a day, we haven't seen any evidence that one way or another is any better.

dogs treats and human foods as a gesture of love. Some of us feel righteous about buying dog biscuits and treats because they seem to be good for dogs, especially their teeth. If you can't resist, then try adding up the calories and fat you're feeding your dog by hand and comparing it with that in his food. If the total of your daily handouts exceeds 10 percent of what's in his food, you're overdoing it.

5. Unless your vet recommends otherwise, you're probably not depriving your dog of good nutrition by sticking with a good-quality dog food. On the other hand, a good balanced supplement isn't likely to hurt, and for some dogs, supplements help coat quality. But the biggest mistake you can make is to throw your dog's diet off-balance by oversupplementing with unbalanced products. Healthy dogs should not need much in the way of supplements.

6. If you provide home-cooked food for your dog, use a trusted recipe designed for nutritional balance. Lady may love to polish off a half-pound of hamburger, but raw meat doesn't even begin to fulfill her nutritional requirements.

"My dog is worried about the economy because Alpo is up to ninety-nine cents a can. That's almost seven dollars in dog money."
— JOE WEINSTEIN

5 Great Recipes for Homemade Dog Biscuits

Vicky Dubois of SeeFido.com has developed these wonderful treat recipes. You will discover that they are fairly easy to prepare. One of Vicky's recipes even fights fleas!

1. Chicken Liver Cookies

2 cups flour

1 cup wheat germ or cornmeal (or ½ cup each)

1 egg, lightly beaten

3 tbsp. vegetable oil

½ cup chicken broth (I use the liver water from boiling the livers)

2 tsp. chopped parsley

1 cup chopped chicken livers, cooked

Preheat oven to 400° F. Combine flour and wheat germ or cornmeal. In separate bowl, beat egg with oil; add broth and parsley, mix well. Add dry ingredients to bowl a little at a time, stirring well. Fold in chicken livers and mix well. Dough will be firm. Turn dough out onto lightly floured surface and knead briefly. Roll out ½ inch thick and cut into shapes. Place on greased cookie sheets an inch apart. Bake 15 minutes or until firm. Store in refrigerator or freezer.

Recipe from Marg MacFadden

2. No Flea Dog Biscuits

Don't use this recipe if your dog has a yeast allergy.

2 cups all-purpose flour

½ cup wheat germ

½ cup brewer's yeast

1 tsp. salt

2 cloves garlic, minced

3 tbsp. vegetable or olive oil

1 cup chicken or beef stock

Preheat oven to 400° F. Grease two to three baking sheets. Combine flour, wheat germ, yeast, and salt. In a large mixing bowl, combine garlic and oil. Slowly stir flour mixture and stock alternately into oil and garlic, beating well, until the dough is well mixed. Shape dough into a ball. On lightly floured surface, roll out dough to ½ inch thick. Using a 2-inch biscuit cutter, cut dough into rounds. Transfer biscuits to prepared baking sheets. Bake 20–25 minutes or until well browned. Turn off heat and allow biscuits to dry in oven for several hours or overnight. Store in refrigerator or freezer.

Researchers studying what dogs like to eat have found that the appetite also by the owners' food preferences, their perception of their pet, and

3. Cheese Bone Cookies

2 cups all-purpose flour

1¼ cups cheese, any kind, shredded

2 garlic cloves, minced

½ cup vegetable oil

4 tbsp. water

Preheat oven to 400° F. Combine flour, cheese, garlic, and oil; knead well. Add water, if needed, to form stiff dough. Roll out on floured surface to ½-inch thickness; cut into shapes. Place on ungreased cookie sheet. Bake 10 to 15 minutes or until bottoms are lightly browned. Cool on wire rack. Refrigerate in airtight container.

4. Liver Cookies

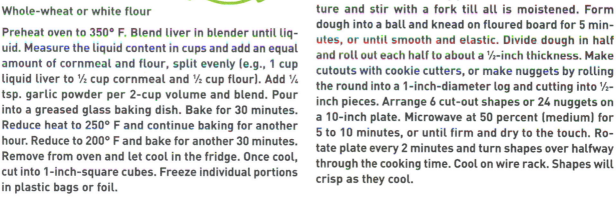

1 lb. beef liver

Garlic powder

Cornmeal

Whole-wheat or white flour

Preheat oven to 350° F. Blend liver in blender until liquid. Measure the liquid content in cups and add an equal amount of cornmeal and flour, split evenly (e.g., 1 cup liquid liver to ½ cup cornmeal and ½ cup flour). Add ¼ tsp. garlic powder per 2-cup volume and blend. Pour into a greased glass baking dish. Bake for 30 minutes. Reduce heat to 250° F and continue baking for another hour. Reduce to 200° F and bake for another 30 minutes. Remove from oven and let cool in the fridge. Once cool, cut into 1-inch-square cubes. Freeze individual portions in plastic bags or foil.

5. Microwave Dog Biscuits

½ cup all-purpose flour

¾ cup nonfat dry milk powder

½ cup quick-cooking rolled oats

¼ cup yellow cornmeal

1 tsp. sugar

⅓ cup shortening

1 egg, slightly beaten

1 tbsp. instant bouillon granules, either beef or chicken

½ cup hot water

Combine flour, milk powder, rolled oats, cornmeal, and sugar in medium bowl. Cut in shortening until mixture resembles coarse crumbs. Add egg to this dry mixture, and stir. Add bouillon to hot water and stir until granules are dissolved. Slowly pour hot broth into flour mixture and stir with a fork till all is moistened. Form dough into a ball and knead on floured board for 5 minutes, or until smooth and elastic. Divide dough in half and roll out each half to about a ½-inch thickness. Make cutouts with cookie cutters, or make nuggets by rolling the round into a 1-inch-diameter log and cutting into ½-inch pieces. Arrange 6 cut-out shapes or 24 nuggets on a 10-inch plate. Microwave at 50 percent (medium) for 5 to 10 minutes, or until firm and dry to the touch. Rotate plate every 2 minutes and turn shapes over halfway through the cooking time. Cool on wire rack. Shapes will crisp as they cool.

of pet dogs is affected by the taste, texture, and smell of the food, and the physical environment in which the dog is eating.

7 Tests to Determine if Your Dog Is Psychic

Your dog is likely to be much more intelligent than you think, and in any event, these experiments will be fun for both you and your dog. Do not keep practicing these tests for hours on end, as the success rate will decline as your dog tires and loses interest. Twenty minutes is about the right length of time. Regular short sessions are much better than a lengthy session every now and again. Be lavish in your praise every time your dog succeeds in any of these tests. They are taken from the excellent *Developing Psychic Communication with Your Pet* by Richard Webster (Llewellyn Worldwide, 2002).

1. Teach your dog to recognize and fetch six different-colored blocks painted with different primary colors. Rearrange the sequence of blocks so that you are sure it is the color the dog recognizes and not the order in which the blocks are positioned. Once you have done this you can mentally decide on a color and send a telepathic message to Elvis, asking him to bring back a particular color. Focus your thoughts on your dog's walking over, choosing the specific block, and bringing it back to you. Your dog may seem puzzled or perplexed at first, as he will be used to your asking for them out loud. However, after a possible slight resistance at first, your dog will fetch the block you are thinking about — if he's really psychic.

2. Sit in a room away from your dog. Close your eyes and think about taking your dog for a walk. Picture yourself making the usual preparations and then stepping out of the house and starting the walk. Visualize your dog and what she would normally be doing at the start of a walk. If your dog is psychic, it is likely that she will be standing excitedly in front of you, ready for a walk, before you have finished thinking about it. This test should be done at a time when you do not normally go for a walk. Reward your dog by taking her for a walk.

3. This is a more advanced test. Sit down quietly somewhere, close your eyes, and send Chester a psychic message asking what he would like to do. You may find that he immediately appears, excited that you are going to do what he wants. You may receive a clear mental impression as to what it is he wants to do. If the mental impression does not come through, follow your pet and see if that provides enough clues for you to carry out the desired response.

4. This fascinating test involves mentally suggesting that your dog do a number of actions. You might, for instance, suggest that she go to the bedroom and fetch your slippers before picking up a plaything so that the two of you can have a game. This works best if the dog is sleeping and the tasks are pleasant ones. Sit down in the same room as your dog and think about the actions you want her to perform. Think about each action in turn, saying mentally to yourself something like this: "I want you to fetch my slippers first, and then go and find your rubber banana so that we can have a game." Start off with imagining one task, and once your dog has done it think of a second task and then a third. In time you will be able to think of a whole series of activities and your psychic dog will faithfully do them all in order.

5. When Captain is out of the room, hide a well-loved toy in a place where he will be able to find it. Call him to you and ask him to find the object. He will first go where the toy is usually kept and will be reluctant to look anywhere else. Think about where you have hidden the toy, and try to send these thoughts to your dog. Telepathically, lead Captain to the object step by step. Be sure that the object is placed in an airtight container so that it can't be detected by

smell. Don't repeat this exercise more than once a day, but be sure your dog can play with the object once it has been found.

6. Get five or six identical boxes and place a well-loved toy inside one of them. Place other items in the other boxes. Close the boxes, mix them up, and then ask your dog to find the box that contains her toy.

7. With your dog out of sight, sit down, close your eyes, and think about giving her a bath. Think about it for at least five minutes. Then call your dog and see if she comes. If she doesn't come or comes to you with an unhappy expression, she has probably read your thoughts. The experiment is considered a failure if your dog bounds up to you in his normal fashion. (This experiment won't work with dogs who love bath time.)

How to Photograph Your Puppy

1. Remove film from box and load camera.

2. Remove film box from puppy's mouth and throw in trash.

3. Remove puppy from trash and brush coffee grounds from muzzle.

4. Choose a suitable background for photo.

5. Mount camera on tripod and check flash and focus.

6. Find puppy and take dirty sock from mouth.

7. Place puppy in prefocused spot and return to camera.

8. Forget about spot and crawl after puppy on knees.

9. Focus with one hand while fending off puppy with other hand.

10. Get tissue and clean nose print from lens.

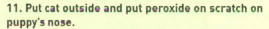

11. Put cat outside and put peroxide on scratch on puppy's nose.

12. Put magazines back on coffee table.

13. Try to get puppy's attention by squeaking toy over your head.

14. Replace your glasses and check camera for damage.

15. Jump up in time to grab puppy by scruff of neck and say, "No, no, outside!"

16. Call spouse to help clean up the mess.

17. Fix yourself a drink.

18. Sit back in chair, put your feet up, sip your drink, and resolve to teach puppy "sit" and "stay" the first thing in the morning.

Lori Sash-Gail photographs her dog Arrow.

Tips for Dealing with Doggy Stains and Odors

If your house smells like Urinetown, try these solutions, provided by the Dumb Friends League.

To clean washable items

1. Machine-wash as usual, adding a pound of baking soda to your regular detergent. If possible, it's best to air-dry these items.

2. If you can still see the stain or smell the urine, machine-wash the item again using an enzymatic cleaner or stain remover such as OxiClean or Carbona Stain Wizard. Follow the package directions.

To clean carpeted areas and upholstery

1. Soak up as much of the urine as possible with a combination of newspaper and paper towels. The more fresh urine you can remove before it dries — especially from the carpet — the simpler it will be to remove the odor. Place a thick layer of paper towels on the wet spot and cover that with a thick layer of newspaper. Stand on this padding for about a minute. Remove the padding and repeat this process until the area is barely damp.

2. If possible, take the fresh urine-soaked paper towels to your dog's designated outdoor "bathroom area" and let your pet see you do it. Don't behave angrily when you do this. Instead, try to project a "happy" attitude to your pet. This will help remind your dog that eliminating is not a bad behavior as long as it's done in the right place.

"My husband and I are either going to buy a dog or have a child. We can't decide whether to ruin our carpets or ruin our lives."
— RITA RUDNER

3. Rinse the accident zone thoroughly with clean, cool water. After rinsing, remove as much of the water as possible by blotting or by using a wet-vac.

4. If you've previously used cleaners or chemicals of any kind on the area, then neutralizing cleaner won't be effective until you've rinsed every trace of the old cleaner from the carpet. Even if you haven't used chemicals recently, any trace of a non-protein-based substance will weaken the effect of the enzymatic cleaner.

5. To remove all traces of old chemicals and clean old, heavy stains in carpeting, consider renting an extractor or wet-vac from a local hardware store. These machines do the best job of forcing clean water through your carpet and then forcing the dirty water back out again. Use only plain water in these machines.

6. Once the area is really clean, you should use a high-quality pet odor neutralizer. These are available at pet supply stores.

7. If the area still looks stained after it's completely dry from extracting and neutralizing, try a good carpet stain remover.

8. If urine has soaked down into the padding underneath your carpet, your job will be more difficult. You may need to remove and replace that portion of the carpet and padding.

To clean walls and floors

1. If the wood on your furniture, walls, baseboard, or floor is discolored, the varnish or paint has been

affected by the acid in the urine. You may need to remove and replace the layer of varnish or paint.

2. Go to your local hardware store for advice on how to remove and replace any varnish or paint.

Helpful hints

If you are having difficulties locating soiled areas with your eyes and nose, use a black light in a darkened room. You'll see the soiled areas, and you can outline them with chalk so you'll know exactly where to clean.

Do not use steam cleaners to clean urine odors from carpets or upholstery. The heat will permanently set the odor and stain by bonding the protein into any fibers. Also, avoid using any cleaning chemicals such as ammonia or vinegar. These don't effectively eliminate or cover the urine odor and may actually encourage your dog to use this area for elimination.

The Cheap-'n'-Easy Dog Bed

Sometimes man's best friends just want a warm, safe spot to curl up and nap. Ready-made dog beds can be expensive, and cleaning them can pose a real challenge. They don't fit in the washer very well, and if you hose them off on the back porch, they stay damp and grow mildew. Tanya Brown of TackyLiving.com has a truly unique solution to this problem — dirty laundry. To make a genuine Tackyliving dog bed, simply heap your laundry on the floor and throw Rover on top. Tanya believes that once you try this method, you and your dog will be so satisfied that you'll never again look at expensive commercial alternatives! Here are some of the benefits of the Cheap-'n'-Easy dog bed.

1. Dirty laundry, the primary component of our dog bed, is readily available in most households and will fit most budgets.

2. The bedding materials get reused, making this an environmentally friendly proposition — something you can truly feel proud of.

3. An average-size load of dirty clothes will provide a warm and comfortable bed for all but the very largest of dogs — and even they can be accommodated with the output of most families.

4. Dogs just love the mingled scents of filthy socks and underwear and will happily wallow in them for hours.

5. The bedding is easily cleaned; simply throw it in the washing machine at regular intervals.

6. If placed next to the dryer, there will be times when the dog bed is toasty warm.

7. The tumbling noise of the dryer will cover up Spot's snoring.

From a single drop of urine, the sniffing dog learns the marking animal's sex, diet, health, emotional state, and even whether it's dominant or submissive, friend or foe.

2 Theories on the Origins of Tail Wagging

Theory 1: There was a time when cats were far larger in size than dogs. These cats possessed fangs that were so large that they were unable to close their mouths fully. While feeding, their mouths remained open, allowing dust, bugs, and other airborne particles to enter. These cats were subject to allergies, hay fever, and colds, which often resulted in violent sneezing fits that disabled the cats for a long period of time. Dogs, which at that time had very large tails, soon discovered that by wagging their tails they could stir up great amounts of dust particles and insects, thereby sending their predators into fits of sneezing.

Theory 2: The ancestors of the modern-day dogs ran in packs. Their ability to communicate with each other was essential to the hunt and to their survival. Using his tail as a signaling device, a dog was able to communicate aggression, submission, or impending conflict. Some experts believe that a wagging tail is an indicator of impending conflict. The science of behaviorism suggests that dogs wag their tails to ward off attackers and that the only trait tail-waggers share is a state of conflict.

Why Dogs Chase Their Tails

Tail chasing is a very common behavior in an active puppy. In an older dog, tail chasing may have different and more serious causes. Here are some reasons that dogs chase their tails:

1. Because the tail is always there. Puppies don't know where their bodies end and the world begins. So a wiggly little tail is definitely intriguing. This is especially true when the puppy has been separated from his littermates and has only himself to play with.

2. Older dogs sometimes chase their tails when they are anxious, bored, or frustrated.

3. Tail chasing can be a symptom of a physical problem such as the presence of fleas or irritated anal glands.

4. Tail chasing can also result when a dog is confined and has his movement restricted.

5. Some breeds such as Bull Terriers, German Shepherd Dogs, and Australian Cattle Dogs are more predisposed to chase their tails, suggesting that this tendency may be an inherited trait.

6. The dog may have canine compulsive disorder. This is a rare condition, but it might be the cause of tail chasing.

7. One good turn deserves another.

Dave Barry's Deep Thoughts on Dog Behavior

Dave Barry is a Pulitzer Prize–winning journalist for the *Miami Herald* and the author of many bestsellers, including *Dave Barry's Greatest Hits*, *Dave Barry's Complete Guide to Guys*, and *Dave Barry Turns 50*. Here are some of Barry's observations on the behavior of his own dogs:

1. "Dogs feel very strongly that they should always go with you in the car, in case the need should arise for them to bark violently at nothing right in your ear."

2. "Most dogs are earnest, which is why most people like them. You can say any fool thing to a dog, and the dog will give you this look that says, 'My God, you're RIGHT! I NEVER would have thought of that!'"

3. "I removed my dogs from the confined, controlled environment of our house and put them outside, where they were free to reveal their hidden lives. I observed them closely for the better part of a day, and thus I am able to reveal here, for the first time anywhere, that what dogs do, when they are able to make their own decisions in accordance with their unfettered natural instincts, is: try to get back inside the house. They spent most of the day pressing sad, moony faces up against the glass patio door, taking only occasional breaks to see if it was a good idea to eat worms."

4. "Dogs employ barking as a vital means of communicating important messages, such as: 'bark.' Barking also serves a vital biological purpose: If a dog does not release a certain number of barks per day, they will back up, and the dog will explode. (Whenever you hear an un-explained loud noise in the distance, it's probably a dog exploding.)"

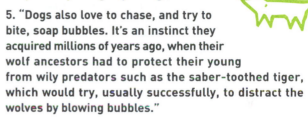

5. "Dogs also love to chase, and try to bite, soap bubbles. It's an instinct they acquired millions of years ago, when their wolf ancestors had to protect their young from wily predators such as the saber-toothed tiger, which would try, usually successfully, to distract the wolves by blowing bubbles."

6. "Magnetism is one of the Six Fundamental Forces of the Universe, with the other five being Gravity, Duct Tape, Whining, Remote Control, and The Force That Pulls Dogs Toward The Groins Of Strangers."

7. "Mousse was a Labrador retriever, which is a large enthusiastic bulletproof species of dog. This is the kind of dog that, if it takes an interest in your personal regions (which of course it does) you cannot fend it off with a blowtorch."

8. "Dogs never scratch you when you wash them. They just become very sad and try to figure out what they did wrong."

9. "Dogs need to sniff the ground; it's how they keep abreast of current events. The ground is a giant dog newspaper, containing all kinds of late-breaking dog news items, which, if they are especially urgent, are often continued in the next yard."

10. "Dogsled-riding is a sport that is relaxing as well as fragrant."

Why Dogs Howl

The origin of dog howling can be traced back to the wolf, whose howling was and is still used to communicate with and locate her pack over long distances. In the domestic dog this characteristic can be attributed to other factors.

1. Howling is a form of communication in dogs. As with the wolf, it is a way for dogs to signal their presence to other dogs who are often located far away. It is common in wolves and coyotes, both relatives of today's domestic dog.

2. Domestic dogs that howl, especially those that howl excessively, are usually doing it because they are bored and lonely. Giving your dog goodies, extra attention, and exercise will generally reduce her need to howl. *Please don't leave your dog outside all night.*

3. Sometimes dogs howl when they hear sirens or other loud, high-pitched sounds like clarinets and flutes. Dogs do this instinctively as a response to what they are hearing, not because the sound annoys them.

4. Dogs will sometimes howl when their humans are singing. This is not an insult to your singing ability — your dog is just proving that he's part of the family.

10 Rules of Etiquette for Traveling with Your Dog

1. **Always call ahead** to make sure an establishment allows dogs.

2. **Only travel with a well-behaved dog** who is friendly to people and especially children. If your dog is uncomfortable around other people, you might consider taking her to obedience classes or hiring a professional trainer before traveling with her.

3. **Please keep your dog leashed.** People who are afraid of dogs will greatly appreciate it, and so will people with leashed dogs. Plus, most hotel owners, restaurant owners, store owners, and festival coordinators require dogs to be on a leash.

4. **Always clean up after your dog.** Pet stores everywhere sell pooper scooper bags. You can also buy sandwich bags from your local grocery store. They work quite well, and they're cheap.

5. **Make sure your dog has relieved herself** before entering a festival or event area. The number one reason that most festival coordinators do not allow dogs is that some dogs go to the bathroom in areas where people might sit.

6. Unless it is obvious, **ask the hotel clerk if dogs are allowed** in the hotel lobby and other common areas.

7. **Never leave your dog alone in your hotel room.** The number one reason hotel management does not allow dogs is that some people leave them in the room alone. Certain dogs, no matter how well trained, can cause damage, bark continuously, or scare the housekeepers. Unless the hotel management allows it, please make sure your dog is never left alone in the room. This is also for your dog's safety — we know of a case in which two dogs were stolen right out of their hotel room.

8. While you are in the room with your dog, **place the Do Not Disturb sign on the door or keep the dead bolt locked.** Many housekeepers are surprised or scared by dogs when they enter a hotel room to clean it.

9. **When your dog needs to go to the bathroom**, take her away from the hotel and the bushes located right next to the hotel rooms. Try to find some dirt or bushes near the parking lot. Some pet-friendly hotels even have a designated pet walk area.

10. **Keep a close eye on your dog** and make sure she does not go to the bathroom in a store. Store owners that allow dogs inside assume that responsible dog owners will be entering their store. Before entering a dog-friendly store, visit your local pet store first. They are by far the most forgiving. If your dog does not have an accident there, then you are off to a great start! If your dog does make a mistake in a store, apologize and offer to clean it up.

10 Dog-Friendly Hotel Chains

Finding a hotel that welcomes dogs can be difficult and stressful, but now Web sites such as Dog Friendly.com and PetsWelcome.com have made this process much easier. Their sites contain listings for dog-friendly hotels all over the United States and numerous countries abroad. The national hotel chains listed here not only welcome dogs but in some cases even provide your dog with complimentary food and water dishes, and their staff will happily direct you to nearby dog parks and dog-friendly attractions.

1. **La Quinta Inns & Suites**:
   lq.com or call 1-800-642-4241

2. **Innworks**:
   innworks.com or call 1-800-800-8000

3. **Howard Johnson**:
   hojo.com or call 1-800-446-465

4. **Holiday Inn**: ichotelsgroup.com
   or call 1-866-655-4669

5. **Motel 6**:
   motel6.com or call 1-800-466-8356

6. **Studio 6**:
   staystudio6.com or call 1-888-897-0202

7. **Red Roof Inn**:
   redroof.com or call 1-800-733-7663

8. **Novotel**:
   www.novotel.com or call
   1-800-NOVOTEL

9. **Sheraton**: www.starwoodhotels.com
   or call 1-888-625-5144

10. **Westin**: www.starwoodhotels.com
    or call 888-625-5144

"Did you ever notice when you blow in a dog's face he gets mad at you? But when you take him in a car he sticks his head out the window!"
— **STEVE BLUESTONE**

Vintage postcard suggesting a special way to celebrate Bagel's Bark Mitzvah

"The other day I saw two dogs walk over to a parking meter. One of them says to the other, 'How do you like that? Pay toilets!'"
— **DAVE STARR**

The Ideal Outdoor Doghouse

DoghousePlans.com, which specializes in designing dog houses for various law enforcement agencies around the country, has come up with wonderful doghouse designs for both family pets and service dogs. Here are some of the attributes needed for the perfect outdoor doghouse.

1. The doghouse should be built so that it is raised off the ground. This allows air to move all around the doghouse.

2. The floors, roof, and walls of the doghouse should be fully insulated.

3. The roof should be on hinges for easy cleaning, and so it can be lifted to any height for increased airflow.

4. The roof should be on a slant so that rainwater easily runs off it and to the ground.

5. All doghouses should have a removable inside wind wall to protect your dog from the wind and restrict the portion of the doghouse where the dog sleeps, so that this part is warmed by the dog's own body heat.

6. It is imperative that doghouses are built in the proper size to fit their canine residents. This way, dogs can maintain sufficient warmth in the house from their own body heat.

19 Things to Consider When Flying with Your Dog

Dogs that are transported in commerce are protected by the Animal Welfare Act (AWA). The U.S. Department of Agriculture's Animal and Plant Health Inspection Service (APHIS) enforces this law. APHIS's shipping regulations help ensure that people who transport and handle dogs covered under the AWA treat them humanely. Airlines and other shippers are affected by regulations established to protect the well-being of animals in transit. APHIS advises that you take the following measures to ensure that your dog travels safely.

1. Take your dog to the vet. Airlines and state health officials generally require health certificates for all animals transported by air. In most cases, health certificates must be issued by a licensed veterinarian who examined the animal within ten days of transport. Ask your veterinarian to provide any required vaccinations or treatments. Administer tranquilizers only if specifically prescribed by your veterinarian and only in the prescribed dosage.

2. If you are traveling abroad, contact the appropriate embassy, governmental agency, or consulate at least four weeks in advance of transporting your pet to determine what their quarantine policies are. You may also contact a full-service travel agency for assistance.

Airline Procedures

3. Dogs must be at least eight weeks old and must have been weaned before traveling by air.

4. Kennels must meet minimum standards for size, strength, sanitation, and ventilation. Kennels must be enclosed and allow room for the animal to stand, sit, and lie in a natural position, and be easy to open, strong enough to with- stand the normal rigors of transportation, and free of objects that could injure the animal. They should be sanitary and have a solid, leakproof floor that is covered with litter or absorbent lining. Wire or other ventilated subfloors are generally allowed; pegboard flooring is prohibited. Kennels also must have rims to prevent ventilation openings from being blocked by other cargo and should all have grips or handles for lifting to prevent cargo personnel from having to place their fingers inside the kennel and risk being bitten. Hint: Get your dog used to his kennel by leaving it open in the house and placing an old sock or other familiar object in it.

5. Instructions for feeding and watering the animal over a twenty-four-hour period must be attached to the kennel. The twenty-four-hour schedule will assist the airline in providing care for your animal in case it is diverted from its original destination. Food and water must be provided to dogs every twelve hours if they are eight to sixteen weeks old. Mature animals must be fed every twenty-four hours and given water every twelve hours.

6. At the time you make your trip reservations, advise the airline directly that you will have an animal with you. Be sure to reconfirm with the airline twenty-four to forty-eight hours before departure that you will be bringing your pet. Advance arrangements are not a guarantee that your animal will travel on a specific flight.

7. Arrive at the airport with plenty of time to spare. If your animal is traveling as a carry-on pet or by the special expedited delivery service, check-in will usually be at the passenger terminal.

8. If you are sending your pet through the cargo system, you will need to go to the airline cargo terminal, which is usually located in a separate part of the airport. Check with your airline for the acceptance cutoff time for your flight. Note that by regulation an animal may be presented for transport no more than four hours before flight time (six hours by special arrangement).

9. Use direct flights whenever possible to avoid accidental transfers or delays.

10. Travel on the same flight as your pet whenever possible.

11. Pug-nosed dogs, such as Boxers and Bulldogs, are more likely to experience breathing problems during

transport. In the summer, choose early-morning or late-evening flights to avoid temperature extremes that may affect your pet. Avoid holiday traveling whenever possible.

12. Carry a leash with you so that you can walk your pet before check-in and after arrival. Do not place the leash inside the kennel or attach it to the outside of the kennel. It may choke your dog.

13. Do not take your pet out of her kennel inside the airport. In keeping with airport regulations and courtesy for other passengers, let your pet out only after you leave the terminal building.

14. Outfit your pet with a sturdy collar and two identification tags. The tags should have both your permanent address and telephone number and an address and telephone number where you can be reached while traveling.

15. Attach a label on the pet carrier with your permanent and travel addresses and telephone numbers.

16. Make sure your pet's nails have been recently clipped to prevent them from hooking onto the carrier door or other openings.

17. Carry a current photograph of your pet. If your pet is accidentally lost, having a current photograph will make the search easier.

18. If you need to file a complaint regarding the care of your pet during transport, contact USDA-APHIS.

19. If your pet should get lost during transport, immediately speak to airline personnel. Many airlines have computer tracking systems that can trace a pet transferred to an incorrect flight. Should there be no report of your animal, contact animal control agencies and humane societies in the local and surrounding areas and check with them daily.

For further information, call 1-800-545-USDA, or visit their World Wide Web site at www.aphis.usda.gov/ac.

4 Ways to Prevent Carsickness in Dogs

If your dog begins yawning, drooling, or whining when she travels in your car, you may be witnessing the first signs of carsickness. Most often carsickness is caused by the stress of being in a car and not the motion of the car. Here are some tips to help you and your dog to have more pleasant car rides.

1. Open the window a little to get some fresh air circulating inside.

2. Make sure your dog can see out the window. Choose a spot in your car — a rear window ledge is fine — where she can get up and look out to see the road up ahead.

3. Train her to be comfortable riding in the car. Begin by just sitting in the car with her and praise her for being good. Next, start and run the engine for a few minutes and continue the praise. Then drive away slowly, praising her all the while. Do this exercise over the course of a few hours, increasing the distance you travel until she can ride in the car without getting sick. Once you've been able to drive for a half-hour without her getting sick, the problem is probably solved. It is best to have someone else in the car with you who can help calm and soothe your dog while you drive.

4. If your dog's reaction to being in the car is severe, try a motion sickness medication and take her to the vet.

16 Questions to Ask Before You Hire a Professional Dog Walker

According to the late Dr. Jeff Proulx and Fawn Pierre of the San Francisco SPCA, dogs need lots of physical and mental stimulation. They also need to spend quality time with people and other dogs. If you're not home to give your dog regular daily outings and companionship, a professional dog walking service may be a good choice for you. You should be comfortable with the person you hire to walk your dog. He or she should have composure, sincerity of purpose, presence, and playfulness. You should also be in agreement about a training philosophy and routine.

The following questions are intended to help you evaluate a potential dog walker. There are no "right" or "wrong" answers. Rather, the questions are meant to inform you of the dog walker's practices — to educate you about how your dog will be treated and handled so you can make an informed decision.

William Wegman's *Dog Walker*, 1990.
Courtesy of William Wegman.

1. Where will you walk my dog?

2. What types of activities do the dogs engage in? Do you walk them on- or off-leash? Will my dog be participating in a supervised playgroup at a designated location?

3. For how long will you exercise my dog (excluding car time)?

4. Do you include obedience training during my dog's walk? If so, how?

5. What sort of punishment and/or rewards do you use?

6. What will you do if my dog does not come or sit when she is called? Likewise, what will you do if my dog jumps on you or someone else?

7. Do you consult with a professional dog trainer? If so, who? What is your philosophy on keeping dogs under control?

8. What is the maximum number of dogs you will walk on an outing? Do you separate dogs according to size? Age? Activity level?

9. What is the protocol for introducing my dog into the group, and for letting my dog off-leash? How do you screen dogs for dog-friendliness?

10. Will you provide any reports or updates on my dog's behavior, either weekly or monthly?

11. In case of an emergency, what plan of action do you have in place? Are you trained in pet first aid or CPR?

Choosing a Pet Sitter

Charlotte Reed has been recognized as the Pet Sitter of the Millennium Year and was inducted into the National Association of Professional Pet Sitters Hall of Fame in 2000. She has shared her expertise with millions of people through her Pet-Owning Made Easy series of booklets and her appearances on ABC's *The View*, *Good Day New York*, CNN, and Fox's *Pet News*, among others. Here are Ms. Reed's suggestions for choosing a pet sitter.

1. Get a referral. Check with your veterinarian, the National Association of Professional Pet Sitters, or Pet Sitters International for a pet sitter in your area.

2. When choosing a potential pet sitter, make sure she has experience dealing with your pet's unique needs.

3. Hire a pet sitter who can relate to your emotional attachment to your dog, preferably someone who has owned a dog.

4. Make sure the sitter meets and interacts with your pet before being hired. See how she and your dog get along. If they don't click, keep looking until you find someone your pet likes.

5. Make sure the sitter is willing to care for your pet your way, regardless of what you request. She should be aware of your dog's daily routine and your expectations, and she should fulfill them.

6. Check that the sitter is bonded and insured. If something happens in your home or to your pet, you want to be sure that you'll receive appropriate compensation.

7. Ask the sitter for a comprehensive service agreement listing services, methods, and rates. Avoid disputes by knowing what services are offered, the time frame for each provided service, and the fee.

8. Ask for references and check them out. It's the best way to find out what level of service the person provides.

9. Discuss an emergency contingency plan with the sitter. Make sure she has your telephone numbers as well as the phone number of a reliable backup pet care provider.

10. Give the sitter the name and number of your vet, other doctors in the area, and organizations that provide emergency service.

11. Inform the sitter about neighborhood dog runs, pet stores, and parks. Your dog will be happier if the provider knows about the area's best spots for walking and playing.

12. Has a dog ever been lost or injured on your walks? What happened?

13. Will walks be delegated to anyone other than yourself (an assistant or associate)? If so, how far in advance of the actual outing with my dog will these arrangements be made?

14. How long have you been walking dogs professionally? Were you trained to manage multiple dogs? If so, where or by whom?

15. Can you provide references from current and former clients? May I contact them?

16. May I observe/accompany you on a walk?

How to Evaluate a Boarding Kennel

Deciding to entrust the care of your dog to a boarding kennel is a huge decision. You will have to do research and ask other dog owners in your area some significant questions. So whether you wish to board your dog at a basic care kennel or an upscale one, here are some things to keep in mind.

1. Decide whether or not you want to board your dog at a kennel or have a caregiver come to your home instead.

2. Ask your veterinarian if she can recommend a reputable kennel. Some veterinarians also board animals — ask other people who go to the same vet if they've had good experiences boarding their pets.

3. Visit the kennel before you bring in your dog for her first stay. If the kennel won't give you a guided tour of the facilities, don't even think about boarding your dog there.

4. When you arrive at the kennel, give it the sniff test. You'll get a sense of how clean the facility is by the intensity of odors.

5. Make sure that the runs are relatively clean but don't look for perfection. Even a great kennel can't keep all the runs clean all the time.

6. Be sure that the kennel provides clean bedding and good ventilation and that it has a caring staff.

7. Get an overall impression about the condition of the kennel, including the kitchen area. Is it well maintained? Are the grounds well cared for?

8. Make sure the kennel is not overbooked. If they are crowded but tell you they will accommodate your dog, don't consider them.

9. Find out if the kennel has medical expertise and how they deal with emergencies.

10. Ask as many questions as you can. Can you leave your dog's favorite toy or blanket? How many dogs are assigned to a staff member? How much individual attention will your dog get? How often will your dog be exercised and groomed? Find out about feeding schedules. If the staff at the kennel sound bored or laugh at your questions, they will probably bring this attitude into the care of the animals.

11. Discuss costs, including any special costs you may incur (such as for the administration of medications).

12. Find out if the kennel is a member of a professional association. You can consult www.petsitters.org to see if the particular kennel you're interested in is listed.

8 Great Web Sites for Free Dog Stuff

1. www.Workingdogweb.com/FreeStuff.htm — free games, dog e-postcards, and products such as calendars, biscuits, treats, screensavers, and software.

2. I-love-dogs.com/freedogstuff.html — free dog lover's e-mail address, your own free dog Web site, and the best dog software to download for free. Choose from screen savers, desktop themes, e-books, and games.

3. Chazhound.com/pet_games.html, Chazhounds Free Dog Page — free dog e-book, games, screen saver, and shareware.

4. www.talktothevet.com/FREE_PET_STUFF/ — free Purina Puppy Care Kit, including an informational video and booklet designed to help you bring out the best in your puppy, and step-by-step, age-appropriate advice on training, veterinary care, and nutrition. You can also get a free pet safety kit, and free samples of Mighty Dog canned food and Nature's Recipe dog food, as well as lots of games and online printable coloring books for kids.

5. www.free-dog-stuff.com/ — high-quality, healthy

5 Ways to Help Your Dog Deal with Divorce

Pet expert Arden Moore is the author of more than a dozen books, including *Dog Parties: How to Party with Your Pup* and *Healthy Dog: The Ultimate Fitness Guide for You and Your Dog.* Moore is the pet columnist for *Prevention* magazine. She can be reached through her Web site: www.byarden.com.

With the divorce rate at about 40 percent, more and more dogs get caught in an emotional tug of war between dueling spouses. Here are some of Moore's suggestions on making the transition easier for your dog.

1. Speak softly and avoid stressing your dog. Yelling, slamming doors, and icy silences can take emotional and physical tolls on ever-loyal dogs. Dogs can actually become physically ill due to heightened levels of stress.

2. To maintain a sense of normalcy for your dog, stick to your routine as much as possible. Dogs are creatures of habit and look forward to their regular activities, such as the Saturday trip to the dog park or eating their favorite food treat.

3. Dogs have actually been surrendered to shelters by one spouse only to find the other spouse, days later, looking for his missing dog. Tragically, sometimes these dogs have already been euthanized. The family pooch should not become a pawn during the divorce process. Rather than using the family dog as a weapon, couples should strive to work out an amicable agreement to share custody. It's better for them and for the dog.

4. If custody of the dog is to be shared, each party should keep copies of the dog's medical records. Furthermore, they will need to keep each other — and their veterinarians — informed of any changes regarding current medical conditions and any prescribed treatments. They should also keep two sets of identification tags that they can switch when they transfer custody of the dog.

5. In a two-dog household it's best to split up the two dogs, especially if they aren't getting along. Each dog may become happier when she is the top dog in her own home.

dog products. This company frowns on commercially processed treats and foods so they will not offer these types of samples.

6. freebies.about.com/cs/dogfreebies — free doggie pick-up bags, a free coupon book from PetSaver with discounts good at a number of online retailers, a sample of Improve supplements, an Animal Poison Hotline magnet, and a free holistic pet care booklet.

7. www.dogomania.com/category/Free_stuff/ —dog calendars, games, e-postcards, screen savers, music, icons, and wallpapers.

8. www.actualfreestuff.com/pets.htm — sample dog treats, a coupon for a free sample of Pro Plan® canned dog food, Pedigree® Puppy Starter Kit can, a sample of Yappy Dog Treats, and an issue of *Good Dog* magazine. Fill out a survey and you can get your dog a free bandana.

11 Things You Should Know About Grooming Your Dog

According to the Animal World Network, grooming your dog accomplishes much more than just making her coat look nice and shiny. Grooming provides you with the opportunity to spend quality time with your dog, combing, brushing, bathing, and generally bonding with her. You will also be able to check your dog closely for any skin irregularities or other problems while grooming her.

Regular grooming makes your pet look better. Additionally, scientific proof shows that grooming improves a pet's health. For aged and convalescing animals, grooming stimulates the circulation. With any pet, grooming causes deep relaxation and a dramatic slowing of heart rate. This helps animals cope better with physical and emotional stresses. Longhaired dogs should be groomed daily, and shorthaired breeds may require grooming only twice a week.

Your dog should find brushing pleasurable. Some people discover that it's difficult to get their pet to submit to regular grooming. Perhaps this is simply because they don't know how their pets like to be brushed. The following guidelines will help make weekly grooming sessions fuss-free.

1. Get dogs used to grooming early in life. Longhaired breeds should be groomed from the time they are puppies. Do not use tranquilizers on a routine basis to calm a nervous dog — this can lead to liver damage.

2. Be sensitive to your dog's likes and dislikes. Dogs often prefer to flop over onto one side for brushing, so don't insist that they sit up or stand. Simply brush on that side first; then gently grab hold of their front and hind legs to roll your dog over and brush the other side.

3. Use appropriate combs and brushes. Use a brush with stiff bristles on one side and wire on the other. If the atmosphere is very dry and full of static, as it often is in winter, moisten your fingers and the brush to reduce the chances of giving your dog electric shocks. For the same reason, it is good to place the dog on a wool rug or a cotton towel.

4. Be gentle and reassuring. Before you begin grooming, stroke Phoebe reassuringly around her head to make her feel safe and secure and let her know that nothing unusual is going to happen. Any time you accidentally knock your dog's knee or shoulder with the edge of the brush, stroke her.

5. Learn to use the brush and your fingers properly. First, run your fingers down your dog's back quite firmly several times to loosen up any dead fur. Then use the wire brush, working down from the head to the tip of the tail, then under the chin, along and around the chest and abdomen, and finally brushing down each leg. Finish up with the bristle side of the brush, using it around the dog's face and then briskly brushing down your dog's back to give her coat a final sheen. Don't use the wire side of the brush on your dog's face, as you could easily poke her in the eye or otherwise hurt her.

6. When dogs are shedding the thick undercoat that insulates them during the winter, don't keep raking hard with the wire side of the brush. You will only make your dog's skin hypersensitive. Don't brush hard on patches of fur that haven't loosened up yet, either.

7. Move your dog's fur aside and

examine her skin closely for fleas, ticks, and any irritations. Look for unusual problems with the coat such as mats, tangles, dandruff, etc. Mats and tangles can be carefully removed while you are grooming.

8. Learn where she likes to be combed and brushed and where she doesn't. All dogs have sensitive areas that need to be groomed a little more gently and carefully than others. By paying special attention to these areas, you will make your dog more comfortable and she won't resist future grooming sessions.

9. Regular grooming is essential to your dog's health and well-being. Regular combing and brushing will keep her coat clean and healthy. It will stimulate her skin and allow natural oils to circulate to the coat. Check for hair loss, inflammation, unusual tenderness, or lumps under the skin. Constant scratching in a particular area may also be an indication of a problem. Check with your veterinarian about any unusual problems or irregularities.

10. Puppies, like children, have short attention spans. They require special consideration. Select a time when your puppy is less energetic. Begin with a short grooming session, about five minutes or so. Talk in a gentle, reassuring tone while grooming to make him feel comfortable. Be sure to check his ears, paws, teeth, and underside during the grooming procedure. This will, in time, make him accustomed to being handled and examined. Eventually, he will be quite comfortable being groomed and will look forward to these sessions.

11. Regular nail trimming is important to your dog's health and well-being. Never use ordinary scissors to trim your dog's nails. Use trimmers that are specially designed for dogs. Hold the dog's paw firmly and cut off the tip of the nail with a single stroke.

Be very careful to stop short of the quick, the blood vessel inside the nail. Cutting the nails right after bathing will make the quick more visible; applying baby oil will serve the same purpose. Follow up by filing your dog's nails smooth.

Why Dogs Don't Use Computers

1. Can't stick their heads out of Windows 95.

2. Fetch command not available on all platforms.

3. Hard to read the monitor with your head cocked to one side.

4. Too difficult to "mark" every Web site they visit.

5. Can't help attacking the screen when they hear "You've Got Mail."

6. Fire hydrant icon simply frustrating.

7. Involuntary tail wagging is dead giveaway that they're browsing www.pethouse.com instead of working.

8. Keep bruising noses trying to catch that MPEG Frisbee.

9. Not at all fooled by chuck-wagon screen saver.

10. Still trying to come up with an "emoticon" that signifies tail wagging.

11. Oh, but they WILL . . . with the introduction of the Microsoft Opposable Thumb.

12. Three words: carpal paw syndrome.

13. 'Cause dogs ain't GEEKS! Now cats, on the other hand . . .

14. Barking in next cube keeps activating *your* voice recognition software.

15. SmellU-SmellMe still in beta test.

16. *Sit* and *stay* were hard enough; GREP and AWK are out of the question!

17. Saliva-coated mouse gets mighty difficult to maneuver.

18. Annoyed by lack of newsgroup alt.pictures.master's.leg.

19. Butt sniffing more direct and less deceiving than online chat rooms.

20. It's too damn hard to type with paws.

How to Bathe Your Dog

Your nose will tell you when your dog needs his next bath. If Barnaby hates water and gives you a rough time about staying in the bathtub, try bathing him outdoors (where he can splash all he wants) in a tub of shallow water. Increase the amount of water each time you bathe him until he seems used to the routine, then reintroduce the indoor bathtub. Chances are, your dog will not scratch or bite you while you are giving him a bath. He will just look at you as if to say, "What did I do to make you punish me?"

Here are some tips to make the bathing experience as enjoyable as possible for both you and your dog. After all, you're both going to get wet — why not have fun?

1. Choose the most comfortable spot for you to bathe your dog. A small dog can be bathed in the kitchen sink, but a large dog may require your bathtub or may need to be bathed outdoors.

2. Have all your supplies at hand. These should include your dog's brush, a small bucket, a hair trap for the drain, a rubber mat for the floor of the tub, a coat conditioner, a couple of towels, one or two washcloths, cotton balls, a gentle hypoallergenic dog shampoo, a hair dryer, and a spray to help detangle your dog's coat if she is especially hairy.

3. Brush your dog's coat before you get her wet. This will help prevent her coat from knotting and will make bathing much easier.

4. Place cotton in your dog's ears so water can't get inside and cause an infection.

5. Rinse your dog with warm water by holding the shower head very close to her body when you spray her. It's a good idea to speak to your dog in a soothing voice to help keep her calm and happy. Never spray water directly into your dog's face.

6. Apply shampoo in small amounts, working from head to tail. Avoid getting soap in her eyes.

7. Get into some of the more difficult-to-reach areas such as between your dog's toes, behind her ears, under her chin, and around the rectum.

8. Thoroughly rinse your dog using warm water. Position one of your hands over her eyes so soap can't get in.

9. Gently squeeze out as much water as you can using your hands and then use a combination of hair dryer and towels to dry your dog.

10. Make sure your dog is perfectly dry before you let her outdoors. If she rolls in the dirt before she's dry, she will need — you've got it — another bath!

"Anybody who doesn't know what soap tastes like never washed a dog."
— FRANKLIN P. JONES

7 Toothbrushing Tips

The health of your dog's teeth is paramount to her overall health and longevity. Her teeth should be cleaned at least twice a week, and she should routinely be given food specifically designed to help keep them clean. If she has tartar or stains that you can't remove, call your vet. Excess tartar and plaque can cause painful periodontal disease resulting in premature tooth loss. Start brushing your dog's teeth when she is still a puppy — let her play with the toothbrush to familiarize herself with it. A lot of dogs like the taste of doggie toothpaste, so apply a liberal amount to her toothbrush. You might even want to give her a taste before inserting the brush in her mouth. This way, she'll be licking her lips and her mouth will be open, making it easier to place the toothbrush inside. *Never* use human toothpaste (especially ones with fluoride) on dogs — it can make them very sick.

1. Choose the correct toothbrush and toothpaste. A long-handled brush with an angulated head and extra-soft bristles makes the ideal brush, but a washcloth can also be used to scrub the paste onto her teeth.

2. Select a time when you and your dog are both relaxed.

3. Place the paste in between the bristles as opposed to the top of the bristles. This will keep the paste on the teeth more effectively.

4. Get yourselves into a comfortable position.

5. Lift her lower lip and begin brushing her teeth using a circular motion just as you would for your own teeth. Be sure that you brush near her gum line; this is where plaque tends to build up most. Hold the brush so that its surface is at a 45-degree angle with the tooth and so that the bristles touch the gum tissue. Brush all the teeth is a similar fashion.

6. If you are cleaning her teeth for the first time, don't use a brush. Let her get acquainted with the feeling of your fingers on her teeth first. Then let her taste a little bit of the toothpaste before you proceed any further.

7. If she is a little fidgety about the process, try starting out slow and gradually increase the number of teeth you brush until she's comfortable.

"The most affectionate creature in the world is a wet dog."
— AMBROSE BIERCE

19 Unusual Dog Products and Services

Yes, these are all for real!

1. **Genetic Savings & Clone** is the acknowledged leader in the emerging pet cloning field. They offer gene banking for cats and dogs as well as wild and/or endangered relatives of cats and dogs. Though they are not yet offering cloning services commercially, they are developing cloning technology for dogs and refining it for cats, having announced the world's first cat clone, CC, in February 2002.

2. The **Pet Phone** allows your pet to answer and hang up the telephone by stepping on a platform (stepping off hangs the phone up automatically). No more long, lonely days for your pet. Call your pet during your lunch break, or just for fun! For pets one pound to hundreds of pounds, the Pet Phone

measures about 13.5 inches by 20 inches at the base, and tapers from 1¼ inches to 5 inches high. Levers under the top board operate the phone.

3. **Pet Chime** is a portable, wireless electronic doorbell that allows your pet to tell you when she needs to come in or go out. The wireless doorbell looks like a paw print and can be placed on the floor or mounted on the wall. When your pet pushes the paw, the chime lets you know what she wants.

4. **KosherPets**'s products are the *only* ones certified kosher by one of the largest and most respected kosher certifying agencies in North America. All of KosherPets's products contain pure and natural ingredients, approved by both the USDA and the Chicago Rabbinical Council.

5. **Doggles**, protective eyewear for dogs, have polycarbonate (shatterproof), antifog lenses that block 100 percent of ultraviolet light and keep out wind and debris. The wraparound frames completely cover the eyes without any gaps to let in stray light or foreign objects. Two adjustable elastic straps keep Doggles on securely during a variety of activities.

6. **Neuticles** are testicular implants for pets. Neuticles should be inserted at the time the dog is neutered but can also be implanted years afterward. Neuticles eliminate any concern that your pet will look neutered. A "Neuticled" pet looks exactly the same after

surgery! Neuticles are available in two models: NeuticleOriginals (rigid firmness) and NeuticleNatural (natural firmness). Each is crafted to replicate the dog's testicle size, shape, weight, and feel. Custom sizing is available.

7. **Secondnature** is a housetraining system offered by Purina, whose staff of dog breeders, trainers, and behaviorists spent years developing it. This safe, effective, and easy program for housetraining puppies includes dog litter and a litter pan specifically designed for a dog's elimination.

8. **Chiengora** (pronounced she-angora) is the name of yarn spun from dog hair. (*Chien* is French for "dog" and *gora* is derived from "angora," the soft fur of a rabbit.) Dog fur is up to 80 percent warmer then sheep's wool. This is an important factor to consider when planning a project with your very special and unique yarn. Dog breeds that make the best yarn are Bouvier des Flandres, Chow Chows, Border Collies, Australian Shepherd Dogs, Shih Tzus, and Newfoundlands.

9. **Pawlish** nail polish provides colored nails for those with tails! Designed specifically for pets' nails, Pawlish is safe and easy to use. And because it's manufactured by OPI, who makes all the dazzling shades you see in nail salons these days, you know that the colors are going to be "pet-i-cularly" fabulous. Only a single coat is necessary, and it's quick-drying and nontoxic, so

both you and your pet can feel good about it! Pawlish is available in six bold, bright colors that will look fetching on most pets.

10. Wheelchairs for dogs can make life a lot easier for dogs suffering from degenerative myelopathy, hip dysplasia, disk or cervical disease, ruptured disk, spinal disorders, or any other problem that affects her hind legs. The chairs are invariably custom-made and consist of a harness that connects your dog to a two-wheeled "back end." Yes, they are cute, but more important, they can restore a vital, even active lifestyle to incapacitated dogs. Made of durable materials, doggie wheelchairs are designed to withstand water, rough terrain, and even the most frenzied of dogs.

11. Soft Paws nail caps for dogs are vinyl nail caps that glue on to your dog's nails to keep them blunt and harmless. This original product helps protect you and your belongings against problem scratching.

12. The Dog Island is the ultimate destination for people who want their dogs to spend the remainder of their lives in complete freedom. More than 2,500 dogs are already enjoying a better life at Dog Island in Tallahassee, Florida. Separated from the anxieties of urban life, dogs on Dog Island live a natural, healthy, and happy life, free from the stress of living among humans. They live with almost limitless space, and tens of thousands of rabbits, rodents, and other natural prey to chase after. To place your dog or to apply for a job working on The Dog Island, visit The-DogIsland.com.

13. A company by the name of **Outrageous International** launched Pipi-Max, "the World's Only Walking, Barking, Drinking, and Peeing Toy Dog!" The remote-controlled Pipi-Max drinks water and then barks before lifting his leg to let you know that he needs to do his business. Pipi-Max is the perfect companion for kids and parents who want a pet who is already house-trained.

14. Formulated with special herbs for breeding females during preheat, heat, gestation, whelping, and lactation, **Bitch Pills** contain the enzyme-producing culture aspergillus for the digestion and assimilation of nutrients. Better prenatal nutrition results in healthier offspring. This product is ideal for pregnant or lactating bitches.

15. The **2004 Dog Poo Calendar** is a calendar unlike any other, containing an entire year of arty images of dog excrement in all shapes and sizes. December, for instance, shows a dog in the snow wearing a Santa hat with his little gift to nature in the foreground. The month of February offers a very special box of Valentine's Day chocolates.

16. The **Super Bark-Free Ultrasonic Trainer** senses constant barking and triggers an ultrasonic tone — inaudible to humans — to help stop this behavior. The device works outdoors over a twenty-five-foot range and is a humane way to stop your dog — or your neighbor's dog — from barking incessantly.

17. PetGems is a new product created by a Chicago-based company called LifeGem, who will take your dog's ashes from an affiliated crematorium and convert them into a diamond. The process involves applying great heat and pressure to the ashes, and it takes about five months to produce. The cost ranges from $2,000 to $13,000 depending on the size of the stone. (LifeGem offers the same bling-bling service for human remains.)

18. CDs for dogs can offer companionship when you can't. Recently, the University of Belfast studied the effects of different types of music on fifty dogs. They learned that heavy metal songs caused dogs to growl while classical music calmed them down. These results inspired a Netherlands-based music distributor called LindeTree to create CDs for pets using nature sounds and music. These two CDs are entitled *Relaxation Music for Dogs and Cats* and *While You Are Gone*. Songs included on *While You Are Gone* are "Wet Kisses," "New Leash on Life," and "Unconditional Love."

19. Summum of Salt Lake City will be happy to mummify your deceased animal in preparation for the afterlife. The procedure costs $20,000 to $50,000 for a medium-size animal. The price includes a bronze statue of your pet.

Soft Paws vinyl nail caps for dogs

Physics for Dogs

Lexiann Grant, an award-winning writer and contributor to multiple regional, national, and international pet newsletters, explains here the elements of Canidae Physics, the nonscience that attempts to explain why dogs act like dogs.

1. **Energy.** How active your dog is when you don't want him to be.

2. **Force.** Influence of your hand on your dog's collar, moving him to a space that he does not want to occupy.

3. **Matter.** Your most valued material possessions; what your dog likes to chew most.

4. **Motion.** The action your dog takes when he moves away from you after you tell him to come.

5. **Laws of Motion. a.** For every creature that moves in a dog's territory other than immediate family and pack, there will be a proportionate bark and chase reaction. **b.** Dogs at rest tend to stay at rest, unless something interesting occurs to wake them, at which point the first Law of Motion occurs.

6. **Mediocrity Principle.** If there is something particularly interesting occurring at a convenient time in his space, a dog will react and tend to keep reacting. If there is nothing interesting, he will become bored and go to sleep or entertain himself by destroying matter.

7. **Black Hole. a.** The craters in your yard that are a direct result of your dog's boredom. **b.** Where dogs hide the evidence of the matter they have destroyed.

8. **Laws of Gravity. a.** Dogs at rest can be used as objects to hold sofas and beds to the floor. **b.** Balls and biscuits thrown into the air are easier to catch on the way down. **c.** Food going down tastes better than when coming back up, but a dog will eat it either way.

9. **Principle of Most Time.** How long it takes a dog to do his business before entering the veterinarian's office.

10. **Quantum Leap.** How high a dog can jump up when he greets you, height being relevant to level of dog's enthusiasm and quality of the clothes you are wearing.

11. **Theory of Bark Limitation.** Each dog is born with a finite number of barks. Owners must attempt to prevent dogs from using all their barks at one time.

12. **Photoelectric Effect.** What happens when your dog is doing something unbelievably smart or cute: you grab the camera, take a picture, and all you capture is a streak of blurry fur.

13. **Superconductivity.** The ability of light-colored fur to stick to dark clothing.

14. **Synergy.** Three dogs together in one household can destroy more matter, dig deeper black holes, and eat more food than three single dogs in three separate households.

15. **Uncertainty Principle.** The more you study and read about dogs, the less you understand their behavior.

16. **Occam's Razor (or Oster's Trimmer).** A dog's philosophy: Reduce everything to its essentials. Keep life simple — eat, sleep, play, and potty on a regular basis.

17. **Paradox.** The worse you feel, the more your dog loves you and tries to cheer you up.

18. **Cosmological Constant.** You are the center of your dog's universe. In his eyes, the sun rises and sets in your smile toward him. Be kind to him, take good care of him, and love him every day of his life.

The Top 10 Major Advances in Dog Health Care

Dr. Wendy C. Brooks, a board-certified specialist in canine and feline practice and a member of the American Academy of Veterinary Dermatology, is the author of *Pet Health Library, The Pet Nutrition Corner*, and *The Pet Pharmacy*. As the educational director for VeterinaryPartner.com, Dr. Brooks provides top-quality, cutting-edge veterinary information to pet owners. Dr. Brooks considers the following to be major advances in the history of canine health care.

1. **Readily available commercially prepared dog food.** Years ago, people simply fed table scraps to their dogs and there was no standardization of what was meant by "complete and balanced" food. Currently, it is almost impossible for a dog to develop a nutritional disease or a disease stemming from bacterial contamination of food. Anyone can go to the local grocery store and buy a reliable, appropriate dog food with decades of research and testing behind it.

2. **The development of antibiotics.** It is hard to imagine a time when even the president's son could not be saved from septicemia resulting from a simple foot wound. Killing bacteria with a pill is a stunning development — antibiotics save millions of lives every year — both canine and human.

3. **Organized and regulated veterinary medicine.** Not only is there an educational program that individuals must follow, but an assortment of certification tests with regular recertification is necessary to demonstrate that a doctor and the facility where she practices are up to federal and state health standards.

4. **The development of modern flea control products.** 1995 marked the beginning of the new generation of flea control products. The ineffective days of sprays and shampoos ended. Though many people still do not know that a flea infestation can be lethal, the efficacy of the new products has created fewer life-threatening circumstances.

5. **Community-funded shelters.** Though your local shelter may not be the nicest facility on the block, having a shelter in your area means that fewer stray and abandoned dogs are roaming the streets and that strays are suffering from fewer diseases. Furthermore, with a system of adoption in place, people can visit their local shelter and bring home a best friend. Imagine what our lives would be like without these facilities.

6. **The development of diagnostic imaging.** Clinical radiology has meant the same for veterinary care as it has for human medicine. Ultrasound technology is of nearly equal importance.

7. **Vaccination against distemper and parvovirus.** There was a time when these viruses marched unchallenged through our communities and left dead and injured dogs in their wake. Now, for less than fifteen dollars, vaccination is available against these horrific viruses. If you don't remember what it was like before these vaccines were available, it might be hard to appreciate the magnitude of their significance.

8. **Rabies control.** There was a time when dogs roamed free and our yards weren't fenced in. But that was before the horrors of rabies ravaged the country. Though there is still no cure for rabies, the widespread vaccination of dogs is an inestimable development.

9. **The recognition of the importance of sterilization.** Spaying and neutering is not just about preventing unwanted puppies. These procedures reduce the risks of certain cancers and infections common to unsprayed and unneutered dogs. Low-cost programs have made sterilization easy for even low-income pet owners.

10. **The microchip ID.** A dog without a collar can still make her way back to her owner only moments after she is found. The microchip is encoded with the owner's information and implanted between the dog's shoulder blades. A found dog can be scanned to obtain information on where she belongs. This device has enabled thousands of dogs to return home and avoid becoming candidates for shelter euthanasia.

20 Pioneers in Dog Care and Medicine

1. During the 1980s **Dr. R. K. Anderson** and his colleague Ruth Foster developed the Gentle Leader head collar. Behavior problems are the number one reason people surrender their dogs to shelters. The Gentle Leader, now worn by over a million dogs in America, has given dog owners a tool that enables them to better deal with behavioral problems in a humane way.

2. **Dr. Jane Bicks** is one of the pioneers of veterinary nutritional/alternative medicine and is recognized nationally as an authority in the natural treatment of animals. She is the executive director of New Product Development and Education for HealthyPetNet, where she oversees all product development and consults with pet industry experts to ensure that HealthyPetNet's cutting-edge formulas meet the highest standards for quality and effectiveness.

3. **Leland E. Carmichael, DVM**, has spent the past forty years at the James A. Baker Institute for Animal Health at Cornell University, where he has served as professor and has done pioneering work in the field of virology as it relates to the dog. He has received several awards, including two Gaines "Fido" Awards (1975, 1980), the American Animal Hospital Award of Merit (1981), the Ralston Purina Small Animal Research Award (1981), and the American Veterinary Medicine Association–American Kennel Club's Career Achievement Award in Canine Research (1994). Discoveries in Dr. Carmichael's lab have led to the identification and treatment of various canine viruses.

4. **Ian Dunbar, DVM**, founder of the Association of Pet Dog Trainers, has been an important promoter of humane dog training and early puppy socialization classes. He is the star of the British television show *Dogs with Dunbar* and has been teaching pet owners to train their dogs humanely and thoroughly for more than thirty years. Dunbar has written numerous books, including *Before and After Getting Your Puppy: The Positive Approach to Raising a Happy, Healthy and Well-Behaved Dog* (New World Library, 2004) and *How to Teach a New Dog Old Tricks* (James & Kenneth Publishers, 1998).

5. **Benjamin Hart, Ph.D., DACVB**, at UC Davis, is one of the founding fathers of the American College of Veterinary Behaviorists (along with Dr. Anderson) and has provided a wealth of research in animal behavior. He is the coauthor of *Perfect Puppy: How to Choose Your Dog by Its Behavior* with his wife and colleague, Dr. Lynette Hart.

6. **Lynette Hart, Ph.D.**, at UC Davis is the head of the Center for Animal Alternatives, a University of California statewide (and worldwide, with their integrated Web site) group that promotes reducing the number of animals needed in research and refining research projects. She is the wife of Dr. Benjamin Hart and has written numerous books with him.

7. **Dr. James Law** received his DVM degree at the Edinburgh Veterinary College in Scotland. He began veterinary instruction at Cornell University in 1968 and brought with him a commitment to rigorous training for veterinarians in America. Law introduced rigor and science to issues of animal and public health, and he is regarded as one of the most influential leaders in veterinary medicine.

8. **Laurie McCauley, DVM**, is considered one of the leading authorities on veterinary rehabilitation and has been referred to as one of the pioneers of veterinary rehabilitation. She is credited with introducing hydro-treadmill therapy to canine rehabilitation. Dr. McCauley has lectured numerous times on the topic of canine rehabilitation, including at the annual convention of the American Veterinary Medical Association. Dr. McCauley is also an instructor at the Animal Rehabilitation Institute, which is the certification program for veterinarians, veterinary technicians, physical therapists, and assistants. She is the owner and operator of TOPS Veterinary Rehabilitation in Grayslake, Illinois.

9. **C. W. Meisterfeld, Ph.D.**, is the leading pioneer of canine psychoanalysis and psychological dog training. He is considered the first canine psychoanalyst expert witness to be recognized and approved in the judicial system of the California Supreme Court. His philosophy of teaching based on mutual respect and trust has earned him many awards.

10. In the late 1940s **Mark Morris, DVM**, discovered that some canine kidney ailments could be successfully managed with a low-protein diet, so he developed a mix to feed affected dogs. His pioneering work to improve nutrition for all dogs led to a line of pet food used by veterinarians. Today these products are called Prescription Diet pet foods. His affiliation with the Hill Packaging company, which manufactured his line of food, allowed him the opportunity of founding the Morris Animal Foundation, dedicated to improving the health of companion animals. A portion of the profits of his line of food products allows his foundation to research animal-related health studies.

11. **Dr. Marvin Olmstead**, professor of surgery at Ohio State University and School of Veterinary Medicine, is the acknowledged leader in the field of total hip replacement surgery. Since 1990, Dr. Olmstead has been performing canine total hip replacement using the BioMedtrix hip system. Dr. Olmstead is a world-renowned surgeon in this field, and he is considered one of the pioneers, having performed this procedure since the early 1970s.

12. **Donald F. Patterson, DVM**, received his degree in veterinary medicine in 1954 at Oklahoma State University. He is responsible for the first genetic clinic for animals and the first course in medical genetics for veterinary students. In 1974 Dr. Patterson obtained support from the National Institutes of Health for a number of research projects, including the studies of genetics of congenital heart disease, metabolic defects, and other genetic diseases of dogs. He was the first person to standardize dog chromosomes and to detect chromosome defects in dogs, which led to the development of the first biochemical and molecular tests for canine genetic disease diagnosis and carrier detection.

13. The "Pavlov's Dog" phenomenon was realized when **Ivan Pavlov** noticed that a dog listening to the footsteps of the person who fed him on a daily basis would begin to salivate before the food actually arrived. Pavlov's description on how animals (and humans) can be trained to respond in a certain way to a particular stimulus paved the way for a new and objective method of studying animal and human behavior. His book *Conditioned Reflexes* is a pioneering work in experimental psychology.

14. **Dr. Richard Pitcairn** is a leading pioneer in the field of veterinary homeopathy. His book *Natural Health for Dogs and Cats*, published in 1982, emphasized the use of homeopathy in animal treatment. Since 1992 he has been teaching a course for veterinarians in the use of homeopathy. Dr. Pitcairn founded the Animal Natural Health Center in 1986 and in 1995 started the Academy of Veterinary Homeopathy along with two other veterinarians.

15. **Karen Pryor** is a behavioral biologist, a pioneering dolphin trainer, and an authority on applied operant conditioning — the art and science of changing behavior with positive reinforcement. She is one of the inventors of "clicker training" for dogs. Her book *Don't Shoot the Dog* has become the bible for many dog trainers, especially those who want to avoid harsh methods.

16. **Allen M. Schoen, DVM**, is considered one of the pioneers in holistic medicine for animals. His practice incorporates an integrative approach, combining the best of natural therapies along with conventional medicine, recommending whatever is felt to be best for your individual animal companion. He is the author of *Kindred Spirits: How the Remarkable Bond Between Humans and Animals Can Change the Way We Live* (Broadway, 2002). His practice incorporates an integrative approach, combining the best of natural therapies with conventional medicine.

17. **James Serpell, Ph.D.**, associate professor of humane ethics and animal welfare, is the director at the Center for the Interaction of Animals and Society in the School of Veterinary Medicine, University of Pennsylvania. His research has focused on human-animal interactions, more specifically the benefits of pet ownership on some aspects of human well-being. He is the author of *The Domestic Dog* and has been a leading researcher in human-animal bonds.

18. **B. F. Skinner** developed the theory of operant conditioning, the idea that people behave the way they do because this kind of behavior has had certain consequences in the past. This theory, which relies on positive and negative reinforcement to model behavior in small steps that would allow a subject to learn complex actions, was applied to the training of all sorts of animals — including dogs. Clicker training is based on operant conditioning.

19. **Dr. Sharon Willoughby** is the founder of animal chiropractic. She is a DVM as well as a doctor of chiroprac-

tic and started Options for Animals, the first school for veterinarians and chiropractors to become certified, thus bringing the two fields together. Dr. Willoughby developed the curriculum and format of the basic certification and advanced animal chiropractic programs. She holds degrees in both veterinary medicine and chiropractic.

20. **Dr. Susan Wynn**, executive director of the Georgia Holistic Veterinary Medical Association, has published several books and is known for pioneering work in the field of nutroceuticals. Her memberships include the American Veterinary Medical Association, the American Holistic Veterinary Medical Association, the American Animal Hospital Association, the International Veterinary Acupuncture Society, the American Association of Veterinary Acupuncturists, and the Georgia Veterinary Medical Association. She has served on two ad hoc advisory panels for the National Institutes of Health and was an invited participant on two international consensus panels dealing with complementary and alternative medicine. She is co-owner and principal author of the AltVetMed Web page.

27 Ways to Tell if Your Dog Is Sick

If you've grown up with dogs, chances are you've developed a sense of knowing when your pooch is under the weather. You've seen her at her best and you know when there are any disturbing changes. But if you are a first-time dog owner, Dr. William O'Reilly, DVM, past president of the Northern New Jersey Veterinary Medical Association and medical director of the Closter Animal Hospital in Closter, New Jersey, suggests that you familiarize yourself with some of the most common signs of illness. (Keep in mind that a healthy dog has a body temperature of 101–102° F, a respiratory rate of 15–20 breaths per minute, a heart rate of 80–120 beats per minute, and will try to hide her illness as well as she can.)

1. Difficulty breathing
2. Loss of appetite
3. Abnormal temperature
4. Disorientation
5. Weakness or lethargy
6. Lack of interest in her surroundings
7. Hiding in a dark place
8. Scratching or chewing at her feet, skin, or coat
9. Persistent coughing or retching
10. Discharge from her eyes
11. Discharge from her ears
12. Inflamed, red, or cloudy eyes

13. Weight loss
14. Persistent diarrhea
15. Difficulty walking
16. Walking in circles
17. Persistent head shaking
18. Persistent ear scratching
19. Unpleasant breath odor and/or swollen gums
20. Harsh-feeling coat; coat with a dull texture; dull and flaky skin
21. Potbelly
22. Soft, foul-smelling stools
23. Blood in the urine

24. Pale mucus membranes
25. Mucus or blood in the stools
26. Repeated vomiting over several days
27. Unusual lumps under the skin

Early twentieth-century French postcard with art by Louise Ibels

12 Great Safety Products for Your Dog

1. **Reflective clothing** such as bandanas, vests, and jackets can keep your dog safe from nighttime drivers. These products are available at numerous stores and Web sites.

2. **Pet Strobes** are lights that attach to your dog's collar. They emit a beam of light that has 360-degree visibility for up to a half mile. Pet Strobes are available at LittleRiverPetShop.com.

3. **Lighted dog collars**, such as the Auroralites Safety Collar, can provide great visibility for your dog at night. These collars are used by search and rescue teams, as well as law enforcement personnel. Available at www.auroralites.com, or call 905-820-2980.

4. **Dog life jackets** double as flotation devices for boating and any other water sport or activity. The Outward Hound life jacket is a high-performance dog flotation jacket. It is available at www.partipoodlepetsupplies.com.

5. With the **Finder System ID tag**, you use your telephone to record all your pertinent contact information into the tag's assigned voice mailbox. When your pet is found, the finder dials the tag's 800 number and enters the tag's six-digit voice mailbox number. The person who finds your dog can hear all the ways you can be contacted. The Finder System ID tag is available from www.familysafety.com, or call 609-266-2605.

6. **Ruff Wear Beacon Mini-Flasher.** The Beacon clips to your pet's collar or to your clothing, giving you peace of mind anytime you and your companion are out and about. Available at LittleRiverPetShop.com.

7. **Dog coats and jackets** become more important as the cold weather arrives. On those cool, damp days and chilly nights, your dog will appreciate a water-repellant, fleece-lined coat to keep him warm and toasty. A variety of these coats can be found at most pet stores.

8. A **safety seat support harness** attaches easily to any seat belt and will keep your dog safe while riding in a car. They are available at 1-800-Pets-Now. Or you can choose the Ruff Rider Roadie Dog Car Restraint Seat Belt, available at www.ruffrider.com.

9. **Auto barriers** keep your pet to the rear of your vehicle, safely away from the driver and passengers. The tubular construction eliminates blind spots, installs in minutes, and fits most SUVs and wagons. Available at www.petcarecentral.com.

10. **Dog gates**, such as the KidCo Gateway, will help keep your dog safe when she is home alone by restricting her movements and protecting her from potentially harmful situations. Dog gates are available at www.petcarecentral.com.

11. The **Indoor Radio Fence** by Petsafe is designed to keep dogs out of restricted or unsafe areas inside your home. Available at www.petsafe.net.

12. **Invisible Fence Brand** combines professional installation, advanced technology, and customized training to keep pets in the yard and out of danger. Available at www.invisiblefence.com, or call 1-800-578-DOGS to find a dealer near you.

First-Aid Kit for Dogs

Before an emergency ever arises, it's a good idea to learn all you can about first-aid techniques and pet health care. Emergency first aid is most effective when it is administered promptly and calmly, and even though it is usually better to take your dog to a clinic or animal hospital or veterinarian, it is important to give your dog immediate care. Below are some of the essential items to keep in your dog's first-aid kit.

- First, you need a kit box to contain all the emergency supplies. A large tackle box with numerous compartments is a great idea.
- Paperwork, including the dog's health record, medications, local and national poison control numbers, regular veterinary clinic hours and telephone numbers, and emergency clinic hours and telephone number
- Examination or surgical gloves (will keep the area sterile and reduce the danger of disease transmission)
- Muzzle (will help you control your dog and protect yourself from possible injury from a fear biter)
- Nonstick Telfa pad bandages (great for open wounds)
- Four-inch gauze sponges
- Cotton balls
- Hydrogen peroxide or rubbing alcohol to clean out an open wound

- Neosporin or a triple-antibiotic (can be applied directly on clean open wounds to reduce contamination)
- Ear syringe to flush out any debris
- Ace self-adhering athletic bandage — three-inch width is best
- White petroleum jelly (Vaseline or similar)
- Eye wash
- Pepto Bismol tablets for gastrointestinal problems
- 25-milligram diphenhydraminine (Benadryl) capsules (for allergies)
- Karo syrup in the event that your dog overdoes it and his blood sugar drops. Dogs with low blood sugar will become weak and nonresponsive and may eventually have seizures.
- Bottle of water in case of dehydration

- Pedialyte or other balanced electrolyte fluid (to aid in restoring your dog's normal body chemistry)
- 1 percent hydrocortisone acetate
- Sterile stretch gauze bandage — three inches by four yards
- Buffered aspirin for pain relief and as an anti-inflammatory
- Dermicil hypoallergenic cloth tape — one inch by ten yards
- Maximum-strength Kaopectate tablets for diarrhea
- Bandage scissors
- Custom splints
- Blanket
- Hemostats or tweezers
- Wound compression pads
- Rectal thermometer
- Ziploc bags
- Any medications that your dog regularly uses

The theobromine in chocolate that stimulates the cardiac and nervous systems is too much for dogs, especially smaller ones. A chocolate bar is poisonous to dogs and can even be lethal.

13 Dog Wound Treatment Basics

Dr. Clive Dalton is the winner of the 1993 Landcorp Communicator of the Year Award and the Sir Arthur Ward Award for agricultural communication. He is the author of more than thirty scientific papers and six books and an honorary life member of the Guild of Agricultural Journalists and Communicators. Visit his Web site at www.lifestyleblock.co.nz. We are grateful to him for the information presented here.

The two main objectives in treating a wound are first to stop the bleeding as quickly as possible, and second to prevent infection. Keep in mind that an open wound is a contaminated wound and it will get infected unless it is cleaned thoroughly and antibiotics are administered. Here are some treatment basics. Remember that any serious injury should always be treated by a veterinarian.

1. Muzzle the dog to protect yourself and anyone who is helping you from being bitten.

2. Wounds should be covered with a clean (sterile, if possible) dressing as soon as possible.

3. Make sure your hands are clean, and wash wounds with disinfectant.

4. If wounds are bleeding, stop the blood flow by applying pressure over a bandage. You can clean up the blood later.

5. Use a nonadhesive bandage to keep splints in place and to prevent and reduce swelling.

6. Don't put bandages on too tightly or the dog's circulation will be affected.

7. If you bandage a limb, leave the foot out to judge the dog's body temperature and amount of swelling.

8. Anything can be used as a splint — for example, a rolled-up newspaper or magazine.

9. To stop bleeding, use external pressure and elevate the body part unless it is fractured.

10. Wash the wound and surrounding skin with running water, working from the center outward.

11. Remove any visible foreign matter and dry the wound with cotton.

12. Keep everything as clean as possible and liberally use disinfectant.

13. If the dog has been impaled, don't pull out the object from the dog's body. This may cause excessive bleeding and the dog may even bleed to death in a short amount of time. Instead, if possible, leave the object for the veterinarian to take care of.

6 Emergency Household Medications Your Dog Might Need

The following is a list of common household human medications that can also be used for dogs. These should be used only when you can't reach your veterinarian immediately. If your vet recommends an over-the-counter drug, find out what the precise dosage should be for your dog. Here are some medications that Dr. O'Reilly recommends keeping on hand.

1. Buffered aspirin for pain relief and anti-inflammatory action

2. Benadryl to treat allergies, insect stings, and itching

3. Dramamine to reduce motion sickness

4. Hydrogen peroxide (two to three teaspoons of a 3 percent solution can be used to induce vomiting after an accidental ingestion of poison)

5. Pepto Bismol for diarrhea, vomiting, and gas

6. Kaopectate to relieve diarrhea

What to Do When You Find a Stray Dog

It's a wrenching scenario for anyone who cares about animals. Once you see any kind of stray pet beside the road it's too late to avert your eyes and drive on, even if you wanted to. After all, what if your own dog or cat were standing there? So before you pull over, Good Samaritan, here are some guidelines from the HSUS on assisting stray animals safely and effectively.

1. Think about your safety first. You can't help an animal if you become injured. Look in your rearview mirror before braking, signal your intentions, pull your car completely off the road, turn off the ignition, set the parking brake, and put on your hazard lights. If you have emergency flares, prepare to use them.

2. Consider the safety of the animal. A strange, frightened, and possibly sick or injured animal may behave unpredictably. A sudden move on your part, even the opening of your car door, may spook him, causing him to bolt — possibly right onto the highway. If the animal looks or acts threatening, or if for any reason you feel uneasy about the situation, remain in your car.

3. If possible, restrain the animal. Create a barrier or use a carrier, leash, piece of cloth, or length of rope to keep the animal from leaving the area. Signal approaching vehicles to slow down if you can't confine the animal, or divert traffic around him if he appears to be injured and is still on the roadway.

4. Use caution when approaching the animal. Should you succeed in getting close enough to capture him, you stand a good chance of being scratched or bitten. Even a small animal can inflict a painful wound, and if you are bitten by a cat or dog whose vaccination status is unknown, you will be advised to undergo preventive treatment for rabies.

5. When approaching the animal, speak calmly to reassure him. Make sure he can see you at all times as you approach, and perhaps entice him to come to you by offering a strong-smelling food such as canned tuna or dried liver.

6. Try to lure the animal into your car with food, close the door, and wait for help. But do this only if you are certain someone will come to get the animal very soon. In most cases it's not a good idea to drive somewhere with a strange dog unrestrained in your car; he may become frantic or aggressive once you're in the car with him. Cats may do the same, as well as lodge themselves under the car seat, from which extracting them can be dangerous.

7. If you're not able to safely restrain the animal, call the local police or an animal control agency. Do so whether or not the animal is injured, and whether or not he appears to be a stray or to be owned (meaning that he is wearing an identification tag or a flea collar or has recently been groomed). If you have a phone in your car, call the local animal care and control agency (in rural areas, call the police or sheriff) and report the situation. Leave your phone or beeper number with the dispatcher and try to get an estimate of how long it may take someone to respond. If possible, stay on the scene to keep an eye on the dog or cat until help arrives. Make sure you report to authorities precisely where the animal is. For example, say "one mile north of Livingston on Highway 101" or "between markers 65 and 66 on the New York State Thruway."

8. If you are able to transport the animal, take him to the nearest animal shelter. Or, if you plan to keep the animal in the event no owner is found, notify animal control that you have the animal or that you have taken him to a veterinary hospital for treatment. You usually can place a free "found" ad in your local newspaper. Keep a copy of the ad to prove your good in-

tentions should any question arise later. To check on any relevant laws in your state, county, or town, contact your local animal control agency, humane society, or SPCA. Many times, the dog or cat you find along the highway will turn out to be unowned, unwanted, and unclaimed. Even so, a person who finds a stray dog or cat doesn't automatically become their owner or keeper — as in "finders keepers"—until he has satisfied certain state and local requirements. In almost every state, the animal is not "owned" by the finder until the holding period for strays (as specified by state or local laws) has expired and the finder has made an attempt to reunite the animal with his original owner and has taken steps — obtaining vaccinations, license, collar, and identification tag — to prove he is now the owner.

9. Don't assume that you are dealing with an irresponsible owner. Good Samaritans who have never lost a cherished companion animal may conclude that the owner of the found dog or cat callously abandoned him or, at the very least, neglected to keep him safely confined at home. But accidents can happen to anyone.

A frantic pet owner may be looking everywhere for their beloved animal.

10. Understand the limitations of animal care and control agencies. Once you have taken the initiative, time, and trouble to rescue a dog or cat along the highway, you may be surprised to find that the rest of the pet care community may not necessarily rush forward to do what you see as its part. For instance, you may take a badly injured stray dog to animal control, only to learn that the agency is unable to provide expensive surgery to treat the dog's injuries and, to relieve him from his suffering, euthanizes him instead. A cat with relatively minor injuries may be kept for only the mandated stray holding period and then euthanized. Virtually all animal control facilities have severe budgetary or space limitations and must make painful decisions on how best to allocate their inadequate resources.

11. Before you take an injured animal to a private veterinary hospital for treatment, be willing to assume financial responsibility for the animal before treatment begins. Good care is not cheap, and many veterinarians have many Samaritans in their waiting rooms every year. Anyone who is committed to saving injured stray animals should discuss these issues in advance with the veterinarian. Fortunately, some states have laws that allow veterinarians to collect from a fund for treating unowned injured animals who have been presented to them by animal control or a Good Samaritan.

12. If you're uncertain about whether or not to assist or keep an animal you see alongside the highway, here's a final word of advice: First, think of what you would want the finder of your animal to do if he happened to find him injured and his collar missing. You'd want him to take your pet to a veterinarian, and you'd want him to try to find you. At the same time, be reasonable about how much you can afford to do for that animal if no owner shows up. Are you willing to add him to your household? Are you willing to return him to his original home if his owner turns up after you've started to form an attachment? Think these issues through in advance — they may stand you in good stead the next time you see that wrenching sight at the side of the road.

"If you pick up a starving dog and make him prosperous, he will not bite you; that is the principal difference between a dog and a man."
— MARK TWAIN

What to Do if You Are Being Attacked by a Dog

According to Brent Ablett, of Animal Control of New Zealand, many dog bites are the result of people reacting incorrectly when they are approached or threatened by a dog. Your initial reaction should be to stop and remain completely still. Avoid eye contact with the dog and speak to her gently. A command such as "sit" or "stay" can be given softly to the dog, because many dogs will obey. All threatening gestures such as yelling at the dog, waving your arm, or rushing at her should be avoided. Here are some things you can do if none of the above works and you are still threatened by an attacking dog.

1. If you believe the attack is full on, reach down and pick up a handful of stones, a shingle, or whatever you can find and throw it at the dog.

2. If that fails, grab your clipboard or briefcase and offer it to the dog, making sure to keep it well away from your body. If the dog is truly aggressive he will grab the object and hold on. In this case, do not let go of the object. If you do, he will soon realize that it is not you and will likely attack again.

3. Normally after he realizes he is having little or no effect he will stop the attack (or at least give you time to plan your next move).

4. Strike the dog only as a last resort. When a dog is in attack mode, pain can further incite him to more violence.

5. Never try to kick the dog when he is facing you (it's reported that a dog can bite ten times before humans can respond).

6. If you are knocked to the ground, remain motionless in the fetal position. Cover your face by crossing your arms over your head.

17 Ways to Avoid Being Injured by a Strange Dog

The best way to avoid being bitten is to avoid dangerous situations. Here are some rules to follow:

1. Never approach a stray or unfamiliar dog, especially one that is behind a fence or in a car or even tied up with a leash.

2. Never pet a dog through a fence.

3. Understand that a wagging tail does not always indicate friendliness.

4. Never pet a strange dog without his owner's permission.

5. Never tease a dog. A threatened dog will often bite.

6. Never hold your face close to a dog.

7. Never pet a dog without letting him see and sniff you first.

Moving an Injured Dog

Dr. O'Reilly reminds us that injured dogs should be moved with great caution. If a dog is in the road or in an otherwise dangerous area, moving her to a safer location is essential. If the area is clear, take a few minutes to assess the dog's condition before you decide to transport her anywhere. Remember to keep yourself safe first.

8. Never startle a dog. No loud noises.

9. Never bother a dog who is sleeping.

10. Never bother a dog who is eating.

11. Never bother a dog who is chewing on a toy.

12. Never bother a dog who is caring for her puppies.

13. Never run from a dog. A dog's natural instinct is to chase you.

14. Never stare a dog directly in the eye. He may feel challenged.

15. Stay as still as possible if approached by a stray.

16. If a dog attacks you, roll into a ball and lie still.

17. Always protect your face, neck, and stomach.

1. Before attending to the dog, be certain that you are not in danger from either the dog or your surroundings. Be sure there is no oncoming traffic, for example.

2. Muzzle the dog for his and your safety. Any dog, no matter how gentle he might seem, has the potential to bite when he is severely injured, frightened, or in pain, so it is important for you to protect yourself from being bitten. If a first-aid kit is not handy you can improvise by using either a rope, a scarf, adhesive tape, or even the dog's leash. Tie the muzzle on top of the nose. Warning: Don't muzzle the dog if he is coughing or vomiting, seems to be having trouble breathing, or is unconscious.

3. Before moving him, check for obvious injuries and treat accordingly. You may have to control the dog's bleeding or give the dog CPR to revive him if he is not breathing before you even consider transporting him.

4. Small dogs can be cradled in your arms while you are moving them. Try to keep the injured side of the dog pressed up against your body. Large dogs can be placed in a blanket or sheet. Keep the dog as flat as possible by supporting the back, head, and pelvis. This is best done by three people, two carrying the dog and the third supporting his body.

5. If you suspect that the dog's back or neck has been injured, try to place the dog on a flat board or other rigid and study material so that the injury doesn't get any worse.

6. Cushion the dog with pillows, towels, clothing, or rolled blankets to prevent him from being jarred during transport.

7. Use the board as a stretcher and take the dog directly to the nearest veterinary facility.

8. Keep the dog warm with a blanket, towel, or clothing.

9. Keep the dog's body as still as possible while transporting.

Vaccinations Every Dog Needs

William O'Reilly, DVM, is the past president of the Northern New Jersey Veterinary Medical Association and medical director of the Closter Animal Hospital in Closter, New Jersey. According to Dr. O'Reilly, dogs should be vaccinated for the first time when they are young puppies (from nine weeks of age — and occasionally earlier) to protect them against a number of important infectious diseases. Here are Dr. O'Reilly's recommendations.

1. The initial vaccine for canine distemper should be at eight weeks and twelve weeks, with a booster one year later and then every two years.

2. The measles vaccine produces antibodies against canine distemper in young puppies. It is used in puppies under eight weeks of age and not repeated.

3. The canine parvovirus vaccine should be given at eight, twelve, and sixteen weeks of age, with a booster in a year and repeated in two years.

4. The canine adenovirus 2 vaccine should be given at eight and twelve weeks. It is repeated in one year and then every two years.

5. Vaccination against bordetell bronchiseptica is given at six to eight weeks of age initially and then every six months in high-risk situations, such as when your dog is going to a kennel.

6. The canine parainfluenza vaccine should be given at eight and twelve weeks and repeated in one year and then every two years.

7. The leptospirosis vaccine should be given at eight and twelve weeks of age and repeated annually.

8. The initial rabies vaccine is given between twelve and sixteen weeks of age and protects for one year. A subsequent vaccine is given after six months of age and protects for three years.

9. Tetanus toxoid is given if your dog exhibits signs of tetanus. Routine preventive vaccination is not recommended for this disease.

Signs of Distemper

According to Animal Health Channel, which was developed and monitored by board-certified veterinarians, canine distemper is a contagious, incurable, and often fatal multisystemic viral disease that affects the respiratory, gastrointestinal, and central nervous systems of dogs. Distemper is caused by the canine distemper virus (CDV). This disease is the leading cause of death in unvaccinated puppies. CDV can also occur in humans, but anyone who has been vaccinated against measles, a related disease, is immune. Here are some of the early signs of distemper to watch out for.

1. A fever of 103 to 106 degrees appearing three to six days after infection

2. Possible eye symptoms including inflammation of the cornea and conjunctiva, lesions on the retina, and inflammation of the optic nerve (this can lead to blindness)

3. Enamel hypoplasia (unenameled teeth erode quickly in puppies whose permanent teeth haven't come in yet — the distemper virus kills all the cells that create teeth enamel)

4. Gastrointestinal symptoms such as loss of appetite or anorexia, diarrhea, and vomiting

5. Hyperkeratosis, or hardening of the foot pads and nose

6. Respiratory symptoms including cough, labored breathing, and pneumonia

7. Dogs almost always develop encephalomyelitis (an inflammation of the brain and spinal cord), the symptoms of which are variable and progressive. Most dogs that die from distemper die from neurological complications such as ataxia, the loss of muscle coordination, depression, increased sensitivity to touch, deterioration of mental abilities and motor skills, seizures, and complete or partial paralysis.

13 Steps to Take if Your Dog Is Stolen

Every year about 5 million companion animals are reported missing. Whether your dog is lost or stolen, the experience can be harrowing and can leave you with feelings of grief, terror, and guilt. Here are some steps you need to take once you realize that your dog is missing.

1. Start looking for your dog as soon as she disappears. Don't rely on Autumn to find her way back to you.

2. Call and whistle to your pet. If he hears you there's a good chance he will respond even if injured.

3. Call the police and ask them for help.

4. Get in your car and start circling your block. Widen your search if you need to by circling the entire neighborhood. Have a family member or friend stay at home to man your phone in case anyone calls you with information or in case your dog reappears. Be sure to look for your dog in her favorite places.

5. Have your neighbors check their yards, garages, basements, etc.

6. Your telephone should be manned twenty-four hours a day. If your dog has an ID tag with your phone number on it, you may very well get a call.

7. Circulate a "lost dog" flyer. Keep it simple and readable. We suggest that you use a bold headline which can read: REWARD: LOST DOG. The flyer should include your dog's description, the date she disappeared, and at least two phone numbers at which you can be reached at all times. Keep at least one of your dog's physical attributes a secret so that you can weed out crank calls from people claiming to have found your dog. If the caller doesn't spot the obvious characteristic that you've omitted, you know that person hasn't found your dog.

8. Put up signs in stores, schools, churches, and community centers including the dog's name, description, and photograph, as well as your name, address, and phone number. Post flyers in local stores throughout your area, veterinary offices, gas stations, restaurants, etc.

9. Contact all local animal shelters, humane societies, veterinary hospitals, and animal control officers immediately.

10. Contact Petfinders at 1-800-666-5778 or any other organization that deals with lost pets. If your dog has been tattooed, contact the National Dog Registry at 1-800-647-3647 or Tattoo-A-Pet at 718-646-8203.

11. Ask delivery persons, garbage collectors, and postal workers in your neighborhood if they have seen your dog.

12. You can try searching the Internet, but this is usually not very effective.

13. Never give up your search. We've all heard stories about dogs being reunited with their owners weeks or even months after they've gone missing.

20 Car Safety Tips for Your Dog

A great deal of care should be taken when you bring your pal along for a car ride. Unless she is properly prepared, you run the risk of seriously injuring your dog as well as yourself and any other passengers. Some dogs like to jump around in the car, while others are happy sticking their heads out the window. Here are the basics of auto travel; for more information, consult the excellent PetsWelcome.com.

1. Get her used to riding in the car when she is a puppy so that she learns not to be afraid.

2. If she is not used to longer excursions, take her on a series of short rides to find out how well she does. Make sure that the first couple of trips are to places she likes. You don't want her associating the car with a negative experience.

3. Be sure to keep her leash firmly in hand whenever she enters or exits from the car. She should always enter the car from the sidewalk side. Be sure that other drivers are aware that you have your dog under control.

4. Be sure she has a current ID tag in the event that she manages to get away.

5. Never let her ride in the front seat. You don't want her climbing on you while you're driving, and you don't want her going through the windshield in case there's an accident or you need to stop suddenly. An air bag can also hurt her severely if it opens for any reason.

6. The best place for her to be in the car is in a travel crate. A sturdy crate or pet carrier should be secured so that it doesn't move around while you're making sharp turns or coming to a sudden stop.

7. If you are on a long trip, be sure that she has been exercised before the journey.

8. You should also make frequent stops to allow her to relieve herself and get a drink of fresh water.

9. If your car doesn't have enough room for a crate, you must use some sort of harness. These are available at most pet stores. A harness with adjustable straps is designed to fasten securely to a standard seat belt.

10. Check behind you frequently. If Molly seems nervous or fidgety, reassure her that everything is okay.

11. If she's a barker you can place a citronella collar around her neck. The citronella emits an unpleasant spray every time she barks.

12. Bring a dish and some water since dogs often get thirsty during car rides.

13. Keep a first-aid kit in your car. See page 334.

14. Make sure that windows are rolled up in such a way that she can't squeeze out.

15. Discourage your dog from jumping out of the car as soon as you arrive home. She may do this in a busy area and get hurt as a result.

16. You can help prevent her from getting carsick if you avoid feeding her within three hours before the ride. It might also be a good idea to not give her water just before you both take off. Hint: You can give your dog ginger if she is getting sick. Some folks also use a couple of licks of vanilla ice cream to cut down on nausea.

17. On long trips it's a good idea for you and your buddy to stop occasionally and stretch your legs.

18. Don't let her stick her head out of the window for long periods, especially in dusty conditions. Dirt may find its way into her eyes, ears, or nose, causing injury or infection. (Goggles may look silly on Lindy — especially if you tie a white silk scarf around his neck — but they will protect his eyes. See "19 Unusual Dog Products and Services," p. 326.)

19. Dogs are at the greatest risk of injury when they are riding in a convertible with the top down or in the back of a pickup truck. Keep your dog out of these situations.

20. Never, ever leave your dog in the car alone during the summer months or whenever it is hot outside. The temperature in a car on a hot day can soar to as high as 120 degrees and might very well kill her.

11 Tips for Deskunkifying Your Dog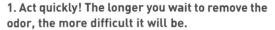

Curious dog + startled skunk = disaster.

Here are some tips to help you deal with this smelly problem.

1. Act quickly! The longer you wait to remove the odor, the more difficult it will be.

2. Put on some old clothes before you even go near your dog. Since skunk spray is an oil, it is very difficult to remove from clothing.

3. Keep your pooch away from his crate or bed until you've dealt with the odor.

4. Try to leave your dog outside the house while the odor is still a problem.

5. If you've been able to locate the exact spot where your dog has been sprayed, try to trim away some of her affected hair.

6. When you wash your dog, wash the affected area only. Washing all over can spread the skunk oils to other areas of your dog's fur.

7. If your dog has a thick double coat you have to act quickly before the sulphuric spray dries on her fur. Otherwise removing the odor completely will be nearly impossible.

8. Once you've bathed your dog you can use a deskunking product such as Skunk-Off. Skunk-Off should stop skunk odor quickly and permanently. It is also safe, nontoxic, and nonirritating.

9. Another method, although questionably effective, for deskunking involves saturating your dog's coat with either tomato juice or mouthwash and then bathing her with a canine shampoo. If you're using tomato juice, you're going to need a lot of it. A couple of cans won't even come close. Groomers point out that if your dog has a light-colored coat, tomato juice will probably turn it pink.

10. A chemist by the name of Paul Krebaum has invented a new and more effective formula for deskunking. Mix 1 quart of 3 percent hydrogen peroxide, ¼ cup of baking soda, and 1 teaspoon of a strong liquid soap such as a dishwashing detergent. After you've mixed these ingredients, wet your dog and massage the solution into her coat. Try to keep the mixture away from your dog's eyes, nose, and mouth. Note: When mixing these ingredients, be sure to do so in an open bowl or bucket. Otherwise they will fizz up, and if you keep the solution in a tight container, it may explode. Furthermore, don't store this mixture — use as much as you need and throw away the rest.

11. To keep skunks off your property you can try either placing mothballs in and around your yard or about five minutes before you let your dog out, especially at night, turn on an outdoor light and make some noise. Both of these methods can scare away skunks.

"Scratch a dog and you'll find a permanent job."
— FRANKLIN JONES

Tips for Ticks

Ticks, such as the brown dog tick, the American dog tick, and the deer tick, are wingless parasites that are found in almost every region of the country. Ticks have spread diseases as diverse as Rocky Mountain spotted fever and Lyme disease. Ticks are most commonly found in the bushes, grasses, and woods that surround our homes. In order for a tick to feed it must attach itself to a warm-blooded animal, such as a dog. The bite that ensues can cause serious harm to dogs. Here are some tips from Dr. O'Reilly for preventing and treating tick bites.

1. Avoid walking your dog in off-trail areas. Ticks live primarily in long grasses and shrubs, so it is a good idea to stick to paths and areas that have been cleared of brush.

2. Before taking your dog outside, treat her coat with either a spray, a dip, or a powder containing pyrethrins. This is an insecticide that contains the tick-fighting ingredient D-limonene.

3. If you find a tick on your dog's body, spray the area with a tick insecticide and then comb your dog's fur with a flea comb. This will remove any ticks that remain on the surface of her coat.

4. Make sure that the tick or ticks are dead before you dispose of them; otherwise they may jump back onto your dog.

5. Watch your dog for a few days to make sure she isn't ill as the result of a tick bite.

> "He that lieth down with dogs **shall rise up with fleas.**"
> — BEN FRANKLIN

> "A reasonable amount of fleas is good for a dog; **it keeps him from brooding over being a dog.**"
> — EDWARD NOYES WESTCOTT

The Best Way to Remove a Tick

Use tweezers, not your fingers. Place the tweezers level with the skin, squeeze, and pull directly up. The tick attaches, it does not embed. If you use your fingers in removing a tick, you may inadvertently compress the swollen abdomen of the tick and facilitate a regurgitation of its contents, which may contain bacteria.

Managing Fleas

Fleas use dogs as hosts to incubate their larvae. These larvae hatch every two to five days and can infest your furniture, carpeting, and bedding. Flea larvae can flourish and thrive only in humid environments, where they are able to become adult fleas. Flea bites are painful and may result in blood loss, irritation, itching, and rashes that can last as long as one year. Treatment and management of fleas involves caring for both the dog and her environment. Dr. O'Reilly suggests that you seek the advice of your veterinarian for issues specific to your dog, but here are some general guidelines to help control fleas.

Treating your dog

1. If you suspect your dog is infested with fleas, you will want to bathe her right away.

2. Run a flea comb through your dog at least twice a week. After each stroke, drown the fleas by submerging the comb in a bowl of hot, soapy water.

3. Although flea collars are only partially effective (the bigger the dog, the less effective they are), they are easy to use and inexpensive. Most collars remain active for about four months, but there are also some longer-acting collars on the market. Collars that contain organophosphorus compounds, or OPs — such as the Prevender — are long-lasting and provide the best protection.

4. Spot-on preparations that are applied directly to your dog's skin contain small quantities of concentrated drugs. Current spot-on preparations such as Advantix, Frontline, and Stronghold are by far the most convenient and effective of the drugs used to treat fleas today. A few drops applied to the skin cause no stress to your dog, are very effective in killing fleas, and are safe and easy to use.

Treating the environment

1. The best way to manage fleas inside your home is by maintaining a clean, well-vacuumed house. This will help to control the mature flea population by killing the larvae and eggs. Vacuum your house weekly and pay close attention to the crevices of couches and chairs and other hard-to-reach areas.

2. Wash your dog's bedding, pillows, blankets, and toys on a weekly basis.

3. Rake up wet leaves and grass clippings and do not store garbage out in the open. These conditions attract fleas.

4. Use a dehumidifier in your home to lower the humidity to safe levels. Try to keep humidity below 50 percent.

5. Before bringing a new pet into the house, inspect her for fleas and treat as necessary. There are many brand-name insecticides formulated as shampoos, aerosols, dips, sprays, dusts (powders), and flea collars for use on pets. All products should be used carefully. Read any insecticide label carefully so that your dog is treated safely.

Fleas can jump 150 times the length of their bodies and accelerate almost 50 times faster than a space shuttle does after liftoff. A female flea can lay as many as 40 eggs per day with more than 2,000 eggs laid in her lifetime.

10 Tips to Help Your Dog with a Fear of Thunder

It's not uncommon for dogs to be frightened by thunder or other loud sounds. These types of fears may develop even though your dog has had no traumatic experiences associated with such sounds. Many fear-related problems can be successfully resolved. If left untreated, however, your dog's fearful behavior will probably worsen. The most common behavior problems associated with a fear of loud noises are destruction and escaping. Here are some things you can do to help your dog overcome or deal with this fear.

1. Create a safe place. Try to create a safe place for your dog to go to when she hears noises that frighten her. But remember, this must be a safe location from her perspective, not yours. Notice where she goes or tries to go when she's frightened and if at all possible, give her easy access to that place. If she's outside and tries to get inside the house, consider installing a dog door. If she tries to get under your bed, give her access to your bedroom. You can also create a "hidey-hole" that's dark, small, and shielded as much as possible from the frightening sound (you can turn on a fan or a radio to help block out the offending noise). Encourage your dog to go to this place when you're home and it's thundering outside. Give her food in that spot and associate other "good things" with that area. Your dog must be able to come and go from this location freely. Confining her in the "hidey-hole" when she doesn't want to be there will only cause more problems. The safe-place approach may work with some dogs, but not all of them. Certain dogs are motivated to move and become active when they are frightened and, unfortunately, hiding out won't help them to feel less fearful.

2. Distract your dog. This method works best when your dog is just beginning to get anxious. Encourage her to engage in an activity that captures her attention and distracts her from behaving fearfully. Start when she first alerts you to the noise and is not yet showing a lot of fearful behavior but is only watchful. Immediately try to interest her in doing something that she really enjoys. Get out the tennis ball and play fetch (in an escape-proof area) or practice some commands that she knows. Give her a lot of praise and treats for paying attention to the game or the commands. As the storm or the noise builds, you may not be able to keep her attention on the activity. Still, it might delay the start of your dog's fearful behavior for longer and longer each time you do it. If you can't keep her attention and she begins acting afraid, stop the process. If you continue, you may inadvertently reinforce her fearful behavior.

3. Try behavior modification. Behavior modification techniques are often successful in reducing fears and phobias. The appropriate techniques are called "counterconditioning" and "desensitization." This means you need to condition or teach your dog to respond in nonfearful ways to sounds and other stimuli that previously frightened her. This must be done very gradually. Begin by exposing her to a level of noise that doesn't frighten her and pair the experience with something pleasant, like a treat or a fun game. Gradually increase the volume as you continue to offer her something pleasant. Through this process, your dog will come to associate good things with the sound she was previously afraid of.

4. Consult your veterinarian. Medication may be available that can make your dog less anxious for short time periods. Your veterinarian is the only person who is licensed and qualified to prescribe medication for your dog. Don't attempt to give your dog any over-the-counter medication or (human) prescription medication without consulting your veterinarian. Animals don't respond to drugs the same way people do, and a medication that may be safe for humans could prove fatal to your dog. Drug therapy alone probably won't reduce fears and phobias permanently. In extreme cases, however, behavior modification and medication used together can be the best approach.

5. Consult an animal behavior specialist. If your dog has severe fears and phobias and you're unable to achieve success with the techniques we've outlined here, you should consult with an animal behavior specialist and your veterinarian.

6. Go to an obedience class. Such classes won't make your dog less afraid of thunder or other noises, but they could help boost her general confidence.

7. Don't attempt to reassure your dog when she's afraid. This may reinforce her fearful behavior. If you pet, soothe, or give treats to her when she's behaving fearfully, your dog may interpret this as a reward for her fearful behavior. Instead, try to behave normally, as if you don't even notice her fearfulness.

8. Don't put your dog in a crate to prevent her from being destructive during a thunderstorm. She'll still be afraid when she's in the crate, and she is likely to injure herself — perhaps even severely — while attempting to get out of the crate.

9. Don't punish her for being afraid. Punishment will only make her more fearful.

10. Don't try to force your dog to experience or get close to the sound she is frightened of. Making her remain close to a group of children who are lighting firecrackers will only make her more afraid, and it could cause her to become aggressive in an attempt to escape from the situation.

7 Things You Should Do if Your Dog Gets Heat Stroke

If your dog exhibits rapid panting, wide eyes, staggering, or signs of weakness, he may very well be on his way to heat stroke, which can result in collapse and may lead to unconsciousness. If you suspect that your dog might be in danger, take his temperature. A rectal thermometer reading above 106° is serious and is an indication that immediate action is called for. Dr. O'Reilly recommends that these steps be taken at once.

1. Get your dog to a cool area immediately.

2. Determine your dog's temperature with a rectal thermometer.

3. Put your dog in a cool — but not ice-cold — tub of running water. You can also spray her with your garden hose. Be sure that the water reaches her skin. The stomach and the inside of her legs are important areas that also need to be cooled.

4. Run ice water over your dog's mouth and tongue, but avoid pouring water directly over her head. Water poured on an overheated dog's head can actually cause brain damage.

5. Let your dog drink small amounts of cool water or lick ice cubes.

6. Keep in mind that small dogs recuperate faster than large dogs.

7. Once your dog's temperature falls to 103°, it is safe to take her to a veterinarian or animal hospital. It is important to get the pet to the veterinarian as soon as possible because even if she appears to be cooled down, internal organs such as the brain, liver, and kidneys can be injured as a result of being overheated.

15 Tips for Keeping Your Dog Safe During a Disaster

According to the Humane Society of the United States, the single most important thing you can do to protect your pets is to take them with you when you must evacuate your home. Animals who are left behind in a disaster can easily be injured, lost, or killed. Animals left inside your home can escape through storm-damaged areas, such as broken windows. Animals turned loose to fend for themselves are likely to become victims of exposure, starvation, predators, contaminated food or water, or accidents. Leaving dogs tied or chained outside in a disaster is giving them a death sentence. Here are some of the HSUS's tips for keeping your dog safe:

1. If you leave your house, even if you think you may be gone for only a few hours, take your animals. Once you leave, you have no way of knowing how long you'll be kept out of the area, and you may not be able to return for your pets.

2. Leave early — don't wait for a mandatory evacuation order. An unnecessary trip is far better than waiting too long to leave safely with your pets. If you wait to be evacuated by emergency officials, you may be told to leave your pets behind.

3. Don't forget ID. Your pets should be wearing up-to-date identification at all times. It's a good idea to include the phone number of a friend or relative outside your immediate area — if your pet is lost, you'll want to provide a number on the tag that will be answered even if you're out of your home.

4. Find a safe place ahead of time. Because evacuation shelters generally don't accept pets (except for service animals), you must plan ahead to ensure that your family and pets will have a safe place to stay. Don't wait until disaster strikes to do your research.

5. Contact hotels and motels outside your immediate area to check their policies on accepting pets. Ask about any restrictions on number, size, and species. Ask if "no pet" policies would be waived in an emergency. Make a list of pet-friendly places and keep it handy. Call ahead for a reservation as soon as you think you might have to leave your home.

6. Check with friends, relatives, or others outside your immediate area. Ask if they would be able to shelter you and your animals or just your animals if necessary. If you have more than one pet, you may have to be prepared to house them separately.

7. Make a list of boarding facilities and veterinary offices that might be able to shelter animals in emergencies; include twenty-four-hour telephone numbers.

8. Ask your local animal shelter if it provides foster care or shelter for pets in an emergency. This should be your last resort, as shelters have limited resources and are likely to be stretched thin during an emergency.

9. If your family and pets must wait out a storm or other disaster at home, identify a safe area of your home where you can all stay together.

10. Keep dogs on leashes and cats in carriers, and make sure they are wearing identification.

11. Have any medications and a supply of pet food and water inside

watertight containers, along with your other emergency supplies.

12. Don't wait until the last minute to get ready. Warnings of hurricanes or other disasters may be issued hours or even days in advance.

13. Call to confirm emergency shelter arrangements for you and your pets.

14. Bring pets into the house and confine them so you can leave with them quickly if necessary. Make sure each pet and pet carrier has up-to-date identification and contact information. Include information about your temporary shelter location.

15. Make sure your disaster supplies are ready to go, including your pet's first-aid kit.

Note: When a disaster strikes, the HSUS Disaster Animal Response Teams (DART) move quickly to assess the damage and evaluate the impact on animals and then to provide the most appropriate support to the local community. They work with local emergency responders, local humane associations and shelters, and local disaster volunteers. The disaster response program is supported by a network of trained and equipped staff volunteers available for nationwide response.

10 Ways to Keep Your Dog Safe on a Hot Day

Your dog needs to be protected during the summer months, when temperatures and humidity remain high. Unlike their human companions, dogs do not have sweat glands all over their bodies; they have them only in their paws. They can't regulate their body temperature by sweating. Panting is the only way your dog can cool off. If your dog's temperature exceeds 102 degrees, she runs the risk of suffering from heat stroke. Signs of heat stroke include excessive panting, drooling, glazed eyes, and sudden weakness. If your dog experiences any of these symptoms, she is in trouble and requires immediate attention. Here are some guidelines, provided by Dr. O'Reilly, to follow to make sure that your dog does not get overheated.

1. If you leave your dog outside, make sure she has a shaded spot to lie in and be sure to give her plenty of fresh, cool water to drink. Make sure that her water bowl is tip-proof.

2. If you can, provide your dog with a small kiddie pool that she can get into and out of easily.

3. Never leave your dog in a parked car. Even if you leave the window open, the temperature in a car can soar to anywhere between 120 and 140 degrees and your dog can suffer the effects of heat stroke in just a few short minutes. Leaving your dog in a parked car in the summertime (and in hot climates all year round) can kill your dog.

4. When exercising your dog, do so during cooler times of the day. The early morning or evening hours are best.

5. No matter when you exercise your dog, be sure that she has an ample supply of water and let her pause to drink frequently.

6. Wetting down your dog prior to an exercise session is a good way to keep his body from overheating.

7. Try to keep your dog's coat as short as possible, but a coat that is too short might make your dog susceptible to sunburn.

8. Don't let your dog get overly heavy. A fat dog has a much more difficult time coping with heat than a dog who is at her proper weight.

9. If you have a short-muzzled breed such as a Pug or a Bulldog, extra precautions have to be taken since their breathing ability is already somewhat impaired. Keep short-muzzled dogs inside in an air-conditioned environment on very hot days or days with exceptionally high humidity. They won't be able to breathe properly if you exercise them outside in such weather and can become extremely sick.

10. Be sure to monitor your dog's temperature and minimize her activity on hot, humid days. You're probably best off keeping your dog inside on extremely hot days.

"Howliday" Hazards: How to Keep Your Dog Safe During the Holiday Season

Many well-intentioned dog owners are unaware of the dangers that holiday events can pose for their four-legged friend. While they wish to include their pet in the festivities, they are often oblivious to the potential problems these occasions can present. Here are some factors to consider when including your dog in celebrations.

Christmas

1. Keep the water stand of your Christmas tree covered. If mixed with water and ingested, the pine sap is poisonous.

2. Keep holiday treats and candies away from your dog's reach and be sure to keep wrapped food items away from your dog as well.

3. Plants such as poinsettia and mistletoe are extremely poisonous to dogs. Be sure to keep these plants out of your dog's reach.

4. Don't put lights on the lower branches of your tree. Your dog may accidentally bite into an ornament or burn himself.

5. Don't use edible ornaments, or cranberry or popcorn strings. Your dog may knock the tree over as it lunges for a new treat.

6. Keep electrical cords away from your pet. Dogs will sometimes chew on them and this can result in a nasty shock or even electrocution.

7. Keep lit candles *completely* out of your dog's reach. An exuberant tail wag or swat of the paw can result in injury to your dog or possibly fire in your home. So keep burning candles on high tables or mantels.

8. Pine needles are sharp and shouldn't be digested. Keep your tree fenced off so that your dog can't go anywhere near this potential hazard.

9. Tinsel can also be dangerous for dogs. If your dog ingests tinsel it may obstruct her circulation and block the intestines. Be sure to pick up any tinsel, ribbon, or ornament hooks before they can cause injury.

10. If your dog receives a holiday gift from a friend or relative, make sure it doesn't pose any hazards.

11. Keep wrapped packages out of your dog's reach for his sake — and yours.

Fourth of July

1. Dogs generally don't appreciate Fourth of July fireworks. Keep your dog inside your home on the Fourth so that she isn't exposed to loud noises that will upset her sensitive ears.

DURING *THE OFF SEASON,* CODY HAD SECRETLY UNDERGONE EXTENSIVE TRAINING AND WAS NOW A CHRISTMAS-PRESENT-SNIFFING DOG.

2. If your dog is in the house and is still bothered by noises, take her to a quiet room and stay with her until she calms down.

3. No matter how much fun you and your guests may be having, never give your dog alcohol.

Thanksgiving

1. Don't feed your dog turkey bones. They can pose a serious choking hazard. Small bones or bone fragments can lodge in his throat, stomach, or intestines.

2. Don't feed your dog poultry skin or gravy. These are rich in fat and can cause serious gastrointestinal upset.

3. Keep a close eye on your dog at the holiday table and be sure that he can't get at the leftovers or go foraging in the garbage.

Note: Try not to change your dog's daily routine. Feeding, walking, and playtime or alone time are important to your dog, and any disruption can cause him stress. Keep your dog by your side or with another family member so he stays out of trouble and can't bother anyone who is skittish around dogs. Also be mindful of the fact that with everyone coming and going, your dog may try to escape the house when the door is open.

How to Winterize Your Dog

Cold weather brings its own safety and health concerns for dogs. Here are some steps Dr. O'Reilly recommends for ensuring that your dog remains healthy in the winter.

1. Give him plenty of fresh water. He's as likely to get dehydrated in the winter as in the summer, and snow is not a good substitute for water, especially if it is yellow.

2. Feed him well and be sure he gets enough extra calories to help him deal with being outside in the cold. He needs the extra energy that these calories provide to keep his body temperature normal.

3. Snow and ice are dangerous since they can cut into the pads of your dog's feet. So, keep Vincent's paws dry by rinsing his feet in warm water after a walk. You can even add a little Vaseline to his foot pads to soften them up and prevent cracking. By the way, doggie snow boots are currently all the rage.

4. Your dog needs to be well groomed in order for his coat to provide the insulation it should. Make sure that the fur around his feet is well trimmed. This will prevent snow from building up between his toes. Towel or blow-dry your dog if he gets wet from rain or snow.

5. Keep him dry, warm, and away from drafts. Seal up any drafty spots around his sleep or rest area and give him blankets to curl up in.

6. Don't leave your dog outside for long periods of time. Dogs are as susceptible to frostbite as humans are. Monitor the temperature of your dog's ears, tail, and feet. Sweaters or coats are great for keeping your dog warm.

7. Make sure that your dog is safe around icy ponds, lakes, or rivers. Snow is also a potential hazard because it can muffle scents and your dog may get lost.

8. Don't leave your dog alone in a car with the engine running. The carbon monoxide emitted from your car's engine can be dangerous if not lethal.

9. Keep him away from antifreeze. It may taste good, but it's a deadly poison. The most likely source of this poison is radiator drainage spots in your garage. *Very important: These should be flushed with water immediately.*

Index

B

"bad dogs": barkers, 102, 203, 206; biters, 188, 205; dog show disqualification, 116; droolers, 209; gassiness, 213; raise insurance costs, 205; snorers, 201

barking: breeds, 102, 193, 203, 206; in the Talmud, 15; understanding and control, 294–295, 299, 327

Barry, Dave, 247, 313

Basenji: description, 172; good for allergy sufferers, 189; history, 172; nickname, 146; traits, 193, 196, 207, 208, 209

Basset Hound: avoid if you have allergies, 189; bad breeding, 223; cost, 217; description, 152, 162, 173; history, 9, 173; long-ear record, 93; stamp, 29, 152; traits, 193, 195, 196, 204, 209

Beagle: cost, 217; description, 148, 162, 173; drug detection, 173; and royalty, 166; stamp, 29, 173; traits, 192, 193, 195, 196, 206, 208, 213; *See also* Pocket Beagle

Bearded Collie, 146, 162, 177, 195, 200, 210

Beauceron, 180

Beauchamp, Richard G., 112

Bedlington Terrier, 162, 168, 189, 209

behavior: books on, 268–269; developmental stages, 270–271; effects of isolation, 295, 298–299; effects of neutering and spaying, 245; fear, 346–347, 350; tail chasing, 312

Belgian Malinois, 85, 158

Belgian Sheepdog, 200, 204

Benjamin, Carol Lea, 285

Bergamasco, 189

Berger de Picard, 180

Bernese Mountain Dog, 156, 162, 195, 200

Best in Show (award): by Breeder of the Year, 144, 145; first given, 38, 103;

process to win, 97, 108; well-known judges, 113, 114, 117; winners 2000–2004, 105–106

Best in Show (movie), 47

Best of Breed (award), 38, 97, 105, 144, 145

Bichon Frisé: cost, 217; description, 152–153, 162; and royalty, 166; traits, 189, 193, 195, 198, 201

Billings, Michele L., 112–113

biology, 141

birth process, 111, 218–219, 241, 244, 247

biting, 188, 205, 249, 260–261, 262, 296, 338

Black-and-Tan Coonhound, 29, 163, 173, 209

Black Russian Terrier, 160, 175

Blind Dogs Connections, 256

blindness: in dogs, 256, 300; guide dogs for humans, 22, 25, 29, 73, 85, 87, 95, 302

Bloodhound: in books and movies, 47, 61; description, 157, 159, 168, 173; evidence used in court, 267; history, 5, 22, 231; traits, 195, 196, 204, 209; war dogs, 79

Blount, Roy, Jr., 71

Bluetick Coonhound, 173, 209

Bobtail. *See* Old English Sheepdog

body language, 282–284

Boerboel, 190

Bolognese, 189, 193

books: on dog behavior, 268–269; on dog care, 264–265; on dog training, 266–267; fiction with dogs, 28, 51, 58–61, 72–74; memoirs about dogs, 4, 64–66, 78; "written" by dogs, 66–67

Border Collie: in books, 64–65; fastest to open car window, 92; hero, 84; life expectancy, 162; traits, 190, 197, 204, 208, 210

Border Terrier, 162, 189, 208

Borzoi, 172, 175, 196, 207. *See also*

Russian Wolfhound

Boston Terrier: cost, 217; description, 151, 162, 165; nickname, 146; as a pit bull, 188; stamp, 29; traits, 193, 195, 201, 203, 204

Bouvier des Flandres, 180, 231

Boxer: in books, 64; cost, 217; description, 149, 162, 231; heroes, 94; stamp, 177; traits, 195, 201, 209, 210, 213

Braque Saint-Germain, 6, 180

Brazilian Mastiff. See *Fila Brasileiro*

breeders: to avoid, 214, 215–217, 220–221, 247; Breeder of the Year Award, 107, 144–145; reputable, 213–214, 221, 224, 225, 246–247

breeding: costs, 219, 222; disorders from bad, 223; dwarfing, 9; history, 3–7; miniaturization, 9; neonatal mortality rate, 219; overbreeding, 214, 218; poodle mixes, 189, 193, 211; selective, 3, 224; your dog, 218–219, 222, 239

breeds: advantages of purebred dogs, 224–225; AKC-recognized, 158–160; and allergies, 189; American, 163–165; for apartment living, 201–202; Asian, 176–178; avoid with children, 194; biting, 188, 205; of the British Isles, 168–171; clumsiest, 190; compatibility with other animals, 208–209, 251; constitutionality of laws, 262; costs for specific, 217–218, 221; for couch potatoes, 193; and dating, 192–193; definition, 108, 158; disadvantages of purebreds, 225; DNA testing to verify, 39; droolers, 209; extinct or near-extinct, 161, 180, 191; French, 180–181; German, 182; good with children, 195; groups (*see* Herding Group; Hound Group; Nonsporting Group; Sporting Group; Terrier Group; Toy Group; Working Group); hairless, 191; and intelligence, 196,

cold, excessive, 351

collars, 6, 9, 22, 238, 292–293, 345

collectibles, 51, 55

Collie: avoid if you have allergies, 189; bad breeding, 223; barking, 206; in books, movies, and television, 40, 41, 45, 51–52, 73; cost, 217; description, 153–154; heroes, 89, 94; nickname, 146; stamp, 29; traits, 192, 195, 204, 210; war dog, 79; wealthiest, 95; *See also* Bearded Collie; Border Collie; Rough Collie; Scottish Border Collie; Smooth and Rough Collie

color, rare, 221

commands, 131, 196, 275, 277, 289

Companion Animal Recovery, 39

compatibility, 208–209, 236, 251

computer games, 133

constellations, 53

contests, 134–135, 229. *See also* sports

Continental Kennel Club, 226–227

Coonhound, 195. *See also* Black-and-Tan Coonhound; Bluetick Coonhound; English Coonhound; Redbone Coonhound

Corgi, 74, 162. *See also* Cardigan Welsh Corgi; Pembroke Welsh Corgi; Welsh Corgi

costs: breeding, 219, 222; insurance, 205; for pets annually, 230; for specific breeds, 217–218, 221; for total life span of dog, 245; what to expect, 247

Coton de Tulear, 166, 189

crates, 297, 342

Crested. *See* Chinese Crested

Crossbreed and Mongrel Club, 228

Crufts Dog Show, 98, 102

Curly-Coated Retriever, 200

Cuvac. *See* Slovensky Cuvac

D

Dachshund: and allergies, 189; bad breeding, 223; in books, 61, 72; cost,

217; description, 148–149, 162, 173, 222; history, 9; popularity, 185; and royalty, 166; traits, 193, 194, 201

Dalmatian: bad breeding, 223; as a circus dog, 197; cost, 217; life expectancy, 162; in movies, 46; nickname, 146; stamp, 223; traits, 194, 197, 204, 210, 213

dance, 125–126, 127

Dandie Dinmont Terrier, 157, 168, 208

dates, dogs and your, 192–193

death and bereavement, 219, 252, 255, 256, 257. *See also* euthanasia

Deerhound. *See* Scottish Deerhound

Deubler, Dr. Josephine, 113

developmental stages, 270–271

dewclaw, 246

deworming, 217, 246

Dibra, Bash, 282, 285

Dickin Medal, 84, 85, 94–95

diet. *See* food for dogs

Dingo, 161

disabilities: assistance dogs, 54, 55, 88, 89 (*see also* guide dogs for the blind); dogs with, 256, 300, 327

Disaster Animal Response Teams (DART), 349

disc-catching, 23, 89, 124–125, 133, 135, 294

discipline, 277. *See also* training

disease and disorders: from bad breeding, 223; blindness, 256, 300; cancer, 218, 223; carsickness, 317; deafness, 219, 223, 301; distemper, 340; eyes, 221, 222, 223; genetic, 220, 221, 223, 246; heat stroke, 347; hip dysplasia, 220–221, 222, 223, 246, 247; prostate disease, 218; in puppies from pet stores, 216, 217; rabies, 10–11; thyroid, 222; transmission to humans, 252; transport of diphtheria serum, 83; uterine or vaginal infections, 218, 222

divorce, 321

Doberman Pinscher: avoid if you have

allergies, 189; bad breeding, 223; best tracker, 92; in books and movies, 47, 49, 58; cost, 217; description, 152, 162; history, 231; and insurance costs, 205; intelligence, 197; nickname, 152; traits, 188, 194, 206, 209, 210, 213; urban legend, 25; war dogs, 22, 79, 81

Dodge, Geraldine Rockefeller, 103, 104, 113–114

dog areas and home shelter: crate, 297, 342; dog bed, 311; doghouse, 238, 315; dog parks, 257, 303–304; fenced yard, 238, 273, 293; not on the bed, 242; puppy-proofing your home, 273

Dog Fanciers' Fund, 256

dog shows: awards and trophies, 104, 116 (*see also* Best in Show; Best of Breed); conformation, 96–99; disqualification, 116; Great American Mutt Contest, 77, 134–135, 229; handlers, 100, 101, 103, 115, 116, 122–123; history, 7, 101–102; how they work, 97, 116, 120; how to find, 99; judges, 100, 109, 112–118, 120; most influential people, 112–118; most prestigious, 77, 98–99, 102–106; movie about, 47; prize money, 107; qualities of good show dog, 118; qualities of good show human, 114; ribbon colors, 113; scoring system, 38, 96, 117; terminology, 108–110, 121; things to bring, 119; virtual, 133; what judges look for, 101; what to wear, 120–121; who's who at, 100; *See also* field trials

dog sitter, 319

Dogue de Bordeaux (French Mastiff), 44, 180, 209

Donaldson, Jean, 266, 267, 285

Downing, Melbourne T. L., 114

dreams, meaning of dogs in, 11

droolers, 209

Dunbar, Dr. Ian, 266, 268, 281, 285, 330

Mastiff: in art, 17; cost, 218; description, 154; history, 3, 5, 6, 16, 22; in movies, 41, 43; proverb, 62; traits, 195, 196, 201, 209; *See also* American Bandogge Mastiff; American Mastiff; American Mastiff (Panja); Bull Mastiff; Dogue de Bordeaux; English Mastiff; *Fila Brasileiro*; Neapolitan Mastiff; Old English Mastiff; Spanish Mastiff; Tibetan Mastiff
Mastin de Español. See Spanish Mastiff
McConnell, Dr. Patricia B., 267, 286
medicine. *See* disease and disorders; health
Meistrell, Lois, 286
mental capability: developmental stages, 270–271; intelligence, 196, 197, 207, 211; memory, 196; psychic ability, 308–309; for tricks, 92; *See also* training
Mexican Hairless Dog. *See* Xoloitzcuintle
microchips, 38, 217, 288, 329
Middle-Asian or Central-Asian Ovtcharka, 109, 174–175, 190
Milbank, Dr. Samuel, 112, 117
Miniature Bull Terrier, 209
Miniature Pinscher, 151, 162, 193, 194, 203, 209, 218
Miniature Poodle, 9, 73, 189, 206
Miniature Schnauzer, 89, 150, 189, 203, 218
Mioritic Sheepdog, 191
Mixed Breed Dog Clubs of America (MBDCA), 228
mixed-breed dogs: advantages, 224; in books and movies, 40, 42, 43, 46, 58, 59, 67, 69, 93, 286; Canine Good Citizens, 229; clubs, 125, 126, 224, 228–229; Great American Mutt Contest, 77, 134–135, 229; heroes, 94; history, 5; registration, 228; steps for choosing, 229–230; wacky, 212; wealthy, 95

Morris Animal Foundation, 302
Mountain Cur, 191
Mountain Dog. *See* Bernese Mountain Dog; Greater Swiss Mountain Dog
movies: about war dogs, 81; acting awards, 93; dog celebrities, 2, 23, 29, 41, 49, 50–52; great dog, 40–48, 50–52, 54–55; really bad dog, 49, 192; that promote animal issues, 49
Mugford, Dr. Roger, 138, 286–287
Munneke, Edi, 287
Murr, Louis, 117
museums, 39
music, 36–37, 43, 44, 327
mutts. *See* mixed-breed dogs
mythological dogs, 6, 7, 9, 10, 16, 179
myths about dogs, 128, 244, 262. *See also* legends; mythological dogs; religious and spiritual beliefs; superstitions

N

names, 39, 250
National Animal Control Association (NACA), 147
National Disaster Search Dog Foundation (NDSDF), 302
National Service Dog Center (NSDC), 302
Native American culture, 13, 16
Native American Indian Dog, 189. *See also* American Indian Dog
Neapolitan Mastiff, 5, 72, 209, 250
neutering and spaying: advantages, 238; development, 329; effects on behavior, 218, 245, 288; in Judaism, 15; myths, 244; as owner's responsibility, 216, 247, 260, 288; stamp, 29
Newfoundland: in books, 67, 73; cost, 218; description, 156; at dog show, 103; hero, 94–95; nickname, 156;

stamp, 29; *Titanic* survivor, 82; traits, 195, 204, 209, 210
New Guinea Singing Dog, 161, 231
news and newspapers, 19, 49, 137–138
Nicholas, Anna Katherine, 117
Nonsporting Group, 38, 104, 105–106, 142, 144, 145
Nordic Spitz. *See* Norrbottenspets
Norfolk Terrier, 162, 170
Norrbottenspets (Nordic Spitz), 187
North American Dog Agility Council (NADAC), 124, 224, 228
North American Mixed Breed Registry (NAMBR), 228
Norwegian Elkhound, 174, 201, 203, 206, 208
Norwich Terrier, 47, 158, 170
NYC Dog, 256–257

O

obedience. *See* training
Old English Mastiff, 92
Old English Sheepdog, 146, 162, 170, 193, 195, 201, 210
older dogs, 248–249
Orthopedic Foundation for Animals (OFA), 220–221, 246, 247, 302
Otterhound, 157, 174, 208
Ovtcharka. *See* Caucasian Ovtcharka; Middle-Asian or Central-Asian Ovtcharka; South Russian Shepherd Dog

P

"papers." *See* registration
Papillon, 146, 154, 162, 167, 193, 197
parks, dog, 257, 303–304
Parson Russell Terrier, 162. *See also* Jack Russell Terrier
paws and nails, 246, 326–327, 351
pedigree, 220, 221, 247
Pekingese: cost, 218; description, 154,

162, 177; history, 5, 9, 177; nickname, 167; and royalty, 9, 167, 177; *Titanic* survivor, 82; traits, 193, 194, 196, 203, 204

Pembroke Welsh Corgi, 152, 170, 202, 218

People for the Ethical Treatment of Animals (PETA), 259, 260

Perro de Presa Canario (Canary Dog), 181

Persian Greyhound. *See* Saluki

personality, 186, 204–205, 246–247, 249

Peruvian Inca Orchid, 189, 191

pests. *See* fleas; skunks; ticks

Petdiabetes.org, 256

Petit Basset Griffon Vendéen (PBGV), 146, 162, 174, 181

Petit Bleu de Gascongne, 181

pets: and bereavement, 252, 257; compatibility of your dog with, 208–209, 251; introduction to the household, 208, 251, 263, 271–273; most common, 131; and smiles, 230; U.S. annual amount spent, 230; *vs.* show dogs, 111

pet stores, do not buy a puppy from, 216–217

Pharaoh Hound, 157, 172, 179, 208

photography, 17, 18, 68–71, 121, 309, 318

Pila. *See* Hairless Khala

Pinscher. *See* Affenpinscher; Doberman Pinscher; German Pinscher; Miniature Pinscher

pit bulls, 188, 194

Pit Bull Terrier, 23, 59, 64, 66, 192. *See also* American Pit Bull Terrier

play, 23, 298, 299. *See also* exercise; sports

Plott Hound, 157, 165, 174, 208, 209

Pocket Beagle, 48

poetry, 31, 66

Pointer, 3, 6, 210. *See also* American Pointer; English Pointer; German

Longhaired Pointer; German Shorthaired Pointer; German Wirehaired Pointer; Spanish Pointer

poisons, 263, 334, 351

Pomeranian, 82, 150, 193, 199, 202, 204, 218

Poodle, 25, 26, 27, 36, 61, 72, 193, 197, 202, 213, 231. *See also* English Poodle; French Poodle; Miniature Poodle; Standard Poodle; Toy Poodle

poodle-mixes, 189, 193, 211

Portuguese Water Dog, 158, 189, 195, 210

postcards with dogs, 22, 86, 93, 185, 315

pound. *See* animal shelters

prairie dog, 211

presidents, quotes from, 20–21

products and services, 60, 326–327, 333

protectiveness, 190–191, 235, 245

proverbs and sayings, 3, 5, 34, 62–63, 301

psychic ability, 308–309

Pug: in books and movies, 46, 65; cost, 218; description, 150, 162, 177; history, 9, 177; nicknames, 146; and royalty, 9, 167; traits, 192, 193, 195, 199, 202, 204

Puli (Pulik), 189, 206

pull records, 135

puppies, 92, 248–249

puppy mills, 213, 214, 215–217

puppy-proofing your home, 273

Q

quiet breeds, 207

R

rabies, 10–11

racetracks and racing, 128

radio, 51

Rainbow Ark, 257

Rainbow Bridge essay, 256

Rat Terrier, 84–85

recipes for biscuits, 306–307

record-breaking dogs, 79, 92–93, 95, 102, 135

Redbone Coonhound, 208, 209

Red Tick. *See* English Coonhound

registration, 217, 220, 247

religious and spiritual beliefs: afterlife, 10, 14, 15; of ancient Egypt, 10, 16, 50; astrology, 8, 9, 186; blessing of animals, 6, 7; burial, cremation, or mummification, 9, 10, 46, 58, 177, 327; chapel for dogs, 7, 15; Christianity, 11, 12, 16; conference on dogs, 7; dog creation theory, 113; Feng Shui, 7; Islam, 10–11; Judaism, 15; sacrifice of dogs, 15; saints, 7, 11; shamanism, 13; Zoroastrianism, 10, 16

rescue organizations, 246, 253, 259

resources: AKC, 107; bereavement helplines, 255; books on dog care, 264–265; books on training, 266–267; dog owner support groups, 256–257; finding a dog show, 99; finding a handler, 115; finding a trainer, 266; junior handler information, 122; national foundations, 302; rescue organizations, 246, 253, 259; safety products, 333; sports groups, 124, 125, 126; training videos, 281; unusual products and services, 326–327; *See also* Web sites

responsibilities of dog owners, 216, 238, 242–243, 247, 252, 260, 288

Retriever. *See* Chesapeake Bay Retriever; Chocolate Labrador; Curly-Coated Retriever; Flat-Coated Retriever; Golden Retriever; Labrador Retriever

Rhodesian Ridgeback, 45, 162, 174, 194, 207, 208, 210

Rin Tin Tin Inc., 54
Roberts, Percy, 117
Rodrigue, George, 18
Rosenberg, Alva, 118
Rottweiler: in books, 58; cost, 218; description, 150, 162; nickname, 150; stamp, 150; traits, 188, 190, 192, 194, 197, 201, 205, 206, 210, 213
Rough Collie, 162
Russian Bear Schnauzer, 175. *See also* Black Russian Terrier
Russian Wolfhound, 92, 175. *See also* Borzoi
Russo-European Laika, 175
Ryan, Terry, 287

S

safety: bite prevention, 296; car travel, 342; during disaster, 348–349; dog theft prevention, 288; excessive heat, 342, 347, 349; on finding a stray, 336; during the holiday season, 350–351; poisons, 263, 334, 351; products, 333; puppy-proofing your home, 263; things you should not do to a puppy, 274; what to do during an attack, 338–339; winter, 351
Saint Bernard: bad breeding, 223; in books, 60, 72, 73; cost, 218; description, 155, 162; in movies, 2, 41, 43, 45; traits, 188, 192, 195, 204, 209; weight pull record, 135
St. Hubert Hound, 5
Saluki, 48, 167, 172, 179, 208
Samoyed: cost, 218; description, 162; history, 175, 187; traits, 195, 201, 208, 210
Scandinavian Hound, 187
scent hounds, 173–174
Schipperke, 202, 203, 218
Schnauzer, 189, 202. *See also* Black Russian Terrier; Giant Schnauzer; Miniature Schnauzer; Russian Bear Schnauzer

Schutzhund, 22, 135
Scottish Border Collie, 44
Scottish Deerhound, 6, 162, 167, 170, 172
Scottish Terrier: in books, 72; cost, 218; description, 155, 162, 170; First Dog, 82; in man-bites-dog story, 19; nickname, 155, 170; traits, 202
Sealyham Terrier, 157, 170, 209
sedate breeds, 193, 198–199, 201–202
Setter. *See* English Setter; Gordon Setter; Irish Setter
Shakespeare, dog quotes, 74
Shar-Pei: avoid if you have allergies, 189; bad breeding, 223; cost, 218; description, 177; history, 5, 7, 177; traits, 196–197, 209; *See also* Chinese Shar-Pei
Sheepdog. *See* Belgian Sheepdog; English Sheepdog; Icelandic Sheepdog; Komondor; Mioritic Sheepdog; Old English Sheepdog; Shetland Sheepdog; Welsh Sheepdog
sheepdogs, 42, 62, 72, 94
shelter. *See* animal shelters; dog areas and home shelter
Shepherd. *See* American Tundra Shepherd; American White Shepherd; Anatolian Shepherd; Australian Shepherd; Caucasian Ovtcharka; Central-Asian Shepherd Dog; German Shepherd; South Russian Shepherd Dog
Shetland Sheepdog, 9, 151, 162, 197, 206, 218
Shiba Inu, 177, 208
Shichon, 189
Shih Tzu: cost, 218; description, 149, 162, 177; good for allergy sufferers, 189; in movies, 47; nickname, 199; and royalty, 167, 177; stamp, 177; traits, 193, 199
Siberian Husky: cost, 218; description, 152, 175, 187; history, 187; and insurance costs, 205; in movies, 48; as

sled dog, 131; traits, 188, 195, 201, 204, 210
sight, sense of, 172, 300
Silky Terrier, 193, 209
Silvani, Pia, 287
singing, 26, 231
Sirius (Dog Star), 48, 53
skunks, 343
Skye Terrier, 42, 72, 157, 170
Sled Dog. *See* Inuit Sled Dog
sled dogs, 61, 65, 83, 129–131
sleeping habits, 248
Sloughi (Arabian Greyhound), 179
Slovensky Cuvac, 191
smell, sense of, 173–174, 178, 229, 311
Smooth and Rough Collie, 170
Smooth Fox Terrier, 170, 171, 209
snoring, 201
social order: alpha dog, 242; and body language, 242, 283, 284; socialization to humans, 221, 240–241, 246, 271–272
Soft-Coated Wheaten Terrier, 170, 189, 210
songs about dogs, 36–37, 43
South Russian Shepherd Dog, 175
space exploration, 82–83, 89
Spaniel, 5, 26. *See also* American Cocker Spaniel; American Water Spaniel; Brittany Spaniel; Cavalier King Charles Spaniel; Clumber Spaniel; Cocker Spaniel; English Cocker Spaniel; English Springer Spaniel; English Toy Spaniel; Irish Water Spaniel; Springer Spaniel; Sussex Spaniel; Tibetan Spaniel; Welsh Springer Spaniel
Spanish Bulldog. *See* Alano Español
Spanish Greyhound, 181
Spanish Mastiff (*Mastin de Español*), 187, 209
Spanish Pointer, 181
Spanish Water Dog (Turkish Dog), 181, 189
spaying. *See* neutering and spaying

speed, 172
Spitz. *See* Finnish Spitz; German Spitz; Japanese Spitz; Norrbottenspets (Nordic Spitz)
Spitz, Carl, 41, 50, 287
Spitz-type dogs, 16
Sporting Group, 38, 104, 105–106, 142, 144, 145
sports: agility, 124, 224; associations, 124, 125, 126, 224; ball-fetching, 92–93; baseball team helpers, 89; disc-catching, 23, 89, 124–125, 133, 135, 294; diving, 93; dogsledding, 83, 129–131, 187; Earthdog, 124; fly-ball, 125; great, 124–126; herding competitions, 125; jumping, 92; lure coursing, 125; musical canine freestyle, 125–126, 127; obedience competitions, 126; Schutzhund, 22, 135; water rescue, 126; weight pull, 135; *See also* field trials
Springer Spaniel, 189, 190, 195, 204. *See also* English Springer Spaniel; Welsh Springer Spaniel
Staffordshire Bull Terrier, 162, 188, 190, 205, 209
Staffordshire Terrier, 170. *See also* American Staffordshire Terrier
Staghound. *See* American Staghound
stains and odors, 310–311
stamps, 29, 55, 150–152, 171–173, 177, 200, 202, 258–259
Standard Poodle: circus, 26; cost, 218; description, 149, 162; good for allergy sufferers, 189; good with children, 195; history, 182; in movies, 47; therapy dog, 88
Standard Schnauzer, 189, 203
stars, 48, 53
strangers, breeds that don't like, 190–191
strays, 336–337. *See also* animal shelters
Strickland, Winifred Gibson, 287
stud fee, 222
superdogs, 30

superstitions, 3, 4, 5
support groups, 256–257
Sussex Spaniel, 170–171, 193

T

tag, identification, 238
tail, 246, 312
Tails in Need, 134, 229
Talbot, 22
taste, sense of, 178, 229
tattoos, 288, 341
taxonomy, 141
teeth, 325
television: animal issues on, 49; dogs in, 42, 43, 46, 47, 48, 51–52, 55–57, 66, 73, 95
temperament. *See* personality
Terrier, 16, 65, 72, 192, 206. *See also* Airedale Terrier; American Hairless Terrier; American Pit Bull Terrier; American Staffordshire Terrier; American Toy Terrier; Australian Terrier; Bedlington Terrier; Black Russian Terrier; Border Terrier; Boston Terrier; Bull Terrier; Cairn Terrier; Dandie Dinmont Terrier; Fox Terrier; German Hunt Terrier (*Jagdterrier*); Glen of Imaal Terrier; Irish Terrier; Jack Russell Terrier; Japanese Terrier; Kerry Blue Terrier; Lakeland Terrier; Little Wire Fox Terrier; Manchester Terrier; Miniature Bull Terrier; Norfolk Terrier; Norwich Terrier; Parson Russell Terrier; Pit Bull Terrier; Rat Terrier; Scottish Terrier; Sealyham Terrier; Silky Terrier; Skye Terrier; Smooth Fox Terrier; Soft-Coated Wheaten Terrier; Staffordshire Bull Terrier; Staffordshire Terrier; Tibetan Terrier; Toy Fox Terrier; Welsh Terrier; West Highland White Terrier; Wire Fox Terrier; Yorkshire Terrier

Terrier Group, 38, 104, 105–106, 142–143, 144, 145
territoriality. *See* aggression; protectiveness
terrorist attacks, 84–85, 88, 95
theft, 288, 341
therapy dogs, 84, 85, 88, 89
thunder, fear of, 346–347
Tibetan Mastiff, 177–178
Tibetan Spaniel, 178
Tibetan Terrier, 5, 162, 178, 189, 209
ticks, 344
Titanic survivors, 82
Toy Fox Terrier, 165, 193
Toy Group, 38, 104, 105–106, 142, 144, 145
Toy Manchester Terrier, 193
Toy Poodle, 92, 162, 189, 193, 194, 199, 206
toys, 23, 298
tracking competitions, 126
trainers, 266, 285–287, 291
training: a blind dog, 300; books on, 266–267; clicker method, 266, 277, 290–291; commands (*see* commands); daily chores, 263; a deaf dog, 301; housetraining, 248, 263, 278, 279–280, 326; jokes, 269; Jolly Routine method, 277; Koehler method, 277; lure method, 125, 277; military, 22, 23; as a mutual process, 263; obedience classes, 238, 242, 291; obedience competitions, 126; play, 277; schools of thought on, 277; Schutzhund method, 22, 136; target stick method, 277; tips, 274, 275–276; videos, 281
traveling with your dog, 314–315, 316–317, 342
treatment of dogs. *See* care and proper treatment; health
Treeing Walker Hound, 174
tricks, 92, 285, 297
Turkish Dog. *See* Spanish Water Dog